教育部哲学社会科学研究重大课题攻关项目：
推动智库建设健康发展研究（17JZD009）

南大智库文丛
李刚 主编

CTTI智库报告(2019)

李刚 王斯敏 冯雅 甘琳　主编

2019 Annual Report on the Development of
CTTI Source Think Tanks

南京大学出版社

中国特色新型智库建设的"下半场"

——南大智库文丛序

2013年4月，习近平总书记对中国特色新型智库建设工作做了重要批示。根据中共中央办公厅、国务院办公厅2015年1月公开印发的《关于加强中国特色新型智库建设的意见》提出的时间表——到2020年实现中国特色新型智库建设总体目标，那么自2013年以来的这五年应属于中国特色新型智库建设的"上半场"，未来三年应该属于新型智库建设的"下半场"。

2016年5月，习近平总书记指出："近年来，哲学社会科学领域建设智库热情很高，成果也不少，为各级党政部门决策提供了有益帮助。同时，有的智库研究存在重数量、轻质量问题，有的存在重形式传播、轻内容创新问题，还有的流于搭台子、请名人、办论坛等形式主义的做法。"（《在哲学社会科学工作座谈会上的讲话》）我们认为习近平总书记的总结仍然是对五年新型智库建设切中肯綮的评估。

经过这五年的实践，我们对新型智库建设的深远意义认识得更加清晰。

第一，新型智库建设成为推动国家治理体系和治理能力现代化的重要抓手和重要路径。什么样的国家治理体系才是现代化的？什么样的治理能力才是现代化的？现代化不光是工具层面的，也应当是价值层面的，现代化的治理体系和现代化的治理能力体现在国家治理的价值、理论、方法、工具所具备的现代性上。以人民为中心的法治化、规范化、科学化、协同化、效用化的治理体系才是现代化的治理体系。综合运用并发挥国家治理体系的最大效用，达到全民福祉的最大化，形成"良好治理"，就是现代化的治理能力。新型智库无疑是观察国家治理体系和治理能力现代性的一个重要指标。加强新型智库建设实质上就是在促进国家治理的现代性成长。

第二，新型智库建设继承了儒家"学为政本"传统，促进了国家治理的科学理性和专业理性。儒家强调"学为政本"，这和黑暗的中世纪欧洲形成了鲜明的对比。有思想家说，中国文明是"早熟"的文明，这是与西方传统对比后得出的结论。秦汉以后，中国就建立了高度理性的非世袭的郡县制和官员任期制。隋唐以后，科举制已经成为官员选拔的主要制度，这比近代欧洲文官制度要早数百年。可以这么说，中古以后，中国国家治理模式就是建立在知识基础之上的贤人政治。但是，近代以来，西方逐渐走向了"学为政本"的国家治理法治化和专业化的路向，中国反而陷入积贫积弱、四分五裂的境况，国家治理不再依赖学术和知识共同体，"学为政本"的传统被迫中断。现代智库虽然起源于西方，却是为数不多的可以嫁接到中国文化传统的一种现代西方国家治理架构。现代智库体现的"学为政本"的贤人政治精神契合中国文化的精神，这就很好地解释了中国知识界为何对建设新智库充满热情。

　　第三，新型智库建设本质是开放言路，建立制度化的"政—知""政—产""政—媒""政—社"意见交通渠道，调动各行业知识精英参与国家治理的积极性。根据我国宪法，人民在国家治理中处于中心地位，但是在国家治理的体系和实践中，决策体系相对封闭，人民参与国家治理的渠道和机会均有限。实际上，不要说普通群众了，即使是高级知识分子，提供给他们参与决策咨询的选项也不多。新型智库建设不仅给政府的内脑——各级各类研究室带来了专业化的决策咨询工作理念，而且通过外脑——高校研究机构、社科院、党校行政学院、主流媒体的智库化转型，使得理论界、社科界、高等教育界的专家获得了制度化的建言献策管道。如果说内脑是新型智库建设中的存量部分，那么外脑就是智库建设中的增量部分。如果说内脑是以往决策咨询的主体，那么现在外脑和内脑则获得了对等的主体地位，虽然它们的话语权并不相等。这种不相等并不是由于到决策中枢的距离远近，而是缘自内脑和外脑的分工和专业素养的不同。在短期和应急决策咨询上，内脑发言权较大，而在长期和基础的决策咨询中，也许外脑话语权更大。决策咨询体系增量主体的扩大促进了国家治理体系的开放性、协商性、民主性、包容性。

　　第四，新型智库建设促进了有利于开展政策辩论的理性第二公共政策空间的成长。互联网的兴起虽然极大地提升了政策辩论的参与度，但是有时候这种参与也是无序的和非理性的,这往往使得正常的政策辩论在网络空间中无法开展。这种情况一方面是由于长期以来民众接受的政策素养教育严重不足,的确不知道如何开展一项严肃的政策辩论;另一方面是因为一部分自媒体人和公众号的写手为吸引眼球无所不用其极,搅乱了正常的政策辩论。而在新型智库建设过程中,政策共同体的要素和边界逐渐明晰,形成了由党委政府、人大政协、政策研究机构、新型智库、主流媒体等部门的专家组成的第二公共政策讨论空间。在这个共同空间中,智库起到了连接器和催化器的作用,推动了理性的公共政策辩论和协商。

正是因为认识到新型智库建设是推动国家治理体系和治理能力现代化的难得机遇,以天下为己任的中国哲学社会科学界才怀着满腔热情和历史使命感积极响应中央的号召,努力推动新型智库建设。

如果从新型智库实体建设来说,我们取得了巨大的成绩。根据中国智库索引的统计,截至 2018 年底,我国已经有 9 大类 706 家智库,分布于 50 多个战略和政策领域。根据规模和研究能力,这些智库分为国家高端智库、省级重点智库和普通专业智库三个层次,其中还包括一些按照"民非"(民办非企业单位)、社团或者企业形式运行的社会智库。另外,在智库的制度建设和运营管理上也探索出不少有益的经验,涌现出很多可圈可点的案例。

2017 年,南京大学中国智库研究与评价中心和光明日报智库研究与发布中心征集评选了一系列值得重视的新型智库建设案例。例如,"复旦发展研究院:始终坚持国际化路径促进传统论坛转型为智库论坛""同济大学财经研究所:智库研究要抓重大现实问题要突出前瞻性——《重新认识和准确定义新时期我国社会的主要矛盾》""北京市信访矛盾分析中心:智库实证研究的佳作——《社会矛盾指数研究》""华中师范大学中国农村研究院:三十年专注农村社会调查——从走村串户到构建大数据智库调查服务平台""浙江师范大学非洲研究院近年来立足中非合作实践需要,成功探索出了一条学科、智库、媒体三位一体的发展路径""江南大学食品安全风险治理研究院旨在打造小而专、小而精、小而强,国际化视野的高校专业智库""长江教育研究院:充分利用人大政协渠道,搭建一流专业论坛,十年如一日专注中国教育现代化",等等。

对照《关于加强中国特色新型智库建设的意见》提出的到 2020 年要实现的总体目标，我们认为新型智库建设"上半场"没有解决好的问题有以下几点。

第一，我国智库产业集中度和产业集群性很低。实体数量的增长并不意味着我国新型智库就形成了"党政部门、社科院、党校行政学院、高校、军队、科研院所和企业、社会智库协调发展"的局面，就形成了"定位明晰、特色鲜明、规模适度、布局合理的中国特色新型智库体系"。总体上说，我国智库机构"散""弱""小"的局面并未发生根本改变，其实由于数量增加了，智库类机构"散""弱""小"的总体情况可能反而更严重，这导致我国智库产业集中度和产业集群性很低。

相反，美国智库产业集中度和产业集群性很高。华盛顿智库街上的近 400 家美国智库中，三分之一以上的智库拥有的全职研究员和职员在百人左右。美国西海岸的兰德公司有员工 1850 人，芝加哥大学的全美舆情研究中心（NORC）有全职研究员和职员 800 余人。可以说，美国智库不仅多，而且单个规模大、研究咨询力量强、影响力大。反观我们的智库，虽然中国社科院全院总人数 4200 多人，有科研业务人员 3200 多人，但这些研究人员分属 31 个研究所、45 个研究中心和 120 个学科，每个研究所（中心）拥有的研究人员平均起来不过 42 人。更关键的在于，这些研究所和研究中心都是独立行政单元，跨所（中心）的协同合作非常困难。这种现象不仅存在于中国社科院，也存在于不少省级社科院。至于高校智库，"散""弱""小"的现象则更严重。C9 高校中的哲学社会科学研究机构动辄数百个，但是其中绝大多数都属非实体非法人的教授课题组，往往会因为教授转会或者退休而"人亡政息"，形成大量"僵尸机构"。可以说，我国智库体系中杂牌军多、正规军少，业余选手多、专业选手少，新智库多、老牌智库少。因此，中央抓国家高端智库建设、省市抓重点智库建设是非常必要的。如果不能把有限的经费和专家资源集中到一起，还是分散发展，那就不可能迅速改变我国新型智库体系"散""弱""小"的局面。

我国的主要专家资源集中在高校系统，但是高校过于重视学科建设，把主要资源都投入学科建设。决定学科建设能否进入一流的主要指标主要包括纵向的项目、学位点、重点实验室、"戴帽子"的各类人才数量、高水平论文和各类奖项的数量等。遗憾的是,新型智库的质量和数量并不在其中,这就导致大部分高校对新型智库建设都不够重视,不愿意投入真金白银。国家在一流高校里认定了14家高端智库(含高端培育智库),有些智库的确发挥了智库的功能,但也有一些智库还是以教学研究为主,转型脚步慢了半拍;还有的高校虽然拿到了国家高端智库建设的入场券,但是并未给予足够重视。

第二,新型智库建设未能有效突破体制上的"三明治瓶颈"。实体数量的增长并不意味着智库研究质量的同步提升和新型体制机制的落地生根,我国智库的治理体制难以突破"三明治瓶颈"。2018年3月,黄坤明同志在国家高端智库理事会扩大会议上的讲话中指出,试点工作以来,中央和有关部门在经费管理、人员出国、奖励激励、会议管理等方面出台了一系列含金量很高的政策,赋予试点单位很大的自主权和政策空间,但不少单位承接、落实还不到位,很多政策仍然悬置。人员管理、薪酬待遇、职称评定、财务管理等方面的掣肘比较突出。

产生这种现象的根本原因是我国大部分智库都是附属型智库。根据中国智库索引的数据,我国智库体系中95％的智库都是母体机构下属的非法人的实体智库和非法人挂靠性质的智库。这些智库外部治理结构类似三明治,三明治的上层是国家/省市部委智库管理部门,中间是母体单位(比如高校和社科院),下层才是智库。之所以称之为智库治理的"三明治瓶颈",是因为国家/省市部委智库管理部门根本无法直接管理这些母体单位下属的非独立智库,而是要通过母体单位(也可以叫平台单位)才能作用到智库。母体单位(平台单位)就像三明治的中间层隔绝了国家/省市部委智库管理部门和非独立智库之间的直接治理联系,国家/省市部委智库管理部门任何政策落地都需要母体单位(平台单位)制定实施细则,或者经过母体单位(平台单位)的认可同意配套相应的落地政策。比如,中央出台的增加经费中专家劳务费用支出比例的意见,如果未经母体单位(平台单位)认可并制定相应的实施细则和财务审批的流程,那么中央的含金量很高的意见就不可能作用于非独立智库(三明治下层),非独立智库望眼欲穿的好政策由于三明治中间层的梗阻就无法落地,政策红利也就无法释放出来。

对于母体单位(平台单位)来说,下属智库只是众多业务单元之一,是否值得为中央/省市部委智库管理部门的政策落实制定配套的细则和流程,还有许多其他考量。以高校为例,学科建设是主要任务,不可或缺,而智库建设属于锦上添花,可有可无。如果要为中央/省市部委智库管理部门的政策落实制定细则、配套资源,就会存在是否会激怒主体院系的问题。如果同意智库增加经费中专家劳务费用支出比例,那么非智库单位要比照执行怎么办? 不同意的话,非智库单位会援例争吵;如果同意的话,科研经费中学校分成势必减少,伤及自身利益。因此,大部分高校都会对中央出台的增加经费中专家劳务费用支出比例的文件采取置之不理的做法。三明治中间层对智库宏观治理影响巨大,可以说对非独立智库而言,母体单位(平台单位)的智库治理才是最直接最关键的,中央/省市部委智库管理部门的智库治理属于天高皇帝远、鞭长莫及。如何破解智库宏观治理中的“三明治瓶颈”呢? 根本解决方法是把非独立智库变成独立法人实体机构。比如南京大学为化解智库治理的“三明治瓶颈”,就让下属的两家省级重点智库——长江产业经济研究院和紫金传媒智库在省民政厅注册为“民非”法人实体智库,这样一来“三明治瓶颈”的中间层就不存在了。独立的法人实体智库可以直接执行中央/省市部委智库管理部门的有关智库治理的政策文件。学校内部其他院系和研究中心也无法援引这两家智库享受的政策红利。同时,为了让这两家智库同时利用学校的资源,南京大学还发文成立了南京大学长江产经研究院和南京大学紫金传媒智库。南京大学通过一个法人实体两块牌子的方式成功化解了智库治理的“三明治瓶颈”。

第三,智库的研究咨询业务过于集中在政策过程的前端,业务模式头重脚轻。政策过程包含议程设置、政策辩论、决策与路演、政策教育、政策评估、政策反馈修正等,这是一个完整的政策环,每个环节都需要智库参加,但是每个环节需要不同层次不同专业的智库参加。如果从国家政策层面来说,在议程设置阶段和政策辩论阶段主要需要高层次高端智库参与,其他层次的智库由于缺乏全局性的视野和经验往往就不适合此项工作。可是在政策评估环节,即使是地方智库也可以从本地区出发对国家政策的执行情况开展评估和反馈。但是由于我们智库考核指标的设置往往给予高层次批示极高的权重,导致几乎所有智库都在思考全国性政策议程设置问题。这种定位错误,造成了大量的重复劳动和无效劳动,如雪片一样飞向北京的内参其实大多数是没有必要的。因此,绝大多数省级智库都不应该把业务重心放到全国性政策议程设置的决策咨询工作上。

相反,大量的专业智库应该把业务模式重心下移和后置,把主要精力放到政策教育、政策评估和政策反馈上来。专业智库角色定位主要不是当"国师"——为党委政府出思想、出概念和出思路,而是应该承担更多的技术性支援工作。专业智库的主要工作是调查研究、采集数据、数据分析、建模计算,是协助政府脚踏实地地落实政策,是用自己的数据、计算能力评估政策和项目的执行情况并及时反馈给政府。对于专业智库来说,可能核心能力并非思想力,而是调查、数据、计算、规划、评估等能力。没有这些核心能力,智库只能开展定性研究,靠拍脑袋为政府出主意,那样业务重心就浮于表面。

第四,智库和政府内部研究机构是"两张皮",供给与需求之间的信息不对称无法消除。智库是政府的外脑,政府内研究机构是内脑。习近平总书记指出,"要加强决策部门同智库的信息共享和互动交流,把党政部门政策研究同智库对策研究紧密结合起来,引导和推动智库建设健康发展、更好发挥作用"(《在哲学社会科学工作座谈会上的讲话》),强调的其实就是内脑和外脑的协同。内脑要指导、引导和推动外脑的对策研究,要解决政策研究和对策研究"两张皮"的问题,要消除需求和供给之间的信息不对称。这个问题之所以未得到有效解决,原因很多。首先,我国智库体系中高校智库比重过大。截至2017年底,CTTI来源604家智库中58%属于高校智库。这种情况得到中国社科院评价院的《中国智库综合评价AMI研究报告(2017)》核心智库目录的印证。该报告确定了166家核心智库,其中高校智库有79家,比重为47%。高校智库往往是由传统学术研究"翻牌"而来,更擅长的是学术研究而非对策研究。高校智库因为固有的师道尊严文化,往往缺乏"客户第一"的服务精神。智库是一种高端的决策咨询服务工作,不管是高端还是低端服务业,只要是服务业,没有"客户第一"的服务精神,那么服务工作就不可能做好。因此,让高校智库主动对接政府研究机构,心甘情愿地为政策研究部门做好技术支援性工作,心甘情愿地为政策研究部门做调查研究、采集数据、分析数据、撰写研究报告初稿，几乎是不可能的。其次，政府政策研究部门恐怕也未必看得上智库，更不愿意和智库共享数据和信息。坦率地说，二者之间也存在竞争关系，政策研究部门也有"教会徒弟饿死师傅"的忧虑。

解决这个问题的主要途径还是智库主动采用嵌入式决策咨询服务模式。嵌入式决策咨询服务模式是我们首次归纳的一个学术概念，指的是智库的对策研究通过嵌入政府政策研究过程解决外脑和内脑的协同问题。嵌入首先说明了智库和政府政策研究部门之间存在着一定距离，存在一定的区别；嵌入也意味着智库的对策研究有独立的价值，有自己独特的属性——和政府政策研究部门相比，智库研究可能更关心中长期问题，更关心基础问题，更关心前瞻性问题。嵌入式决策咨询服务包括政策过程的嵌入、决策咨询流程的嵌入、决策咨询场景的嵌入和政策共同体的圈层嵌入。政策过程的嵌入是指智库应该嵌入一个政策的完整过程，和内脑开展紧密合作，从议程设置、政策辩论、决策与推广、政策执行、政策教育、政策评估和政策反馈全过程的参与和发挥作用，不仅要关心政策文本的产生，还要促进政策文本的落地以及落地后的效果。决策咨询流程的嵌入是指要在调查研究、数据采集、数据分析、分析研判和撰写报告等过程中都和内脑紧密合作，充分发挥智库技术支援的优势，服务内脑的政策研究。决策咨询场景的嵌入是指积极参加领导的调研活动、决策咨询会议和政策路演活动，获得决策咨询活动的现场感与语境，如此才能了解政策产生的前因后果。政策共同体的圈层嵌入是指智库要和政府决策者、政策研究部门形成密切的联系，产生强烈的互信关系，这是其他三种嵌入的前提，也是结果。当然，政策共同体中并非只有决策者和政策研究者（内脑），还包含其他的要素，智库要和这些要素之间都形成密切的圈层嵌入。如果智库能实现四种形式的嵌入，那么就有可能解决对策研究脱离实际、不接地气、没有市场的困境，成为党委政府想得起、用得上、离不开的智库。

第五，智库成果认定与激励的指挥棒设计不合理。成果认定与激励制度是引导智库发展的指挥棒，但目前这个指挥棒设计不够合理，是制约智库健康发展的主要问题之一。我国智库成果认定标准非常单一，从我们收集到的各种认定奖励文本来看，各类智库都看重批示的行政级别，无论是折算成文章还是直接奖励金钱，都是行政级别越高的批示得奖越重。这种做法简单粗暴,必然导致智库只愿意为决策者服务而不是为决策过程服务,必然导致智库只愿意为高端决策者服务而不是为基层治理服务,必然导致智库只愿意着力揣摩领导意图的政策研究而不是基于客观事实基础的政策研究。其实,智库所承担的大量政策评估、政策宣传等工作都不会产生批示,但是这些技术支援性工作恰恰是政府更需要的。因此,这些工作都应该纳入智库成果的认定范围。政策评估等工作政府会以横向项目的形式交给智库,而在我们的智库考核体系中,横向项目恰恰是最不受重视的。我们认为,对于国家高端智库和省级重点智库而言,的确批示的权重应该大一些,因为这些智库的主要功能是咨政建言。可是对于大多数专业智库而言,用专业能力为党委政府提供技术性支援工作往往不会产生批示,对它们而言,批示就不应该是主要考核指标。

上述五大问题能否解决好,决定了新型智库建设"下半场"的成效。新型智库体系建设要解决智库产业的集中度和产业集群性问题,实体化和法人化是解决体制机制创新、克服"三明治瓶颈"的重要途径,业务重心下移和后置是解决智库浮于表面、注重形式传播问题的重要思路,而推行嵌入式决策咨询服务模式是解决政策研究与对策研究衔接、发挥内脑和外脑协同研究效应的重要选择,智库成果认定与激励措施的调整则始终是最重要的保障。

2017年,我被批准承担教育部哲学社会科学研究重大课题攻关项目——"推动智库建设健康发展研究"(项目编号:17JZD009)。此后,我带课题组调研了一些智库和智库管理部门,它们反映的情况引发了我上述思考。恰逢"南大智库文丛"又有新书出版,考虑到原来的丛书序已经和形势有所脱节,故以此文作为"南大智库文丛"的新序。"南大智库文丛"在南京大学出版社的大力支持下已经出满10种。其中4种已经重印,这对我们也是很大的鼓舞。《CTTI智库报告(2018)》是我们中心和光明智库共同推出的第三份报告,报告用中英双语种出版,目的是向海外宣传中国特色新型智库建设的成就,展示中国智库的群体风采。

南京大学中国智库研究与评价中心被智库界称为"智库的智库",我们中心的使命就是研究中外智库发展的规律,促进中国智库共同体的发展,为智库交流搭建平台，为中国智库培养管理人才，为我国智库和公共政策研究机构提供管理咨询服务。

经过数年的努力，我们中心取得了一些成绩。

第一，我们和光明日报社共同开发了"中国智库索引"。CTTI 系统是具有智库垂直搜索、智库数据管理和智库在线智能评价三位一体的具有自主知识产权智库信息系统。目前收录 706 家智库、12299 名专家、19071 次智库会议和咨询活动记录、120303 项智库研究成果记录。CTTI 成为我国找智库、找专家服务和找专家成果的第一平台。

第二，我们和光明日报社共同创立了"中国智库治理论坛"。2016 年 12 月，第一届年会在南京大学召开，与会代表近 700 人。2017 年 12 月，第二届年会在北京召开，与融媒体峰会一起进行，与会代表预计 300 人，实际到会 700 余人。2018 年 12 月，第三届年会在南京召开，实际到会代表近 800 人。经过三届年会，论坛对促进我国新型智库共同体建设起到了积极作用。

第三，我们编撰了中英文对照的《CTTI 智库报告》和工具书《中国智库索引》，这些书已经被国内数百所高校图书馆以及海外的不少东亚图书馆和著名智库，如华盛顿布鲁金斯学会、基辛格研究中心等采购收藏。

第四，南京大学中国智库研究与评价中心是我国最早在博士生招生目录上设立智库研究方向的博士生培养项目单位。我们智库中心已经培养了 4 名智库专业博士毕业生，为促进智库和公共政策研究机构管理成为一个专门的学术领域做出了应有的贡献。

李　刚

2019 年 9 月 5 日

各章节作者名单

章节名称		执笔者
导言　新型智库建设与国家治理体系现代化		李　刚
上篇	专题一　国家高端智库与省市重点新型智库建设进展	吕诚诚 马雪雯
	专题二　新型智库成为决策咨询新生力量	黄　静 徐　路
	专题三　新型智库传播能力有了长足进步	丁炫凯
	专题四　智库在对外关系中扮演重要角色	徐　路 向　君
	专题五　新型智库网络与智库共同体的形成	冯　雅
	专题六　国家与学术：新时代智库研究进展	甘　琳
下篇	一、CTTI 三期系统简介	邹嘉晨
	二、2019 年度 CTTI 来源智库证书更新与新智库增补	崔　妍
	三、CTTI 来源智库人力资源特征	
	四、CTTI 来源智库产出数据分析	吕诚诚
	五、CTTI 来源智库分政策领域数据扫描	韦芷晴 王　蕾 卢柯全
	CTTI 来源智库目录（2019）	崔　妍

目　录

下　篇　中国智库索引来源智库报告

Content

Part One   Research on the Construction of New Think Tanks with Chinese Characteristics from 2015 to 2019

Part Two   Chinese Think Tank Index Source Think Tanks Report

导言：新型智库建设与国家治理体系现代化

2013 年 4 月 15 日，习近平总书记对智库建设做出重要批示，明确提出"中国特色新型智库"建设目标，要求智库积极为中央科学决策提供高质量智力支持。2013 年 11 月，十八届三中全会《中共中央关于全面深化改革若干重大问题的决定》进一步明确提出"加强中国特色新型智库建设，建立健全决策咨询制度"。经过紧张的起草和意见征集，2014 年 10 月 27 日，《关于加强中国特色新型智库建设的意见》提交"深改组"第六次会议审议，习近平总书记就智库建设再次发表重要讲话，他强调，要从推动科学决策、民主决策，推进国家治理体系和治理能力现代化、增强国家软实力的战略高度，把中国特色新型智库建设作为一项重大而紧迫的任务切实抓好。2015 年 1 月 20 日，新华社公开播发了中办、国办印发的《关于加强中国特色新型智库建设的意见》。五年来，新型智库建设是决策咨询系统和哲学社会科学界最热门的议题，新型智库建设也取得了令人瞩目的成就，也暴露了一些发展中的问题。中共十九届四中全会再次强调了国家治理体系和治理能力现代化的命题，为新型智库发展提供了前所未有的历史机遇。

一、新型智库建设契合了中国深厚的理性政治与学为政本的文化传统

中国特色新型智库建设是健全完善决策体制机制的一项重要改革举措，是得到理论界、高教界、新闻传播界和广大知识分子阶层衷心拥护的一项重要政策。

之所以如此，首先这是一项基于中国深厚文化传统的正确决策。陈寅恪曾经指出："窃疑中国自今日以后，即使能忠实输入北美或东欧之思想，其结局当亦等于玄奘

唯识之学，在吾国思想史上，既不能居最高之地位，且亦终归于歇绝者。其真能于思想上自成系统，有所创获者，必须一方面吸收输入外来之学说，一方面不忘本来民族之地位。这两种相反而适相成之态度，乃道教之真精神，新儒家之旧途径，而二千年吾民族与他民族思想接触史之所昭示者也。"（陈寅恪《冯友兰〈中国哲学史〉下册审查报告》）

智库这个概念是"舶来品"，来自西方社会，但是它之所以在当代中国政治生活中产生如此巨大的反响，得到知识阶层的广泛支持，原因就在于智库契合了中国的政治文化传统和知识分子的士大夫传统。

中国作为有上下五千年历史的文明古国，他的政治文化在西周时期已经摆脱了蒙昧的巫术政治文化，春秋战国时期又历经了诸子百家思想争鸣的洗礼，已经建立了理性的政治文化传统。比如，韩非法家就是一种极其冷静和极其理智的基于计算的政治理论。春秋战国事情统治阶级之间竞相募士、养士和用士，出现了稷下学宫这样著名智囊机构。汉代的太学是世界上第一所规模上万人的国立大学，也是汉代官僚集团的主要来源。隋唐时期确立了科举取士的传统，此后无论朝代如何变迁，但是士农工商的四民顺序却从未改变，倚重文人集团治理国家的格局几乎没有根本的变化。

也正因为养士和用士的理性政治传统，古代中国的知识阶层也以天下为己任，强调学术经世致用。"为天地立心，为生民立命，为往圣继绝学，为万世开太平"的横渠四句也就成为一代又一代中国士大夫阶层的价值追求。

这就是新型智库建设这项重大改革举措深得知识阶层拥护的"文化基因"，这个文化基因包含两个相辅相成的序列，一方面是政治理性主义传统，另一方面是士阶层的为往圣继绝学，为万世开太平的知识报国传统。智库在中国的兴起，恰恰符合陈寅恪阐述的西学东渐的机理——一方面吸收输入外来之学说，一方面不忘本来民族之地位。也可以说，智库并非舶来品，是我们文化自信的写照，它在中国社会有深厚的文化基础。因此，可以说新型智库倡议是一项合意程度极高，契合了中国的深厚历史文化传统，具有丰沛生命力和影响力的一项战略决策。

二、新型智库建设主要阶段性成果

观念性成果是普及了现代智库的概念和知识，智库从一个小众的陌生词汇变成了我国政治文化生活的热词，为我国决策咨询体系的现代化创造了良好的氛围。这大大促进了党委政府建智库用智库的热情，对提升我国的决策科学性，完善决策机制有极大的好处。

其次，我国从中央到省市地方建立一批智库机构，据不完全统计，截至 2019 年 2 月，中央和省市部委办局以红头文件批准成立的各级各类重点智库已经有 383 家。截至 2019 年 12 月，CTTI 来源智库已经达 848 家。也就是至少从数量上，我们国家的智库仅少于美国。848 家 CTTI 来源智库拥有研究人员 14241 位，27699 次活动记录，157394 件各类成果。

再次，在智库实体建设的同时，规章制度也逐渐形成体系。据 CTTI 中心马雪雯统计，截至 2019 年 4 月，共有 27 个省级行政区先后出台了本省新型智库建设的实施意见或办法，并在其中提出了省级重点（高端）智库的建设规划，将重点智库建设工作纳入了规范化、法制化的进程。数十家研究型大学制定了智库成果认定的标准和考核指标体系。另外，智库在理论创新、决策咨询、舆论引导、社会服务和公共外交方面都深入嵌入我国的政治文化体系，正在起着不可或缺的作用。同时，智库研究队伍迅速成长，智库研究成果也呈现爆发性增长，对中外不同时期智库的认识逐渐深入。本报告分几个专题详细阐述了新型智库建设的成果。

当然，新型智库建设中也出现了过热化现象，形式主义泛滥。也出现了个别智库和咨询公司打着智库旗号敛财创收，甚至为利益集团摇旗呐喊的极个别现象。这非常值得重视。但是，那种从根本上质疑新型智库建设必要性和紧迫性是完全错误的。

三、新型智库建设唤醒了决策咨询共同体的身份认同、专业认同和职业认同

中国共产党向来注重政策研究。早在 1930 年 5 月做寻乌调查期间，毛泽东就从

理论上总结了调查研究与马克思主义世界观之间不可分割的关系。他在这次调查期间写下的《调查工作》一文中，对调查研究活动提出过许多重要的理论观点，其中最著名的是"没有调查，没有发言权"这一论断。1941 年 8 月 1 日，毛泽东在起草《中共中央关于调查研究的决定》时表示："党内许多同志，还不了解没有调查就没有发言权这一真理。还不了解系统的周密的社会调查，是决定政策的基础。还不知道领导机关的基本任务，就在于了解情况与掌握政策，而情况如不了解，则政策势必错误。"1948 年 3 月 20 日是毛泽东在杨家沟度过的最后一天。动身前毛泽东决定对前段工作做个暂时的了结，为中央发出《关于情况的通报》。只有党的政策和策略全部走上正轨，中国革命才有胜利的可能。政策和策略是党的生命，各级领导同志务必充分注意，万万不可粗心大意。"1948 年 9 月党中央在西柏坡成立了"中央政策研究室"，彭真任主任，全部工作人员有 23 名，主要任务是起草文稿和调查研究。1949 年以后，中国共产党依然保持了先开展调查研究然后决策的民主集中制模式，也创造了走村住户的"蹲点"和解剖麻雀等调查研究新方式，但是由于党内政治生态紊乱，调查研究经常流于形式，脱离实际的决策很多，导致一系列重大政策失误，直到"文革十年"决策咨询体系完全停摆。改革开放后，为应对改革开放过程中出现的新形势、新问题，提高政府决策的科学化水平，中国共产党大力恢复决策咨询和调查研究体系，建立了党委系统的政策研究室和政府系统的研究室。以国务院发展研究中心（1980 年成立）、中共中央政策研究室（1981 年成立）、中国现代国际关系研究所（1980 年成立）为代表的各级党政部门下属的发展研究中心、政策研究室、研究所等决策咨询机构纷纷建立、发展。应该说经过近 40 年的发展，中国共产党建立了以党委政策研究室和政府研究室为主体，社科院、党校行政学院为辅助的完整的、系统的内部调查研究和决策咨询体系，也就是党委政府的"内脑"系统。但是这个系统一直缺乏一个明确的身份认同，有时叫"文字工作者"，有时叫"幕僚"，有时叫"智囊"，《关于加强中国特色新型智库建设的意见》为党委政府的"内脑"系统赋予了一个现代的全球性的身份认同标签——"智库"。这个身份认同标签还被其他系统，比如高校、科研院所、大型国企的政策性研究机构援用,这样我国就形成了包括"内脑"和"外脑"两类主体构成的具有明确身份认同、专业认同和职业认同的"智库界"。

这必然会促进决策咨询分工的细化,有利于提升我国决策咨询工作的专业化、职业化和科学化。党委政府内的研究室系统发生了分工上的细化,一部分继续以往的以文稿服务为主,另一部分则逐步摆脱烦琐的文稿服务,把主要精力放到政策研究和政策服务上。高校的哲学社会科学研究机构以政策研究为主要任务的都明确了智库身份,学科建设任务淡化,智库研究比重大大加强。各级社科院有的还提双轮驱动,有的干脆只提智库功能。市场化的咨询公司也分化出一部分专门服务党委政府决策咨询工作专业化智库性质的咨询公司。这样,我国就出现了一个横跨党委政府、高校社科院等体制内研究部门和市场化咨询公司的多元化的"智库共同体",各类机构以服务党委政府决策咨询为主要任务,拥有统一的身份认同、专业认同和价值认同。这是新型智库建设的一大硕果。

四、新型智库成为发展协商民主的主渠道之一

习近平同志指出:"人民通过选举、投票行使权利和人民内部各方面在重大决策之前进行充分协商,尽可能就共同性问题取得一致意见,是中国社会主义民主的两种重要形式。"《中共中央关于坚持和完善中国特色社会主义制度 推进国家治理体系和治理能力现代化若干重大问题的决定》指出:"坚持社会主义协商民主的独特优势,统筹推荐政党协商、人大协商、政府协商、政协协商、人民团体协商、基层协商以及社会组织协商,构建程序合理、环节完整的协商民主体系,完善协商于决策之前和决策实施之中的落实机制,丰富有事好商量、众人之事由众人商量的制度化实践。"2014年9月,习近平同志在庆祝人民政协成立65周年大会上的讲话指出各类智库是十种协商渠道之一。这非常明确地赋予了新型智库作为协商民主主渠道的地位。因此,从政治上来说,新型智库建设就不仅仅是服务党委政府决策咨询的工具性功能,还具备了发扬社会主义协商民主的政治功能。新型智库也具备了团结和联系知识界的统一战

线功能，是群众路线的一种切实机制。

五、新型智库建设催生了哲学社会科学的"智库范式"

中国共产党一直提倡哲学社会科学必须经世致用。革命战争时期，毛泽东同志强调"纤笔一枝谁与似？三千毛瑟精兵。"笔杆子和枪杆子一样都是革命武器。

改革开放以来我们大规模输入西方哲学社会科学概念和思潮，在丰富我们的知识体系同时也损害到中国哲学社会科学的自主性和有效性，加上评价体系唯西方主流期刊为主，一度再次形成了"言必称希腊"的错误倾向。中央及时地提出了"关于加快构建中国特色哲学社会科学的意见"，核心命题就是解决中国主体性和解决中国问题的有效性问题。哲学社会科学贵在求真，贵在求用。求真体现在哲学社会科学的"哲学范式"（学术范式），求用体现在它的"智库范式"。如果我国的哲学社会科学不能发展出自己的"智库范式"，那么，哲学社会科学的"知行合一"问题就没有彻底解决。新型智库建设找到了哲学社会科学从哲学范式到智库范式的创造性转换路径，哲学范式和智库范式都是加快构建中国特色哲学社会科学所不可或缺的。经过五年的新型智库建设，哲学社会学科的智库范式已经具备如下几个特征。

第一、智库范式体现在研以致用的"知行合一"特征。智库是基于事实的独立的公共政策和战略研究机构，公共政策分析追求规范性和实证性的目的是指向政策分析的可操作性。智库不仅重视"知"，强调"真知"和"实知"，而且要在理论和实践之间，要在学术界和实务界（政界、产经界、媒体等）之间承担沟通、创造性转换、双向反馈，使哲学逻辑指导实践逻辑，使实践逻辑刺激哲学逻辑的演化。如果说哲学范式关注的是事物或者现象的理论逻辑，那么智库范式关注的更多是实践逻辑。智库范式的知行合一特征就体现在智库学者能够根据理论界或者自身发现的事物发展的客观规律，根据社会经济基础和上层建筑的实际环境，提出切实可行的政策组合和政策实施路径，从而达改变世界的鹄的。

第二、智库范式还体现在研究的"需求导向性"和"强烈的问题意识"。康德有一句名言："位我上者,灿烂星空;道德律令,在我心中。"对于康德而言,哲学研究从来没有考虑实用,超越和永恒才是他的追求。而智库范式的逻辑起点是"问题意识",智库的研究具有"临床医学"的属性,很多智库研究直接导致政策变革和社会变革。

第三、智库范式体现在咨询与研究并重。现代咨询业兴盛于工商管理领域,主要咨询形式包括公司的战略咨询、风险管理咨询、技术咨询、财务咨询、IT 咨询等。改革开放以来,我国的管理咨询产业也取得了长足的进步,但是面向党委政府的决策咨询工作既无亮眼的理论建树,也无大量的案例积累,究其原因就是因为我国智库建设滞后,传统的决策咨询机构,比如政府内部的政策研究室忙于繁重的日常事务根本无暇也没有专业人员从事决策咨询的案例积累和理论研究。对于大多数智库来说,决策咨询和政策研究同等重要,甚至有时难以区别哪些工作是咨询,哪些工作是研究。一般而言,政策分析和政策研究处于政策过程的前端,政策议程的设置的理论基础、数据基础、必要性分析、政策规划等是政策研究的主要内容。而决策咨询侧重政策实施的可行性分析、实施路径分析、实施方案制定、政策解读等政策路演实务。

第四、智库范式还体现在智库具有强烈的经营意识。哲学范式并不赞成对学术研究过程加以"经营",学术研究的成果形式相对简单,论文和著作是主要的两种形式。学术成果的传播交给学术期刊,学术共同体自身并不可以去"吆喝"自己的研究成果。智库不同于学术机构,它的组织文化更类似现代咨询公司的组织文化,而非大学的组织文化。本质上,大部分智库都是一种特殊类型的咨询公司,智库和咨询公司的形式区别有两条,智库是非营利的,而咨询公司是营利,智库从事的公共政策研究咨询,主要服务对象是政府。因此,许多一流的智库都学习咨询公司的营运模式,比如智库强调自己的机构治理,强调研究产品的设计,强调研究产品的传播,强调研究员的绩效考核等等。

六、中共十九届四中全会为新型智库建设赋予了时代责任和历史机遇

《中共中央关于坚持和完善中国特色社会主义制度 推进国家治理体系和治理能力现代化若干重大问题的决定》从六个方面阐述"坚持和完善党的领导制度体系"，分别是"建立不忘初心、牢记使命的制度""完善坚定维护党中央权威和集中统一领导的各项制度""健全党的全面领导制度""健全为人民执政、靠人民执政各项制度""健全提高党的执政能力和领导水平制度"和"完善全面从严治党制度"。这个六个方面制度的解构性与有机性联系构成了党的领导制度体系。"建立不忘初心、牢记使命的制度"是价值观，是核心理念，是思想领导，是制度性思想，是整个领导制度体系的逻辑起点、历史起点、实践起点，这个思想制度是统领整个党的领导制度体系的，是灵魂与本体所在。"完善坚定维护党中央权威和集中统一领导的各项制度"和"健全党的全面领导制度"是党的领导制度体系主体内容，是马克思列宁主义政党区别与资产阶级政党的根本标志，中国革命的历史和社会主义建设的历史反复证明了，党中央权威、党的全面领导是取得中国革命胜利和社会主义现代化建设成功的关键所在，每一次挫折都和集中统一领导制度遭到侵蚀和破坏有极大的关系。"健全为人民执政、靠人民执政各项制度"阐明了党的领导制度体系的构筑基础，是合法性的来源。"健全提高党的执政能力和领导水平制度"是"坚持和完善党的领导制度体系"主要内容，执政党的执政能力与领导水平决定了党的领导制度体系是不是具有旺盛生命力，是不是具有现代效能，是不是具有坚强领导力的关键。而"完善全面从严治党制度"强调的是党的自我治理，确保党的领导不忘初心、确保党中央权威和集中统一领导、确保党的全面领导制度、确保为人民执政、靠人民执政等各项制度落到实处。

坚持和完善党的领导制度体系的基本途径主要是"科学执政""民主执政"和"依法执政"，民主执政是根本，依法执政是遵循，科学执政是关键。《决定》相关段落从领导方式、决策机制与激励机制三个方面论述了提升党的执政能力和领导水平的内涵。《决定》认为党的领导包括"把方向、谋大局、定政策、促改革"四个方面。《决定》指出：

"健全决策机制，加强重大决策的调查研究、科学论证、风险评估，强化决策执行、评估、监督。"可以清晰地看到，《决定》是从"政策过程"的科学性上来阐述执政能力的内涵。如果从政策科学的视角而言，"把方向、谋大局、定政策、促改革"就是战略管理、议程设置、决策与政策落实。科学执政则是指整个政策过程必须符合规律、符合实际、政策供给合理，实施过程坚强有力，评估监督贯彻全过程，及时反馈，及时进行政策中期调整。

"坚持和完善党的领导制度体系，提高党科学执政、民主执政、依法执政水平"的时代要求为对新型智库建设提出了更高了的要去。"健全决策机制，加强重大决策的调查研究、科学论证、风险评估，强化决策执行、评估、监督。"赋予了新时代中国特色新型智库建设丰富的内容和具体的任务。可以说"四中"全会决定虽然一个字没有提及智库，但是却突出了加强中国特色新型智库建设的战略性、基础性、迫切性和必要性，对新型智库建设的政治性、科学性、政策性、公共性等提出了更高的要求。因此，十九届四中全会以后，中国特色新型智库建设不仅不应该被淡化，而是应该加强，应该以更高的目标和更高的标准，加强内涵发展和内容创新。

新型智库建设是国家治理体系和能力现代化的有机组成部分，科学执行离不开用智库，离不开切实发挥智库的功能。显然，新型智库建设下一步的重点是克服形式主义，是克服新瓶装旧酒路径，是数量建设转向内涵发展，是加强内容创新，是加强决策咨询等智库核心能力建设，是加强制度建设和体系建设。

上　篇

2015 年～2019 年中国特色新型
智库建设专题研究

专题一　国家高端智库与省市重点新型智库建设进展

党的十八大以来，以习近平同志为核心的党中央高度重视新型智库建设，不断从战略高度审视国家智力资源，为我国新型智库建设做出了一系列战略部署和顶层设计。国家高端智库建设作为中国特色新型智库建设的示范工程，已于 2015 年 11 月正式启动，25 家机构成为首批国家高端智库建设试点单位[2018 年 3 月，根据党中央关于深化党和国家机构改革的部署，中央党校和国家行政学院进行整合，组建成新的中央党校（国家行政学院），25 家试点单位变更为 24 家]。按照中央要求，国家高端智库建设试点工作由中宣部牵头，全国哲学社科规划办具体规划，各试点单位牢牢把握直接为中央决策服务这一根本任务，着力加强全局性、战略性、前瞻性问题研究，为党和国家事业发展做出了重要贡献。

与此同时，为响应《关于加强中国特色新型智库建设的意见》中强调的"有条件的地方先行开展高端智库建设试点"，全国各省（自治区、直辖市）参照国家高端智库试点工作，相继出台地方性的新型智库建设实施意见，划分省级重点智库范围，并给予经费资助。各省市逐渐加快智库建设进程，初步形成了以国家高端智库为引领，以省市级重点智库为支撑，以其他专业性智库为补充，布局合理、分工明确的地方智库发展体系，为服务地方决策咨询、实现地方治理体系与治理能力现代化提供智力支持。

一、国家高端智库建设进展

自国家高端智库建设试点工作启动以来，备受瞩目的 24 家国家高端智库试点单位发展迅速，以建设成为"国家亟需、特色鲜明、制度创新、引领发展"的高端智库为目标，不断探索有利于发挥智库咨政建言、理论创新、舆论引导、社会服务、公共外交五大功能的管理体制和运行机制，为服务党中央决策、服务党和国家工作大局发挥了重要作用。经过 4 年多的建设，试点单位在体制机制改革、决策服务、舆论引导、对外交流等方面工作取得了明显进展和成效，为探索中国特色新型智库建设路径积累了丰富经验。

（一）试点任务有序展开，持续推进

1. 政策供给着力体制机制创新

政策支撑是国家高端智库参与决策过程、推进智库体系建设的先决条件。我国智库坚持高起点推进、高标准建设，以体制机制创新为突破口，制定一系列科学合理的政策文件，搭建高端智库建设的基本制度框架，为我国高端智库规范化管理和运行提供基本遵循。2013 年，党的十八届三中全会通过了《中共中央关于全面深化改革若干重大问题的决定》，明确提出"加强中国特色新型智库建设，建立健全决策咨询制度"。这表明中国特色新型智库建设已经被纳入全面深化改革的总体布局当中。2014 年 10 月，习近平总书记在中央全面深化改革领导小组第六次会议上强调，要从推动科学决策、民主决策，推进国家治理体系和治理能力现代化、增强国家软实力的战略高度，把中国特色新型智库建设作为一项重大而紧迫的任务切实抓好。随后，中共中央办公厅、国务院办公厅于 2015 年 1 月印发《关于加强中国特色新型智库建设的意见》（以下简称《意见》），提出实施国家高端智库建设规划，并指出新型智库要深化组织管理体制、研究体制、经费管理制度、成果评价和应用转化机制、国际交流合作机制五方面管理体制改革。《意见》还明确了智库建设的重大意义、基本原则、总体目标和发展格局等，成为我国新型智库建设的首份发展纲要。2015 年 11 月，中央全面深化改革领导小组第十八次会议审议通过了《国家高端智库建设试点工作方案》（以下简称《试点工作方案》），《试点工作方案》从试点智库的入选条件、认定程序，到试点单位运行管理的具体措施，对高端智库试点各项工作予以明确。同时，中宣部研究起草的《国家高端智库管理办法（试行）》（以下简称《管理办法》）和财政部出台的《国家高端智库专项经费管理办法（试行）》，分别对国家高端智库的组织管理方式和经费管理给予制度化安排,国家高端智库建设的蓝图逐渐清晰、明确。国家高端智库建设作为中国特色新型智库建设的示范工程,承担着探索体制机制改革创新的重要任务,为促进智库高质量发展探寻新路、积累经验。

2. 国家高端智库理事会充分发挥决策指导职能

按照中央要求,国家高端智库实行理事会制度,在全国哲学社科规划领导小组下设立国家高端智库理事会。国家高端智库理事会作为国家高端智库建设的议事机构和评估机构,承担着把握战略方向、审议重大决策、指导科研规划、实施监督评估等职责,具体负责审议高端智库建设的发展规划和规章制度,提出国家亟须解决的重点研究任务,并定期开展国家高端智库的综合评估工作。同时,各试点智库也陆续成立国家高端智库理事会,牢记服务中央决策、服务党和国家工作大局的核心使命,定期召集理事会成员进行经验总结和工作部署,在做好理事会统筹规划工作的同时,充分发挥其决策指导职能,加强工作的宏观指导和督促推动,切实把国家要求和部署落到实处。

3. 四类高端智库协同创新发展

2015年12月,国家高端智库试点工作启动会在北京举行,会议公布了25家机构(现变更为24家)入选首批国家高端智库建设试点单位。这24家试点单位涉及经济、科技、法律等7种类型,涵盖公共政策、宏观经济、科技发展、国家治理、国防和军队建设、党的建设等20多个重点研究领域,整体呈现出类型广泛、特色鲜明的结构样貌。

24家入选智库机构共分为以下四类:[①]

第一类是9家党中央、国务院、中央军委直属的综合性研究机构,其中8家属于正部级单位,只有中央编译局属于副部级单位。其中,中国社会科学院(以下简称"中国社科院")是中共中央直接领导、国务院直属的国内哲学社科研究的最高学术机构

---

① 以下24家国家高端智库基本信息均从智库官网发布的资料和官方媒体报道的新闻中获得。

和综合研究中心，中国科学院则是中国科学技术领域的最高咨询与研究机构，军事科学院是中央军委领导下的军事科研核心机构，以上3家机构都在各自领域拥有强有力的话语权。新华社作为国家通讯社，是党和国家话语的"发声筒"，更是拥有庞大全球信息采集分析研判网络和一大批专家型编辑记者的首家高端媒体智库。中央编译局作为党中央直属的理论工作机构，在2018年与中央党史研究室、中央文献研究室进行职能整合，组建中央党史和文献研究院，接续原中央编译局国家高端智库建设试点工作，但对外仍保留中央编译局牌子，承担党的思想理论建设和国家意识形态建设等重要职责。

第二类是依托大学和科研机构的12家专业性智库。12家专业性智库中有6家均来自"双一流"高校，分别为北大、清华、人大、复旦、武大和中山大学。中国社科院的2家直属研究机构入选，可以看出中国社科院前期决策咨询工作备受认可。2家部委直属正厅级单位入选，它们分别依托国家发改委和商务部，主要为中央提供宏观经济、经贸研究等方面的决策研究与咨询服务；中国现代国际关系研究院（以下简称"现代院"）从事综合性国际问题研究，全院15个研究所中有10个属于国别研究所，涉及范围几乎覆盖了世界所有国家和地区，能够为"一带一路"建设、人类命运共同体等议题提供更为系统的决策方案；上海社会科学院（以下简称"上海社科院"）是全国最大的地方社会科学院，它的入选能够有效评估国家战略的地方落实效果，为地方科研机构建设高端智库探寻可行道路。12家专业智库涉及领域广泛，涵盖世情、国情、民情等重点议题，也体现出我国对国际关系、港澳局势、法治建设、社会治理等方面的高度关注。

第三类是依托大型国企的智库，只有中国石油经济技术研究院（以下简称"经研院"）1家。经研院作为中国石油集团的直属科研机构，承担集团公司综合信息开发和发展战略研究的重要决策职能，重点聚焦国家能源安全和战略资源开发研究，以及对未来能源行业发展规律的预研预判，对推进落实国家能源发展战略行动计划发挥了关键性的决策咨询作用。

第四类是 2 家基础较好的社会智库,分别是中国国际经济交流中心(以下简称"国经中心")和综合开发研究院(中国·深圳)(以下简称"综研院")。2 家高端智库虽然属于社会性质的,但都曾为国家重大战略性问题出谋划策。例如:国经中心高质量完成《共建"一带一路":进展、贡献和展望》的基础起草工作,此文件成为第二届"一带一路"国际合作高峰论坛大会官方权威文件。[1] 综研院,又称"中国脑库",是经国务院总理批准成立,在业务上接受国务院研究室指导的独立研究咨询机构。综研院积极承担我国与刚果共同规划实施的黑角经济特区规划任务,对黑角经济特区的产业规划、空间规划、投资可行性研究做出了巨大贡献。

首批入选的四大类 24 家国家高端智库试点单位发展方向各异,这种选择体现了我国对党的建设、国际战略、全球治理、宏观经济、科技创新、区域协调发展、国防建设等领域的高度关注和决策需求,引导高端智库研究与国家和社会发展方向结合起来、与国家重大决策需求结合起来、与决策部门重点工作结合起来,做到供需对接、精准服务。

(二) 创新体制机制,激发智库发展内生动力

1. 治理结构不断优化,为智库发展创造新生长点

智库建设 4 年多以来,各试点单位不断深化治理结构改革,推进体制创新,目前基本建立起由智库理事会决策、学术委员会把关、首席专家领衔负责,以服务决策为导向、以科研人员为中心、以课题项目为纽带的内部治理机制。理事会承担高端智库的组织领导、监督评估和决策指导职能,一般由拥有不同专业背景的政府官员、专家学者、社会活动家组成,为把握智库建设的战略方向提供有力保障。学术委员会负责高端智库学术规划、科研协调和学术审议等各项具体事务,委员会主任一般由首席专家兼任,切实发挥科研指导和学术决策作用。例如:国经中心设立理事长会,并搭建

---

① 国经中心举办"一带一路"系列丛书发布会[EB/OL]. [2019 - 06 - 28]. http://www. cciee. org. cn/Detail. aspx? TId=7&newsId=16761.

了理事长会领导下的中心学术委员会、咨询委员会、基金董事会和执行局的"三会一局"管理架构。

此外，国家高端智库还按照现代智库的管理模式和运行规律对内设部门进行整合，有效统筹资源力量，激发智库内在动力。如中国社科院在原有 11 个机构的基础上，初步构建了以院综合性智库为统领、以 21 家专业化智库为重点、以 30 多家所（院）级研究单位为支撑的"三位一体"智库建设体系。① 中国科学院设立咨询顾问委员会，按照综合管理、学部支撑、科学研究、交流传播和科教融合 5 个板块，构建新型智库组织体系；同时，中国科学院组建的具有独立法人地位的科技战略咨询研究院（以下简称"中科院战略咨询院"），拥有 13 个非法人单元，这些非法人单元既是中科院战略咨询院网络化战略发展的需要，更是中科院战略咨询院创造新生长点的关键。② 中国工程院在院主席团与院常务会的领导下组建了"智库咨询工作委员会"，将其作为全院战略咨询工作的主管单位；成立战略咨询中心，将其作为高端智库建设的核心支撑机构。新华社依托中国经济信息社、瞭望周刊社、新华网思客、参编部、新闻研究所等设立 6 个一级研究中心，并制定"1＋8"基础性文件，初步形成科学合理、层次分明的整体建设方案。③ 北京大学国家发展研究院（以下简称"北大国发院"）建有 11 家研究中心，其中 2 家挂靠教育部，7 家挂靠北大，利用年检制度和退出机制对评估不合格的中心予以整顿甚至撤销。上海社科院设立了全国第一个专门开展智库研究的"智库研究中心"，努力成为"智库的智库"。综研院及时调整部门管理架构，改组成立"智库研究与信息部"和"智库交流与合作部"，加强智库研究与国际合作交流水平。

---

① 中国社会科学院国家高端智库建设工作座谈会在京举行[EB/OL].[2018-05-30].http://www.china.com.cn/opinion/think/2018-05/30/content_51531972.htm.

② 战略咨询院非法人单元情况交流暨发展研讨会召开[EB/OL].[2018-09-07].http://www.cas.cn/yx/201809/t20180907_4663030.shtml.

③ 王斯敏，杨谧，张胜等.让中国智库"领头雁阵"振翅高飞——国家高端智库建设试点工作开展一周年纪实[N].光明日报,2016-12-02.

2. 以制度建设为抓手，为智库长远发展架梁设柱

为了贯彻落实国家层面的智库建设指导意见，各试点单位积极落实科研领域放管服改革，针对经费管理、人事管理、绩效考评、成果激励等方面研制并出台了较为明确、具体的制度规定，逐渐释放制度红利，深化推进决策咨询体制改革。

第一，智库顶层制度设计为高端智库建设指明了发展方向。例如：国务院发展研究中心（以下简称"国研中心"）、中国社科院、中国工程院、中央编译局、中山大学粤港澳发展研究院等智库均制定了《＊＊国家高端智库建设试点工作方案》或《＊＊高端智库管理实施细则》等文件，对智库建设的职能定位、组织架构、职责分工、课题管理、成果管理、奖励评估等做出了明确规定。

第二，智库经费管理制度改革赋予了智库人才更大的科研自主权。例如：中国工程院、中央编译局、北大国发院、国经中心等智库纷纷出台《＊＊高端智库专项经费管理细则》，建立规范的经费监管制度和多元化的经费投入机制，并对各归口管理部门和职能部门的职责分工予以明确。综研院也积极探索新型经费管理办法，加大绩效支出和优秀成果奖励，提升经费使用效率，形成了智力竞相迸发、科研活力四射、高质量成果不断涌现的建设局面。[①]

第三，智库项目管理制度改革促进了项目的规范化管理和高质量成果产出。例如：中央党校（国家行政学院）制定出台了《中央党校（国家行政学院）国家高端智库建设项目组管理办法》，以公益服务为导向，增强科研项目组的灵活性和竞争力。中国宏观经济研究院（以下简称"宏观院"）针对每种课题分别制定管理办法，将纵向课题细分为重大课题、重点课题、应急课题、常规课题、基本科研业务费专项资金课题和战略平台课题等6种，明确了每类课题的立项、验收与结项程序和责任追责要求等。国经中心则制定《中国国际经济交流中心基金课题管理办法》，对基金课题的原则、总体

---

①　郭万达.以体制机制创新激发智库活力[N].光明日报,2019－08－05(016).

目标、管理部门与职责、管理流程、评审程序、成果转化等做出具有可操作性的设计。[①]

第四,智库成果评价激励机制改革激发了科研人员生产高质量成果的积极性。例如:军事科学院专门制定了《军事科学院高端智库决策咨询类科研成果奖励细则(试行)》,明确了智库决策咨询类成果奖励的原则、范围、标准等。北大国发院和经研院分别制定了《＊＊高端智库专项奖励经费管理办法》和《＊＊高端智库成果奖励办法》,明确奖惩机制,建立规范高效、公开透明、监管有力的成果评选与科研业绩激励办法,充分调动科研积极性,鼓励科研人员多出成果、出好成果。

由此可见,当前高端智库制度创新正从组织方式创新向管理方式创新不断推进。下一步制度体系改革应更加重视人员的激励,完善选人用人留人机制,分类推进人才评价机制改革,实现对高质量成果的认可和兑现,激活智力资源。除此之外,高端智库还需对智库建设过程中的信息公开、会议管理、人才发展、政府采购、政策评估、舆论引导、对外交流等方面制定更为具体、更具可操作性的实施细则,切实为高端智库的长远发展搭建内部管理制度框架。

3. 专精尖研究团队基本形成,为攻克难题打牢地基

形成内外兼备、专兼结合的多层次人才梯队。中国科学院统筹院内外资源,组建出由专业化核心研究队伍、客座研究队伍和网络化合作研究队伍构成的人才格局。中国工程院逐渐形成以院士为核心的战略咨询领军队伍、以专家为骨干的咨询研究队伍和专业化战略咨询支撑研究团队,采取"强核心、大协作、开放式"的方式不断培养和造就优秀的战略咨询人才队伍。[②] 中央党校(国家行政学院)按照专职为主、专兼并行的原则,实施"名师工程",全校(院)拥有近400位专职教研人员、高中级领导干部、国家高端智库特约研究员和党校系统科研专家等。军事科学院不断完善首席

---

① 王斯敏,焦德武,张胜等.不负使命、奋发有为 以高端成果服务国家决策——国家高端智库建设经验交流会发言摘登[N].光明日报,2019-07-01.
② 常理.科技强国助圆民族复兴梦[N].经济日报,2018-06-05(013).

专家和特聘首席专家管理办法,目前已初步形成了一支以两院院士、首席专家领衔,国家人才奖励对象为中坚,高水平科研创新团队、科研骨干为支撑的高素质军事科研人才方阵。国防大学则以"名师工作室"为标志,以杰出教授为龙头,以杰出中青年专家、学科学术带头人为中坚力量,以优秀中青年教研骨干、教研人才为基础,合力打造"六大层次"人才培养体系。[①] 商务部国际贸易经济合作研究院(以下简称"商务部研究院")注重海外专家的引进,选聘知名跨国公司总裁为特聘专家充实专家力量,如集保全球总裁彼德·迈凯(Peter Mackie)和雀巢公司全球高级副总裁兼供应链总裁克里斯·泰亚斯(Chris Tyas)等。综研院建立市场化、社会化选人用人机制,大量引进海外留学人员,人才队伍日益完善。

探索中国特色的"旋转门机制"。中国科学院建立特聘研究员制度,积极探索外聘战略咨询项目首席专家、核心专家、客座研究员的"旋转门"机制。[②] 2019 年 9 月,人大国发院特聘 4 位高级研究员和 80 位专聘研究员,其中这 4 位高级研究员均是从中央部委或其他政府部门引进的专家型官员,增进了智库与决策部门之间的联系和沟通,打造中国式"旋转门"。由此看出,高端智库已然开始探索并试行"旋转门机制",尝试通过专家与政府官员的互动交流从而建立稳定、直接的对接机制,但智库与决策部门之间的合作联动还不够,信息共享机制不健全,双方的对接和互动有待进一步深化。

注重多形式培养。中科院战略咨询院自 2017 年开始设立院长青年基金资助项目,2017、2018 年已连续资助 40 余人。北大国发院和复旦大学中国研究院等将智库研究成果纳入绩效考核,还专门为智库研究人员单独开辟研究员职称序列。军事科学院先后携手北京、广州等地共建军民融合协同创新和人才培养平台,还为 40 余名科技领军、学科拔尖人才培养对象聘请院士带教,实现人才共育共用。中国社科院国

---

① 罗金沐. 百望山下听惊雷[N]. 解放军报,2018 - 07 - 19(001).

② 建设专业队伍　发现培养人才　战略咨询院年终专题之六:人才篇[EB/OL]. [2018 - 02 - 10]. http://www.casisd.cn/ttxwl/zlyjytt/201802/t20180210_4946903.html.

家金融与发展实验室对杰出青年学者除了给予奖励外,还会根据需要为其招聘助理研究员,甚至成立专门的研究中心。人大国发院采用筛选机制,对特定人才进行1～2年的孵化培养以检验其咨政建言的能力和水平。综研院建立内部职称制度,以能力和业绩为导向,把成果质量、需求方评价作为考核依据,还为青年人才发展创造条件,如由有能力的年轻人担任课题组组长、鼓励年轻人参与媒体评论、提供海外名校实习机会等。

4. 经费来源多元化,助力智库长效稳定发展

多数国家高端智库除了依托中央财政拨款,还通过创立基金会、完善经费管理制度等方式扩大资金来源,加强自有资金积累,并且注重绩效导向的经费管理,提升经费使用的效率和效益。

第一,创立基金会。国研中心实施"一体多翼两重"的智库外交工作机制,其中中国发展研究基金会是"两重"之一,也是国研中心发起设立的全国性公募基金会,用于支持政策研究和学术交流活动。人大国发院创设国家高端智库研究基金,一部分用于保证本院资金的有效流动,另一部分则以母基金形式,注入运作资金,满足持续性发展需求。中山大学粤港澳发展研究院设立霍英东港澳研究基金,用于博士生创新研究资助计划、高层次人才引进专项资助计划和出国(境)学术访问交流资助计划。上海社科院新成立了"上海社会科学院智库建设基金会",建立长期跟踪研究、持续滚动资助、后端奖励的新型科研资助模式,为高端智库建设提供更加充足的经济保障。综研院设立了综研软科学发展基金会和马洪经济研究发展基金会,前者资助本院自主研究课题并出版著作,后者发挥资源优势为地方经济发展提供智力支持,协力巩固"一体两翼"格局。

第二,以绩效为导向的经费投入机制。北大国发院建立健全高端智库专项奖励经费管理办法,实行经费管理容错机制,专门调整财务管理系统,并通过社会捐赠设立系列学术荣誉称号,如"发树学者""发树讲席教授""木兰青年学者""金光讲席教授"等,专门奖励有突出成果和杰出贡献的科研人员。中国社科院国家全球战略智库基本形成以成果的务实管用为导向、以快速反应和战略应对相结合、以国际视野和国内热点相互动、以专题对策和基础理论相促进的工作格局,实行以课题为导向、"养智不养人"的经费管理模式。① 现代院强调经费要用于奖励真正为国家提供真知灼见的战略成果上,让"板凳甘坐十年冷"的专注研究者获得更多褒奖。

5. 创新科研组织与管理模式,着力提升快速响应能力

推进科研组织方式创新。高端智库普遍采用项目制管理模式整合资源,加强重大专项课题研究的策划组织,开展跨学科、跨单位的联合研究,集聚队伍、集中力量,提高智库研究的科学性,如中央党校(国家行政学院)、中央编译局、人大国发院、综研院等。除此之外,中国社科院积极探索重大科研项目协同研究、重大形势分析集体研判、重大专项问题多角度建言的科研工作机制。中国科学院将学部与实体相结合,发挥学部学术引领功能,建立由规划职能部门、战略研究平台和专业研究机构、科技创新基地战略研究组、研究所战略研究组等共同构成的多层次、系统性、网络型院战略研究体系,形成以任务为引领的矩阵式、网络化研究模式。军事科学院内部开展军事理论人员和军事科技人员"捆绑式"研究,组建融合型科研队伍,积极探索"跨域联合、集中办公、封闭运行、全面保障"的重大任务协同攻关科研组织模式,充分发挥理技融合优势。②

强调层次化、灵活化管理。宏观院实行院、所两级独立管理,横向课题细分为重点课题、应急课题、常规课题等6类,并针对每种课题分别制定管理办法。到目前为止,科研管理领域的管理办法和制度规定已有25项之多。人大国发院打破终身制管理模式,以项目为中心配置人员、经费和其他研究条件,实行"计件薪酬制",就是将研究任务分解为更详细的工件,按完成的质量和数量支付报酬,有效调动研究人员的主动性和积极性。

---

① 中国社会科学院国家全球战略智库.经费花在关键处　科学管理促发展[N].光明日报,2019-07-01(010).
② 董晓巍.优势资源向作战研究倾斜[N].解放军报,2019-05-14(002).

注重成果全过程管理。中国工程院、宏观院等针对重大项目实行前端控制，以召开项目启动会、选题研讨会、月度务虚会的形式对项目质量进行把关。军事科学院坚持课题全流程化的节点管理，强化对科研立项、研究开展、结题上报等关键环节的监督，确保高质量高标准完成智库成果；还注重科研指导，全力做好"选题环节把准方向、研究环节提供组织保障、报送环节精准规划渠道、转化环节提出完善建议"等工作。中国社科院国家金融与发展实验室实行科研例会制度，邀请决策部门、监管当局、金融机构资深从业人员集思广益，借助"外脑"把控成果质量。但是，从整体上看，智库成果的质量管理仍需进一步规范，成果质量控制关卡仍较为松懈，下一步必须明确高端智库成果管理标准，推进重大课题的全流程细化管理，加强关键节点监督，切实提高智库研究水平。

（三）围绕大局服务决策成为高端智库基本共识

1. 职能定位彰显决策价值

首批高端智库试点单位通过整合优势资源，强化决策咨询职能，逐渐探寻到适合自己的发展道路，努力彰显独特的智库价值。中国科学院集科研院所、学部、教育机构于一体，确立了"民主办院、开放兴院、人才强院"的发展战略。中国工程院充分发挥多学科、跨部门的综合优势，持续推进"创新引领、国家倚重、社会信任、国际知名"的国家高端智库建设，努力打造"顶天立地"的高端智库战略格局。[①] 中央党校（国家行政学院）积极发挥"学校、阵地、机构、智库"四位一体作用，确定了建成"党的最高学府、走在前列的党的思想理论高地、在全国处于领先地位的党的社科学术殿堂、党和国家知名的高端智库"四大发展目标。中国社科院国家全球战略智库以对策研究型智库为定位，主攻"一带一路"、全球战略、周边安全研究等科研领域。商务部研究院以政策研究咨询为主攻方向，聚焦商务中心工作，在服务决策、智库外交、舆论引导三

---

① 李晓红. 屹立时代潮头 书写创新华章[N]. 中国科学报，2019 - 06 - 03(001).

驾马车的带动下,积极发挥咨政建言、国际交流和对外发声等方面的智库作用。①

2. 研究领域聚焦决策需求

国家高端智库为避免同质化竞争,不断探索自身科研发力点,总体上都聚焦在重大思想理论研究、重大决策部署研究、重大现实问题研究和重大专题研究等 4 方面内容。通过对中国智库索引(CTTI)收录的国家高端智库政策研究领域进行统计,我们发现:(1)以国研中心、中国社科院、上海社科院、宏观院、人大国发院为代表的高端智库更趋向于宏观经济与产业发展、市场经济与财政政策等领域;(2)以军事科学院和国防大学为代表的军队智库将国防政策、军事政策和安全政策研究作为主攻方向;(3)以现代院、中国社科院国家全球战略智库等智库则关注国际外交、"一带一路"、全球文化、人类命运共同体等领域;(4)以新华社为代表的传媒智库关注互联网管理、公共文化、新闻政策等领域;(5)以中央党校(国家行政学院)和中央编译局为代表的党政部门智库则以党的建设、意识形态研究为主要任务。

从机构个体层面来看,各试点单位研究重点又存在差别。中国科学院以解决重大科技战略和政策问题为导向,实施世界科技前沿研判与中国重大科技突破前瞻研究等三大重点突破任务,以及适应新科技革命与产业革命的科技体制变革研究等五大重点培育任务,支持开展前瞻性、储备性前沿探索任务。宏观院更注重调研,目前已与全国 9 个地方的发改委建立合作,设立国情调研基地,开展地方经济发展、产业经济、能源经济等 10 大领域研究。人大国发院更依托学科优势,注重理论创新,确立了经济治理与经济发展、政治治理与法治建设、社会治理与社会创新、公共外交与国际关系四大研究领域。中央编译局围绕马克思主义理论与当代实践、当代世界社会主义前沿问题等 5 个重点研究领域,专门细化设置了 10 个部门开展分领域智库研究。

---

① 商务部国际贸易经济合作研究院.打造对外话语体系　提升智库国际形象[N].光明日报,2019-07-01(011).

但从总体来看,高端智库仍面临研究站位不高、前瞻性研究不够、专深研究力度不足等问题。有鉴于此,必须牢记高端智库服务中央决策这一中心任务,聚焦关系全局、关系长远的重大问题,想国家当下之所急、谋国家未来之所需,夯实基础研究,着力形成一批有战略远见、有思想深度、可信可靠的研究成果。

3. 积极服务国家重大战略任务

高端智库担负着为中央提供决策服务的根本任务,必须紧紧围绕国家重大战略、重大任务、重大工作,深入开展前瞻性、针对性、储备性政策研究。4 年来,各试点单位围绕"十三五"规划、"一带一路"建设、国家安全等重大议题,推出了大量有思想深度、有实际价值的成果,为中央决策做出不少贡献。

踊跃参与"十三五"规划重大课题。"十三五"规划开局之年恰逢国家高端智库试点工作正式启动。中央为了集聚智库专家智力、广泛征集规划意见,特委托 42 家机构协助完成"十三五"规划任务,并最终完成了 31 项"十三五"规划重大课题项目和 117 份专题研究报告,其中就包括国研中心、中国社科院、中国科学院、北大国发院等高端智库试点单位。[①] 例如:国研中心 2015 年承担的 17 项中央交办的研究课题中,就有 10 项是关于"十三五"规划的重大课题。[②] 2016 年 3 月,来自北大国发院、上海社科院、中国社科院国家金融与发展实验室、国防大学的 4 位国家高端智库首席专家围绕政府工作报告、"十三五"规划纲要草案等文件进行讨论,积极发表看法、建言献策。

协同助力"一带一路"建设。国研中心发起成立的"丝路国际论坛"和"丝路国际智库网络"是在全球范围内构建"一带一路"智库合作网络的较早尝试。复旦大学中国研究院成立数字一带一路研究中心(DBRC),从新技术新产业的视角研究"一带一路"。中国科学院自 2013 年以来率先打造"人才、平台、项目"相结合的"一带一路"科

①　王斯敏.让中国智库"领头雁阵"振翅高飞[N].光明日报,2016 - 12 - 02(001).
②　李伟.以改革创新为动力　深入推进国家高端智库建设[N].光明日报,2015 - 12 - 03(016).

技合作体系,实施"发展中国家科教合作拓展工程"和"一带一路"科技合作行动计划,发起倡议并联合40多个国家和地区的科教机构和相关国际组织成立了"一带一路"国际科学组织联盟(ANSO)。[①] 中国工程院与"一带一路"沿线32个国家建立合作关系,构建了"一带一路"国际工程科技合作基本框架,并聚集院内百余位院士开展研究。上海社科院通过创办丝路信息网、"一带一路"上海论坛、"一带一路"研究英文刊物、"一带一路"大数据库等,更好地服务"一带一路"建设。国经中心在"一带一路"建设历程中的决策贡献更为突出,受国家发改委委托完成"孟中印缅""中老""中缅"经济走廊等重大交办任务,中心多位领导直接参与了"一带一路"课题工作;同时,国经中心还编撰并发布了"一带一路"系列丛书,为推进"一带一路"走深走实、实现高质量发展贡献力量。

军队理技融合的"二次创新"。军事科学院重新调整了关于战争与作战问题研究、条令法规编修等方向的重点科研任务,缩减了偏离主业的研究课题,增设了关于战争形态、作战样式等军队实战课题,还提出了"一园多点"协同创新的总体布局,初步构建出军事科研大联合、大开放、大协作的工作局面。[②] 国防大学着力打造国家安全高端战略智库,搭建了国家安全工程实验室、中国国家安全问题研究中心、军民融合深度发展研究中心等平台,围绕党、国家和军队重大战略需求展开课题研究、战略研判、人才培训和国际交流工作。

4. 嵌入政策过程直接服务国家高端决策

根据《试点工作方案》要求,国家高端智库试点单位可通过由全国哲学社科规划办主办的《国家高端智库报告》内刊将智库成果直报中央,借助直通渠道嵌入政策过程。同时,允许并鼓励各试点单位通过自有渠道将重要成果报送至相关部门。例如:上海社科院设立了《新智库专报》《国际问题专报》《舆情信息》三种专报,为中央和上

---

① 吴月辉.集科技之优势　造福一带一路[N].人民日报,2017 - 05 - 10(002).
② 新华社解放军分社.建设高水平军事科研机构[EB/OL].[2019 - 05 - 23].http://mil.gmw.cn/2019 - 05/23/content_32858037.htm.

海市委市政府领导提供更全面的决策参考。中科院战略咨询院还创办了《科技智库报告》《科技决策参考》《科技前沿动态》三大内刊和《科技前沿快报》《科技政策与咨询快报》两大快报以支撑决策服务。中山大学粤港澳发展研究院通过《粤港澳研究专报》《港澳社情舆情动态》《粤港澳研究观点摘报》《全球湾区动态》等内参报送成果。

除报送内参之外，高端智库还通过参与文件起草、参加内部座谈会、建立合作平台、人员借调交流等方式嵌入政策过程，为中央决策提供智力支撑。例如：中国科学院与国务院研究室依托中科院战略咨询院共建中国创新战略和政策研究中心，依托国务院研究室成果利用转化渠道和中科院战略咨询院综合研究集成平台，针对国家创新战略和宏观政策提供更多前瞻性、建设性的咨询建议。① 中山大学粤港澳发展研究院邀请具有丰富决策咨询经验、社会知名度高的退休或离职政府官员进入理事会，设立专门负责对接联络事务的行政副院长，还不定期邀请相关部门官员开展讲座活动，院内智库专家主动走进决策部门提供咨询建议、参与方案编制、合办专家座谈会等，选派青年学者到决策部门开展短期借调工作，到港澳工作部门短期参与专题研究等。②

（四）多元主体强劲发声，舆论引导有理有力

1. 品牌矩阵逐步成型

打造独特的智库产品体系逐渐成为国家高端智库标新立异、提升智库社会影响力的关键推动力。当前，各试点单位不断整合优势资源，通过举办学术论坛、创办精品书刊、编撰系列皮书、搭建特色平台等形式，促进优秀成果的发布与转化，着力打造独具特色的智库品牌矩阵。

第一，主办/承办国家级重大学术论坛。如国研中心自 2000 年以来，多次主办

① 科技战略咨询研究院.高端人才政策座谈会在战略咨询院举行[EB/OL].［2017－12－01］.http://www.bjb.cas.cn/gzjz/201712/t20171201_4905547.html.
② 中山大学粤港澳发展研究院.加强供需对接　提升研究实效性[N].光明日报,2019－07－01(011).

"中国发展高层论坛"这一国家级大型国际论坛,该论坛也是我国政府领导、中外商界领袖、专家学者之间进行高层对话与研讨的重要平台。① 国经中心从 2009 年开始,已经连续举办五届"全球智库峰会",围绕全球治理、经济全球化、"一带一路"建设等议题进行深入交流。中国科学院定期举办"战略与决策高层论坛"和高端智库建设品牌活动"国家高端科技智库大讲堂",初步形成由学部学术年会、科学与技术前沿论坛、小型高端论坛、各学部学术论坛等组成的多层次高水平学术交流体系。中国工程院自 2013 年以来,每年定期在深圳召开"战略性新兴产业培育与发展论坛",并发布年度《中国战略性新兴产业发展报告》,在全行业引发热烈反响。北大国发院举办了"中国经济观察报告会""格政"和"国家发展论坛"三个智库品牌活动,牵头组织"中美经济对话"和"中美卫生对话"等活动,并于 2018 年开始举办"国家发展青年论坛",为青年智库人才提供交流平台。宏观院形成了国宏宏观经济论坛、国宏大讲堂、国宏学术茶座等系列学术品牌,有力推动中国特色宏观经济理论创新。

第二,创办精品书刊和专题皮书。如中国工程院创办 *Engineering* 和《中国工程科学》两种工程综合类学术期刊,其中《中国工程科学》是中国工程院国家高端智库成果的重要展示窗口。宏观院创办了《宏观经济研究》《中国能源》《经济管理文摘》等 6 大学术期刊,并以学术丛书、年度文集和年度报告的形式展示智库成果。北大国发院设有《经济学》(季刊)和 *China Economic Journal* 两大刊物,为我国经济学科发展搭建海内外成果展示与交流平台。综研院创办《国家高端智库观察:中国经济月报》和英文研究动态 *CDI Newsletter* 两份专刊,将其报送至国内相关政府部门、重点智库、国际智库和跨国企业,还以年报、综研丛书、综研快参、开放导报、综研报告等形式发布一批公开出版物,海内外影响力大幅度提升。

第三,举办特色活动、搭建指数平台。综研院开办了"银湖沙龙"和"CDI 资本沙

---

① 360 百科.中国发展高层论坛[EB/OL].[2019-03-21].https://baike.so.com/doc/6721689-6935742.html.

龙"活动,其中"CDI资本沙龙"是依托国家高端智库,为行业专家、投资者、企业家等搭建的一个高端、专业、小众、封闭的交流平台;还与英国 Z/Yen 集团联合编制"全球金融中心指数",适时发布《中国金融中心指数(CDI CFCI)报告》。除此之外,北大国发院还搭建了"中国投资者情绪指数""中国消费者信心指数""中国创新创业区域指数"等一系列指数平台,以指数报告的形式展现中国经济发展态势。

2. 智库专家积极作为

越来越多的高端智库在国际重要场合亮相发声,阐述中国观点、提出中国主张,这已然成为我国公共外交中一种不可或缺的力量,中国智库的国际影响力和知名度也不断提升。例如:2018年4月4日,美国政府公布了对我国输美的1333项、价值约500亿美元的产品加征关税清单。次日上午,来自发改委的国经中心和宏观院专家便围绕中美经贸关系展开讨论,纷纷发表自己的观点。[①] 此外,国经中心举行中美经贸关系高端研讨会,国经中心理事长曾培炎针对中美经贸问题进行客观理性分析,以强硬的语气回击错误观点。综研院院长樊纲专门接受央视英语频道专访,解读 G20 杭州峰会各项议题,还多次接受彭博电视采访,分析人民币汇率以及资本管制相关问题,并在"博鳌亚洲论坛""伦敦阿斯班世界经济年会""伦敦北京大学120周年校庆海外典礼"等会议及主流媒体上发表观点。[②] 商务部研究院实行主动发声、借力发声、合作发声"三位一体"的外宣模式,组建由政商学媒界专业人士组成的特聘专家委员会,增强对外话语体系的有效性和针对性。[③] 国经中心以中美、中欧、中日、中韩系列"二轨"对话为载体,积极应对复杂多变的国际经贸形势,坚定维护国家利益,努力发出中国声音。

① 中国国际经济交流中心.国家发改委两大高端智库讨论中美经贸关系[N].中国改革报,2018-04-05.
② 刘艺婷,张蔚.2016年年报[M].中国(深圳)综合开发研究院:2016.
③ 商务部国际贸易经济合作研究院.打造对外话语体系 提升智库国际形象[N].光明日报,2019-07-01(011).

3. 传播形式愈加丰富

建设 4 年多来,国家高端智库借助报刊、网站、微信公众号等媒体平台,广泛宣传智库重要成果和有突出贡献的智库专家,不断提升智库影响力和公信力。瞭望智库作为新华社国家高端智库的公共政策研究中心,目前已逐渐构建出以公共政策研究团队及系列政策研究委员会为研究基础,以《瞭望研报》等研究型内参为内核,以"智库客户端集群"为新兴传播和交互矩阵的新型智库传播模式。① 宏观院开设"国宏高端智库"微信公众号,完成了内网网站、外网中文网站和外网英文网站的"三网"建设。复旦大学中国研究院提出"三个平台发力",分别是举办"思想者论坛"线下活动、搭建"观察者网"线上平台和创建"观视频"思想短视频品牌,三大平台协同作战,构建"'互联网+'+智库"模式。上海社科院成立科研成果传播办公室,开办院网、院报和院微信公众号,开设专栏、定制频道,充分发挥传统媒体和新兴媒体的融合优势,形成了极具影响力的"四位一体"传播网络。综研院利用新媒体开设"综研国策""综研观察""澎湃问政"三大评论专栏,呼吁公众参与,以扩大社会影响力和公共传播力。

二、省市重点新型智库建设进展

为深入贯彻落实中办、国办印发的《意见》,在国家高端智库的带动引领下,各省(自治区、直辖市)不断探索适应地方智库发展规律的改革良策,尝试培育和发展一批省级重点新型智库和行业性智库,逐渐形成结构合理、功能齐全的省级重点智库方阵。

(一)智库管理制度逐步完善

1. 新型智库建设基础文件陆续出台

中办、国办《意见》下发后,各省(自治区、直辖市)结合地方特点,纷纷制定了地方

---

① 梁现瑞,李欣忆等.四川与 5 家高端智库达成战略合作[EB/OL].[2019 - 10 - 27]. https://sichuan. scol. com. cn/ggxw/201910/57368365. html.

新型智库建设指导意见，为省重点智库建设提供了基本遵循。据统计（截至 2019 年 12 月），目前约有 30 个省（自治区、直辖市）先后出台了新型智库建设意见，发布时间大多集中在 2015～2017 年这三年，智库管理工作主要由省委宣传部或决咨委（办）负责。例如：江苏省出台的《关于加强江苏新型智库建设的实施意见》指出，"到 2020 年，重点建设一批支撑国家和区域发展的专业化高端智库"。江苏省作为全国率先出台地方性新型智库建设基础文件的省份之一，反应早、起步快、强度大，为全国其他省市加快推进新型智库建设做出表率。河南省出台的《关于加强中原智库建设的实施意见》提出，"到 2020 年，争取 2～3 个智库进入国家专业化高端智库行列，打造 5～8 个在中西部乃至全国有影响的专业智库"，目标明确，态度坚定。

　　随着地方新型智库建设意见的陆续出台，部分地区也开始提出建设省级重点智库的目标，针对省级重点智库的建设方案和管理办法也随之发布，如江苏、黑龙江、云南、山东等。江苏省制定《江苏省新型智库建设与管理暂行办法》，从管理机制、课题与项目、人员与经费、考核激励等方面做出具体规定，为全省智库规范化管理和运行提供指导。湖北省委宣传部于 2016 年 6 月 3 日发布《湖北省新型智库建设方案》，依托武汉大学、华中科技大学、省社科院、省委党校等 10 家单位组建的十大重点新型智库入选。湖南省委办公厅、湖南省政府办公厅于 2015 年 7 月 14 日联合印发《关于加强湖南新型智库建设的实施意见》，指出"建设一批在全省乃至全国具有一定影响力的省级重点智库"，并于同年 9 月，湖南省委宣传部印发了《湖南省省级重点智库管理办法》。除此之外，安徽省出台的《安徽省重点智库管理办法（试行）》、北京市出台的《首都高端智库试点单位建设管理办法》等政策文件均对地方重点智库的职责、任务、成果报送、经费管理、考核与评估等内容做出明确规定。

　　2. 行业性智库政策文件步步跟进

　　中办、国办印发的《意见》中提出，统筹推进党政部门、社科院、党校行政学院、高校、军队、科研院所和企业、社会智库协调发展，形成定位明晰、特色鲜明、规模适度、布局合理的中国特色新型智库体系。在国家层面，教育部印发的《中国特色新型高校智库建设推进计划》,中宣部、民政部等 9 部门联合印发的《关于社会智库健康发展的若干意见》以及中国科协印发的《中国科协关于建设高水平科技创新智库的意见》等行业性智库政策文件已陆续出台。地方政府也紧跟国家步伐,相继制定针对高校智库、科技创新智库、社会智库和党校智库等行业性智库的重点培育建设方案。例如:辽宁省教育厅印发《辽宁省高等学校新型智库建设实施方案(试行)》,并于 2019 年 1 月公布了 20 家首批辽宁省高等学校新型智库名单。2018 年,陕西省教育厅印发《陕西高校新型智库管理办法》,随后经高校遴选推荐、教育厅形式审查,认定 2018 年度陕西高校新型智库 22 家。2018 年 4 月,由云南省科技厅研究起草的《云南科技创新智库建设和运行管理办法(试行)》正式实施,对 24 家云南科技创新智库进行重点培育。同时,云南省教育厅出台《云南高校新型智库建设实施方案(试行)》,并于 2014 年下半年确定 14 家智库获立项建设、3 家智库获培育建设,建设期内获得省财政给予的 80~100 万的建设经费支持。

3. 智库配套政策文件加速制定

为进一步提高省级重点智库的内部治理水平,各省份还制定出台了一系列专项管理办法与实施细则,主要涉及专项资金管理、专家队伍建设、考核与评估等,为重点智库的规范管理与营运起到了专业指导和监督作用。

一是新型智库专项经费管理政策。智库经费的合理使用影响着新型智库规范化运营与管理成效,在财政部出台的《国家高端智库专项经费管理办法(试行)》的总体指导下,北京、黑龙江、江苏、安徽、宁夏等地陆续出台了适应本地发展的专项经费管理办法,明确了专项资金的资助额度、开支范围、预算管理和使用监督等具体内容。除此之外,广西、湖北、重庆、河北等地还设立了决策咨询成果奖,评奖范围更侧重应用对策研究。

二是新型智库专家队伍建设政策。人才队伍是智库建设的核心竞争力。为了进一步加强省级重点智库人才队伍的建设与管理,充分发挥智库专家的决策主力作用,部分省(自治区、直辖市)制定了人才资助计划或管理办法,如山东省制定《关于加快智库高端人才队伍建设的实施意见》，黑龙江省教育厅制定《"龙江学者支持计划"管理办法》，河南省出台《"中原学者"管理办法》等，明确了智库专家的聘任条件及范围、工作职责、奖励机制、成果考评等具体要求。

三是新型智库考核评估政策。为了有效监督和评价省级重点智库建设成效，各省市制定智库评估工作方案，完善了监督考核机制，包括详细的考核评估指标体系、重点智库名单动态调整和后备智库制度等。例如：在浙江省政协第221号重点提案办理工作座谈会上，审议通过《浙江省新型智库评估指标体系》，逐渐形成了浙江省智库工作大框架。2016年12月，江苏省出台《江苏省新型智库管理与考核评估试行办法》，明确由江苏省智库建设办公室负责智库考核工作，实行"重点高端智库5年一考核、重点培育智库3年一考核"的动态考核机制，并进一步明确了智库考核评价指标和具体的实施细则。

总体上，我国的智库政策环境正在日益得到改善，但各省市的政策落实情况不一，推进改革的做法和力度也不尽相同，存在政策落实"最后一公里"的现象。从政策制定层面来看，仍有部分地区受社会经济发展水平、智库建设基础、思想认识等条件的限制，尚未落实重点智库的建设规划工作，部分地区针对省级重点智库专门的配套政策和保障措施还未得到完善，重点智库的准入条件、建设标准、经费管理、评估方法、淘汰机制还未专门制定管理方法加以明确。从政策实施层面来看，地方部门往往因邻里交流不足、上下沟通不畅造成政策难以落地。因此，智库建设不应流于形式，更应该聚焦内容创新与质量提升，充分借助制度优势，深化体制机制改革，为国家重大战略和地方经济发展提供更好的决策支持。

（二）智库治理机制发挥实效

1. 省级智库理事会着力抓好规划协调工作

地方性的智库理事会作为省级重点智库的统筹管理部门，一般由各省智库管理部门牵头组建，负责广泛联系省内智库，开展政策协调、工作推进、战略规划、考核评估等协调指导与管理服务工作。据不完全统计，全国约有14个省一级政府设立新型

智库建设的统筹管理部门,其中有 6 家成立省级新型智库理事会,例如:2017 年,由
江苏省委宣传部牵头组建的新型智库理事会是指导全省新型智库建设的议事机构和
评估机构,理事包括省委省政府各部门成员与江苏省 9 家重点高端智库和 15 家重点
培育智库负责人。① 2018 年,北京市成立首都高端智库理事会,制定了《首都高端智
库理事会议事规则》,同时北京大学、中共北京市委党校(北京行政学院)、中国人民大
学首都发展与战略研究院等首都高端智库建设试点单位也均已成立理事会。河北省
成立河北省哲学社会科学工作(新型智库建设)领导小组和新型智库理事会,其中领
导小组负责统筹协调处理有关河北哲学社会科学发展的重大问题,而智库理事会以
议事决策为主要职能,统筹协调全省社科力量,借智借力服务好河北智库建设。

　　由此看出,省级智库理事会等智库主管部门相继成立,在智库发展规划、决策指
导、考核评估等方面充分发挥作用。接下来,包括智库理事会在内的省级智库主管部
门更应强化供需联络与渠道对接,建立健全面向决策部门的课题认领制度,以出成果
为第一目的,指导监督智库研究团队的选拔、管理和考核工作,协助智库以高质量成
果咨政辅政。此外,智库主管部门在保证省内智库整体协调发展的基础上,更应加强
指导和管理的针对性,着力形成一批结构合理、特色鲜明的智库建设后备梯队。

　　2. 重点智库报送渠道更加稳定畅通

　　省级重点智库除了编撰著作、发布研究报告、内部座谈讨论、媒体采访等方式建
言献策以外,还会将成果以特定渠道定期或不定期地编发给省委研究室、省政府研究
室、省委宣传部等政府部门。报送渠道一般包括:一是智库管理部门指定的内参,如
首都高端智库理事会秘书处(社科联)主办的内刊《首都高端智库报告》、江苏省委宣
传部智库办专门面向省重点高端和培育智库编印的《智库专报》、辽宁省委省政府咨
询委员会和辽宁省委政策研究室主办的《咨询文摘》、四川新型智库领导小组办公室

---

① 江苏智库网.关于成立江苏省新型智库理事会的通知[EB/OL].[2017 - 05 - 09]. http://
www.jsthinktank.com/tongzhigonggao/201705/t20170509_4064465.shtml.

《智库成果专报》等；二是省级重点智库专有内部刊物，以江苏省为例，省社科联依托
39家决策咨询研究基地和全省社科界知名专家编辑的《决策参阅》、省社科院编发报
送的《决策咨询专报》、省委党校（省行政学院）编发的《研究报告》以及长江产业经济
研究院编发的《长江产经决策咨询报告》等。由此看出，各省级重点智库依托指定内
参和自创内刊，能够更为规范、有序、直接地进行成果报送，智库主动服务中央和地方
决策的职能得到有效发挥。

此外，省级重点智库除采用传统内参报送的方式嵌入政策过程以外，更应拓展新
的服务决策渠道，积极承接决策部门委托、交办的科研任务，积极开展文件起草、讲学
培训、舆情调研、国际交流等工作，使智库研究全方位融入决策、服务决策。

（三）省级重点智库发展思路更加清晰

1. 智库培育模式各具特色

政策试点是中国特色的政策实施举措，是落实国家战略和政策思想的有效途
径。[①] 习近平总书记在全面深化改革领导小组第三十五次会议上针对推动改革试点
工作提出了明确要求，强调"坚持试点先行，分类分层推进""搞好制度设计，有针对性
地布局试点"。这表明抓好试点是改革破局、创新开路的关键一招，对改革全局意义
重大。据初步统计（截至2019年12月），全国共有21个省（自治区、直辖市）先后开
展重点新型智库试点培育工作，由省哲学社会科学规划办公室、省委宣传部、省决策
咨询委员会、省社科联等单位统筹指导，建设周期3～5年，资助金额在10～100万/
家不等（见表1.1）。

地方治理现代化的多层治理结构要求不同类型、不同层级智库的参与，从纵向上
看，省级重点智库体系可分为两种模式：一是单一的"重点/培育"模式。这种模式是
全国大多数地区的智库培育模式，典型代表有辽宁、黑龙江、广东、宁夏等；二是"重点
-培育"模式。江苏、安徽等地按照"先培育、后遴选"的思路，选择一批中央和地方决

---

① 陈振明，黄元灿.推进地方新型智库建设的思考[J].中国行政管理，2017(11):43-49.

策急需、基础较好的专业智库作为培育单位加以扶持，从而形成结构合理、优势集聚的省级重点智库建设梯队。根据各省（自治区、直辖市）官方公布的重点智库名单，结合中国智库索引数据库（CTTI），发现高校智库占比最高，其次是党政部门智库、社科院智库等官方智库，这种布局与各地普遍形成的高校智库为基础、政府智库为主导的新型智库发展格局基本吻合。①

表 1.1　省级重点智库实体建设情况

省份	重点智库名称	主管/指导单位①	数量②
北京	首批首都高端智库建设试点单位	首都高端智库理事会	14
黑龙江	黑龙江省重点培育智库（共两批）	黑龙江省委宣传部	20+6
吉林	吉林省级新型智库建设试点单位	吉林省委宣传部	8
辽宁	辽宁省首批省级重点新型智库	辽宁省委省政府决策咨询委员会	27
江苏	江苏省重点高端智库	江苏省宣传部牵头，江苏省哲学社会科学规划办公室指导	10
江苏	江苏省重点培育智库		16
山东	首批重点新型智库建设试点单位	山东省哲学科学规划办公室	15
安徽	安徽省重点智库	安徽省委宣传部	10
安徽	安徽省重点培育智库		5
河北	河北省首批新型智库试点单位	河北省哲学科学规划办公室	9
河北	河北省新型智库重点培育单位		5
湖北	湖北省十大新型智库	湖北省委宣传部	10
湖北	湖北省十大改革智库	湖北省委政策研究室（省改革办）	10
湖南	湖南省首批省级重点智库建设单位	湖南省委宣传部	7
湖南	湖南省专业特色智库		26
江西	首批省级重点智库建设单位	江西省委宣传部	17
广西	广西特色新型智库联盟重点智库	广西壮族自治区决策咨询委员会	22
重庆	重庆市综合高端智库建设试点单位	重庆市委宣传部	6

---

①　陈振明，黄元灿.推进地方新型智库建设的思考[J].中国行政管理，2017(11)：43-49.

续表

省份	重点智库名称	主管/指导单位	数量
四川	四川首批新型智库	四川省委宣传部	22
浙江	浙江省高端智库建设试点单位	浙江省委宣传部牵头，浙江省新型智库工作联席会议统筹指导，浙江省社科联设秘书处	5
	浙江省新型重点专业智库		13
	浙江省重点培育智库		8
云南	云南省首批重点培育新型智库	云南省委宣传部	30
青海	青海省级重点智库	青海省委宣传部	5
宁夏	第一批自治区级重点培育智库	宁夏回族自治区党委宣传部	3
广东	广东省重点智库	广东省委宣传部	15
贵州	贵州省首批新型特色智库	贵州省委宣传部	4
内蒙古	内蒙古自治区首批高端智库试点单位	内蒙古自治区党委宣传部	6

注：① 表中"主管/指导单位"根据《管理办法》印发单位、重点智库名单发布单位、重点智库遴选工作负责单位等发挥统筹协调作用的管理部门进行确定，具体以真实情况为准。

② 由于各省区市重点智库建设名单对外公布程度不同，表中"数量"属于不完全统计，且不考虑智库名单中存在重复的情况，准确数据以官方公布名单为准。

2. 智库发展体系逐渐形成

面对纷繁复杂的国际国内形势，智库所承担的决策任务也是高度综合的，绝不是任何单一学科或机构可以单独完成的，需要不同类型、不同层次的智库参与其中。在这样的背景下，多层次、多元化智库发展体系的建设至关重要。当前，新型智库体系构建面临前置动力不足、智库主体发展不平衡、智库研究动力和合力不够、成果对接机制不畅等困境，[①]各省市加快顶层设计和整体谋划，对重点新型智库进行分层分类建设，逐渐形成符合地方智库运行规律的发展体系。

从总体格局来看，部分省市已初步构建出以国家高端智库为引领，以省级重点智库为支撑，以高校智库、科技创新智库、社会智库等行业性智库为补充的省级智库发

---

① 刘德海.新型智库体系的内涵特征与建构思路[J].智库理论与实践,2017,2(04):2-8.

展新格局。例如:江苏省已搭建起"10 家重点高端智库＋16 家重点培育智库＋50 家决策咨询类研究基地"的战略布局,基本形成了研究特色显著、研究领域多元、综合型与专业型智库共同发展的总体格局。湖南省提出,到 2020 年,初步形成一个以省级重点智库为主导,以高校智库、科技创新智库、企业智库、社会智库为补充的新型智库体系。① 广西壮族自治区构建出以决策咨询委员会为统筹、智库联盟为协调、六类智库建设为主体、四种服务平台为支撑的"1＋1＋6＋4"特色新型智库体系。

为统筹推进全省各类智库协调发展,各省(自治区、直辖市)分批遴选中央决策急需、关系发展全局的行业性智库作为专项培育单位加以扶持。以高校智库、科技创新智库和社会智库为例,据不完全统计(截至 2019 年 12 月),全国共有 13 个省(自治区、直辖市)明确发布省级高校新型智库建设名单,7 个省(自治区、直辖市)公布省级科技创新智库或研究基地的重点建设名单,着力打造深度融合的专业智库工作格局,扎实开展决策咨询和建言献策活动,为党委政府和地方经济发展提供高效服务。

一是省级重点高校智库建设。省教育厅或省教委作为省级重点高校智库的归口管理部门,负责省级重点高校智库的评选、认定和指导工作。从表 1.2 可看出,云南、辽宁、甘肃等省份已公开发布首批省高校新型智库重点培育名单。例如:上海市依托地方高校智库同城协同机制,构建出"内环—中环—外环"的上海高校智库网络,内环是由上海市教卫工作党委、上海市教委专项资助的 30 家上海高校智库,中环是上海高校智库内涵建设计划入选机构(培育型智库),外环是其他活跃智库机构。② 浙江省自 2016 年启动了高校新型智库建设工程,至今已确定 2016 年度首批 15 家和2018 年度第二批 13 家高校智库,逐步形成特色鲜明、布局合理、彰显浙江特色的省内高校系统新型智库体系。

---

① 湖南省人民政府门户网站.关于加强湖南新型智库建设的实施意见[EB/OL].[2015 - 07 - 30].http://www. hunan. gov. cn/hnyw/zwdt/201507/t20150730_4755791. html.

② 沈国麟.同城协同:上海高校智库建设实践探索[J].社会科学文摘,2018(10):119 - 120.

表 1.2　省级重点高校智库实体建设情况

省份	省级重点高校智库名称	数量
浙江	浙江省新型高校智库（共两批）	15＋13
吉林	吉林特色新型高校智库立项建设单位（2015、2016 年两批）	22(2015) 18(2016)
	吉林特色新型高校智库立项培育单位（2015、2016 年两批）	9(2015) 7(2016)
江苏	江苏高校人文社会科学校外研究基地	20
	江苏高校人文社会科学校外研究基地培育点	15
云南	云南高校新型立项建设智库	14
	云南高校新型立项培育智库	3
陕西	陕西高校新型智库	22
安徽	安徽省教育厅高校智库	16
辽宁	辽宁省高等学校新型智库	20
宁夏	宁夏自治新型高校智库	8
甘肃	甘肃省高校精准扶贫智库	5
	甘肃省高校新型智库（人文社会科学）	20
上海	上海高校智库	30
天津	天津市高校智库（共两批）	12＋8
江西	江西省高校重点基地	53
福建	福建省高校特色新型智库（共三批）	9＋15＋20

注：表中"数量"属于不完全统计，且不考虑智库名单中存在重复的情况（如吉林），准确数据以官方公布名单为准。

二是省级重点科技创新智库建设。为落实中央和省委决策部署，结合中国科协相关要求，省科技厅或省科协联合省级学会、系统科协、高校科协、企业科协等，建设一批高水平科技创新智库或研究基地（见表 1.3）。例如：2017 年 5 月，山东省科协印发的《山东省科协关于建设高水平科技创新智库的实施意见》指出，到 2020 年计划建成以山东省创新战略研究院为"小中心"，以所属省级学会、市级科协科技创新智库和战略合作的高等院校、科研单位等为创新战略研究基地的"大外围"科技创新智库体系。2017年9月,陕西省科技厅印发《陕西科技智库体系建设方案》,提出"平台＋基地＋中心"的智库体系建设方案,建立以陕西省科学技术情报研究院为依托单位,以11家陕西省软科学研究基地为支撑的陕西科技智库体系。[①] 吉林省科协自2018年扎实推进省科协科技智库智汇工程建设,已基本构建出由20家基地组成的省科协决策咨询服务体系。

表1.3　省级重点科技创新智库实体建设情况

省份	省级重点科技创新智库名称	数量
江苏	江苏省科协科技创新智库基地(共三批)	13＋18＋10
云南	首批云南科技创新智库	24
吉林	吉林省科技创新智库基地(共两批)	12＋8
陕西	陕西省软科学研究基地	11
黑龙江	省科协科技创新智库研究基地	16
广西	广西壮族自治区科技智库	5
重庆	市新型科技智库建设试点单位	19

三是省级重点社会智库建设。从总体上来看,当前全国各省(自治区、直辖市)的社会智库建设还处于探索和起步阶段,社会智库数量少、规模小。但部分省(自治区、直辖市)已开始重视社会智库建设,将社会智库健康发展纳入新型智库发展体系之中。例如:2018年3月,江苏省民政厅等9部门联合下发《关于江苏社会智库健康发展的实施意见》,进一步细化全省社会智库发展的任务要求和工作举措。同时,江苏省对社会智库实行与社科类社会组织相同的"双重管理体制",即由民政部门和业务主管单位双重负责、双重管理。山东省民政厅起草制定了《关于促进社会智库健康发展的实施意见(征求意见稿)》,于2019年开展省级重点社会智库建设试点工作,计划

---

① 侯燕妮.我省将建设科技智库体系[N].陕西日报,2017-09-14(002).

到 2020 年培育发展 10 个左右的省级重点社会智库。因此,地方政府应加大社会智库政策倾斜力度,大力扶持一些基础较好的社会智库,为民间智库力量深度嵌入社会治理体系提供更好的外部条件。

3. 省域智库联盟初显规模

省域智库联盟是依托省委省政府、省重点高校、党政部门、企业等单位,通过共建平台、共享资源、协作研究,共同发起成立的智库联合体,旨在协调整合各联盟成员的优势资源,促进政产研学媒协同发展、智政良性互动,典型代表有湖南、山东、黑龙江、广西等。例如:经山西省民政厅批准,国内第一家省级智库行业协会——山西省智库发展协会(三晋智库联盟)成立,由山西社科院主管,汇集全省高校、科研机构、国有企业和各界专家学者成立的公益性、非营利性独立法人社团。① 来自甘肃省的 25 家党政机关、院所高校、科技企业、行业协会、新闻媒体机构的 40 多家智库自愿联合发起成立省内首个以科技创新为主旨的新型智库联盟——甘肃省科技创新智库联盟。2019 年 1 月,河南省高校智库联盟揭牌成立,该联盟是由全省高校智库自愿参加的应用对策型研究平台,首批由河南省 46 所高校的 65 家智库组成,旨在搭建信息共享、科研协作、成果交流的合作平台。山东社科院发起并联合省内重点智库、各地市社科院等成立了山东智库联盟,还同步开通了山东智库联盟网站、微信公众号和微博,创办《智库交流》月报,举办"泰山智库讲坛",为联盟成员协作交流、资源共享提供有效渠道。广西壮族自治区党委政策研究室和自治区政府发展研究中心牵头组建广西特色新型智库联盟,实行联席会议制,分设高校智库、企业智库等 6 个联络处,已搭建出由 16 家理事单位、22 家广西重点特色智库、160 家智库联盟成员单位和 106 位智库专家组成的综合性联盟体系。②

---

① 中国日报山西记者站.山西省智库发展协会成立[EB/OL]. [2017 - 01 - 07]. http://cnews.chinadaily.com.cn/2017 - 01/07/content_27890114.htm.

② 资料来自广西决策咨询网官方发布信息。

三、对国家高端和省市重点新型智库建设的几点建议

经过 4 年多的建设,国家高端和省市重点智库建设取得重要进展和显著成效,充分发挥了试点单位的示范、引领、带动作用。随着中国特色社会主义进入新时代,我国智库应抓住重要战略机遇期,勇担使命、展现更大作为。面对新形势新任务,中国特色新型智库建设更要在"中国特色"和"新型"两个概念上下功夫。"中国特色"是要解决中国发展中的现实问题,"新型"是要求智库在体制机制创新上有所突破。只有利用现代智库的思维,围绕党和国家中心工作、党中央重大决策部署、社会热点问题,继续深化智库在人财物管理、科研组织、项目管理、成果评价与应用转化、国际交流合作等方面的管理体制改革,才能使新型智库建设取得更大成效。

(一) 明晰功能定位,注重内容创新

习近平总书记指出:"智库建设要把重点放在提高研究质量、推动内容创新上。"明确功能定位是加强新型智库内涵式建设的首要任务。把握正确方向,明晰职能定位,体现中国特色、社会主义特色,着力深化重大问题研究,坚持高标准定位、高质量发展。一方面,智库定位要体现"中国特色",围绕大局、找准定位,牢牢把握正确政治方向、价值导向,紧紧围绕党和国家事业面临的突出矛盾和问题,深入开展战略性、前瞻性研究,注重调查研究,夯实基础研究,精准对接中央决策需求,为国家宏观战略规划和地方改革发展精准施策。另一方面,智库定位要彰显"新型",从解决"重机构、重编制、重级别"等根本问题出发,将体制机制改革作为智库实现新突破的着力点。多数智库从属于实体机构的二级单位,管理体制受母体单位的严格控制。因此,只有从中独立出来,进行实体化建设,充分释放科研、人事、财务等管理的自主权,才能真正实现智库内涵式发展。[①]

(二) 全方位融入决策服务,实现智政无缝沟通

做好决策对接工作是我国智库更好地服务中央和地方决策的关键,更是推进中

---

① 李刚.实体化是新型智库建设的方向[J].科学与管理,2017,37(04):8.

国特色决策支撑体系建设的重要环节。第一，充分发挥理事会的政策协调、决策指导作用，深化与决策部门的沟通交流，力促决策部门在信息公开、项目采购、人员互访、成果反馈等方面采取更主动、有效的措施，实现供需双向发力。决策部门要乐于"借智"，完善政府信息公开制度和成果反馈机制，不定期向智库传达中央精神和决策诉求，转变决策部门的"高姿态"角色，为智库研究提供便利；智库要善于"寻路"，主动走进决策部门，拓展新的服务决策渠道，积极开展文件起草、方案策划、舆情调研、讲学培训、国际交流等工作，使智库研究全方位融入决策、服务决策。第二，懂得有效把握时机，将"适时为上"作为智库对内建言和对外发声的关键准则。适时的成果推介能有效提高智库成果产生较大影响力的机会，迅速获得决策部门和社会公众的关注和认同，实现智库成果的快速转化。

（三）完善选人用人留人机制是第一要务

人才是智库建设的第一资源，更是智库长效发展的内原动力。我国智库应把培育人才作为基础工程，建立健全科学合理的选人用人留人机制，充分激活智力资源。第一，鼓励智库积极引进高端外部人才。首先，必须探索并解决传统科研单位的编制不够灵活的问题，允许智库在一定范围内超编引进高端专家或紧缺型专业人才，为特殊紧缺型人才开辟绿色通道；其次，必须提升引进人才的选拔标准和管理力度，着重聘请一些具有丰富决策咨询经验的专家型官员和海外智库专家，切实提升决策服务水平。第二，建立灵活高效的用人机制。首先，注重培养一批行业领军人物，充分发挥首席专家、青年骨干等高端人才的示范引领作用；其次，以研究项目为纽带，强化自身建设，打造专业过硬的创新团队，提高应急决策快速响应能力。第三，创新人才评价与激励方式。首先，分类推行人才评价机制改革，加强对智库人才建言献策成果、优秀报刊文章、参与外事外宣工作等成果的支持和认可；其次，注重高端成果补偿，提供职称评定、称号评授等方面的公平待遇，为智库研究人员开辟优质的成长空间；最后，加大优秀人才的非物质奖赏力度，通过派遣出国交流、项目经费支持、配备科研助理、人才计划优先推荐等措施，调动智库人才工作积极性，形成多劳多得、优劳优得的鲜明导向。

（四）加强智库全球合作网络建设

放眼全国,中国智库"走出去"的步伐不断加快。加强智库全球范围的深入合作,是"开门办智库、开放办智库"的应有之义,更是中国智库融入世界话语体系、参与全球治理的有效途径。第一,我国智库要围绕"一带一路"国际合作高峰论坛、中国发展高层论坛、中国国际进口博览会等重大国际性会议,积极组织筹办多类型、多层次的专题智库活动,开展多边国际交流与合作,把"中国产品"带出去、"中国思想"传出去、"中国声音"发出去。第二,支持有条件的智库在海外设立分支机构或研究基地,为优秀智库人才提供海外交流实习机会,双方积极筹办国际性学术论坛,并与国际知名媒体加强合作,扩大中国在国际舞台上的话语权和影响力。第三,搭建海内外智库合作组织和交流平台,如"一带一路"国际智库合作委员会,借助机制化合作关系打通国家信息共享和人才交流通道,为推动全球治理、促进多轨外交、加强全球思想对话提供组织保障。第四,针对国内外热点、重点、难点问题,支持与海外智库在合作网络框架下广泛开展合作研究、委托研究、联合研究,为全球治理提供"中国方案"。第五,针对前瞻性、预见性、应急性重大议题,积极参与国际学术活动,牵头组织国际大科学计划,并鼓励引进国际知名智库专家,搭建全球人际关系网络,广交深交一批信得过、用得上的国际友人,实现思想汇聚、信息共享、数据互联,让我国智库为构建人类命运共同体贡献出更多中国思想、中国价值和中国力量。

（五）突破体制机制障碍,提升治理效能

党的十九届四中全会突出强调了对坚持和完善中国特色社会主义制度、推进国家治理体系和治理能力现代化的总体要求。中国特色新型智库作为现代国家治理体系的重要组成部分,应将改革重心放到突破体制机制堵点上来。从机构设置、职能转变、编制调整等方面找准切入点,加大重点领域体制机制研究和改革力度,助力破解深层次矛盾和问题。这要求我国智库必须尽快破除"科研转化率底、人才引进留住难、职称体系固化、编制体制制约生产活力"等体制机制壁垒,从根本上激活科研单位

内在动力，形成符合智库运行特点、活力高效的现代智库管理体制。因此，可尝试遴选一批不同类型的非实体化研究院（所、中心），开展专项改革试点工作，对这些试点机构赋予事业单位独立法人资格，不纳入机构编制核定范围，借助"市场契约"方式来管理，自负盈亏，实现企业化管理、市场化运营。① 这种现代法人治理结构能够充分释放智库在机构设置、专家选聘、员工社招、酬薪分配等方面的自主权，更有利于实现科研成果转化和社会效益最大化，激发智库活力和科研人员创造力，促进治理效能提升，推进"中国之治"走向新境界。

---

① 王晓菲."四不像"机构管理难题在济"破冰"［N］.济南日报,2019－12－06(A03).

专题二　新型智库成为决策咨询新生力量

　　2014 年 10 月 27 日,中央全面深化改革领导小组第六次会议召开,会议审议了《关于加强中国特色新型智库建设的意见》。习近平总书记强调,我们进行治国理政,必须善于集中各方面智慧、凝聚最广泛力量。改革发展任务越是艰巨繁重,越需要强大的智力支持。要从推动科学决策、民主决策,推进国家治理体系和治理能力现代化、增强国家软实力的战略高度,把中国特色新型智库建设作为一项重大而紧迫的任务切实抓好。① 2015 年 1 月 20 日,中共中央办公厅、国务院办公厅印发《关于加强中国特色新型智库建设的意见》(以下简称《意见》)并明确指出,中国特色新型智库是党和政府科学民主依法决策的重要支撑,是国家治理体系和治理能力现代化的重要内容,是国家软实力的重要组成部分,②这为中国特色新型智库建设与决策咨询服务指明了方向。5 年来,中国特色新型智库一直肩负着引导共识、咨政启民的责任,取得了令人瞩目的成就,各级各类智库机构奋发有为,聚焦决策需求、嵌入政策过程服务决策,众多智库成果转化为公共政策、转化为社会生产力,已成为政策共同体的重要成员之一,并成为我国协商民主和政府科学决策的重要补充,③在很大程度上为提升国家治理体系与治理能力现代化水平、增强国家软实力做出了重要贡献。

---

① 人民网—中国共产党新闻网.习近平为何特别强调"新型智库建设"? [EB/OL].[2019 - 12 - 2]. http://theory. people. com. cn/n/2014/1029/c148980 - 25928251. html.

② 新华社.中共中央办公厅、国务院办公厅印发《关于加强中国特色新型智库建设的意见》[EB/OL].[2019 - 12 - 2]. http://www. gov. cn/xinwen/2015 - 01/20/content_2807126. htm.

③ 王辉耀.提高新型智库的决策咨询能力[J].新西部,2017(8):85.

一、决策咨询是新型智库的首要功能

中国自古就有"以智辅政"的传统，门客、谋士、师爷、幕僚、言官、谏议大夫以及翰林院等智囊制度及机构历史悠久。古语有云"众力并则万钧不足举也，群智用则庶绩不足康也"，充分肯定了聚民智和智囊制度的重要意义。中国传统文人士大夫也以咨政建言为应尽之责并以此为荣，有"如欲平治天下，当今之世，舍我其谁"的豪言壮语，有"家事国事天下事，事事关心"的家国情怀，更有"鞠躬尽瘁，死而后已"的奉献精神。文人谋士充当君王的智囊，以自身丰富的知识、经验和智慧，运筹帷幄，决胜千里，甚至直接参与决策，影响历史发展方向与进程。中国悠久的咨政传统，为"现代化"咨政服务奠定了良好的文化基础和氛围，新型智库与古代智囊一脉相承，可以看作对中国"以智辅政"传统以及士大夫精神的继承与发扬，同时也是对西方咨询机制的学习与借鉴。

当前，全面深化改革进入攻坚期，经济增长阶段进入转换期，国家治理体系和治理能力现代化建设以及政府职能转变等要求，使得各级政府对民主决策、科学决策、依法决策以及决策正确度的要求越来越高。① 伴随着中国和平崛起，国际环境日益复杂，国内经济社会结构不断变化，寻求咨政服务和智力支持成为不少政府的选择。如为更好地实现疫情防控，湖北省委书记应勇多次召开座谈会，多次听取治疗救治、心理危机干预、应急管理、法律服务等领域的专家以及一线医务工作者关于医疗救治和疫情防控的意见建议，并在2020年2月25日的专家智囊团座谈会上明确表达"湖北和武汉作为全国疫情防控的重中之重和决胜之地，打赢阻击战，需要全方位多角度倾听专家意见"②。向外"借智"能够帮助政府应对复杂的决策环境，提升决策水平，其中智库是政府重要的借智对象。

① 人民网—中国共产党新闻网.习近平为何特别强调"新型智库建设"？［EB/OL］.［2019-12-2］.http://theory.people.com.cn/n/2014/1029/c148980-25928251.html.

② 上观新闻.湖北防控指挥部再调整，省委书记应勇面对"智囊参谋"说：请大家直言不讳［EB/OL］.［2019-12-2］.https://www.jfdaily.com/news/detail? id=216448.

　　《意见》指出:"中国特色新型智库是以战略问题和公共政策为主要研究对象、以服务党和政府科学民主依法决策为宗旨的非营利性研究咨询机构",并且明确中国特色新型智库具有"咨政建言、理论创新、舆论引导、社会服务、公共外交等重要功能",提出"健全中国特色决策支撑体系,大力加强智库建设,以科学咨询支撑科学决策,以科学决策引领科学发展"[1]。由此可见,中国特色新型智库本质上是决策咨询机构,咨政建言(决策咨询)是新型智库的首要功能,其核心任务就是聚焦经济社会发展中的战略问题和政策性问题,基于扎实的理论基础和科学的研究方法进行深入分析和研判,为党和政府的决策提供支撑。

　　进入全面深化改革历史新阶段的中国,为新型智库的发展提供了肥沃土壤,党的十八届三中全会从顶层设计、制度建设等方面为智库发展指明了方向,并且为智库拓展提供了广阔舞台。[2] 这 5 年来,各级各类智库建设都取得了显著成效,随着智库治理结构不断优化、制度建设持续完善、研究团队建设完善、科研组织与管理模式持续创新,智库发展内生动力不断增强,智库发展体系逐步形成,围绕大局服务决策已经成为智库,尤其是高端智库的共识,逐步形成了研究领域聚焦决策需求、积极服务国家重大战略任务、嵌入政策过程服务决策的智库咨政局面,可以说新型智库已经融入国家决策的开放性平台之中,成为中国政策决策体制的一部分。[3]

二、新型智库成为政策共同体的重要成员

　　政策支撑是智库参与决策过程、推进智库体系建设的先决条件。第一章已对各级智库管理制度进行了详细的梳理分析,目前智库建设发展的基础政策、行业性文

---

　　① 新华社.中共中央办公厅、国务院办公厅印发《关于加强中国特色新型智库建设的意见》[EB/OL].[2019 - 12 - 2].http://www.gov.cn/xinwen/2015 - 01/20/content_2807126.htm.

　　② 人民网—中国共产党新闻网.习近平谈建设新型智库:改革发展任务越重越需要智力支持[EB/OL].[2019 - 12 - 2].http://cpc.people.com.cn/xuexi/n/2015/0121/c385475 - 26422432.html? tdsourcetag=s_pcqq_aiomsg.

　　③ 人民网.公开出版智库成果　发挥智库研究作用[EB/OL].[2019 - 12 - 2].http://world. people.com.cn/n1/2016/0826/c1002 - 28668345.html.

件、配套文件都在步步跟进,智库政策环境正在日益得到改善,其中不乏对智库决策咨询服务体制的完善,支持鼓励智库咨政建言。《意见》明确了"落实政府信息公开制度;完善重大决策意见征集制度;建立健全政策评估制度;建立政府购买决策咨询服务制度"①等保障制度,为新型智库参与政府决策制度保障体系奠定了基石。部分省市据此建立了决策咨询制度,如山东省发布的《山东省人民政府决策咨询特聘专家工作规则》(鲁政字〔2018〕205号),明确了决策咨询专家参与政府决策工作的职责范围、工作规范等相关规则。② 还有省市将智库服务纳入政府采购,如2016年发布的《河北省省级政府购买决策咨询服务管理办法(试行)》,提出"省级政府购买决策咨询服务遵循按需购买、以事定费、公开择优、合同管理的基本原则",明确界定了购买主体、承接主体和购买内容等事项。③

不断完善的智库决策咨询服务体制,拓展了智库服务决策的渠道,加深了智库嵌入决策过程的程度。虽然不同智库因自身的性质和特点,参与政府决策的广度、深度以及方式有所差异,但总体而言,新型智库已经成为政策共同体的重要成员,不同类型智库各施所长、各尽所能、各尽己责,在决策中发挥着越来越重要的作用。本章将结合公共政策参与主体和智库影响力的三个结构层次(决策/核心影响力、精英/中心影响力和大众/边缘影响力)④,对智库在政策共同体中与其他政策参与主体的关系以及发挥的作用进行分析。

(一)直接服务核心决策者

1. 专家受邀授课培训

当前,我国已建立起从中央到地方的层次清晰的干部学习培训体系,从国家层面

---

① 新华社.中共中央办公厅、国务院办公厅印发《关于加强中国特色新型智库建设的意见》[EB/OL].[2019-12-2]. http://www.gov.cn/xinwen/2015-01/20/content_2807126.htm.
② 山东省人民政府关于印发山东省人民政府决策咨询特聘专家工作规则的通知[EB/OL].[2019-12-2]. http://zfgb.m.iqilu.com/gbszfwj/201811/01/722154.html.
③ 河北省人民政府网站.我省出台省级政府购买决策咨询服务管理办法[EB/OL].[2019-12-2]. http://www.hebei.gov.cn/hebei/11937442/10761139/13656795/index.html.
④ 朱旭峰.中国思想库——政策过程中的影响力研究[M]北京:清华大学出版社,2009,32.

看,党的十六大以来就形成了中央政治局集体学习制度,2002 年至今开展了 139 次集体学习,平均 40 天一次,近 200 位全国各领域的顶尖专家学者汇聚中南海,成为这个特殊课堂的讲师。中国共产党第十九届中央政治局集体学习目前共开展 19 次,①不少智库专家受邀进行授课,如 2019 年 11 月 29 日清华大学教授薛澜就我国应急管理体系和能力建设授课讲解,并提出意见和建议。受邀成为中央政治局集体学习讲师的专家学者,多结合决策需求、时事热点等,充分发挥自身的研究专长,深入浅出地为中央决策层阐明理论,呈送智库成果。

地方层面的常规干部培训一般由党校系统承担,各级党校(包含各地党校行政学院智库)经常就国家和地方重大方针政策和文件精神,为领导干部开办培训班和研讨班。如中共中央党校和国家行政学院一般在国家重大政策出台前夕举办省部级干部专题研讨班,集中讨论党的建设和执政党的路线、方针政策,②从宏观上对与会干部的执政理念和决策思路进行引导。此外,邀请专家解读时政热点议题也成为不少政府的选择,智库专家积极投身政府的专题培训工作,同样能够直接与决策者对话,实现咨政建言。如上海社会科学院经济研究所专家受邀为内蒙古自治区人大信息工作培训班讲授"一带一路"的相关内容,③增强了内蒙古信息调研工作人员的大局意识,引导其关注热点、难点问题,提高内蒙古自治区信息调研工作水平,从而推动科学决策。

2. 呈报决策咨询内参

结合自身的研究专长和当前的时政热点,形成研究成果并上报内参是当前很多智库实现决策参考的主要方式。截至 2019 年 3 月,根据 CTTI 系统的 706 家来自智库填报的内参和批示数据,共有内参数据 7976 条、批示数据 2005 条。自 2013 年

---

① 中央领导机构资料库. 中央政治局集体学习(十九届)[EB/OL]. [2019 - 12 - 2]. http://cpc. people. com. cn/n1/2017/1025/c414940 - 29608670. html? from＝singlemessage.

② 严丽莎. 智库对我国政府决策过程的影响力探究[J]. 企业导报,2015(01):82 - 83.

③ 孙伟丽. 当好决策助手　发挥智库作用——自治区人大常委会办公厅研究室在土右旗举办全区人大信息工作培训班[J]. 内蒙古人大,2017(07):40.

习近平总书记对中国特色新型智库建设做出重要批示以来,智库内参的年报送量和批示量均呈逐年递增的趋势,特别是 2015 年《关于加强中国特色新型智库建设的意见》出台之后,智库报送内参数量呈爆发式增长(详见图 2.1)。

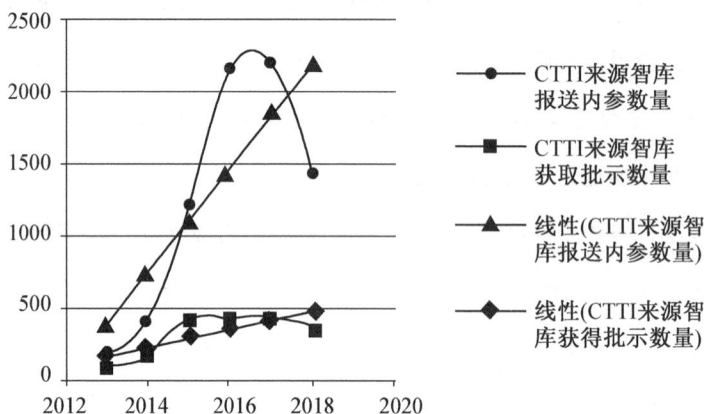

图 2.1　CTTI 来源智库内参报送和批示年份分布

　　其中高校智库(在 CTTI 来源智库中占比超过 65%)内参报送数量和获得批示数量最多(具体各类型智库内参报送、获得批示数量见图 2.2),如中国人民大学国家发展与战略研究院自 2016 年以来凭借学校的中办信息直报点等内参渠道累计向中央报送内参 1000 余份。据不完全统计,200 余份内参得到党和国家领导人批示,约三分之一的成果被有关部门采纳,转化为国家重大决策。[1]　内参报送和获得批示数量紧随其后的是党政部门智库、社科院智库和党校行政学院智库,这三类智库内参报批比均高于高校智库,他们与政府部门拥有更加密切的关系,如中国创新战略和政策研究中心由中国科学院与国务院研究室依托中科院战略咨询院共建,依托国务院研究室转化渠道和战略咨询院综合研究集成平台,针对国家创新战略和宏观政策提供

---

　　① 严金明:努力建设成为中国特色新型智库引领者[EB/OL].[2019 - 12 - 2]. http://www. sohu. com/a/305968792_345245.

前瞻性、建设性的咨询建议;①而上海社科院与不少中央部门建立了研究和咨询对接机制,进一步完善常态化的智库咨询服务;中央党校的内参《思想理论内参》和《研究报告》可直接报送中央政治局、中央书记处以及中办、国办等中央决策层。

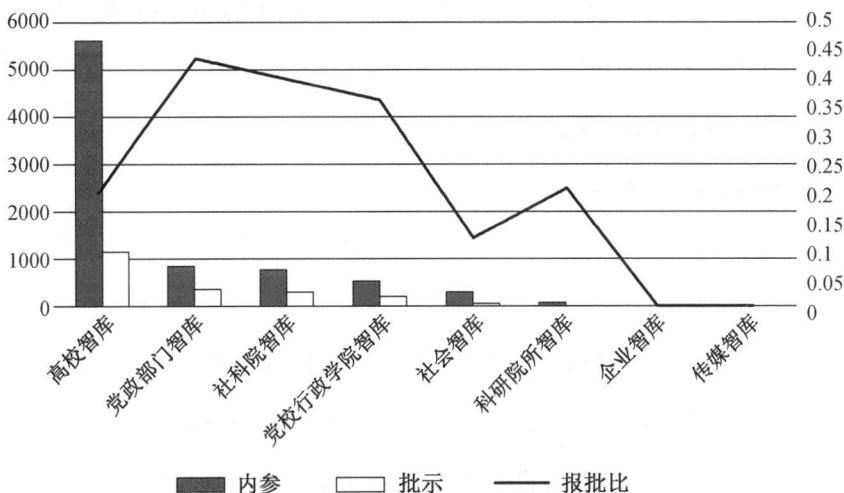

图 2.2 CTTI 来源智库内参报送、获得批示数量及报批比

3. 承接政府咨询课题

智库承接政府咨询课题大体分为两类:一是领导指示圈示课题,研究成果直接报送领导参阅。不少省、市设立了领导指示圈示课题,如贵州省通过省社科院开展省领导指示圈示课题申报、招标和行政委托相结合的方式组织专家对圈示课题开展研究;广州市社科规划办每年开展"领导圈题"活动,课题成果最终直接呈送相关领导。二是政府部门课题,研究成果直接报送委托部门及相关领导参阅。如中国旅游研究院西部旅游发展研究基地(陕西师范大学地理科学与旅游学院)承接了西安市政府专家决策咨询委员会的重点课题,启动了《以文化旅游促进乡村振兴战略实施研究》的研究工作,聚焦文化和旅游如何有效助力乡村振兴发展问题。承接课题便于智库开展

---

① 科技战略咨询研究院. 高端人才政策座谈会在战略咨询院举行[EB/OL]. [2019 - 12 - 2]. http://www.bjb.cas.cn/gzjz/201712/t20171201_4905547.html.

点对点、定制式咨询服务，深化智库与决策部门的沟通交流，政府可以更好地向智库传达决策诉求，智库可以获得更加深入的决策信息，及时获取成果反馈，实现供需双向发力、精准服务。如中国旅游研究院西部旅游发展研究基地在调研和报告撰写过程中多次与西安市政府专家决策咨询委员会、西安市文化和旅游局、西安市农村工作局等部门交流沟通，确保报告内容满足决策需要。

（二）直接参与决策过程

1. 参与政策文件起草

各省市政府发展研究中心、政策研究室等党政部门智库是本地重大政策文件的主要起草机构，截至 2019 年底，CTTI 数据库收录了 69 个党政部门智库，他们承担了本地重大政策制定、理论调研、文件草拟等任务，如山东省宏观经济研究院近三年以来累计承担或参与重要文稿和规划意见等 400 余项，参加省委省政府重大调研活动 200 余次，为省委省政府决策提供了有力的智力支持，为地区经济建设以及社会发展做出了积极贡献。

而随着政府立法第三方起草工作的兴起，近年来其他类型的智库也更多地参与到政策文件起草工作中。如国家行政学院文化政策与管理研究中心承担了《公共文化服务保障法》《公共图书馆法》的起草研究工作，以及《推动特色文化产业发展的指导意见》《关于贯彻落实〈国务院关于推进文化创意和设计服务与相关产业融合发展的若干意见〉的实施意见》《中办、国办关于加快构建现代公共文化服务体系的意见》等文化领域的重磅文件的代拟工作；中国工程院等 10 余家研究机构的 32 位院士及数百名工作人员参与了《交通强国建设纲要》的编制工作；[①]天津大学国家知识产权战略实施研究基地受邀参与《知识产权强国战略纲要（2021—2035 年）》制定工作，承担"提升知识产权服务水平"专题研究，完成了相应的政策文本，并为《知识产权强国

---

① 中国网. 新闻办就《交通强国建设纲要》有关情况举行发布会［EB/OL］.［2019 - 12 - 2］. http://www. gov. cn/xinwen/2019 - 09/24/content_5432724. htm.

战略纲要(2021—2035 年)》的制定提供了厚实、全面的理论支撑和数据支撑。

此外,"第三方立法"领域也涌现出很多新的尝试和探索,如贵州省确立了《贵州省政府立法第三方起草和评估办法》①,从法制层面明确了第三方参与政府立法的程序和规范。地方政府通过定向委托或是公开招标等方式将地方立法和政策文件起草工作交托给高校智库、社会智库等智库团队。2018 年 3 月 1 日,湖南省发改委与湖南师范大学签订《〈湖南省洞庭湖条例〉立法委托服务合同》,委托湖南师范大学生态环境保护法治研究中心负责立法草案起草工作,该智库团队基于前期的研究成果,前往常德、岳阳、益阳三市开展立法调研,形成《湖南省洞庭湖条例(送审稿)》,并于2019 年 7 月通过了湖南省人大常委一审。又如武汉大学环境法研究所《基于风险的环境治理多元共治体系研究》专题报告对环境多元共治相关立法、执法和司法文件和方案草案的审议和通过提供了重要的参考,咨询报告《〈青海省生态环境损害赔偿制度改革实施方案〉草稿及其编制说明》,被青海省委办公厅、省政府办公厅采纳。

2. 提供专家咨询意见

除智库团队整体参与决策过程外,智库专家"单兵作战"主要通过以下两种形式发挥作用。一是入选政府咨询专家库。为更好地提升政府决策能力和治理能力,各级政府设立了多种类型的决策咨询工作专家库,有综合性专家库,如山东省人民政府决策咨询特聘专家库和四川省立法专家库,涉及经济、文化、生态等多个领域,为全省的重大决策提供咨询服务;也有较为专业的专家库,如海南旅游专家库,聚焦旅游领域。智库专家进入政府咨询专家库,发挥个人才智,履行专家义务,对政策方案进行合理性论证,辅助政府决策,如广州市决策咨询专家库自成立以来共参与了市委、市政府工作部门的各类研讨会、评审会、咨询论证会等千余次,提出咨询建议数千条,为

---

① 贵州省人民政府.《贵州省政府立法第三方起草和评估办法》(第 181 号)[EB/OL].[2019 - 12 - 2]. http://www. guizhou. gov. cn/zwgk/jbxxgk/fgwj/szfwj _ 8191/szfl _ 8192/201801/t20180115 _ 1090639. html.

提高政府决策质量提供了有力支持。[①] 二是出席咨询论证会议。为更好地集民智、听民意，立法决策要进行集体咨询论证，通过举办听证会、交流会、座谈会等各类方式广泛征求意见，其中专家意见尤其受重视，如广州市政府工作部门的专题工作会议时常邀请专家参与，在政策文件讨论、政策可行性分析、政策的风险评估等环节听取专家意见。

（三）参与塑造政策环境

学者、专家、媒体和社会公众等都是公共决策的参与者，在不能直接服务于政策制定者时，另辟蹊径成为很多智库的选择。智库以书刊、报告等形式公开研究成果，以会议、论坛等方式进行公共对话，传播智库思想，引起学者、媒体、社会公众的关注和讨论，促进政策共同体中其他成员的参与，形成舆论影响力，间接实现咨政建言目的，服务政府决策。

一是创办发行精品书刊、专题报告等出版物。出版图书、报告，公开发行刊物，是智库向社会公开智库成果，传播智库思想的重要途径。如国家发改委宏观经济研究院共发行《宏观经济研究》《经济管理文摘》等6个学术刊物，并以学术丛书、年度文集和年度报告的形式对宏观经济领域的众多问题展开解读，展示智库成果；中国工程院创办 Engineering 和《中国工程科学》两种工程综合类学术期刊，其中《中国工程科学》是中国工程院国家高端智库成果的重要展示窗口；盘古智库结合"一带一路"专题出版了《"一带一路"国际合作精华30问》和《"一带一路"节点国家态度研究》丛书等学术著作，发布专题研究报告，为国际合作过程中遇到的问题提供专业而深入的解读，助益推动"一带一路"合作，深化相关人群对"一带一路"的认知。

二是主办/承办学术会议、学术论坛等交流活动。学术会议、学术论坛是展示智库成果的重要平台，与会人员在此进行深层次交流，展开思想碰撞，结合议题探寻解决之道，凝聚共识，共同发声，引发舆论，持续性系列活动还可以形成品牌效应和规模

---

① 王龙. 广州市智库参与地方政府决策过程中的问题与对策研究[D]. 兰州大学，2018.

效应,进一步扩大社会影响力。如中国科学院定期举办"战略与决策高层论坛"和高端智库建设品牌活动"国家高端科技智库大讲堂",初步形成由学部学术年会、科学与技术前沿论坛、小型高端论坛、各学部学术论坛等组成的多层次高水平学术交流体系;上海社会科学院、新华社国家高端智库、复旦发展研究院、全球化智库和上海社会科学院智库建设基金会自2016年以来,每年联合主办"上海全球智库论坛",来自世界十多个国家的智库和专家汇聚一堂,共同探讨当年全球化和智库发展的热点问题,交流思想、凝聚智慧、形成共识、形成影响。

三是与媒体平台通力合作实现共赢。媒体对重大政策进行独立分析的能力有所欠缺,在进行新闻报道和评论时需要借助智库的研究成果和观点,[①]而智库的大众传播力和影响力远比不上媒体,在这方面智库与媒体合作可以实现共赢,因而双方都拥有较强的合作意向。如媒体方面主动谋求智库支持,人民网、光明网等媒体平台都设有专家解读政策专栏,邀请智库专家分析政策,并关注、挖掘、转载优秀的智库成果。2019年11月12日,浙江大学社会治理研究院"中国县域社会治理指数模型暨2019年浙江省县域社会治理十佳县(市)区"成果,受到了人民网、凤凰网、中新社等多家媒体的报道与关注。而智库也积极利用媒体平台,如国家高端智库/中国(深圳)综合开发研究院利用新媒体开设"综研国策""综研观察""澎湃问政"三大评论专栏,呼吁公众参与以扩大社会影响力和公共传播力。智库与媒体的积极合作,让智库成为媒体专业观点的来源,媒体成为智库政策主张、思想观点的传播载体和推动力量,共同形成推动决策的社会氛围。

三、嵌入政策过程有力促进了决策的科学性与规范性

公共政策的过程复杂而漫长,政府在公共决策过程中,尤其是重大决策过程中,

---

① 王里. 美国智库在政府决策中的作用及启示[EB/OL]. [2019 - 12 - 2]. http://www. qunzh. com/qkzx/gwqk/jczx/2017/201714/201707/t20170720_32692. html.

从前期的议题发起、内容制定,中期的执行落实,到后期的决策评估、政策反馈都给智库提供了广阔的参与空间。新型智库努力嵌入政策过程,决策咨询服务贯穿整个公共政策过程,发挥智力支撑、舆论引导、沟通桥梁等作用。下面从政策形成、政策执行和政策评估三个过程阶段分析新型智库决策咨询在公共决策中的作用。

(一)推动政策制定的民主化科学化

智库已经成为政府决策链上不可缺少的一环,但当前阶段智库发挥咨询作用主要是在政策形成过程中,[①]截至2019年3月,通过对CTTI来源智库内参成果和批示所对应的"政策过程阶段"进行人工标引和分析(见图2.3),除去内容或摘要不可见的保密内参1311项和批示25项后,得到内参数据6665条、批示数据1980条,其中智库所报内参成果对应"议程设置和政策建议过程阶段"占比高达93%,获得批示量占比达94%,可见智库目前决策咨询的重心还多集中在政策形成过程,[②]其作用体现在启发议程设置、保障民主决策、促进科学决策三个方面。智库通过引导关注社会议

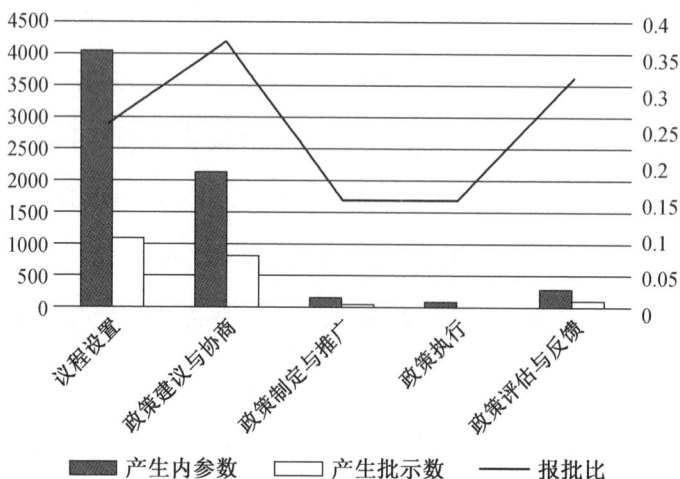

图2.3 我国智库报送内参和获得批示对应政策过程各阶段分布及报批比

① 李婉芝.智库在公共政策过程中的作用分析[D].湖北大学,2012.
② 王传奇,李刚,丁炫凯.智库政策影响力评价中的"唯批示论"迷思——基于政策过程理论视角的研究[J].图书与情报,2019(03):11-19.

题启发议程设置,提供科学依据和解决方案,在政策论证和审议阶段发挥专家咨询作用,从而提升政策制定的科学性和民主性。

1. 双管齐下参与议程设置

政策议程设置是决策过程的起始阶段,也是最为核心的环节之一。政府资源的有限决定了仅有部分议题能够进入正式政策议程,如何让民众关心的、社会发展需要的议题入选,是智库在议程设置阶段的咨政任务。政策议程一般包括政府议程和公众议程,智库启发公共政策议程设置即通过这两种议程类型产生作用。

一是参与政府议程。政府议程属于正式的官方议程,是指政府关注到某些社会问题,然后将其纳入政策讨论的过程,[①]官方、半官方智库或直接参与政府议程,或接受政府委托,或自主开展调研,将调研成果通过内参、课题、建议提案等多种形式送达政府部门,从而被纳入政府议程。如中南财经政法大学法治发展与司法改革研究中心专家徐汉明的《检察长列席审判委员会制度的探索与发展》报告,被最高检《领导参阅件》采用,并被纳入重要立法建议。

二是引导公众议程。公众议程是指社会问题引起公众关注的过程,从而影响政府议程设置,如近几年疫苗事件引起社会广泛关注,推动了《中华人民共和国疫苗管理法》的出台。政策研究有助于在议题进入严肃讨论之前重新界定问题的边界和实施干预的维度,[②]智库在公众议程中便有着类似的"启智"和"聚焦"作用,即从专业角度澄清相关概念,对议题进行聚焦和界定,引导公众的价值观念,形成有利于被决策者采纳的舆论氛围。

2. 为民发声促进民主协商

民意是决策过程中的活性炭,能去除影响决策效果的有害杂质——那些未曾看

---

①　杨宏山.从精英驱动到互动创设:中国政策议程设置的制度发展[J].国家治理,2019(30):13 - 18.

②　罗什福尔、科布.问题界定的政治学:形成政策议程[M].堪萨斯大学出版社,1994:10 - 15.

到的风险、没能觉察的隐患,[①]增强决策透明度和公众参与度是民主决策的必然要求。政府现已建立了提案、会议、座谈、听证、公示、咨询、民意调查等多种民主协商方式,尽力做到贴近实际、贴近生活、贴近群众,但在现实的公众意见表达过程中,难免存在发表意见渠道不够便利,公众意见纷杂矛盾、不成体系、不易被政府采纳等问题。

智库在收集民意、表达民意方面可以起到桥梁、过滤器以及润滑剂的作用。智库开展民意调研,充当政府与民众之间的桥梁,可以更加广泛、全面且有针对性地收集信息,增加民意传递渠道;对公众观点和社会现实进行科学的整理分析,可以过滤庞杂的无效意见,最终形成精简专业的调研报告,更加准确有效地将社会公众的利益诉求传达给政府,实现国家、公众和专家三种力量的理性沟通。如安徽省高校管理大数据研究中心2018年参与安徽省高校师生满意度调查,共调查了27所高校,学生15051人,老师1355人,分析师生对于高等教育质量的满意程度,对我国高等教育的政策与实施、管理与教学、支持与服务等各方面现状进行了全面系统的梳理,切实传达了政策相关者的意见。又如江南大学食品安全风险治理研究团队结合食品安全问题,先后对20多个省(自治区、直辖市)90多个地级市进行了实地调查,访谈4万多名基层干部群众、400多家食品生产经营企业,形成了《从农田到餐桌,如何保证"舌尖上的安全"——我国食品安全风险治理及形势分析》调研报告,被《新华文摘》全文转载,并被光明日报总编室《情况反映》2018年第128期收录,呈送中共中央办公厅、国务院办公厅,将人民的声音传达给政府;同时国内主流网络媒体与主要新媒体门户网站也不同程度地转载了该调查报告,转载的网络新闻超过1000条,引起社会关注和舆论讨论,进一步增加了公众参与度,推动了更广泛的民意表达。

3. 基于研究提出科学建议

随着对决策科学化的要求越来越高,专家咨询和论证已经成为政府决策的必要环节,不少政府在政策文件制定前成立专家咨询组,如2019年10月广东省政府成立

---

① 本报评论部.科学决策要有"效果意识"[N].人民日报,2016-8-4(005).

了包含 38 名国内著名专家学者和企业家在内的"十四五"发展规划专家委员会,负责对广东省推进高质量发展提供咨询意见和建议,对发展规划编制实施进行咨询论证等,以提高广东省发展规划制定实施的科学化水平。

此外,智库还注重把握时机、主动服务,积极开展立法调研、文件起草、方案策划等工作,使智库研究全方位融入决策、服务决策。智库密切关注大政方针,基于扎实专业的研究基础,把握承接政府课题等机会,为决策提供依据乃至决策方案。如2018 年,我国新一轮税改正式启动,中国家庭金融调查与研究中心利用在全国范围开展的中国家庭金融调查(CHFS)和中国小微企业调查(CMES)数据研究结果,为税改过程中的政策制定提供了客观依据;陕西经济研究中心承接并完成了《铜川市大气污染防治条例》立法调研报告和《铜川市饮用水水源地保护条例》立法调研报告,为铜川市多项立法工作提供依据。

2018 年 11 月,习近平总书记在上海第一届国际进口博览会上表示,支持长三角区域一体化发展并上升为国家战略,[①]南京大学长江产业经济研究院、复旦大学长三角研究院、华东师范大学长三角一体化研究中心、浙江大学中国农村发展研究院等多家智库基于自身的研究基础从构建区域创新共同体、长三角乡村一体化振兴、长三角地区政府数据开放等不同角度对长三角一体化建设提出了相关方案。多种方案的汇集本身就是一个政策方案选择过程,有助于科学决策,而不同智库围绕同一主题的交叉研究,能够扩展政府决策思路,提升决策的全面性、可行性和科学性。在此过程中,智库也能充分发挥自身的专业优势,获得决策部门的关注和认同,实现智库成果的快速转化。如专注于长三角一体化研究 20 余年的南京大学长江产业经济研究院专家团队,近年来围绕"长三角一体化发展策略"这一方向展开深度的系列研究,产生了很多专业性和操作性都很强的建议方案,提出的 2 个具体建议——"建立沪宁合产业创

---

① 新华网.习近平在首届中国国际进口博览会开幕式上的主旨演讲(全文)[EB/OL].[2019 - 12 - 2]. http://www. xinhuanet. com/2018 - 11/05/c_1123664692. htm.

新带"和"建设一体化发展的区域股权交易市场"，被《长江三角洲区域一体化发展规划纲要》采纳，咨询报告《统一市场建设：长三角一体化的使命与任务》被《国家社会科学基金项目成果要报》2019 年第 39 期刊发并上报中央领导。

（二）政策教育广泛凝聚社会共识

政策未能达到预期结果，其原因有时并不在于政策本身，而在于政策不能被公众理解，不能执行到位。《关于加强中国特色新型智库建设的意见》提出"发挥智库阐释党的理论、解读公共政策、研判社会舆情、引导社会热点、疏导公众情绪的积极作用"，可见把握正确舆论导向，积极进行舆论引导，开展政策宣传解读，增进社会公众认同，是智库义不容辞的责任。

1. 聚焦政策热点，引导公众关注方向

很多智库，尤其是高端智库，以对党和国家重大方针政策的全方位、多视角的分析解读为己任，如中国人民大学国家发展与战略研究院以《政策观察》和《一张图读懂系列》为平台，密切关注国家大政方针、重要会议精神与各部委动态及走向，进行独家解读。智库科学解读可以将公众的注意力引导到符合政策目标、符合社会稳定与发展大局、符合广大人民群众利益的方向上来，[1]如党的十九大召开时，中国网与盘古智库联合推出"砥砺奋进　开启新征程"——智库解读十九大系列专题，[2]从依法治国、绿色发展等多个角度阐述解读十九大报告和相关议题，发表了《十九大将是实现新的千年辉煌的里程碑》《十九大报告：依法治国在中国特色社会主义建设中的定位是什么》《践行绿色发展理念，建立保护环境的长效机制》等多篇解读报告，引导公众关注十九大提出的新发展理念。

2. 解读政策条款，帮助公众理解内容

互联网时代，各式各样的政策解释喷涌而出、层出不穷，需要高端智库发挥作用，

---

① 肖昊宸.智库要着力发挥舆论引导功能[EB/OL].［2019 - 12 - 2］. http://www. cssn. cn/index/index_focus/201607/t20160712_3117257. shtml.

② 中国网."砥砺奋进　开启新征程"——智库解读十九大系列专题[EB/OL].［2019 - 12 - 2］. http://www. china. com. cn/opinion/think/node_7252830. htm.

提供权威精准的政策解读。① 智库充分发挥自身专业性和权威性优势,通过出版专著、发布研究报告、发表专栏评论、以专家身份接受媒体采访等方式,精准解读政策,从而让社会公众更加全面、准确、深刻地理解政策,推进政策落地。在众多的政策解读传播渠道中,通过媒体发布解读报告、开展专家评论是最迅速高效的手段,智库可以通过自有媒体平台或者人民网、光明网等重要平台的专家解读政策栏目,将深奥晦涩的政策转换为公众更易理解的要点,为政策宣传寻找舆论落点,如《长江三角洲区域一体化发展规划纲要》发布后,中国政府监管与公共政策研究院专家第一时间接受新华社采访,解读了纲要中的部分亮点。

3. 凝聚社会共识,营造良好政策氛围

智库的专业性、权威性以及大多数智库的独立性,让智库的政策宣传相较于政府更容易获得公众的信任和认可,因而也能取得更好的舆论效果。对于重大的政策和议题,很多智库会对其进行更深一步的研究分析,某些议题成为多家智库的共同选择,在CTTI2019年智库成果征集中我们发现,"扶贫""一带一路""乡村振兴"等主题得到了多家智库的关注。对于同一议题的多角度深入研究,有助于澄清政策概念,有助于公众了解政策目的和意义,从而凝聚共识,营造良好氛围。如2017年~2019年,武汉大学经济发展研究中心与光明日报社聚焦"新时代、新理念、新体系""新时代文化强国战略"和"全球治理体系变革与中国主张"三个主题,联合举办了三届珞珈智库论坛,以主旨演讲和圆桌对话的形式展开,围绕国家亟须和中央重大决策部署,帮助树立正确的应对世界格局变化的历史观、大局观、角色观,积极推进经济和社会的创新发展。②

(三) 政策评估推进政策及时调整改进

公共政策评估是国家治理现代化必不可少的组成部分,我国公共政策评估起步

---

① 张倪.中国智库:探索新职能　履行新担当[EB/OL].[2019 - 12 - 2].http://www.chinado.cn/? p=4504.

② 光明日报.光明日报社与武汉大学联合主办第三届珞珈智库论坛[EB/OL].[2019 - 12 - 08].http://about.gmw.cn/2019 - 10/14/content_33229975.htm.

较晚,总体而言,仍处于探索阶段。党的十八大以来,政策评估越来越受到中央和各级地方政府的重视,越来越受到社会各界的关注,党的十八大报告和十八届三中全会通过的《中共中央关于全面深化改革若干重大问题的决定》明确指出,要"健全重大决策社会稳定风险评估机制",①②党的十八届四中全会则把"风险评估"确定为重大行政决策法定程序的重要环节;③党的十九届四中全会通过《中共中央关于坚持和完善中国特色社会主义制度　推进国家治理体系和治理能力现代化若干重大问题的决定》,进一步提出"健全决策机制,加强重大决策的调查研究、科学论证、风险评估,强化决策执行、评估、监督"。④

党的十八大、十八届三中全会和四中全会提出的"风险评估"是一种事前评估,即在决策执行前对政策可行性进行评估,使政策方案更加全面、周延,更具可行性,类似政策执行阶段的咨询论证,如黑龙江省公共健康安全及医改策略研究高端智库构建了基于 ProModel 的医保制度仿真系统模型,并模拟研究实施不同政策方案下医保制度的优化状况,探讨医保制度多目标优化的途径及政策选择。党的十九届四中全会提到的"决策评估、监督"则是事后评估,是对政策执行效果进行评估,从而为政策变化、政策改进和新政制定提供依据,帮助政府优化政策资源配置,提高政策运行的科学性和准确性,这也是本节要讨论的政策评估的内涵。

根据 CTTI 来源智库截至 2019 年 3 月的内参成果和批示对应的政策过程阶段的分析,对应政策评估阶段的智库内参成果占比不到 5%,而与此相对的是该阶段内

---

①　人民网.胡锦涛在中国共产党第十八次全国代表大会上的报告[EB/OL].[2019 - 12 - 2].http://cpc. people. com. cn/n/2012/1118/c64094 - 19612151 - 7. html.

②　新华社.中共中央关于全面深化改革若干重大问题的决定[EB/OL].[2019 - 12 - 2]. http://cpc. people. com. cn/n/2013/1115/c64094 - 23559163 - 13. html.

③　新华社.十八届中央委员会第四次全体会议公报[EB/OL].[2019 - 12 - 2]. http://www. gov. cn/xinwen/2014 - 10/23/content_2769791. htm.

④　新华社.中共中央关于坚持和完善中国特色社会主义制度　推进国家治理体系和治理能力现代化若干重大问题的决定[EB/OL].[2019 - 12 - 2]. http://www. gov. cn/zhengce/2019 - 11/05/content_5449023. htm.

参报批比远高于其他阶段,这说明我国政府对智库参与政策评估与反馈的需求有很大上升空间。① 近年来,智库已经在政策评估方面做出了很多努力和尝试,不断提升政策评估水平。

1. 持续追踪,有效评估政策落地效果

公共政策的执行效果需要专业团队进行长期的跟踪评估,政策评估的能力和水平也反映决策咨询机构向政府建言献策的能力和水平,评估人员需要具有较高的专业素质,智库的人才队伍构成和政策参与经验,在政策评估方面具有显著优势,高校智库、社会智库等非党政部门智库可以成为优秀的第三方政策评估者。当前不少智库团队或受邀或主动参与到政策效果的跟踪评价中,如兰州大学管理学院受甘肃省食品药品监督管理局委托,对"十三五"以来甘肃省食品药品安全治理绩效进行第三方评估,评估团队从《国家"十三五"规划纲要165项重大工程项目》关于"食药安全"工程项目的中期实施情况、《甘肃省"十三五"规划纲要》"平安甘肃"工程关于健全食品药品安全可追溯制度的中期实施情况以及《甘肃省"十三五"食品药品安全规划》目标任务的中期实施情况三个方面展开,开展实地调研,形成《甘肃省食品药品安全"十三五"中期治理绩效评估报告》,该报告对"十三五"以来,甘肃省食品药品安全治理绩效做出了科学全面客观的评估,对存在的问题进行了整理,明确"十三五"后期工作的新发力点,提出具体的、有针对性的对策和建议。又如陕西师范大学教育实验经济研究所从2013年~2016年对西部16个贫困县216所农村小学的243名老师及其所教的近10000名五年级学生开展了多项跟踪调查,明确贫困地区农村小学实施教师绩效工资政策落实情况,形成了《研究完善贫困农村地区小学教师绩效工资的政策建议》,通过智库自身的《政策研究简报》上报,得到教育部重视,为教师绩效工资制度改革提供了依据。智库可以充分发挥自身的专业优势,秉承科学开放的理念,基于广泛

---

① 王传奇,李刚,丁炫凯.智库政策影响力评价中的"唯批示论"迷思——基于政策过程理论视角的研究[J].图书与情报,2019(03):11-19.

全面的调研,充分考察公共政策与基层实际匹配度,对公共政策的适应性和绩效进行评价。[①]

2. 深入调研,探究政策落实欠佳原因

尽管各级政府科学决策、依法行政的能力不断提升,但仍有不少公共政策制定或执行不当,或由于社会经济环境等发生变化而变得不合时宜。智库可在全面客观调查的基础上对收集的数据、材料进行分析整理,撰写政策评估报告,反馈相关责任主体态度,分析总结政策利弊,推断探究失利原因,提出修订调整意见,甚至直接参与政策的后续调整工作,及时化解利益相关方的矛盾,进一步促进政策公平、民主,提高政策效率。如广东国际战略研究院联合北京大学企业大数据研究中心针对民企参与"一带一路"项目建设不足的现实情况,对广东省 14500 家民营企业进行调研,覆盖广东省 21 个地级市,29 个市、区(县),基于一手的微观企业调查数据,就民企参与"一带一路"建设的现状、参与意愿、存在问题以及背后的原因等进行深入剖析和总结,形成《民企参与"一带一路"建设:"强意愿、不迈步"的成因与对策》报告,为接下来发挥民企力量推动"一带一路"建设,实现合作共赢提出了搭建可落地实施的产学研平台、设立中国境外投资"一站式"管理模式等对策建议。又如中共贵州省委党校针对铜仁市思南县易地扶贫搬迁政策落实存在的难题,在思南县易地扶贫板桥镇安置点等多个安置点进行了问卷调查与深入访谈,形成了《铜仁市思南县易地扶贫搬迁的真正难题及其破解之策》,被省级内参《贵州决策咨询》2019 年第 1 期采纳,并获得贵州省委书记孙志刚和贵州省政协副主席罗宁肯定性批示,为后续异地扶贫搬迁的政策制定提供了借鉴。

3. 全面分析,总结成功经验提供借鉴

智库开展公共政策评估与反馈工作,除了发现已有政策存在的问题与不足,提出改进意见之外,还会对一些创新的、成功的政策经验进行总结,并结合本地实际因地

---

① 刘西忠.社会智库参与国家治理的路径创新[J].中国国情国力,2018(01):20-22.

制宜地提出推广建议。智库对试点政策及时进行评估反馈,有助于进一步完善政策,促进政策经验迅速推广,如浙江省县域医共体试点工作开展半年后,浙江大学社会治理研究院课题组基于县域医共体绩效、能力以及组织、制度等维度,对这项工作进行了第三方独立评估,总结了试点工作的成功经验,并进一步提出了推进全省县域医共体建设的政策建议,其中9条政策建议被浙江省委办公厅、省政府办公厅《关于全面推进县域医疗卫生服务共同体建设的意见》采纳,先进经验得到充分肯定,并很快转化为公共政策。

四、小结

经过几年的发展,新型智库服务政府决策咨询的方式不断丰富完善,在议程设置、政策形成、执行落实、评估反馈等公共政策过程中发挥了越来越重要的作用,现已成为党和政府科学民主决策的重要智囊、服务社会改革的重要参谋。新型智库做到了坚持深入调研,服务基层;广泛汇集民意,服务群众;前瞻专业研究,服务发展;聚焦热点难点,服务大局,并已成为政策共同体的重要成员,是国家治理体系和治理能力现代化的重要智力支撑。今后,面对全球化不断深入发展的新局面和我国经济社会快速发展的新问题,新型智库要进一步提升决策咨询服务的水平和能力,打造具有国内外影响力和竞争力的中国特色新型智库品牌,继续为促进国家治理现代化水平提升和完善现代化国家治理体系添砖加瓦。

专题三 新型智库传播能力有了长足进步

2015 年 1 月中共中央办公厅和国务院办公厅印发了智库建设的指导性文件《关于加强中国特色新型智库建设的意见》(以下简称《意见》),指出:"鼓励智库运用大众媒体等多种手段,传播主流思想价值,集聚社会正能量","加强中国特色新型智库对外传播能力和话语体系建设,提升我国智库的国际竞争力和国际影响力"。《意见》中的这两句话,既表明了新型智库的传播功能,也对新型智库传播做了两方面要求:一是面向国内传播,承担起党和政府治理助手的责任,做好理论阐释、政策解读、舆情研判、疏导公众情绪等工作;二是面向境外做好国际传播,发挥公共外交的功能,"中国特色新型智库需具备开展国际合作交流的良好条件"。一方面,中国新型智库通过成果传播中国声音、塑造中国形象,提升官方机构和国内媒体在国内民众和国际传媒系统内的信任度;另一方面,中国智库可以通过传播活动,在国内、国际上科学设置政策议程,提升话语权、影响舆论走向,服务国家战略部署。[①]

一、智库传播赋能的重要性

(一)智库传播助力凝聚政策共识

智库作为政策研究与咨询机构,需要借助各类渠道传播智库思想,来达到引导舆论、启迪民智、影响决策以及树立智库品牌的目的。[②] 智库传播包含传播意识、传播内容、传播渠道等方面,可以贯穿咨政建言、政府决策、国家治理的全过程。

---

① 丁炫凯.中国特色新型智库传播力评价体系研究[D].南京:南京大学,2018.
② 冯雅,李刚.新型智库传播现状与优化策略研究——基于 CTTI 来源智库媒体影响力的实证分析[J].图书与情报,2019(3):20-28.

　　智库的传播意识是智库采取传播行动的前提。① 在决策前,智库传播一方面通过长期以来集中智库专家提出的新思想和新理念,收集、分析大量真实科学客观的数据信息,借助数据挖掘工具与统计分析方法等有效的研究手段提升政策研究水平,为决策提供良好的信息基础、专业建议和权威咨询;②另一方面依照科学的理论方法,"深入实际、深入群众、深入基层,倾听群众呼声,掌握真实情况,广泛调研,潜心研究",通过对群众智慧的集中收集、梳理加工,真实反映民意,广泛集中民智,为党和政府决策提供新视角,打开新路径,在一定程度上影响决策。③

　　智库的传播内容承载着智库观点。在决策过程中,一方面智库是一种相对稳定的政策研究和咨询机构,是政策过程中的一个重要参与者,可以通过参与重大决议和政策的起草,参与调研直接为政府决策建言献策,智库的传播内容表现出较高的学理性、专业性、可信度、可靠度,直接影响决策;④另一方面智库传播面向社会公众,正确阐释重大决策,做好公共政策话语的转换工作,增强社会公众对重大决策的信任感和理解度,引导民间智慧和社会力量深度参与政府决策,通过构建各种制衡机制推进政府民主进程,减少不和谐因素,进而自觉地贯彻落实,实现决策效益的最大化,促进经济增长和社会进步。⑤

　　智库的传播效果源于智库的传播渠道。在决策后,为达到智库的社会化、大众化、普及化的传播效果,一方面智库传播利用新媒体技术,借助网络平台、主流媒体、第三方平台等社交媒体,打造多元化的传播渠道,以亲民的方式和渠道传播智库思想,为受众提供互动平台,从而达到影响社会公众的目的,有利于政策的进一步推行;另一方面在与社会公众交流互动的过程中,智库传播实现了社会民意的利益表达和

---

　　① 冯雅,李刚.新型智库传播现状与优化策略研究——基于CTTI来源智库媒体影响力的实证分析[J].图书与情报,2019(3):20-28.

　　② 张欣,池忠军.发挥智库在公共治理中的作用[J].理论探索,2015(1):95-98.

　　③ 邵景均.加强中国特色新型智库建设[J].中国行政管理,2017(12):5.

　　④ 朱旭峰,苏钰.西方思想库对公共政策的影响力——基于社会结构的影响力分析框架构建[J].世界经济与政治,2004(12):21-26.

　　⑤ 邵景均.加强中国特色新型智库建设[J].中国行政管理,2017(12):5.

传递，纠正了社会舆论中存在的短视、片面或偏激的观点，并将公众意见或建议反馈给政府，进一步修正政策方案，会更容易得到社会的一致认同，形成有利于政策被决策者采纳的社会舆论，从而影响政府的公共决策，有助于政策出台后的执行。

智库传播在政策制定的前中后期发挥着重要桥梁和纽带作用。不仅有利于完善国家治理体系，提升国家治理能力，还通过互联网、新媒体等新兴传播手段最大程度地争取民意对公共决策的支持，起到咨政启民、理论阐释、政策解读、疏导公众情绪等作用。①

（二）智库传播着力讲好中国故事

中国智库要传播中国声音，塑造中国形象，承担起国家对外传播软实力的重要任务，提升国家软实力，扩大国际影响力和话语权，发挥对外传播中思想发动机的功能，为我国经济社会发展营造良好的国际环境。目前，智库国际传播主要从以下三个方面参与全球治理体系构建。

一是构建"中国话语体系"。长久以来，在中国的传播实践中，一方面，主流官方媒体充当核心行动主体的角色，但是由于受到政治、意识形态、文化、宗教等因素的影响，特别是国际社会对这一主体的信任不够，西方社会对中国官方媒体传播内容的客观性、真实性、完整性充满质疑，大大影响了对外传播的效果与效率，这就为智库预留了发挥功能的空间；另一方面，要发挥中国智库的主观能动性。过去的 20 多年，全球盛名的达沃斯论坛、香格里拉论坛、全球财富论坛都是欧美一流智库和相关机构在主导。中国智库要发挥主观能动性，就需要从国家战略传播的高度去建好智库，科学设置国际政策议程、在国际舞台提升话语权、影响国际舆论走向等。②

二是实施"走出去"战略。智库国际传播要对外发出中国声音，讲好中国故事，整合国际资源，参与到全球治理体系中。智库传播以平等对话、理性交流、破立并举的

---

① 冯雅，李刚.新型智库传播现状与优化策略研究——基于 CTTI 来源智库媒体影响力的实证分析[J].图书与情报，2019(3)：20 - 28.

② 丁炫凯.中国特色新型智库传播力评价体系研究[D].南京：南京大学，2018.

方式主动回应国际社会的关切;把握对外传播的时机与场合,在重大外交事件前后,积极影响国际舆论;在充分发挥自身研究长处的基础上,积极参与国际学术理论探讨与学术话语权构建,参与国际议题的探讨;对外传播国家价值,服务国家战略目标的实施。[①]

三是打造国际化品牌。中国智库要树立全球意识和品牌意识,将智库建设纳入国家外交大战略的体系中来运作,建立健全适合智库发展的体制和机制,找到一条适合中国国情的智库发展道路,增强智库国际传播能力,争夺智库国际话语权。智库传播通过品牌建设,利用品牌效应,借助品牌影响力,提高智库国际传播力,从而直接影响智库应对全球性问题和处置国际事务的能力,特别强调智库研究视角应该不断向国际议题扩展,通过组建全球性或地区性智库网络,不断扩大自身的全球化影响。[②]中国积极推动构建人类命运共同体,促进"一带一路"国际合作,参与和引领全球治理体系变革,因此,做好智库的国际传播,发挥公共外交的功能,是让世界了解中国、认识中国、接受中国,增强中国话语权,不断提升增加国家软实力的重要途径。[③]

二、基于 CTTI 来源智库的传播现状分析

智库影响力的提升和话语权的获得与智库机构传播紧密相关,成果发布渠道、宣传推广阵地的多样化加强了智库机构、决策机构、学术研究机构、国内外大众的交流机会,更多的机构、个人了解智库研究成果、智库机构理念,最终达到决策咨询、参与治理的目的。

当前,互联网成为信息传播的主要媒介。智库机构借助传统网站、新媒体平台传播研究成果,充分发挥互联网平台交互性、及时性、适用性强的优势,提高了传播效

①　尹朝晖.我国智库国际传播力建设的路径论析[J].领导科学,2016(4):59-62.
②　丁炫凯.中国特色新型智库传播力评价体系研究[D].南京:南京大学,2018.
③　中共中央宣传部.习近平新时代中国特色社会主义思想学习纲要[M].北京:人民出版社,2019.

率,增强了智库品牌的影响力。CTTI 数据库收录了诸多传播渠道的数据信息,主要包括:相关报道平台(纸媒、新闻网站、电视)、机构网站、新媒体平台(微博、微信等)。本报告选取 2018 年入围 CTTI 来自智库 706 家的网站和新媒体平台建设情况进行分析。

(一) 传播平台统计分析

根据统计,CTTI 数据库中的 706 家智库机构,拥有机构专属网站 503 家,创建微信公众号平台有 339 家,创建机构官方微博的有 101 家。

表 3.1 呈现不同类型智库统计网站、微信、微博建设情况。党政智库、党校、社科院智库传统网站建设起步早,受政务公开等因素影响,网站建设占比额度较高;企业智库、社会智库、媒体智库较其他智库类型在利用微信平台宣传优势明显;在微博平台的使用上,除媒体智库外,其他各类型的智库提升空间较大。

全媒体传播平台的建设可以满足个性化政策研究需求的同时,也可以提升具有国际影响力的专业型智库传播水平。长江产业经济研究院是国家高端智库建设培育单位、江苏省首批重点高端智库,通过构建多渠道的新型传播方式,不断拓展自媒体平台的运营能力,及时交流最新的学术资讯与研究成果,成功树立智库品牌形象。截至 2019 年 12 月 12 日,其官方网站共发布新闻通知 409 篇,首席专栏 298 篇,专家观点 514 篇,圆桌会议相关文章 149 篇,媒体文章 101 篇,研究报告 7 篇及 45 本系列著作的获取链接,其官方公众号共发布原创内容 419 篇,平均每篇文章的阅读量 1200+。

社会智库的传播理念相较于其他类型智库更灵活多变。以盘古智库为例,多平台、立体化、高效率的传播矩阵为智库的内外宣传提供了有力保障。盘古智库的专业媒体团队与国内外主流媒体建立了良好的合作渠道,能够协调一大批有影响力的大V、自媒体发声,通过各类媒体资源的调配,为智库发声。成立 6 年来,盘古智库搭建了"盘古智库""盘古智库印度研究中心""盘古智库东北亚研究中心""老龄与未来""智行院"等传播矩阵,培养了一大批"会发声"的青年学者与"爱阅读"的优质受众。目前,盘古智库共拥有自媒体平台 13 个,合作主流媒体 50+、自媒体 100+,连接专家350＋,网络平台累计粉丝数339万,百度相关新闻量155万篇,谷歌中英文相关新闻66.3万篇,媒体转载及报道13.2万篇,自媒体平台发文数量8000篇。这种横向传播平台丰富、纵向传播平台数量繁多的传播平台矩阵正成为媒体智库、社会智库的传播主流配置。

表3.1 CTTI来源智库网站、微信、微博平台建设情况(各类型)

智库类型	CTTI来源智库总数量	创建网站		创建微信		创建微博	
		总数量	占比	数量	占比	数量	占比
党政智库	69	63	91.30%	38	55.07%	14	20.29%
社科院智库	51	47	92.16%	24	47.06%	12	23.53%
党校智库	48	34	70.83%	23	47.92%	2	4.17%
高校智库	441	301	68.25%	200	45.35%	40	9.07%
军队智库	6	1	16.67%	2	33.33%	0	0%
科研院所智库	34	23	67.65%	12	35.29%	7	20.59%
企业智库	8	5	62.50%	6	75.00%	3	37.50%
社会智库	36	24	66.67%	23	63.89%	14	38.89%
媒体智库	13	5	38.46%	11	84.62%	9	69.23%

表3.2 CTTI来源智库网站、微信、微博平台建设统计(各地区)

省份	CTTI来源智库数量	创建官方网站		创建微信公众号		创建微博		三种渠道都创建的数量
		数量	占比	数量	占比	数量	占比	
北京	207	147	71.01%	104	50.24%	44	21.26%	31
天津	41	27	65.85%	16	39.02%	2	4.88%	2
河北	19	13	68.42%	7	36.84%	1	5.26%	1
山西	3	1	33.33%	0	0.00%	0	0.00%	0
内蒙古	6	4	66.67%	2	33.33%	1	16.67%	1
辽宁	14	9	64.29%	4	28.57%	0	0.00%	0
吉林	13	8	61.54%	6	46.15%	1	7.69%	1
黑龙江	12	8	66.67%	5	41.67%	1	8.33%	1

续表

省份	CTTI 来源智库数量	创建官方网站		创建微信公众号		创建微博		三种渠道都创建的数量
		数量	占比	数量	占比	数量	占比	
上海	81	57	70.37%	45	55.56%	13	16.05%	11
江苏	43	31	72.09%	21	48.84%	7	16.28%	4
浙江	17	15	88.24%	11	64.71%	3	17.65%	3
安徽	7	5	71.43%	2	28.57%	0	0.00%	0
福建	10	8	80.00%	0	0.00%	0	0.00%	0
江西	15	11	73.33%	4	26.67%	1	6.67%	1
山东	15	13	86.67%	6	40.00%	1	6.67%	1
河南	5	3	60.00%	3	60.00%	1	20.00%	1
湖北	27	21	77.78%	17	62.96%	4	14.81%	4
湖南	28	19	67.86%	13	46.43%	3	10.71%	2
广东	24	20	83.33%	23	95.83%	5	20.83%	5
广西	5	5	100.00%	2	40.00%	1	20.00%	1
海南	10	6	60.00%	1	10.00%	0	0.00%	0
重庆	18	15	83.33%	7	38.89%	2	11.11%	1
四川	16	11	68.75%	5	31.25%	5	31.25%	2
云南	12	6	50.00%	5	41.67%	0	0.00%	0
贵州	5	2	40.00%	2	40.00%	1	20.00%	0
西藏	3	3	100.00%	1	33.33%	0	0.00%	0
陕西	24	17	70.83%	9	37.50%	2	8.33%	1
甘肃	16	9	56.25%	11	68.75%	2	12.50%	2
青海	4	4	100.00%	2	50.00%	0	0.00%	0
宁夏	4	3	75.00%	4	100.00%	0	0.00%	0
新疆	2	2	100.00%	0	0.00%	0	0.00%	0

表 3.2、图 3.1、图 3.2、图 3.3 呈现 CTTI 来源智库中按照省份统计的网站、微信、微博建设情况。从绝对数量上看，同时具有机构网站、微信平台、微博平台的，北京、上海优势明显，符合当前新型智库发展趋势的客观事实；从建设比例方面看，各省份智库的网站建设情况好于微信平台建设，微博平台建设有待进一步加强。

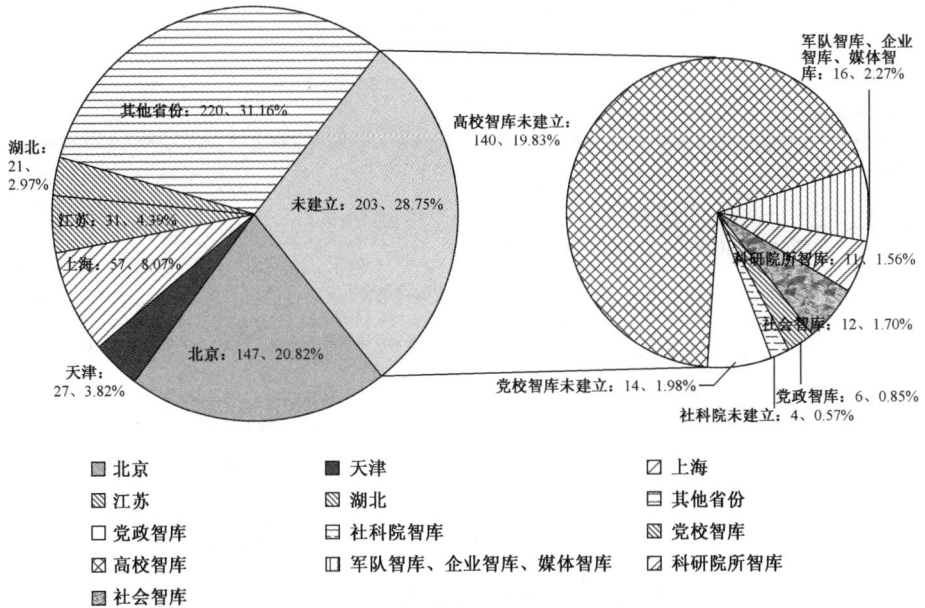

其他省份：220、31.16%

湖北：21、2.97%

江苏：31、4.39%

上海：57、8.07%

天津：27、3.82%

北京：147、20.82%

未建立：203、28.75%

高校智库未建立：140、19.83%

军队智库、企业智库、媒体智库：16、2.27%

科研院所智库：11、1.56%

社会智库：12、1.70%

党校智库未建立：14、1.98%

党政智库：6、0.85%

社科院未建立：4、0.57%

▨ 北京	■ 天津	▨ 上海
▨ 江苏	▨ 湖北	▤ 其他省份
□ 党政智库	▤ 社科院智库	▨ 党校智库
▨ 高校智库	□ 军队智库、企业智库、媒体智库	▨ 科研院所智库
▨ 社会智库		

图 3.1 CTTI 来源智库网站建设情况

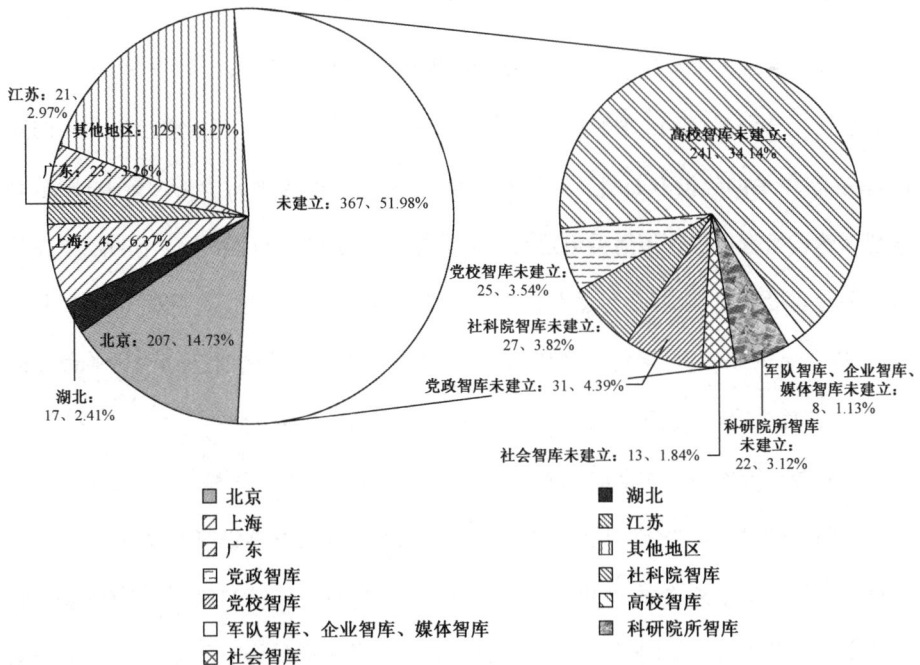

江苏：21、2.97%

其他地区：129、18.27%

广东：23、3.26%

上海：45、6.37%

北京：207、14.73%

湖北：17、2.41%

未建立：367、51.98%

高校智库未建立：241、34.14%

党校智库未建立：25、3.54%

社科院智库未建立：27、3.82%

党政智库未建立：31、4.39%

军队智库、企业智库、媒体智库未建立：8、1.13%

科研院所智库未建立：22、3.12%

社会智库未建立：13、1.84%

▨ 北京	■ 湖北
▨ 上海	▨ 江苏
▨ 广东	▤ 其他地区
□ 党政智库	▨ 社科院智库
▨ 党校智库	□ 高校智库
□ 军队智库、企业智库、媒体智库	▨ 科研院所智库
▨ 社会智库	

图 3.2 CTTI 来源智库微信建设统计

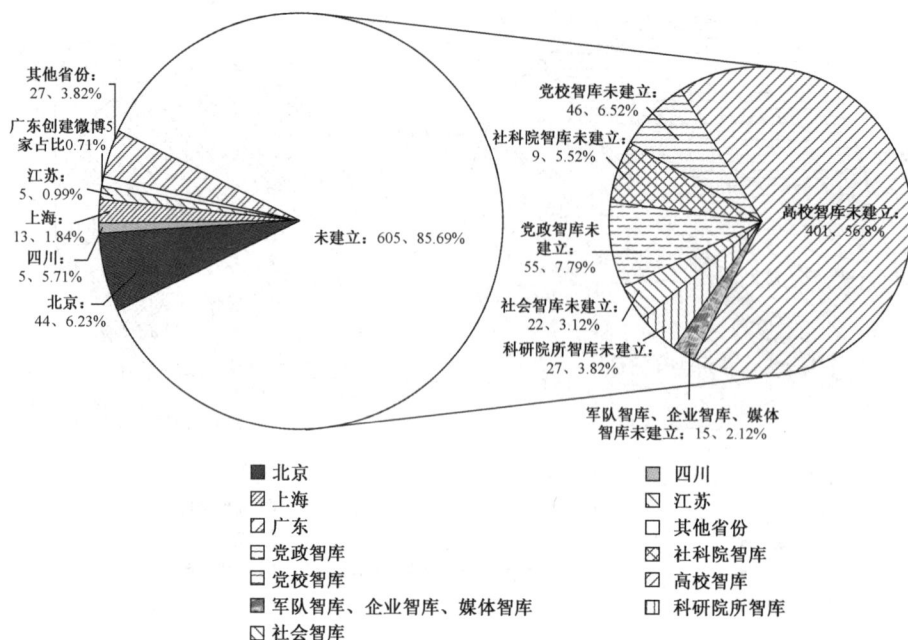

图 3.3 CTTI 来源智库微博建设统计

表 3.3 呈现国家高端智库、国家高端智库建设培育单位的网站、微信、微博建设情况统计。与全部 CTTI 来源智库平均数据相比,首批国家高端智库经过几年的建设,在传播渠道的建设方面明显处于领先地位,相关数据远远高于平均数值;国家高端智库建设培育单位在传播渠道建设方面数据略好于平均数值,优势不明显。在具体的平台建设方面,微博平台建设有待进一步加强。相比海外智库新媒体平台,善于利用 Twitter 和 Facebook 等加强传播力度,影响社会舆论和政府决策,其平台传播速度快、传播受众准、互动反馈及时,与微博平台有共性优势。

知名海外智库面向大众的传播理念也影响我国新型智库传播理念。以中国人民大学重阳金融研究院为例,其将传播与运营放在与研究同等重要的位置,坚持智库不仅仅是为领导层服务的理念,更是要将智库带来的信息传播给大众,人大重阳在精心运营中英文双语官网的同时,还不断拓展和提升自媒体平台的运营能力,在微信公众号和新浪微博等平台搭建了"人大重阳"传播矩阵,及时传递更新最新、最权威的学术研究成果。目前,微信公众号自创建以来,到 2019 年 12 月 12 日共发布了原创作品 144 篇,每篇文章的阅读量 1000＋。人大重阳的微博粉丝 90 万＋,每日阅读量 10000＋,让智库在更大的群体中有了更深远的影响。

表 3.3　国家高端智库、国家高端智库建设培育单位网站、微信、微博统计

类别	智库总数量	创建网站		创建微信		创建微博	
		数量	占比	数量	占比	数量	占比
全部 CTTI 来源智库	706	503	70.94％	339	47.81％	101	14.25％
国家高端智库	25	23	92.00％	17	68.00％	10	40.00％
国家高端智库建设培育单位	15	15	100.00％	9	60.00％	2	13.33％

(二) 传播平台传播力综合评价分析

本报告评价样本来源是 2018 CTTI 来源智库的 706 家的网站和新媒体平台建设情况的数据。评价指标体系分两级,包括 3 个一级指标(官方网站传播、微信公众号传播、微博传播),14 个二级指标,包括网站整站日均 IP、整站日均 VP、微信公众号平均阅读量、微博粉丝量、转发量等指标(详见表 3.4)。采用层次分析、熵权法相结合的评价方法(层次分析法是解决多目标复杂问题的系统决策分析方法,根据主观经验判断各个指标对研究目标影响程度的大小来确定指标权重的大小,主观性较强;熵权法是根据指标变异性的大小来确定客观权重,利用信息熵计算指标的熵权,以对层次分析法确定的指标权重进行调整,从而得出客观、符合实际需要的评价结果)。用层次分析法确定指标的权重,同时采用熵值定权法对确定的权重进行修订,使得赋权更加可靠。

表3.4 智库传播力综合评价指标体系

智库传播力综合评价指标体系		
	指标	单项指标
智库传播力评价	官方网站	整站日均 IP
		整站日均 VP
		百度权重
		移动权重
		百度流量预计
		索引量
		百度收录
		百度反向链接
	微信公众号	平均阅读量
		原创文章数
	官方微博	平均点赞数
		平均转发量
		粉丝数
		平均评论数

具体步骤:

第一步:层次分析赋权

(1)构造成对判断矩阵(对指标重要性逐对比较,即对每两个指标 g_i 和 g_j 判断哪一个重要,g_i 与 g_j 的重要性之比为 r_{ij})

$$\begin{bmatrix} r_{11} & r_{12} & \cdots & r_{1n} \\ r_{21} & r_{22} & \cdots & r_{2n} \\ \cdots & \cdots & \cdots & \cdots \\ r_{n1} & r_{n2} & \cdots & r_{nn} \end{bmatrix}$$

(2)成对判断矩阵标准化。

$$\overline{r_{ij}} = \frac{r_{ij}}{\sum_{k=1}^{n} r_{kj}} \quad (i, j = 1, 2, \cdots n)$$

（3）将标准化的矩阵按行相加。

$$\overline{w_i} = \sum_{j=1}^{n} \overline{r_{ij}} \quad (i = 1,2\cdots n)$$

（4）将矩阵$\overline{w} = (\overline{w_1}, \overline{w_2}, \cdots, \overline{w_n})$标准化

$$w_i = \frac{\overline{w_i}}{\sum_{j=1}^{n} \overline{w_j}} \quad (i = 1,2,\cdots,n)$$

第二步：熵权法赋权

现有 m 个待评项目，n 个评价指标，形成原始数据矩阵 $A = (a_{ij})_{m \times n}$

$$A = \begin{bmatrix} a_{11} & a_{12} & \cdots & a_{1n} \\ a_{21} & a_{22} & \cdots & a_{2n} \\ \cdots & \cdots & \cdots & \cdots \\ a_{m1} & a_{m2} & \cdots & a_{mn} \end{bmatrix}$$

其中，a_{ij} 为第 j 个指标下第 i 个项目的评价值。

对于某一评价指标，信息熵为：

$$e_j = -k \sum_{i=1}^{m} p_{ij} \cdot \ln p_{ij} \quad (i = 1,2,\cdots,m; j = 1,2,\cdots,n)$$

式中 $p_{ij} = \dfrac{a_{ij}}{\sum\limits_{j=1}^{m} a_{ij}}$, $\quad k = 1/\ln m$ 。

根据信息熵的基本原理，指标的信息效用价值取决于该指标熵值与 1 的差，则指标的熵权为：

$$W_j = (1 - e_j) / \sum_{j=1}^{n} (1 - e_j) \quad (j = 1,2,\cdots,n)$$

于是，得到评价指标的熵权向量：$W = (W_1, W_2, \cdots, W_n)$

第三步：组合权重

兼顾层次分析法（AHP）和熵权法的优缺点，取二者之所长，将层次分析法（AHP）和熵权法相结合得到评价指标的组合权重：

$$\overline{W} = \left\{ \frac{W_1 w_1}{\sum\limits_{j=1}^{n} W_j w_j}, \frac{W_2 w_2}{\sum\limits_{j=1}^{n} W_j w_j}, \cdots, \frac{W_n w_n}{\sum\limits_{j=1}^{n} W_j w_j} \right\} = (\overline{W_1}, \overline{W_2}, \cdots \overline{W_n})$$

显然,组合权重$\overline{W_j}$与w_j和W_j都应尽可能相近,根据最小相对信息熵原理,有

$$\min M = \sum_{j=1}^{n} \overline{W_j}(\ln \overline{W_j} - \ln w_j) + \sum_{j=1}^{n} \overline{W_j}(\ln \overline{W_J} - \ln W_j)$$

拉格朗日乘数解上述优化问题,得到优化组合权重:

$$\overline{W} = \left\{ \frac{(W_1 w_1)^{0.5}}{\sum_{j=1}^{n}(W)_j w_j)^{0.5}}, \frac{(W_2 w_2)^{0.5}}{\sum_{j=1}^{n}(W_j w_j)^{0.5}}, \cdots, \frac{(W_n w_n)^{0.5}}{\sum_{j=1}^{n}(W_j w_j)^{0.5}} \right\}$$
$$= (\overline{W_1}, \overline{W_2}, \cdots \overline{W_n})$$

基于 AHP‐熵权法的指标权重计算结果为:

整站日均IP	整站日均PV	百度权重	移动权重	百度流量预计	索引量	百度收录	百度反向链接	平均阅读数	原创文章数	平均点赞数	平均转发量	粉丝数	平均评论数
0.49	0.49	0.79	0.77	0.71	0.57	0.97	0.60	0.74	0.84	0.27	0.25	0.82	0.36

第四步:计算评价得分

将得到的优化组合权重,带入下面公式中,即得到 m 个待评价项目的评价得分结果:

$$F = A^* \overline{W} \quad (i=1,2,\cdots,m; j=1,2,\cdots,n)$$

其中$\overline{W}$为优化组合权重;A^*为智库传播力评价指标值。

由于综合评价指标体系中的各评估指标计量单位不同,在构建指标时首先应该统一评估指标的量纲。研究对采集到的数据进行无量纲化,把各项指标中最大值取作1,其他数据按最大值进行比例计算。用标准化的数据乘以该指标的权重,求和得到各智库样本的网络传播力综合指数(具体各智库机构传播力得分不公布)。表3.5呈现各得分排名智库类型的分布情况,表中与总体情况系数相比可以体现排名段内该智库传播平台建设总体情况。

在排名1～100名的智库机构中,智库传播平台传播力成绩从高到低为:媒体智库、企业智库、党政智库、社会智库、军队智库、科研院所智库、社科院智库、高校智库、党校行政学院智库。在排名1～200名的智库机构中,智库传播平台传播力成绩从高

表3.5　CTTI来源智库传播平台传播力评价分段排名统计表

智库类型		党政智库	社科院智库	党校行政学院智库	高校智库	军队智库	科研院所智库	企业智库	社会智库	媒体智库
总数		69	51	48	441	6	34	8	36	13
占比		9.77%	7.22%	6.80%	62.46%	0.85%	4.82%	1.13%	5.10%	1.84%
排名1~100名 各类型数量	数量	18	7	2	49	1	5	3	8	7
	占比	18.00%	7.00%	2.00%	49.00%	1.00%	5.00%	3.00%	8.00%	7.00%
	与总体比系数	1.84	0.97	0.29	0.78	1.18	1.04	2.65	1.57	3.80
排名1~200名 各类型数量	数量	31	14	14	104	1	11	4	13	8
	占比	15.50%	7.00%	7.00%	52.00%	0.50%	5.50%	2.00%	6.50%	4.00%
	与总体比系数	1.59	0.97	1.03	0.83	0.59	1.14	1.77	1.27	2.17
排名1~300名 各类型数量	数量	49	22	28	157	1	12	4	17	10
	占比	16.33%	7.33%	9.33%	52.33%	0.33%	4.00%	1.33%	5.67%	3.33%
	与总体比系数	1.67	1.02	1.37	0.84	0.39	0.83	1.18	1.11	1.81
排名1~400名 各类型数量	数量	57	40	33	215	2	15	6	20	12
	占比	14.25%	10.00%	8.25%	53.75%	0.50%	3.75%	1.50%	5.00%	3.00%
	与总体比系数	1.46	1.38	1.21	0.86	0.59	0.78	1.32	0.98	1.63
排名1~500名 各类型数量	数量	60	49	39	283	2	21	7	27	12
	占比	12.00%	9.80%	7.80%	56.60%	0.40%	4.20%	1.40%	5.40%	2.40%
	与总体比系数	1.23	1.36	1.15	0.91	0.47	0.87	1.24	1.06	1.30
排名1~600名 各类型数量	数量	69	51	48	356	2	25	7	30	12
	占比	11.50%	8.50%	8.00%	59.33%	0.33%	4.17%	1.17%	5.00%	2.00%
	与总体比系数	1.18	1.18	1.18	0.95	0.39	0.87	1.03	0.98	1.09
排名1~706名 各类型数量	数量	69	51	48	441	6	34	8	36	13
	占比	9.77%	7.22%	6.80%	62.46%	0.85%	4.82%	1.13%	5.10%	1.84%
	与总体比系数	1.00	1.00	1.00	1.00	1.00	1.00	1.00	1.00	1.00

到低为：媒体智库、企业智库、党政智库、社会智库、科研院所智库、党校行政学院智库、社科院智库、高校智库、军队智库；在排名1～300名的智库机构中，智库传播平台传播力成绩从高到低为：媒体智库、党政智库、党校行政学院智库、企业智库、社会智库、社科院智库、高校智库、科研院所智库、军队智库。总体而言，媒体智库、党政智库、企业智库传播力得分整体较高，高校智库、军队智库得分较低。

三、智库传播存在问题和对策建议

（一）存在问题

1. 自身传播的意识不够强

就目前来看，大部分智库对传播的重要性依然认识不足，传播意识相对薄弱，且往往选择用大量笔墨对研究成果进行宣传报道，忽视了对智库自身的介绍以及传播，社会大众对智库了解认识的机会不多。

值得注意的是，不同性质、不同地域智库的传播意识、传播特征存在较大差异。从智库的性质来说，由于高校智库可以直接借助所在高校的传播平台和体系，因此其对各类媒体利用率较高，媒体报道数量在各类智库中最多；党政军智库、科研院所智库则由于更加接近决策中心，研究成果易有涉密限制，因此相应的媒体报道数量较少，更加倾向于通过内参报送等渠道扩大影响；与其他各类智库相比，社会智库的数量最少，但在新媒体与网络的应用上最为自由灵活。从智库所在地域上说，经济发达的地区往往更加关注新型智库的建设问题，这就为智库的发展提供了良好的外部环境和稳定的资金来源，这些地区的智库的传播意识相对较强、媒体利用率更高、方式更加灵活、内容更加多样。

智库机构与单纯学术机构的一个重要区别是学术机构强调"板凳要坐十年稳""两耳不闻窗外事"，较少关注公共关系的营造。[①] 但除少数具有保密性质的智库外，

---

① 李刚，郭婷婷.智库嵌入式决策咨询服务模式[J].智库理论与实践，2019(4):1-6.

绝大多数智库都需发挥智库的传播功能,构建智库与大众、政府、企业、媒体、学术机构的合作关系。传播力是智库的生命线,传播效率的高低直接关乎智库的生存发展。但在媒体高度发达的今天,不应由于类型与地域的不同而产生传播意识上的过大差异。

2. 传播水平有待提高

(1) 未能打造基于自身功能定位的传播机制

近年来,新型智库建设取得了长足的发展。但一些完全不具备资格的营利性的机构也借此蜂拥而起,摇身一变成为"智库",出现智库泛化的现象,大大影响了新型智库建设的质量。有些智库则尚未确定自己发展的方向,还停留在"什么是热点,就研究什么""跟着任务走"的阶段。这些都反映出部分智库对自身认识不够全面、定位不够清晰,有计划、有重点地提升自身的传播力更是无从谈起。

(2) 传播内容的产出同实际需要未能完全匹配

当前国内国际形势极端复杂多变,外交、军事等多个关键领域需要更加专业化的智力支持,正是智库积极回应国家需求、吸引公众关注的重要契机。但部分智库依旧难以脱离传统研究范式的窠臼,在专属智库的研究方法论上突破不多,研究视野领域不够全面深刻,高水平、高质量的专业化智库数量仍然不足,有影响力的传播内容产出较少。

(3) 传播内容的表现力不强,吸引力不够

目前,部分智库的传播内容主要以新闻稿的形式加以呈现,在极易产生同质化问题的情况下,只能将学术产出、会议活动等智库的基本动态进行简单展示,理念功能、思想体系、研究特色等智库的核心特征未能得到实质性宣传。

3. 传播渠道较为单一,传播体系尚未完善

尽管新媒体的发展开辟了广阔的传播空间,但部分智库在传播渠道的选择上依旧较为单一。从类型看,受资金成本、传播能力以及智库性质等方面的影响,智库自媒体的建设力度较为薄弱,其宣传以网络平台为主,其中又以新闻门户型网站的分量

最重。从级别上看，由于主流媒体往往具有一定的影响力以及公信力，大多数智库仍然倾向于选择主流媒体作为传播渠道，在一定程度上影响智库传播的大众化、社会化。

传播渠道的多样性以及实际利用上的单一性之间的矛盾，反映了当前我国智库运用各类媒体平台不够灵活全面，无论是智库自媒体的建设还是与主流媒体的合作等都存在利用率不足、不全面、不深刻的问题。

（二）对策建议

随着全媒体融媒体时代的来临，如果智库不能充分适应全新的媒体环境，利用多种渠道提升传播效率，那么智库的传播效果将大大降低，也就无法满足新型智库的建设要求。

1. 提升智库传播意识

自觉的传播意识是新型智库开展一切传播活动的前提。欧美智库除了认识到传播的重要性，还应与媒体建立良好的合作关系。此外，他们也致力于加强与媒体的合作与融合，通过自身的外联部门，积极主动地将科研的最新动态以及对政策的见解发送给媒体，许多智库研究员也频繁出现在新闻媒体上，对时事政策、重大事件公开发表评论，常规性地开展传播活动。

一是设立专门传播部门或任命传播专员。欧美智库一般都会选择设立专门部门，常设智库总监负责总体协调智库传播事宜，投入大量的资源来增加媒体曝光度，提升智库的社会形象。如布鲁金斯学会就拥有一支经验丰富的智库传播团队，该团队花费大量时间和精力更新网站上的智库信息，并实时监控网站数据流量，确保智库在知名媒体上的高曝光率。我国新型智库中，党政智库、党校社科院智库一般都由宣传部或者分管宣传工作的相关人员负责智库传播，但智库传播不是其主要工作职责；高校智库由于一般都是高校内设机构，不具备专业的宣传力量，智库传播工作成为高校智库行政办公人员兼职工作；社会智库具有灵活的运营机制，一般都会专人负责智库传播。

二是打造多元智库传播场景。智库传播不仅包括发布研究报告，还应该包括参与政府调研活动、参加决策咨询活动和政策路演活动等。一方面，通过举办各类智库活动、参与政府决策工作场景，全面了解政策产生的前因后果，与政府建立良好的互动关系，对传播智库观点有积极作用。另一方面，通过打造这类智库传播场景，了解政府部门信息为接下来的研究确定具体方向做准备。因为很多领导的讲话都有两个版本，一个是现场口头的版本，另一个是书面的文字版本。有时候这两个版本之间差异大，很多重要信息、观点和意见，领导在做报告时说了，但是这些信息不适合向全社会公开。如果智库研究仅仅根据书面稿进行，势必会造成很多"误读"和"误判"。[①]因此，多元的智库传播场景也是智库和政府信息互动的有效场所。

三是加大与媒体的合作交流。智库机构和智库学者都应注重和媒体的关系，打造智库品牌。[②] 智库要有意识地利用媒体宣传，了解媒体、期刊、报纸的智库版并加以利用，扩大自身影响力，实现智库与媒体的双赢。智库机构或者智库专家成为媒体集中采访的对象往往在两个时间节点上，一是当普遍被关注的问题产生新的变化时，二是当出现全新的热点事件时。[③] 智库专家通过媒体传播他们的研究成果和观点，智库也可以随时向主流媒体推荐最新研究成果，主流媒体的报道可以吸引受众的注意力，产生巨大影响力，大大提高智库传播水平。

2. 提高智库传播内容质量

智库高质量的传播内容是智库传播力提升的核心因素。一方面，智库的传播内容应从社会环境与受众需求出发，既要影响决策层，又要注重与不同阶层、不同群体的社会大众近距离接触。如《人民日报》就经常通过图解新闻、漫画新闻、短片新闻等通俗易懂的形式，对一些深度的智库研究报告进行解读，使其被更广泛的群体了解、接受。另一方面，要注意传播内容的时效性。如发生重大国际事件、某一形势发生重大转变等关键时刻，即可以通过发表文章、接受媒体采访等形式传播影响。

---

① 李刚,郭婷婷.智库嵌入式决策咨询服务模式[J].智库理论与实践,2019(4):1-6.
② 甘琳,李刚.IP建设是提升智库品牌竞争力的关键[J].出版参考,2018(9):12-16.
③ 丁炫凯.中国特色新型智库传播力评价体系研究[D].南京:南京大学,2018.

提高智库传播内容质量,可以从以下三个方面努力:

一是形成特色鲜明的智库研究领域。诸如中国社会科学院、国务院发展研究中心等这类国家级综合性智库,研究团队、资源丰富,研究领域广。其他绝大部分智库都应该充分考虑自身优势,集中资源优势打造智库研究领域品牌。长江产业经济研究院致力于经济领域的研究,聚焦中国经济运行、产业经济、金融发展、中国宏观经济、开放经济和企业发展战略六大方向,通过对长三角乃至国内经济的长期研究,掌握经济发展的脉络趋势,清晰、鲜明解答经济发展问题,特设的"圆桌会"板块内容涵盖国内经济热点话题解读、中国发展模式探析,与国际发展接轨等重点内容,形成研究领域明确、脉络清晰、层次鲜明的新型智库传播模式。

二是持续推出优质的智慧产品。智慧产品的设置要充分体现三个"结合":结合热点政策、结合重大战略、结合外部需求。2019 年 12 月,国家刚刚颁布《长江三角洲区域一体化发展规划纲要》,长江产经研究院就发布了相关经济学分析研究论文,站在国家乃至全球的视角探究长三角一体化的重要性以及实施策略,与境外的一些智库高频发布"瘦身"文章、大量使用图片而忽视学术严谨性只顾抢占先机博取眼球的情形大相径庭。中国人民大学重阳金融研究院连续五年紧跟中央"一带一路"倡议,持续发布"一带一路"研究成果。从 2014 年的《欧亚时代:丝绸之路经济带建设蓝皮书 2014—2015》到 2016 年的《"一带一路"与国际贸易新格局:丝绸之路经济带智库蓝皮书 2015—2016》,再到 2019 年的《"一带一路"这五年的故事》,不仅为"一带一路"倡议建言献策,更重要的是向世界展示了中国作为一个新兴大国,如何带动周边沿线国家共同建设"一带一路"基础设施,如何在经济、文化等方面相互促进、相互融合等历程,切实助力"一带一路"倡议实施的形象。

三是加强传播内容的质量控制。形成特色鲜明的研究领域解决传播内容设置是源头问题,推出高质量的智慧成品是结果呈现,那中间环节的质量控制就是一个实现的过程路径。传播内容的质量控制不仅包括研究报告等文本的质量控制,还包括会议会务等智库活动产品的过程控制,看似不大的问题反映的是质量控制能力不足。

小问题也会影响智库专业化的品牌形象和影响力。文档管控是智库品牌建设不可或缺的环节。实际上,对一个智库研究报告或一个智库项目来说,从开始介入工作到工作推进全过程的活动记录和资料都具备保存价值,智库应设置专门人员和场所管理存放这些文件和档案(包括纸质的和电子的),将其按照一定的归档模式整理存放好,为下一次咨询工作做参考方便备查。[①]

3. 打造多元化传播渠道

面对"互联网＋"时代传播环境的变化,智库应该从更接近大众的方式入手,直接与大众交流,了解趋势,满足大众的需求。美国的布鲁金斯学会、兰德公司、英国的海外发展研究所等,也都经历了从政策圈、学术圈向大众圈发展的过程。改善传统的单一化传播平台,搭建新型立体化传播平台,整合实体传播平台,社交网络传播平台,增加用户的参与度和体验感,实现智库传播平台的全面优化。一方面,重视智库机构的官方网站建设,网站是信息传播的主阵地,从收集到的数据可以看出,很多智库机构的官方网站处于"瘫痪"状态,属于僵尸网站。经常出现不可访问,没有及时更新等情况,有的智库甚至没有自己的官方网站。与国外的著名智库机构相比,网站入链数,总链数,网页的浏览量和访问率等都存在很大差距,中国智库的网站建设还有很长一段路要走[②];另一方面,建设有特色的智库新媒体平台,及时更新研究成果,用多语种发布内容,并将内容分门别类,打破语言障碍,吸引全球受众访问,浏览内容,不断增强微信公众号,官方微博的功能,增加关键字检索功能,社交媒体功能,个性化服务功能,该平台可接受受众进行信息反馈,能够与用户在第一时间保持沟通,互动,提高用户参与度,极大程度上简化了发布信息的方式,简单易行,互动性强,扩大智库传播范围,跟踪受众的浏览情况,分析受众的阅读倾向,可提供点对点的个性化服务,满足受众的个性化需求,提升网站、新媒体平台的传播力水平。

---

① 李刚,郭婷婷.智库嵌入式决策咨询服务模式[J].智库理论与实践,2019(4):1-6.
② 丁炫凯.中国特色新型智库传播力评价体系研究[D].南京:南京大学,2018.

专题四　智库在对外关系中扮演重要角色

　　2014 年 11 月,习近平总书记在中央外事工作会议上的讲话明确了中国大国外交的定位,标志着我国进入了大国外交的新时代。党的十八大以来,以习近平同志为总书记的党中央把握国际形势新变化,积极推进外交理论和实践创新,提出一系列新思想、新理念、新举措,推进中国特色大国外交开创新局面。[①] 智库作为对外关系的"参谋"和"尖兵",承担了宣传国家政策、参与国际事务和舆论引导等重要使命。在中国特色大国外交的新形势下,我国智库纷纷加快了国际化步伐,不断加深国际合作,重视对经济、政治、军事、科教文化等多领域全球性课题的研究,为大国外交出谋划策,智库逐渐成为国与国之间沟通交流的重要桥梁,并为大国外交提供智力支撑。

一、新时代外交战略的新变化

　　随着中国综合国力的大幅提升,中国已经成为全球治理舞台中的建设性力量,这为中国全面、深度参与全球治理提供了难得的历史机遇,但也给中国带来了来自经济全球化方面的诸多压力、风险和挑战。伴随着世界多极化、经济全球化、社会信息化、文化多样化,全球发展不平衡现象加剧,贫富分化日益加大,霸权主义、强权政治、新干涉主义、保护主义、民粹主义、恐怖主义、种族主义思潮泛滥,地区冲突和局部动荡频繁发生,非法移民、粮食安全、气候变化、能源资源短缺、网络安全、核扩散等复杂问题亟待解决,这些弊端导致全球问题不断产生和积累,出现世界秩序失调的状态。为

---

　　① 齐鹏飞.改革开放 40 年"中国特色大国外交"的发展历程和基本经验[J].学海,2019(01):5 - 18.

有效解决危机、应对全球性挑战、改变制度僵局，国际社会有必要对全球治理体系进行实质性变革，推动构建与经济全球化相一致的全球治理体系。①

党的十九届四中全会对"坚持和完善独立自主的和平外交政策，推动构建人类命运共同体"做出精辟论述，这既是推进全球治理格局变化、提升我国国际话语权的战略抉择，同时也是回应国际社会期待、承担大国责任的必然要求。习近平总书记深刻洞悉全球治理变革大势，提出"我们将从世界和平与发展的大义出发，贡献处理当代国际关系的中国智慧，贡献完善全球治理的中国方案，为人类社会应对 21 世纪的各种挑战做出自己的贡献"的理念，并在政治、经济、外交等领域展开丰富的实践活动。②

第一，在政治领域，中国积极推广中国全球治理的新理念和治理方案。2016 年在杭州举办的 G20 峰会上，习近平总书记针对世界经济、金融、贫困治理等议题，提出中国的解决方案，阐释了中国的全球治理哲学。③ 2017 年，习近平总书记在达沃斯经济论坛开幕式上提出，"坚持与时俱进，打造公正合理的治理模式"，世界经济论坛创始人兼执行主席施瓦布也表示，"世界正进入多极化转型时期，达沃斯论坛更加期待中国声音，期待倾听习主席诠释中国如何在国际事务中施展有责任的领导力"。在 2017 年金砖国家领导人厦门峰会上，习近平总书记指出："加快全球经济治理改革，提高新兴市场国家和发展中国家代表性和发言权，为各国发展创造良好外部环境。"2018 年，在南非约翰内斯堡举行的金砖国家工商论坛上，习近平总书记提出"坚持多边主义，完善全球治理"的主张。2019 年，在中法全球治理论坛闭幕式上，习近平总书记指出"要坚持共商共建共享的全球治理观，坚持全球事务由各国人民商量着办，积极推进全球治理规则民主化"④。

---

① 金灿荣,石雨松.习近平的全球治理理念[J].太平洋学报,2019,27(10):10-20.
② 邱昌情.全球治理与中国国家治理能力建设研究[J].广西社会科学,2019(03):30-37.
③ 欧阳向英,李燕.当代中国的全球治理观[J].观察与思考,2019(06):65-72.
④ 新华网."平语"近人——习近平关于全球治理的重要论述.[EB/OL].[2019-12-2].http://www.xinhuanet.com/politics/2015-11/16/c_128433360.htm

第二，在经济领域，中国主张国际经济金融组织应切实反映国际格局变化，扩大新兴市场国家和发展中国家的代表性和话语权，促进全球治理体系更加完善，从而代表大多数国家的切身利益。中国近年来提出的"一带一路"倡议、建设金砖国家新开发银行、建设亚洲基础设施投资银行、设立丝路基金、出台中非"十大合作计划"等多项倡议，这些多边机构的设立和运行既帮助维护了国际金融秩序的稳定，也为发展中国家的国内基础设施建设提供了重要的资金保障。① 如"一带一路"倡议作为中国为改善全球经济治理体系、促进全球共同发展繁荣提出的方案，截至2019年8月底，中国已与136个国家和30个国际组织签署了195份共建"一带一路"倡议框架下的合作协议，②这其中大部分的合作对象都是发展中国家。从某种意义上说，多边机构的兴起反映了新兴国家群体性崛起这个大趋势，体现了世界政治格局的深刻变化，也预示着国际秩序和全球治理体系正迎来一场大变革。

第三，在外交领域，中国领导人科学分析当前的国际局势，合理定位中国的国际地位，在此基础上适时调整我国对外政策和对外战略，制定了符合国情、世情的国际战略。2014年11月，在中央外事工作会议上，习近平总书记就提出，"中国必须要有自己特色的大国外交，中国的对外工作要有鲜明的中国特色、中国风格、中国气派"。这意味着中国正式确立了大国外交的定位，中国进入了大国外交的新时代。在理论创新方面，中国提出了中国梦并深刻阐述其世界意义，提出构建新型国际关系和全球伙伴关系网络，打造人类命运共同体，建立正确义利观等。在实践创新方面，中国努力构建全球伙伴关系网络，拓展全方位外交布局，深入参与全球治理，积极贡献中国方案，加强公共外交和人文交流，增强国家软实力。③

值得关注的是，公共外交作为外交工作的重要方面，在习近平新时代中国特色社

① 朱旭.全球治理变革与中国的角色[J].当代世界与社会主义，2018(03):158-165.
② 贾平凡.欢迎世界搭乘"中国号"快车.[EB/OL].[2019-12-25].http://ydyl.people.com.cn/n1/2019/1017/c411837-31405030.html
③ 张启群.十八大以来中国特色大国外交研究[D].山东师范大学，2018.

会主义外交思想指引下也得到前所未有的重视。党的十八大报告提出"扎实推进公共外交和人文交流",随后党的十九大报告进一步提出"加强中外人文交流,以我为主、兼收并蓄,向世界展现真实、立体、全面的中国,提高国家文化软实力"。我国在公共外交领域开展了各类宣传推介活动,针对参与全球治理现代化建设,推动全球治理体系变革等重大问题从各个层面进行了全方位分析,让国际社会能深入、全面地了解中国在新时代的全球治理理念、行动与作用。同时,在公共外交体系中,智库外交往往起到智力和信息中枢的重要作用,被称作公共外交的"大脑""思想工厂"和"议程设定者",被赋予宣传国家形象和国家政策、参与公共事务和舆论宣传等重要使命。新形势下我国智库纷纷加快了国际化步伐,不断加深国际合作,重视地区安全问题、国际经济问题等全球性课题的研究,在交流与合作过程中不断开辟新平台。

二、发挥自身优势,积极投身外交活动

　　纷繁复杂的国际形势以及中国在国际舞台上扮演的日趋重要角色对智库提出了新要求。本部分以《CTTI智库报告(2018)》的分类方法为参考,对党政部门智库、社科院智库、党校行政学院智库、企业智库、社会智库和传媒智库类等类型智库在外交活动中发挥的积极作用展开分析。①

(一)党政部门智库

　　在中国特色新型智库建设中,党政智库具有举足轻重的地位和意义。党的十八届三中全会以来,党政部门智库积极贯彻中央加强中国特色新型智库建设的精神,结合自身定位与专业特长,在外交政策研究、公共外交事务参与方面积极探索。②

　　如在外交政策研究方面,中国现代国际关系研究院长期以来在国际战略、世界政治与经济、中国与各国双边外交、国际涉台港澳问题等方面积极开展综合性及专项性

---

① 李刚,王斯敏,邹婧雅.CTTI智库报告(2018)[M].南京:南京大学出版社,2019.
② 程同顺,王虹.党政决策部门与智库信息共享机制研究[J].学习论坛,2018(05):61-66.

研究工作。该院自 2001 年起已经连续 19 年发布战略黄皮书《国际战略与安全形势评估》，对国际形势和国际热点问题进行了全面梳理、系统总结和深刻阐释，为我国外交政策的制定和外交战略的实施提供借鉴和参考。此外，该院还主办《现代国际关系》《国际研究参考》等知名刊物，定期输出理论研究成果，向党中央、国务院献言献策。①

在参与公共外交事务方面，国务院发展研究中心与伊斯兰合作组织代表团、中日经济协会、印度国家转型委员会等机构展开国际交流，就中国发展经验、多边贸易体制、双方机构间合作等内容进行交流，充分发挥公共外交的作用。而上海国际问题研究院则通过与世界银行举办了"世行与中高收入国家合作：IEG 评估例证"研讨会，并受外交部委托举办"叙利亚问题的出路与前景"国际研讨会，配合第三轮中日韩北极事务高级对话举办第五届北太平洋北极研究共同体会议，发挥智库服务国家总体外交和上海地方外事的功能。②

（二）社科院智库

社科院作为党委、政府领导下的专门从事哲学社会科学研究的机构，在新型智库建设中拥有独特优势。在国家对中国特色新型智库全面部署下，中国社会科学院以及省级、地市级社会科学院积极参与公共外交活动，起到了"思想库"和"智囊团"的作用。

如在理论建设方面，中国社会科学院聚焦我国"一带一路"对外战略，进行了一系列理论研究，先后发布了《"一带一路"定位、内涵及需要优先处理的关系》《"一带一路"建设与东盟地区的自由贸易区安排》《"一带一路"与亚洲一体化模式的重构》《21世纪海上丝绸之路：目标构想、实施基础与对策研究》《中美丝绸之路战略比较研

① 忻华. 智库、外交政策和地缘政治［M］. 南京：南京大学出版社，2019. 173－197.
② 上海国际问题研究院 2018 年年报.［EB/OL］.［2019－06－19］. http://www. siis. org. cn/Content/Info/4U7TFMX4XBYM

究》①等一系列专题研究,对"一带一路"沿线国家分国别进行了国情、经济、投资、双边关系等方面全面深入的研究和分析,为实施"一带一路"倡议提供了重要参考。而广东省社会科学院国际问题研究所结合区域经济特点,完成《"广东—东盟"战略深化研究》《粤港澳大湾区世界级城市群建设研究》《粤港澳大湾区文化比较研究》《关于广东海洋经济重大问题的研究》等40多项广东省级重大决策咨询课题,多项研究成果获得广东省委省政府主要领导的肯定性批示并转化为政府文件执行。同时,该院编著《粤港澳大湾区建设蓝皮书(2019)》《南亚资本合作研究》等书籍20多本,学术及社会影响力稳步提升。②

在信息保障服务方面,上海社会科学院作为首批国家高端智库试点单位之一,与香港贸发局联合发布了《"一带一路"中外合作园区发展报告》,③立足自身地方特色,探讨内地企业在"一带一路"相关国家设立的经贸合作区建设的背景及具体成效,提出进一步推动我国境外经贸合作区的思路和政策建议。同时该院积极发挥高端智库平台的优势,与中国国际经济交流中心合作共建了"一带一路"大数据库(又称为"丝路信息网"),该数据库涵盖"一带一路"相关国家和众多城市,包括丝路国家库、丝路城市库、文献数据库、统计数据库、投资项目库、经济运行报告库、中国国策库等9个子数据库,为各级政府、企业以及参与"一带一路"建设的国家提供信息平台。④

(三) 党校行政学院智库

党校智库是新时代中国特色新型智库的重要组成部分,在服务党委和政府科学决策、推进国家治理体系和治理能力现代化建设中作用日益凸显,一些党校行政学院智库通过在一系列外交活动中发挥宣传和推介在作用,成为对外宣传平台、对外交流

　① 中国社会科学网.中国社科院发布"一带一路"系列研究成果.[EB/OL].[2015-7-14].http://www.cssn.cn/xspj/xspj_yw/201507/t20150701_2056540.shtml? COLLCC=3991738916&.
　② 李涛.地方社科院加强新型智库建设研究[J].云南社会科学,2016(06):1-7.
　③ 人民网.上海社科院发布"一带一路"系列研究成果丝路信息网打造大数据库.[EB/OL].[2017-5-19]https://www.sohu.com/a/141728319_114731
　④ 田祚雄.地方社科院智库建设的现实困境与发展路径[J].理论月刊,2016(10):136-141.

合作平台和高端智库国际合作平台。①

以中共中央党校②为例，该校通过举办研讨会、论坛、智库座谈、学员交流、发表演讲、召开媒体招待会等多种形式，向外国政界、学界、社会各界积极宣介"一带一路"倡议等外交理念，介绍中国治国理政实践和改革开放相关成就。在 2017 年金砖国家领导人会晤期间，该校先后在福建泉州和南非约翰内斯堡与中宣部共同成功举办"金砖国家治国理政研讨会"③。此外，该校积极构建高端智库国际合作交流平台，不断拓展对外智库交流渠道，与主要周边国家、"一带一路"沿线国家、"金砖国家"的相关知名智库建立了交流合作关系，不断推动我国外交政策的执行和外交战略的落实。

地方党校在国际交流中"请进来"与"走出去"两方结合，充分发挥了传播我国外交理念和对外政策的积极作用。中共浙江省委党校智库长期与澳大利亚新南威尔士大学、巴黎政治大学、新加坡公共服务学院等海外知名高校保持合作伙伴关系。在"请进来"方面，接待过来自美国、俄罗斯、法国等国家的多批国（境）外代表团，在"走出去"方面，校领导多次率团赴美国、澳大利亚、捷克等国开展公务交流、专题调研、参加国际学术会议。

（四）高校智库

高校作为中国特色新型智库体系的重要一环，在学术研究资源、教师人才储备、公共外交平台建设上具有一定优势。部分高校智库基于自身优势资源，建立起一批专业外交智库，如复旦大学美国研究中心、华东师范大学周边合作与发展协同创新中心、四川大学南亚研究中心、浙江师范大学非洲研究院等机构在各自领域成果丰硕。④

① 刘大可.党校行政学院智库建设的现状与对策[J].中共福建省委党校学报,2015(06):46-57.

② 光明网.党校行政学院智库:百舸争流中力争上游[EB/OL].[2016-12-27].http://epaper.gmw.cn/gmrb/html/2016-12/27/nw.D110000gmrb_20161227_5-06.htm

③ 金砖国家治理国理政研讨会[EB/OL].[2017-8-19]http://www.china.com.cn/news/node_7250622.htm

④ 刘峰.我国高校智库公共外交功能的建设路径思考[J].高校教育管理,2017,11(05):75-80.

如复旦大学美国研究中心基于自身的学术资源优势,专注于美国政治和外交、军备控制和地区安全、美国社会和文化、美国亚太安全战略、美国经济和中美关系等六个研究方向,每年与美国太平洋论坛合作举办"中美关系与地区安全"战略对话,并建立起美国研究数据库和国际关系研究数据库,为我国对美国外交战略和外交政策做了大量前期调研和理论研究基础工作。

又如延边大学基于地缘优势成立了朝鲜半岛研究院。① 该院作为我国最早成立的研究朝鲜半岛的机构之一,聚焦朝鲜半岛各个研究领域的问题,开办了《东疆学刊》,并与朝鲜金日成综合大学、韩国首尔大学、韩国学中央研究院、日本早稻田大学等国内外知名高校和学术机构建立了广泛的学术交流合作机制。而内蒙古财经大学则充分利用区位优势,建立"中蒙俄经济走廊"和"草原丝绸之路经济带"并展开研究,同时组建"中蒙合作发展研究院"、中蒙商学院等多个国际合作平台和研究中心,更好地推动我国"一带一路"倡议的施行。

(五) 传媒智库、企业智库和社会智库

传媒智库、企业智库和社会智库等综合型智库分别从各自的视角在我国对外战略的进程中发挥作用。如媒体智库利用自身优势资源和媒体网络,在全球舞台上传递中国声音,在塑造国家形象、传播中国政策、推进对外战略方面发挥着重要的作用。相较于政府智库和高校智库,媒体智库最大的优势是了解基层、贴近实际,自备强力传播平台,具有丰富传播经验,可以通过有效传播,提升智库产品的知名度,扩大智库成果的影响力。新华社致力构建融通中外的话语体系,与18家联合国所属机构建立了高层往来关系,并吸纳部分专家学者作为智库重点联系对象,开办国家高端智库论坛,不断扩大国际影响,加强国际智库合作。凤凰国际智库②通过吸纳上千位国际问

---

① 延边大学朝鲜半岛研究院[EB/OL].[2019 - 12 - 06]. https://baike. so. com/doc/26420341 -28556849. html

② 光明网. 凤凰国际智库发布国别报告与千人专家数据库.[EB/OL].[2016 - 1 - 19]. http://theory. gmw. cn/2016 - 01/19/content_18565912. htm

题及国际经济的学者智囊、100 多位海外观察员，推出了《先行军》《战略家》《与世界对话》三个文字栏目及《大国小鲜》视频栏目，将自身打造成为全球智库观点的传播平台。①

而阿里研究院作为企业智库，从消费领域入手，利用大数据技术研究全球电子商务发展现状，为中国企业"走出去"提供指导，为我国"一带一路"倡议的推广做海外市场调研。中国石油经济技术研究院总结海外投资环境多年研究成果，出版了《"一带一路"油气合作国别报告》系列成果，为"一带一路"区域内各国能源投资和合作研究提供了重要参考。②

此外，察哈尔学会作为社会智库积极参与国际议题的设置，与韩国国际安保交流协会开展上海和平论坛、荷兰国际关系研究所和德国对外文化关系协会举办公共外交国际论坛、斯德哥尔摩国际和平研究所开展"中日东海冲突的危机管控"为主题的察哈尔圆桌会议等活动。③ 根据 CTTI 来源智库案例，盘古智库汇总了长期以来服务"一带一路"倡议的实践经验，发表了《"一带一路"国际合作精华 30 问》以帮助中国企业和机构开展国际合作。④

三、智库服务外交工作的主要路径

智库作为国家软实力的重要载体和国际竞争力的重要因素，其目标是提升国家软实力和国际影响力。对内需要"服务决策"，在研究上"早半步""适度超前"，以提升外交政策质量，服务国家战略。⑤ 近年来，中国特色新型智库在习近平新时代中国特

---

① 黄楚新，王丹.媒体智库:发展路径与关键[J].新闻与写作,2016(01):13-16.
② 丁炫凯，徐致远.我国互联网企业智库成果量化分析——以百度、阿里巴巴、腾讯(BAT)为例[J].图书馆论坛,2016,36(05):17-24.
③ 赵新利，于凡.民间智库如何开展公共外交——以察哈尔学会的实践为例[J].对外传播,2016(05):19-21.
④ 钟曼丽，杨宝强.社会智库成果传播能力及影响机理分析[J].情报杂志,2017,36(08):39-46.
⑤ 何亚非:中国智库要多方位为外交服务.[EB/OL].[2019-12-25].https://opinion.huanqiu.com/article/9CaKrnJYmQu

色社会主义外交思想指引下,在咨政建言外交工作、深度参与外交活动、积极引导国际舆论等方面的优势日渐显现,为开创中国特色大国外交新局面注入了鲜活力量。

（一） 智库为新时代外交工作咨政建言

1. 智库成为新时代外交政策的孵化器

一国要在国际关系中处于优势地位,除了对传统硬实力的重视外,还必须充分重视软实力。世界各国开展公共外交实际上就是软实力的角逐,而智库作为思想创新的源泉,是国家软实力的策源地。国际关系中频繁而畅通的智库型公共外交,可为国家的整体外交提供创新性和前瞻性的战略思想支持。智库通过积极发挥自身在知识加工和生产上的资源优势,帮助决策者对政策进行充分的论证与评估,进而体现外交决策机制的科学化,从而在国家对外战略的制定过程中起到孵化器作用。

在外交政策制定上,很多智库的学术成果被采纳并体现在我国的外交政策上。如中国国际问题研究院作为中华人民共和国外交部直属专业研究机构,近年来先后出版《普京大外交:面向 21 世纪的俄罗斯对外战略 1999—2017》《国际秩序演变与中国特色大国外交》《国际形势和中国外交蓝皮书(2019)》《CIIS 研究报告》并主办期刊《国际问题研究》(中英文版)等在国内外有较大影响的理论成果。而察哈尔学会则通过《公共外交季刊》《察哈尔快讯》等期刊,以及"察哈尔外交与国际关系丛书""察哈尔外交与国际关系丛书"等学术著作,对中国公共外交理论与实践的发展及国际关系社会智库等领域深入研究,并在朝鲜半岛问题、中韩中朝双边关系、中日关系上积极作为。此外,中国国际问题研究院和上海国际问题研究院还在中国针对欧洲主权债务危机的政策等多个外交问题上,积极服务中国领导者的外交决策,推动了 2015 年中欧战略对话,奠定了第 17 次中国欧盟领导人会晤联合声明的基础。

智库作为外交政策的孵化器,还通过提出和应用新思想,推动协商沟通。以智库服务"一带一路"倡议为例,2016 年 7 月,人大重阳金融研究院和德国国际合作机构(GIZ)合作举办"中国—哈萨克斯坦'一带一路'智库对话"并开展系列交流活动,取得良好成效，①中国（深圳）综合开发研究院为肯尼亚蒙巴萨基里菲特殊经济区、毛里求斯晋非合作区、朝鲜南浦综合保税区等多个项目提供规划咨询服务，为中国企业参与"一带一路"建设提供了帮助。

2. 智库成为重大事件应对策略的"高参"

智库作为专业化政策研究机构，在一系列重大对外关系中，通过分析国际形势和开展实地调研，为应对外交政策提供了理论指导和调研准备，给出战略构想和政策建议。

以智库在中美关系中的作用为例，近年来国际局势发生历史性变化、中美关系面临重要选择的重大关口，如美国战略界对中国的焦虑感日益增强，特朗普政府对中国不断施加压力，对此中国智库必须提出应对方案，强化对中美关系良性发展的理念引领。对中国智库学者来说，一方面要争取与知华派、友华派的合作，共同平衡对华极端鹰派势力的扩张，另一方面要主动化解美国对华态度中的误解，保持中美智库对话及互信建设。如中国与全球化智库（CCG）、中国国际问题研究院、中国现代国际关系研究院、清华-卡内基全球政策中心、察哈尔学会、海国图智等智库持续就美国特朗普时期的新政以及一系列民众关心的话题发表看法、举办研讨会和论坛、撰写调查报告，梳理特朗普政府的执政脉络，为我国对美政策提出建议。

布鲁金斯学会的李成曾表示："如果中美经济相互依赖是两国关系的压舱石，中美学术交流就是两国关系发展的坐标仪，两国智库的沟通应该是中美关系的报警器、缓冲带和减压器。"北京大学国际战略研究院通过与美国布鲁金斯学会合作开展北阁对话年会，邀请具有丰富政治经验、深厚学术修养和广阔战略视野的国内外前政要及知名专家莅临北京大学，共同探讨国际形势和世界政治的前景，就未来中美是否可能在经济和技术层面实现"脱钩"，以及变化中的全球秩序等重大战略和热点问题展开

---

① 金鑫，林永亮."一带一路"建设中的智库交流——"一带一路"智库合作联盟建设实践及发展前景[J].当代世界，2019(05):27-30.

探讨。此外,盘古智库通过发布《美国当选总统特朗普候任期观察报告》详细记录了特朗普的执政准备,并举办"中美关系大格局与中日关系的展望"等研讨会,探讨中美关系对世界格局的影响,通过智库报告等多种渠道上报,得到相关决策部门的重视。

再以英国"脱欧"问题为例,商务部所属国际贸易经济合作研究院及时关注热点,其第一时间发布的《英国"脱欧"对我国经贸领域多变权利义务的影响》报告获得中央领导的关注与肯定性批示。而中国国际经济交流中心围绕英国"脱欧"后的中欧贸易关系开展了多次研讨会,并把研讨成果发表在内部刊物《智库言论》《研究报告》中上达有关决策部门。此外,上海国际问题研究院等智库也分别对英国"脱欧"问题展开了一系列前瞻性的学术探讨,并得出了多角度、多层次的研究成果,为我国决策部门的应变、应急、政策制定提供了强有力的智力支撑。

(二) 深度参与外交活动

1. 智库成为大国外交活动的"尖兵"

党的十八大以来,面对复杂多变的国际形势,中国特色新型智库已经成为中国特色大国外交的参与者和推动者,不但能为政府的外交事务提出建议,而且自身积极参与外交事务,通过与国外智库沟通、对话和交流,积极参与各类官方外交对话中,从而塑造良好中国形象,助推中国理念走向世界,增强中国国际话语权和感召力。

近年来,很多智库尤其是国家高端智库顺势而为,在诸多国际智库合作机制中的作用日趋凸显。如中国社会科学院已搭建与中东欧 16 国的智库合作网络,与东盟国家形成了固定的智库交流机制,还与二十国集团(G20)、上海合作组织、金砖国家等成员国知名智库建立经常性合作机制。[1] 如在 2019 年举办的亚洲文明对话大会中,中国社科院会同有关国家智库在会议中发起多边合作倡议,推动"构建亚洲命运共同体智库伙伴关系"计划,与相关单位签署《亚洲文明交流互鉴建设智库伙伴关系》意向

---

① 　王斯敏,张胜. 为中国特色大国外交贡献力量.[EB/OL].[2019 - 12 - 25]. http://ex. cssn. cn/zk/zk_rdgz/201808/t20180802_4522597. shtml? COLLCC=1916704892&.

书，并会同有关国家智库开展包括亚洲文明互鉴、人类命运共同体建设、"一带一路"与亚洲文明共同体建设等首批多边联合研究项目，这些案例充分表明智库已积极参与外交事务，成为我国对外战略实施过程中的重要参与方。

2. 智库成为"二轨外交"的主力之一

在外交领域，一般来说外交官的身份很重要、正式、权威且敏感，但同时也会有许多限制，双方往往会因为身份的正式和敏感，或多或少都会受到一些心照不宣的天然限制。而智库相较官方外交和民间交流有着更大的灵活性和专业性，作为政府外交活动的重要补充，通过积极承担二轨外交职能，促进国家或地区之间重大利益问题的沟通协商，为对话合作提供纽带，并努力在冲突与争端中寻求建设性的解决方案。

近年来，我国智库在助力公共外交方面积累了很多有益经验。如在各类大型多边国际会议过程中，新型智库积极作为，配套举办国际智库会议，平等交流、凝聚共识、营造氛围、提出建议，为会议成功举办提供了重要的智力支持。围绕这些外交议程，中国智库还发起成立了国际性的智库联合体，与相关国家智库合作开展课题研究、共同举办研讨会等。

在 G20 峰会中，T20（即 G20 智库峰会）充当了二十国集团领导人峰会的"友好大使"。自 2013 年以来连续召开 T20 会议，会议已经吸引了超过了千名全球智库学者，在世界各地举办多轮会议，相关研究成果为决策层传递了有效的信息，为 G20 会议的召开做出了很好的铺垫，引起了广泛的国际关注。如人大国发院重阳团队作为 G20 智库峰会（T20）共同牵头智库，积极配合领导人参加 G20 峰会等重大主场外交和领导人高访活动，受邀在主要官方媒体发表评论。

在金砖国家合作过程中，一般会在金砖国家峰会召开之前举行智库论坛，由举办领导人会晤的国家主办，各国智库相关成员参会，讨论金砖合作未来发展路径，深化金砖合作机制。根据《德班宣言》，2013 年 3 月五国智库牵头单位在峰会期间成立了"金砖国家智库理事会"，2014 年以来每年在金砖峰会前召开理事会会议。如金砖国家智库合作中的中方理事会是金砖国家智库理事会的中方牵头单位，目前涵盖了 88

名理事和 90 家理事单位,其中既包含官方智库,也吸收了民间智库。该中方理事会自成立以来创办了"万寿论坛",主办了十余场金砖合作相关研讨会,并发布了"智库金砖系列丛书",使智库合作之声成为金砖合作的美好和声。智库论坛不仅同金砖各国智库开展联合研究和学术交流,还致力于同其他新兴市场国家和发展中国家智库交流合作,不断促进新型南南合作的达成。

(三) 积极引导国际舆论

习近平总书记曾指出,"要加强国际传播能力建设,精心构建对外话语体系,发挥好新兴媒体作用,增强对外话语的创造力、感召力、公信力,讲好中国故事,传播好中国声音,阐释好中国特色"①。我国智库坚持中国立场、世界眼光,增强战略思维、紧跟世界前沿,积极面向世界、走向世界,开门办智库、开放办智库,积极开展国际交流合作,积极开展多种形式的智库外交、智库外宣,助力国家提升公共外交能力,增强国际影响力和话语权。②

1. 传播新时代外交理念,塑造新时代国家形象

国家形象作为本国与他国交往的靓丽名片,能在一定程度上反映本国在国际社会中的地位,而通过智库开展公共外交是改善国家形象重要而又高效的方式。近年来,我国各类智库通过与国际社会积极互动,讲好中国故事、阐述中国方案,深入答疑解惑,努力向全世界展现真实、全面、开放的中国。③

近年来,中国通过平等相待的全方位外交,以全新的国际形象站在了世界舞台的中央,并以自身发展的成功经验参与全球治理,与世界分享发展成果,如"一带一路"倡议从提出、到实施再到开花结果,渐渐成为世界经济复苏的助推器之一。自 2016 年提出"一带一路"倡议以来,作为"一带一路"民心相通工作的重要组成部分,智库交

---

① 人民网:习近平的新闻舆论观.[EB/OL].[2019 - 12 - 28].http://paper.people.com.cn/rmrbhwb/html/2016 - 02/25/content_1656513.htm

② 靳诺.中国特色新型高校智库的建设和发展[J].中国高等教育,2019(20):4 - 6.

③ 唐小松,景丽娜."一带一路"背景下公共外交与中国国家形象构建[J].公共外交季刊,2017(02):22 - 27+173.

流在过去几年蓬勃发展，为推动政策沟通、增进民心相通、促进务实合作发挥了独特作用，日益成为"一带一路"建设中的一道靓丽风景线。2015年4月，中共中央对外联络部牵头成立"一带一路"智库合作联盟；截至2019年5月，该联盟已拥有国内成员单位138家、国外成员单位114家。智库联盟秘书处及成员单位先后赴沿线60多个国家访问，与对方智库共同举办多规格、多主题的各类研讨活动，系统介绍"一带一路"倡议发展情况，让各方认识到"一带一路"倡议不但对中国发展有利，而且对沿线国家、相关国家乃至全世界的发展都有利。此外，该联盟还邀请国外知名智库专家来华开展专题研讨，并鼓励国内外专家学者深入探讨"一带一路"倡议，深化沿线国家民众对"一带一路"倡议的了解。①

在"人类命运共同体"外交理念传播过程中，新华社作为国家高端智库，围绕我国一系列对外战略和外交重要活动，第一时间组织智库专家发声解读，并综合运用全媒体传播形态，充分发挥海外传播优势，重点稿件集中在美、英、法、德等19个G20成员所在地的主流媒体发布。而春秋发展战略研究院则推出"观察者网"，网站以"中国关怀，全球视野"为口号，邀请我国著名政治学者、经济学家、知名媒体人以及外籍嘉宾等，通过深度报道和独家评论的形式，打造中国自己的发声渠道。而第一财经研究院、封面智库、凤凰国际智库、光明智库、瞭望智库等多家传媒智库也纷纷利用全媒体技术手段，"讲好中国故事"，向海外宣传我国国家形象，打造热点话题，营造良好的国际舆论氛围。

根据CTTI来源智库数据，目前共有17家智库从事"一带一路"领域的研究，涉及国际旅游资源开发、高端人才培养、中外经贸与文化交流、国际商务合作等多个研究方向。其中，中国社会科学院、中国国际问题研究院、中国科学院、国家信息中心、中国宏观经济研究院等国家级智库发布了一系列理论研究成果，为有关决策部门提

---

① "一带一路"智库合作联盟秘书处."一带一路"建设中的智库交流——"一带一路"智库合作联盟建设实践及发展前景.［EB/OL］.［2019 - 10 - 25］. http://world. people. com. cn/n1/2019/0521/c187656 - 31096114. html

供了理论支持,并在国际上召开了一系列学术研讨会,成为"一带一路"倡议传播的主力军之一。此外,凤凰国际智库等媒体智库还成为"一带一路"智库传播新渠道,利用外文网站,微信等自媒体平台不断提升国际影响力。

2. 参与国际政策辩论,引导国际舆论

全球化时代,一个国家在国际上是否受其他国家的公众欢迎,与其所传递的思想和价值观以及其所采取的传播策略密切相关。在错综复杂的国际新形势下,我国智库勇于站在国际舞台上阐明中国主张,通过一定的舆论媒介向社会进行信息传递,积极提高舆论的传播力、引导力、影响力、公信力。[①]

如在中美贸易摩擦事件中,中国智库从国际关系、经济贸易、国际法等多个领域为相关决策者献言献策,就中美贸易摩擦展开分析,预判中美局势走向,表明中国立场,对美方无理寻衅予以有力反击。面对美方的寻衅和无理要求,中国宏观经济研究院、国务院发展研究中心等智库的专家学者发表文章,或者接受媒体采访,分析中美经济贸易形势,有效缓解市场的恐慌情绪,对内起到了稳定民心、增强市场信心的作用,对外表明了中国不怕打压的坚定底气,以争取国际社会的理解与尊重。在美国为主的西方媒体鼓动"中国威胁论"的形势下,中国智库能利用海外发声渠道,传递中国的真实形象,打破西方媒体妖魔化中国的企图,传播和平发展理念,引导舆论,为中国制造稳定的国际发展环境。同时,智库专家利用全媒体平台,通过专著、论文、访谈、纪录片等多种形式开展各种宣传推介活动,帮助西方民众客观认识中国,展现国家形象。

而在南海危机中,中国社科院、中国人民大学国家发展与战略研究院、武汉大学国际法研究所等多家智库纷纷站出来,从历史、国际法权威等角度捍卫中国领土主权。在外交实践中,智库能快速响应,先发制人,利用广播、电视、互联网等社交平台主动发声,制造有利于我国的国际舆论导向。如南海仲裁案期间,复旦大学中国研究

---

① 王莉丽.从"智库公共外交"看智库多元功能[N].中国社会科学报,2014 - 04 - 11(A04).

院和观察者网联合推出视频《南海仲裁案真相》，该视频通过优酷、腾讯等平台播出，几天内点击量就近 500 万，英文版上传至 YouTube 网站，由美国最大的互联网媒体《赫芬顿邮报》发布，被包括菲律宾在内的多国网站转载。国防大学、军事科学院智库专家从军事战略视角出发，揭露了美国、菲律宾在南海仲裁案中的无理要求，系列文章《南海仲裁案十问十答》等在互联网上被广泛转载。新型外交智库利用国内外媒体"发声"，有力扭转了国际社会在南海仲裁案上对中国的偏见。此外，中国社会科学院国家全球战略智库首席专家傅莹还在我国南海危机中通过发表长文《关于南海争议和南海紧张的缘由》，被海内外媒体广泛转载，扭转了当时国际上对南海问题的误解。

四、对策建议

"修之于天下，其德乃普。"习近平外交思想作为新时代我国对外工作的指导思想，是推动中国特色大国外交的根本遵循和行动指南。中国智库建设应以习近平外交思想为指引，在实践中不断探索和创新，努力为中国特色大国外交贡献力量，现提出如下建议：

（一）加强公共外交智库的品牌建设

品牌建设是推动智库高质量发展的重要路径之一，而智库品牌是其质量和信誉的体现，具有很高的辨识度，[①]在智库服务公共外交工作过程中，良好的智库品牌能够更方便与外界接驳，得到国际互认互信，推进全球背景下的文化交流与互鉴。公共外交智库的品牌建设应以专业和优质的研究成果为基础，以质量为导向，不断拓展新视野、新思路、新格局，为公共外交智库的发展注入新动能。[②] 第一，树立品牌意识，塑造品牌形象。把握规范、严谨、专业的公共外交智库定位，在公共外交实践中主动树立和培养品牌意识，积极塑造和维护品牌形象，全面把握公共外交智库品牌的核心

---

① 刘清. 关于智库品牌建设的若干思考和认识[J]. 智库理论与实践，2019，4(01)：25 - 29.
② 郭庆松. 着力"三大建设"打造智库品牌[J]. 智库理论与实践，2017，2(05)：10 - 14.

价值观并贯穿于整个品牌建设中。第二,突出品牌优势,彰显品牌特色。以我国独特的外交理论与实践经验为支撑,对公共外交问题开展长期深入的研究,对公共外交成果进行深刻的研讨与反复的提炼,依据研究专长,开发优势学科,打造拳头产品,发挥智库在公共外交领域的意见领袖作用,形成具有我国特色、符合我国国情、顺应时代主流的特色智库品牌。① 第三,增强品牌竞争力,扩大品牌影响力。广纳贤才,吸收国内外公共外交领域的专家学者,打造一支通识型公共外交智库人才储备梯队;积极发表研究成果、决策内参,拓宽决策咨询成果转化的渠道,形成高质量的公共外交智库产品;同时开阔视野,聚焦全球问题,创新思路,与时俱进,在公共外交领域中形成以人才为核心,以产品为支撑,以创新为引领的公共外交智库的品牌建设。②

(二) 推进智库的全媒体建设

推进智库的全媒体建设是当前我国智库建设的一个新的着力点。全媒体多元化的传播渠道可以为智库研究成果的推介提供更多机遇。第一,对智库的全媒体建设规划统筹设计。立足我国战略和发展全局,构建研究体系,明确研究方向,创新研究成果传播机制,建立长效成长机制和可持续发展机制,同时建立依法依规的管理标准,审慎对待智库成果内容的传播。③ 第二,创新传播手段和传播载体。除了传统纸媒、会议论坛、学者访问外,通过开发网站、App、小程序,制作电子刊物,开通微博、微信、Facebook、Twitter、Youtube 等形式多样的网络媒体传播渠道,打造智库的全媒体传播平台,提高智库传播效能。④ 第三,重塑智库成果形态和服务。对接传统媒体,灵活利用网络媒体传播平台,汇聚各方资源智慧,吸收、整合数据资源,开展系统深入的研究并开发成数据成果,形成生产和传播于一体的智库成果生产方式,更好地服务

① 周湘智.智库建设应走向品牌化[N].中国社会科学报,2014-08-01(B02).
② 李雪.地方社科院智库建设的形势和问题及天津社科院的思路和举措——天津社会科学院党组书记、院长新方华访谈录[J].经济师,2020(01):6-8.
③ 郑佳欣.以全媒体智库建设推进党报集团全面转型[J].南方传媒研究,2018(02):55-59+54+2.
④ 施蕾蕾.研究与传播的融合:新时期媒体型智库成果生产模式分析[J].情报杂志,2019,38(06):187-193+173.

政府决策需求。①

（三）构建全方位的国内外智库对话合作机制

智库对话在中国外交工作中发挥着越来越重要的作用,通过构建全方位的国内外智库对话合作机制,进一步加深国际交流与合作,有助于汲取他国经验智慧,广泛传播中国声音,推进公共外交工作的开展。② 一方面可加强国内智库间的交流与合作,通过加强跨学科合作,畅通国内各领域智库专家学者和各种人才的对话合作渠道,共建、共享智库成果,打造相关研究领域的学术共同体;另一方面,应加强国内智库与国际智库间的交流与合作,如通过社交媒体的交互式对话,把我国智库的思想成果与洞见在国外网络媒介上及时准确地表达出来,扩大智库对话交流范围,③也可通过构建合作平台,倡导平等的对话合作机制,吸引国外智库的专家学者走进来和鼓励我国智库的专家学者走出去,就共同关心的问题开展深入合作研究。

（四）增强国际议题参与和设置能力

近年来,中国更加积极地参与全球治理,并向世界展示中国智慧和中国风采。智库可通过强化国际议题参与和设置能力,提高我国智库的国际交往能力、国际感召力和国际影响力,④倡导世界全面客观地看待中国,让世界对我国的外交理念产生共通、共鸣、共情。第一,坚定文化自信,拓展全球视野。可通过创新服务方式,加强全球舆情动态研究,⑤提高我国智库的政策供给能力,积极提出中国观点、中国倡议,为全球问题的解决贡献中国方案。第二,强化"中国参与"和"中国创建"意识。积极担任国际组织的轮值主席或为国际组织提供会议准备、政策建议,主动参与和主导多边

① 李雪.媒体融合发展趋势下新型智库成果推广体系创新探索——广东省社会科学院副院长、研究员章杨定访谈录[J].经济师,2018(09):6-7.
② 陈晨晨.善用智库平台推进智库外交——以2017年4月"习特会"前中美智库系列对话会为例[J].对外传播,2017(05):13-15.
③ 王莉丽.智库公共外交:概念、功能、机制与模式[J].社会科学文摘,2019(05):112-114.
④ 毛跃.加强智库建设提升国际话语权[J].智库时代,2017(02):46.
⑤ 柯银斌,吕晓莉.国外智库国际化成功经验及启示[J].智库理论与实践,2016,1(05):48-55.

机制的议程设置,搭建智库交流合作平台,积极获得国际舞台的话语空间。① 第三,广泛布局研究机构,提高议题针对性。借鉴国外优秀智库的运营模式,建立我国相关智库的海外分支机构,深入研究当前国际关系背景下目标受众国的关注热点,拓展具有前瞻性的研究领域,产出具有前瞻性的思想产品,有针对性地提出切合当前世界形势和国际社会关心的议题。

---

① 张骥,方炯升.中国外交安全智库国际话语权分析[J].国际展望,2018,10(05):75-94,160.

专题五　新型智库网络与智库共同体的形成

共同体是指具有共同的利益基础和价值观念,而且这些共同性质能够深刻地作用于其他成员的群体。[①] 自从习近平总书记提出"建设中国特色新型智库"的倡议以来,我国各类型智库机构如雨后春笋般,为智库共同体的出现与发展奠定了基础。随着智库的蓬勃发展,不同类型、不同主题、不同区域的智库在本领域、本地区逐渐形成了一定规模的智库网络。与此同时,智库与决策者、社会团体、媒体、社会公众等的互动交流越来越频繁。智库网络与智库之间交流共同推动了智库共同体的形成与发展,智库网络以"合纵连横"之势,充分汇聚智库力量,为智库共同体形成之基石;智库交流聚"智"力、汇"智"才、集"智"识,多维度为智库赋能,为智库共同体发展之动力。智库网络的兴起,日益频繁的智库交流,促进了智库共同体的发育,完善了我国新型智库体系,加快了我国新型智库的专业化和行业化进程。

一、多维聚力形成了各具特色的智库网络

我国新型智库的迅速发展促进了智库网络的形成。智库网络可看作智库、相关政策研究机构组成的一种关系形式。作为维系智库本行业内关系的重要平台,智库网络可以为智库的发展提供必要服务与重要保障,有着为智库发展提供资金支持、提高智库传播能力、为智库发展提供组织和管理建议以及促进智库间资源信息共享的重要作用,还有助于推动智库共同体建设。根据我国新型智库发展实际,我国智库网络可以分为政府主导型、系统型、平台型以及联盟型四种形态,不同的智库网络有着

[①]　李义天.共同体与政治团结[M].北京:社会科学文献出版社,2011:19.

不同的特点。

（一）政府主导型网络凝聚高端"智"力

　　建设"中国特色新型智库"已被提升至国家战略的高度,政府的重视与鼓励是我国新型智库发展的一大重要机遇。因此,在我国智库网络发展过程中,由政府部门主导创立的智库网络是一大特色。"政府主导型网络"主要是指以国家高端智库、各省市级重点智库等为代表的网络形态。这类智库网络由政府主导创立,受到官方认可,因而拥有较高的资源保障,打破了智库的地域、性质、学科的界限,网络的稳定性较高;网络宗旨主要是着眼于"重点建设一批具有较大影响力和国际知名度的高端智库"的目标,智库网络成员大都是经千挑万选,发展状况良好或拥有较大发展空间的智库"翘楚",拥有较强实力,政策转化率相对较高。因此,政府主导型智库网络成为凝聚高端精英智库资源的智库网络形式。

1. 国家高端智库网络凝聚国内领先力量

　　国家高端智库网络是指由国家高端智库建设试点单位和国家高端智库建设培育单位构成的智库网络,凝聚了国内各领域领先的智库力量。2015 年年初开始,中宣部在深入调研的基础上研究制定《国家高端智库建设试点工作方案》。2015 年 12 月 1 日,国家高端智库建设试点工作会议在京召开,标志着试点工作正式启动,会议强调着力建设一批国家亟须、特色鲜明、制度创新、引领发展的高端智库,推动我国智库建设实现新发展。首批国家高端智库建设试点单位共 25 家。2017 年,中宣部公布了 13 家国家高端智库建设培育单位。在 2018 年的党和国家机构改革中,中央党校和国家行政学院的职责整合,组建新的中央党校(国家行政学院),25 家试点单位遂变更为 24 家。由此,形成了"24＋13"国家高端智库网络,包括党中央、国务院、中央军委直属的综合性研究机构,依托大学和科研机构的专业化智库,企业智库和社会智库等多种智库类型,研究范围涵盖政治、经济、思想、科技、军事、法律等多个领域。

　　为了进一步扩大智库内部治理自主权,提高资源配置效率,激发智库的活力,中宣部等部门出台了一系列政策文件,为试点工作搭建了初步的制度框架:2015 年,中宣部研究起草了《国家高端智库管理办法（试行）》，与财政部共同制定了《国家高端智库专项经费管理办法（试行）》，作为高端智库运行管理和专项经费管理的基本规范。2016年1月，为便于中央有关决策部门了解国家高端智库相关情况，有针对性地交办研究课题，推动供需之间有效对接，中宣部社科规划办发布《首批国家高端智库建设试点单位简介》，从机构概况、研究队伍、研究领域和主要成果、成果转化载体、研究支撑条件、组织架构和管理制度、国际合作交流等方面对高端智库建设试点单位进行介绍。

同时，为加强国家高端智库的协调管理，服务高端智库创新发展，经中央批准，在全国哲学社会科学规划领导小组下设立国家高端智库理事会，作为国家高端智库建设的议事机构和评估机构。国家高端智库理事会的成立对于国家高端智库的发展与智库网络凝聚力的提升有重要意义，理事会充分发挥了引导管理、统筹协调功能，积极打通咨政渠道，增强智库间的联系。2016年10月，理事会第二次全体会议召开，听取各试点单位工作汇报并进行测评，对下一阶段工作提出要求。为了增强咨政研究的针对性、有效性、务实性，理事会向十几家中央决策部门征集研究选题，形成并发布《2016年国家高端智库选题方向和重点课题》。2017年1月，为提升国家高端智库品牌形象，扩大社会影响，推进国家高端智库建设试点工作扎实深入开展，国家高端智库理事会组织设计了国家高端智库标识，①并公布了《国家高端智库标识使用规范》，明确了国家高端智库标识的使用情形和场合。2019年6月，全国哲学社会科学工作办公室在深圳召开国家高端智库建设经验交流会，国家高端智库负责人深入学习贯彻习近平总书记关于中国特色新型智库建设的重要论述，就各自在服务决策、舆论引导、对外交流等方面的做法及体制机制改革经验进行了充分交流研讨。

作为"智库国家队"，国家高端智库网络集合了国内最精锐的智库力量，智库类型

---

① 全国哲学社会科学工作办公室. 国家高端智库标识设计说明[EB/OL]. [2019 - 12 - 03]. http://www. npopss - cn. gov. cn/n1/2017/0103/c219469 - 28995832. html.

多样,覆盖广泛,特色鲜明;智库网络有具有实体性质的理事会和工作会议、严密的组织管理制度、稳定的资金支持,为全国新型智库建设积累了宝贵经验,发挥了良好的示范作用。

2. 省市重点智库网络集聚区域优势力量

随着《关于加强中国特色新型智库建设的意见》出台,以及国家高端智库建设试点工作开展,各省市纷纷着手开展本省市的新型智库建设工作,培养本区域内的重点智库,由此形成了各个省市重点智库网络。例如,2016 年 4 月,由河北省委宣传部批准成立九家首批新型智库试点单位。2016 年 9 月,山东省委宣传部下发《关于公布山东省重点新型智库建设试点单位名单的通知》,遴选确定 15 家智库作为首批重点新型智库建设试点单位。2017 年 12 月,江西省委宣传部发出《关于遴选首批省级重点智库的通知》,并于 2018 年公布了 17 家重点智库名单。2017 年 8 月,黑龙江省委宣传部组织开展了黑龙江省重点智库培育工作,最终研究决定设立 20 家省首批重点培育智库;2018 年 9 月,面向全省公开组织开展第二批重点培育智库遴选工作,11 月公布了黑龙江省第二批 6 家重点培育智库。2018 年 5 月,浙江省启动新型智库遴选工作,并于 9 月公布了 13 家浙江省新型重点专业智库和 8 家浙江省重点培育智库,以 5 年为期建设重点智库,从而形成了新型重点专业智库与重点培育智库互补的智库发展格局。与之相类似的还有北京、江苏、湖南、广东、安徽、湖北、重庆、四川等地都制定本地区智库建设的《意见》或《方案》,组织开展试点工作,从而形成了省级重点智库网络。除了省级重点智库网络之外,部分县市的重点智库同样构成了智库网络。例如 2017 年 5 月,滁州市公布了 4 家重点智库和 4 家重点培育智库;2018 年 3 月,连云港市公布了 9 家首批重点智库;2018 年 4 月,南京市公布了首批 6 家重点新型智库。

此外,部分省市还成立了重点智库建设工作指导管理机构。例如江苏省设立了新型智库建设工作指导委员会,下设江苏省新型智库建设办公室,负责新型智库建设事宜,并在 2017 年 5 月成立江苏省新型智库理事会,作为指导全省新型智库建设的议事机构和评估机构。四川省成立了由省委、省政府领导下的新型智库建设领导小组，负责四川新型智库建设工作的议事协调机构，并设立四川新型智库建设专家委员会作为领导小组专门的学术咨询机构。

各省市为促进本地区新型智库的建设与发展，制定了一系列的政策，因此各省市重点智库网络往往与国家高端智库网络一样，拥有一定的资金与政策支持，较为完善的管理与评估制度以及更为畅通的咨政通道。省市重点智库网络的形成一方面起到了较强的引导和标杆作用，为本地新型智库建设积累经验；另一方面也有助于集合本地区的优势智库力量与智库资源，推动当地智库共同体建设，拢指合拳，形成区域智库合力，更高效地服务于当地政府决策。

（二）系统型网络富集行业"智"力

系统型智库网络主要由国家部委或是相关部门倡导成立的某一系统（行业）内的智库构成。《关于加强中国特色新型智库建设的意见》提出中国特色新型智库的发展要做到规模适度、布局合理，并将新型智库划分了七个类型：党政部门、社科院、党校行政学院、高校、军队、科研院所和企业与社会智库。不同类型的智库往往拥有不同的特点与隶属关系，而同类型智库则具有较大的相似性。因此在我国新型智库建设热潮中，不同系统、不同类型的智库相互联系，形成了系统型网络。由于"条块分割"的管理体系，与政府主导型网络的"块状"形态不同，系统型网络属于"条状"网络形态。例如，由国务院发展研究中心和部分省区市、计划单列市和省会城市发展研究中心（研究室）共同发起成立全国政策咨询信息交流协作机制，建立了"联席会议"制度，每年召开政策咨询工作会议，促进全国政策咨询信息交流与协作。

系统型网络往往具有较强的行业属性，由相同领域、行业的智库组成，因此网络的政策领域相对更为集中，成员间的行业差距、学科差距更小；网络稳定性相对较高；其网络宗旨往往是在相关部门指导下，以促进相关系统工作和相关行业发展为目标。例如2014年，教育部印发的《中国特色新型高校智库推进计划》中提到"以2011协同创新中心和人文社会科学重点研究基地建设为抓手，重点打造一批国家级智库"，这可看作教育系统的智库网络。除了国家级的教育系统智库网络,部分省市教育系统也建立了相应的智库网络。2015 年,甘肃省教育厅(高校工委)启动实施了甘肃高校精准扶贫智库建设,并于 10 月公布了 5 家甘肃省高校精准扶贫智库,瞄准全省精准扶贫、精准脱贫工作展开深入研究,并为政府扶贫决策提供智力支持。2018 年 8 月,福建省教育厅遴选确定 20 个福建省高校特色新型智库。

在教育系统中,还形成了某一领域的智库网络。例如教育部国别和区域研究备案中心组成了教育系统有关国别和区域研究的智库网络。2011 年 11 月,教育部区域和国别研究培育基地项目启动;2015 年 1 月,教育部出台《国别和区域研究基地培育和建设暂行办法》;2017 年 3 月,出台了《国别和区域研究中心建设指引(试行)》;2018 年 11 月,教育部国别和区域研究备案中心第四次交流会议暨非洲中心建设专题研讨会在浙江师范大学召开,外交部非洲司、教育部国际司、浙江省教育厅等相关部门领导,以及来自全国 147 家教育部国别和区域研究备案中心的负责人、学者参加会议。建设国别和区域研究备案中心旨在服务国家的外交战略,以高校的研究为国家外交发展提供咨询,促进高校发展成为国家重要决策的"智囊团"和"思想库"。

除了教育系统的智库网络之外,还有文化、科技、交通等系统的智库网络。例如,2016 年 4 月,文化部办公厅开展了年度文化艺术智库项目申报工作,以项目申报的形式促进文化艺术智库体系建设;11 月,文化部文化科技司组织的文化艺术智库项目集体开题会在贵州举行,首批 4 个文化艺术智库项目集体开题,标志着"文化艺术智库体系建设工程"正式启动。此外,文化部还通过相应的评选程序,推出"智库联系点",以符合条件的省级艺术研究院所为依托,聚集社会各方文化艺术研究力量。此后于 2017 年、2018 年,文化部继续开展了文化艺术智库项目申报工作,依托文化艺术智库体系形成了文化艺术智库网络,不仅为当地文化艺术建设提供决策咨询,其中具有典型性和示范作用的研究成果也可为国家文化艺术建设提供决策参考。2018 年 2 月,交通运输部出台了《关于促进交通运输新型智库发展的实施意见》,明确提出要依次按照部属、行业、社会不同圈层的智库,进行分类指导,分类推进各类智库发展,力争用五年左右的时间,在铁路、公路、水运、民航、邮政及综合交通运输等领域建设一批新型智库,并开展部级新型智库试点工作,由此可形成交通系统的智库网络。

(三)平台型网络汇聚广泛"智"力

平台主导型智库网络主要依托于某一平台形成,智库网络受平台影响较大,例如智库网络的稳定性、网络成员之间的凝聚力、网络成员的资格要求,与前两者网络类型相比具有更大的不确定性。因此,平台型网络往往具有较强的可扩容性,可以在更大范围汇聚智库资源。平台型网络的产生一方面得益于信息技术的发展;另一方面,由于党和政府的大力支持,各类型智库数量不断增长,体系架构不断优化,质量不断提升,在很大程度上刺激了各类智库研究与评价机构的发展。因此,平台型网络可按平台的功能进行分类,常见的平台型智库网络有依托研究评价型平台而建立的智库网络、依托服务型平台而建立的智库网络、依托管理型平台而建立的智库网络。

评价型平台网络主要依托相关智库研究评价机构而形成的智库网络。2016年12月,由光明日报社、南京大学主办,光明日报智库研究与发布中心、南京大学中国智库研究与评价中心承办的"2016中国智库治理论坛"在南京举行,我国首个智库垂直搜索引擎和数据管理平台——中国智库索引(CTTI)发布,并公布首批入选智库名录。截至2019年12月,全国共有848家CTTI来源智库融入了一个共建共治共享,线上线下良性互动的智库网络中。同时,光明日报社与南京大学共同主办的"中国智库治理论坛"从2016年开始已连续举办4届,累计数千人参会。以"中国智库治理论坛"和"中国智库索引"为纽带,848家CTTI来源智库构成的智库网络共同推动了新型智库共同体建设。此外,上海社会科学院智库研究中心推出的《中国智库报告》年度系列,包含500余家智库在内的智库备选池同样构成了一个以研究评价平台为纽带的智库网络。

服务型平台网络主要依托服务型平台而建立,智库参与该网络主要是利用平台的服务功能。以新浪智库平台为例,在新浪平台上线后,有国内外数十家优秀智库入驻,不仅为合作智库在新浪网上提供了具有增值能力服务的独立展示空间,同时还成为智库、政府、企业项目对接的高效通道,构建"线上＋线下"一体化服务体系,从而将智力资源转变为信息增值服务的产品,更好地服务社会。

管理型平台网络往往由智库主管部门倡导建立。智库主管部门依托相关信息平台,达到管理、服务、引导智库发展的目的。例如 2018 年 9 月,民航局出台《关于加强民航局新型智库建设的实施办法》,提出建设信息化的民航局新型智库管理服务平台。平台将依托民航局网站建设,具备政策研究需求发布、智库成员登记注册、研究申报、信息发布、项目管理与评估五大功能;为打造开放式的民航局新型智库格局,民航局对智库成员实行登记注册制管理,分为智库成员单位或智库个人成员两种类型,在平台登记注册,经过审核后完成认证。通过平台,可以发布政策研究方向,加强信息交流,实现资源共享,也可促进智库成员之间加强横向交流和联合研究。该平台既是决策部门借智引智的平台,也是智库与决策部门沟通交流的平台、智库成果传播转化的平台。在该平台登记会员单位或个人则构成了以民航局新型智库管理服务平台为纽带的智库网络。由于平台带有一定的管理性质,有严格的注册认证体系,因此,该类型的平台型网络相比与其他平台型网络具有更强的凝聚力。

(四) 联盟型网络吸纳专业"智"力

联盟指多个行动者集中资源,并在联合行动期间积极沟通以实现共同目标,是一种网络形式。自党的十八大以来,中央从国家治理体系和治理能力现代化的高度,把新型智库建设工作提上重要议程。中国特色新型智库建设进程的有力推进,为智库联盟的发展带来了契机。近年来,我国智库联盟建设劲头十足,这促使智库联盟成为国内最为普遍、分布最广的网络形态之一。联盟型智库网络的宗旨或目的往往十分明确,一般由智库自发成立,为的是集合某一地区、某一行业,乃至某一学科的智库力量和资源,搭建智库信息、资源、成果共享的交流合作平台,共同促进该地域或该领域的发展,对整合地区智库资源,吸纳专业智库力量,推动智库共同体建设有重要价值。例如 2014 年 1 月,由南京市政协指导的南京智库联盟成立,按联盟章程独立运行。作为非营利松散型智库联合体,南京智库联盟坚持高端定位,实行会员加盟制,主要工作任务包括决策咨询、沟通联系、信息共享、研究协作、资政议政、决策评估、人才培养、对外交流八项,对整合南京地区乃至长三角地区的智库资源有重要意义。2015年4月,"一带一路"智库合作联盟成立,旨在为各研究机构搭建信息共享、资源共享、成果共享的交流平台,提高"一带一路"研究水平,同时联盟具有解读政策、咨政建言、推动交流的高端智库职能。

与政府主导型网络和系统型网络不同,大部分联盟型网络虽没有官方背景,但往往有较为完整的组织架构。一般而言,联盟型网络的成员资格限制相对较小,网络规模可大可小,研究领域较为集中,网络凝聚力与稳定性相较于平台型网络要高。由于是智库自发组成,开展活动的形式和频率的相对限制较少。从目前我国智库联盟发展的实际情况看,可分为多种不同的类别。例如按照不同的地域、研究领域、行业、学科、智库属性等组建而成的智库联盟形成了不同的联盟型网络。总体来看,目前我国智库联盟发展呈现以下几个特点:

1. 智库联盟数量增长迅速

总体而言,智库联盟数量近几年有了较大突破。国内较早的智库联盟组织如广东智库联盟成立于2010年,武汉智库联盟成立于2012年。在2013年之后,智库联盟有了爆发性的发展,如图5.1所示。随着《关于加强中国特色新型智库建设的意见》《国家高端智库建设试点工作方案》出台,智库联盟依托新型智库建设进程的稳步推进,进入了高速发展时期。2015年~2018年,国内成立了70余家智库联盟。2019年上半年已经有越南研究智库联盟、河南省高校智库联盟、江苏新智库联盟、长三角地区党校(行政学院)智库联盟等数家智库联盟成立。截至2019年12月,国内已经建成的智库联盟已有百余家,这百余家智库联盟可以为不同地区、不同领域、不同类型的智库提供一个交流合作的平台,打破智力孤岛,提高智库之间的协同创新能力和政策服务能力。从智库性质层面来讲,不同类型的智库,如高校智库、社会智库、党政军智库、企业智库等根据自身不同性质组成了不同性质的智库联盟。例如国家级或省级高校智库联盟;党校系统联盟(如山东省党校系统智库联盟、长三角—珠三角党校智库合作联盟),企业智库联盟(如中央企业智库联盟)和社会智库联盟(如蓝迪国际智库平台)等。相同性质的智库组成联盟有利于同一系统间智库信息的交流,但也容易形成智库条块分割的现象,不利于更大范围内的智库交流合作。

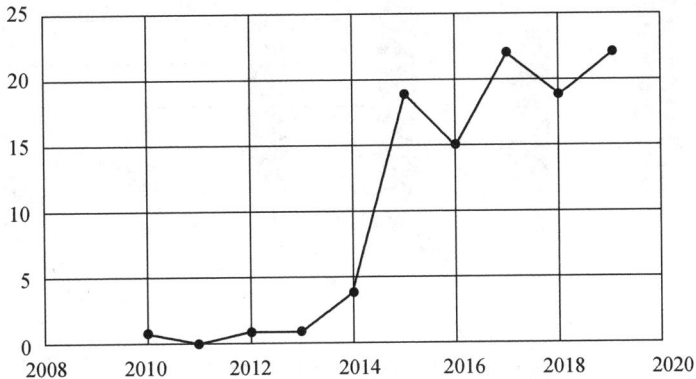

图 5.1　2010 年～2019 年智库成立数量

2. 智库联盟呈现地域化特点

从智库联盟涉及的地域来看,目前国内主要有全国性智库联盟、省级智库联盟、区域性智库联盟、市县级智库联盟以及国际性智库联盟。国际智库联盟主要是由我国智库倡导成立的,有外国智库加入的智库联盟。区域性智库联盟主要是跨省市的区域联盟。具体联盟数量如图 5.2 所示。从地域层面来讲,国内目前有广东、广西、云南、湖南、山东、江苏、贵州、甘肃等地成立的省级智库联盟;南京、苏州、武汉、黑河等地成立市级智库联盟;甚至部分县、区也成立了相应的智库联盟。如 2015 年,由浙江省宁波市象山县委政研室、宁波工程学院象山研究院、象山天一智库共同发起组建的象山智库联盟,是全国首家县级层面智库联盟;2018 年,深圳宝安区成立了宝安区智库联盟。除了省市区之外,还有部分跨区域的智库联盟,如中国沿边省区新型智库战略联盟、全国"一带一路"沿线城市智库联盟、宁镇扬智库联盟,以及长三角、珠三角、京津冀等地区智库机构组成的智库联盟。

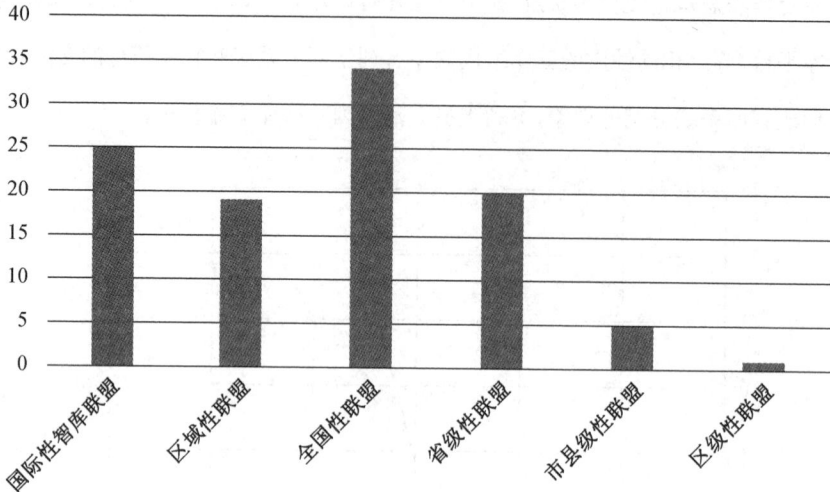

图 5.2 不同地域范围的智库联盟数量

3. 智库联盟运行机制有待完善

智库联盟能有效避免单一智库"散兵作战"的劣势及"孤岛"现象，克服短板效应，产生合作共赢的效果。但目前我国智库联盟绝大部分是以线下实体形式存在，并无专门的智库联盟网站，仅有少数在线下联盟的基础上建立了线上交流合作平台。这与国外众多智库联盟相比，还有较大差距。线下智库联盟以实体化形式运营，容易受到地点、时间、经费、人数等多方面的限制；且各类智库联盟数量众多，联盟成员从几个到上百个不等，这也为联盟的管理运行带来不便。智库联盟的活动较为单一，主要以会议、论坛形式出现。但由于大部分智库成立时间较短，且部分智库年会以两年一次或是三年一次的频率召开，智库联盟成员之间联系较弱。特别是涉及地域广、成员数量较多的智库联盟，如何保证智库联盟的凝聚力，增强智库成员的归属感是智库联盟必须要考虑的问题。部分智库联盟在成立之初，便公布了智库章程与目标，但是并没有与之相适应的智库成果评价、验收、转化等机制。仅靠一年或几年一次的智库年会，对于增强智库之间的合作、加强人才交流、促进成果转化的帮助比较有限。智库联盟仅有联盟之名，而无联盟之实，智库之间的交流合作还停留在表面，这不仅与智库联盟成立的初衷相悖,也在一定程度上造成了智力资源的浪费。

二、高水准的智库交流活动促进了智库网络的发育

　　随着我国新型智库建设进程的加深,智库机构数量的增加,智库网络逐渐形成,不同区域、类型的智库之间,智库与其他机构之间的交流日益频繁,逐渐常态化。智库论坛、智库会议、智库培训、智库调研等是当前智库交流的主要形式。智库交流是促进智库之间相互了解,维系和谐、可持续的智库网络的关键步骤。

(一)品牌论坛成为网络节点

　　《关于加强中国特色新型智库建设的意见》出台后,各类型智库机构在党和政府的支持下进入建设发展的热潮。智库交流往往紧随智库发展,在智库建立发展之初,部分智库论坛陆续开设。经过几年的发展,部分智库论坛参与人数逐年增加,论坛规模逐渐扩大,品牌效应开始显现。国研智库论坛是在国务院发展研究中心指导下,依照国务院发展研究中心打造"国际一流高端智库"的发展目标,举全中心之力,由国务院发展研究中心直属单位中国发展出版社主办,国研智库(国研文化传媒集团股份有限公司)、中国发展观察杂志社承办的高端论坛,由国研智库论坛年会,国研智库新年论坛,国研智库月度论坛、行业论坛、地方论坛及国际对话组成。[①]自创办以来,国研论坛举办了数十场高端论坛。国研智库论坛充分发挥智库作用,在解读国家政策、传播智库声音、促进科学决策与服务经济社会健康发展方面起到了积极的作用。历届论坛均取得了丰硕成果,产生了良好的社会影响,目前已成为国内智库领域的标志性论坛,全媒体影响力位居中国学术领域论坛影响力排行榜前列。[②]

　　为推动中国智库治理现代化、专业化和科学化,南京大学中国智库研究与评价中

---

　　① 新华网.国研智库论坛[EB/OL].[2019－12－03].https://baike.baidu.com/item/国研智库论坛/22315266? fr=Aladdin.

　　② 中国网."国研智库论坛·第五届年会(2018)"即将在京举行[EB/OL].[2019－12－08].http://ydyl.china.com.cn/2018－11/22/content_74198020.htm.

心、光明日报智库研究与发布中心特倡议成立了"中国智库治理论坛"，并决定在每年
12 月份召开年会。每年年会邀请中央及各省市智库管理部门领导、中国智库索引
（CTTI）来源智库、智库研究界著名专家学者和部分媒体参与论坛，自 2016 年至今累
计 2000 余人参会，成为我国智库界的"阿斯彭思想节"。"中国智库治理论坛"既是一
场学术盛宴，又是思想的盛会，同时也是来源智库优秀成果的发布会。自 2017 年开
始，"中国智库治理论坛"面向智库征集优秀成果，旨在通过遴选推介优秀智库研究成
果，集中展现中国特色新型智库咨政启民、为国建言的价值追求与坚实成绩，并特别
指出参选成果的作者来源不受限制，可由某一智库独立完成或多家智库合作完成，鼓
励智库联盟及合作网络积极参选，评选结果及评选情况将向相关管理部门专报报送。
论坛的荣誉供给机制对提高智库积极性，宣传智库先进经验，增强智库网络凝聚力有
重要意义。

　　"珞珈智库论坛"由武汉大学和光明日报社联合举办，自 2017 年至今已连续举办
3 届，会议以主旨演讲和圆桌对话形式展开，主要围绕国家亟须和中央重大决策部
署，立足武汉大学学科和科研优势，搭建智库服务与政策对接的平台，积极推进经济
和社会的创新发展。每年会议都有来自学界、政界、实业界、金融界、智库机构的专家
学者齐聚武汉珞珈山，共话我国发展的新时代。推动我国新型智库体系建设，需要着
力增强智库在议程设置、舆论宣传、统筹协调等方面的能力，离不开智库与媒体的通
力合作，珞珈智库论坛就是国内知名高校与中央主流媒体通力合作的代表之一。①

　　"中国南方智库论坛"是贯彻落实中共广东省委、广东省人民政府《广东省建设文
化强省规划纲要（2011—2020）》和《广东省哲学社会科学"十二五"发展规划》，推进广
东省文化强省建设重要项目之一，同时也是广东省文化建设领域的重点项目和社科

---

　　① 光明日报. 光明日报社与武汉大学联合主办第三届珞珈智库论坛[EB/OL]. [2019 - 12 - 08].
http://about. gmw. cn/2019 - 10/14/content_33229975. htm.

发展盛事。①"中国南方智库论坛"举广东省社科界之力,广邀国际、国内知名专家、学者聚集广州展开一年一度的专题讨论,至今已成功举办8届,形成了"新"(体现新起点、新趋势、新机制、新优势)、"特"(广东特色乃至中国特色)、"高"(理论高度、决策研究高度)的特点,已逐步建立起智库品牌公信力与影响力,成为政、商、学界交流对话的重要平台,为实现广东"三个定位,两个率先"总目标做出了应有的贡献。

此外还有中国浦东干部学院和光明日报社共同主办的"中国特色新型智库建设"高层论坛,上海社科院等机构主办的"上海全球智库论坛",复旦大学和智库论坛秘书处主办的"中国大学智库论坛"等知名论坛都在国内形成了较大的影响力。从目前论坛的举办情况看,我国智库论坛已经形成了较强的连续性,逐渐常规化,参与智库论坛的人数、单位、机构等逐年上升。特别是部分开设较早的智库论坛经过几年时间的发展沉淀,积累了较丰富的办会经验,形成了较成熟的办会模式,在智库界甚至社会上形成了明显的品牌效应。因此,品牌智库论坛往往成为智库界目光的焦点,成为智库观点与思想交锋、碰撞、交流的重要平台,具有显著的引导和汇聚作用,为智库共同体不断提供发展势能。

(二) 组织会议是智库网络的主要功能

除了部分受到整个智库界关注的高端品牌论坛之外,各地区、各机构举办了多种规模,多样类型、多元主题的年会、论坛、研讨会、咨询会、座谈会等智库会议。"一会一主题,一会一焦点"的灵活的会议主题设置在很大范围上覆盖了智库建设、研究中涉及的主题,适应社会关切的重点、难点、热点。组织会议成为智库网络的主要功能。

部分省市积极召开了本区域的智库会议,搭建区域内智库联络交流的平台。江苏智库峰会是由江苏省委宣传部、江苏省社科联主办的全省智库交流高端平台,也是

---

① 中国社会科学网.打造中国高端智库论坛品牌[EB/OL].[2019-12-08].http://www.cssn.cn/zt/rwln/whzt/lb/201601/t20160105_2811296.shtml.

江苏智库界每年一度的"思想盛宴"，①自 2016 年至今已经连续举办 4 届，旨在加强智库间交流与协作，提高智库研究质量，促进江苏新型智库建设。从第三届智库峰会开始，还组织评选智库实践、智库研究的优秀案例，以推动智库多出高质量的实践成果。

行业性的智库会议重点关注了本行业、本领域内的发展动向，团结了行业内的智库精英力量。例如"互联网与国家治理智库论坛"从 2014 年至今已成功举办了 6 届，并从 2015 年开始发布《互联网与国家治理年度报告》，旨在推动互联网与国家治理领域的学术研究和决策服务，搭建跨学科交流、碰撞和合作的长效机制，充分发挥互联网与国家治理研究领域的社会服务和专家智库作用。

智库会议逐渐成为打破行业壁垒，沟通不同领域智库资源，促进跨机构、跨行业智库合作交流的重要平台。浙江舟山群岛新区研究中心（CZZC）于 2019 年 3 月 10日正式策划启动了"周末智库沙龙"（SZS）这一产生智力的新平台。经过不断地探索与努力，"周末智库沙龙"基本形成了半个月举行一期，每期规模在 25 人左右的工作规律，邀请来自政府部门、高校、各行业有关专家领导参加，是具有 CZZC 特色的系列研讨活动。截至目前，CZZC 已经成功举办了 11 期"周末智库沙龙"。每期沙龙不仅气氛热烈、观点纷呈，更反映了智库供给智力的水平，不仅注重对国家战略举措、时政热点的研究和探讨，同时聚焦对舟山群岛新区建设发展问题的剖析和解答，充分发挥了新型智库提供智力支持、献言献策的作用。

此外，不定期召开的座谈会、研讨会、咨询会等以其灵活机动的优势弥补了定期年会在会期与主题上的限制。在我国新型智库共同体的形成过程中，类型多样的智库会议是智库交流的最重要也是最常见的形式之一。这些丰富多彩的智库会议成为团结本行业、本地区智库力量，促进智库资源流通的重要平台。

---

① 新华日报.第四届江苏智库峰会在宁举行[EB/OL].［2019－12－08］.http：//xh.xhby.net/mp3/pc/c/201912/06/c719648.html.

（三）组织培训是智库网络促进自我发展的重要路径

在我国新型智库建设进程中，部分智库机构积累了一定的智库建设经验，形成了较为成熟的智库运作模式，同时也涌现了一大批拥有先进理念、观念的智库专家。培训是给受训者传授其完成某种行为必需的思维认知、基本知识和技能的过程。智库培训是智库专家向智库从业者或智库机构传授智库观点、智库理念以及智库研究方法的重要途径与方式，同时也是智库共同体交流的重要形式。例如江苏省社科联成立江苏省智库研究与交流中心，主要承担开展智库理论研究、推进研究基地发展、组织智库成果交流、智库人才培训、指导并支持市县社科联智库建设工作等职能，多次承担省委宣传部、省社科联共同主办的江苏智库峰会的具体组织工作，举办多期江苏青年智库学者培训班和江苏青年智库学者沙龙，在省内外重要媒体推出众多智库研究成果，有力地推动了江苏新型智库发展。2019 年 11 月，由江苏省委宣传部指导，江苏省社科联主办，江苏智库研究与交流中心具体组织的江苏高层次智库专家研修班在清华大学继续教育学院举行，来自江苏省重点高端智库、省重点培育智库、省决策咨询研究基地等机构的首席专家或骨干专家，和省委研究室、省政府研究室、省发改委、省工信厅等省新型智库理事会单位职能处室负责人等近 60 人参加。①

"智库能力与新型智库建设高级研修班"由中国科学院文献情报中心《智库理论与实践》编辑部主办，至今已成功举办了 4 届，研修班师资包括国家有关部门智库专家、企业智库专家、研究机构、高校相关智库专家和学者等，围绕新型智库核心能力建设主题展开专深讲解和互动交流，旨在加强中国特色新型智库核心能力建设，推进国家治理体系和治理能力现代化，解决新型智库建设理论与实践发展中面临的新问题。

首届"国际顶尖智库高级研修班"开设于 2017 年，由全球化智库（CCG）、宾夕法尼亚大学智库研究项目（TTCSP）、宾大沃顿中国中心主办，南京大学中国智库研究

---

① 江苏省哲学社会科学界联合会. 江苏高层次智库专家研修班在清华大学举行［EB/OL］.［2019 - 12 - 08］. http://www. js-skl. gov. cn/news/9598. html.

和评价中心协办,至今已举办 3 届,旨在通过借鉴国际顶尖智库管理经验和战略规划,促进我国智库界、学术界专家与智库顶级专家的深度交流,持续提升我国智库建设的专业化和管理创新水平。

近些年各地区智库相关部门和机构纷纷举办培训班,邀请著名智库专家担任讲师,或是参观访问著名智库机构,学习智库建设经验与技能;或是针对新型智库建设的重大问题如"智库职能发挥""新型智库建设""智库传播""智库人才培养"等话题进行深度交流。可见,智库培训已经成为智库网络交流与加强联系的形式,起到了很好的理念传递作用,是智库网络实现自我发展的重要路径。

(四) 频繁的走访调研增强智库网络的连接性

相互访问和考察调研是机构间交流的重要形式。随着各类新型智库先后建立,智库之间、智库与其他机构之间的互访和调研逐渐频繁,成为促进新型智库交流合作的重要方式,大大增强了智库网络的连接性。按调研双方性质主要有以下几种:

一是智库之间互访调研。这是智库之间相互学习、交流信息、交流合作项目、交流人才较为有效和常见的途径。智库之间相互了解新型智库的体制机制、运营模式、团队氛围、研究成果,通过"取经"吸收和学习更多对传统智库转型升级有启发的新型智库建设经验,建立智库建设与研究共识,从而为开展务实合作奠定基础。

二是智库与高校、企业等非智库机构之间的调研交流活动。智库之"智",在国在民,智库与非智库单位的沟通交流是智库充分发挥职能的前提。以中国人民大学重阳金融研究院为例,每年有数十次访问或接待国内不同研究机构、高校、媒体等活动。这些活动是智库与非智库单位建立联系的重要方式,为增进双方了解、建立更长远的合作提供了一个相互了解的途径。

三是政府部门与智库之间的调研访问活动。政府部门调研智库机构主要是调研新型智库建设情况,听取智库建设经验,了解智库建设难点;或是听取智库政策意见。部分省市智库主管部门会组织专门智库调研组对下辖智库的建设情况定期调研评估。例如:上海市曾组建由上海市哲学社会科学规划办牵头,联合上海市教卫工作党委、上海市决策咨询委员会办公室等部门组成的新型智库建设调研小组,调研上海市高校智库建设情况,通过调研工作的沟通与交流,加深了政府部门对高校智库建设成果、存在瓶颈等方面的了解,也在智库与政府间搭建起了一座沟通桥梁。

四是国内智库与国外机构的互访活动。随着我国智库的国际影响力逐渐提高,国际"朋友圈"逐渐扩大,国内智库访问或接待国外机构、国外专家学者越来越频繁,这有助于国内智库主动与国际接轨,了解国际先进的智库理念、研究焦点,及时了解国际智库发展大势。例如在 2015 年到 2019 年间,全球化智库接待了德国、日本、印度、美国、古巴、英国、以色列等多个国家地区的访问团;同时也积极"走出去",访问了美国商会、美国商务部、英国发展研究智库、美国进步中心等诸多国外机构,积极了解国际形势,与西方智库交流智库建设经验等。

智库调研的一个重要目的是增加调研双方相互了解。双方无论是吸取经验,畅谈合作,还是了解智库建设进展与发展痛点难点,都将有助于充分认识智库建设现状,取长补短,挖掘智库发展潜力,促进智库共同体的形成,更深入推进新型智库建设。

三、智库共同体协同创新为智库建设提质增效

在我国新型智库建设进程中,智库共同体的形成对于促进智库要素的整合、智库平台的融合,形成分类分层、协调有序的新型智库发展体系有重要意义。通过智库共同体,可以在一定程度上避免智库研究的同质化、碎片化等问题,使智库资源利用最大化;同时以课题研究和学术研讨为纽带,集聚跨地区、跨部门、跨体制、跨专业、跨行业的优质智库资源,形成智库合力,弥补单个智库的短板弱处,打造"强强联合、优势互补、开放融合"的多元协同智库建设新机制,达到"1+1>2"的效果,创造智库建设与发展的新格局。

(一) 智政互通,咨政建言谋实谋势

不同类型的智库有助活跃我国智库行业,产生"鲶鱼效应",但不同智库往往受性

质、资源、区域等多方面因素影响而呈现不同的发展状态,例如在我国新型智库体系中,党政军智库、科研院所等相比高校智库、社会智库更接近决策中心,掌握更多智库资源,咨政渠道较为畅通。一方面,智库共同体有效缓解了个体智库差异,搭建政智交流合作的桥梁,促进政智互通;另一方面,智库共同体作为智库的"plus"版,在提供咨政服务时,同样必须紧跟时事热点,聚焦大势,主动适应社会环境变化,切合国家大政方针及战略的调整。咨政建言只有谋实谋势,才能充分发挥智库共同体咨政之职。

例如,为了进一步发挥河南省高校智库联盟的平台优势以及"共商、共建、共享"的作用,展示高校智库的研究成果,更好地服务河南经济社会发展大局,2019 年 11 月 25 日,河南省高校智库联盟召开了成果发布会,32 所高校的 43 个智库提交展示成果 132 项。这次成果发布会给予了智库与实际工作部门面对面的对接和交流的机会,有利于破解智库建设中智库与应用长期"分离、两不靠"的老大难问题和瓶颈制约,缓解部分智库关门做学问、自弹自唱甚至自娱自乐的窘况。河南省高校智库联盟召开的成果发布会搭建了政府与智库之间的桥梁和纽带,如果在此基础上形成每个厅局与若干智库对接,长期合作,彼此依赖的协作格局,将在很大程度上破解智库发展难题。

又如为促进中韩(盐城)产业园的高质量发展,"沿海发展智库"与中韩(盐城)产业园建设办公室主动对接,构建交流协作机制,通过联席会议、实地调研、专家研讨、宣传推介等有效沟通机制,提出诸多咨询建议,共建"中韩产业合作联合研究中心";编写的《中韩(盐城)产业园建设实施方案》获江苏省政府发文确认;此外,还协力中韩(盐城)产业园举办各类国际、国内论坛,在共享各类信息的同时共同推进园区的高质量发展。

（二）智媒互联，舆论引导及时发声

传播技术与媒体平台的不断发展是当今社会的重要特点之一。对于智库而言,充分利用媒体是智库传播的重要途径。通过与媒体平台合作,智库更快、更广泛的发布智库成果,提升和扩大自身影响力与知名度,更好地发挥自身职能。目前,智媒联合与合作,甚至智媒融合,已经成为融媒体时代智库发展的重要趋势,在实践中,我国新型智库共同体积极与媒体平台、网络平台合作,建立"线上＋线下"的智库传播格局。

以粤港澳大湾区发展广州智库为例,该智库依托 4 家高校 6 个广州市人文社科重点基地,集聚各高校的学科人才力量,以自身科研优势和特色研究领域为主导,发挥整体优势开展决策研究,为形成高质量成果提供了坚实的保障;同时高度重视创新智库媒体联动机制,积极引导社会舆情;加强与《光明日报》《中国社会科学报》《广州日报》、光明网、大洋网等媒体合作,探索"智库＋媒体"联动机制,以专版、专题、专栏等形式,围绕粤港澳大湾区建设等相关主题,组织策划专家访谈,及时发出智库声音,引导社会主流舆论。《粤港澳大湾区发展规划纲要》于 2019 年 2 月 18 日发布,2 月21 日该智库就组织华南理工大学党委书记章熙春等专家进行专题阐释,在《光明日报》"光明视野"版面上整版刊发《粤港澳大湾区:打造最具竞争力的国际科创中心》,充分显示了智库的敏锐度,积极发挥了释政启民的职能。

（三）智学互助，智库研究谋深谋远

智库不是单纯的学术研究机构,但学术研究为智库研究提供了理论与学术基础,专业性的思考是智库研究的出发点。智库研究相比学术研究更具应用性和实践性。因此,在我国智库共同体的发展过程中,同样注重智库研究与学术研究相互促进,相辅相成,并在学术研究的基础上深化智库研究的应用性、政策性、前瞻性与战略性。例如为了响应国家战略的指示,促进多式联运运输结构改革,推动以铁路为核心的多式联运转型发展,上海交通运输协会多式联运分会与中国(上海)自贸区供应链研究院共同推进"基于铁路运输的多式联运综合评价指标体系研究",以多式联运协会为领导单位,组建成立了基于铁路运输的多式联运指标体系评价领导小组,并协同长三角三省一市的主要铁路货场和管理部门联合实施。该研究从铁路视角出发,评价我国运输结构调整背景下的多式联运发展现状,并结合长三角三省一市的实际运输数据进行分析与建议,通过产学研融合的方法为铁路视角下我国多式联运的发展提供

了独到的见解。

为深化政府、学者与大众之间的沟通，加强学生群体、青年学者与资深专家之间的交流，提升青年学者服务国家需要的自觉意识，道德发展智库举办了"道德发展智库月系列活动"；围绕"伦理道德发展的文化战略"核心议题先后举办了"新中国70年伦理道德发展的'中国问题'及其前沿理论"杰出青年学者智库论坛、"新中国70年伦理道德发展的文化轨迹和文化规律"长江学者智库论坛、"伦理道德发展的文化战略"道德发展智库国际论坛。道德发展智库月系列活动是一场立足伦理学学科又超越伦理学学科范围的系列对话活动，具有思想深度、内容广度和战略高度，赢得了政府决策者、青年学者、国内专家、海外学者的广泛参与，参与者们为智库建设提供了宝贵的决策意见和智力支持。

（四）智声海外，中外对话崭露头角

《关于加强中国特色新型智库建设的意见》提出要"加强中国特色新型智库对外传播能力和话语体系建设，提升我国智库的国际竞争力和国际影响力。建立与国际知名智库交流合作机制，开展国际合作项目研究，积极参与国际智库平台对话。"总体来说，经过几年的发展，我国智库的国际影响力较之前有了较大提升。在我国新型智库共同体的形成发展过程中，在很大程度上帮助智库发挥了公共外交的职能以及促进了我国智库国际话语权的建立。

"上海全球智库论坛"首次举办于2014年，目前已举办5届。"2019年上海全球智库论坛"由上海社会科学院、"一带一路"智库合作联盟、中国宏观经济研究院、复旦大学、上海全球城市研究院和万里智库等共同主办，本届论坛以"中国的新开放与全球智库创新"为主题，来自中国、美国、德国、英国、荷兰、新加坡、日本、罗马尼亚、丹麦等国70余家智库的近200位专家学者参加了研讨。中国国际经济交流中心举办"全球智库峰会"，中国社会科学院和俄罗斯国际事务委员会主办的"中俄高端智库论坛"，由中国人民大学、光明日报、"一带一路"智库合作联盟主办的"中国智库国际影响力论坛"等都成为我国智库发出"中国声音"，讲好"中国故事"，促进中外智库交流，引领智库研究和创新发展的重要学术品牌和传播平台。

除了积极举办会议论坛等交流活动,我国智库也积极提出"中国主张"。天津大学生物安全战略研究中心为推动构建全球生物安全命运共同体,制定生物科学家行为准则,承办了许多重要国内外会议,通过一系列努力,"生物科学家行为准则范本"现已成为联合国《禁止生物武器公约》专家会议题,正式列入会议工作计划,展现了我国在全球生物安全治理中的示范与引领作用。

此外,我国智库主动作为,积极倡导成立智库国际联盟,促成智库国际合作。以复旦发展研究院金砖国家研究中心为例,中心于2019年初承担金砖国家大学联盟秘书处工作之后,校领导、发展研究院院领导、中心主任及工作人员一起召开工作会议,由领导部署这一年的工作安排和计划,确定了这一年的工作重点。通过2019年一年的努力,秘书处在建章立制、治理架构、代表性平台、核心产品四个方面取得重大突破,实现大学联盟的稳健运行,在主要合作伙伴中形成显著的影响力,进一步巩固和提升中方在金砖国家大学联盟为最主要代表的金砖国家教育领域务实合作中的声望和影响力。

我国新型智库的繁荣发展,智库之间交流不断深入,智库网络日益扩大,这些都为新型智库共同体的形成奠定了基础。打造新型智库共同体,是充实中国特色新型智库体系的重要一环,有助于集中优势智力资源,提高智库之间的协同创新能力,服务社会重大需求,为政府提供政策建议,推动智库研究与政府决策良性互动。但目前我国智库共同体建设仍处于发展初期,存在着合法身份有待认证,共同体体系有待完善,共同体运作缺乏平台支撑,网络桎梏有待破除,共同体凝聚力较低、功能较弱等问题。新型智库共同体的发展与新型智库建设相辅相成,是一项长期性系统性的工程,必须打破地域、学科、性质、领域、机构、形态的限制,使之成为一个有机整体,才能充分发挥智库共同体的聚合、交流、咨政作用。

专题六　国家与学术：新时代智库研究进展

国家需求是我国哲学社会科学发展的主要动力,是驱动学术前沿发生变化的重要力量。知识界积极响应国家各项政策,集中力量投入多样化科研资源,服务于国家重大项目,推动研究领域由"冷"变"热",从学术边缘走向学术前沿,从小众研究走进大众视野。中国特色新型智库建设是推进国家治理体系和治理能力现代化的重要途径。党中央有关中国特色新型智库建设的战略部署激发了社会科学工作者智库研究的热情,近5年智库研究的数量和质量都了新飞跃,充分体现了新时代学术服务新时代国家建设的社会科学发展新特征。

一、国家需求驱动学术发展

国家政策反映现实社会最迫切需求,是社会科学各界的密切关注点。国家政策与学术发展关系紧密且相互促进发展。政治环境和国家政策变化多次影响哲学社会科学前沿发展,近年来由学术边缘走向学术前沿的"智库研究"力证了这一良性推动机制。

（一）国家重大战略需求——建设中国特色新型智库

2013年4月15日,习近平总书记对智库建设做出重要批示(以下简称"4·15批示"),提出建设"中国特色新型智库"的重大战略部署。① 2013年11月,十八届三中全会《中共中央关于全面深化改革若干重大问题的决定》明确提出"加强新型智库建

---

① 李刚,丁炫凯.习近平治国理政思想是新型智库建设的指针[J].智库理论与实践,2016,1(02):
1-7.

设,建立健全决策咨询制度",将"4·15 批示"主要内容写入中央文件。因此,理论界和智库界将 2013 年看作建设"中国特色新型智库"的元年。2014 年"中办"下发《关于加强中国特色新型智库建设的意见》(以下简称《意见》)的第 65 号文件,但这份文件并未向全社会公开印发,现在提及的多为 2015 年 1 月 20 日由中共中央办公厅、国务院办公厅公开印发的《意见》。《意见》明确指出,中国特色新型智库是党和政府科学民主依法决策的重要支撑,是国家治理体系和治理能力现代化的重要内容,是国家软实力的重要组成部分。[①] 该《意见》是中央关于建设中国特色新型智库的第一份专门文件,对构建中国智库发展新格局、深化管理体制改革、健全制度保障体系、加强组织领导等方面都做出了说明。[②] 2015 年 11 月,中央财政部与中共中央宣传部为贯彻落实中央《意见》相继出台《国家高端智库专项经费管理办法(试行)》(财教[2015]470号)、《国家高端智库建设试点工作方案》(中宣发[2015]37 号)等文件。总体而言,以上文件基本奠定了中国特色新型智库建设理论基础,完成了体制机制建设,规划了新型智库建设路径,明确了智库人财物具体管理办法。各省、自治区、直辖市和各部委积极响应中央号召,根据本地区本行业实际情况统筹安排新型智库建设。2015 年后,部分省市和国家部委出台新型智库建设相关文件。[③④] 党的第十九届四中全会审议通过《中共中央关于坚持和完善中国特色社会主义制度、推进国家治理体系和治理能力现代化若干重大问题的决定》(以下简称《决定》),全面总结了新中国国家制度和国家治理体系建设的历史性成就,集中概括了中国特色社会主义制度和国家治理体系的显著优势,提出了坚持和完善中国特色社会主义制度、推进国家治理体系和治理

---

① 新华社. 中共中央办公厅、国务院办公厅引发《关于加强中国特色新型智库建设的意见》[EB/OL]. http://www.gov.cn/xinwen/2015－01/20/content_2807126.htm,2018－11－09.

② 李国强,徐蕴峰. 学习习近平"智库观",推动中国智库建设健康发展[J]. 智库理论与实践,2017,2(02):1－10.

③ 教育部. 教育部关于印发《中国特色新型高校智库建设推进计划》的通知[EB/OL]. http://old.moe.gov.cn//publicfiles/business/htmlfiles/moe/s7061/201404/164598.html,2018－11－10.

④ 人民网—人民日报. 关于社会智库健康发展的若干意见[EB/OL]. http://politics.people.com.cn/n1/2017/0505/c1001－29255043.html,2018－11－05.

能力现代化的总体要求和总体目标，部署了坚持和完善支撑中国特色社会主义制度的根本制度、基本制度、重要制度的重大任务，是坚持和完善中国特色社会主义制度、推进国家治理体系和治理能力现代化的政治宣言和行动纲领。① 《决定》提出"健全决策机制，加强重大决策的调查研究、科学论证、风险评估，强化决策执行、评估、监督"② 对我国新型智库建设工作具有直接的重大指导意义。由国家政策引导的新型智库建设在全国范围内兴起并不断推向高潮。理论界和学术界加紧围绕智库建设的理论研究、行动研究和案例研究开展应急研究。

（二）国家科研基金牵引智库研究走向学术前沿

国家各类科研基金项目指南向知识界明确表达国家意志，牵引学术发展方向。根据 2011 年至 2018 年国家级社科基金和教育部社科基金公布的各项项目指南和立项课题，智库类研究主体数量增长较快（见表 6.1）。相关智库项目指南多分布于图书馆、情报与文献学（34%）、国际问题研究（19%）、管理学（15%）和政治学（13%）

表 6.1　国家级/教育部社科基金项目指南与立项课题中智库研究的数量统计

智库研究项目指南/立项课题数（单位：个）		2011 年	2012 年	2013 年	2014 年	2015 年	2016 年	2017 年	2018 年
国家级社科基金	项目指南	1	1	3	3	14	6	9	3
	立项课题	3	2	1	10	21	8	10	9
教育部社科基金	项目指南	0	0	1	0	0	0	1	0
	立项课题	0	0	7	3	14	1	5	3

---

① 机关党委，国务院发展研究中心举行学习贯彻党的十九届四中全会精神宣讲报告会[J/OL]. http://www.drc.gov.cn/zxxw/20191122/353-223-2899792.htm, 2019-11-22.

② 新华社.中共中央关于坚持和完善中国特色社会主义制度　推进国家治理体系和治理能力现代化若干重大问题的决定[EB/OL].[2019-11-05]. http://www.chinanews.com/gn/2019/11-05/8999040.shtml.

等（见图 6.1）。在立项课题统计中，智库相关课题分布更加广泛，与图一统计结果相比较，图 6.2 出现了许多涉及智库研究的新学科，比如"出版学""法学""医学"和"计算科学"等。以上数据说明在国家政策和国家牵引学术发展工具的指引和支持下，不

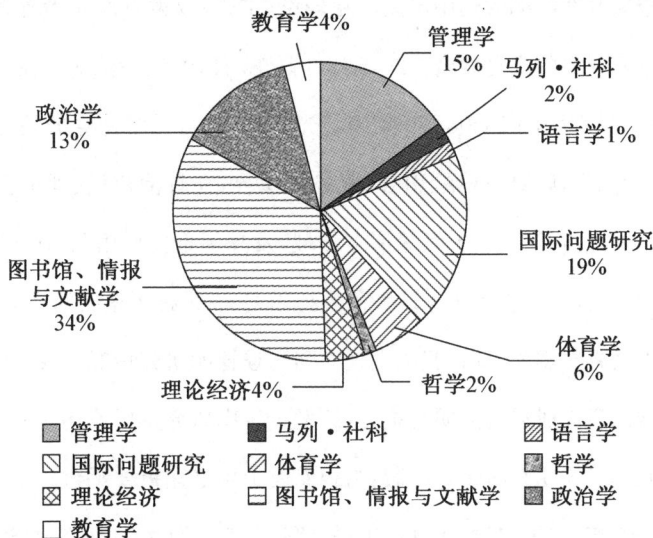

图6.1 国家级和教育部社科基金项目指南中智库研究所在学科分类

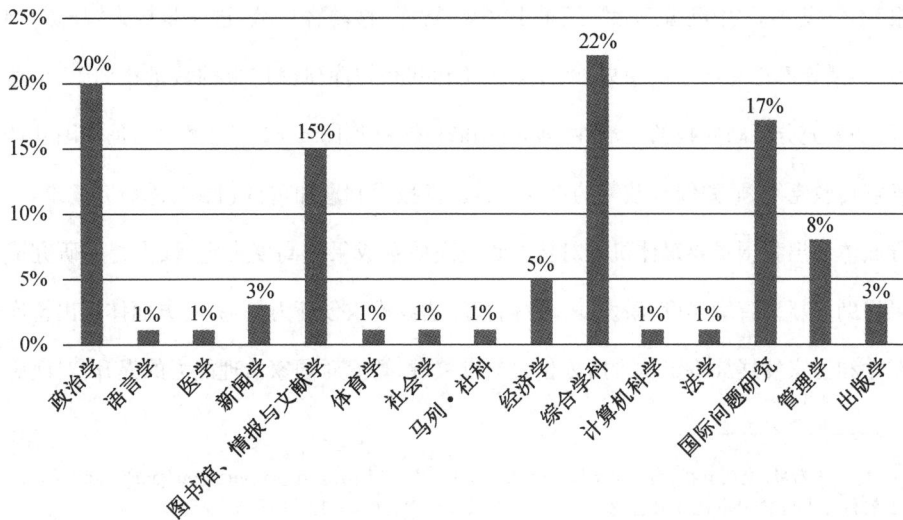

图6.2 国家级和教育部社科基金立项课题中智库研究所在学科分类

同学科学者主动投入力量开展智库研究，从多方面推动智库研究从学科交叉边缘走向学术舞台、理论舞台、媒体舞台的中心位置。

（三）党报党刊大力宣传智库研究成果

我国党报党刊在鲜明表达中国共产党理论、主张、政策方面充当着重要角色，也是展示重要学术成果的高光舞台。2019 年 6 月 16 日，习近平总书记在写给《光明日报》创刊 70 周年的贺信中写道，"70 年来，《光明日报》自觉坚持党的领导，坚持与真理同行、与时代同步，团结、联系、引导、服务知识界，在政治建设、理论创新、道德引领、教育启迪、文化传播、科学普及等诸多领域，发挥了重要作用"。在传播智库建设重要性工作中，党报党刊作为国家政策落实抓手之一，发挥了重要的推动作用。通过中国知网报纸文献数据库，统计我国党报党刊刊登智库研究情况。我国党报自 2003 年开始刊登智库研究成果，《光明日报》持续发布智库研究重要论述，并于 2014 年 12 月 25 日专门设立《光明日报·智库版》为智库舆论场搭建重要平台。① 《新华日报·智库版》于 2015 年 6 月 9 日推出，以"走进社科名家，关注社科动态，推送智库报告"为编辑理念，主要有"智库出品""社科名家""智库论坛""决策眼"等栏目。② 《经济日报》不仅设立了"中经智库版"，还推出"中经智库"移动客户端，进一步扩大智库影响力，传播智库思想产品。中央、地方党报党刊刊登智库研究成果的数量在 2015 年达到顶峰，充分反映党报的政治性、即时性和宣传性（见图 6.3）。党报党刊是中国共产党宣传政党纲领、路线和政策的重要工具。党报党刊愈加重视刊载智库研究成果，一方面体现出我国重要媒体机构对智库研究高质量成果的高度肯定，认为智库研究成果将助力新型智库建设、激发知识界向智库建设投入创新力量，另一方面体现出智库在党和国家发展战略定位中所处位置愈发关键，智库对国家治理能力的提升，对政府

---

① 王斯敏. 光明日报《智库》版与读者见面[EB/OL]. http://epaper.gmw.cn/gmrb/html/2014-12/25/nw.D110000gmrb_20141225_5-01.htm? div=-1, 2014-12-25.
② 邱雪莲. 新华日报《智库》版. [EB/OL]. http://jsdjt.jschina.com.cn/special/Selection2015/Forum/xhrb/201605/t2815407.shtml, 2016-05-16.

科学决策能力的改善,对社会舆论引导作用的加强和对在国际舞台软实力的展现发挥着重要作用。

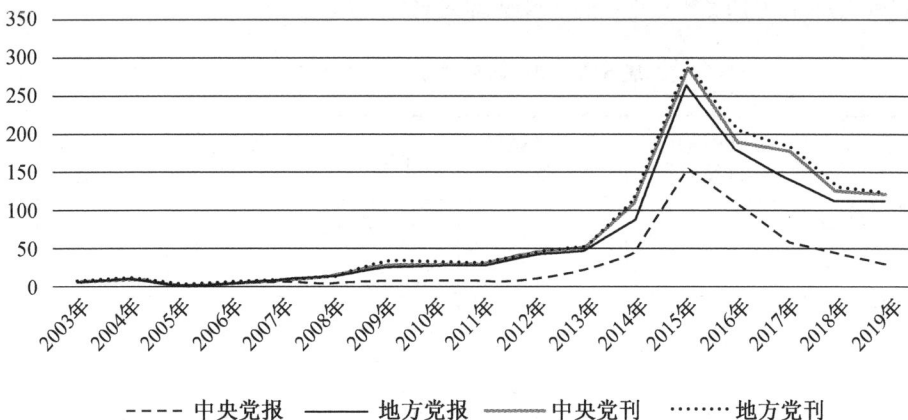

图6.3　中央/地方党报刊登智库研究成果情况统计

二、学术发展积极响应国家政策——智库研究成果实现突破性增长

中国哲学社会科学的发展路径与国家政治紧密相关,各专业领域依据国家现实发展需要、国家政策调整研究资源配置,优先解决国家所需、所急。智库研究从学术边缘走向学术前沿是知识界积极响应国家政策的有力证明。统计智库研究文献和专著数量能够最直观地反映这一明显变化。

利用中国知网期刊数据库,以"智库""智囊团""思想库""内脑""布鲁金斯学会"为篇名检索,共得到7000多篇文献。通过剔除不相关文献、重复文献、新闻报道等冗余文献之后,共得到6359篇有效文献。随着年份增长,智库研究文献增长数量和速度出现显著变化。表6.2显示,国内学者自二十世纪八十年代初开始进行智库研究。直至2008年,智库研究文献量长期偏低,反映出智库研究一直处于研究边缘,少有人问津。2009年至2014年期间,智库研究文献量显著提高且一直处于增长状态,但这一时期文献增长速度远不及2015年至今智库研究文献增速。2015年智库研究文献量大约是2014年文献量的两倍,至此之后,智库研究文献量一直居高。图6.4清晰展现在 2015 年前后,即 2015 年 1 月 20 日中央颁布《意见》前后,智库研究文献量实现突破性增长。这一明显标志说明,国家政策强力驱动智库研究从学术边缘走向前沿阵地,知识界向该领域投入研究资源,推动该研究领域不断发展。

表 6.2　智库研究文献量年份分布表

年份	文献量（篇）	累计文献量（篇）	年份	文献量（篇）	累计文献量（篇）
1981 年	1	1	2001 年	6	127
1982 年	3	4	2002 年	9	136
1983 年	2	6	2003 年	12	148
1984 年	4	10	2004 年	37	185
1985 年	2	12	2005 年	24	209
1986 年	4	16	2006 年	37	246
1987 年	5	21	2007 年	28	274
1988 年	6	27	2008 年	40	314
1989 年	3	30	2009 年	107	421
1990 年	2	32	2010 年	130	551
1991 年	2	34	2011 年	102	653
1992 年	6	40	2012 年	159	812
1993 年	5	45	2013 年	224	1036
1994 年	7	52	2014 年	388	1424
1995 年	12	64	2015 年	718	2142
1996 年	11	75	2016 年	1110	3252
1997 年	6	81	2017 年	1127	4379
1998 年	9	90	2018 年	1140	5519
1999 年	17	107	2019 年	840	6359
2000 年	14	121			

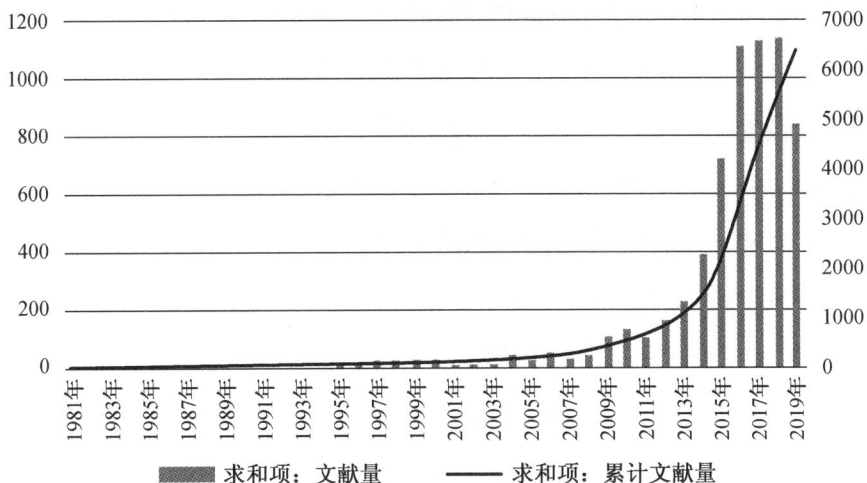

图 6.4　智库研究文献增长趋势

　　通过读秀图书数据库，统计智库研究专著数量变化，其年份分布如图 6.5 所示。2015 年前后智库研究专著数量较前一阶段显著增长。智库研究文献和专著数量在 2015 年出现突破性增长说明，知识界意识到智库研究对国家决策咨询能力发展的重要价值，自觉意识逐渐凸显。

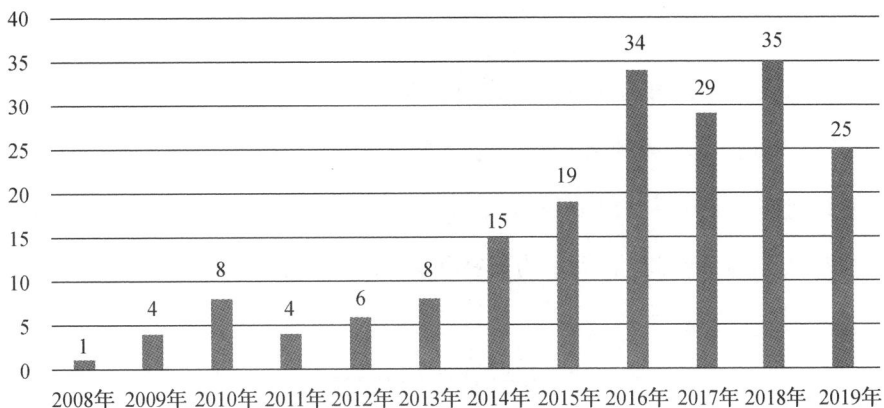

图 6.5　智库研究专著数量年份分布

三、推进我国智库知识体系制度化进程

随着决策咨询专业化和现代智库的发展，西方智库研究已走上制度化道路。西方智库研究拥有稳定数百人核心作者群体，70％智库研究文献发表在水平较高的国际学术期刊上，受到政治学、公共管理学、教育学、图书馆与情报学等学科硕士生、博士生的密切关注，建立连续性、专业性国际智库学术会议，涉及地域范围越来越广。[①]西方智库研究制度化明确两大指向，一是将智库作为政治现象和管理现象，从学术层面探讨其丰富的理论内涵；二是将智库作为实践综合体，从操作层面探索改善智库管理实践的方式方法。西方智库研究已嵌入主流社会科学的常态化研究。制度化、常态化的智库研究将为智库建设发展提供一片沃土。

（一）明确智库知识体系基本构成是首要前提

2016 年 5 月 17 日，习近平总书记在哲学社会科学座谈会上发表重要讲话，强调"要加快构建中国特色哲学社会科学，按照立足中国、借鉴国外、挖掘历史、把握当代、关怀人类、面向未来的思路，着力构建中国特色哲学社会科学，在指导思想、学科体系、学术体系、话语体系等方面充分体现中国特色、中国风格、中国气派。"[②]构建具有自身特质的学科体系、学术体系、话语体系，我国哲学社会科学才能形成自己的特色和优势。

智库既是学术机构，也是现代咨询业的重要部分。[③] 高水平智库建立学术成果转化机制，利用学术成果帮助政府提升决策科学性和政治理性，有效发挥智库咨政建言、理论创新、舆论引导、公共外交和社会服务的五大职能。研究智库发展各个方面，促进智库知识体系[④]制度化形成，为国家决策咨询战略提供重要支撑。智库知识体

---

① 李刚，甘琳，徐路.智库知识体系制度化建构的进程与路径[J].图书与情报，2019(03)：1 - 10，72.

② 新华社.习近平主持召开哲学社会科学工作座谈会[EB/OL].http://www.xinhuanet.com//politics/2016 - 05/17/c_1118882832.htm，2016 - 05 - 17.

③ 尹开国.现代咨询业的概念和分类探讨[J].图书情报工作，2002(09)：84 - 87.

④ 严建新.国内几种科学知识体系结构的评述[J].科学学研究，2007(01)：19 - 25.

系是关于智库话语体系、学科体系、学术体系和职业发展体系的有机结合。构建智库话语体系体现中国智库发展的历史和实践，争取在国际舞台拥有中国智库话语权，充分表现习近平总书记强调的中国特色、中国风格、中国气派。加强智库学科体系建设，开拓智库研究领域，嵌入基础学科体系，设置智库研究核心课程，撰写智库研究相关教材，培养智库研究高水平人才，牵动智库走向国内主流学术圈，为国家现代化智库发展打下坚实的学科基础。学术体系以学术组织、学术期刊和学术活动等要素为主要内容，设立智库研究学术委员会，有助于规划、组织和协调全国或地方性智库研究与评价工作；搭建智库研究成果发表平台，有助于智库研究长期稳定占据主流学术期刊选题席位；定期连续举办智库学术活动，有助于扩大智库学术影响力、提升智库媒体影响力，①形成智库学术活动制度化。打造智库职业发展体系，源源不断地向国家政府部门、研究机构和智库输送高端人才，推进智库管理制度化、规范化和科学化进程。②

智库知识体系从话语体系、学科体系、学术体系和职业发展体系四条路径，助力智库发展，达成国家现代化智库建设目标，改善国家现代化治理体系，加大力度建设我国政治理性化，提升国家现代化治理水平，支持国家决策咨询战略稳步前进。

（二）智库话语体系初步形成

智库话语体系是指智库在公开场合表达的思想理论或观点主张中概念、句式、志趣、情感、立场等信息集合体，带有话语智库的鲜明风格和强烈政治属性，经过多年积累、沉淀和锤炼得来，是智库不懈努力构建的成果。③ 虽然我国智库建设起步较早，可追溯至 20 世纪 80 年代，以国务院发展研究中心（1980 年）、中共中央政策研究室（1981 年）、中国现代国际关系研究院（1980 年）等决策咨询机构的成立为标志，但单

---

① 朱瑞博，刘芸.智库影响力的国际经验与我国智库运行机制［J］.重庆社会科学，2012，（03）：110-116.

② 唐庆鹏.论现代智库的成长逻辑及其对我国的启示［J］.社会主义研究，2015(01)：139-147.

③ 欧阳兵.习近平中国特色新型智库建设思想中的话语体系构建［J］.学习论坛，2017，33(06)：5-10.

纯依靠党委政府内智库为核心的决策咨询模式难以提升我国现代化治理能力。借助信息政策研制模型，开展循证政策研究，大力发展专业高端智库建设势在必行。2015年初国内大规模开展智库建设之时，国内现实情况是智库知识储备严重不足，缺乏对智库历史发展、现代智库运营管理的基本认识。

以 2015 年为分界线，对比 1981 年至 2014 年与 2015 年至 2019 年不同阶段智库研究关键词的变化，分析国内智库研究演化路径。通过关键词词频统计，运用二八定律，确定前一阶段高频关键词共现频次为 15 次及以上，后一阶段高频关键词共现频次为 60 次及以上。利用 UCINET 软件绘制图 6.2 中不同阶段的高频关键词共现聚类图谱，并据此做出高频关键词聚类统计（见表 6.3）。通过计算图 6.6 中两张图谱的网络密度和关键词点度中心性可知，前一阶段高频关键词共现网络（网络密度为0.4397）较后一阶段（网络密度为 0.6677）更为松散。通过计算各阶段高频关键词点度中心性并观察图 6.6 和表 6.3 可知，1981 年至 2014 年智库研究以国外智库为研究对象，尤其是美国和日本智库，并探究智库基本功能、智库与政府间关系、新型智库创新和发展等问题。2013 年前后国内知识界举办多场智库相关会议、论坛和研讨

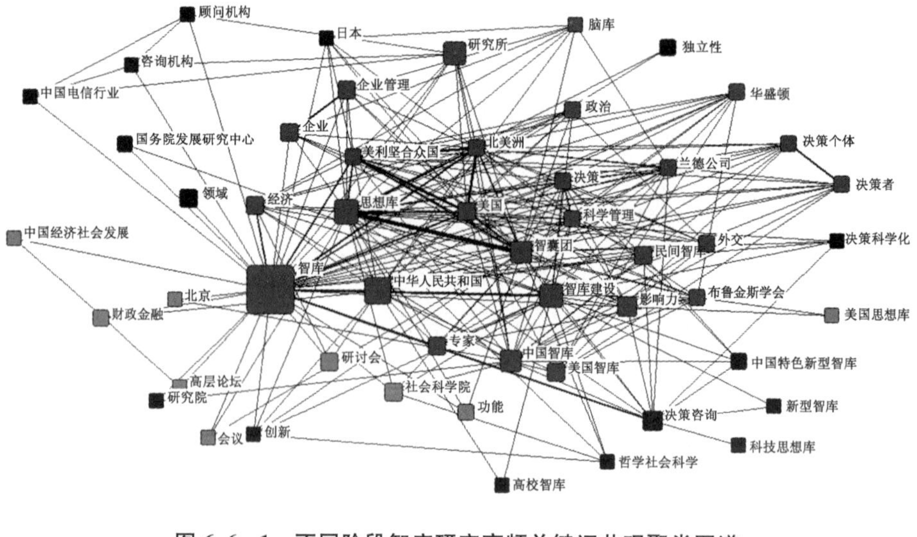

图 6.6-1   不同阶段智库研究高频关键词共现聚类图谱

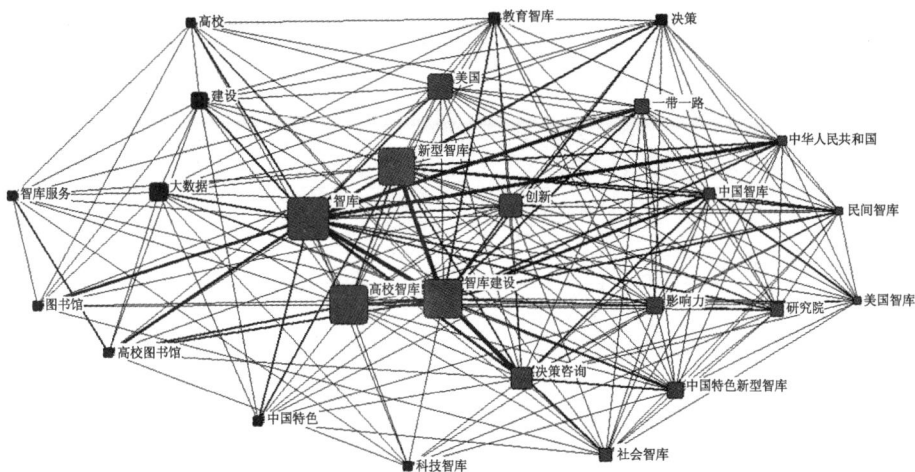

图 6.6‑2 不同阶段智库研究高频关键词共现聚类图谱

会,产生重要会议综述文献。2015 年～2019 年智库研究出现新气象,智库研究聚类更加集中,高校智库研究占据重要一席,图书馆在智库服务方面发挥重要功能;智库发展紧紧跟随时代脉搏,与"大数据""一带一路"等社会热点紧密结合;智库研究类别细分化愈加明显,科技智库、社会智库和民间智库建设成为知识界聚焦点。

表 6.3 不同阶段智库研究高频关键词聚类表

1981 年～2014 年

聚类 1	聚类 2	聚类 3		聚类 4
顾问机构	中国经济社会发展	脑库	决策	独立性
中国电信行业	北京	研究所	兰德公司	决策科学化
咨询机构	财政金融	企业管理	决策个体	中国特色新型智库
日本	高层论坛	企业	决策者	新型智库
国务院发展研究中心	研讨会	美利坚合众国	科学管理	决策咨询
领域	会议	北美洲	智囊团	科技思想库

续表

1981 年～2014 年

聚类 1	聚类 2	聚类 3		聚类 4
研究院	社会科学院	政治	民间智库	哲学社会科学
创新	功能	华盛顿	外交	高校智库
	美国思想库	经济	智库建设	
		思想库	中华人民共和国	
		美国	智库	
		中国智库	专家	
		美国智库	影响力	
		布鲁金斯学会		

2015 年～2019 年

聚类 1	聚类 2	聚类 3		
高校	智库服务	美国	创新	高校智库
教育智库	大数据	一带一路	中国智库	智库建设
决策	高校图书馆	中华人民共和国	民间智库	影响力
建设	中国特色	新型智库	智库	研究院
图书馆	科技智库	美国智库	决策咨询	中国特色新型智库
		社会智库		

经历将近四年的初期探索,国内知识界就智库的属性、特征、历史发展与演变、西方智库的历史和实践等基本问题给出了答案,国内智库研究主题逐渐聚焦于智库专业性方面。专业性要求智库具备"规制性""自治性"和"权威性"的基本特征。智库"规制性"研究帮助机构厘清基本职能和特殊职能,确定智库基本性质、资质、职责和权益;智库"自治性"研究为机构成立、管理和营运赋能,设置基本职能机构,如学术委员会、咨询委员会和理事会等;智库"权威性"研究声明智库负有的崇高社会责任,为国家赢得国际话语权,为社会建设提供具有科学性和客观性的咨询建议。但以上研究尚未影响到国际智库界。相比于西方智库研究论断对我国智库研究的影响而言,

例如智库独立性、"旋转门机制"和"第五种权利说"等，凝聚中国特色、中国风格和中国气派的新型智库话语体系尚未形成。

（三）智库学科体系具有显著的跨学科特征

智库研究属于跨学科研究领域，涉及学科知识广泛，包括政治学、管理学、传播学、国际关系、图书情报与档案、历史学和教育学等一级学科。智库研究学科体系的建立以多学科基本理论和研究方法为基础，逐渐形成自己的核心知识体系和训练体系。建立智库学科体系是智库知识体系发展的重要路径，有助于稳定智库研究的前沿地位，有助于源源不断地培养智库专业高层次人才，有助于促进智库研究嵌入主流社会科学。

根据中国知网硕博士论文数据库统计，自 2004 年至 2019 年共有 233 篇硕博士论文与智库研究紧密相关。同样，2015 年后这一数量较前一阶段显著增长。2015 年至 2019 年，共计 179 名硕士生和博士生研究智库相关选题（详见图 6.7），学科背景呈现多样化、细分化的特征，其中行政管理、公共管理和国际关系等政治学学科的硕

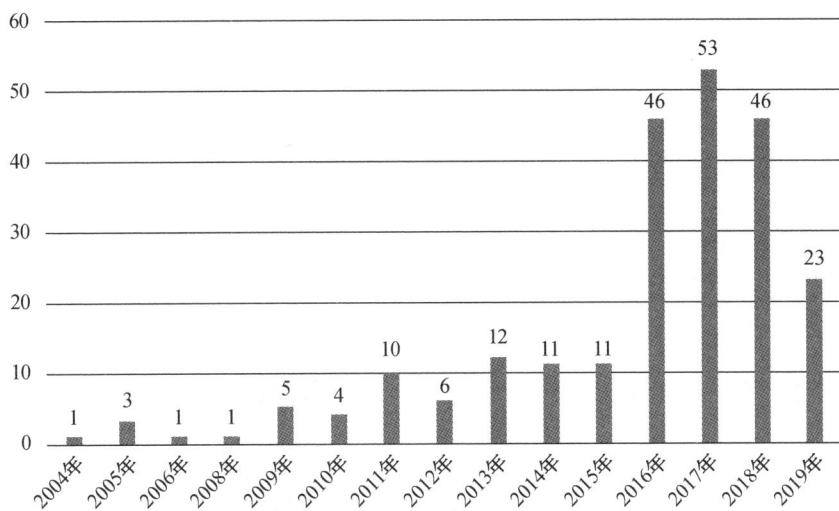

图 6.7　智库研究硕博士论文年份分布表

博士论文占比最多；其次是教育学（包括教育经济与管理、高等教育学、比较教育学等）、图书情报与档案学和新闻传播学三类学科占比较重（详见表6.4）。根据长尾效应，涉及智库研究的头部学科占比较重，尾部学科占比较轻且十分松散，表明智库研究具备前学科阶段的典型特征。

表 6.4　智库研究硕博士论文学科分布统计

学科	文献量	学科	文献量	学科	文献量	学科	文献量
行政管理	64	政治学理论	5	教育史	2	社会学	1
公共管理	41	档案学	4	比较制度学	2	思想政治教育	1
国际关系	18	世界史	3	法政策学	2	体育人文社会学	1
教育经济与管理	12	英语语言文学	3	比较政治学	1	哲学	1
高等教育学	11	法学	2	科学技术哲学	1	政治学	1
情报学	10	工商管理	2	科学社会主义与国际共产主义运动	1	中外政治制度	1
国际政治	8	马克思主义中国化研究	2	马克思主义法学	1	公安学	1
新闻传播学	8	外交学	2	马克思主义理论	1	法律	1
图书馆学	7	教育学	2	农业信息管理	1	德语语言文学	1
比较教育学	6	管理科学与工程	2	软件工程	1		

构建智库学科体系，将智库研究嵌入政治学、管理学、图书情报学、经济学和教育学等社会主流学科，需要主流学科专家学者、一流高校和著名研究机构共同重视，共同努力，促进智库研究嵌入主流学术圈。

以2015年智库研究文献数量实现突破增长为界限，对6359篇智库研究文献作者分阶段分析，运用普莱斯定律确定了不同阶段核心作者群体。由表6.5可知，2015年至2019年智库研究核心作者数量较前一阶段大大增加，从42人增长至90人，且出现了在一级学科研究领域享有极高声誉的学者，如清华大学的薛澜、朱旭峰，人民大学的王文、王莉丽，等等。2015 年以前核心作者合作网络密度为 0，说明这一时期智库研究核心作者尚未形成合作网络。虽然 2015 年至 2019 年核心作者合作网络密度也较小(0.0058)，但已形成较小合作规模。图 6.8 证明核心作者合作网络中至少已有 7 类小团体网络。国内智库研究共同体已形成一定规模，且具有不断扩大的良好趋势，为智库研究制度化奠定基础，他们将作为智库知识体系建设、智库运营管理的重要咨询顾问。

表 6.5　不同阶段核心作者对比

	核心作者	文献量	核心作者	文献量	核心作者	文献量	核心作者	文献量	核心作者	文献量	核心作者	文献量
	王莉丽	15	薛澜	7	李树林	5	陈广猛	4	李桢	3	王辉耀	3
	王文	13	陈圻	6	张志强	5	陈向阳	3	吴天佑	3	朱有志	3
	徐晓虎	9	韦磊	5	王力	4	李安方	3	李婧	3	傅曦	3
1981年至2014年	李伟	8	卫思宇	5	张新霞	4	李光	3	王春法	3	刘益东	3
	朱旭峰	8	王荣华	5	王颖	4	朱毅凯	3	赵可金	3	王丁凤	3
	陈一新	7	金家厚	5	夏春海	4	崔树义	3	高尚全	3	王小海	3
	李国强	7	王丁凤	5	曹升生	4	胡乐明	3	紫石	3	孙志茹	3
	王文	29	李清刚	8	史明睿	7	郭华	6	田山俊	6	徐维英	5
	李刚	29	朱旭峰	8	侯书漪	7	孙鸿飞	6	陈开敏	5	刘大可	5
	张旭	13	文少保	8	吴瑛	6	张广汇	6	卜雪梅	5	周洪宇	5
	申劲婧	13	丁炫凯	8	杨再峰	6	郭子睿	6	柏必成	5	沈进建	5
2015年至2019年	张舜栋	12	程煜	8	王莉丽	6	李国强	6	张大卫	5	王伟光	5
	李凌	12	苗绿	8	彭焱	6	杨国梁	6	刘春艳	5	万劲波	5
	曹如中	11	邱均平	8	于丰园	6	郑军卫	6	陈赟畅	5	李丽	5
	李伟	10	马岩	7	武慧娟	6	王灵桂	6	黄长伟	5	张宏宝	5
	任福兵	9	付睿	7	傅广宛	6	杨茜	6	潘燕婷	5	俞贺楠	5
	任恒	9	陈海贝	7	韩万渠	6	杨宝强	6	周湘智	5	李宏	5

续表

	核心作者	文献量	核心作者	文献量	核心作者	文献量	核心作者	文献量	核心作者	文献量	核心作者	文献量
1981年至2014年	王辉耀	9	易本胜	7	韦磊	6	黄东升	6	梁宵萌	5	潘教峰	5
	谭玉	9	刘志光	7	张涛	6	王世伟	6	张象林	5	薛惠锋	5
	卓翔芝	9	赵蓉英	7	杨东升	6	张述存	6	张冬梅	5	许烨	5
	伊林甸甸	9	徐路	7	胡燕	6	刘颖	6	王清莲	5	丁元竹	5
	赵雪岩	9	廉立军	7	袁曦临	6	安婧宜	6	储节旺	5	郑荣	5

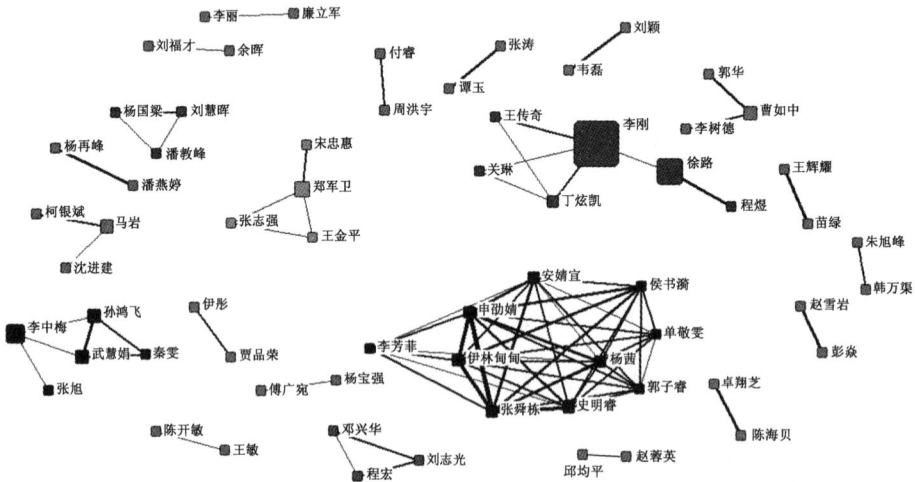

图6.8　2015年至2019年智库研究核心作者合作网络共现聚类图谱

经统计，20015年至2019年发文作者所属机构数量（2708家）是前一阶段数量的（821家）三倍之多。各地各层次科研机构、高校和政府部门等纷纷投入智库研究的浪潮中，智库研究领域开始出现百家甚至千家争鸣的盛况。图6.9统计了不同阶段发文数量排名前20的机构，结合发文机构整体情况，1981年至2014年，高校占发文机构比例大幅度提升，尤其是"双一流"大学积极推动和支持相关学院、研究中心展开智库研究。国家和地方社科院、研究院（所）发文数量虽有大幅度增长，但占发文机构整体比例略有下降。相反，民间研究机构和其他机构占发文机构整体比例有所上升，但发文总量不及前者。南京大学、中国人民大学重阳金融研究院、上海社会科学院智库研究中心、国务院发展研究中心、中国国际经济交流中心等持续围绕智库展开研究，而中国科学院及其下属机构、武汉大学、吉林大学、《智库理论与实践》编辑部等机构则在 2015 年之后开始展现研究实力。

1981 年至 2014 年智库研究机构合作网络十分松散，基本上属于各自为阵的状态，网络中清华大学公共管理学院和国际关系学院公共管理系的中心性最为突出，浙江省委内部合作、中国人民大学学院间合作较为频繁。2015 年至 2019 年，智库研究机构合作网络发生巨大变化。网络密度大大提高，网络链接数大大增加，出现了以中国科学院及其下属机构、南京大学中国智库研究与评价中心、武汉大学信息管理学院、吉林大学信息资源研究中心等小团体，机构内部合作、机构间合作更加频繁（见图6.10）。就目前发展趋势看，智库研究嵌入主流学术圈并非难事，嵌入主流社会科学、构建完备智库学科体系、出版专业性核心教材尚需一段时日。

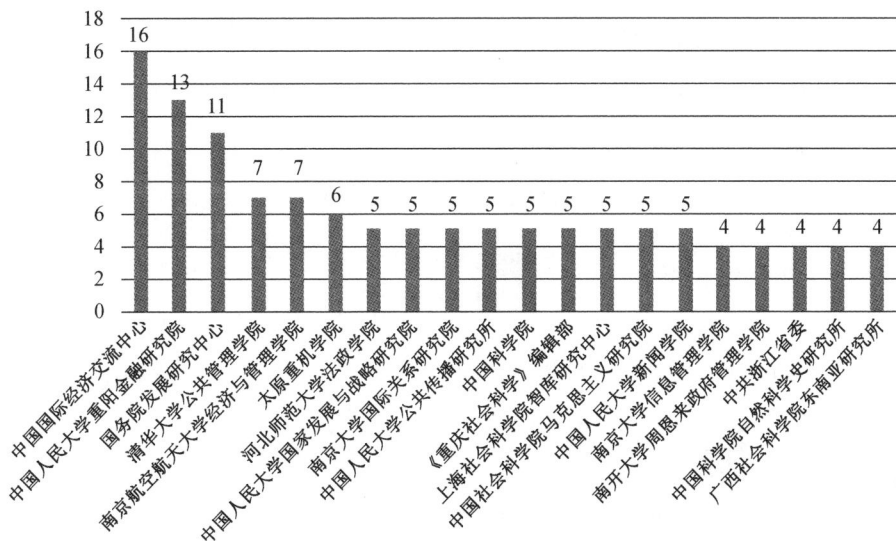

图 6.9‑1 不同阶段智库研究发文机构统计
1981 年至 2014 年发文机构统计（前 20 名）

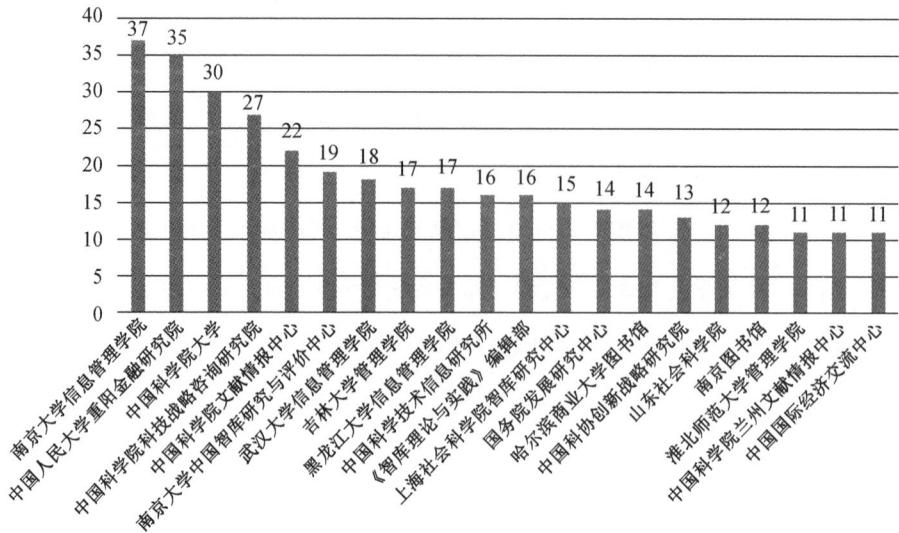

图 6.9‑2　不同阶段智库研究发文机构统计
2015 年至 2019 年发文机构统计（前 20 名）

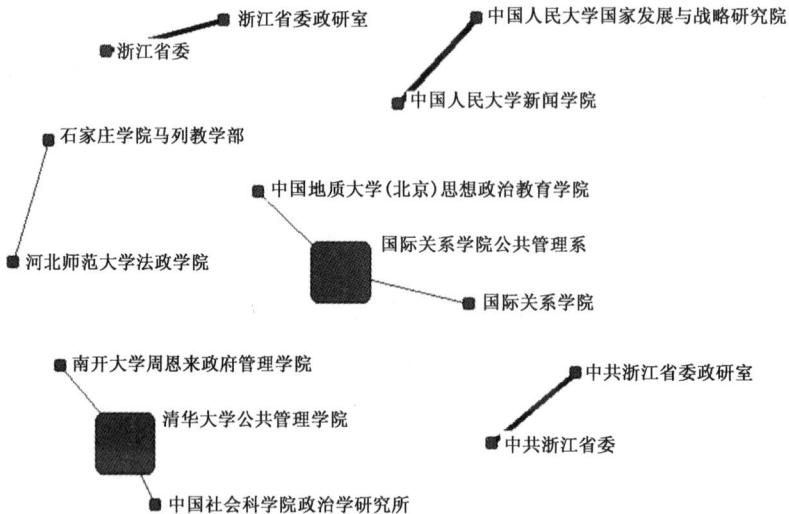

图 6.10‑1　不同阶段智库研究机构合作网络共现聚类图谱

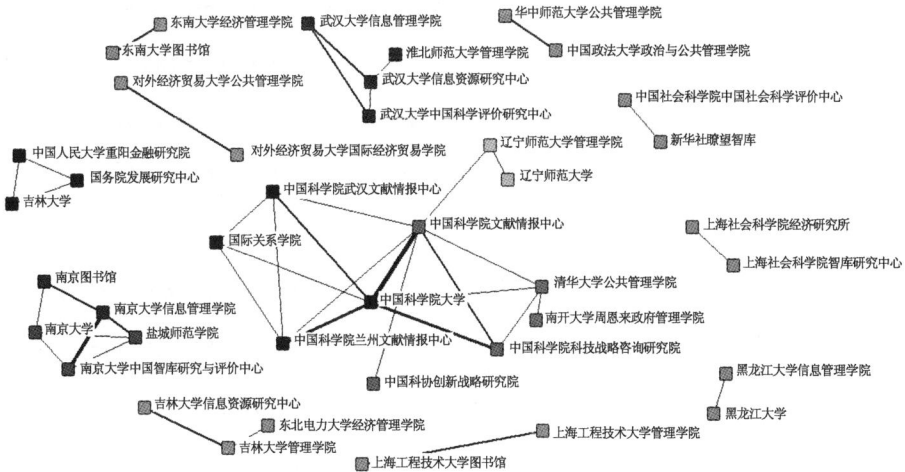

图 6.10 - 2　不同阶段智库研究机构合作网络共现聚类图谱

（四）智库学术体系和职业发展体系显露雏形

构建智库学术体系，建立智库相关学术组织，创办智库研究学术期刊，定期组织开展智库研究学术活动，帮助智库研究人员和管理人员进一步规划职业发展体系，为智库知识体系制度化提供可持续发展的根本保障。

目前，国内尚未成立全国性质的智库研究一级学会，也未在政治学会、管理学会或中国图书馆学会下设智库研究专业委员会。全国智库研究、评价工作的规划、组织、协调和开展缺乏统一性和合法性。智库学术研究组织的建设基本是一片空白，从全国到地方建立专业性、统一性和科学性的智库学术组织工作仍需投入更多优质资源和力量。建设智库学术组织，为全国智库研究者搭建交流平台，促进智库研究成果的创新与应用，真正让智库研究成果效用最大化。

《智库理论与实践》创办于 2016 年 2 月，是国内唯一一份专业性智库研究期刊，致力于探索智库理论、支撑智库建设、指导智库实践、传播智库成果。[①] 在三年多的

---

① 智库理论与实践. 智库理论与实践—信息公告［EB/OL］. http://zksl. cbpt. cnki. net/WKD/WebPublication/wkList. aspx? columnID=5e39458d - 27b4 - 4fe0 - 92fa - 83ab3d0d6976，2019 - 05 - 14.

时间里，该期刊已刊登智库研究论文超过 300 篇，为智库研究打造了专业发表平台。学术刊物"一枝独秀"难以长期吸引稳定的作者群体，难以形成制度化的高层次发表平台。

据统计，1981 年至 2014 年刊载智库研究文献期刊共计 612 种，CSSCI 期刊共计 117 种；2015 年至 2019 年刊载智库研究文献期刊共计 1226 种，CSSCI 期刊共计 173 种。由此可知，国内不同层次学术期刊均开始重视智库研究文献的成果发表，尤其是图书馆学、情报与文献学、管理学、政治学、经济学、教育学、综合社科类期刊。例如，《人民论坛》《图书馆论坛》《中国行政管理》《经济学动态》等（详见表 6.6）。高质量学术出版物重视智库研究，认可智库研究方法的科学性和规范性，研究成果具有重要影响力。为建设智库理论体系夯实基础，为扩大智库学术体系影响力提供理论依据，为加强智库学科体系建设提供重要参考，为规划智库职业发展体系指明方向。

表 6.6　不同阶段 CSSC 期刊刊载智库研究文献数量统计（前 30 名）

2015 年至 2019 年				1981 年至 2014 年			
CSSCI 核心期刊	文献量	CSSCI 核心期刊	文献量	CSSCI 核心期刊	文献量	CSSCI 核心期刊	文献量
人民论坛	89	图书与情报	12	人民论坛	19	国际经济评论	4
情报杂志	61	出版发行研究	11	国外社会科学	17	红旗文稿	4
图书情报工作	26	高校教育管理	10	中国行政管理	12	情报科学	4
现代情报	22	江苏高教	10	马克思主义研究	9	情报理论与实践	4
情报资料工作	21	中国高等教育	10	国际展望	8	图书情报工作	4
图书馆论坛	21	重庆大学学报（社会科学版）	10	情报资料工作	8	云南社会科学	4
教育研究	20	南京社会科学	9	现代国际关系	8	中国高等教育	4
情报理论与实践	20	宁夏社会科学	9	经济学动态	6	中国科技论坛	4
高教探索	19	国家教育行政学院学报	8	社会科学战线	6	中国软科学	4

续表

2015 年至 2019 年				1981 年至 2014 年			
CSSCI 核心期刊	文献量	CSSCI 核心期刊	文献量	CSSCI 核心期刊	文献量	CSSCI 核心期刊	文献量
情报科学	18	国外社会科学	8	外交评论（外交学院学报）	6	高校教育管理	3
图书馆学研究	16	教育发展研究	8	教育发展研究	5	管理学刊	3
中国行政管理	16	科技与出版	8	世界经济与政治	5	国际论坛	3
国际经济评论	15	经济社会体制比较	7	中国高教研究	5	国际新闻界	3
旅游学刊	14	科学管理研究	7	比较教育研究	4	行政论坛	3
中国高教研究	13	中州学刊	7	当代世界与社会主义	4	经济社会体制比较	3

　　"中国智库治理论坛"由光明日报社和南京大学创办，以智库研究和智库专业建设为目的的全国连续性会议。该论坛已成功举办三届，每届都有将近 800 人参会，是智库业界的年度盛会。根据中国智库治理论坛 2016 年至 2018 年历届参会者统计信息（见表 6.7），参会人员主要来自智库管理部门，国家高端智库和党政军智库，党校、行政学院、社科院系统，高校智库管理部门，社会、媒体、科技和企业智库，高校智库，各类参会人员人数每年都有所增长。这说明"中国智库治理论坛"影响力越来越大、辐射面越来越广。智库研究、智库营运、智库建设等方面的工作已经成为某些智库论坛参会者的工作职责和职业发展路径。

表 6.7　中国智库治理论坛 2016 年至 2018 年历届参会者相关统计

参会人员类别	2016 年	2017 年	2018 年
智库管理部门	32	36	35
国家高端智库和党政军智库	37	51	100
党校、行政学院、社科院系统	72	75	82

续表

参会人员类别	2016 年	2017 年	2018 年
高校智库管理部门	48	50	54
社会、媒体、科技和企业智库	74	72	78
高校智库	498	476	394
学术支持单位	26	29	33
外国专家	1	1	1

国家需求与学术发展之间联系紧密，相互影响。1949 年后，党中央不断制定政策、采取措施，大力推动哲学社会科学发展。哲学社会科学是人们认识世界、改造世界的重要工具，是推动历史发展和社会进步的重要力量，其发展水平反映了一个民族的思维能力、精神品格、文明素质，体现了一个国家的综合国力和国际竞争力。一个国家的发展水平，既取决于自然科学发展水平，又取决于哲学社会科学发展水平。一个没有发达的自然科学的国家不可能走在世界前列，一个没有繁荣的哲学社会科学的国家也不可能走在世界前列。坚持和发展中国特色社会主义，需要不断在实践和理论中探索、用发展着的理论指导发展着的实践。在这个过程中，哲学社会科学在服务国家需求方面具有不可替代的重要地位。国家需求成为哲学社会科学发展的重要驱动力。

在这一机遇下，智库研究积极向国家政策靠拢，满足国家发展的战略需求，推动自身走向研究前沿阵地。新时代智库研究已向前迈出重要一步，智库研究成果实现突破性增长、研究共同体不断扩大、研究主题不断向前沿推进、研究网络不断扩展、研究交叉性不断加深。这是国家政策引导智库研究不断发展的重要体现。新时代智库研究必须根据国家政策和哲学社会科学发展战略，不断推进学科体系、学术体系、话语体系和职业发展体系建设和创新，利用知识体系推动我国新型智库建设。

下　篇

中国智库索引来源智库报告

一、CTTI 三期系统简介

（一）CTTI 系统的建设历程

为全面描述、全面收集智库数据，提供数据整理、数据检索、数据分析、数据应用的功能，更好地服务中国特色新型智库建设，在中共江苏省委宣传部的指导下，南京大学中国智库研究与评价中心率先提出开发"中国智库索引"（以下简称"CTTI"）的设想，并得到了光明日报智库研究与发布中心的积极响应。自 2015 年起，双方发挥各自优势，通力合作，共同研究开发 CTTI 系统。

经过前期的系统开发，CTTI 已经拥有较为完备的数据字段，并于 2016 年 9 月 28 日正式上线发布，开放给被收录的所有来源智库录入数据。一年多的运营过程中，CTTI 收集到了大量来自各类智库和管理部门的实际需求，发现智库信息管理工具的缺乏已严重制约智库机构的日常管理。因此，2017 年 5 月，南京大学中国智库研究与评价中心与光明日报智库研究与发布中心联合课题组决定进一步完善 CTTI 的数据字段，优化系统功能，以满足上述需求。两个中心提出合力打造一款面向智库 IT 治理的增强型数据信息工具，CTTI Plus 版本应运而生。CTTI Plus 版不仅仅聚焦智库的定量评价，也着眼于满足智库信息管理的业务需要。在课题组的共同努力下，CTTI Plus 于 2017 年底完成更新与上线测试工作，并从 2018 年起投入使用。同年 5 月，由光明日报智库研究与发布中心和南京大学中国智库研究与评价中心联合主办的"2017CTTI 智库最佳实践案例（BPA）发布暨智库评价系统研讨会"在南京召开，会上专门举行了 CTTI Plus 系统发布及上线仪式，再次获得了国内智库同行及专家学者的热切关注，新版系统也得到更广范围的推广和利用。

CTTI 系统经过前两期建设，已经具有了智库检索、专家检索、成果检索、活动检索和 MRPAI 评价的功能。通过在线填报的机制，CTTI 目前已收集了大量的智库建设及成果数据。但是，随着越来越深入 CTTI 系统建设，我们发现 CTTI 系统还有着更大的提升空间。在反复调研和探索后，我们确定了 CTTI 三期建设目标，三期系统研发的重点在于提高用户友好性和系统功能的实用性，同时大力建设云智库内部评价，在收录智库数据、检索智库数据、智库评价的基础上，实现云智库管理机构、专家的横向考核评价对比。为了维护系统的稳定性和现有数据的可靠性，CTTI 三期版本的核心功能将延续 CTTI 前两期的设计，进一步强化 SaaS 服务，升级检索功能，完善数据导出功能，优化数据统计与管理功能，并且增加便捷的数据分析工具。

（二）CTTI 系统的总体架构

目前，CTTI 的总架构除了本地主系统外，还包含智库云管理功能和智库共同体机制两个方面。其中，用户权限分配采用多级叠加的星型结构，用户身份和权限描述拓扑结构如图 7.1 所示。

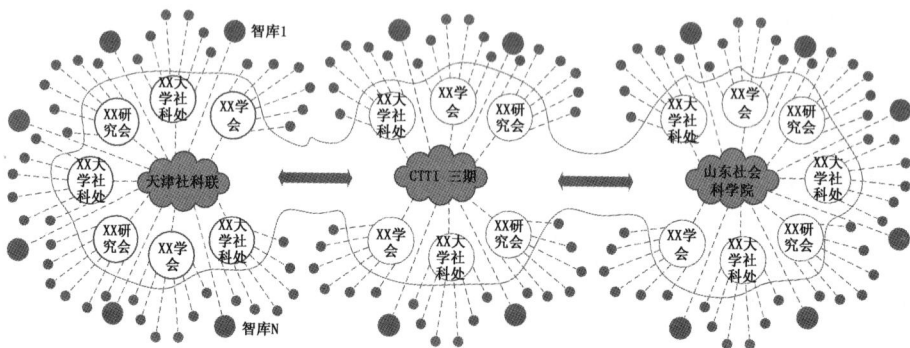

图 7.1　CTTI 三期功能架构拓扑图

曲线所标定的核心区域为智库共同体用户和智库云用户，曲线外部的点代表云智库。CTTI 将为中国智库共同体提供网络化的线上信息共享平台，并通过智库云功能进一步描述智库管理的层级。

CTTI 三期还预留了各智库机构自建系统数据同步入口，支持将各智库机构自建系统的数据,通过定制开发合入 CTTI 系统。

1. CTTI 系统的共同体

为了打造中国新型智库线上联盟,共享智库建设成果,CTTI 引入了智库共同体机制。智库共同体旨在为有志推进我国新型智库交流合作的智库机构和智库管理部门提供一个实体化的网络资源平台。智库共同体成员将以政府管理部门、事业单位和非营利单位法人为主。成员机构将享有系统所有数据和功能的使用权,同时 CTTI 将协助其在本地部署系统、建立本地智库云,并保证系统内数据的日刷新,如图 7.2 所示。

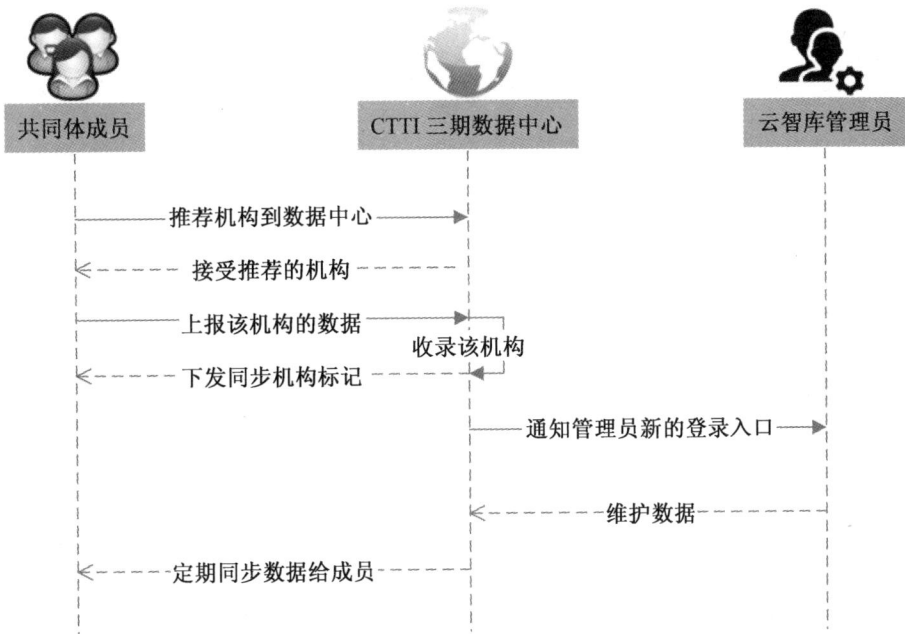

图 7.2　CTTI 三期数据交互机制

对于共同体成员自行增加的智库,可通过系统内流程推荐到 CTTI 来源增补资源池,并赋予适当权重。共同体成员的本地数据分为两部分:CTTI 系统收录的机构和专家数据将由 CTTI 向共同体成员每日刷新;共同体成员自建机构和专家数据在本地进行维护,以保障数据安全性和私密性。当共同体用户推荐的智库被纳入

CTTI 来源智库名录时,CTTI 将一次性收录该智库所有数据,并与其他来源智库统一管理日刷新到共同体本地系统。

为与共同体成员现有管理信息系统兼容,我们还支持成员单位前台界面的风格定制,并提供数据交换接口,以便与现有系统对接和交换数据,同时将以单点登录的方式实现所有共同体成员管辖下的前台用户统一登录。

目前,已有天津社科联和山东省社会科学院两家单位成为 CTTI 智库共同体成员,并且已经完成本地的系统部署。

2. CTTI 系统的智库云

为了满足广大智库管理部门在实际工作中的业务需求,在总结前期经验的基础上,经过对大量智库机构和智库管理单位的实地走访调研,CTTI 增设了智库云功能。智库云功能是将 CTTI 系统完善的智库数据字段、先进的数据库架构以及科学的智库评价算法面向广大有数据管理需求的机构或部门开放,以线上大数据资源托管平台的方式为广大智库机构和管理部门提供数据管理服务,旨在为不具备智库数据管理系统设计和研发能力的用户提供成熟的智库管理和索引服务,可以让普通机构、单位通过开通智库云同样拥有中国智库索引系统的数据管理和评价功能(如图7.3 所示)。

开通智库云
等于在不用部署本地硬件资源的情况下拥有一套CTTI三期系统

CTTI智库云用户系统
为不具备本地化部署条件的智库管理机构和大型智库提供服务

智库云用户
享有CTTI的高可信资源而无需单独部署,不占用本地硬件资源

图 7.3　智库云管理系统

 智库云用户可以自行添加机构用户和专家用户，从而实现对管辖对象的管理。同时，云用户享有 CTTI 的高可信资源而无需单独部署，不占用本地硬件资源，而且 CTTI 所有的更新和升级云用户均可享有。但需要强调的一点是，为保证数据安全，所有智库云之间的数据都是相对独立的，即智库云用户的所有数据只对该智库云框架内的所有云智库账号开放，并不面向公众开放。智库云管理员可以通过创建云智库的方式将下属智库单位和专家纳入智库云中统一管理。拥有云智库账号权限就相当于在 CTTI 中建立一片私有空间，独立维护机构、专家、项目、成果、活动等智库信息，并可以对云智库内的机构、专家进行管理、评价、考核。每一个云智库管理员都可以对辖区内智库的建设情况一目了然（如图 7.4 所示）。

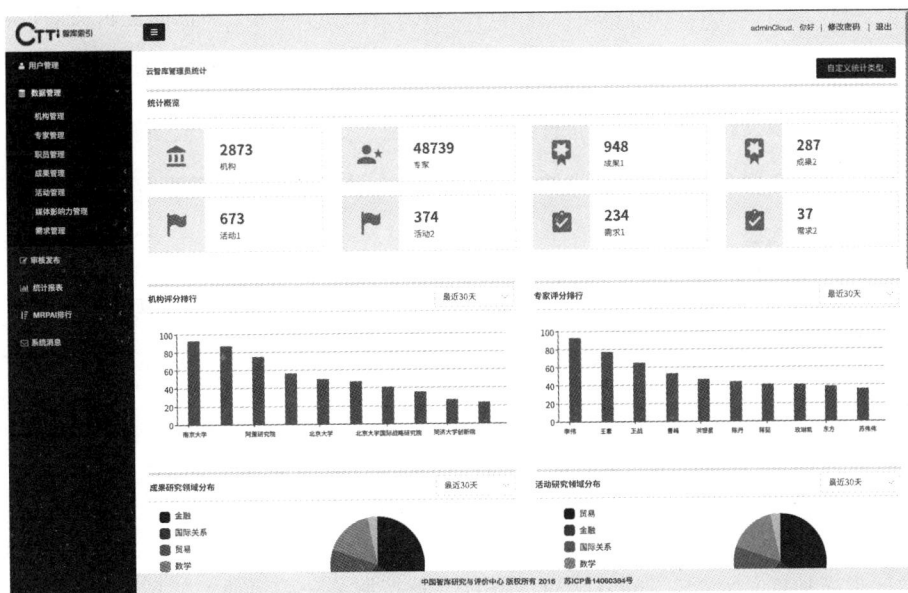

图 7.4　智库云管理界面

 CTTI 将以 360 度的智库贡献视角，全面公正地协助各云智库开展日常工作。随着智库云的全面铺开，智库界将逐渐形成统一的数据管理标准，该标准与 CTTI 测评算法无缝对接，使智库评价切实作用于智库日常管理，从而达到评价与管理的相互促进，以及评价方法与管理水平的双螺旋上升。

（三）CTTI 的主要功能

1. 检索功能

CTTI 系统首页主要实现检索功能，可完成包括机构检索、专家检索、项目检索、成果检索、活动检索及需求检索等检索任务。CTTI 系统自上线以来，受到了智库界的广泛关注，在充分调研智库界专家、学者需求的基础上，CTTI 三期在检索功能上做出了一个全新的升级。CTTI 三期强化高级检索功能，根据不同的检索对象，细化检索的颗粒度，增加模糊匹配、精确匹配、与或关系组合等操作，协助使用者更加快速、准确地检索到目标对象，旨在建设符合学术人士检索习惯的智库搜索引擎。

CTTI 的检索方式包括模糊检索、精确检索以及多条件组合检索。

单一检索条件的多值检索，只需要以空格为分隔条件；对于多值间逻辑关系，系统会自动默认为"或"操作，所有输入类型的检索字段均支持选择模糊和精确检索；多条件组合检索支持用户选择多条件间的逻辑关系——全"与"或者全"或"，全"与"表示所有条件全面命中则显示查询结果，而全"或"表示多条件中只需要命中任意一个则显示查询结果。

除此之外，在成果、活动、需求的检索中，CTTI 三期会支持多种类检索和单种类检索，其中多种类检索时，检索字段仅显示所有成果的公共属性字段；而单种类检索时，将显示更加丰富的字段供用户进行精确的检索。

CTTI 最终检索结果以列表形式呈现，结果条目按照命中权重即检索字段匹配率从高到低排序。

考虑到智库研究的特点，CTTI 三期还支持按照某一政策研究领域来检索机构或者专家。以机构检索任务为例，用户如果想要在 CTTI 系统首页检索某一政策研究领域的机构，可以在左侧的列表里面勾选对应的研究领域，然后再进行相关检索（如图 7.5 所示）。

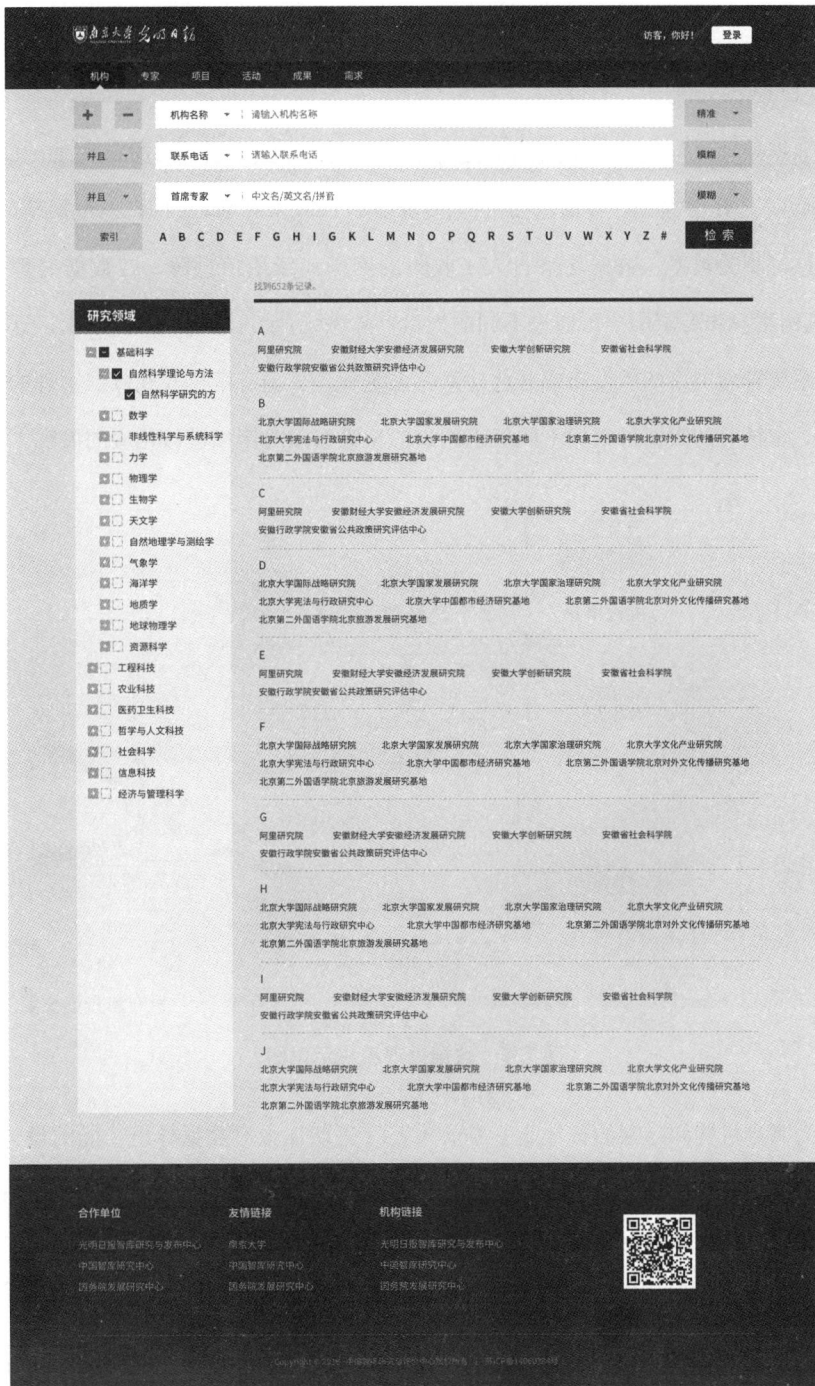

图 7.5　检索界面示意图

2. 数据管理功能

（1）数据处理

数据处理流程主要实现的功能包括数据的录入、修改、审核、发布和维护（如图7.6所示）。其中"数据"不仅包括机构、专家、项目、成果和活动数据，也包括新闻、需求信息等相关数据。数据均来自人工收集的网络或纸质信息源。在数据处理流程中，机构用户和专家用户可通过不同的入口登陆系统，录入对应字段的数据。这些数据经系统管理员审核后发布或开放检索。系统管理员拥有审核权和数据管理的最高权限。审核后的数据可根据不同级别用户的检索权限对用户进行相应的展现。

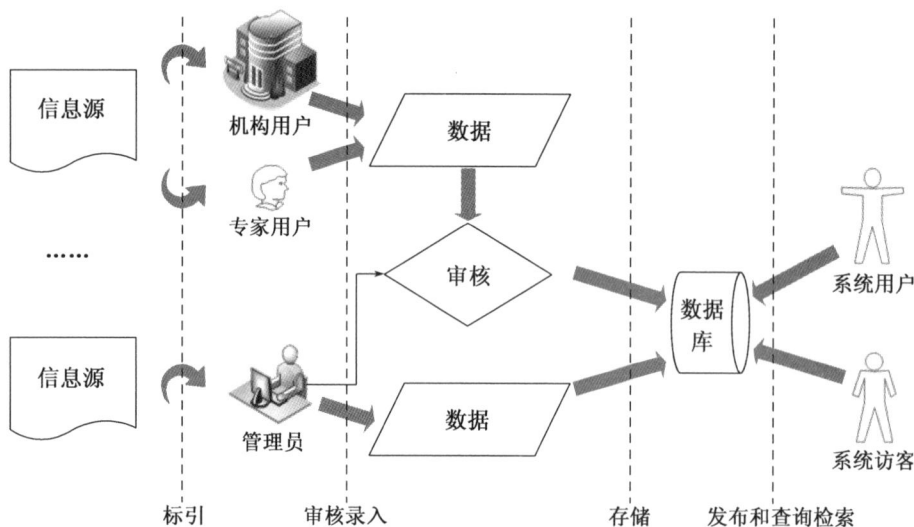

图 7.6 数据处理流程示意图

为满足机构和专家的日常业务需求，CTTI三期加强对数据导出功能的设计，机构、专家、项目、成果、活动、影响力等38类数据均支持横向和纵向双路径导出。机构和专家不仅可以轻松填报数据，还能够一键导出所填数据，用于其他业务场景。

（2）数据统计与管理

CTTI致力于服务新型智库共同体，成为各智库和智库专家进行数据管理的好帮手。CTTI三期加强了对数据统计与管理功能的升级，希望通过提供多种不同类型、不同维度的统计结果展现方式,增强数据识别效果,传递有效信息,让机构和专家更加直观地观察数据状态,更加方便快捷地管理数据,完成日常管理工作。各来源智库以及他们的智库专家利用 CTTI 三期系统,可以直观地看到项目、成果、活动等各项数据的统计,并且可以根据其实际需要选择生成相应的统计图表。以机构账号为例,机构管理员登录系统后不仅可以直观清晰地看到该机构收录的专家、项目、论文、活动、需求等各项数据的统计信息,还能根据本机构的实际情况,选择不同类型的数据来生成趋势图或者分布图(如图 7.7 所示)。这些统计信息和图表能够帮助忙碌的机构管理人员从繁琐复杂的信息解放出来,更加快速高效地分析本智库的建设状况和发展趋势。

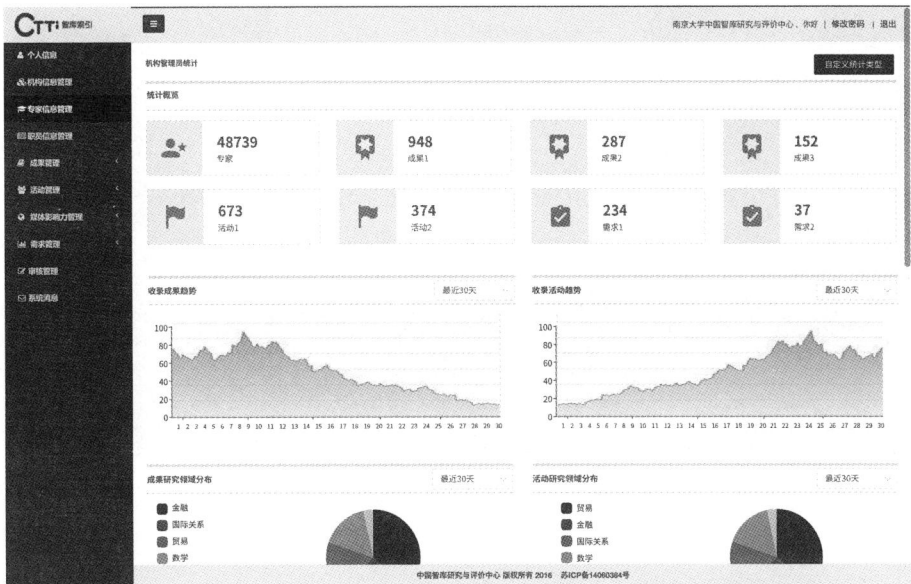

图 7.7 机构数据统计与分析功能界面

(3)专家个人知识管理

CTTI 一直在探索如何更好地服务智库专家、辅助专家便捷地管理自身智库知识成果,所以 CTTI 三期新增了专家个人知识管理的功能,专家可以通过 CTTI 系统掌握个人的智库建设贡献。

专家不仅能够便捷地在 CTTI 系统里录入相关数据，还能根据自己的需求导出系统数据，并且可以一键生成个人知识管理界面，用于各种资质申报或考核需求。例如，专家可以自由选择近一年或几年的数据，也可以自由选择需要展示的基本信息和成果类型，然后匹配生成自己的履历（如图 7.8 和图 7.9 所示）。

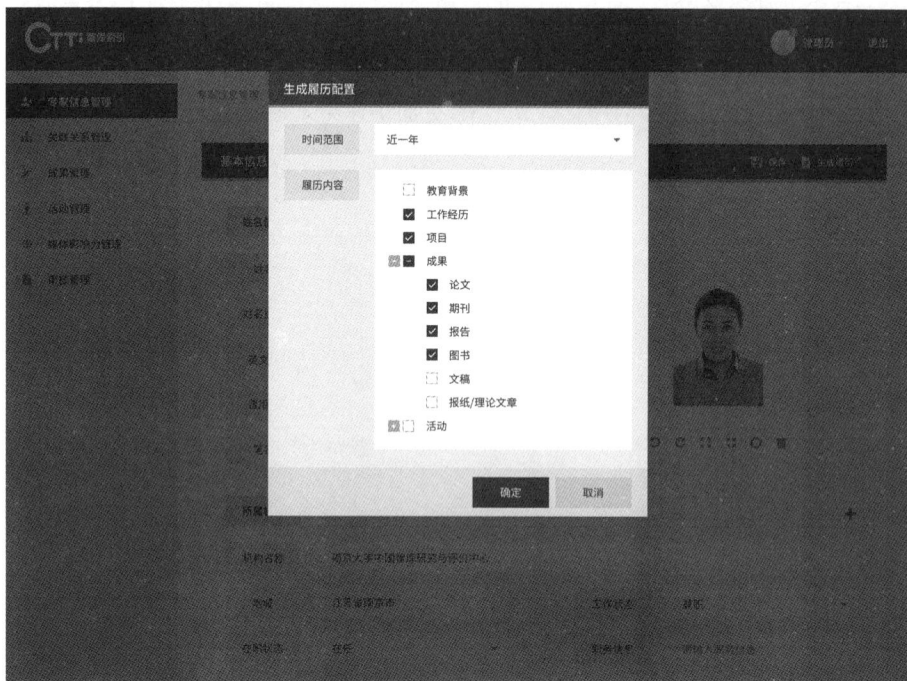

图 7.8　专家个人知识管理展示界面

（4）云智库数据分析

CTTI 系统采用主流的大数据分析技术，已实现对智库数据进行离线数据统计、分析和挖掘功能，力争从不同角度对智库机构和专家进行客观评价和排序，主要包括智库间的横向对比、专家间的横向对比，以及展示智库和专家自身在各个领域的发展趋势，旨在为党和政府提供决策服务，为指定领域内的政策咨询提供数据支撑。图 7.10 为 CTTI 所提供的一些图表的示例。

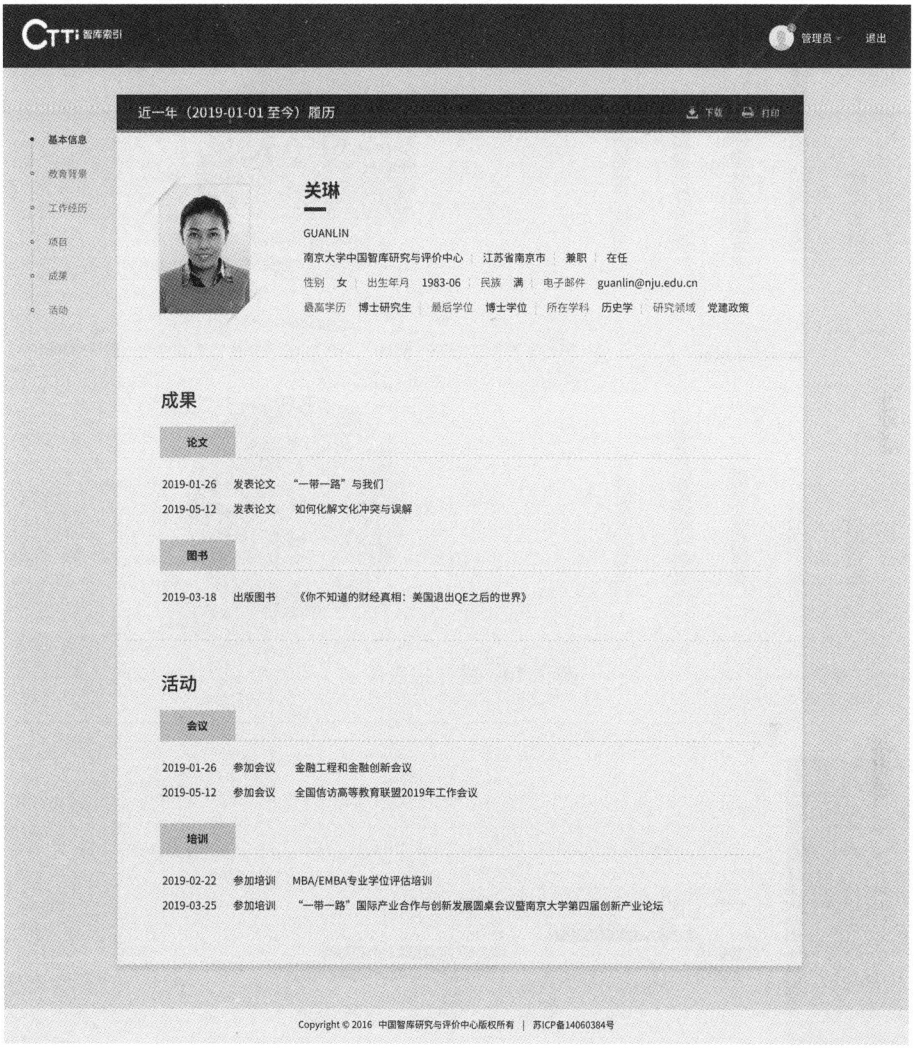

图 7.9　专家个人知识管理展示界面

　　CTTI 三期继续优化数据分析功能,在原有统计报表的基础上开发了基于页面操作的便捷查询统计工具,智库研究人员可以通过组合查询更有针对性地进行专项分析研究(如图 7.11 所示)。

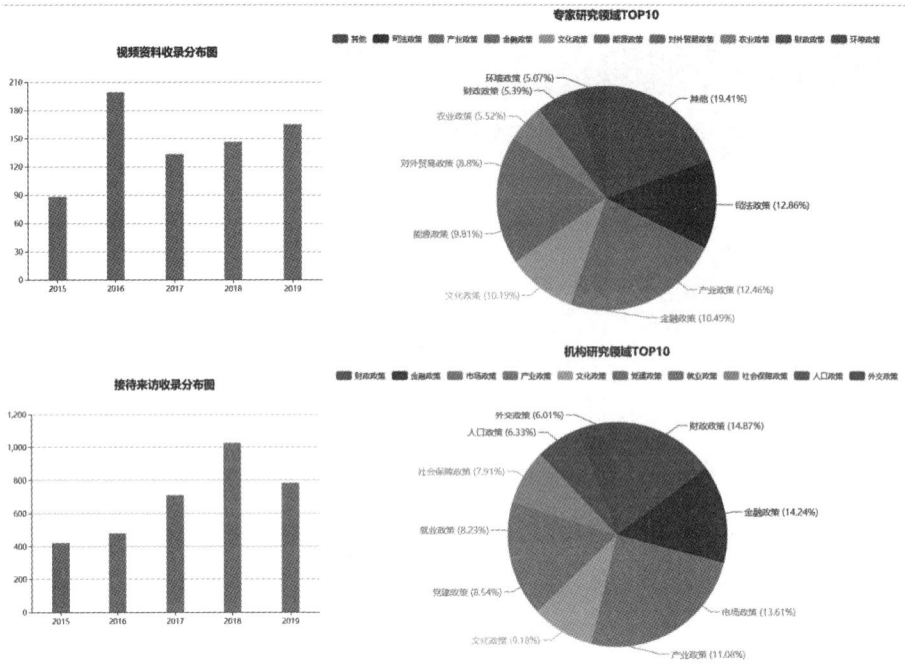

图 7.10　统计报表图例

图 7.11　组合查询工具展示界面

3. 多样化的评价功能

(1) CTTI 评价基本原则

CTTI 智库测评是以第三方身份对智库机构运用资源方式的能力和效益进行"过程—结果"导向型评价。在项目的实施过程中,我们借鉴第四代评价理论的相关方法,同时结合智库评价领域的具体实际,将以下几点确立为智库评价的基本原则。

① 实施评价的目的是为智库提升管理质量提供专业服务,而不是生产治理权和话语权。

② 评价是评估者向被评价对象学习的过程,是一个对话交流的过程,评价者与被评价对象需要共同参与评价过程,而不是单方面的训导与规范。

③ 评价是基于数据的系统分析,无数据则无法测量,无法获得数据的智库,不在评价范围之内。对评价中数据的解读要客观、准确,不能歪曲评价分析的结果。

④ 评价过程必须公正公开,结果可核查可重复,及时回应社会问责。同时,评价者具备核心的业务能力。

⑤ 尊重机构的商业秘密、保护人的隐私、严守国家秘密的安全底线。

⑥ 一切为了公共福祉,以非营利的形式在一定范围内公开共享评价结果。

(2) MRPAI 评价指标

CTTI 数据库字段是对智库机构、专家、项目、成果、活动、媒体影响力的"画像",是描述智库的元数据格式和标准"词汇",从理论上说词汇越丰富,"画像"越准确。基于这些数据字段,我们希望运用数据科学的专业技能,结合现代智库管理的专门知识,对 CTTI 来源智库的数据开展定量和定性相结合的分析,把结果提供给智库共同体。需要注意的是,在选择和确定测评指标时,我们并不是涵盖数据库每一个数据字段,而是有所选择。具体而言,我们在确定测评指标时主要关注以下几项原则:

① 指标数据颗粒度与可获得性相适应。我国新型智库建设虽已取得一定成效,但各智库的工作差异性极大,原始数据形式多样。另外,我国智库数据累积性不强,数据管理意识欠缺,除了教育部重点基地有规范的数据填报制度外,大部分机构并无

长期的数据积累。针对这种情况,为了鼓励智库填报 CTTI,降低填写数据的难度,大部分数据库字段都专门设置了合理数量范围的必填数据项。因此,在确定 MRPAI 指标时必须结合 CTTI 字段的实际数据情况,考虑数据的可获得性,具体遵循以下流程:

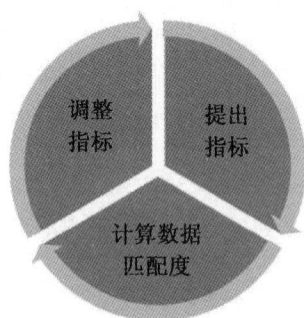

图 7.12　MRPAI 指标选择流程

最初,将提出的指标逐一输入系统进行匹配,如果数据的可获得性不足 80%,则舍弃或者降低指标的颗粒度。比如关于智库专家指标,原本希望对智库专家的职称和年龄结构进行评价,但是经过数据匹配发现,该字段数据的获取量未能达标,而90% 的智库都填写了专家数量和年度预算,所以这两个值就被确定为衡量智库资源(R 值)的基本指标。

② 指标数据的关键性、代表性和表达性要显著。选取的指标必须是体现智库属性的关键性、代表性的字段。智库的属性主要体现在完善的治理结构、强烈的政策影响倾向、积极主动地运用论坛和会议等形式扩大公共影响力、深入调研深入实际等方面,因此从反映这些属性的内参、批示、研究报告、项目、会议、调研等字段中,选取了较多的指标,体现了指标突出智库属性的倾向性。

③ 指标要具备客观性与系统性。指标的客观性有两层含义,一是指标和 CTTI 数据字段一样,是对智库真实属性的揭示,是由最具客观性的字段综合而来;二是指标取值具有客观性,并不是估值等主观性强的数值。指标的系统性是指各种指标之间存在严密的逻辑关系。比如 MRPAI 五个一级指标体现了投入产出的绩效逻辑。

④ 指标体系必须起到以评促建的作用,要符合当下新型智库建设的现状。如果说 2013 年以来中国特色新型智库建设取得了一定成效,那么未来几年将是新型智库建设的"攻坚"阶段,是实现新型智库建设的高质量发展的关键阶段。但同时我们也要承认,仍存在对智库建设规律认识不到位,智库运行不够规范化、不够流程化等诸多问题。因此,我们不能依据国际标准或者不符合我国智库实际建设情况的标准来测评智库,否则容易挫伤被测评智库的积极性,难以起到以评促建的鼓励性和肯定性作用。

依据以上原则,我们确定了 5 个一级指标,24 个二级指标。5 个一级指标分别是 M(治理结构)、R(智库资源)、P(智库成果)、A(智库活动)、I(智库媒体影响力),命名为智库 MRPAI 测评指标,MRPAI 属于结果导向的智库效能测评体系,它可以从两大维度来测评智库:一是资源占用量;二是资源的运用效果,也就是效能。它既能测量智库的体量、产量,也能测评智库的效能,还可以测量智库属性的强弱。因此,MRPAI 体系符合指标选择的诸多原则,可以对 CTTI 来源智库进行有效测量。

从二级指标看,当我们单纯关注 R 指标时,可以测量智库预算的大小和人员的多寡,毫无疑问资金雄厚,专家和行政人员多的智库是体量大的智库。当我们单独关注 P 指标时,可以测量智库研究成果的多少,显然成果多的智库是好智库。当我们单独关注 A 指标时,可以测量智库开展活动的多少,不能说活动多的智库就是好智库,但是活动少的智库一定是智库特征不明显的智库,这样的智库更像大学里的研究中心,或者政府的政策研究室,虽然有一定的学术和政策影响力,但智库属性可能比较弱。当我们单独关注 I 指标时,可以测量智库被媒体报道的数量和社会影响力大小,媒体影响力是智库发挥咨政启民作用的途径之一,也是衡量智库水平的重要指标。

当 P 类的 P1、P2、P5 加上 A 类和 I 类指标之总值都比较高时,我们一般认为该智库的智库属性比较强。当我们将智库的产出除以资源后,得到的结果就是智库的效能。因此,MRPAI 也可以测量智库的效能。

表 7.1 MRPAI 智库测评指标及其赋值

一级指标	代码	二级指标	代码	计分规则	分值
治理结构	M	理事会（董事会）	M1	有则赋值	15
		学术委员会	M2	有则赋值	10
		咨询/顾问委员会	M3	有则赋值	10
		管理团队/首席专家	M4	有则赋值	10
		国家高端智库	M5	是则赋值	100
智库资源	R	年度预算	R1	≤100 万	20
				每增加 10 万赋值 x 分	1
		科研人员	R2	≤10 人	40
				每增加 1 人赋值 x 分	2
		行政人员	R3	≤5 人	20
				每增加 1 人赋值 x 分	1
		网络资源	R4	有中文门户	20
				有英文门户	8
				有微信公号	8
				有官方微博	5
				有专门数据采集平台	10
智库成果	P	单篇内参（无论是否被批示）	P1	按篇赋值	2
		被批示内参	P2	正国级/每条	30
				副国级/每条	20
				省部级/每条	10
				副省部级/每条	5
		智库主办/承办期刊	P3	每种 CSSCI 来源刊	20
				每种普通期刊	10
				每种通讯/内参集	8
		图书（正式出版）	P4	每种赋值	2
		研究报告	P5	每份赋值	4

续表

一级指标	代码	二级指标	代码	计分规则	分值
治理结构	M	《人民日报》《光明日报》《求是》杂志	P6	每篇赋值	5
		论文	P7	CSSCI 来源刊论文/每篇	1
				SSCI/A&HCI 收录/每篇	2
				CSCI/EI 收录/每篇	1
				其他普通论文/每篇	0.5
		纵向项目	P8	纵向—国家社科重大/教育部社科重大	10
				纵向—国家社科重点/国家自科重点	6
				纵向—国家社科一般项目/青年项目	4
				纵向—省部级项目	2
				纵向—其他	0.5
		横向项目	P9	每项基本分 2＋每 10 万赋值 1 分值	
智库活动	A	会议	A1	主办承办全国性会议/每次	10
				省市自治区一级会议/每次	5
				国际性会议/每次	10
				其他会议/每次	3
		培训	A2	全国性培训活动/每次	8
				其他层次培训	2
		调研考察	A3	接受副国级领导以上调研活动/每次	15
				接受省部级领导/专家调研/每次	5
				接受其他层次领导/专家调研/每次	2
				外出调研考察	1

续表

一级指标	代码	二级指标	代码	计分规则		分值
智库媒体影响力	I	报纸新闻报道	I1	中央级		5
				省部级		4
				地方级		3
				境外媒体		2
				其他媒体		1
		电视新闻报道	I2	中央级		5
				省部级		4
				地方级		3
				境外媒体		2
				其他媒体		1
		网络新闻报道	I3	中央级		5
				省部级		4
				地方级		3
				境外媒体		2
				其他媒体		1

指标权重的分配有多种方式，MRPAI采取的是直接赋值法，这样的好处是易于理解，直观公开，可复核。被评价者可以根据既定的算法直接复核所得数值是否准确，评价主客体之间的对话性好坏。但是对评价的要求比较高，不仅赋值要比较合理，而且测评系统也要保证精确。否则就无法及时回应被评价者的质疑。

表7.1指标赋值采取了德尔菲法，先后进行了4轮专家调查，合计98位领导和专家接受了问卷调查。以下是对赋值的说明。

表7.1中MRPAI二级指标赋值考虑了以下几点情况：

① M1－M4对智库结构的测评只考察是否有内部管理机构，而没有考察这些机构运转是否正常。这符合我国新型智库建设的现状，先看有没有这些内部机构，以后测量时再看运转是否规范。因此分值并不高，满分仅45分。M5则是对已经被列为

国家高端智库的特别赋值,是对这种地位的一种肯定。

② R1 考察的是年度预算。考虑到我们智库普遍规模偏小,年度经费 100 万元是常态,因此没有再区分年度预算 100 万以下的智库。小于等于 100 万的,统一赋值 20 分,每增加 10 万元增加 1 分。

③ R2-R3 是人员指标及其赋值。我们没有区别全职和兼职,原因是人事制度改革,加上智库专家大部分属于弹性工作制度,单从工作时长与任务多少较难区分全职还是兼职。因此,小于等于 10 位科研人员的机构统一赋值 40 分,然后每增加 1 人赋值 2 分。行政团队小于等于 5 人规模的为 20 分,每增加 1 人赋值 1 分。随着系统数据的日益规范,日后这部分数据在填报时可能需要提供相应的证明材料,各智库还应尽快完善员工聘任合同。

④ R4 网络资源其实也可以看成智库的建设成效。我们把网站等看作跟办公场所一样的基础设置。现代智库对办公室场所要求不高,如果智库不填这个数据,真实性也无从复核,因此,对于人、财、物、网,R4 舍弃了对有形物质办公条件的测量,而是把重点放在网络条件上。这几个指标都是可核查的,具有可操作性。鉴于我国大多数智库对网站建设的关注不够,对社交媒体的运用更是非常陌生,所以这个指标也只是根据"有/无"进行赋值,没有考虑质量之高下。

⑤ P 指标中,内参、批示和研究报告的赋值比较高。被询问的专家普遍认为这是反映智库决策影响力的主要指标,分值应该加大。这也是建智库的主要目的。目前这个数值是根据专家的意见调高的。对于大部分省级智库而言,拿到国家级领导人的批示并不容易,所以正国级领导批示的分值反而对普通智库的总分影响不大。由于 MRPAI 测评侧重的是分类排序,是把相同层次的智库放在一起比较,那么这样的赋值相对公平。为了鼓励写内参,凡是发表在省部级以上内参集(内部报送性连续出版物),如《光明内参》等,无论是否被批示都予以赋值。给予 P6 指标较高的分值体现了《人民日报》《光明日报》和《求是》在我国政策话语体系中的特殊地位,如果能在这些报刊上发文章,也意味着政策影响力和公众影响力的扩大。

⑥ MRPAI 测评指标体系给予了智库活动成果比较重要的地位。高层次、高水平的论坛和会议是智库发挥影响力的重要途径,这也是智库区别于传统研究机构的重要特征。世界著名智库几乎都是会议中心,几乎都是重大政策路演的主要平台。因此,对于智库举办的全国性会议和国际性会议赋值比较高。虽然"搭台子、请名人"这种不良风气确实存在,但这只是少数。会议不仅可以传播信息,而且是智库拓展研究网络、政策网络的主要渠道之一。

调研考察是具有中国特色的智库研究方法。没有调查研究就没有发言权,大数据分析也无法替代亲身实地调查。因此,MRPAI 测评指标对此类活动也给予较高的分值。

⑦ I 指标考察的重点在于智库的媒体影响力。无论在国内还是国外,媒体影响力一直是智库界关注的重点,计算全国性或国际性的重要报纸、杂志、电视等传媒的引用率也是最为常见的公开评价。这是因为智库不同于传统的学术研究机构,传播与研究对智库而言同等重要,因而在电视、报纸、网络上露面或发表看法被认为智库影响力的重要体现。目前,我们暂时仅将报纸、电视及网络上传播的新闻报道纳入评价范围,这三种媒介在智库传播中的应用及影响范围更为广泛,有一定质量保障。同时,按报道级别高低赋予不同分值,中央级是最具权威性的,因此赋予最高分值。

(3) MRPAI 测评系统

MRPAI 测评系统是 CTTI 系统后台的一个系统。MRPAI 测评系统深刻理解了MRPAI 指标体系、赋值和排序规则,运用了先进的排序算法,也包含一些基本的机器学习功能,能够做到对来源智库进行即时测评。MRPAI 测评系统既可以综合排序,也可以分不同类型排序。

另外,MRPAI 测评系统还有查询功能和数据统计分析功能,不仅能够准确定位智库和专家,而且可以统计出每个智库或者每位专家 MRPAI 指标的具体得分情况。这样就可以清楚地分析来源智库各分值之间的比例,也就可以揭示智库在管理、资源、成果、活动等具体方面的强弱,对改善智库管理有极大帮助。

CTTI 系统设置了灵活可配的定制化评价功能——将 MRPAI 测评系统指标项分值做成了可调整的参数形式。这样评价主体(可能是智库管理部门、研究者、有特定需求的用户)在登录系统后,可依据评价目标和侧重点自行选择数据维度,调用不同的算法,从而得出不同的个性化的排序结果。

需要说明的是,目前 MRPAI 测评系统布置在后台,前台暂时无法查阅,这样可以比较好地保护机构和专家测评数据安全,尊重专家个人隐私。未经机构和专家本人同意,CTTI 项目组不会向任何第三方透露详细测评结果。

(4) 主观评价功能

CTTI 评价是一种多因子的评价模型,其评价包含几十个,甚至上百个因子,尽可能最大限度地提升智库评价的真实性。就智库评价而言,专家对智库的主观评价也是一个不可或缺的维度。所以,CTTI 系统在 MRPAI 算法的基础上,又引入了专家的主观评价。

CTTI 系统现已收录一万多名专家,并将这些专家都纳入智库主观评价资源池中。CTTI 系统后台开发了问卷调查的功能,将以邮件通知的方式将待评价的智库列表及此次评价的维度以问卷链接的形式发送至各专家,专家登录系统对这些智库打分,再由高级用户或系统管理员将主观评价结果与客观的定量评价结果做综合计算,进而对这些智库作完整的综合评估。

(四) CTTI 系统的主要特征

CTTI 的用户群体包括政府、企业事业单位、社会团体等,由于这些用户有大量的政策研究、咨询需求,但是它们未必知道谁是最恰当的解决方案提供者,而智库也常无法寻找到目标客户,造成智库功能发挥受限。CTTI 的设计目标之一就是解决这种信息不对称情况。CTTI 作为一个智库的"垂直搜索引擎"(专业搜索),以完备的字段作为支撑,结合多角度查询的方式,全方位展示查询结果,实现对智库机构从内部架构到外部活动、从人员组成到成果发布的立体式展示;实现对智库各种信息的智能分析，促使用户快速准确检索到目标信息，可为课题找专家、为专家找课题，从而消除智库和用户之间的"信息不对称"。CTTI 的成功上线填补了我国智库数据管理和在线评价工具的空白，为我国智库评价工作提供了基础数据，理清了新型智库评价这项集机构评价、成果评价、人员评价以及活动评价的复杂工作的头绪，并引导这项工作趋于理性和客观。但需要指出的是，CTTI 评价的目的是服务来源智库，我们一直把遴选、采集数据、测评看成我们向来源智库学习与沟通的过程，评价结果也主要为来源智库、管理部门和学术界提供一定参考。

与此同时，应当明白 CTTI 并不是对西方某个成熟产品的模仿，而是一项基于中国体制优势的一项自主创新。具体体现在以下几个方面：

1. 设计理念

（1）数据采集

CTTI 建立了共建共享的数据采集机制，重视数据的客观性和准确性。目前，系统采集数据的方式有三种：① 依靠来源智库和专家自主填报的方式；② 南京大学中国智库研究与评价中心人工收集；③ 网上数据自动抓取。其中第一种方式是主流，数据由智库机构管理员或者专家本人录入，提交给 CTTI 后台审核，每一条数据都经过后台审核准确无误才提交到数据库。这种数据采集机制表面上因为人工投入巨大，实际上由于采用了时下最流行的"众包"（众筹）模式，数据共建共享，数据采集成本分摊到每一个参与者，反而是比较低廉的，且由于是人工模式，数据的准确性大大提高。此外，为减少人为干扰影响力数据的情况，CTTI 每个智库每个专家的影响力数值除后台管理员填报的少数字段外，都是根据填报的数据自动计算出影响力数值的。

（2）功能布局

CTTI 创新了用户分层服务模式。CTTI 的用户除了有需要利用智库的党和政府的政策研究机构，负责智库注册、业务指导的民政局、宣传部等部门，智库管理员和专家等机构内部用户，还有大学、媒体、科研院所等学术宣传单位，各种企业等营利部门,以及一般的公众。CTTI针对不同层次的用户,设计了分层服务方案,给予针对性的服务,不同层次用户访问到的数据层次和类型有所不同。例如,各种统计图标、统计工具在设计时就充分考虑了行政管理部门的需要。在数据的呈现与导出方面,充分考虑了智库的需要,智库和专家可以很方便地在 CTTI 中进行数据管理与导出。又比如为了方便系统管理员的风险应急管理,CTTI 提供了瞬间关闭某一智库全部数据而不影响其他智库数据的功能。这样即使个别智库数据出现敏感问题,也不需要关闭整个系统。

2. 数据体系

CTTI 在一定意义上建立了中国特色新型智库的统计指标体系和元数据标准。经过三期的反复调研,从共同体成员、广大用户以及智库管理部门的实际需求出发,我们对各类对象字段再次扩充、改造,完善数据体系,旨在最大程度上与广大用户现有管理系统,如与"全国普通高等学校人文社会科学研究管理信息系统"对接,也为未来建立国际通行的智库行业数据标准打下基础。目前,CTTI 系统涵盖的上千个字段实现了对智库基本信息、专家信息、项目信息、成果信息、活动信息、影响力信息的各种属性的全面覆盖,给出了立体的智库各要素画像。这些数据字段可以成为今后其他智库系统开发的元数据。

3. 灵活性

CTTI 系统拥有很强的灵活性以应对智库的复杂特征。一是灵活可配的定制化评价。MRPAI 测评系统可自主赋值算法支持时间范围可配置、评价指标可配置、分值权重可配置。共同体成员、智库云成员等高级用户或者系统管理员能够根据实际需求,自动配置 MRPAI 算法。二是数据字典可动态扩充。智库涉及字段众多,且很多字段内容在建设过程中都存在定义不准确、不完善的情况。因此,字段的可扩充性对于系统的成熟完善,以及是否能准确、充分描述智库来说有重要意义。CTTI 三期系统开发智库字段数据智能归一化功能,支持自动提取智库字典的用户输入情况,并根据管理员的映射设置,自动将满足条件的输入文本转换成映射的数据字典,实现数据字典动态扩充。

4. 安全性

CTTI系统和数据安全性达到了准金融数据安全级别。在部署方案上,CTTI将应用服务器与数据服务器分开部署,采用内外网隔离的方案,公网用户只能访问应用服务器,无法直接访问数据服务器,保证了数据的安全性;在通讯协议方面,CTTI使用https的SSL加密协议,保证所有请求数据在传输的过程中都是加密的,防止攻击者通过拦截篡改请求内容来非法访问系统。由于CTTI收录的数据众多,为了防止系统数据被轻易的窃取,CTTI在反扒网方面也做了应对设计,采用了B/S架构并以科学的权限设置和角色分配,保障信息的可用性和可控性,一般访客访问系统只能查询到最基本的数据,无法看到系统的全貌。

经过多年的建设和升级,CTTI现已发展成为集智库搜索、智库数据管理、在线智能评价功能于一体的集成信息管理系统。随着CTTI在国内外的影响力日益显著,以及智库共同体成员和智库云的不断增加,系统数据增量必将迎来一个快速发展的阶段。届时,凭借一万多名专家组成的学术共同体资源,结合灵活可定制的客观定量评价功能,CTTI将成为智库界兼具检索、管理与评价功能的重要工具,助力我国新型智库建设向前推进。

二、2019 年度 CTTI 来源智库证书更新与新智库增补

（一）CTTI 来源智库证书换发

自 2016 年 12 月"中国智库索引"(CTTI)首批来源智库名单发布以来,我中心于 2017 年和 2018 年先后开展两次增补工作,截至 2018 年 12 月已收录来源智库 706 家。对于正式入选来源智库名单的智库,我中心与光明日报智库研究与发布中心联合颁发证明文件。值得注意的是,CTTI 来源智库目录是动态系统,一定年限后会进行部分调整,数据更新的及时与否是目录调整的重要依据之一。截至 2019 年 3 月,首批来源智库(2016 年入选)和第一批增补智库(2017 年增补)的入选证书有效期(2017 年 1 月～2018 年 12 月)已过,因此,我中心于 2019 年 3 月开展 CTTI 来源智库证书换发工作。经过与各家来源智库四个多月的联系和沟通,截至 2019 年 7 月,共收到《CTTI 来源智库证书换发基本信息采集表》207 份。经审核,这 207 家智库均能积极主动向 CTTI 填写数据,充分保证了 CTTI 数据的及时性、完整性。于是,我中心于 2019 年 9 月通过邮寄的方式向这 207 家智库颁发铭牌,铭牌有效期是 2019 年 1 月 1 日至 2022 年 12 月 31 日(见图 8.1)。

图 8.1　CTTI 来源智库铭牌

（二）2019年度 CTTI 来源智库目录增补

　　中国特色新型智库是国家治理体系的重要组成部分，现代智库建设方兴未艾。南京大学和光明日报社一直坚持 CTTI 的公益性质，致力于推动建设共建、共享的中国新型智库共同体，服务于国家治理体系和治理能力的现代化建设。为了使 CTTI 来源智库目录能够比较准确地反映新型智库发展的形势，经研究决定，启动 2019 年 CTTI 来源智库增补工作，仍然沿用智库主动申请、数据填报、专家评审、摸底调研相结合的方式，严格把关增补智库的质量，严格执行智库增补的遴选程序与要求。

1. 增补要求

　　坚持首批来源智库入围标准不变，参照以下七方面考量，如表 8.1，尤其注重的是否实体化运行，是否有良好的政策研究咨询能力与成果。凡是被各省市和中央部委认定为省部级重点和重点培育智库（政策研究基地）者优先考虑。

表 8.1　来源智库遴选参考指标

	具体内容	量化指标
政治要求	遵守国家法律法规	
学术基础	近 2 年来，智库专职研究人员在学术刊物上发表过学术论文	近 2 年内，专职研究人员在 CSSCI 来源期刊或者人民日报、光明日报理论版发表文章人均 1 篇以上
领域要求	有特色鲜明、长期关注的决策咨询研究领域	
组织形式	相对稳定、运作规范的实体性研究机构	有机构成立批文或其他证明文件
	健全的治理结构	有组织章程，设立理事会、学术委员会等组织
资源保障	一定数量的专职和兼职研究人员与行政人员	有 1～2 名领军人物，5 人以上的全职研究员和 5 人以上的兼职研究员与研究助理
	有保障、可持续的资金来源	年度经费 30 万元以上
	固定的办公场所与基本设备	50 平方米以上独立办公室

续表

	具体内容	量化指标
运行与成果	正常开展研究、咨询、会议活动	每年举办的活动不少于 3 场
	提交研究成果	每年至少正式发布(或向用户提交)3 份以上研究报告和 3 篇以上报刊文章
	网站和新媒体	有独立的网站,微信(或者微博)等新媒体公众号
	智库连续出版物	有期刊、内参等印本或电子版简报等出版物
国际合作与交流	有开展国际合作交流的条件,有望产生一定的国际影响	

2. 增补规则

高校智库由各高校科研管理部门推荐或智库机构自荐,若由高校下属智库机构自荐,须该校科研管理部门同意。为确保对来源智库的公平性,我们对每家高校的 CTTI 来源智库的数量做了一些规定,但那些实力雄厚、特色鲜明、成果丰硕、活跃度高、机制灵活的高校智库不受此限制。此外,针对入选智库数量较少的地域、类型、政策领域,我们在增补时对其进行充分考量,并给予适当倾斜。

3. 增补程序

申请增补智库填写申请表——资格审查——为符合标准的智库建立 CTTI 帐号——初选智库填写数据——数据审核——筛选出数据质量和数量达到 CTTI 来源智库标准的智库——CTTI 来源智库增补专家组审核——公布增补名单,颁发来源智库证明文件。

4. 增补过程

2019 年 9 月 16 日,CTTI 团队在官网(https://cttrec.nju.edu.cn/)发出《2019CTTI 来源智库增补启事》,本年度增补工作正式启动。申请增补的智库需填写《2019CTTI 来源智库增补申请表》并提交证明材料。《申请表》重点考察智库的机构层次、政策研究领域、人力与经费资源、旗舰成果与活动、主管/母体单位科研管理部门推荐意见，能够较为全面地考察智库运行的情况。来源智库增补工作得到了智库界和各级科研管理部门的大力支持。武汉大学、华南理工大学、西南大学、陕西师范大学等校均合理发挥了科研处的统筹能力，以学校为单位进行宣传、组织、筛选、向 CTTI 增补工作组递交申请表。截至 2019 年 10 月 20 日，工作组共收到电子、纸质申请材料 371 份。经南京大学中国智库研究与评价中心及光明日报智库研究与发布中心联合调研、讨论、审定，工作组初步遴选出 133 家合格智库。不少智库因为智库属性不足而落选，具体原因主要有研究人员数量不足、内参和批示数量过少、缺乏政策研究领域、仅有学术成果等。

初选工作完成后，增补工作组给通过初选的智库发放 CTTI 的账号和密码，并发函邀请初选智库进行数据采集。数据填写的数量、质量既是二次评估的重要依据之一，也是各智库今后利用 CTTI 进行自我数据管理的重要基础，因此，大多数智库高度重视并认真填写。与此同时，面对上百家智库提交的海量数据，我中心组织多位工作人员在 CTTI 后台对数据进行逐条审核，确保了数据的合理性、有效性、正确性。在多方努力下，历时近一个月，截至 2019 年 11 月 30 日，初选智库积极踊跃、严谨细致地录入了机构、专家、成果、活动等多种类型的大量珍贵数据，有力地支持了 CTTI 增补工作的展开。

数据采集截止之后，工作组随即组织专家团队以数据填报情况、增补申请表和调研结果为依据，以数据的科学性、完整性和相应竞争力为标准，对初选合格的智库进行二次评估。针对未能及时提供足够有效数据以供专家评审的 3 家智库，工作组将其排除在增补名单之外。

经过以上各环节的工作，最终确定本年度 CTTI 增补智库共 130 家，通过率为35%，如此高标准、严要求的增补过程有助于实力强劲的智库脱颖而出、成功增补，也保证了 CTTI 来源智库的质量始终保持在较高的水准。按智库类型来看，本次增补了高校智库 119 家、党政部门智库 2 家、科研院所智库 2 家、传媒智库 2 家、企业智库

2 家、社会智库 2 家、党校行政学院智库 1 家;按机构层次来看,有国家高端(高端培育)智库 4 家,省部级重点(重点培育)智库 59 家,教育部哲社重点研究基地 1 家,教育部国别研究基地 8 家。

另一方面,天津市社科联与南京大学、光明日报自 2016 年建立战略合作。按照三方战略合作协议,2019 年天津地区 CTTI 来源智库增补工作由天津市社科联负责组织实施,按数据填报、增补申报和增补评审三个阶段组织开展来源智库增补,得到了天津各智库机构及上级主管单位的积极响应。天津市社科联于 2019 年下半年启动了 CTTI-TJ 数据填报工作。截至 11 月下旬,天津市各智库机构严谨细致地录入了机构基本信息、专家、活动、成果等数据,有力支持了后续增补评审工作。在此基础上,天津市社科联按照 CTTI 来源智库增补要求,结合天津实际,确定增补申报原则,开展增补申报工作。至申报截止,共收到 9 家单位的近 30 个智库的申请书,基本涵盖了天津市主要高校及部分社会智库机构。经形式审查、初步审定和修改后,遴选出候选智库参与增补评审。为确保增补评审公平公正,天津市社科联反复推敲,制定了详细增补评审方案。通过资质评审、量化评分、MRPAI 计分三个环节,并经会议研究决定,总得分排于前 12 位的智库推荐为 CTTI 来源智库。

最终,在原有 706 家智库的 CTTI 来源智库名单的基础上,加上本年度新增补的 130 家来源智库,以及天津地区推荐的 12 家智库,CTTI 现有正式来源智库 848 家。

5. 新增补智库特点

本年度的智库增补工作受到了各界的热烈响应,收到的增补申请数量为历年之最。相较往年,今年通过增补的智库呈现出以下鲜明的特点:

一是学术基础好。据统计,新增来源智库近三年内平均有 8.6 个国家级科研项目、19.4 个省部级科研项目,撰写了 9.9 本专著、53.9 篇 CSSCI 来源期刊。当然,这其中不乏大量高校智库的贡献,同时我们也欣喜地发现不少非高校智库在智库建设过程中也很重视学术研究的价值,如南方电网能源发展研究院有限责任公司近三年内共有 29 个省部级及以上的项目、4 本专著和 9 篇高质量的论文。但是,如何将理论研究与对策应用研究相结合，产出学理性强、实践价值高的研究成果，仍是值得思考的问题。

二是成立年限久。据统计，新增补智库中有 22 家成立了 5～8 年，有 28 家成立了 8～15 年，还有 11 家智库成立已超过 15 年。这些历史较为悠久的智库多为高校智库和科研院所智库，它们长期深耕某一专业领域，积累了较为丰厚的研究资源，因此得以在特定的政策研究领域中发挥影响力，如成立于 1976 年的云南省生态环境科学研究院坚持以"支撑决策、服务社会"为己任，在水污染防治、大气和土壤环境保护、生态保护与修复、重金属污染防治、环境规划、应对气候变化等领域形成了专业优势，部分研究成果达到国内先进水平。

三是咨政能力强。据统计，新增补智库在三年内平均撰写内参 19.5 份，平均获得省部级以上批示 8.0 个。虽然有极个别智库凭借一己之力提高了均值，如复旦大学国际问题研究院三年内撰写内参 232 份，获得省部级以上批示 33 个，但均值仍能证明新增补智库实力强、成果多，作用不可小觑，是 CTTI 来源智库的重要组成部分。

四是影响力广泛。一方面，据统计，新增补智库在近三年内平均主办或承办了近十次全国性或省部级会议，说明智库在国内的该行业领域内有一定感召力和影响力，致力于搭建同行之间学习交流的平台。另一方面，新增补智库中有 41 家现已加入智库联盟，表明国内正在形成良性互动的智库共同体。而且，有个别智库加入了国际性的智库联盟，如国家市场监督管理总局发展研究中心加入了"一带一路"国际智库合作联盟，华侨大学华侨华人研究院加入了印度尼西亚研究联盟，他们在国际舞台上讲中国故事，正是中国特色新型智库发挥公共外交功能的体现。

（三）增补后 CTTI 来源智库机构信息透视

1. CTTI 来源智库地域分析

首先，按照中国行政区划标准，CTTI 来源智库地区分布情况如图 8.2 所示。就整体情况而言，华北地区、华东地区在数量方面的优势较为明显，仅这两个地区的来

源智库共占据入选智库总量的一半以上。其中,华北地区共有 305 家机构被 CTTI
系统收录,占所有入选机构数量的 36.0%;华东地区以 227 家紧随其后,占总数的
26.8%;华中地区以 87 家位列第三,占比为 10.3%;其余几个地区的来源智库数量
相对均衡。在 2019 年增补工作中,华东、华北地区的智库后备力量充足,再次扩大了
数量优势;广东省的华南理工大学、广东外语外贸大学、暨南大学有多家智库成功入
围,华南地区的智库占比也由此从 2018 年的 5.92% 显著提升到 7.4%,从 2018 年的
第七位跃升至第四位。

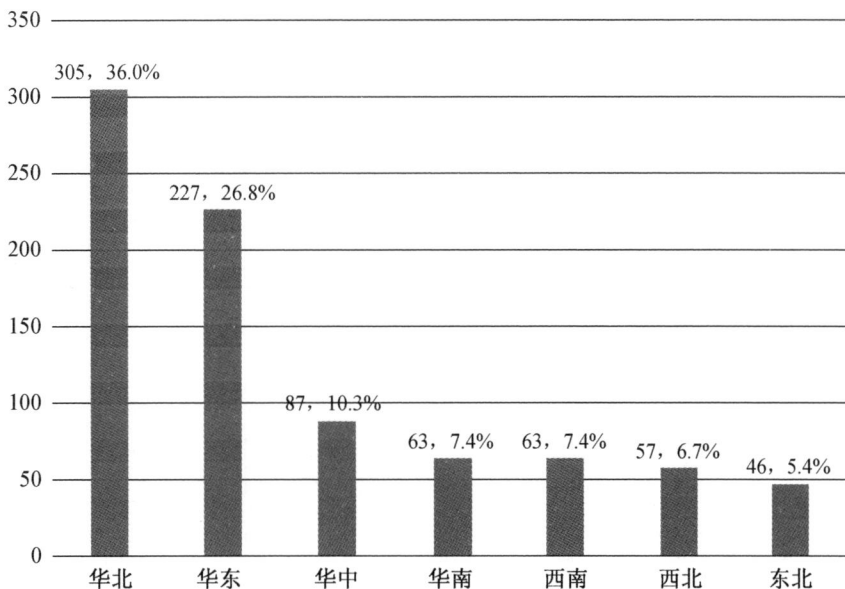

图 8.2　CTTI 来源智库地区统计图

其次,如图 8.3,和往年相比,来源智库排名前四的省份分布情况没有变化,仍是
北京市、上海市、天津市、江苏省。其中,北京市原有 197 家智库入选,2019 年增补的
智库数量也位居各省第一,现共有 219 家来源智库,进一步巩固了榜首地位。这与北
京市特殊的政治、经济和文化地位密不可分。上海市、天津市和江苏省入围智库数排
名紧随其后。往年第五的湖南省降为第六,广东省跻身前五,这仍和前文提到的华南

理工大学、广东外语外贸大学不无关系，2019 年广东省增补了 20 家来源智库，实现了量的突破。与此同时，湖北省、陕西省、浙江省、重庆市等地也不断壮大自己的智库队伍，入选智库数均达到 20 家。此外，山东省、吉林省、河北省、江西省、云南省、黑龙江省、福建省、安徽省、海南省、河南省、西藏自治区均有智库通过 2019 年的增补，因此智库数量上均有一定程度的提升。四川省、甘肃省、辽宁省、内蒙古自治区、广西壮族自治区、宁夏回族自治区、贵州省、山西省、青海省、新疆维吾尔自治区没有新增补智库，因此智库数量和去年相同。不难发现，拥有较多智库的省份均有诸多层级较高的高等院校，而智库较少的省份在高等院校的数量和质量上均有所不足，即此图虽是来源智库省份统计图，同时也反映了科教资源的分配。

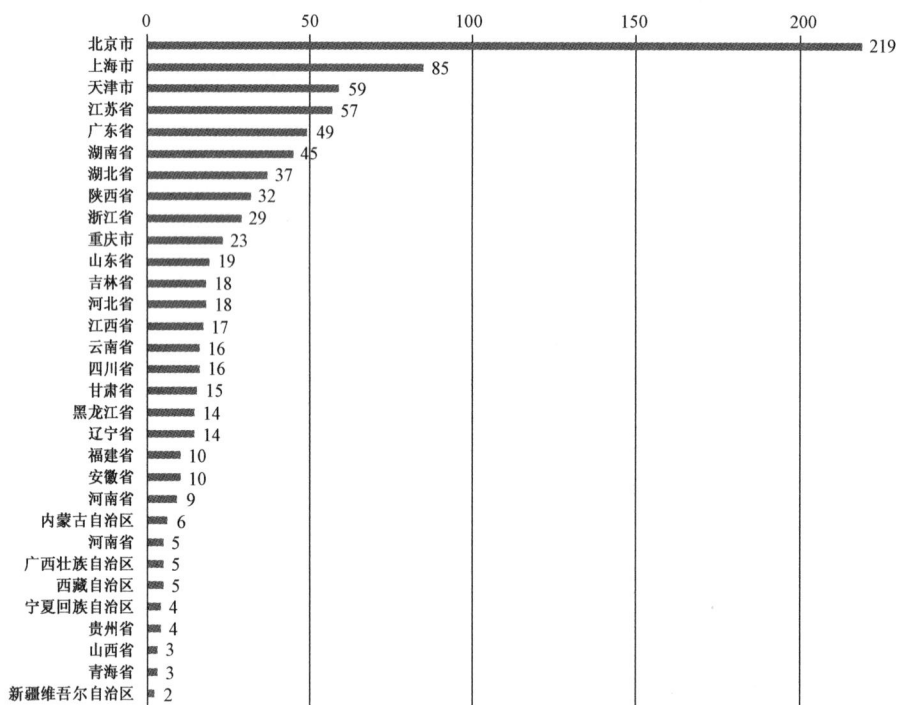

图 8.3　CTTI 来源智库省份统计图

2．CTTI 来源智库类型分析

根据图 8.4 可知，高校智库依旧是来源智库最主要的类型，共 572 家，占来源智库总量的 67%；党政部门智库 71 家，占 8%；社科院智库 51 家，占 6%；党校行政学院智库 49 家，占 6%；社会智库 38 家，占 5%；科研院所智库 36 家，占 4%；传媒智库 15 家，占 2%；企业智库 10 家，占 1%；军队智库 6 家，占 1%。

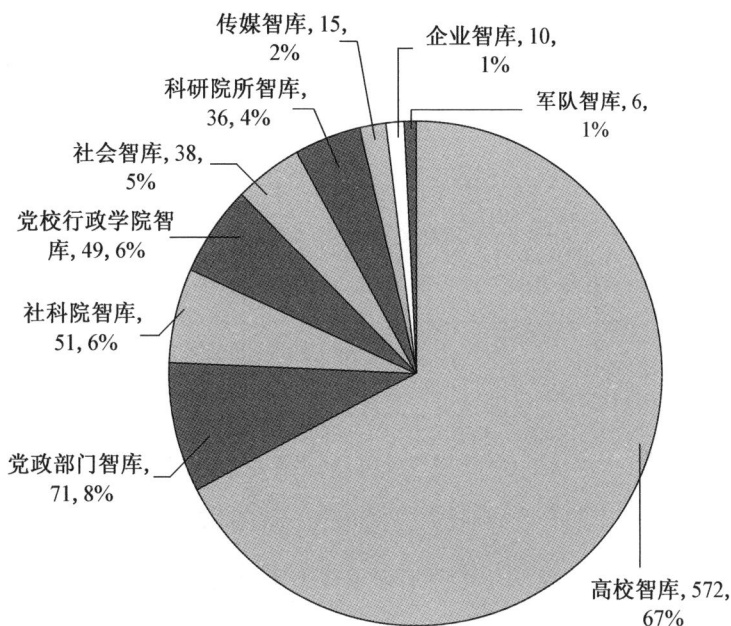

图 8.4　CTTI 来源智库类型统计图

从智库类型分布的整体情况看，各类智库所占比例几乎没有太大变化，相较去年，仅有高校智库占比有所增加，从 62% 提升到 67%。正如前文所述，高校智库是2019 年新增来源智库的主力军，其中华南理工大学、广东外语外贸大学、武汉大学新增来源智库均超过 5 家，再次扩大了高校智库这一群体的队伍。相较于高校智库，社会智库、传媒智库、企业智库、军队智库占比不变，党政部门智库、社科院智库、党校行政学院智库、科研院所智库 2019 年增补数量较少，所以在占比上均有所下滑。这反映出高校智库仍是国内智库界的主力军，其次是行政系统内的智库，民间智库仍是少数群体成员。

3. CTTI 来源智库研究领域分析

特色化和专业化是智库发展的方向，智库研究的分工也愈来愈细致。通过分析来源智库的研究领域，并将各研究领域按照智库研究主体数量的多少进行排序，如表8.2 所示，来源智库的研究领域非常广泛，涉及 53 个研究领域。这里需要说明的是，这些来源智库既存在只研究特定领域的，即一家智库专攻某个特定研究领域；也存在部分智库有多个研究领域，即一家智库涉猎多个研究领域。产业政策、金融政策、文化政策、财政政策、市场政策、外交政策是较为热门的研究领域，均有超过 100 家智库聚焦这些领域，且每一领域都体现出不同类型智库的研究力量。由此说明，大部分来源智库将研究中心放在经济、文化、外交等重大问题上，显然，这和我国的发展国情是息息相关的：以经济建设为中心是立国之本，是国家兴旺发达、长治久安的根本要求；文明，特别是思想文化是一个国家、一个民族的灵魂，要坚定文化自信；随着我国国际地位的提升，更要对外讲好中国故事。其次，社会保障政策、科技政策、社会建设与社会政策、司法政策、资源政策、对外贸易政策、农业政策、环境政策、安全政策也得到了较多智库的关注。但是针对水利政策、监察政策、统战政策、审计政策、药品政策、公安政策展开研究的智库比较少。行业智库发展不充分，这些行业的政策研究水平就上不去，比如前一段时间一部关于药品的电影揭露了进口药品的天价问题，推动了《药品管理法》的修订，这在一定程度上反映了智库圈对药品政策缺乏关注度和影响力，因此，一些重要领域的智库建设仍需加强。

按智库类型来看，高校智库凭借所依托的学科和专业优势，拥有大量智力资源，对各类政策均有不同程度的研究。相比之下，军队智库主要聚焦军事政策、国防政策、安全政策、外交政策、科技政策等几个研究领域，智库研究逐渐呈现精细化的特点。企业智库、社会智库、传媒智库等智库，除较少涉及党建政策、监察政策、公安政策等领域外，其他多数研究领域均有涉及，体现了智库研究的广泛性和多样性。

表 8.2 CTTI 来源智库研究领域统计表

	党政部门智库	社科院智库	党校行政学院智库	高校智库	军队智库	科研院所智库	企业智库	社会智库	传媒智库	汇总
产业政策	15	25	7	121	0	10	5	15	4	202
金融政策	14	21	8	98	0	3	2	13	4	163
文化政策	6	23	8	90	0	1	1	9	6	146
财政政策	17	14	7	69	0	4	3	11	3	128
市场政策	8	16	6	62	0	3	4	9	4	112
外交政策	3	8	2	78	1	1	1	11	2	107
社会保障政策	11	21	5	45	0	1	0	6	1	90
科技政策	6	5	3	41	1	18	3	9	3	89
社会建设与社会政策	4	4	7	63	0	1	0	4	2	85
司法政策	4	11	2	59	0	1	1	2	2	82
资源政策	8	7	4	48	0	6	1	5	2	81
对外贸易政策	8	8	2	50	0	1	2	7	1	79
农业政策	5	18	4	41	0	5	1	3	1	78
环境政策	8	6	3	47	0	5	1	4	1	75
安全政策	2	3	0	57	2	0	1	5	0	70
意识形态政策	2	12	21	29	0	0	1	1	1	69
城乡建设政策	5	12	2	34	0	3	0	7	1	64
党建政策	4	8	34	18	0	0	0	0	0	64
人口政策	6	13	3	36	0	2	0	3	0	63
高等教育政策	4	2	0	51	0	1	1	2	1	62
民族政策	0	7	4	41	0	0	0	4	0	58
互联网管理政策	1	3	3	34	0	2	4	5	4	56
就业政策	7	12	5	25	0	0	1	3	3	56
服务业政策	4	8	1	23	0	3	2	7	2	50
能源政策	6	4	0	30	0	3	2	3	1	50
消费政策	4	8	1	27	0	0	1	4	2	47
工业政策	4	10	0	22	0	3	1	4	1	45

续表

	党政部门智库	社科院智库	党校行政学院智库	高校智库	军队智库	科研院所智库	企业智库	社会智库	传媒智库	汇总
宗教政策	1	8	2	28	0	0	0	3	1	45
网络安全政策	1	2	3	25	0	3	1	3	2	40
基础教育政策	5	2	0	25	0	1	1	4	1	39
劳动政策	3	8	2	21	0	0	0	3	1	38
医疗卫生政策	6	5	2	20	0	1	1	2	1	38
高端制造业政策	6	6	1	15	0	4	0	5	0	37
住房政策	1	8	2	16	0	1	1	5	0	34
民政政策	4	6	3	17	0	1	0	0	0	31
海洋政策	4	1	0	16	0	4	0	5	0	30
交通政策	2	2	0	19	0	1	0	3	1	28
国防政策	0	2	1	14	4	0	0	4	0	25
新闻政策	1	2	0	14	0	0	0	0	8	25
林业政策	1	4	0	11	0	3	1	1	1	22
军事政策	0	0	0	8	5	0	0	2	0	15
人事政策	2	3	2	8	0	0	0	0	0	15
健康政策	1	3	0	7	0	1	1	0	0	14
出版政策	2	1	0	8	0	0	0	1	1	13
食品政策	2	2	0	8	0	0	0	0	0	12
港澳台政策	0	0	1	8	0	0	0	3	0	12
广播电视政策	1	2	0	7	0	1	0	0	1	12
水利政策	0	2	0	3	0	3	0	2	0	10
监察政策	1	0	1	8	0	0	0	0	0	10
统战政策	2	1	2	4	0	0	0	1	0	10
审计政策	1	3	1	4	0	0	0	0	0	9
药品政策	0	1	0	4	0	2	0	0	0	7
公安政策	2	0	0	4	0	0	0	0	0	6

三、CTTI 来源智库人力资源特征

（一）CTTI 来源智库人力总体情况

智力资源是一个国家、一个民族最宝贵的资源，也是智库建设最重要的资源。布鲁金斯学会前董事会主席约翰·桑顿说："任何智库的成功，首先取决于所拥有的专家的实力。"[①]智库在于"智"字，"智"源于一流的专家学者、强大而高效的研究团队、背景多元的专家队伍。人才队伍既包括领军人物和杰出人才，为决策咨询提供权威、科学的建设性意见，推动智库研究，还包括稳定的运营团队，确保智库的日常工作有效进行。

表 9.1 CTTI 收录人员类型及学历统计表

每家智库平均人数	全职/兼职	人员类型	学历	人数占比
14.3	全职	研究人员	博士研究生	78%
			硕士研究生	14%
2.4	兼职		本科	7%
			其他	1%
0.9	全职	行政人员	/	

据 CTTI 后台统计，如表 9.1，CTTI 共收录两种类型的智库人员，分别是行政人员和研究人员（即专家），研究人员又分为全职研究员和兼职研究员。

如上表所示，每家智库平均拥有 14.3 位全职研究员和 2.4 位兼职研究员。按学

---

① 智库的核心价值是什么？——访布鲁金斯研究院理事会主席约翰·桑顿[J]. 决策信息，2009(8):50-52.

历来看,拥有博士学历、硕士学历、本科学历和其他学历的研究人员分别占比 78％、14％、7％和 1％,学历分布总体呈"倒金字塔型"。这一方面说明了来源智库的专家们大多接受过长期、系统的学术训练,拥有较为突出的智力优势,聚焦专业的研究领域,为智库持续发挥功能提供稳定、持续的智力支撑;另一方面说明了诸多高校智库对于研究人员的学历要求较高,但在研究过程中,前期的诸多工作如信息采集、问卷调查、数据分析无须博士学历的加持。正如许多国外知名智库那样,研究团队的学历理应呈"金字塔型",一位高级研究员配置多名研究助手从事基础性工作,以此合理配置人力资源,提高人员利用效率。因此,相比之下,可以说来源智库过于追求研究员的学历,忽略了人才梯队配比的重要性,存在一定程度上的"学历过剩"问题。

如上表所示,每家来源智库平均仅拥有 0.9 位全职行政人员,因数量过少,在此也不再对学历做统计,当然这很可能是因为较多智库未填写、未填全行政人员信息,实际行政人员数量应略大于这个数值。在美国,智库的行政人员数量与研究员数量之比约为三比一,中国智库却与之相反,行政人员数量远远小于研究员数量,这导致了行政人员的工作量过于饱和,许多非研究性工作无法展开。值得注意的是,智库行政人员的力量不可小觑,唯有在配备一定数量的专业行政人员的前提下,智库才能做好对内运营和管理、对外交流与传播。在 CTTI 系统中,全球化智库共录入 49 位全职行政人员,在合理分工之下,分别负责财务、运营、新媒体等工作,维持全球化智库的良好运转,协助智库在国内乃至国际上占据一席之地。

（二）专家学科分析

如图 9.1,我们也统计了专家所在学科的情况,可知这些专家分布在 13 个学科领域。其中,三分之二的专家都是来自经济学、法学或管理学,占比分别为 26％、23％和 17％。除这三类学科外,文学和工学专家各占 7％,历史学和哲学专家各占5％,教育学、理学、医学、艺术学、农学、军事学这几个学科的专家都不足 5％。可见,我国新型智库的专家学科结构比较单一,主要集中在人文社会科学专业领域,自然科学和高精尖技术领域的专家较少,也就是说,智库专家多为文科学者,技术驱动的智库研究和科技问题显得较为棘手,这必然会导致在对应的政策研究领域中缺乏一定数量和质量的智库研究成果,显然难以适应科技兴国的时代背景。可喜的是,以"区块链"为例在 CTTI 中进行检索,得到 13 条活动记录和 59 条成果记录。区块链是一个新兴的概念,本不存在这一研究领域,而 CTTI 的检索结果说明有部分专家能够灵敏地追踪热点话题,挣脱自己的学科限制,及时地展开跨领域、跨行业的研究。的确,对智库专家来说,深耕自己擅长的研究领域非常重要,同时更要"接地气",关注时事,关注最新的研究动向,当好政府的耳目、尖兵和参谋。

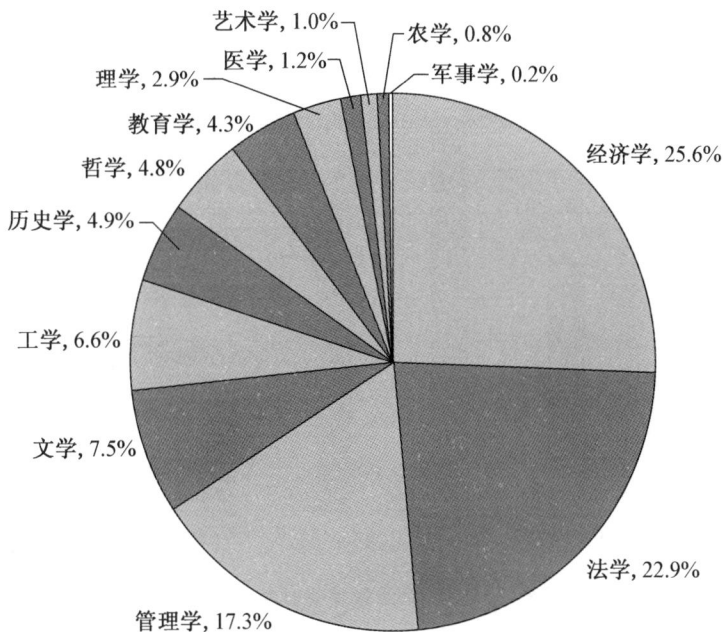

图 9.1　CTTI 来源智库专家所在学科统计图

（三）专家年龄分析

经过 2019 年的数据填报,截至目前,CTTI 已收录专家 14241 位,对填写了有效数据的 13802 位专家进行年龄统计(见图 9.2),专家的年龄类似于正态分布,均值为 48.3 岁,40 岁~50 岁的专家人数最多,约占三分之一,其次是 50 岁~60 岁,占比为

30.6％,30 岁～40 岁、60 岁～70 岁的专家也有一定数量,30 岁以下的青年专家和 70 岁以上的老年专家占比很少。这一点和外国智库的情况相吻合,在美国,智库的专家大多都是 50 岁左右的高校教授或曾在政府任职的领导。一方面,智库研究人员需要具备一定的社会阅历,才能对经济社会发展中的重大问题有思考、有见解,展开战略性、前瞻性、全局性的研究;另一方面,年龄的增长意味着人脉资源的积累,拓宽了智库服务的渠道和途径,能够缩短研究成果进入决策的时间。因此,毋庸置疑中年专家是智库研究人员的中坚力量。当然,作为未来的中流砥柱,青年专家厚积薄发、潜力无限,并且对于新生事物和时事热点的嗅觉更为敏感,也是研究力量的重要组成部分。

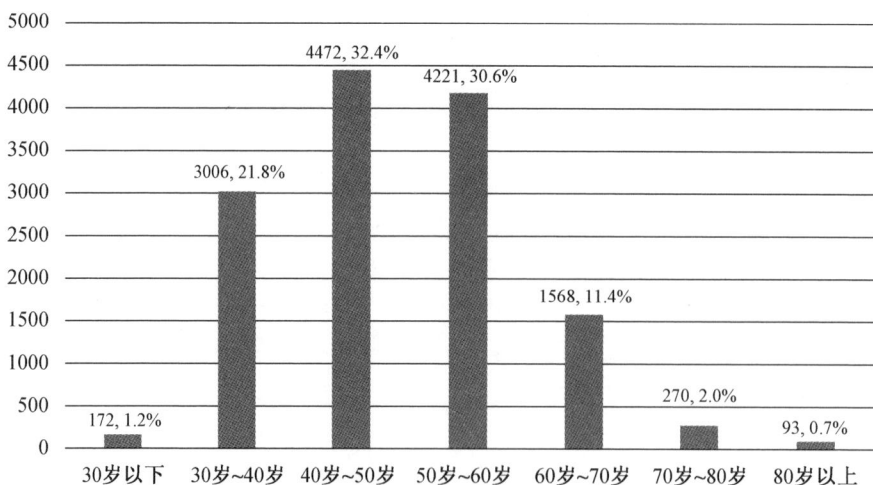

图 9.2　CTTI 来源智库专家年龄统计图

四、CTTI 来源智库产出数据分析

截至 2019 年 12 月 6 日，CTTI 共收录机构 848 家，成果 142943 项，活动 23907 场。因此，CTTI 系统涵盖了类型全面、总量巨大的智库数据，基本上能够满足学者对智库信息检索的不同需求。

（一）CTTI 来源智库成果数据分析

1. 来源智库成果数据总体分析

通过对 CTTI 各子数据库的全部数据进行统计，我们发现成果数据体量最大，涵盖类型最多，涉及范围最广。其中，论文数量达到 69469 篇，约占成果总数的 48％，其次分别是项目、报纸文章、单篇内参、报告，占比分别为 17.83％、9.32％、7.60％、7.32％（见图 10.1）。以上五类成果共占全部数据的 90.67％，由此可见，当前论文仍是最主流的智库成果产出形式，成果载体较为固定，但类型相对比较丰富。

2. 来源智库成果数据类型分析

CTTI 系统共设置了 13 类智库成果。以下对论文、单篇内参、项目、报告和报纸文章等五类主要成果分别进行数据分析。

（1）论文类成果数据分析

论文一直是来源智库收录的最主要成果类型。本节对 CTTI 全部收录论文数据进行统计，对论文的类型分布、层次分布、学科分布、发文机构等展开详细分析。在此说明，由于一篇论文存在被多个核心期刊目录收录的情况，因此我们以统计各核心期刊目录收录来源智库论文的篇次为最终结果。

从论文类型来看，97.11％属于期刊论文，而会议论文、学位论文分别占比

视频资料, 798, 0.56%　电子出版物, 290, 0.20%　单篇内参, 10869, 7.60%

其他出版物, 514, 0.36%

项目, 25484, 17.83%

通讯, 978, 0.68%

内参集, 296, 0.21%

图书, 10041, 7.02%

期刊, 422, 0.30%

报告, 10459, 7.32%

论文, 69469, 48.60%

报纸文章, 13323, 9.32%

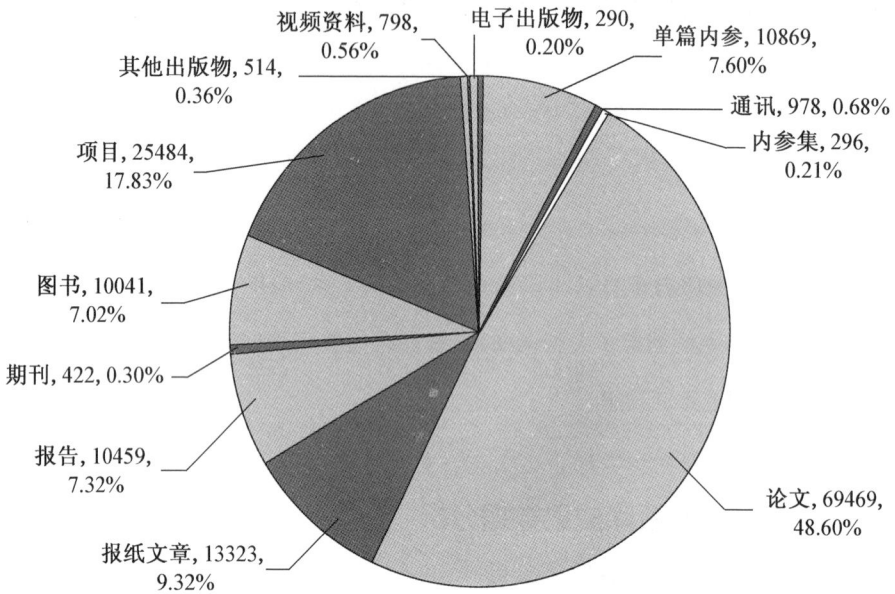

图 10.1　来源智库成果类型统计图

2.53%、0.36%（见图 10.2）。期刊论文占据极大比重，可见学者多数仍以发表期刊论文为主，以会议论文促进智库交流的活动仍然较少。

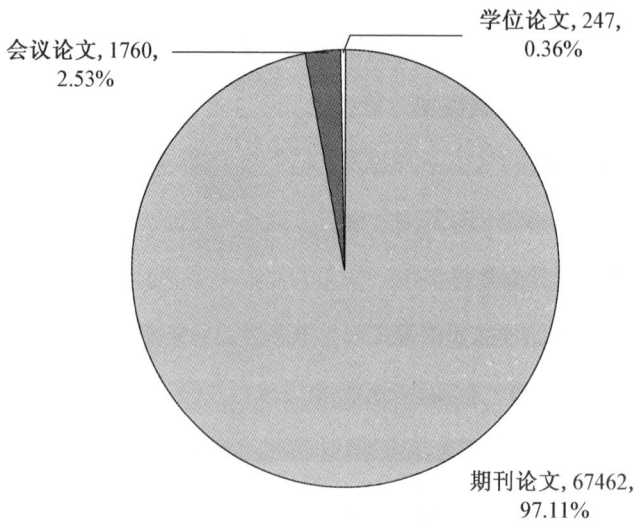

会议论文, 1760, 2.53%　　　　　学位论文, 247, 0.36%

期刊论文, 67462, 97.11%

图 10.2　来源智库论文类型统计图

从论文层次来看，来自 CSSCI 期刊的论文数量最多，占比约 54.04％，已超过全部论文的一半，其次是发表在普通期刊上的论文，占比 36.53％，剩余论文大多刊发在 SCI、SSCI、EI 等国际顶级期刊，占比 1％～5％（见图 10.3）。与 2018 年来源智库论文统计结果相比，CSSCI、SCI、SSCI 期刊论文数均有所提升。因此，值得肯定的是，来源智库在学术研究方面功底扎实，实力颇高，但也侧面反映出我国智库评价科研水平仍以论文、奖项为主，"以刊评文"形象仍然存在，"破五唯"工作仍然是加快质量导向的学术评价治理体系建设的关键。

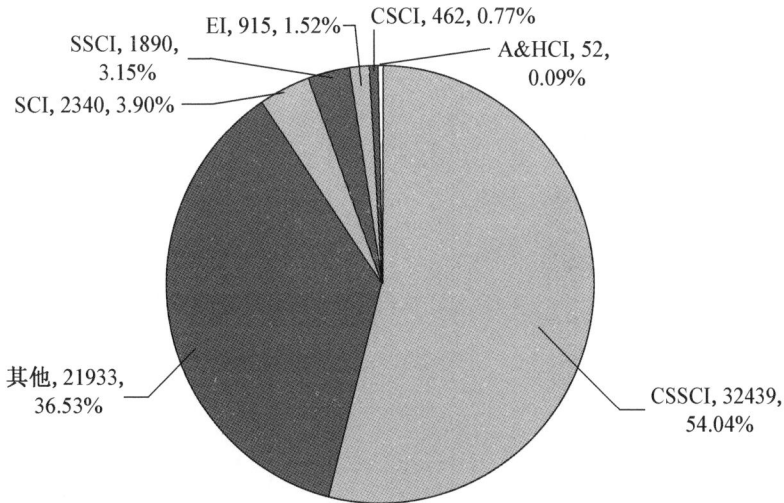

图 10.3　来源智库论文层次统计图

从论文学科分布来看，一是学科领域较为集中。来源智库发表论文多数分布在管理学、经济学、法学、教育学、政治学等领域，前三名均超过 1000 篇，合计占比超过65.7％；二是学科范围涉及广泛。其中不乏交通运输工程、能源科学技术、材料科学、航空航天科技等自然科学领域，占比虽然不高，但能体现出来源智库的不断拓展以及接纳范围的扩大（见图 10.4）。新型智库建设不再仅仅是哲学社会科学领域学者的专属研究方向，更是全社会专家跨界交流的重要议题。智库研究涉及的问题是复杂综合的，需要来自全国，甚至全球的智库专家共同探讨、合作交流，加快推进我国新型

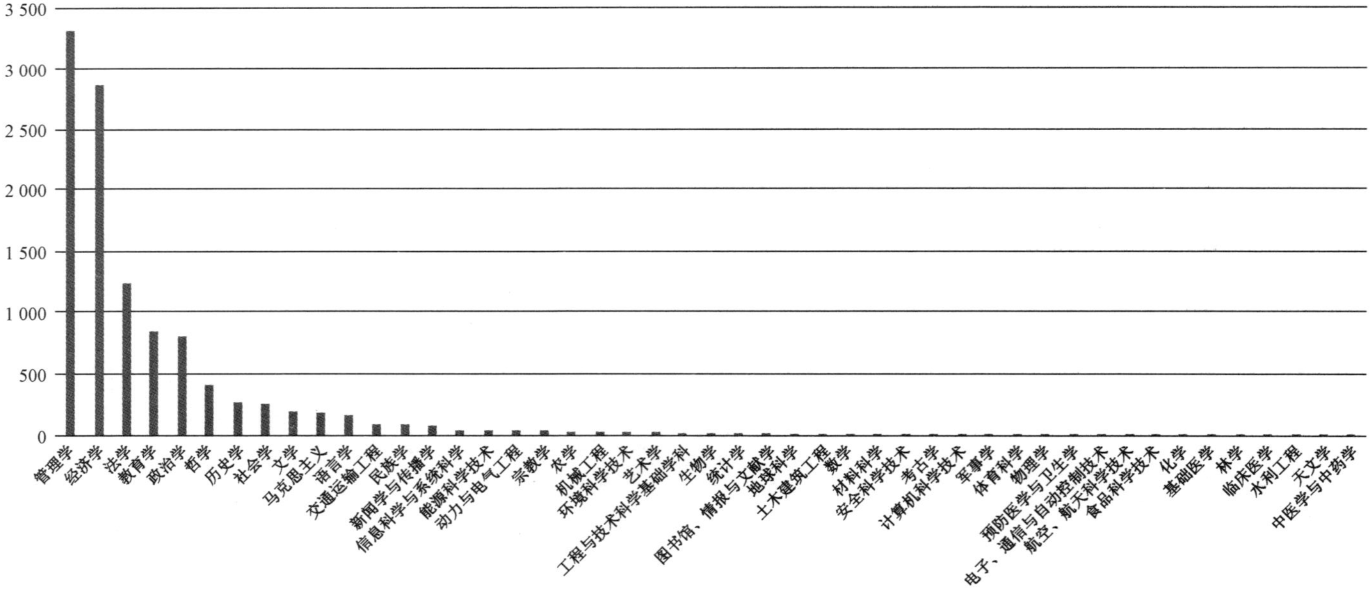

图 10.4 来源智库论文学科分布统计图

智库共同体建设。

从发文机构所在省份来看,来自北京、湖北的智库机构发文量最多,均超过 4000 篇;其次是上海、湖南、天津、广东的智库机构发文量在 2000 篇~3000 篇,江苏紧随其后,发文量接近 2000 篇。从全国范围来看,收录文献多集中在以湖北、湖南为代表的华中地区,以北京、天津为代表的华北地区,以江苏、上海为代表的华东地区以及以广东为代表的华南地区,其中陕西、青海等西部地区收录文献较少。因此,西北部、东北部以及部分南部省份的智库应进一步提高智库研究质量和创新水平,可借助特色资源优势与国内外顶尖智库共建交流平台、合办主题会议、聘请优秀专家,加快推进智库建设。

(2)单篇内参批示情况分析

内参是我国智库最具特色且最为重要的决策咨询成果。从当下的智库评价指标体系来看,内参批示情况仍是体现智库服务中央决策和地方经济发展的关键指标,能够直观反映出新型智库的决策服务水平。根据 CTTI 收录的单篇内参批示数据,统计出单篇内参 10869 篇。由于内参批示存在一篇内参被多位领导批示的情况,因此本节以被各级别领导批示的总篇次为统计标准。经过统计,内参受正国级领导批示 185 篇次(占 6.72%),获得副国级领导批示 263 篇次(占 9.55%),获得省部级领导批示 1975 篇次(占 71.71%),获得厅(司/局)级领导批示 292 篇次(占 10.60%)(见图 10.5)。其中 8283 篇内参属于提交但未获得回应的单篇内参,当然其中不排除保密因素,有些内参被批示了但来源智库并未填报。由此可见,内参报告质量仍然不够高,咨政决策能力需进一步提升,智库政策研究与决策部门需求之间仍存在一定程度的错位。因此,各来源智库更应该提升决策服务的针对性和主动性,以提高内参成果的"批示度"为主要任务,而不能简单地以追求智库内参"提交量"为目的。

值得注意的是,截至目前,CTTI 共收录论文 69469 篇,单篇内参 10869 篇,两者之比约为 6∶1。可见,论文仍然是智库最主要的产出成果,主要是因为国内智库多由学术研究机构转化而来,智库专家也以教授、研究员等专业学者为主,这既体现了中国特色,同时也为智库建设带来了不少挑战。当前学术机构的主要功能仍是教学、

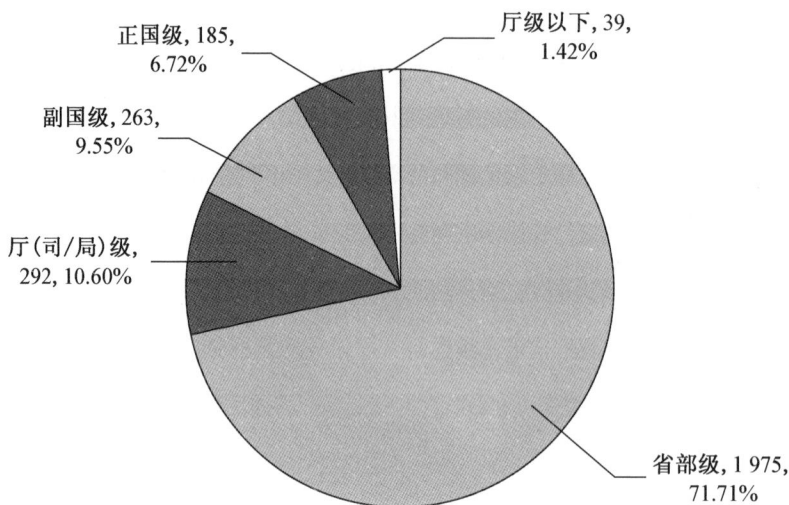

图 10.5 来源智库单篇内参批示情况统计图

科研和社会服务，而合格的智库至少需要具备咨政建言、理论创新、舆论引导、社会服务和公共外交这五大功能，但学术机构职能定位的转变不是一蹴而就的，学术机构转型智库更是一项复杂的系统工程，需要其在科研组织、资源分配、成果鉴定、考评激励等方面实现体制机制改革，这也是激发智库专家的研究热情、促进高质量成果产出的关键。

（3）项目类成果数据分析

科研课题是智库针对研究问题开展的一系列复杂的、系统的学术活动，一般包括政府支撑的纵向科研课题，来自企事业单位合作完成的横向科研课题以及机构自筹的科研课题。CTTI 收录的纵向课题主要以省部级课题为主，占比约 47.16％，其次分别是国家社科一般项目/青年项目（占 15.54％）、国家社科重大项目/教育部重大项目（占 7.08％），比例基本与 2018 年持平。横向课题共收录 6992 项，文科项目总数远远超过理科项目，总数相差 4 倍之多。其中，文科项目（经费≥5 万）的数量最多，其次是文科项目（经费≥1 万）和文科项目（经费≥15 万）；理科项目（经费≥2 万）数量最多，其次是理科项目（经费≥10 万）和理科项目（经费≥25 万）（见图 10.6）。

由此可见,来源智库承担横向课题的积极性不断提升,多数集中在 20 万以下的小规模项目(见图 10.7)。来源智库仍需心无旁骛,保持潜心研究的奉献精神,脚踏实地地对待基础性研究;同时,对于以服务决策为主要任务的新型智库,科研项目的成果转化仍是各来源智库亟须解决的问题。

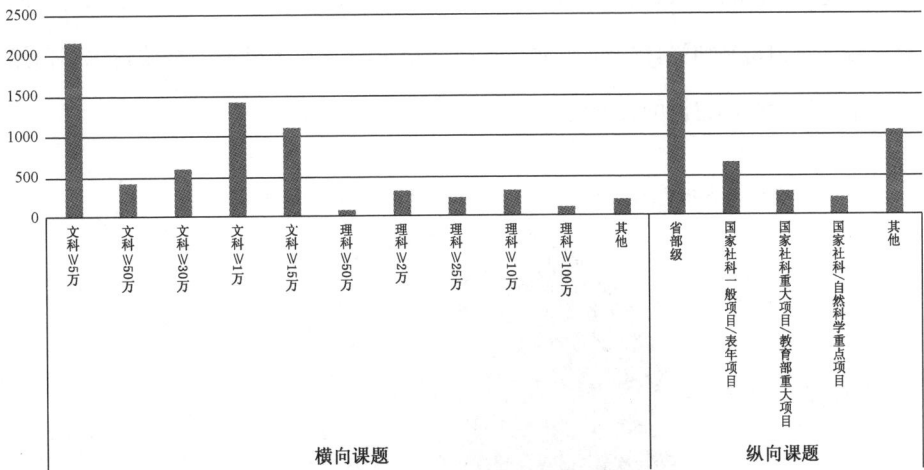

图 10.6 来源智库项目类成果统计图
注:本图表只列出横、纵向课题,未列出机构自筹课题和其他类型课题。

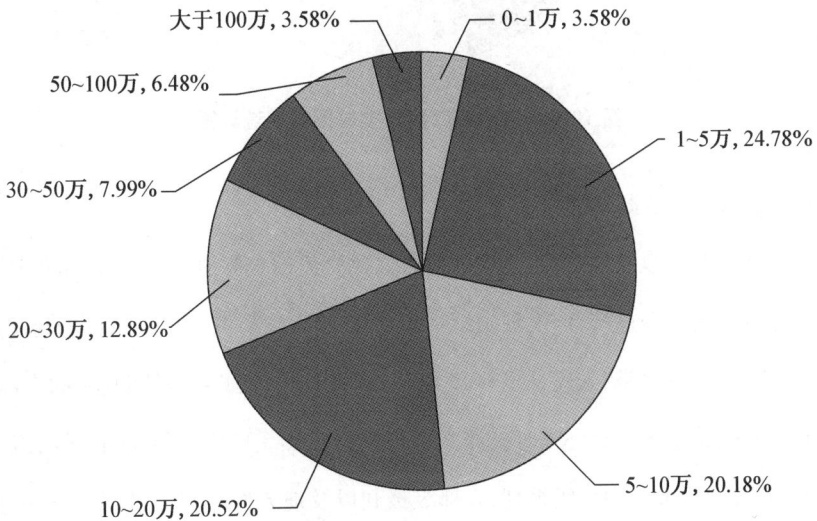

图 10.7 来源智库项目经费统计图

（4）报告类成果数据分析

科研报告是对智库成果系统性总结的一种形式,也是来源智库重要的成果载体,包括研究报告、咨询报告、调研考察报告和其他。经过统计,研究报告所占比重最多,约 55.16％,其次是咨询报告（占 39.53％）和调研考察报告（4.72％）（见图 10.8）。由此可见,研究报告数量仍然很多,咨询报告所占比重较去年有所提升,来源智库的决策咨询意识得到加强,提升咨政报告的撰写质量以及报告成果的有效转化率仍然是各来源智库内涵建设的关键内容。

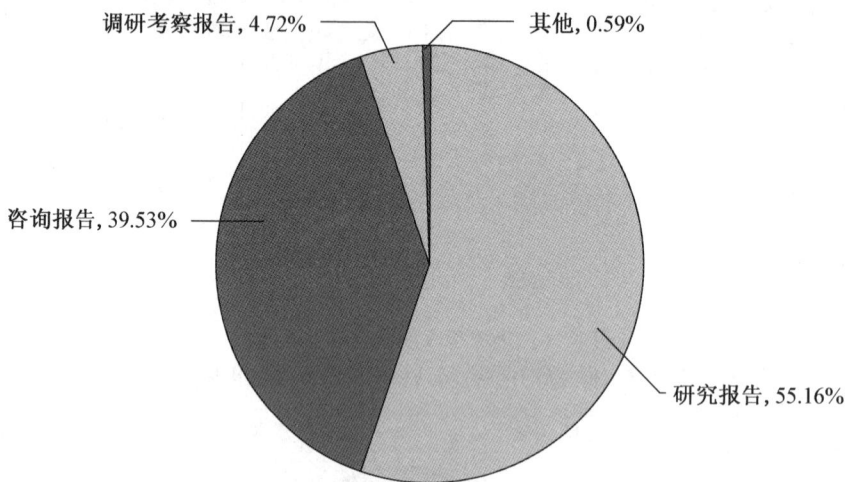

图 10.8　来源智库报告类成果类型统计图

（5）报纸文章数据分析

报纸作为党和政府的喉舌,是中国对外文化交流的重要窗口,也是智库及时对外发声的主要平台。经过统计,发现报纸文章共计 13323 篇,其中《光明日报》刊发量最多,达到 729 篇;其次是《人民日报》495 篇和《经济日报》171 篇,紧随其后的有《中国社会科学报》《检察日报》《环球时报》《文汇报》等（见图 10.9）。CTTI 收录的报纸文章来源范围广泛,涉及中央级报刊、省部级报刊以及地方性报刊等,排名前三的均是中央级报刊,可见中央级党报党刊已经成为智库最看重的舆论宣传阵地。但报纸

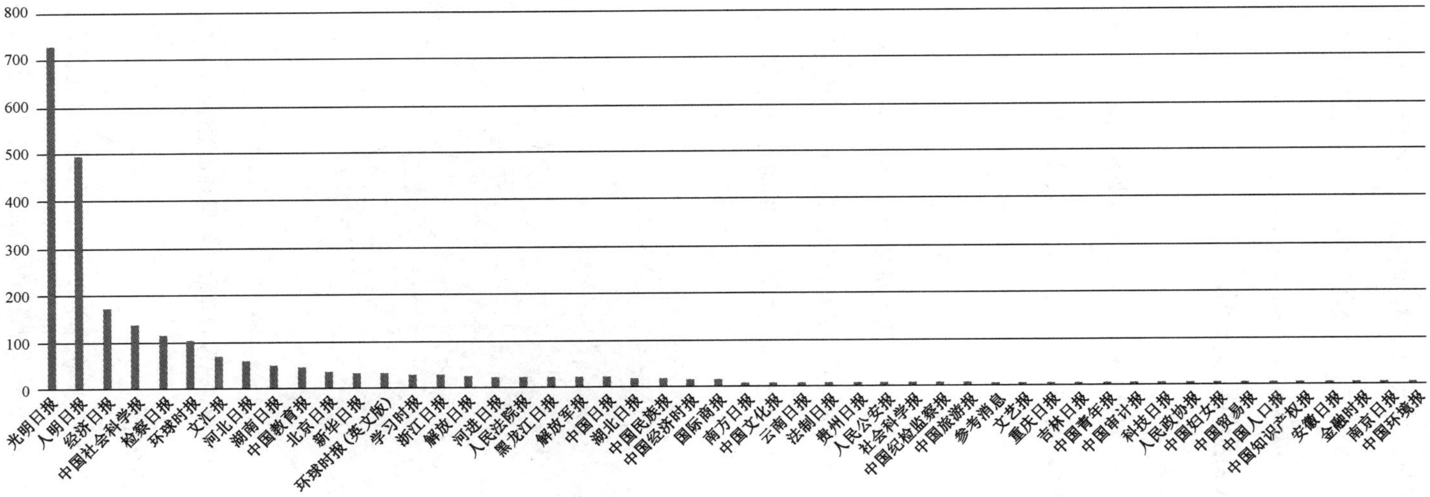

图 10.9 来源智库报纸文章数据统计图（前 50）

发文量与论文数相比差距仍然很大，来源智库应该更为积极主动地在传统报纸类媒体上发表观点、引导舆论，借助媒体的力量将智库成果广泛传播出去，进而提升来源智库的决策影响力和社会话语权。

（二）CTTI 来源智库活动数据分析

1. 来源智库活动类型分析

CTTI 来源智库的活动类型主要包括机构会议、考察（调研）活动、培训活动和接待来访活动四类。经过统计发现，举办机构会议较多，共举办 12961 场，占比约 54.21％，平均每家智库每年举办 5 场会议；其次分别为考察（调研）活动 4017 次（占 16.8％）、接待来访活动 3768 次（占 15.76％）和培训活动 3161 次（占 13.22％）（见图 10.10）。各来源智库开展活动的积极性仍然很高，通过举办各类活动可以增强与海内外智库或专家的交流合作，不断学习借鉴优秀智库建设的模式、经验及其先进的手段和方法，培养或引进高水平智库人才，进而提升智库自身的能力、水平和国际影响力。

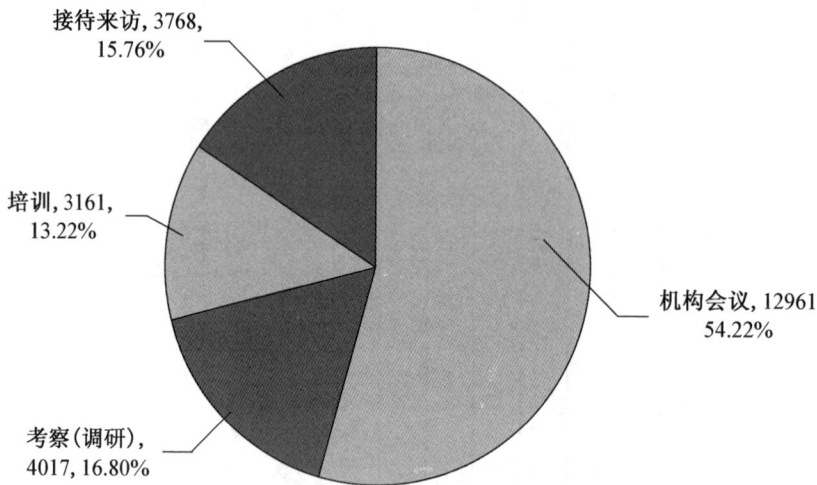

图 10.10　来源智库活动类型统计图

2. 来源智库会议类型分析

根据上一节的统计结果发现，来源智库的活动类型以举办会议为主，通过对举办国际/国内会议的类型进行汇总分析，发现智库举办正式会议较多，国内会议以讲座、研讨会、论坛等形式为主,部分智库是以座谈会、专题讨论会、专业会议等形式举办,形式类型多样,分布广泛;国际会议以研讨会、论坛为主,总体数量较少。除此之外,来源智库尝试以峰会、餐会、沙龙、发布会的新兴类型搭建交流平台,为各领域智库专家提供了思想交叉碰撞的机会和新颖的沟通体验(见图10.11)。但是,以政策研发为目的的头脑风暴型专家会议仍然较少,一定程度上影响着政策研制的深度和广度,智库在提升研究质量、推动内容创新上仍需多加重视。

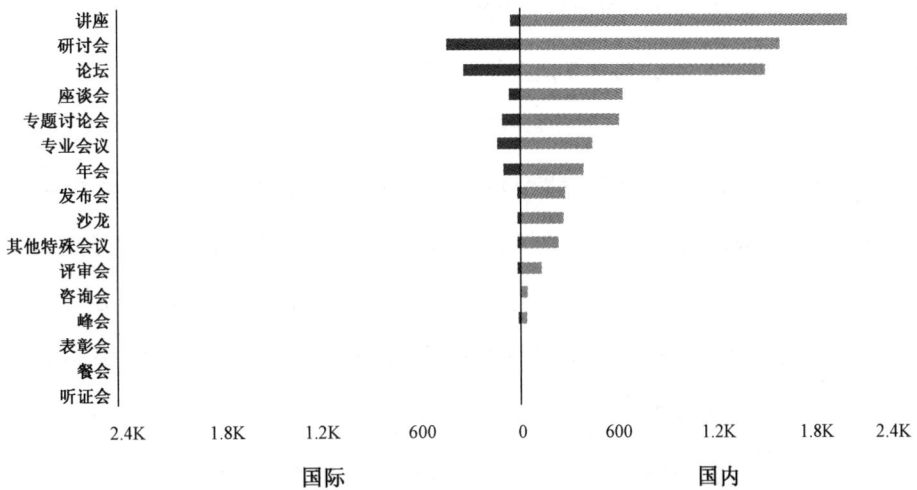

图 10.11　来源智库国内外会议类型统计图

综上可见,CTTI 来源智库的产出成果类型多样,发表在顶级期刊的成果数量不断增加,收录的论文涵盖管理学、经济学、社会学等 47 个不同的学科领域;单篇内参的批示层次得到进一步提升,省部级以上批示数量达到新高;各来源智库承担纵向课题的积极性居高不下,低于 20 万的小规模横向课题数量实现大规模提升;咨询类报告相比去年有所增加,智库的决策服务意识逐渐加强;党报党刊已然成为智库最看重的舆论宣传阵地,但来源智库专家在中央级报刊上发声的主动性和积极性仍然缺乏;来源智库积极举办各类型活动,讲座、研讨会、论坛等会议形式更受欢迎,同时以峰会、餐会、沙龙为主的小规模新型会议形式也开始出现,逐渐形成智库市场的新型互动交流格局,有助于营造更好的思想交流环境,助力新型智库可持续健康发展。

五、CTTI 来源智库分政策领域数据扫描

智库研究的专业性、科学性、前瞻性与政治性是智库影响力的关键因素，同时也是智库发挥职能，传递智库思想与观点的基石。目前，我国新型智库研究关注社会大事要事，紧跟国家大政方针，涉及众多领域，呈现出专业化、特色化的发展趋势。本报告以 CTTI 来源智库为例，延续往年原则，结合科学合理的评价体系与来源智库填报数据情况，从"宏观经济与国际贸易领域""产业与金融领域""区域国别研究领域"等17 个方面展示我国新型智库在不同政策领域的影响力，总结先进经验。本次测评主要以产出影响力为导向，将成果、活动与媒体影响力这 3 个指标赋值按 5∶3∶2 比例分配计算，得到产出影响力分值，即 PAI(产出影响力分值)＝0.5×P(Product)＋0.3×A(Activities)＋0.2×I(Impact)，作为各政策领域内智库产出影响力排序的依据。本次测评时间范围为 2017 年 1 月至 2019 年 12 月，对所有 CTTI 来源智库在该时间范围内数据的填报情况进行分析，其中有 650 家智库填写有较为充分、准确的数据。基于数据可利用性及准确性原则，本次测评对象主要以这 650 家智库为主，各表格中 PAI 值按公式"PAI＝0.5×P＋0.3×A＋0.2×I"计算得出，P、A、I 三个值为原始值。

为保护各智库信息，我们仅公布各类测评中产出影响力分值较高的智库测评分析结果，且本次发布的数据只是一级指标数值，不涉及二级指标得分的具体数值，也绝不向第三方透露相关数据。各智库若需具体得分详情，可以以机构名义发送正式函件至邮箱 ctti@nju.edu.cn，南京大学中国智库研究与评价中心将会为来函机构导出相关测评结果。

（一）宏观经济与国际贸易领域

我国经济已由高速增长阶段转向高质量发展阶段,经济高质量发展成为政策当局制定经济政策、对外贸易政策的重要出发点。为满足党和政府政策制定的需要,领域内智库聚焦地区经济发展、国际或区域贸易等问题,结合自身的资源优势,对全国及当地经济社会运行中的热点难点问题展开了大量调查研究,产出了大批优秀成果。例如,复旦大学中国经济研究中心的《天秤币无太平:中国应对数字加密货币商业化从严监管》、吉林大学数量经济研究中心的《振兴东北的根本途径在于改变政治生态》《关于东北地区经济振兴与脱贫攻坚协调推进的政策建议》等。表 11.1 展示了该领域 PAI 值较高的 20 家智库。

对外经济贸易大学国际经济研究院以科研为立院之本,重点在基础理论研究、国家政策研究、商业咨询服务三个层面开展研究工作,主要涉及世界经济和中国对外经济贸易等诸多领域。该院下设有九个研究中心,即亚洲经济研究中心、台港澳经济研究中心、欧洲经济研究中心、中国-俄罗斯/独联体研究中心、中国东盟经济研究中心、加工贸易研究中心、国际发展与创新研究中心、中国资本运营研究中心、国际新能源战略研究中心。研究院以国际的眼光、开放的思维、海纳百川的胸怀,积极开展对内对外交流与合作,每年组织出版的《中国外商投资报告》《中国出口产业国际竞争力报告》受到学界、政府、社会的普遍认同和广泛好评。

山东省宏观经济研究院在推进新型智库建设中始终坚持服务决策的价值追求,遵循"善谋善成、以智辅政"的科研理念和理论联系实践的科研作风,以"支撑党委政府科学决策的重要智囊、服务全省发展改革的参谋助手"为自身定位,坚持"区域性、对策型"特色发展路径,深度参与政府决策过程,全面提高智库影响力,直接参与重大决策的研究、论证、制定和解读宣传,不断增强研究成果的实际应用成效,着力提升服务决策的层次水平,不断延伸智库功能,提升智库建设格局,积极服务社会、服务基层。为了进一步促进交流发展,2018 年该院与中国宏观经济研究院等 20 家国内知名智库共同发起成立了"中国宏观经济智库联盟"。近三年来,该院累计参加省委省政府重大调研活动 200 余次,省委省政府累计采用专报信息 45 条,一大批科研和调研成果获得省领导批示,许多研究成果内容和观点被政府部门采用,进入相关政策文件,为省委省政府决策提供了有力的智力支持,为全省产业和地区经济建设以及社会发展做出了积极贡献。

表 11.1　宏观经济与国际贸易领域智库 PAI 值评分 Top20

（按名称首字母音序排列）

智库名称	PAI	P 值	A 值	I 值
北京交通大学国家经济安全研究院	172.4	103	371	48
对外经济贸易大学国际经济研究院	261.5	523	0	0
对外经济贸易大学国家（北京）对外开放研究院	188.25	299.5	127	2
对外经济贸易大学中国世界贸易组织研究院	118.95	232.5	9	0
复旦大学中国经济研究中心	512.6	970	92	0
河北省发展和改革委员会宏观经济研究所	293	586	0	0
华中科技大学张培刚发展研究院	137	274	0	0
吉林大学数量经济研究中心	465.55	779.5	220	49
暨南大学广州南沙自由贸易试验区研究基地	232.05	436.5	46	0
南开大学政治经济学研究中心	176.45	320.5	54	0
山东省宏观经济研究院	270	516	30	15
商务部国际贸易经济合作研究院	170	340	0	0
上海对外经贸大学国际经贸治理与中国改革开放联合研究中心	560.5	1121	0	0
上海海事大学中国（上海）自贸区供应链研究院	241	482	0	0
天津财经大学天津市自由贸易区研究院	279.2	538	34	0
武汉大学经济发展研究中心	151.25	254.5	80	0
西安交通大学中国（西安）数字经济发展监测预警基地	139	278	0	0
西北大学陕西宏观经济与经济增长质量协同创新研究中心	129.1	141	66	194
中国财政科学研究院	256	506	10	0
中南财经政法大学中国收入分配研究中心	185.8	329	71	0

（二）产业与金融领域

产业与金融领域聚焦产业与金融体系在转型、融合中出现的问题。随着"十三五规划""供给侧改革""一带一路"及"中国制造 2025"等导向性政策的相继出台，实体产业与金融领域的融合愈加紧密，融资租赁为产业的结构化转型提供了强大推力。如何从中国经济发展的重大现实需求出发持续实现产业与金融领域的深度融合，是产业与金融领域智库面临的重要课题。根据产业与金融领域智库填报的数据，系统自动计算出 PAI 值较高的 20 家产业与金融领域智库，如表 11.2 所示。

党的十九届四中全会要求加快完善社会主义市场经济体制，加强资本市场基础制度建设，健全具有高度适应性、竞争力、普惠性的现代金融体系，有效防范金融风险。中国企业营运资金管理研究中心以独创的"基于渠道管理的营运资金管理理论"和"创新的资本效率与财务风险分析体系"为支撑，持续开展中国上市公司资本效率与财务风险调查，引领资金管理理论创新的发展。研究中心在此基础上，努力实现科教融合、产业协同、理实一体，充分发挥理论创新对人才培养和社会服务的协同带动功能，成为我国资金管理领域的"文献库""信息库"和"案例库"。

同样作为高校智库的中国人民大学重阳金融研究院，同时也是中国金融学会绿色金融专业委员会的秘书处，旨在为绿色生产、消费和发展绿色金融，推进市场导向的绿色技术创新建言献策。研究院发布的《中国绿色金融研究报告 2018》由中国人民大学和中国工商银行共同牵头，深度研究了中国绿色金融各个阶段各个领域的重大理论、政策和热点焦点问题，为绿色金融的未来发展梳理总结了历史经验。表11.2 中中国人民大学重阳金融研究院的 A 值得分为 1122，说明重阳金融研究院注重通过参与决策咨询会议等形式为政府提供智力支持，且以召开具有影响力的智库论坛峰会来传播新型智库理念并提高智库自身的影响力。

在这一领域除了高校智库，还有企业智库。苏宁金融研究院作为一流的企业智库代表，是该领域内活跃性较高的智库，对内为苏宁集团提供战略支持，对外为第三方提供定制化的研究咨询服务。苏宁金融研究院拥有以企业为主体、市场为导向、产学研深度融合的技术创新体系,对于提升产业基础能力和产业链现代化水平具有指导意义。除此之外,苏宁金融研究院还专门设立了数据管理的日常工作岗,安排专人负责更新和维护智库各项数据系统和信息平台的信息,提高智库信息现代化管理的水平。

表 11.2　产业与金融领域智库 PAI 值评分 Top20

（按名称首字母音序排列）

智库名称	PAI	P 值	A 值	I 值
北京大学汇丰金融研究院	144.5	64	375	0
北京工业大学北京现代制造业发展研究基地	330.75	661.5	0	0
福建师范大学竞争力研究中心	159.3	291	46	0
河北金融学院德融研究院	264	306	370	0
华南理工大学广州市金融服务创新与风险管理研究基地	112.45	171.5	89	0
机械工业经济管理研究院	797	1594	0	0
江南大学中国物联网发展战略研究基地	89.85	106.5	114	12
南京财经大学现代服务业智库	136	272	0	0
南京大学长江产业经济研究院	1371.45	1051.5	2575	366
南开大学经济与社会发展研究院	526.1	760	459	42
苏宁金融研究院	952.05	1735.5	281	0
天津财经大学工商管理研究中心	133.4	244	38	0
天津财经大学无形资产评价协同创新中心	395.8	704	146	0
天津财经大学中国滨海金融协同创新中心	230.4	426	48	15
天津商业大学现代服务业发展研究中心	239.5	479	0	0
西南财经大学中国家庭金融调查与研究中心	379.15	467.5	150	502
浙江大学中国跨境电子商务研究院	108.25	69.5	243	3
中国海洋大学中国企业营运资金管理研究中心	4923.9	9804	29	66
中国人民大学重阳金融研究院	821.05	966.5	1122	6
中南财经政法大学产业升级与区域金融湖北省协同创新中心	1203.25	1518.5	956	786

（三）区域国别研究领域

　　区域国别研究是全面客观看待外部世界问题、进行科学合理的国际比较的重要前提之一，是中国从地区性大国向全球性大国发展进程中的必然需要。高校智库不断增强服务国家大局的使命感和责任感，充分发挥语言、经济贸易等重要学科基础及地域与人才优势，为国家制定发展战略、政策措施提供智力支持，已经成为区域国别研究领域内的主要力量之一。表 11.3 展示了该领域 PAI 值较高的 12 家智库。

　　浙江师范大学非洲研究院是在教育部、外交部支持下于 2007 年成立的中国高校首个综合性、实体性非洲研究院，经过十多年的发展已成为有一定影响力的中国非洲研究机构与国家对非事务智库。研究院围绕国家发展大局与中非合作大势，以"当代非洲发展问题""新时期中非合作关系"为重点研究领域，深入开展基础理论与应用对策研究。一直以来，研究院注重品牌建设，编辑出版了教育部哲学社会科学年度报告《非洲地区发展报告》及研究院专业期刊《非洲研究》，在国际上主办"中非智库论坛""中非媒体智库研讨会"等一系列具有一定影响力的学术会议，打造中国非洲研究重要品牌。研究院还努力开展学术研究，夯实智库发展基础，以学术研究激活智库研究，出版了《非洲研究文库》、在国内外重要期刊上发表文章等。基于此，研究院一直都有较强的智库成果产出能力，主动向国家各部委提交各类咨询报告，多篇报告获国家领导人批示或被《教育部高校智库专刊》录用。

　　上海外国语大学中东研究所于 2000 年 12 月被教育部批准建立为教育部人文社会科学重点研究基地。研究所注重团队建设，逐步建立起具有优势和特色的研究队伍，把应用对策研究与基础研究有机地结合起来，把社会科学课题与人文科学课题结合起来，既与中央有关部委保持经常性联系、沟通，做好咨询服务工作，也推动了具有中国特色的阿拉伯学、伊斯兰学的整体构建。而且，研究所在打好学术基础的同时不断促进成果转化。近三年来，研究所发表了近百篇学术论文，并出版了《伊朗伊斯兰共和国经济现代化研究》《中东热点的冷观察》《世界主要国家安全体制机制研究》等重要学术著作，具备较强的理论研究能力。此外，三年来研究所上报了 60 余篇内参，积极建言献策，做好决策咨询服务。

表 11.3　区域国别研究领域 PAI 值评分 Top12

（按名称首字母音序排列）

智库名称	PAI	P 值	A 值	I 值
北京外国语大学二十国集团研究中心	100.95	142.5	99	0
北京外国语大学加拿大研究中心	103.3	119	146	0
北京外国语大学英国研究中心	166.25	253.5	109	34
复旦大学美国研究中心	482.15	304.5	819	421
华东师范大学俄罗斯研究中心	170.3	223	196	0
吉林大学东北亚研究中心	152.4	303	3	0
上海大学土耳其研究中心	106.6	69	173	101
上海外国语大学中东研究所	918.75	822.5	487	1807
同济大学德国研究中心	172.9	179	278	0
延边大学朝鲜半岛研究院	214.9	410	33	0
云南大学缅甸研究院	103.9	119	148	0
浙江师范大学非洲研究院	622.8	635	927	136

（四）国际关系与外交政策

全球化密切了国与国之间政治、经济、文化等领域的联系，国家间的合作与竞争在不断深化。部分智库针对国际事务、国际热点、国家外交政策等领域进行研究，并为决策机构提供政策参考，对外交政策产生了重要影响。表 11.4 展示了 PAI 值较高的 10 家智库。

周边合作与发展协同创新中心于 2012 年由华东师范大学牵头，北京大学和复旦大学共同参与建设的协同创新平台，并与上海国际问题研究院建立了协同关系。中心多年来侧重于中国周边地区的区域、国别研究，强调这一研究领域的整体性，通过建有专门的历史资料库以及两个专业数据库，为将决策咨询与学术研究合为一体提供数据支持。此外，中心还高度重视国际学术交流与合作，已在美国威尔逊国际学者中心和俄罗斯国立高等经济大学设立工作室。同属于华东师范大学的俄罗斯研究中心成立于1999年,2000年成为教育部人文社会科学重点研究基地。基地建设十年来,共承担各类科研项目44项,总经费1100万元,出版学术专著50部,发表核心期刊论文300余篇,获省部级优秀成果奖15项。基地在苏联史、俄苏文学研究史、俄罗斯转型、俄罗斯外交等方面形成了研究特色,并取得了公认的研究成果。

全球化智库(CCG)是北京东宇全球化智库基金会注册的智库机构品牌,是国内领先的社会智库型全球化研究机构。CCG成立于2008年,总部位于北京,在国内外有近10个分支机构或海外代表处,"以全球视野为中国建言,以中国智慧为全球献策",致力于中国的全球化战略、全球治理、人才国际化和企业国际化等领域的研究,目前拥有全职智库研究和专业人员近百人。CCG是中联部"一带一路"智库联盟理事单位,中央人才工作协调小组全国人才理论研究基地,人社部中国国际人才专业委员会所在地,财政部"美国研究智库联盟"创始理事单位且拥有博士后科研工作站资质,并被联合国授予"特别咨商地位"。CCG每年出版10余部研究著作,包括与社科文献出版社合作出版发布的《中国企业国际化报告》《中国留学发展报告》《中国海归发展报告》《中国国际移民报告》《海外华人华侨专业人士报告》《中国区域人才竞争力报告》等具有国内外影响力的蓝皮书。此外,CCG还承担国家多个部委的课题和举办多个论坛及智库研讨会,具备一定的影响力。

表11.4　国际关系与外交政策PAI值评分Top10

（按名称首字母音序排列）

智库名称	PAI	P值	A值	I值
北京外国语大学公共外交研究中心	137.15	239.5	58	0
广西大学中国-东盟研究院	187.95	313.5	104	0
海国图智研究院	424.1	401	726	29
华东师范大学国家话语生态研究中心	175.65	217.5	211	18

续表

智库名称	PAI	P 值	A 值	I 值
华东师范大学周边合作与发展协同创新中心	3068.85	5011.5	1877	0
暨南大学华侨华人研究院	305.05	507.5	159	18
盘古智库	985.5	384	2523	183
全球化智库	2362.7	2878	2021	1587
上海外国语大学中国国际舆情研究中心	442	884	0	0
云南大学周边外交研究中心	724.9	1386	85	32

（五）党的建设与国家治理领域

党的十八大以来，机关党建工作面临的形势任务发生了很大变化。以习近平同志为核心的党中央对全面从严治党、加强机关党的建设做出一系列重要部署，推动机关党建取得显著成效。特别是十九大后，党的建设与国家治理领域智库持续围绕"新时代党的建设""坚持和加强党的全面领导""全面从严治党""加强党的长期执政能力建设、先进性和纯洁性建设"等重要议题，不断推进党建理论创新，加强基层党建工作的总结与思考。根据党的建设与国家治理领域智库所填报的数据，系统自动计算出PAI 值较高的 20 家的智库，如表 11.5 所示。

在国家治理方面，领域内智库紧紧围绕"国家治理体系和治理能力现代化"重要议题，探讨制度建设以及国家治理现代化理论基础与实现路径。中国社会科学院上海市人民政府上海研究院围绕国家战略和上海作为全面深化改革前沿所承担的重要任务开展工作，围绕改革发展的重大理论和现实问题，努力建设成为高端思想库（智库）、高端人才培养基地、高端国际交流合作平台和高端国情调研基地。研究院重视宣传引领工作，积极在人民网、光明网、解放日报、文汇报、新华网等媒体上发表多篇文章，围绕国家战略、全面深化改革等重要问题展开论述。研究院还打造了智库品牌讲座活动"人文社科高端讲座""上海研究院智库大讲堂"，以讲座深化智库服务，塑造自身形象，成为传播人文知识、交流智库思想的有效方式。此外，研究院积极参与国际交流,承办"中韩人文学"论坛,联合主办了中日马克思主义研究高端对话会,老龄化、临终关怀和社会政策国际学术研讨会,还前往土耳其、希腊访问交流,与巴斯大学签署合作谅解备忘录等,通过搭建国际交流平台,不断加强对外宣传,了解外国情况,研究国际形势。

作为高校智库,东南大学中国特色社会主义发展研究院切实发挥了高端思想库和智囊团的作用,在决策咨询、理论创新、媒体传播等方面有较突出表现,先后承担国家重大工程项目 1 项、国家社科基金一般项目近 10 项。党的十九大召开后不久,研究院围绕新时代政治建设组织撰写了系列理论文章,并于《光明日报》2017 年 10 月 24 日第 12 版整版刊发。研究院目前在《人民日报》《光明日报》《经济日报》等相关领域顶级报刊共发表理论文章 20 余篇,在《新华日报》《群众》等省级媒体共发表理论文章 40 余篇。研究院也注重加强理论宣传,通过新媒体、接受媒体专访、参与政策解读、召开研讨会(座谈会)等多种方式,助力推动理论宣传深入人心。例如,研究院专家发表的多篇理论文章被"学习强国"等媒体转载传播,录制的"思政微课堂"系列视频在"学习强国"江苏学习平台、中国江苏网同步上线,还有 2 位专家参与了"'两聚一高'在江苏——智库专家、媒体老总环省行"系列访谈活动,分别与徐州和淮安市委书记面对面交流探讨产业升级、创新创业、城市建设等议题,并提出政策建言。此外,研究院围绕中国特色新型城镇化、科技与产业创新、党的十九届四中全会等主题举办大型高层论坛 7 次,交流研讨会 40 余次,其中 2 次活动获《新华日报》智库版整版报道,产生了广泛社会影响。

同为高校智库的北京大学国家治理研究院是由北京大学、复旦大学、吉林大学共同发起,联合中山大学以及财政部财政科学研究所(后更名为"中国财政科学研究院")建立起的四校一院协同创新单位。"国家治理研究丛书"是研究院的代表成果,目前已出版 11 本,是研究院与国家治理协同创新中心落实协同创新科研任务、推动相关优秀成果转化与应用而形成的国家治理和深化改革专门问题的研究著作。北京大学国家治理研究院始终紧紧围绕全面深化改革的总目标和国家治理现代化的重大迫切需求，通过自身的研究力量与社会各界紧密合作，促成多领域、跨学科交融，来承担解决政府治理、市场治理、社会治理乃至全球治理等多方面重大问题的科学研究，为国家治理的相关人才培养、学科建设和社会服务提供智力支持。研究院正努力建成"国家急需、世界一流、制度先进、贡献突出"的中国特色新型智库机构，为推进国家治理现代化和"双一流"大学的建设贡献力量。

表 11.5　党的建设与国家治理领域智库 PAI 值评分 Top20

（按名称首字母音序排列）

智库名称	PAI	P 值	A 值	I 值
北京大学国家治理研究院	565.85	803.5	547	0
北京市信访矛盾分析研究中心	601.15	1014.5	313	0
东南大学中国特色社会主义发展研究院	742.4	1423	103	0
湖南大学国家腐败预防与惩治研究中心	77.65	95.5	99	1
华中科技大学国家治理研究院	150.85	186.5	192	0
吉林大学廉政研究与教育中心	181.2	246	194	0
江西师范大学管理决策评价研究中心	218	371	71	56
南开大学中国特色社会主义经济建设协同创新中心	156.45	289.5	39	0
南开大学中国政府与政策联合研究中心	189.85	309.5	63	81
上海市人民政府发展研究中心	101.5	158	75	0
四川大学中国西部边疆安全与发展协同创新中心	149.7	294	9	0
天津工业大学天津法治信访研究基地	89.6	130	82	0
天津师范大学国家治理研究中心	183.55	144.5	371	0
天津师范大学应急管理研究中心	123.5	247	0	0
武汉大学党内法规研究中心	96.5	147	62	22
西安交通大学改革试点探索与评估协同创新中心	115.75	207.5	40	0

续表

智库名称	PAI	P 值	A 值	I 值
云南大学边疆民族问题智库	165	330	0	0
浙江财经大学中国政府监管与公共政策研究院	125	196	90	0
中国行政体制改革研究会	129.75	85.5	22	402
中国社会科学院上海市人民政府上海研究院	702.55	688.5	967	341

（六）社会治理与社会保障领域

　　党的十九大报告指出,要加强社会治理制度建设,完善党委领导、政府负责、社会协同、公众参与、法治保障的社会治理体制,提高社会治理社会化、法治化、智能化、专业化水平,积极打造共建共治共享的社会治理格局。社会治理研究领域内智库积极响应党和政府对社会治理的新要求,结合自身专业能力,聚焦医疗、卫生、社会保障等重要问题,对社会治理、民生建设、公共政策进行了研究,为解决实际问题提供智力支持。表 11.6 展示了领域内 PAI 值较高的 20 家智库。

　　南京大学紫金传媒智库以"舆论与社会心态"为主要研究方向,聚焦国内外重大政策出台、关键事件发生后民众在舆论与社会心态方面的变化,围绕国家在互联网与传媒发展、社会风险与公共危机等问题进行长期跟踪研究,精准高效地建言献策,助推经济、社会和文化发展。近三年来,智库陆续举办多场品牌论坛,如"紫金信访高层论坛""紫金青椒论坛""紫金传媒论坛"等,在国内智库界产生了一定的影响力;打造了以"大数据"研究为核心竞争力的系列智库产品,如《2015 中国股市风潮调查中期报告》《中国民众的经济信心指数报告(2015—2016)》《中国 A 股上市公司创新指数报告(2016)》等。

　　武汉大学社会保障研究中心作为国家"985 工程"二期建设项目中的社会保障研究创新基地,产出影响力成绩较为显著。围绕医疗卫生与工伤保险、养老保险、社会福利与救助、医养融合等研究方向,研究中心率先树立品牌意识,有机结合高校特点、学科特征及咨政方向，利用专业优势，打造自身的旗舰产品《中国社会保障改革与发展报告》、CSSCI来源期刊《社会保障研究》以及重要活动"珞珈社保研究生论坛"，通过旗舰产品、品牌活动不断提高智库品牌号召力、社会影响力。

　　暨南大学广州市舆情大数据研究中心依托传统研究优势，重点强化技术平台建设，以构建统一的"数据湖泊"和细分的"数据仓库"为手段，以提升现代组织的"数据治理"能力为目标，以增进大众的"信息福利"为旨归，聚焦"重大理论难题、重大现实挑战、重大社会关切"。研究中心定期编写《广东舆情动态》，与凯迪网络合作出版《舆情观察》，策划出版了"舆情与社会管理黄皮书"。研究中心发布的国庆阅兵系列调查、世博会民意调查、亚运会系列调查、"骆家辉上任驻华大使认知与评价调查""数说财经"调查等成果，受到国内外众多媒体的广泛关注。作为中宣部直报点之一，研究中心向中宣部报送信息多篇，获得采纳80余篇。在服务地方方面，研究中心连续多年联合南方舆情数据研究院举行"粤治"论坛；由研究员编辑推出的《粤治新篇》全面介绍了广东这个改革开放前沿阵地在推进政府治理能力现代化方面的探索成果。

表 11.6　社会治理与社会保障领域 PAI 值评分 Top20

（按名称首字母音序排列）

智库名称	PAI	P 值	A 值	I 值
华中科技大学健康政策与管理研究院	111.4	157	95	22
暨南大学广州市舆情大数据研究中心	258	345	185	150
暨南大学经济与社会研究院	199.5	141	430	0
江西省情研究中心	359.6	712	12	0
江西师范大学中国社会转型研究协同创新中心	391.1	747	28	46
兰州大学循证社会科学研究中心	184.25	280.5	130	25
南京大学紫金传媒智库	486.4	784	276	58
南京理工大学江苏人才发展战略研究院	300.85	594.5	12	0

续表

智库名称	PAI	P值	A值	I值
南京医科大学健康江苏研究院	311.55	424.5	213	177
山东大学卫生管理与政策研究中心	281.75	419.5	240	0
上海大学基层治理创新研究中心	274.65	442.5	178	0
上海交通大学第三部门研究中心	140.95	126.5	259	0
上海交通大学舆论学研究院	172	344	0	0
天津体育学院全民健身研究智库	127	227	45	0
武汉大学全球健康研究中心	404.25	484.5	500	60
武汉大学社会保障研究中心	353.75	641.5	98	18
西安交通大学社会治理和社会政策协同创新研究中心	115.1	155	22	155
燕山大学河北省公共政策评估研究中心	605.2	1202	14	0
浙江大学社会治理研究院	164.7	258	119	0
中南大学人力资源研究中心	188.05	314.5	68	52

（七）城乡发展与区域协调发展领域

近年来,我国在统筹城乡发展、推进新型城镇化方面取得了显著进展,但是也存在城乡要素流动不顺畅、公共资源配置不合理等亟待解决的问题。部分智库聚焦城乡发展过程中的经验与问题,展开了相关政策研究。在区域协调方面,《国民经济和社会发展第十三个五年规划纲要(2016—2020)》就已将区域协调发展摆在了突出的战略位置,反映出中央对当前区域发展形势的一种重要判断。自此,部分智库结合自身专业领域,对推动区域协调发展,推进区域一体化等问题展开理论研究与实践探讨。表11.7展示了领域内PAI值较高的25家智库。

其中,华东师范大学中国现代城市研究中心表现不俗。三年来,该研究中心积极申报重要项目,以项目为依托,深耕城市地理、城市社会等方面的理论研究,学术著作、咨询报告、期刊论文、媒体建言多点发力。2019年上半年,该研究中心已出版了7

部学术著作,发表了 40 余篇中外文论文成果,接受了《光明日报》《新华日报》等重要媒体采访,发表专家建言。例如,研究中心重要研究成果《长江经济带城市协同发展能力指数报告(2019)》,对长江经济带 110 个地级及以上城市的协同发展能力进行了系统分析,提出了提升城市协同发展能力的对策建议,得到了学界、政界、商界的高度肯定,荣获了"上海市第十四届哲学社会科学中国特色社会主义理论优秀成果"二等奖,其主要研究结论也被中央电视台、新华网、人民网、新浪网、凤凰网等国内主流媒体广泛报道,并被 Erdkunde、《改革》《人民论坛》《长江流域资源与环境》等中外学术杂志刊发。

　　盐城师范学院沿海发展智库聚焦沿海高质量发展目标,在努力做好理论研究的基础上,深入参与实践工作,不断促进理论研究成果向实践层面的转化。在理论研究上,该智库紧紧围绕海洋经济和沿海产业发展理论创新,在《人民日报》《光明日报》《群众》等刊物发文 17 篇,出版《江苏省海洋经济发展战略研究》等 5 部专著,在社科文献出版社连续出版 5 期《沿海发展研究》集刊。在实践工作中,该智库还在服务中韩(盐城)产业园高质量发展方面探索了智库的多重服务功能,深度参与中韩(盐城)产业园建设当中,组织了政产学研专门队伍,并与产业园签订正式协议,建立运行通畅高效的合作机制。其后,该智库聚焦"产业转型升级、环境保护利用、园区发展与体制机制创新"等方向进行专题研究,向盐城市委市政府、江苏省委宣传部智库办提交了系列决策咨询报告,提出切实可行的建议举措,并协助中韩(盐城)产业园建设办起草提交《中韩(盐城)产业园建设实施方案》,在其中发挥了重要的服务咨询作用。

　　粤港澳大湾区研究院作为由广东省委宣传部牵头,多家政府机构和社会团体合作共建的区域发展研究院,聚集了粤港澳政商学研资顶尖力量,努力打造国际知名、国内一流的高端智库,助力粤港澳大湾区成为国际一流湾区和世界级城市群。研究院在国际化背景下,根据大湾区经济的发展规律,依托省发改委、省港澳办和省社科院的资源优势,搭建大湾区科研和服务平台,并联合国内国际知名高校、科研机构专家团队,为区域政府决策提供参考,强化科学决策能力。目前研究院已出版粤港澳大湾区蓝、白皮书,并开通了粤港澳大湾区研究的专报通道。

表 11.7　城乡发展与区域协调发展领域 PAI 值评分 Top25

(按名称首字母音序排列)

智库名称	PAI	P 值	A 值	I 值
安徽财经大学安徽经济发展研究院	973.1	1687	428	6
安徽大学创新发展研究院	995.55	1861.5	216	0
北京联合大学北京学研究基地	253.2	462	48	39
重庆工商大学长江上游经济研究中心	257.1	363	252	0
重庆智库	164.35	327.5	2	0
广东外语外贸大学广东国际战略研究院	1066.9	1847	436	63
广东外语外贸大学粤港澳大湾区研究院	298.4	404	276	68
广州大学广州发展研究院	205.35	326.5	101	59
河北工业大学京津冀发展研究中心	1037.3	1822	421	0
华东师范大学长三角区域一体化研究中心	245.95	423.5	114	0
华东师范大学中国现代城市研究中心	1070.35	1377.5	1000	408
淮阴工学院苏北发展研究院	336.1	671	2	0
黄河科技学院中国(河南)创新发展研究院	534.4	478	540	667
江苏省社会科学院区域现代化研究院	341.85	644.5	60	8
江西师范大学江西经济发展研究院	165.95	274.5	95	1
江西师范大学苏区振兴研究院	455.1	764	129	172
南通大学江苏长江经济带研究院	418.05	602.5	116	410
内蒙古自治区发展研究中心	1263.3	2339	198	172
区域现代化研究院	272.5	545	0	0
陕西师范大学中国旅游研究院西部旅游发展研究基地	187.2	353	33	4
上海交通大学中国城市治理研究院	403.45	423.5	575	96
西北大学中国西部经济发展研究中心	193.15	276.5	121	93
盐城师范学院沿海发展智库	255.5	466	65	15
浙江大学中国西部发展研究院	377.45	644.5	184	0
中南财经政法大学城乡社区社会管理湖北省协同创新中心	8934.3	15181	3364	1673

（八）法律与司法政策

习近平总书记在中央全面依法治国委员会第一次会议上提到，"要紧紧抓住全面依法治国的关键环节，完善立法体制，提高立法质量。要推进严格执法，理顺执法体制，完善行政执法程序，全面落实行政执法责任制。要支持司法机关依法独立行使职权，健全司法权力分工负责、相互配合、相互制约的制度安排。要加大全民普法力度，培育全社会办事依法、遇事找法、解决问题用法、化解矛盾靠法的法治环境"。科学立法、严格执法、公正司法、全民守法，推进依法治国一直是国家治理现代化的重要举措。法律与司法政策研究领域内智库针对立法、司法、执法、守法各项重要议题，依托相关专业学科开展了不同方向的研究与决策咨询，表 11.8 展示了 PAI 值较高的 20家智库。

领域内不乏研究法治发展宏观战略的智库，中南财经政法大学法治发展与司法改革研究中心是其中重要代表之一。研究中心按照"高起点、跨越式、重协同、建机制"的思路，为中央和地方立法与决策提供高质量的咨询服务。研究中心重点关注社会治理法治研究、基本公共服务保障法治研究、公共安全法治保障研究、网络社会治理法研究、法治评估研究、司法体制改革等重要研究方向，产出了许多重要成果。其中，《检察长列席审判委员会制度的探索与发展》是研究中心的重要成果之一，该文就检察长列席审判委员会制度等重大问题进行了深入研究，为深化落实这一制度提供了可借鉴思路，最后该文被最高检察院《领导参阅件》采用，被纳入重要立法建议。

南京师范大学中国法治现代化研究院也是研究法治发展宏观战略的重要智库之一。该院重点围绕推进法治中国建设、深化法治江苏建设的重要理论和实践问题，深入开展法治发展战略、法治政府、法治社会、司法改革与现代化、中国法治国情调查等领域的理论和决策咨询研究。该院不仅在《人民日报》《光明日报》《求是》等国家级主流媒体上发表理论文章，还积极组织"学习贯彻党的十九大精神"智库报告会、"把社会主义核心价值观融入法治建设"智库报告会、"让法治成为江苏发展核心竞争力的重要标志"智库研讨会、"新时代社会主要矛盾深刻变化与法治现代化"高端智库论坛等重要活动,不断提高智库的知名度和影响力。

此外,部分智库依托自身优势,不断向专业化、精准化、精确化方向发展,在研究问题上做准做精,为专门法律领域提供强有力的智力支持,如知识产权研究、环境法研究等。中南财经政法大学知识产权研究中心是研究知识产权的杰出代表之一,其积极参与国家和地方的立法和司法咨询,承担实际部门的应用研究课题,采取多种形式为社会提供法律服务和法律咨询,致力打造全国知识产权研究的"思想库"和咨询服务基地。天津大学国家知识产权战略实施研究基地、广东中策知识产权研究院等也是知识产权研究方向的重要智库,这些智库的精品成果都为知识产权强国建设提供了重要的参考借鉴。在环境法研究方向中,武汉大学环境法研究所成绩显著,其作为我国环境法治建设的重要智库,在国家环境法治建设中起到了极其重要的作用,先后承担了全国人大、国家发改委、环境保护部、国土资源部、水利部委托的重要项目,经常性地向国家立法机关、行政部门和司法机关提出关于国外环境法的最新研究成果及相关信息,还密切跟踪国际环境公约和谈判的动态,多次派员参与《联合国海洋法公约》《生物多样性公约》《国际汞公约》等国际条约相关议题的现场谈判和对案准备等工作。研究所还成为国内环境法学术交流的重要力量,先后创办"珞珈环境法论坛""珞珈环境法讲坛""珞珈环境法茶座"等高端学术交流平台。

表 11.8　法律与司法政策 PAI 值评分 Top20

（按名称首字母音序排列）

智库名称	PAI	P 值	A 值	I 值
北京大学国际知识产权研究中心	179.55	202.5	261	0
广东外语外贸大学区域一体化法治研究中心	200.5	342	97	2
广东外语外贸大学土地法制研究院	155.35	128.5	303	1
广东中策知识产权研究院	165.85	275.5	55	58
华东政法大学司法学研究院	118.4	226	18	0

智库名称	PAI	P 值	A 值	I 值
华南理工大学广东省地方立法研究评估与咨询服务基地	143.2	286	0	1
吉林大学犯罪治理研究中心	137.25	274.5	0	0
南京理工大学江苏省知识产权发展研究中心	117.5	134	161	11
南京师范大学中国法治现代化研究院	1336.05	2410.5	436	0
深圳大学港澳基本法研究中心	537.4	435	569	746
天津大学国家知识产权战略实施研究基地	374.3	353	654	8
武汉大学国际法研究所	2330.8	4616	76	0
武汉大学环境法研究所	385.75	663.5	180	0
中南财经政法大学法治发展与司法改革研究中心	873.9	998	379	1306
中南财经政法大学知识产权研究中心	936.4	1437	599	191
中南大学教育立法研究基地	122.7	177	114	0
中南大学人权研究中心	123.85	130.5	148	71
中南大学医疗卫生法研究中心	118.75	136.5	157	17
中南大学知识产权研究院	248.2	269	249	195
中南大学中国文化法研究中心	261.3	364	225	59

（九）公共安全领域

公共安全是总体国家安全的重要组成部分,以保障人民生命财产安全、社会安定有序和经济社会系统的持续运行为核心目标。习近平总书记在中共中央政治局第二十三次集体学习中强调,要牢固树立安全发展理念,自觉把维护公共安全放在维护最广大人民的根本利益中来认识,扎实做好公共安全工作,努力为人民安居乐业、社会安定有序、国家长治久安编织全方位、立体化的公共安全网。部分智库紧紧围绕国家或地区公共安全领域重大需求,结合自身优势和特色,为各项公共安全决策的制定出谋划策,提供解决公共安全问题的理论基础和技术发展方向。表 11.9 展示了领域内PAI 值较高的 5 家智库。

江苏警官学院江苏省公共安全研究院充分发挥公安智库与公安政法机关紧密联系的体制优势，突出专业优长和服务实战的价值导向，高质量推进智库建设。该院着力打造国际执法安全合作与海外利益保护研究特色品牌，完成了 14 个国家国情分析、安全风险与执法安全合作研究报告和 3 个国家警务体制研究报告。另外，该院通过开办国内警务研究交流的品牌活动"中国现代警务改革论坛"，成为凝聚各方智库为公安工作献计献策的重要平台。该院还重视理论创新与舆论引导，加强与媒体合作，讲好平安中国建设故事，围绕党的十九大、全国公安工作会议、十九届四中全会等重大活动，及时召开智库研讨会，组织专家第一时间发声，有效引导舆论。

随着我国经济社会的快速发展，保障食品安全是当前全面贯彻落实科学发展观、建设和谐社会的重要内容之一，也是一项非常紧迫的公共安全治理工作。江南大学食品安全风险治理研究院致力食品安全风险治理问题研究，立足现实场景和具体问题，通过实证调查与案例分析，展开系列研究，取得了一系列重要成果。该院发表的《从农田到餐桌，如何保证"舌尖上的安全"——我国食品安全风险治理及形势分析》系统梳理了我国食品安全治理的生动实践和创新举措，深入分析了食品安全面临的严峻挑战，提出了相关对策建议，成果全文刊载于《光明日报》，后又被"求是网"、《新华文摘》、"环球网"等重要媒体转载，产生了较广泛的影响力。

表 11.9 公共安全领域 PAI 值评分 Top5

（按名称首字母音序排列）

智库名称	PAI	P 值	A 值	I 值
公安部现代警务改革研究所	631.6	904	560	58
江南大学食品安全风险治理研究院	800.6	1187	239	677
江苏警官学院江苏省公共安全研究院	925.8	1440	596	135
天津科技大学食品安全战略与管理研究中心	104.85	138.5	92	40
中国人民公安大学首都社会安全研究基地	162.4	275	79	6

（十）文化政策领域

文化是民族生存和发展的重要力量。党的十八大以来，以习近平同志为核心的党中央坚持社会主义先进文化前进方向，以坚定的文化自信和高度的文化自觉大力建设社会主义文化强国。领域内智库围绕文化发展的新问题、新要求，开展民族文化、地方文化、语言文化、建筑文化、传媒、历史等多个方面的政策研究，为坚定文化自信、锐意进取创新，推动文化体制深入改革建言献策。表 11.10 展示了 PAI 值较高的 20 家智库。

东南大学道德发展智库立足人文科学、社会科学、自然科学的交叉研究与理论整合，聚焦"道德国情与道德前沿"，研究和解决中国伦理道德发展的重大理论和现实问题。成立至今，该智库在政府决策咨询、高端理论研究、道德国情调查、高端研究报告、国际合作交流、高端学术论坛等方面业已取得丰硕成果。最具标志性的原创成果是"中国道德国情大型数据库建设"项目，包括《中国伦理道德发展数据库》和《江苏省道德发展状况测评体系》两项内容。同时，为了更好地吸收国内外资深专家学者的理论建议、倾听政府部门的决策意见、探讨道德发展的现实难题，该智库举办"道德发展智库月系列活动"，扩大了智库理论成果影响力，拓宽了智库成果转化途径。

湖北大学中华文化发展湖北省协同创新中心是"文化传承类"省级协同创新中心。近年来，该中心紧紧围绕"文化发展"做文章，不断凝聚学术队伍，搭建协同创新平台，打造了《文化发展报告》系列蓝皮书、文化发展系列集刊、思想文化史书系、《资政建言》、举办文化发展论坛和大型学术会议、建设中华文化发展智库平台等 6 大品牌。以文化发展论坛和大型学术会议为例，该中心已成功举办了 7 届"世界文化发展论坛"、6 届"中国文化发展论坛"、3 届"湖北文化发展论坛"。同时，举办"首届美德伦理高端论坛""深入推进中华优秀传统文化传承发展工程湖北实施专家专题研讨会""中国特色哲学社会科学体系建设座谈会""第二届中国社会科学伦理学专家高端论坛""国际价值哲学论坛"等高层次国际、国内学术会议 70 余场。

苏州大学东吴智库文化与社会发展研究院以高度的文化使命和文化自觉，主动承担东吴文脉和江南文脉传承发展的重要使命。近年来，为抓紧保护和抢救苏州现有文化资源，东吴智库采用口述史研究方法，对现有苏州名家进行访谈记录并制作专题片。现已推出"东吴名家·艺术家系列""东吴名家·名医系列"丛书和纪录片 10 余部。此外，"对话苏州"系列活动是该智库的品牌活动，旨在加强学术界和实务界的有效沟通，实现学者、党政领导和企业家的直接对话和交流，现已持续举办 5 年，成为苏州市委、市政府确立发展战略、制定发展规划、实现科学决策的重要学术咨询平台，也是推动智政对话互动、促进苏州创新发展的重要品牌。

表 11.10 文化政策领域智库 PAI 值评分 Top20

（按名称首字母音序排列）

智库名称	PAI	P 值	A 值	I 值
北京大学国家对外文化交流研究基地	142.7	128	75	281
北京外国语大学北京中外文化交流研究基地	177.8	262	156	0
北京外国语大学国际中国文化研究院	916	1424	680	0
北京外国语大学国家语言能力发展研究中心	242.15	443.5	68	0
东南大学道德发展智库	606.85	993.5	337	45
湖北大学中华文化发展湖北省协同创新中心	192.2	274	184	0
湖南师范大学道德文化研究院	417	627	299	69
华东师范大学中国现代思想文化研究所	183.5	313	90	0
南京大屠杀史与国际和平研究院	492.75	646.5	551	21
南京艺术学院紫金文创研究院	230.05	216.5	406	0
内蒙古大学蒙古学研究中心	173.45	317.5	21	42
陕西师范大学西北历史环境与经济社会发展研究院	114.1	144	97	65
上海外国语大学中国外语战略研究中心	122.3	228	27	1
苏州大学东吴智库文化与社会发展研究院	457.8	909	11	0
天津大学中国文化遗产保护国际研究中心	125.25	250.5	0	0
武汉大学国家文化发展研究院	292	578	10	0

续表

智库名称	PAI	P值	A值	I值
武汉大学媒体发展研究中心	741.2	805	1037	138
西藏民族大学西藏文化传承发展协同创新中心	414.05	795.5	39	23
中南大学中国村落文化研究中心	181.55	344.5	9	33
中南大学中国作协网络文学委员会中南大学研究基地	104.45	165.5	45	41

（十一）教育政策领域

　　教育智库作为中国特色新型智库的重要构成，在服务国家教育决策、促进教育改革发展中发挥着重要作用。新时代中国特色新型教育智库扮演着教育决策的智囊团、教育改革的思想库、教育政策的评论员、教育实践的引导者、教育发展的评估者、高端人才的储备库、教育交流的联络站、正面舆论的策源地等多重角色，并发挥有咨政建言、理论创新、实践引领、人才培养、数据储备、舆论引导等主要功能。[①] 表11.11展示了该领域内PAI值较高的10家智库。

　　华东师范大学国家教育宏观政策研究院站在国家宏观战略的高度，以国家重大需要为导向，针对经济产业布局、社会发展与制度创新等重大问题，从经济、产业、区域、社会等多角度全方位地对教育问题开展综合研究。研究院创办有《国际教育政策观察》《教育信息观察》等刊物，撰写专著《中国经济转型中高等教育资源配置的制度创新》等十余本。此外，依托国家教育决策支持系统，研究院在三区三州精准扶贫、教师编制问题研究、公民办教师待遇调查、长三角教育一体化研究、长江经济带教育创新研究、全国教师数据分析等方面，近2年先后提交80余篇专报，获国家领导、教育部和上海市领导批示近60次，10余篇研究报告被各级政府采纳。

---

① 中国昌，程功群.中国特色新型教育智库的角色定位及建设路径[J].教育文化论坛,2019(1)：130-130.

　　基于教育大数据推动教育实践改进、发挥教育监测评价对教育决策的支撑作用是当前教育改革与发展的重要趋势。中国基础教育质量监测协同创新中心连续多年承担了教育部委托的国家义务教育质量监测工作,通过组织专业力量分析各省监测结果,提炼各省存在的主要问题,向国家、地方各级教育行政部门持续提供教育质量监测结果报告,积极探索推动各级政府运用监测结果提升教育治理水平、促进教育内涵发展的路径,形成了"监测—反馈—整改—提升"的闭环式工作机制,推动了省政府对地方教育的治理。

　　浙江大学中国科教战略研究院始终瞄准国际工程教育发展前沿,立足国内新工科建设,聚焦工程教育改革,开展特色智库研究工作。该院与中国工程院教育委员会合作编译的《国际工程教育前沿与进展》是国内第一本译介国际工程教育研究进展的主题刊物,内容分为研究报告、前沿观察、会议预告、活动要闻和报刊文摘五个版块,报道国外工程教育研究与政策的最新发展动态,为国内从事工程教育研究和实践的专家学者、政策制定与相关管理者提供参考借鉴。

表 11.11　教育政策领域智库 PAI 值评分 Top10

（按名称首字母排序）

智库名称	PAI	P 值	A 值	I 值
北京师范大学中国教育与社会发展研究院	1762.9	3524	3	0
北京师范大学国际与比较教育研究院	249	453	75	0
北京师范大学中国基础教育质量监测协同创新中心	337.65	313.5	603	0
华东师范大学国家教育宏观政策研究院	848.05	1276.5	480	329
华东师范大学基础教育改革与发展研究所	300.5	453	206	61
华东师范大学课程与教学研究所	464.35	699.5	382	0
厦门大学高等教育发展研究中心	380.7	731	28	34
上海师范大学国际与比较教育研究院	249.35	347.5	252	0
长江教育研究院	264.9	522	13	0
浙江大学中国科教战略研究院	396.1	682	163	31

（十二）生态文明领域

　　坚持和完善生态文明制度体系，促进人与自然和谐共生是党的十九届四中全会做出的重要指示。生态文明建设是关系中华民族永续发展的千年大计，必须践行绿水青山就是金山银山的理念，坚持节约资源和保护环境的基本国策，坚持节约优先、保护优先、自然恢复为主的方针，坚定走生产发展、生活富裕、生态良好的文明发展道路，建设美丽中国。该领域智库不断总结传统发展过程中的弊端，创新发展思路，为生态文明体系的建设贡献智力支持。表 11.12 展示了领域内 PAI 值较高的 10 家智库。

　　南京信息工程大学气候与环境治理研究院聚焦气候变化与环境治理的科学问题、经济发展问题以及公共政策问题，重点围绕气候变化、环境污染、雾霾治理、低碳发展、气候政策和生态文化六个方面展开学术研究、决策咨询和政策服务，在气候与环境治理领域发出江苏声音，支撑国家决策。智库研究关注气候变化的全球化，从国际化的视角看待气候变化的影响以及污染防治方法，从法律、经济、道德基础、外交政策等视角展开深入探讨。在中国社会科学出版社、科学出版社等权威出版社出版发行《正义的排放：全球气候治理的道德基础研究》《中国参与国际气候合作的价值立场研究》等近 10 部著作。

　　国家海洋局海洋发展战略研究所下设海洋权益与法律、海洋政策与管理、海洋经济与科技、海洋环境与资源四个研究室，在海洋发展战略、政策、法律、权益和海洋经济、环境资源等研究领域取得多项研究成果。多年来，研究所及其专家一直参加各类双边与多边海洋法律事务的外交磋商，为政府相关部门提供法律与政策咨询服务。该研究院组织专家起草了《中国海洋 21 世纪议程》《中国海洋事业的发展》《全国海洋经济发展规划纲要》《海南省海洋经济发展规划》《中国海域海洋划界研究》《中国专属经济区和大陆架政策图集》《海洋国策研究文集》等重要文件。除了出版著作和公开发表论文外，研究所每年度《中国海洋发展报告》的发布暨中国海洋发展高层论坛，受到政府机构、学术界以及社会的重视和高度评价。

表 11.12　生态文明领域智库 PAI 值评分 Top10

（按名称首字母排序）

智库名称	PAI	P 值	A 值	I 值
成都理工大学自然灾害防治与地质环境保护研究智库	383.6	682	142	0
国家海洋局海洋发展战略研究所	126.5	250	5	0
湖南师范大学生态环境保护法治研究中心	166.75	279.5	90	0
济南大学山东龙山绿色经济研究中心	97.25	185.5	15	0
暨南大学广州区域低碳经济研究基地	97.05	120.5	110	19
暨南大学资源环境与可持续发展研究所	128.25	213.5	65	10
江西财经大学江西省生态文明制度建设协同创新中心	155.1	247	100	8
南京信息工程大学气候与环境治理研究院	168	303	55	0
上海交通大学国家海洋战略与权益研究基地	89	64	150	60
浙江理工大学浙江省生态文明研究中心	435.05	686.5	272	51

（十三）能源与基础设施领域

　　能源行业的创新发展，需要强化基础研究，拓展实施若干重大科技项目，突出关键共性技术、现代工程技术。[①] 基础设施的发展是区域经济发展的重要条件。近年来，该领域智库立足自身优势，积极开展相关研究，表 11.13 选取了 PAI 值较高的 8 家智库。

　　北京交通发展研究中心于 2002 年 1 月经北京市委、市政府批准成立。研究中心的主要职责是开展北京城市交通发展战略、政策和规划的研究。该研究中心设立了城市交通运行仿真与决策支持北京市重点实验室、城市交通节能减排检测与评估北京市重点实验室、城市交通北京市国际科技合作基地、国家能源计量中心（城市交

---

　　① 张晓强.坚持创新开放合作　推动中国基础设施和能源产业高质量发展[J].全球化,2018(11):5-10,132.

通），于 2006 年通过了 ISO 9001 认证，以其雄厚的技术实力及现代化的管理，为北京市政府及相关部门提供了高质量的咨询服务，为北京创建现代化交通体系提供了强有力的技术支持。同属于北京交通大学的北京物流信息化与服务科学研究基地，承担了国家自然基金重大、重点项目、国家"973"项目、国家"863"计划等各类项目 160余项，累计科研经费 3400 余万元；取得了国家级科技进步奖 1 项（2010 年）、北京市科学技术奖三等奖 2 项（2012 年、2003 年）、商业科技进步奖一等奖 1 项（2008 年）等重要奖项。研究基地为北京市"十五""十一五"和"十二五"物流发展规划的制定等提供的决策咨询服务，为国家和北京市的物流和信息领域的重大服务科学问题做出突出贡献，并逐步形成了鲜明特色的物流和信息化理论与方法体系——新兴 IT 技术下物流管理与工程理论与方法。

电力规划设计总院（简称"电规总院"）是一所具有 60 多年发展历程的国家级高端咨询机构，是中央编办登记管理的事业单位，主要面向政府部门、金融机构、能源及电力企业提供产业政策、发展战略、发展规划、新技术研究以及工程项目的评审、咨询和技术服务和组织开展科研标准化、信息化、国际交流与合作等工作。结合服务政府、行业的定位和长远发展需要，电规总院提出了"能源智囊、国家智库"的发展愿景和建设"国家级高端能源咨询机构和专业智库"的战略目标。近年来先后完成国家"十三五"能源发展规划、电力发展规划能源国际合作专项研究和雄安新区能源发展规划等重大规划研究，参与国家与地方、能源电力体制改革等重要政策研究，承担能源电力监管的支持性任务，组织落实行业重大系统性工程，深度参与能源国际合作，为建设绿色低碳、安全高效的现代能源体系提供了高质量的智库研究支持。未来，电规总院将以智慧为核心，以创新为动力，努力打造成世界一流的能源智库和国际咨询公司，与各界同仁携手努力，共同推进全球能源向清洁低碳可持续发展转型，促进人类永续发展。

表 11.13　能源与基础设施领域 PAI 值评分 Top8

（按名称首字母音序排列）

智库名称	PAI	P 值	A 值	I 值
北京交通大学北京交通发展研究基地	1338.25	1643.5	1721	1
北京交通大学北京物流信息化研究基地	177.25	210.5	240	0
电力规划设计总院	715.65	1198.5	388	0
国网能源研究院	504.05	914.5	156	0
南方电网能源发展研究院有限责任公司	139.75	210.5	115	0
上海海事大学上海国际航运研究中心	840.05	1426.5	350	109
天津大学亚太经合组织可持续能源中心	220.95	188.5	421	2
西安交通大学陕西经济研究中心	139.7	231	72	13

（十四）信息与科技领域

进入 21 世纪以来，面对世界科技革命和产业变革的新形势，站在我国发展的新起点，习近平总书记做出"中国要强盛、要复兴，就一定要大力发展科学技术，努力成为世界主要科学中心和创新高地"的重要判断，强调"实现建成社会主义现代化强国的伟大目标，实现中华民族伟大复兴的中国梦，我们必须具有强大的科技实力和创新能力""要打通基础研究和技术创新衔接的绿色通道，力争以基础研究带动应用技术群体突破"。近年来，通过实施核心技术攻坚战略，我国在多项网络信息技术的研发与应用上取得突破。根据信息与科技领域智库填报的数据，系统自动计算出 PAI 值较高的 15 家智库，如表 11.14 所示。

其中，作为高校智库的华东师范大学全球创新与发展研究院致力科技全球化与中国创新、地缘科技与国家安全等方面的战略研究，近年来面向国家重大战略需求，持续深入地进行全局性、基础性、前瞻性研究，并随时承接相关领域的国家课题，为中央和国家科学决策服务，为解决重大现实问题提供理论支撑。

同为高校智库的南京航空航天大学工业和信息化智库评价中心紧密围绕工业和

信息化系统的重大问题及智库评价展开学术研究，为工信系统的重要问题及智库的绩效评价提供精准数据和决策支持，打造新型高校智库研究平台，有效促进工信系统智库事业的发展。为充分发挥资源优势和情报分析优势，评价中心对43万余篇人工智能领域研究论文的外部特征和内容特征进行可视化分析，深入挖掘了该学科国内外发展态势，为"双一流"背景下的人工智能学科发展提供了精准数据和决策支持。此研究的部分成果已撰写为论文《ESI高被引论文视角下人工智能研究的发展与创新》并获得2019年度江苏省科技情报学会成果一等奖、华东科学技术情报成果二等奖。

江西省科学院科技战略研究所围绕省委省政府重大决策及江西省经济和社会发展对科技的需求，为全省各级政府、行业企业、科研院所、高等院校等社会各界提供科技战略研究、科技咨询、科技查新及知识产权分析评议等科技服务，为江西省科技、经济、社会发展的宏观决策、创新驱动发展提供有效支撑。同时，为更好地提供服务，研究所先后与中科院科技战略咨询研究院、中科院文献情报中心、中国科学技术发展战略研究院等建立合作关系，实现了科技情报资源的共享、专家人员的互动交流和科研项目的协同攻关。

作为企业智库，阿里研究院依托阿里巴巴集团海量数据、深耕中小企业前沿案例、集结全球商业智慧，以开放、合作、共建、共创的方式打造具有影响力的商业知识平台。其口号为"阿里研究，洞察数据，共创新知"。研究院自2007年4月成立以来，与业界顶尖学者、机构紧密合作，聚焦电子商务生态、产业升级、宏观经济等研究领域，共同推出 SPI-core、SPI、EDI、CCI 及数据地图等多个创新性数据产品、大量信息经济领域研究报告，以及数千个经典小企业案例总结。面对数字经济发展带来的治理问题，阿里研究院通过举办新经济智库大会，聚焦新技术、新经济、新治理、新智库、新担当、大未来等关键议题，深入思考数字经济的价值测度、创新与竞争等问题，交流探讨关于数字经济和治理的前沿思考与重大洞见，为阿里乃至社会的数字经济发展提供理论支撑。

表 11.14   信息与科技领域智库 PAI 值评分 Top15

（按名称首字母音序排列）

智库名称	PAI	P 值	A 值	I 值
阿里研究院	91	176	10	0
杭州电子科技大学浙江省信息化发展研究院	59	110	12	2
湖南省科技战略研究中心	58.25	116.5	0	0
华东师范大学全球创新与发展研究院	410.6	761	87	20
华南理工大学重大科技项目与平台实施效果第三方评估智库	121.8	231	21	0
淮北师范大学安徽省高校管理大数据研究中心	104.35	150.5	97	0
吉林大学中国科技政策与科技管理研究中心	90	132	80	0
江西省科学院科技战略研究所	519	1017	35	0
南京航空航天大学工业和信息化智库评价中心	177.2	322	54	0
清华大学技术创新研究中心	60.9	93	48	0
山东省科技发展战略研究所	124.15	166.5	89	71
乌镇智库	103	142	100	10
武汉大学发展研究院	96.6	192	2	0
中国科学院科技战略咨询研究院	50.5	101	0	0
中智科学技术评价研究中心	104	208	0	0

（十五）扶贫政策与"三农"问题

党的十九大报告指出,农业农村农民问题是关系国计民生的根本性问题,必须始终把解决好"三农"问题作为全党工作的重中之重。2019 年的中央一号文件强调,要牢固树立农业农村优先发展政策导向,把落实"四个优先"的要求作为做好"三农"工作的头等大事,优先考虑"三农"干部配备,优先保障"三农"资金投入,优先安排农村公共服务。根据扶贫政策与"三农"领域智库填报的数据,表 11.15 展示了领域内PAI 值较高的 10 家智库。

华中师范大学中国农村研究院是从事农村与农民问题研究的专门性学术机构,

也是教育部人文社会科学百所重点研究基地之一。研究院坚持以田野调查为基础，以实证研究为导向，承担了一系列国家重大课题，产出了一批高水平研究成果。特别是自 2010 年以来研究院连续七年均在《中国社会科学》(中英文版)发表学术论文，其中中文发表 6 篇，占政治学学科总发文量的 22.2%，学术影响力较大。目前，研究院已经形成了"一主三辅"为主要架构的田野调查体系，调查类型涵盖"百村观察"、村庄调查、家户调查、口述史调查等，并同步建立起拥有海量农村调查资料的数据存储平台"中国农村发展智库系统"。

浙江大学中国农村发展研究院成立于 1999 年，全称为浙江大学农业现代化与农村发展研究中心，英文简称"CARD"，中文简称"卡特"，是国家教育部首批建设的国家人文社会科学重点研究基地，也是直属浙江大学的一个跨学科、开放性的教学科研和政策咨询机构。浙大"卡特"的发展目标是：以习近平新时代中国特色社会主义思想为指引，以服务国家"三农"发展重大战略为导向，以平台建设为载体，以人才培养为根本，以科学研究为抓手，以体制机制为保障，以学科交叉融合为路径，立足浙江、服务全国、辐射全球，推动农林经济管理与相关学科的交叉融合，通过若干年努力，建设成为拥有世界一流学科、一流科研水平和一流社会服务能力的人文社科研究基地和高端专业智库。

党的十九届四中全会提出深化农村集体产权制度改革，发展农村经济，完善农村基本经营制度。安徽农业现代化研究院是安徽农业大学汇聚多学科智力资源、协同多家研究机构建立的"三农问题"的综合智力服务平台。研究院积极围绕中央"三农"领域重点工作内容展开研究，形成了多项研究成果，得到当地政府的认可和采纳。研究院将进一步发挥多学科交叉研究的优势，广泛整合各类资源，形成集战略谋划、前瞻研判、资政启智、政策评估、舆论引导于一体的高端专业智库，着力打造安徽省委、省政府农业现代化建设决策咨询的"思想库"和安徽省各级政府和有关部门制定"三农"政策的"智囊团"。

表 11.15　扶贫政策与"三农"领域智库 PAI 值评分 Top10

（按名称首字母音序排列）

智库名称	PAI	P 值	A 值	I 值
安徽农业大学安徽农业现代化研究院	311.25	616.5	10	0
东北农业大学现代农业发展研究中心	126.75	201.5	60	40
东北师范大学中国农村教育发展研究院	176.9	331	38	0
湖南省农村发展研究院	64	128	0	0
华中师范大学中国农村研究院	4389.3	8391	626	30
吉首大学民族地区扶贫与发展研究中心	52.65	85.5	33	0
南京农业大学金善宝农业现代化研究院	249.5	499	0	0
西北师范大学精准扶贫与区域发展研究中心	54.9	105	8	0
浙江大学中国农村发展研究院	645.9	789	504	501
浙江农林大学中国农民发展研究中心	67.6	122	22	0

（十六）"一带一路"领域

自"一带一路"提出以来，"一带一路"从倡议变为行动，从理念转化为实践，如今已成为当今世界规模最大的国际合作平台和最受欢迎的国际公共产品。"一带一路"强调互联互通，合作共赢，"政策沟通、设施联通、贸易畅通、资金融通、民心相通"这"五通"不断推动"一带一路"沿线国家深化多方面合作交流。至今，"一带一路"倡议仍然是国家发展的重要议题，也是许多智库研究的重点话题。根据"一带一路"领域智库填报的数据，表 11.16 展示了领域内 PAI 值较高的 10 家智库。

西安交通大学"一带一路"自由贸易试验区研究院以"服务陕西，立足西部，面向中国，全球视野"为宗旨，在陕西省委省政府的大力支持下，整合国内外优质智力资源，通过制度创新与任务牵引，探索形成"多边、开放、创新、共享"的政智共生、资政启智的生态平台。研究院相关研究成果通过《要情专报》《决策建言》（西安交大自贸区研究院专刊）等渠道呈送国家和省市有关部门，有力促进了"中央法务区"、知识产权证券化交易所建设构想的落地,切实推动自贸试验区重点工作。另外,本着"开放、包容、创新、协调、互补"的理念,研究院举办了"中国(陕西)自由贸易试验区发展论坛",为政、产、学、研、用搭建前沿高端智库交流平台,还组织专家参加国务院参事室、新华社中国经济信息社、海南省社会科学界联合会及各级政府部门、研究机构举办的专题研讨会,不断提供高质量的决策咨询服务。

北京第二外国语学院中国"一带一路"战略研究院直接为"新丝绸之路经济带"和"21世纪海上丝绸之路"国家战略服务,搭建广阔的国际合作交流平台。研究院在"一带一路"沿线国家和地区围绕国别研究、投资与安全、人文与外交、语言战略与政策长期等方向开展长期研究,以"一带一路"研究简报、"一带一路"蓝皮书、"一带一路"论坛、"一带一路"课题等形式重点服务中央和国家部委及"一带一路"沿线国家使领馆,充分发挥了自身在"一带一路"的互联互通工程中的决策咨询作用,为"一带一路"建设提供了核心支持。

国观智库成立于2013年,是国内有名的独立智库之一。智库坚持"行知·致远"的发展理念,用知行合一、行稳致远的态度和时间致力于中国的安全、繁荣和稳定,研究领域聚焦于"一带一路"倡议和境外投资、海洋战略与蓝色经济、边疆治理与全球反恐。国观智库坚持"应用研究为导向、信息研究为基础"的研究思维,组建起一支上百人的研究队伍,通过独立报告、政府专报、媒体内参等形式为决策层建言献策,并参与外交部、发改委、国家海洋局等众多中央政府的相关重大战略课题研究,其研究成果得到决策层的高度肯定。同时,国观智库作为研究"一带一路"领域的智库,构建了国内第一个全球海洋战略舆情环境研究体系及数据库,并积极推动"一带一路"沿线国合作与发展系列对话会,实现智库职能的"知行合一"。

表 11.16 "一带一路"领域智库 PAI 值评分 Top10

（按名称首字母音序排列）

智库名称	PAI	P 值	A 值	I 值
北京第二外国语学院中国"一带一路"战略研究院	231.85	268.5	254	107
复旦大学一带一路及全球治理研究院	142.4	127	175	132
国观智库	148.3	110	235	114
海南大学"一带一路"研究院	165.05	116.5	158	297
江苏师范大学"一带一路"研究院	209.6	324	156	4
内蒙古财经大学中蒙俄经济走廊研究协同创新中心	636.1	1031	402	0
西安交通大学"一带一路"自由贸易试验区研究院	367.35	583.5	142	165
云南大学"一带一路"沿线国家民族问题智库	197.75	386.5	15	0
浙江万里学院宁波海上丝绸之路研究院	108.9	101	194	1
中国丝路智谷研究院	310.6	235	369	412

（十七）综合型智库

除了上文提及的 16 大主要研究领域之外，还有一类综合型的智库，主要由各个地方党校/行政学院、社会科学院等组成。综合型智库与其他领域智库不同，往往展开的是跨学科、多领域、综合性的研究。CTTI 来源智库共有 51 家综合型智库，各省社科院在 51 家综合型智库中占 61%。

天津社会科学院按照中央关于构建中国特色哲学社会科学的指示精神和天津市委的要求，在习近平新时代中国特色社会主义思想指引下，以智库建设为中心，努力将自身建设成坚强的马克思主义理论阵地、哲学社会科学研究基地、综合性高端智库。该院现设有天津市中国特色社会主义理论体系研究中心、天津市舆情研究中心、市情研究中心、天津历史文化研究中心、京津冀协同发展研究中心、社会治理研究中心、东北亚区域合作研究中心 7 个智库型研究中心。在多个智库型研究中心的支撑下，天津社会科学院承担了一大批国家和天津市的研究课题，多次受到国家和天津市的各种奖励。此外，该院也十分重视学术交流，与国内外高校和科研机构建立广泛的学术联系，与俄罗斯、日本、韩国等东北亚国家的学术机构开展长期深入的学术交流与合作。

宁夏社会科学院是宁夏回族自治区唯一的综合性哲学社会科学研究机构，是自治区重要的哲学社会科学研究基地。宁夏社科院主办有《宁夏社会科学》《回族研究》《西夏研究》3 个学术期刊和《宁夏史志》《新智库》2 个内部出版物。该院编发的《决策咨询》《呈阅件》等，发挥着决策建议"直通车"的作用，在体现智库成果多样性、时效性和促进智库成果转化方面，发挥了不可替代的作用。经过多年发展，宁夏社会科学院逐渐形成了以宁夏重大现实问题研究课题为品牌，以蓝皮书为平台，以重大项目为支撑，以修志编史和古籍整理为主要抓手，以学术期刊为重要载体的社科研究体系。宁夏社会科学院现有回族学、西夏学、地方历史文化、应用经济学、社会学、政治学法学、生态文明、文化学、民族文献学九大学科，形成了具有支撑作用、较强优势和具有良好发展前景的基础学科、重点学科和扶持学科，建立了以首席专家、学科带头人、学科骨干为主的多层次学科人才梯队。

河北省社会科学院是河北省委、省政府直属事业单位，是社科研究、理论宣讲机构和社团机构。近年来，该院坚持以习近平新时代中国特殊色社会主义思想为统领，注重学科体系和人才队伍建设，积极发挥学科门类齐全、科研人才密集的优势，主办《河北学刊》《经济论坛》《社会科学论坛》3 本公开发行刊物，以及《河北社会科学》《智库成果专报》《决策参考》等刊物，并与省委宣传部联合主办《党委中心组理论学习通讯》《理论信息》等内部刊物。同时，河北省社会科学院广泛开展国际学术交流与合作，不断提高科研和管理水平，截至目前，已同世界主要国家和港台地区近 30 个科研机构和大学建立起长期稳定的学术交流与合作关系。

各个综合型智库也为促进地区发展，针对地方问题进行了多项调研，多个优秀成果获得了省委领导的肯定性批示并被决策采用。例如，中共黑龙江省委党校（黑龙江行政学院)的《加快黑龙江省煤炭城市转型发展对策研究》《关于促进黑龙江省新型农业经营主体规范发展的建议》、安徽省社科院的《中央和安徽省委重大决策部署舆情信息跟踪研究》、中共山东省委党校(山东行政学院)的《"招才引智"要在精准上下功夫——以滨州吸引大学生"回流"为例》,中共贵州省委党校(贵州行政学院)的《促进民间投资:从深圳做法到贵州建议》《铜仁市思南县易地扶贫搬迁的真正难题及其破解之策》等。

CTTI 来源智库目录（2019）

（按照机构首字母拼音顺序排列，不分先后）

（一）党政部门智库（71家）

北京市信访矛盾分析研究中心

财政部关税政策研究中心

财政部国际财经中心

重庆市经济信息中心（重庆市综合经济研究院）

当代世界研究中心

福建省人民政府发展研究中心

公安部公安发展战略研究所

公安部公安发展战略研究所城市警务研究中心

公安部现代警务改革研究所

国家发展和改革委员会国际合作中心

国家发展和改革委员会宏观经济研究院

国家海洋局海洋发展战略研究所

国家教育发展研究中心

国家市场监督管理总局发展研究中心

国家税务总局税收科学研究所

国家体育总局体育科学研究所

国家卫生计生委卫生发展研究中心

国家卫生计生委医院管理研究所

国家新闻出版广电总局广播影视发展研究中心

国家应对气候变化战略研究和国际合作中心

国家知识产权局知识产权发展研究中心

国土资源部油气资源战略研究中心

国网能源研究院

国务院发展研究中心

河北省财政科学与政策研究所

河北省发展和改革委员会宏观经济研究所

机械工业经济管理研究院

吉林省人民政府发展研究中心

江苏省人民政府研究室

江西省情研究中心

教育部高等学校社会科学发展研究中心

辽宁省人民政府发展研究中心

南京大屠杀史与国际和平研究院

内蒙古自治区发展研究中心

农业部农村经济研究中心

全国党的建设研究会

山东省创新战略研究院

山东省宏观经济研究院

商务部国际贸易经济合作研究院

上海市发展改革研究院

上海市教育科学研究院

上海市浦东改革与发展研究院［中国（上海）自由贸易试验区研究院］

上海市人民政府发展研究中心

生态环境部环境与经济政策研究中心

司法部预防犯罪研究所

天津滨海综合发展研究院

天津市科学学研究所

统一战线高端智库

浙江省发展规划研究院

中共中央编译局

中共中央编译局马克思主义研究部

中共中央编译局世界发展战略研究部

中国财政科学研究院

中国城市和小城镇改革发展中心

中国国际问题研究院

中国国土资源经济研究院

中国教育科学研究院

中国劳动保障科学研究院

中国老龄科学研究中心

中国旅游研究院

中国浦东干部学院长江三角洲研究院

中国浦东干部学院领导研究院

中国浦东干部学院中国特色社会主义研究院

中国青少年研究中心

中国人民银行金融研究所

中国人事科学研究院

中国统计学会（国家统计局统计科学研究所）

中国文化遗产研究院

中国现代国际关系研究院

中国新闻出版研究院

中华人民共和国民政部政策研究中心

（二）社科院智库（51家）

安徽省社会科学院

北京市社会科学院

重庆社会科学院

重庆市生产力发展中心

创新型城市发展与评估研究院

福建省社会科学院

甘肃省社会科学院

广东省社会科学院

广西社会科学院

贵州省社会科学院

海南省社会科学院

河北省社会科学院

河南省社会科学院

黑龙江省社会科学院

黑龙江省社会科学院　东北亚战略研究院

黑龙江省社会科学院　黑龙江社会发展与地方治理研究院

湖北省社会科学院

湖南省社会科学院

吉林省社会科学院

江苏省社会科学院

江苏省社会科学院　区域现代化研究院

江西省社会科学院

辽宁社会科学院

南京市社会科学院

内蒙古社会科学院

宁夏社会科学院

青海省社会科学院

区域现代化研究院

山东社会科学院

陕西省社会科学院

上海社会科学院

四川省社会科学院

天津社会科学院

西藏自治区社会科学院

新疆社会科学院

云南省社会科学院

浙江省社会科学院

中国社会科学院

中国社会科学院财经战略研究院

中国社会科学院当代中国马克思主义政治经济学创新智库

中国社会科学院当代中国研究所

中国社会科学院国家金融与发展实验室

中国社会科学院国家全球战略智库

中国社会科学院欧洲研究所

中国社会科学院上海市人民政府上海研究院

中国社会科学院社会发展战略研究院

中国社会科学院世界经济与政治研究所

中国社会科学院台湾研究所

中国社会科学院意识形态研究智库

中国社会科学院中国文化研究中心

中国社会科学院中国-中东欧国家智库交流与合作网络

（三）党校行政学院智库（49 家）

安徽行政学院安徽省公共政策研究评估中心

甘肃行政学院

国家行政学院

国家行政学院电子政务研究中心

国家行政学院发展战略与公共政策研究中心

国家行政学院决策咨询部

河北行政学院

湖南省科技战略研究中心

山东行政学院

陕西省行政学院

云南跨越式发展研究院

中共安徽省委党校

中共北京市委党校　北京行政学院

中共重庆市委党校　重庆市行政学院

中共福建省委党校　福建行政学院

中共甘肃省委党校

中共广东省委党校　广东行政学院

中共广西区委党校　广西行政学院

中共贵州省委党校　贵州行政学院

中共海南省委党校　海南省行政学院

中共河北省委党校

中共河南省委党校　河南行政学院

中共黑龙江省委党校　黑龙江省行政学院

中共湖北省委党校　湖北省行政学院

中共湖南省委党校　湖南行政学院

中共吉林省委党校　吉林省行政学院

中共江苏省委党校

中共江苏省委党校　江苏党的建设理论与实践创新研究院

中共江西省委党校　江西行政学院

中共辽宁省委党校

中共内蒙古自治区委员会党校　内蒙古自治区行政学院

中共宁夏区委党校　宁夏行政学院

中共青海省委党校　青海省行政学院

中共山东省委党校

中共陕西省委党校

中共上海市委党校　上海行政学院

中共四川省委党校

中共天津市委党校　天津行政学院

中共天津市委党校　新时代创新型与服务型政府建设研究中心

中共天津市委党校　新时代天津党的建设决策研究中心

中共天津市委党校　新时代现代化经济体系建设研究中心

中共西藏自治区委党校　西藏自治区行政学院

中共新疆维吾尔自治区委党校　新疆行政学院

中共浙江省委党校　浙江行政学院

中共中央党校

中共中央党校党的建设教研部

中共中央党校国际战略研究院

中国行政体制改革研究会

中央社会主义学院中国政党制度研究中心

（四）高校智库（572家）

安徽财经大学经济发展研究院

安徽大学创新发展研究院

安徽农业大学安徽农业现代化研究院

北京大学国际战略研究院

北京大学国际知识产权研究中心

北京大学国家对外文化交流研究基地

北京大学国家发展研究院

北京大学国家治理研究院

北京大学汇丰金融研究院

北京大学文化产业研究院

北京大学宪法与行政法研究中心

北京大学中国都市经济研究基地

北京第二外国语学院北京对外文化传播研究基地

北京第二外国语学院北京旅游发展研究基地

北京第二外国语学院首都对外文化贸易研究基地

北京第二外国语学院中国"一带一路"战略研究院

北京服装学院首都服饰文化与服装产业研究基地

北京工业大学北京社会管理研究基地

北京工业大学北京现代制造业发展研究基地

北京航空航天大学高等教育研究院

北京航空航天大学工信部工业和信息化法治战略与管理工信部重点实验室

北京航空航天大学中国航空工程科技发展战略研究院

北京交通大学北京产业安全与发展研究基地

北京交通大学北京交通发展研究基地

北京交通大学北京人文交通、科技交通、绿色交通研究基地

北京交通大学北京物流信息化研究基地

北京交通大学国家经济安全研究院

北京交通大学首都大学生思想政治教育研究基地

北京交通大学中国马克思主义与文化发展研究院

北京理工大学北京经济社会可持续发展研究基地

北京联合大学北京学研究基地

北京农学院北京新农村建设研究基地

北京师范大学国际与比较教育研究院

北京师范大学首都教育经济研究院

北京师范大学首都文化创新与文化传播工程研究院

北京师范大学智慧学习研究院

北京师范大学中国基础教育质量监测协同创新中心

北京师范大学中国教育与社会发展研究院

北京师范大学中国收入分配研究院

北京体育大学冬奥文化研究中心

北京体育大学国家体育总局体育产业研究基地

北京体育大学中华民族传统体育研究院

北京外国语大学北京中外文化交流研究基地

北京外国语大学二十国集团研究中心

北京外国语大学公共外交研究中心

北京外国语大学国际中国文化研究院

北京外国语大学国家语言能力发展研究中心

北京外国语大学海湾阿拉伯国家研究中心

北京外国语大学加拿大研究中心

北京外国语大学日本研究中心

北京外国语大学英国研究中心

北京外国语大学中德人文交流研究中心

北京外国语大学中东欧研究中心

北京外国语大学中外教育法研究中心

北京信息科技大学北京市知识管理研究基地

北京语言大学北京文献语言与文化传承研究基地

成都理工大学四川矿产资源研究中心

成都理工大学自然灾害防治与地质环境保护研究智库

城市绿色发展研究中心

重庆大学城乡建设与发展研究院

重庆大学公共经济与公共政策研究中心

重庆大学国家网络空间安全与大数据法治战略研究院

重庆大学经略研究院

重庆大学可持续发展研究院

重庆大学中国公共服务评测与研究中心

重庆工商大学长江上游经济研究中心

重庆市高校维护稳定研究咨政中心

大理大学云南宗教治理与民族团结进步智库

大连海事大学"一带一路"研究院

大连外国语大学东北亚研究中心

大庆师范学院大庆精神与龙江西部经济社会发展研究中心

东北财经大学经济与社会发展研究院

东北大学中国东北振兴研究院

东北农业大学现代农业发展研究中心

东北师范大学东亚研究院

东北师范大学中国农村教育发展研究院

东南大学道德发展研究院

东南大学反腐败法治研究中心

东南大学江苏省青少年工作研究基地

东南大学江苏省社区矫正损害修复项目研究基地

东南大学交通法治与发展研究中心

东南大学人民法院司法大数据研究基地

东南大学现代管理会计创新研究中心

东南大学艺术大数据与中国艺术发展评价研究中心

东南大学中国高质量发展综合评价研究院

东南大学中国特色社会主义发展研究院

对外经济贸易大学国际经济研究院

对外经济贸易大学国家（北京）对外开放研究院

对外经济贸易大学教育与开放经济研究中心

对外经济贸易大学全球价值链研究院

对外经济贸易大学中国世界贸易组织研究院

福建师范大学竞争力研究中心

复旦大学复旦发展研究院

复旦大学国际问题研究院

复旦大学美国研究中心

复旦大学人口与发展政策研究中心

复旦大学上海市高校智库研究和管理中心

复旦大学亚太区域合作与治理研究中心

复旦大学一带一路及全球治理研究院

复旦大学政党建设与国家发展研究中心

复旦大学中国经济研究中心

复旦大学中国研究院

甘肃政法大学西北民族地区侦查理论与实务研究中心

广东财经大学国民经济研究中心

广东财经大学珠三角科技金融产业协同创新发展中心

广东外语外贸大学广东国际战略研究院

广东外语外贸大学国际移民研究中心

广东外语外贸大学加拿大研究中心

广东外语外贸大学区域一体化法治研究中心

广东外语外贸大学土地法制研究院

广东外语外贸大学外语研究与语言服务协同创新中心

广东外语外贸大学粤港澳大湾区研究院

广西大学广西创新发展研究院

广西大学中国-东盟研究院

广西民族大学广西知识产权发展研究院

广州大学广州发展研究院

贵州大学贵州省大数据产业发展应用研究院

贵州大学中国-东盟研究中心

国际关系学院公共市场与政府采购研究所

国际关系学院国际战略与安全研究中心

哈尔滨工程大学黑龙江区域创新驱动发展研究中心

哈尔滨工业大学"一带一路"人才战略智库

哈尔滨工业大学黑龙江省双创智库

哈尔滨医科大学黑龙江省公共健康安全及医改策略研究智库

海南大学"一带一路"研究院

海南大学海南低碳经济政策与产业技术研究院

海南大学海南国际旅游岛发展研究院

海南大学海南省南海政策与法律研究中心

杭州电子科技大学高教强省发展战略与评价研究中心

杭州电子科技大学浙江省信息化发展研究院

河北大学河北省生态与环境发展研究中心

河北大学河北省文化产业发展研究中心

河北大学跨文化传播研究中心

河北工业大学京津冀发展研究中心

河北金融学院德融研究院

河北经贸大学河北省道德文化与社会发展研究中心

河北经贸大学京津冀一体化发展协同创新中心

河北经贸大学社会管理德治与法治协同创新中心

河北省软科学研究基地:河北师范大学现代服务与公共政策研究基地

河北师范大学长城文化安全研究中心

河南大学中原发展研究院

黑龙江大学黑龙江省文化发展战略研究中心

黑龙江大学龙江振兴发展研究中心

黑龙江大学文化发展战略协同创新高等研究院

黑龙江大学中俄全面战略协作协同创新中心

湖北大学湖北文化建设研究院

湖北大学中华文化发展湖北省协同创新中心

湖北经济学院碳排放权交易湖北省协同创新中心

湖北省中国特色社会主义理论体系研究中心中南民族大学分中心

湖南大学国际贸易研究智库

湖南大学国家腐败预防与惩治研究中心

湖南大学金融发展与信用管理研究中心

湖南大学廉政研究中心

湖南大学民政部政策理论研究基地

湖南大学岳麓书院国学研究与传播智库

湖南大学中国产业金融协同创新中心

湖南大学中国文化软实力研究中心

湖南工商大学湖南省廉政建设协同创新中心

湖南师范大学"一带一路"文化交流与传播研究中心

湖南师范大学道德文化研究院

湖南师范大学湖南省汉语国际推广研究院

湖南师范大学社会主义核心价值观研究院

湖南师范大学生态环境保护法治研究中心

湖南师范大学生态文明研究院

华北电力大学北京能源发展研究基地

华东交通大学高铁与区域发展研究中心

华东理工大学能源经济与环境管理研究中心

华东理工大学社会工作与社会管理研究中心

华东师范大学长三角区域一体化研究中心

华东师范大学俄罗斯研究中心

华东师范大学国家话语生态研究中心

华东师范大学国家教育宏观政策研究院

华东师范大学基础教育改革与发展研究所

华东师范大学课程与教学研究所

华东师范大学全球创新与发展研究院

华东师范大学上海人口结构与发展趋势创新研究基地

华东师范大学上海终身教育研究院

华东师范大学中国文字研究与应用中心

华东师范大学中国现代城市研究中心

华东师范大学中国现代思想文化研究所

华东师范大学周边合作与发展协同创新中心

华东政法大学华东检察研究院

华东政法大学司法学研究院

华东政法大学中国法治战略研究中心

华南理工大学公共外交与跨文化传播研究基地

华南理工大学公共政策研究院

华南理工大学广东旅游战略与政策研究中心

华南理工大学广东省地方立法研究评估与咨询服务基地

华南理工大学广东省社会治理研究中心

华南理工大学广州市金融服务创新与风险管理研究基地

华南理工大学广州特大城市风险治理研究中心

华南理工大学金融工程研究中心

华南理工大学科技革命与技术预见智库

华南理工大学粤港澳大湾区发展广州智库

华南理工大学政府绩效评价中心

华南理工大学重大科技项目与平台实施效果第三方评估智库

华侨大学华侨华人研究院

华中科技大学非传统安全研究中心

华中科技大学国家治理研究院

华中科技大学健康政策与管理研究院

华中科技大学张培刚发展研究院

华中师范大学国家文化产业研究中心

华中师范大学中国农村研究院

淮北师范大学安徽省高校管理大数据研究中心

淮阴工学院苏北发展研究院

黄河科技学院中国(河南)创新发展研究院

吉林大学创新创业研究院

吉林大学东北亚研究中心

吉林大学犯罪治理研究中心

吉林大学国际关系研究所

吉林大学廉政研究与教育中心

吉林大学社会公正与政府治理研究中心

吉林大学数量经济研究中心

吉林大学司法数据应用研究中心

吉林大学中国国有经济研究中心

吉林大学中国科技政策与科技管理研究中心

吉林大学中国人口老龄化与经济社会发展研究中心

吉林大学中国文化研究所

吉首大学民族地区扶贫与发展研究中心

济南大学山东龙山绿色经济研究中心

暨南大学产业经济研究院

暨南大学广州南沙自由贸易试验区研究基地

暨南大学广州区域低碳经济研究基地

暨南大学广州市舆情大数据研究中心

暨南大学华侨华人研究院

暨南大学经济与社会研究院

暨南大学经纬粤港澳大湾区经济发展研究院

暨南大学资源环境与可持续发展研究所

江南大学食品安全风险治理研究院

江南大学中国物联网发展战略研究基地

江苏第二师范学院教育现代化研究院

江苏海事职业技术学院"一带一路"应用型海事人才研究院

江苏警官学院江苏省公共安全研究院

江苏师范大学"一带一路"研究院

江西财经大学江西全面建成小康社会决策支持协同创新中心

江西财经大学江西省生态文明制度建设协同创新中心

江西财经大学江西省战略性新兴产业发展监测、预警与决策支持协同创新中心

江西理工大学有色金属产业发展研究院

江西师范大学管理决策评价研究中心

江西师范大学江西产业转型升级发展研究中心

江西师范大学江西经济发展研究院

江西师范大学苏区振兴研究院

江西师范大学中国社会转型研究协同创新中心

昆明理工大学云南综合交通发展与区域物流管理智库

昆明学院昆明科学发展智库

兰州财经大学丝绸之路经济研究院

兰州大学阿富汗研究中心

兰州大学丝绸之路经济带建设研究中心

兰州大学西北少数民族研究中心

兰州大学循证社会科学研究中心

兰州大学中国政府绩效管理研究中心

兰州大学中亚研究所

辽宁大学东北地区面向东北亚区域开放协同创新中心

辽宁大学东北振兴研究中心

辽宁大学转型国家经济政治研究中心

民政部-华东师大中国行政区划研究院

南昌大学江西发展研究院

南昌大学旅游规划与研究中心

南昌大学中国中部经济社会发展研究中心

南京财经大学现代服务业智库

南京大学长江产业经济研究院

南京大学长江三角洲经济社会发展研究中心

南京大学非洲研究所

南京大学华智全球治理研究院

南京大学社会风险与公共危机管理研究中心

南京大学中国南海研究协同创新中心

南京大学紫金传媒智库

南京航空航天大学工业和信息化智库评价中心

南京理工大学江苏人才发展战略研究院

南京理工大学江苏省知识产权发展研究中心

南京农业大学金善宝农业现代化研究院

南京师范大学中国法治现代化研究院

南京信息工程大学江北新区发展研究院

南京信息工程大学气候与环境治理研究院

南京医科大学健康江苏研究院

南京艺术学院紫金文创研究院

南开大学滨海开发研究院

南开大学当代中国问题研究院

南开大学经济一体化与全球治理研究中心

南开大学经济与社会发展研究院

南开大学日本研究中心

南开大学希腊研究中心

南开大学亚太经济合作组织（APEC）研究中心

南开大学政治经济学研究中心

南开大学中国公司治理研究院

南开大学中国特色社会主义经济建设协同创新中心

南开大学中国政府与政策联合研究中心

南通大学江苏长江经济带研究院

内蒙古财经大学中蒙俄经济走廊研究协同创新中心

内蒙古大学蒙古国研究中心

内蒙古大学蒙古学研究中心

宁波大学东海研究院

宁波大学海洋教育研究中心

宁夏大学回族研究院

宁夏大学中国阿拉伯国家研究院

青海大学青海省情研究中心

清华大学布鲁金斯公共政策研究中心

清华大学公共管理学院智库研究中心

清华大学国际关系研究院

清华大学国情研究院

清华大学技术创新研究中心

清华大学卡内基全球政策中心

清华大学科技发展与治理研究中心

清华大学全球可持续发展研究院

清华大学现代管理研究中心

清华大学中国应急管理研究基地

清华大学中国与世界经济研究中心

山东大学当代社会主义研究所

山东大学孔子学院研究中心

山东大学山东发展研究院

山东大学山东区域金融改革与发展研究中心

山东大学卫生管理与政策研究中心

山东大学县域发展研究院

山东大学犹太教与跨宗教研究中心

山东大学政党研究所

山西财经大学资源型经济转型协同创新中心

山西大学管理与决策研究所

山西大学晋商学研究所

陕西师范大学"一带一路"建设与中亚研究协同创新研究中心

陕西师范大学扶贫政策与评估研究中心

陕西师范大学教育实验经济研究所

陕西师范大学土耳其研究中心

陕西师范大学西北国土资源研究中心

陕西师范大学西北跨境民族与边疆安全研究中心

陕西师范大学西北历史环境与经济社会发展研究院

陕西师范大学语言资源开发研究中心

陕西师范大学中国旅游研究院西部旅游发展研究基地

陕西师范大学中国西部边疆研究院

上海财经大学公共政策与治理研究院

上海财经大学上海国际金融中心研究院

上海财经大学中国产业经济研究中心

上海财经大学中国公共财政研究院

上海财经大学中国自由贸易试验区协同创新中心

上海大学毒品与国家安全研究中心

上海大学基层治理创新研究中心

上海大学拉丁美洲研究中心

上海大学土耳其研究中心

上海大学智库产业研究中心

上海对外经贸大学国际经贸治理与中国改革开放联合研究中心

上海对外经贸大学上海 WTO 事务咨询中心

上海海事大学上海国际航运研究中心

上海海事大学中国(上海)自贸区供应链研究院

上海交通大学城市科学研究院

上海交通大学第三部门研究中心

上海交通大学改革创新与治理现代化研究中心

上海交通大学国家海洋战略与权益研究基地

上海交通大学国家文化产业创新与发展研究基地

上海交通大学世界一流大学研究中心

上海交通大学文化创新与青年发展研究院

上海交通大学舆论学研究院

上海交通大学中国城市治理研究院

上海交通大学中国海洋装备工程科技发展战略研究院

上海师范大学国际与比较教育研究院

上海外国语大学丝路战略研究所

上海外国语大学英国研究中心

上海外国语大学中东研究所

上海外国语大学中国国际舆情研究中心

上海外国语大学中国外语战略研究中心

上海政法学院"一带一路"安全研究院

上海政法学院上海合作组织研究院

深圳大学城市治理研究院

深圳大学港澳基本法研究中心

深圳大学中国海外利益研究院

沈阳师范大学人力资源开发与管理研究所

首都经济贸易大学北京市经济社会发展政策研究基地

首都师范大学北京基础教育研究基地

四川大学南亚研究所

四川大学社会发展与西部开发研究院

四川大学中国西部边疆安全与发展协同创新中心

四川大学中国藏学研究所

苏州大学东吴智库文化与社会发展研究院

苏州科技大学城市发展智库

天津财经大学法律经济分析与政策评价中心

天津财经大学公共经济与公共管理研究中心

天津财经大学工商管理研究中心

天津财经大学金融与保险研究中心

天津财经大学天津市自由贸易区研究院

天津财经大学无形资产评价协同创新中心

天津财经大学中国滨海金融协同创新中心

天津财经大学中国经济统计研究中心

天津城建大学天津城镇化与新农村建设研究中心

天津大学国家知识产权战略实施研究基地

天津大学教育科学研究中心

天津大学社会科学调查与数据中心

天津大学生物安全战略研究中心

天津大学亚太经合组织可持续能源中心

天津大学灾难医学研究院

天津大学中国传统村落与建筑文化传承协同创新中心

天津大学中国绿色发展研究院

天津大学中国文化遗产保护国际研究中心

天津大学中国智慧法治研究院

天津公共部门信息服务评价与治理中心

天津工业大学天津法治信访研究基地

天津科技大学能源环境与绿色发展研究中心

天津科技大学食品安全战略与管理研究中心

天津理工大学循环经济与绿色发展研究中心

天津理工大学中国重大工程技术"走出去"投资模式与管控智库

天津农学院乡村振兴研究院

天津商业大学现代服务业发展研究中心

天津师范大学国家治理研究中心

天津师范大学区域发展战略与改革研究所

天津师范大学应急管理研究中心

天津师范大学自由经济区研究所

天津市基础教育决策服务研究中心

天津体育学院全民健身研究智库

天津外国语大学"一带一路"天津战略研究院

天津外国语大学东北亚研究中心

同济大学财经研究所

同济大学德国研究中心

同济大学可持续发展与新型城镇化智库

同济大学中国战略研究院

武汉大学党内法规研究中心

武汉大学发展研究院

武汉大学国际法研究所

武汉大学国家文化发展研究院

武汉大学湖北政治建设研究院

武汉大学环境法研究所

武汉大学经济发展研究中心

武汉大学经济外交研究中心

武汉大学媒体发展研究中心

武汉大学全球健康研究中心

武汉大学社会保障研究中心

武汉大学信息资源研究中心

武汉大学质量发展战略研究院

武汉大学中国边界与海洋研究院

武汉大学中国传统文化研究中心

武汉大学中国语情与社会发展研究中心

武汉大学中国中部发展研究院

武汉大学主流意识形态建设与教育研究基地

西安交通大学"一带一路"自由贸易试验区研究院

西安交通大学改革试点探索与评估协同创新中心

西安交通大学欧亚经济(论坛)与全球发展研究院

西安交通大学陕西经济研究中心

西安交通大学社会治理和社会政策协同创新研究中心

西安交通大学丝绸之路国际法与比较法研究所

西安交通大学丝绸之路经济带研究协同创新中心

西安交通大学新媒体与社会治理研究中心

西安交通大学知识产权研究中心

西安交通大学中国(西安)数字经济发展监测预警基地

西安交通大学中国管理问题研究中心

西北大学陕西宏观经济与经济增长质量协同创新研究中心

西北大学丝绸之路文化遗产保护与考古学研究中心

西北大学中东研究所

西北大学中国西部经济发展研究中心

西北工业大学西部国防科技工业发展研究中心

西北师范大学"一带一路"战略与教育发展研究中心

西北师范大学甘肃省文化资源与华夏文明建设研究中心

西北师范大学精准扶贫与区域发展研究中心

西北政法大学反恐怖主义研究院

西北政法大学民族宗教研究院

西南财经大学金融安全协同创新中心

西南财经大学中国家庭金融调查与研究中心

西南财经大学中国金融研究中心

西南财经大学中国西部经济研究中心

西南大学俄语国家研究中心

西南大学公共文化研究中心

西南大学教育政策研究所

西南大学农村经济与管理研究中心

西南大学三峡库区经济社会发展研究中心

西南大学统筹城乡教育发展研究中心

西南大学希腊研究中心

西南大学西南民族教育与心理研究中心

西南大学伊朗研究中心

西南交通大学西部交通战略与区域发展研究中心

西南科技大学四川循环经济研究中心

西南石油大学四川石油天然气发展研究中心

西南政法大学人权研究院

西藏大学西藏可持续发展研究所

西藏民族大学南亚研究所

西藏民族大学西藏文化传承发展协同创新中心

厦门大学东南亚研究中心

厦门大学高等教育发展研究中心

厦门大学宏观经济研究中心

厦门大学台湾研究院

厦门大学中国能源政策研究院

湘潭大学地方立法与区域社会治理研究中心

湘潭大学公共管理与区域经济发展研究中心

湘潭大学毛泽东思想研究中心

湘潭大学政府绩效评估与管理创新研究中心

湘潭大学中国共产党革命精神与文化资源研究中心

燕山大学河北省公共政策评估研究中心

燕山大学河北省设计创新及产业发展研究中心

燕山大学区域经济发展研究中心

延边大学朝鲜半岛研究院

盐城师范学院沿海发展智库

云南财经大学公共政策研究中心

云南财经大学印度洋地区研究中心

云南财经大学云南省防灾减灾智库

云南大学"一带一路"沿线国家民族问题智库

云南大学边疆民族问题智库

云南大学缅甸研究院

云南大学文化发展研究院

云南大学沿边开放与经济发展智库

云南大学云南开放经济与产业发展智库

云南大学周边外交研究中心

浙江财经大学中国政府监管与公共政策研究院

浙江大学"一带一路"合作与发展协同创新中心

浙江大学创新管理与持续竞争力研究中心

浙江大学非传统安全与和平发展研究中心

浙江大学公共政策研究院

浙江大学金融研究院

浙江大学民营经济研究中心

浙江大学社会治理研究院

浙江大学中国科教战略研究院

浙江大学中国跨境电子商务研究院

浙江大学中国农村发展研究院

浙江大学中国西部发展研究院

浙江工业大学中国中小企业研究院

浙江理工大学浙江省生态文明研究中心

浙江理工大学浙江省丝绸与时尚文化研究中心

浙江立法研究院暨浙江大学立法研究院

浙江农林大学中国农民发展研究中心

浙江师范大学非洲研究院

浙江万里学院宁波海上丝绸之路研究院

郑州大学社会治理河南省协同创新中心

中国传媒大学国家传播创新研究中心

中国传媒大学首都传媒经济研究基地

中国海洋大学海洋发展研究院

中国海洋大学日本研究中心

中国海洋大学中国企业营运资金管理研究中心

中国科学技术大学安徽大数据应用协同创新中心

中国科学技术大学科技创新与区域发展研究中心

中国矿业大学中国城市公共安全管理智库

中国民航大学临空经济研究中心

中国民航大学中国民航环境与可持续发展研究中心（智库）

中国农业大学国际发展研究中心

中国农业大学国家农业农村发展研究院

中国农业大学中国土地政策与法律研究中心

中国人民大学重阳金融研究院

中国人民大学国家发展与战略研究院

中国人民大学民商事法律科学研究中心

中国人民大学人口与发展研究中心

中国人民大学社会转型与社会治理协同创新中心

中国人民大学刑事法律科学研究中心

中国人民大学中国财政金融政策研究中心

中国人民公安大学首都社会安全研究基地

中国社会科学院大学高校思想政治工作创新发展中心

中国政法大学法治政府研究院

中国政法大学人权研究院

中国政法大学司法文明协同创新中心

中国政法大学中国行政体制改革研究中心

中南财经政法大学产业升级与区域金融湖北省协同创新中心

中南财经政法大学城乡社区社会管理湖北省协同创新中心

中南财经政法大学法治发展与司法改革研究中心

中南财经政法大学反恐怖主义研究中心

中南财经政法大学知识产权研究中心

中南财经政法大学中国收入分配研究中心

中南大学地方治理研究院

中南大学教育立法研究基地

中南大学金属资源战略研究院

中南大学两型社会与生态文明协同创新中心

中南大学人力资源研究中心

中南大学人权研究中心

中南大学社会稳定风险研究评估中心

中南大学统一战线参政议政工作室

中南大学医疗卫生法研究中心

中南大学应用伦理学研究中心

中南大学知识产权研究院

中南大学中国村落文化研究中心

中南大学中国文化法研究中心

中南大学中国作协网络文学委员会中南大学研究基地

中南林业科技大学湖南绿色发展研究院

中山大学国家治理研究院

中山大学南海战略研究院

中山大学粤港澳发展研究院

中央财经大学公共采购研究所

中央财经大学绿色金融国际研究院

中央财经大学首都互联网经济发展研究基地

中央财经大学中国财政发展协同创新中心

中央财经大学中国银行业研究中心

中央文献翻译研究基地

最高人民检察院检察研究基地东南大学民事检察研究中心

（五）军队智库（6 家）

北京系统工程研究所

国防科学技术大学国防科技与军民融合研究中心

国防科学技术大学国防科技战略研究中心

国防科学技术大学国际问题研究中心

中国人民解放军国防大学

中国人民解放军军事科学院

（六）科研院所智库（36 家）

北京科学学研究中心

国家测绘地理信息局测绘发展研究中心

湖南省农村发展研究院

江苏省科学技术情报研究所（江苏省科学技术发展战略研究院）

江苏省苏科创新战略研究院

江西省科学院科技战略研究所

联合国教科文组织国际工程教育中心

辽宁省科学技术情报研究所科技发展战略研究中心

青岛市科技发展战略研究院

山东省科技发展战略研究所

上海国际问题研究院

上海科学技术政策研究所

上海市科学学研究所

首都科技发展战略研究院

水利部发展研究中心

天津市经济发展研究院

西部资源环境与区域发展智库

冶金工业经济发展研究中心

云南省生态环境科学研究院

浙江省科技信息研究院（浙江省科技发展战略研究院）

中国电子信息产业发展研究院

中国工程院

中国航天工程科技发展战略研究院

中国环境科学研究院

中国科协创新战略研究院

中国科学技术发展战略研究院

中国科学技术信息研究所

中国科学院

中国科学院科技战略咨询研究院

中国科学院预测科学研究中心

中国社会科学院生态文明研究智库

中国石油经济技术研究院

中国信息通信研究院

中国信息与电子工程科技发展战略研究中心

中国艺术研究院文化发展战略研究中心

中国中医药信息学会中医药智库分会

（七）企业智库（10家）

阿里研究院

北京市长城企业战略研究所

电力规划设计总院

国家开发银行研究院（金融研究发展中心）

国网江苏省电力有限公司经济技术研究院

南方电网能源发展研究院有限责任公司

苏宁金融研究院

腾云智库

中国管理科学研究院专家咨询委员会

中信改革发展研究基金会

（八）社会智库（38家）

北京国际城市发展研究院

察哈尔学会

长江教育研究院

长沙市现代产业发展研究会

重庆智库

东中西部区域发展和改革研究院

广东财经大学华南商业智库

广东亚太创新经济研究院

广东中策知识产权研究院

国观智库

海国图智研究院

海南亚太观察研究院

蓝迪国际智库

辽宁省软科学研究会

盘古智库

全球化智库

上海春秋发展战略研究院

上海福卡经济预测研究所有限公司

上海华夏社会发展研究院

上海金融与法律研究院

上海新金融研究院

深圳市现代创新发展研究院

桐乡市乌镇智库

万博新经济研究院

新丝绸之路经济研究院

"一带一路"百人论坛

雨花台红色文化研究院

知远战略与防务研究所

中国（海南）改革发展研究院

中国国际经济交流中心

中国金融四十人论坛

中国经济体制改革研究会

中国领导科学研究会

中国南海研究院

中国企业改革与发展研究会

中国丝路智谷研究院

中智科学技术评价研究中心

综合开发研究院（中国·深圳）

（九）传媒智库（15家）

第一财经研究院

封面智库

凤凰国际智库

光明日报文化产业研究中心

光明智库

广州日报数据和数字化研究院

红网智库

经济日报社中国经济趋势研究院

瞭望智库

南方舆情数据研究院

南风窗传媒智库

南京政务舆情研究院

盛京汇智库

人民网新媒体智库

新华通讯社

Introduction: The Construction of a New Type of Think Tanks and the Modernization of China's National Governance System

On April 15, 2013, General Secretary Xi Jinping made important instructions on the construction of think tanks, explicitly proposing the target of "building a new type of think tanks with Chinese characteristics" and requiring think tanks to actively provide high-quality intellectual support for scientific decision-making in the CPC Central Committee. In November 2013, the Third Plenary Session of the 18th CPC Central Committee put forward *Decision of the CPC Central Committee on Several Major Issues in Deepening Reform in an All-round Way*, further proposing to strengthen the construction of new think tanks with Chinese characteristics, and to establish and improve the decision-making consultation system. After intensive drafting and collection of opinions, on October 27, 2014, *Opinions on Strengthening the Construction of New Think Tanks with Chinese Characteristics* was submitted to the sixth meeting of the "Central Leading Group for Comprehensively Deepening Reforms" for deliberation. General Secretary Xi Jinping made another important speech. He stressed that the construction of a new type of think tanks with Chinese characteristics should be earnestly implemented as a major and urgent task from the strategic height of promoting scientific and democratic decision-making, modernizing the national governance system and capability, and enhancing the soft power of the entire country. On January 20, 2015, the Xinhua News Agency publicly broadcast *Opinions on Strengthening the Construction of New Think Tanks with Chinese Characteristics* issued by the General Offices of the CPC Central Committee and the State Council. During the past five years, the construction of new think tanks, which has made remarkable achievements but also exposed some problems in its development, was always the hottest topic in the decision-making consultation system and among the community of philosophy and social sciences. The Fourth Plenary Session of the 19th CPC Central Committee once again emphasized the modernization of the country's governance system and capability, providing unprecedented historical opportunities for the development of new think tanks.

1   The Construction of a New Type of Think Tanks Conforms to China's Profound Cultural Tradition of Rational and Learning-Oriented Politics

The construction of a new type of think tanks with Chinese characteristics is an important reform measure to improve and perfect the decision-making system and mechanism. It is also an important policy wholeheartedly supported by the communities of theoretical study, higher education, news and communication and the majority of intellectuals.

First of all, this is a correct decision based on China's profound cultural tradition. Chen Yinque once pointed out, "I suspect that since today, even if China can faithfully import the ideas of North America or Eastern Europe, such ideas should not surpass Xuan Zang's knowledge-based learning, since they cannot occupy the highest position and will eventually wither away in China's history of ideas. If one can really establish a system of his own ideas and even make some breakthroughs, he must, on the one hand, absorb foreign ideas and, on the other hand, attach importance to the ideas of his own nation. These two opposite but complementary attitudes are the true spirit of Taoism and the traditional approach of the new Confucianism, and are also revealed by the history of ideological communication between China and other nations for over 2, 000 years. " (Chen Yinque, from *Review of History of Chinese Philosophy Second Volume* by Feng Youlan)

The concept of think tank is "imported" and comes from the Western society. However, the reason why it has caused such a stir in contemporary Chinese political community and is widely supported by the intelligentsia is that think tanks conform to China's political and cultural tradition and the intellectual scholar-officials tradition in feudal China.

As an ancient civilization with a history of more than 5, 000 years, China's political culture evolved out of the barbaric witchcraft in the Western Zhou Dynasty (1046BC – 771BC). In the Spring and Autumn Period (770BC – 476BC) and the Warring States Period (475BC – 221BC), China witnessed the Hundred Schools of Thought and established a rational political and cultural tradition. For example, Han Fei, as a representative of Legalism, proposed an extremely calm and rational political theory based on calculation. During the same period, the ruling classes competed with each other in recruiting, cultivating and using intellectuals, and a famous think tank, Jixia Academy, emerged. The Imperial College of the Han Dynasty (202BC – 220) was the first national university in the world with a capacity of over ten thousand students and was also the main source of bureaucrats. The Imperial Civil Examination System was established in the Sui (581 – 619) and Tang (618 – 907) Dynasties. The rank order of scholars, peasants, artisans and merchants was fixed from then on, and there had been little fundamental change in the pattern of scholars governing the country.

Because of the rational political tradition of cultivating and using intellectuals, the ancient Chinese intellectuals also took the whole world as their own duty and emphasized the application of theoretical knowledge to practice. "Establishing a value system for the whole society, ensuring a happy life for people, inheriting and innovating the achievements of sages, and laying the foundation for lasting prosperity" has been the value pursuit of Chinese intellectuals generation after generation.

This is the "cultural gene" that helps this major reform win the support of the intellectual class. Such gene contains two complementary sequences, one is the tradition of political rationalism, the other is the tradition of knowledge serving the country. The rise of think tanks in China is exactly in line with the mechanism of Western ideas spreading to the east elaborated by Chen Yinque. Also, think tanks, having a profound cultural foundation in Chinese society, are not foreign products but a reflection of our cultural confidence. Therefore, this initiative is a strategic decision with a very high degree of agreement and abundant vitality and influence that agrees with China's profound historical and cultural traditions.

2　Main Stage Achievements in the Construction of New Think Tanks

The conceptual achievement is to popularize the concepts and knowledge of modern think tanks, transforming it from a novel word into a hot one in China's political and cultural community and creating a good atmosphere for the modernization of China's decision-making consulting system. This will greatly ignite the enthusiasm of the Party committees and the governments to build and use think tanks, which has great benefits for improving scientific decision-making and its mechanism.

Second, China has established a number of think tanks from the central government down to all other levels. According to the incomplete statistics, as of February 2019, there were 383 key think tanks at all levels and of all types approved by the central and provincial ministries and offices with official documents. As of December 2019, the number of CTTI source think tanks has reached 848. That is to say, the number of China's think tanks is only less than that of the United States. All CTTI source think tanks employ 14,241 researchers, carry out or participate in 27,699 activities, and have obtained 157,394 various achievements.

Thirdly, in the process of building think tanks, the rules and regulations are gradually systematized. According to the statistics by Ma Xuewen of the CTTI Center, as of April 2019, 27 provinces had successively issued implementation opinions or measures for the construction of new think tanks and proposed the construction plans for provincial key (high-end) think tanks, bringing their construction into standardization and legalization. Dozens of research-oriented universities have developed criteria and evaluation index systems for the recognition of think tank achievements. In addition, think tanks are deeply embedded in China's political and cultural system and are playing an indispensable role in terms of theoretical innovation, decision-making consultation, public opinion guidance, social services and public diplomacy. At the same time, the research team of think tanks has grown rapidly, the research results of think tanks have also shown explosive growth, and the understanding of think tanks in different periods at home and abroad has gradually deepened. This report elaborates on the achievements of the construction of the new type of think tanks in several aspects.

Inevitably, overheating and formalism appeared in the process of construction.

There have also been a few cases in which individual think tanks and consulting companies used the name of think tanks to amass money or even give support to some interest groups, which should be paid close attention to. However, it is totally wrong to fundamentally doubt the necessity and urgency of building a new type of think tanks.

3 The Construction of a New Type of Think Tanks Has Awakened the Identity of the Decision-Making Consultation Community in Terms of Status, Majority and Profession

The CPC has always attached importance to policy research. As early as May 1930 during the field visit in Xunwu, Mao Zedong theoretically summarized the inseparable relationship between investigation and the Marxist world outlook. In his article "Work on Investigation and Research" written during that time, he put forward many important theoretical viewpoints on investigation and research activities, the most famous of which is the assertion that "no investigation, no right to speak". On August 1, 1941, when drafting the "Decision of the CPC Central Committee on Investigation and Research", Mao Zedong said: Many comrades in the Party do not understand the truth that "no investigation, no right to speak". They do not understand that systematic and thorough social investigation is the basis for policy decisions. They do not know that the basic task of leaders is to understand the situation and master the policies because failure to understand the situation will lead to wrong policies. March 20, 1948 was the last day Mao Zedong spent in Yangjiagou. Before leaving, he decided to make a temporary summary of the previous work and issue a "Notification of the Situation" for the central government. Only when the Party's policies and strategies are all on the right track can the Chinese people win the revolution. Policies and tactics are the life of the Party. When leading comrades at all levels leaders must pay full attention to them and should never be careless. In September 1948, the CPC Central Committee set up the "Central Policy Research Office" in Xibaipo, with Peng Zhen as its director and 23 staff members, whose main tasks were drafting manuscripts and conducting researches. After 1949, the CPC still maintained democratic centralism and adhered to the mode of investigation first and decision-making after. It also created new ways of investigation and research such as on-site visits and analyzing typical cases. However, investigations and studies sometimes were often only formalistic, and some decisions were divorced from reality, resulting in some major policy mistakes. During the "Cultural Revolution", the decision-making consultation system was completely suspended. After the launch of reform and opening up, in order to cope with the new situation and new problems in the process and to make government decisions more scientific, the CPC has vigorously restored the system of decision-making consultation and investigation and research, and has established the policy research office of the Party Committee and the one of governments. Development research centers, policy research centers, research institutes and other decision-making consultation bodies under the guidance of the CPC and governments at all levels have been established and developed one after another, represented by the Development Research Center of the State Council (established in 1980), the Policy Research Office of the CPC Central Committee (established in 1981) and the China Institute of Modern International Relations (established in 1980). After nearly 40 years of development, the CPC has established a complete and systematic internal research and decision-making consultation system, that is, the "Internal Brain" of the CPC Committee and the governments, with the Committee's policy research offices and the government ones as the main body and the

Academy of Social Sciences, Party schools and schools of administration as the auxiliary. However, once referred to as "writers", "staff" or "brainpower", the system has always lacked a clear identity. *Opinions on Strengthening the Construction of New Think Tanks with Chinese Characteristics* endows the "Internal Brain" system with a modern global identity, "Think Tanks". This has also been used by other systems, such as universities, research institutes and policy research institutions of large state-owned enterprises. In this way, China has formed a "think tank community" with specific identity in terms of status, majority and profession, including "Inner Brain" and "Outer Brain".

This will definitely promote the division of labor in decision-making consultation and is conducive to promoting China's decision-making consultation to be more specialized, professional and scientific. Part of the research office system within the Committee and the governments continues to provide manuscript service, while the other part gradually focuses on policy research and service. The philosophy and social sciences research institutions in colleges whose main task is policy research have made clear their identity of think tanks. Their task of discipline construction has been cut down, and the work of think tank research has been greatly strengthened. Some CASS still offer dual services, while others only serve as think tanks. Market-oriented consulting Companies have also split up into some branches, specializing in serving the Party committee and the governments in respect of decision-making consultation. In this way, a diversified "think tank community" has emerged in our country, with all kinds of institutions taking decision-making consultation of the Committee and the governments as their main task and having a unified identity of status, majority and profession. This is a great achievement in the construction of a new type of think tanks.

4   The New Think Tanks Have Become One of the Main Channels for Developing Democratic Consultation

Xi Jinping pointed out: Our people exercise their rights through elections and voting, and all parties conduct full consultation before making major decisions and reach consensus on common issues as much as possible. These are two important forms of socialist democracy in China. *The Decision of the Communist Party of China (CPC) Central Committee on Some Major Issues Concerning How to Uphold and Improve the System of Socialism with Chinese Characteristics and Advance the Modernization of China's System and Capacity for Governance* points out: "We will maintain the unique advantages of socialist consultative democracy and coordinate consultations at all levels, including political parties, the National People's Congress, the government, the Chinese People's Political Consultative Conference, civil organizations, community-level organizations and social organizations. We will build a system of democratic consultation with reasonable procedures and complete phases, improve the implementation mechanism of consultation before and during decision-making, and enrich the institutionalized practices of consultation for all. " In September 2014, at the general meeting to celebrate the 65th anniversary of the founding of the Chinese People's Political Consultative Conference, Xi Jinping pointed out in his speech that various think tanks are one of the ten channels for consultation and clarified the status of new think tanks as the main channel. Therefore, politically speaking, the construction of a new type of think tanks not only functions as the provider of decision-making consultation service, but also can promote socialist consultative democracy. The new think tank can also unite intellectuals and is a practical mechanism of the mass line.

5   The Construction of New Think Tanks Has Given Birth to the "Think Tank Paradigm" of Philosophy and Social Sciences

The Communist Party of China has always advocated that philosophy and social sciences must be put into practice. During the revolutionary war, Mao Zedong stressed that "what is this slim pen similar to? Three thousand crack troops. " The pen and the gun are both revolutionary weapons.

Since the launch of reform and opening up, we have massively imported concepts and thoughts of Western philosophy and social sciences, which enriches our knowledge system but also damages the autonomy and effectiveness of Chinese philosophy and social sciences. In addition, the evaluation system is dominated by Western mainstream journals, forming the erroneous tendency of "Greek thought must be referred to". The central government promptly put forward the *Opinions on Accelerating the Construction of Philosophy and Social Sciences with Chinese Characteristics*, whose core is to solve the problem of Chinese subjectivity and improve the effectiveness of addressing Chinese problems. Philosophy and social sciences focus on seeking truth and application. Seeking truth is embodied in their "philosophical paradigm" (academic paradigm) and seeking application in "think tank paradigm". If China cannot develop its own "think tank paradigm", then the problem of "unity of knowing and doing" in philosophy and social science will not be completely solved. The construction of a new type of think tanks has found a creative way to transform philosophy and social sciences from philosophy paradigm to think tank one, both of which are indispensable for accelerating the construction of philosophy and social sciences with Chinese characteristics. After five years of construction, the think tank paradigm has shown the following characteristics.

First, "unity of knowing and doing". Think tanks are independent public policy and strategy research institutions based on facts. Public policy analysis pursues standards and evidence in order to make policies operable. Think tanks not only attach importance to "knowledge" ("true knowledge" and "real knowledge"), but also undertake communication, creative transformation and two-way feedback between theory and practice, and academic and practical circles (political, industrial and economic circles, media, etc.), so that philosophical logic guides practical logic and the latter stimulates the former. The philosophical paradigm focuses on the theoretical logic of things or phenomena, while the think tank one focuses more on practical logic. The characteristic of "unity of knowing and doing" is that scholars can put forward feasible policy combination and implementation according to the objective laws of development of things discovered by theoretical circles or themselves, and according to the economic foundation and superstructure of the society so as to change the world.

Second, "demand-oriented" and "a strong awareness of problems". Kant once said that "Two things filled my heart with wonder and fear: the starry sky above me and the moral law in my heart." He believes that philosophical research does not need application and pursues transcendence and eternity. However, the logical starting point of the think tank paradigm is "the awareness of problems", with attributes similar to those of clinical medicine, as many think tank studies directly lead to policy changes and social changes.

Third, attaching equal importance to consultation and research. Modern consulting industry thrives in business management. The main forms of consultation include strategies, risk management, techniques, finance, IT, etc. Since the launch of reform and opening up, China's management consulting industry has also made great progress. However, the decision-making consultation for the Party Committee and the governments has neither brilliant theoretical achievements nor abundant case accumulation. The reason is that the construction of think tanks lags behind, and traditional decision-making consultation institutions, such as the policy research offices within the governments, are busy with daily affairs and have neither time nor professionals that can be devoted to case accumulation and theoretical research. For most think tanks, decision-making consultation and policy research are equally important, and sometimes it is difficult to distinguish between consultation and research. Generally speaking, policy analysis and research are at the early stage of the policy process. The theoretical basis, data basis, necessity analysis and policy planning for setting the policy agenda are the main contents of policy research, while the decision-making consultation focuses on the feasibility analysis, implementation analysis, implementation plan formulation, policy interpretation and other policy roadshows.

Fourth, a strong sense of management. The philosophical paradigm does not approve of "managing" academic research whose results are relatively simple with papers and works as the two main forms. Meanwhile, academic journals assume the function of disseminating academic achievements while academic communities themselves cannot "sell" their research achievements. The organizational culture of think tanks is more similar to that of modern consulting firms than that of universities. In essence, most think tanks belong to a special type of consulting companies. There are two differences in form between think tanks and consulting firms: think tanks are not for profit, while consulting firms seek profit; think tanks focus on public policy research and consultation with governments as their main target. Therefore, many first-class think tanks learn from the operation mode of consulting companies, such as emphasizing their own institutional governance, product design, product dissemination, and performance evaluation of researchers.

6   The Fourth Plenary Session of the 19th CPC Central Committee Has Given the Construction of a New Type of Think Tanks the Responsibility of the Times and Unprecedented Historical Opportunities

The Decision of the Communist Party of China (CPC) Central Committee on Some Major Issues Concerning How to Uphold and Improve the System of Socialism with Chinese Characteristics and Advance the Modernization of China's System and Capacity for Governance elaborates on "adherence to and improvement of the Party's leadership system" from six aspects: 1) establishing the system of remaining true to our original aspiration and keep our mission firmly in mind; 2) improving systems for firmly upholding the authority and centralized leadership of the CPC Central Committee; 3) perfecting the overall leadership system of the Party; 4) perfecting the systems that govern for and by the people; 5) perfecting the system that improves the Party's capacity of administrating and leading; 6) perfecting the system that comprehensively strengthens party self-discipline. The deconstructive and organic connection of these six aspects constitutes the party's leadership system. "Establishing the system of remaining true to our original aspiration and keeping our mission firmly in mind" is the value concept, the core idea, the ideological leadership, the institutional thought, and the logical, historical and practical starting point of the whole leadership system. This ideological system is the leading system of the whole party and is the soul and essence. Improving systems for firmly upholding the authority and centralized leadership of the CPC Central Committee and perfecting the overall leadership system of the Party are the main contents of the party's leadership system and are the fundamental differences between Marxist-Leninist parties and bourgeois parties. The history of the Chinese revolution and socialist construction has repeatedly proved that the authority and the overall leadership of the CPC Central Committee are the key to the victory of the Chinese revolution and the success of socialist modernization as each setback is closely related to the erosion and destruction of the centralized and unified leadership system. Perfecting the systems that govern for and by the people clarifies the foundation and legitimacy of the party's leadership. Perfecting the system that improves the Party's capacity of administrating and leading is the main content of "adhering to and improving the party's leadership system". The governing party's capacity of administrating and leading determines whether the party's leadership system has strong vitality, modern efficiency and strong leadership. Perfecting the system that comprehensively strengthens party self-discipline emphasizes the party's self-governance to ensure the implementation of the above systems.

The basic ways to uphold and improve the party's leadership system are "scientific administrating", "democratic administrating" and "administrating according to law", which are the foundation, the guidance, and the key respectively. The relevant paragraphs of the *Decision* discuss the connotation of improving the capacity of administrating and leading from three aspects: leading approaches, decision-making mechanism and incentive mechanism. The *Decision* holds that the Party's leadership includes four aspects: to maintain the direction, to master the overall situation, to set the policy and to promote the reforms. The *Decision* points out that we will improve the decision-making mechanism; enhance the investigation and research, scientific argumentation and risk assessment of major decisions; and strengthen the implementation, assessment and supervision of decisions. It can be clearly seen that the *Decision* elaborates on the connotation of administrating ability from the scientificity of policy process. From the perspective of scientific policy, "to maintain the direction, to master the overall situation, to set the policy and to promote the reforms" means strategic management, agenda setting, decision-making and policy implementation. Scientific governance means that the whole policy process must conform to the law and the reality, provide reasonable policies, carry out firm and effective implementation, evaluate and supervise the whole process, give timely feedback and make timely mid-term policy adjustments.

"Upholding and perfecting the party's leadership system and improving the capacity of scientific and democratic administration according to law" puts forward higher requirements for the construction of new think tanks. "Improving the decision-making mechanism; enhancing the investigation and research, scientific argumentation and risk assessment of major decisions; and strengthening the implementation, assessment and supervision of decisions" endows with rich contents and specific tasks the construction of new think tanks with Chinese characteristics in the new era.

Although the *Decision* does not mention think tanks, it highlights the strategy, foundation, urgency and necessity of strengthening the construction of new think tanks and puts forward higher requirements for the construction in terms of politics, scientificity, policies and publicity. Therefore, the construction of a new type of think tanks with Chinese characteristics should not be downplayed, but its connotation development and content innovation should be intensified with higher goals and stricter standards.

The construction of new think tanks is an integral part of the modernization of the country's governance system and capabilities. Scientific implementation cannot be carried out without think tanks. Obviously, the next step in the construction of a new type of think tank is to overcome formalism, to overcome the path of old wine in new bottles, to turn quantitative construction to connotative development, to strengthen content innovation, to strengthen the core capacity building of think tanks such as decision-making consultation, and to strengthen system construction.

Part One

Research on the Construction of New Think Tanks with Chinese Characteristics from 2015 to 2019

Topic 1 Building Progress of New National High-End and Provincial & Municipal Key Think Tanks

Since the 18th National Congress of the CPC, the Party Central Committee led by Xi Jinping has attached great importance to the building of new-type think tanks, reviewed the intellectual resources of the country from a strategic perspective, and made a series of strategic deployments and top-level designs for the building of new-type think tanks in China. As a demonstration project for the building of new-type think tanks with Chinese characteristics, the building of national high-end think tanks was officially launched in November 2015. Twenty-five institutions were the first to be included in the trial project of the building of national high-end think tanks [in March 2018, according to *Decision of the CPC Central Committee on Deepening the Reform of Party and State Institutions*, Party School of the CPC Central Committee and the National School of Administration were combined to form a new Party School of the CPC Central Committee (National School of Administration), and 25 pilot institutions became 24]. Based on the requirements of the central government, the pilot project of the building of national high-end think tanks is led by the Publicity Department of the CPC, and the National Planning Office of Philosophy and Social Science is in charge of specific plans. Each pilot institution should make serving directly for the decision-making of the central government as its fundamental task and strive to do researches on overall, strategic and foresighted problems, making due contributions to the development of the Party and the country.

Meanwhile, in response to the advice in *Opinions on Strengthening the Construction of New Think Tanks with Chinese Characteristics* that "regions capable of building high-end think tanks can do so ahead of others", provinces (including autonomous regions and municipalities) throughout the country have introduced opinions on building local new-type think tanks with reference to national high-end think tanks (pilot) work. They have made clear the range of provincial key think tanks and provided financial support. They have gradually accelerated the pace of building think tanks, initially forming local think tank development systems led by national high-end think tanks, supported by provincial or municipal key think tanks, and supplemented by other professional think tanks, with a reasonable layout and clear division of labor. The systems can provide intellectual support for local policy-making consulting and the modernization of local governance systems and capabilities.

1 Building Progress of National High-End Think Tanks

Since the launch of the national high-end think tank pilot project, the 24 high-profile national high-end think tank pilot institutions have developed rapidly. They set the goal of building high-end think tanks that are "needed by the country, having distinctive characteristics and innovative mechanisms and conducive to development." They have explored management systems and operating mechanisms which can help think tanks to play their five major functions, namely policy-making consulting, theoretical innovation, guidance to public opinion, social service and public diplomacy. In the process, they have served importantly to policy-making of the Party Central Committee and to the overall work of the Party and the country. After over four years of construction, the pilot institutions have made significant progress and achievements in system reform, decision-making services, public opinion guidance and foreign exchanges, accumulating rich experience for building new-type think tanks with Chinese characteristics.

1.1   Pilot Projects Are Carried Out Orderly in Sustainable Manner

1.1.1   Policy Supply Focuses on Institutional Innovations

Policy support is a prerequisite for national high-end think tanks to participate in decision-making and promote the construction of think tank systems. China's think tanks start from a high starting point and follow high standard of construction. Taking institutional innovations as a breakthrough, they have formulated a series of scientific and reasonable policy documents, built a basic system framework for the construction of high-end think tanks, and provided basic compliance for the standardized management and operation of China's high-end think tanks. In 2013, the Third Plenary Session of the 18th Central Committee of the CPC adopted the *Decision of the Central Committee of the Communist Party of China on Some Major Issues Concerning Comprehensively Deepening the Reform*, which clearly put forward that "strengthen the construction of new-type think tanks with Chinese characteristics and establish a sound decision-making consulting system." This shows that the construction of new-type think tanks with Chinese characteristics has been included in the overall layout of comprehensively deepening reform. In October 2014, General Secretary Xi Jinping emphasized that we should promote scientific and democratic decision-making, advance the modernization of national governance system and capabilities, enhance the soft power of the country, and make the building of new-type think tanks with Chinese characteristics an important and urgent task and carry it out effectively at the sixth session of the Central Leading Group of Comprehensively Deepening Reform. Subsequently in January 2015, the General Office of the CPC Central Committee and the General Office of the State Council issued *Opinions on Strengthening the*

Construction of New Think Tanks with Chinese Characteristics (hereinafter referred to as *"Opinions"*), which proposed the implementation of the national high-end think tank building plan and pointed out that new-type think tanks should deepen the reform of their management system in five areas: organization and management system, research system, fund management system, results assessment and application system and international exchange and cooperation system. It also clarified the significance, basic principles, overall objectives and development pattern of think-tank building, which became the first development outline for the construction of new-type think tanks in China. In November 2015, the 18th session of the Central Leading Group of Comprehensively Deepening Reform adopted the *"Pilot Working Plan for National High-end Think Tank Building"* (hereinafter referred to as the *"Pilot Working Plan"*). It clearly laid out rules for various tasks of high-end think tanks, from selection criteria for pilot think tanks and affirmation procedures to specific measures of operation and management of pilot institutions. At the same time, the *Regulations of National High-End Think Tanks (Trial)* (hereinafter referred to as *Regulations*) drafted by the Publicity Department of the Central Committee of the CPC and the *Management Methods of Special Fund of National High-End Think Tanks (Trial)* issued by the Ministry of Finance lay out institutional arrangements for organization, operation and fund management of national high-end think tanks respectively. The blueprint for building national high-end think tanks has gradually become clear and accurate. As a demonstration project for the construction of new-type think tanks with Chinese characteristics, the construction of national high-end think tanks undertakes the important tasks of exploring reform and innovation of systems and mechanisms, and seeking new paths and accumulating experience for promoting high-quality development of think tanks.

1.1.2   Give Full Play to the Role of the Board of Directors of National High-End Think Tanks in Decision-Making Guidance

According to the requirements of the central government, the national high-end think tanks follow a board of directors system. The board of directors of national high-end think tanks is established under the leadership of the National Planning Office of Philosophy and Social Science. As the deliberative and appraisal agency for the building of national high-end think tanks, the board of directors of national high-end think tanks is responsible for fixing strategic directions, reviewing major decisions, guiding scientific research, planning and carrying out supervision and evaluation. It is in charge of evaluating the development plan, regulations and rules of building high-end think tanks, locating key research tasks that the country urgently needs to carry out and assessing comprehensively national high-end think tanks on a regular basis. Meanwhile, the pilot think tanks have also established boards of directors of national high-end think tanks, keeping in mind the core mission of serving the decision-making of the central government and the overall work of the Party and the country. They convene members of the board of directors on a regular basis to summarize experiences and deploy works. While carrying out overall planning, they also fully play their role in decision-making guidance, strengthen the macro guidance and supervision of the tasks, and effectively implement the national requirements and arrangements.

1.1.3   Coordinated Innovation and Development of Four Types of High-End Think Tanks

In December 2015, the pilot project of national high-end think tanks kick-off meeting was held in Beijing. The conference announced that 25 institutions (now 24) were the first to be included in pilot institutions of national high-end think tank construction. The 24 pilot institutions specialize in 7 areas, including economics, science and technology, law, etc. , covering more than 20 key research areas such as public policy, macroeconomics, sci-tech development, national governance, national defense and army building, and party building. Overall, they are broad in varieties while each having distinctive features.

The 24 pilot institutions can be divided into the following four categories:

The first category is nine comprehensive research institutions directly subordinate to Party Central Committee, the State Council and the Central Military Commission. Eight of them are ministerial-level institutions, and only Compilation and Translation Bureau of the CPC Central Committee is a vice-ministerial-level institution. Among them, the Chinese Academy of Social Sciences (hereinafter referred to as CASS) is the highest level academic institution and comprehensive research center for philosophy and social science research domestically under the direct leadership of the CPC Central Committee and directly subordinates to the State Council. The Chinese Academy of Sciences is the highest-level consulting and research institution in the field of science and technology. The Academy of Military Sciences is a core institution for military research under the leadership of the Central Military Commission of the CPC. The above-mentioned three institutions have strong voices in their respective fields. As the national news agency, Xinhua News Agency is a "voice tube" for the Party and the nation. It is also the first high-end media think tank with a huge global information collection, analysis, research and judgment network and a host of expert editors and reporters in China. As an institution dedicated to theoretical work directly subordinate to the Party Central Committee, Compilation and Translation Bureau of the CPC Central Committee has integrated with the Party History Research Center of the CPC Central Committee and the Party Literature Research Center of the CPC

Central Committee in 2018 to form Party History and Literature Research Institute of the CPC Central Committee, which will replace the former Compilation and Translation Bureau of the CPC Central Committee to work as a national high-end think tank pilot institution. However, Compilation and Translation Bureau of the CPC Central Committee still preserves its name externally and bears such important duties as building thoughts and theories of the Party and national ideological construction.

The second category is 12 professional think tanks supported by universities and scientific research institutions. Six of them are from " Double First-Class " universities, including Peking University, Tsinghua University, Renmin University of China, Fudan University, Wuhan University and Sun Yat-sen University. Two research institutions directly subordinate to the Chinese Academy of Social Sciences are included, which shows that former decision-making consulting provided by the Chinese Academy of Social Sciences is well recognized. Two department-level research institutions directly subordinate respectively to the National Development and Reform Commission and the Ministry of Commerce are included, which mainly provide decision-making researches and consulting services in the field of macroeconomic and economic and trade research to the central government. China Institute of Contemporary International Relations (hereinafter referred to as CICIR) is dedicated to comprehensive research on international issues. 10 of its 15 institutes study countries, covering almost all countries and regions in the world, which enables it to provide more systematic policy-making plans to issues such as the construction of the "Belt and Road" and the community with a shared future for mankind. Shanghai Academy of Social Sciences (hereinafter referred to as SASC) is the largest academy of regional social sciences in China. Its inclusion can effectively evaluate the implementation effect of national strategies in regions and explore viable ways for local scientific research institutions to build high-end think tanks. These 12 professional think tanks cover a wide range of fields, including key areas like world situation, national conditions, and conditions of the people. This reflects China's great concern to international relations, the situations in China's Hong Kong SAR and Macao SAR, the construction of the rule of law, and social governance.

The third category is the think tank under large state-owned enterprises. This category only includes China National Petroleum Corporation Economic and Technological Research Institute (hereinafter referred to as CNPCETRI). As a research institute directly under CNPC, it is responsible for important decision-making of the group company in comprehensive information development and development strategy research. It focuses on researches of national energy security and development of strategic resources, making pre-research and estimates of the development rules of future energy industry and playing a key role in providing decision-making consulting to the implementation of action plan of national energy development strategy.

The fourth category is two social think tanks with good foundation—China Center for International Economic Exchanges (hereinafter referred to as the CCIEE) and the China Development Institute (Shenzhen, China) (hereinafter referred to as the CDI). Although they belong to social think tanks, they have given advice to national issues of great strategic importance. For example, CCIEE has drafted the preliminary version of *The Belt and Road Initiative: Progress, Contributions and Prospects* with high quality, which is the official authoritative document for the second Belt and Road Forum for International Cooperation. CDI, also known as "China's brain bank", is an independent research and advisory body established with the approval of the Premier of the State Council and led by the State Council Research Office. CDI actively undertakes the task of planning the Pointe Noire Special Economic Zone jointly implemented by China and Congo, making great contributions to the industrial planning, spatial planning and research of investment feasibility of the Pointe Noire Special Economic Zone.

The first included 24 national high-end think tank pilot institutions in 4 major categories have different development directions. The choice reflects China's great concern to party building, international strategy, global governance, macroeconomics, technological innovation, regional coordinated development and national defense construction and the needs to make policies in these fields. China will guide the research of high-end think tanks to suit the development of the country and society, the need of major national decision-making, and the core work of the decision-making divisions, achieving link-up between supply and demand and targeted service.

1.2   Innovate Systems & Mechanisms, Motivate Endogenous Power of Think Tanks

1.2.1   Constantly Improved Governance Structure Creates New Growth Points for Think Tanks

Over four years since the start of the construction, pilot institutions have constantly deepened reform of governance structure and promoted system innovation. At present, an internal governance mechanism featuring decision-making by the board of directors of think tanks, checking by academic committee, major responsibility by chief experts, policy-making serving orientation and research personnel at the center, with projects serving as connections is basically established. The board of directors is in charge of organizing and leading high-end think tanks, supervision and evaluation and guiding decision-making. It is generally composed of government officials, experts, scholars, and social activists of different professional backgrounds, providing a strong guarantee for construction direction of think tanks. The academic committee is responsible for various specific issues, such as academic planning, scientific research coordination, and academic review of high-end think tanks. The director of the committee is usually served by the chief expert, playing the role of scientific research guidance and academic decision-making. For example, CCIEE has set up a board of directors and central academic committee, advisory committee, fund board and executive agency under the leadership of the board of directors, forming a management structure of "three committees and one agency".

In addition, the national high-end think tanks also integrate the internal departments, effectively coordinate resources, and stimulate the internal motivation of think tanks following the management mode and operation rules of modern think tanks. For example, on the basis of original 11 institutions, the Chinese Academy of Social Sciences has preliminarily built a "trinity" think tank construction system with comprehensive think tanks as the leader, 21 professional think tanks as the focus and over 30 research units as the support. The Chinese Academy of Sciences has established an advisory committee and built new organization system of think tanks with five segments: comprehensive management, division support, scientific researches, communications and exchanges, and integration of science and education. At the same time, Institutes of Science and Development set up by Chinese Academy of Sciences operates as an independent legal entity hereinafter refered to as the (ASISD). The fact that it has 13 unincorporated units is needed for it to embark on networked strategic development, and to create new growth points. The Chinese Academy of Engineering has organized Working Committee for Think Tank

Consulting under the leadership of the presidium and Board of Managing Directors of the Academy, making it in charge of the strategic consultation work of the Academy. It has also set up Strategic Consulting Center to work as the core supporting mechanism for the construction of high-end think tanks. Xinhua News Agency, with the support of China Economic Information Service, Outlook Weekly, Thinker of Xinhuanet, Editorial Department Reference News, News Research Institution, etc. , has established six first-level research centers and formulated the "1 + 8" basic documents, initially forming a scientific and well-bedded overall development plan. National School of Development of Peking University (hereinafter referred to as NSD) has 11 research centers, of which 2 are affiliated to the Ministry of Education, and 7 are affiliated to Peking University. With an annual check system and exit mechanism, it reorganizes or even disqualifies a center if it fails an assessment. The Shanghai Academy of Social Sciences has established the first "think tank research center" dedicated to think tank researches, striving to become "a think tank for think tanks". CDI has promptly adjusted the structure of division management and established Think Tank Research and Information Department and Think Tank Exchange and Cooperation Department through reorganization to strengthen international cooperation and exchanges.

1.2.2   Take Institutional Improvement as an Effective Means, Lay Foundation for Long-Term Development of Think Tanks

To implement the guidance for building national-level think tanks, pilot institutions have actively conducted the reform to streamline administration, delegate power and improve regulation and services in the field of scientific research, formulated and issued clear and specific regulations for funds management, personnel management, performance appraisal, and achievement stimulation. These measures help to release dividends of system gradually and deepen the reform of decision-making consulting system.

First, the top-level system design of think tanks points out the development direction for the building of high-end think tanks. Think tanks, such as Development Research Center of the State Council (hereinafter referred to as DRC), the Chinese Academy of Social Sciences, the Chinese Academy of Engineering, Compilation and Translation Bureau of the CPC Central Committee, and the Institute of Guangdong, Hong Kong and Macao Development of Sun Yat-sen University, have all formulated *Work Plan for Pilot Institution of National High-End Think Tank Construction* Or *Enforcement Regulation for the Management of Special Funds for High-End Think Tanks* to make clear function orientation of think tank construction functions, organizational structure, assignment of responsibilities, management of research subjects, result management, and reward assessment.

Second, reform of fund management system of think tanks gives think tank talents greater autonomy in scientific research. Think tanks, such as the Chinese Academy of Engineering, Compilation and Translation Bureau of the CPC Central Committee, NSD, and CCIEE, have all issued *Special Management Rules for High-End Think Tanks* to establish rule-based fund supervision system and diversified fund investment mechanisms, and clear responsibility of departments in charge of centralized management and functional departments. CDI has also actively explored new methods for fund management, increased performance expenditures and awards for outstanding achievements, improved the efficiency of fund use, forming a situation in which intellectual activities are thriving, scientific researchers are vibrant, and high-quality results are constantly emerging.

Third, reform of management system of think tank projects has promoted standardized management of projects and the appearance of high-quality results. For example, Party School of the CPC Central Committee (National School of Administration) has formulated and issued *Management Methods of Project Teams of High-End Think Tank Construction of Party School of the CPC Central Committee (National School of Administration)*. The *Methods* is public-service-oriented and aims to enhance flexibility and competitiveness of scientific research project teams. Academy of Macroeconomic Research (hereinafter referred to as AMR) has formulated management measures for each project. It subdivided longitudinal projects into major projects, key projects, emergency projects, conventional projects, special fund projects of basic research operating expense, and strategic platform projects, and clarified procedures for approval, acceptance inspection and closing of each project and requirements for accountability. CCIEE has formulated Management Measures for Fund Project of China Center for International Economic Exchanges to make an operable design of the fund project's principles, overall goals, management departments and responsibilities, management processes, review procedures and achievement transformation.

Fourth, reform of incentive mechanism of assessment of results of think tanks has stimulated the enthusiasm of scientific researchers to produce high-quality results. For example, Academy of Military Sciences has formulated Detailed Rules for Awarding Research Results in Decision-Making Consulting of High-End Think Tanks in Academy of Military Sciences (Trial), which clarifies the principles, scope, and standards for awarding results of decision-making consulting of think tanks. NSD and CNPCETRI have respectively formulated *Management Measures of Funds for Special Award of High-End Think Tanks* and *Measures for Awarding Achievements of High-End Think Tanks*, clarifying reward and punishment mechanisms. These measures help to establish standardized, efficient, open and transparent ways for evaluating results and rewarding scientific research achievements that can be supervised effectively. They encourage enthusiasm of scientific researchers and motivate them to produce more outstanding results.

It can be said that institutional innovation of high-end think tanks is shifting from innovation in organization to innovation in management. The future institutional innovation should pay more attention to personnel motivation, improving mechanisms for selecting, appointing and preserving personnel. Measures should also be taken to promote reform of the mechanism of talent evaluation, recognizing and rewarding high-quality results, and activating intellectual resources. Moreover, high-end think tanks need to formulate more specific and operable rules for information disclosure, conference management, talent development, government procurement, policy evaluation, public opinion guidance and external exchanges during the process of building think tanks. This can effectively consolidate internal management systems and framework for the long-term development of high-end think tanks.

1.2.3 Top and Specialized Research Teams Basically Formed to Lay Solid Foundation for Tackling Difficult Problems

We have formed a multi-tiered talent pipeline with both part-time and full-time personnel boasting high morality and sophisticated skills. The Chinese Academy of Sciences has formed a talent structure composed of professional core research team, visiting research team and networked cooperative research team with talents within the Academy and outside it. The Chinese Academy of Engineering has gradually formed leading team of strategic consulting with academicians as the core, a counseling studies team with experts as the backbone, and a professional research team for strategy consultancy. Adopting a mode of "powerful core, extensive collaboration, and open frame", it aims to cultivate and create excellent talent team for strategy consultancy. Party School of the CPC Central Committee (National School of Administration) has implemented "Famous Teachers Project" under the principle of making full-time researchers as the main body while hiring part-time researchers. The School has nearly 400 full-time teaching and research personnel, top and middle-level officials, contract research fellow of national high-end think tanks and experts from Party School system. Academy of Military Sciences has constantly improved managenment methods to chief experts and distinguished chief experts. At present, a high-quality talent matrix of military research led by academicians of the Chinese Academy of Sciences and the Chinese Academy of Engineering and chief experts, mainly composed of recipients of national awards for talents and supported by high-level scientific research innovation teams and research talents. The National Defense University has built "Top Teacher Studio". It works to construct six-tiered personnel training system with outstanding professors as leaders, excellent young and middle-aged experts and academic leaders as the backbone force, and prominent young and middle-aged teaching and research talents and teaching and research personnel as basis. Chinese Academy of International Trade and Economic Cooperation (hereinafter referred to as CAITEC) pays attention to the introduction of overseas experts and invites CEOs of famous multinational companies as specially-invited experts to enhance the capacity. By now, it has invited CEOs such as Peter Mackie, CEO of CHEP Global, and Chris Tyas, senior vice president of Nestle Corporation and president of the supply chain. CDI has established a market-oriented and socialized mechanism for selecting and hiring personnel. It has introduced a large number of overseas students, with its talent team becoming better and better.

We are exploring the "revolving door mechanism" with Chinese characteristics.

The Chinese Academy of Sciences has set up a system of specially appointed researchers, actively exploring the "revolving door mechanism" of chief experts, core experts and visiting researchers recruited externally for strategy consultancy. In September 2019, National Academy of Development and Strategy of Renmin University of China specially hired 4 senior researchers and 80 full-time researchers. The 4 senior researchers are expert officials introduced from central ministries or other government departments, enhancing communications between think tanks and decision-making departments, and helping to create a Chinese-style "revolving door". This shows that high-end think tanks have begun to explore and try out the "revolving door mechanism", trying to establish a stable and direct combination mechanism through the interaction of experts and government officials. However, the cooperation between them is still not enough, the mechanism of information sharing is not perfect and bilateral connection and interactions need to be further deepened.

We pay attention to multi-form cultivation. CASISD has set up Dean Funding Project for Youth since 2017. In 2017 and 2018, it has funded more than 40 people. NSD of Peking University and the China Institute of Fudan University have incorporated research results of think tanks into the performance appraisal and have created a separate sequence of technical titles for think tank researchers. Academy of Military Sciences has worked with Beijing, Guangzhou and other places to carry out military-civilian collaborative innovation through integration and build platform for personnel training. It has also invited academicians to teach over 40 champions in the field of science and technology and top-notch personnel to achieve shared education and utilization. In addition to awarding outstanding young scholars, National Institution for Finance and Development of the Chinese Academy of Social Sciences has recruited assistant researchers for them according to their needs and even set up special research centers. National Academy of Development and Strategy of Renmin University of China employs a screening mechanism to incubate specific talents for 1~2 years and then test their ability to provide consulting service and give advice. CDI has established an internal system for technical title, which is guided by ability and performance and uses the quality of results and evaluation of the demand side as factors for assessment. It has also created conditions for the development of young talents, for example designating capable young people as leaders of research group, encouraging young people to participate in media comments, and providing opportunities for internship at famous overseas universities.

1.2.4   Diversified Sources of Funds to Help Long-Term and Stable Development of Think Tanks

In addition to central fiscal appropriation, most national high-end think tanks have established foundations and improved fund management system to expand the sources of funds and accumulate their own funds. They also focus on performance-oriented fund management to improve the efficiency and effectiveness of fund use.

First, set up foundations. DRC implements a diplomatic working mechanism of "one body, multiple wings and two platforms". China Development Research Foundation is one of the "two platforms" and a national public-raising foundation initiated by DRC to support policy researches and academic exchanges. National Academy of Development and Strategy of Renmin University of China has created a research fund for national high-end think tanks. Part of the fund is used to ensure the effective flow of funds of the Academy, and others are kept in the form of mother fund used for capital operation to meet the needs of sustainable development. The Institute of Guangdong, Hong Kong and Macao Development of Sun Yat-sen University has established the Huo Yingdong Hong Kong and Macao Research Fund, which is used for subsidizing doctoral students' innovative research, high-level talent introduction and overseas academic visits and exchanges. The Shanghai Academy of Social Sciences has set up "Think Tank Building Foundation of Shanghai Academy of Social Sciences". It creates a new model of scientific research funding featuring long-term tracking study, rolling funding and back-end rewards to provide adequate economic support for the construction of high-end think tanks. CDI has founded Development Foundation for Soft Science of CDI and Ma Hong Economic Research and Development Foundation. The former supports the independent research projects of CDI and publishing of works. The latter provides intellectual support for local economic development with its resources and works together with other institations consoldate.

Second, performance-oriented fund investment mechanism. NSD has established and improved management methods of special reward of high-end think tanks, carried out a fault-tolerant mechanism for fund management, specially adjusted the financial management system, and established a series of academic honorary titles through social donations, like "Fashu Scholars", "Fashu Chair Professor", "Mulan Young Scholars" and "Golden Light Chair Professor". These are titles designated to reward scientific researchers with outstanding achievements and contributions. The National Institute of Global Strategy of Chinese Academy of Social Sciences has basically formed a pattern in which fund use is results-oriented. Rapid response and pragmatic treatment are given equal importance, attention should be given to both international vision and domestic hot topics, and special countermeasures and basic theories are required to promote each other. The fund management is project-oriented, which stresses "cultivation of intelligence rather than people". CICIR stresses that funds should be used to reward strategic achievements that truly provide insights to the country, and dedicated researchers who devote wholeheartedly should get more awards.

1.2.5   Innovate Organization and Management Mode of Scientific Research, Focus on Improving Ability to Make Rapid Response

Promote innovation in organization of scientific researches. High-end think tanks generally adopt a project-based management mode to integrate resources, strengthen planning and organization of major special subjects, carry out interdisciplinary cooperated research, gather teams and strengths, and make the researches of think tanks more scientific. Party School of the CPC Central Committee (National School of Administration), Compilation and Translation Bureau of the CPC Central Committee, National Academy of Development and Strategy of Renmin University of China and CDI belong to this category. In addition, the Chinese Academy of Social Sciences actively explores research mechanisms, such as cooperative research of major scientific projects, collective research and judgment of major situations, and multi-angle suggestions for major special issues. The Chinese Academy of Sciences combines Academic Divisions with the entities, plays the academic leading role of Academic Divisions, and establishes a multi-layered, systematic and internet-based strategic research system composed of function-planning department, strategic research platforms and professional research institutions, strategic research teams of sci-tech innovation bases, and strategic research teams of research institutes. It aims to form a matrix-structured and internet-based research mode led by tasks. The Academy of Military Sciences encourages researchers of military theories and military science and technology to work together and has established a research organization mode for tackling major tasks cooperatively, which features cross-domain cooperation, centralized office, closed operation and comprehensive support, with an aim of tapping the advantages of both skills and theories.

Attach importance to hierarchical and flexible management. AMR manages the academy and institutes independently. It divides horizontal projects into 6 categories: key projects, emergency projects, conventional projects and so on. It manages them with different methods. So far, there have been more than 25 management methods and regulations for scientific researches. National Academy of Development and Strategy of Renmin University of China has abolished the system of lifelong tenure. It allocates personnel, funds and other research resources based on the projects and payment is made according to the "number of qualified products". This decomposes research tasks into more detailed work pieces, and payment is decided on the quality and quantity of pieces done, mobilizing the initiative and enthusiasm of researchers.

Pay attention to the whole process management of results. The Chinese Academy of Engineering and AMR implement front-end control over major projects and control project quality by convening kick-off meetings, topic selection seminars, and monthly theory-discussing meetings. The Academy of Military Sciences sticks to node management of the full process of projects and strengthens supervision of key links, such as project approval, research development, and final report to ensure think tank results meet high quality and high standard. It also lays emphasis on guidance to scientific research and strives to ensure correct direction for topic selection, provide organizational guarantee to researches, design accurate channels to submission, and give suggestions for improvement in transformation. National Institution for Finance and Development of the Chinese Academy of Social Sciences holds regular meetings for scientific research, invites decision-making departments, regulatory authorities and experienced practitioners in financial institutions to pool wisdom, and utilizes "external intelligence" to ensure the quality of results. However, on the whole, the quality management of think tank results needs to be further regulated, and the quality control of results is not rigorous enough. Going ahead, management standards of results of high-end think tanks must be clarified, and measures should be taken to promote full-process detailed management of major projects, strengthen supervision of key nodes and effectively improve the research ability of think tanks.

1.3   Serving Policy-Making Based on Overall Situation Becomes Basic Consensus of High-End Think Tanks

1.3.1   Function Positioning Manifests Value of Policy-Making

The first high-end think tank pilot institutions, through integrating superior resources and strengthening the role of policy-making consulting, have gradually explored a path of development suited to themselves and strived to demonstrate the unique value of think tanks. The Chinese Academy of Sciences is a combination of scientific research institution, Academic Division, and educational institutions, which has established a development strategy of "building the Academy with democracy, flourishing the Academy through opening-up, and strengthening the Academy with talents". The Chinese Academy of Engineering gives full play to the comprehensive advantages of having multiple disciplines and trans-departments, continues to promote the construction of national high-end think tanks that are led by innovation, relying on the nation, trusted by society, and internationally renowned, and strives to build an "indomitable" strategic pattern of high-end think tanks. Party School of the CPC Central Committee (National School of Administration) has actively played the quaternity role of school, front, institutions and think tanks. It has set four major goals: becoming the best educational institution of the Party, the leading highland of the Party's ideology and theory, the leading academic hall of the social sciences of the Party, and a high-end think tank of the Party and nation. National Institute of Global Strategy of Chinese Academy of Social Sciences positions itself as a think tank dedicated to countermeasure research. It focuses on such scientific research fields as the Belt and Road Initiative, global strategy, and peripheral security research. CAITEC focuses on providing consulting to policy research and the work of business center. Driven by consulting service, think tank diplomacy, and public opinion guidance, it actively plays its role in providing advice to policy-making, international exchanges, and external publicity.

1.3.2 Focus on Research of Policy-Making Needs

In order to avoid homogenous competition, national high-end think tanks keep on exploring their own research and development strengths. In general, they focus on four aspects: major researches on ideology and theory, policy-making and deployment, major practical problems and major special topics. According to the statistics on research fields of the national high-end think tanks included in the Chinese Think Tank Index (CTTI), we found that: (1) think tanks like DRC, the Chinese Academy of Social Sciences, Shanghai Academy of Social Sciences, the Macro Academy and National Academy of Development and Strategy of Renmin University of China tend to focus on macroeconomics, industrial development, market economy and fiscal policy; (2) military think tanks like the Academy of Military Sciences and National Defense University make national defense policy, military policy and security policy as the main research fields; (3) think tanks like CICIR and National Institute of Global Strategy of Chinese Academy of Social Sciences focus on international diplomacy, the Belt and Road Initiative, global culture, and the community of shared destiny for mankind; (4) media think tanks represented by Xinhua News Agency focus on management of Internet, public culture and news policy; (5) think tanks of the Party and government represented by Party School of the CPC Central Committee (National School of Administration) and Compilation and Translation Bureau of the

CPC Central Committee mainly focus on party building and ideological research.

From the perspective of individual institutions, the research focus of each pilot institution is different. The Chinese Academy of Sciences is dedicated to resolving major issues of scientific and technological strategies and policy and implementing such major tasks as studying and judging world's scientific and technological frontiers and prospective study of China's major science and technology. It also studies reform of the scientific and technological system suitable for new technological revolution and industrial revolution and supports the implementation of forward-looking and preparatory front exploration tasks. AMR pays more attention to research and has established cooperation with 9 local development and reform commissions to set up national condition research bases and carry out research in 10 areas like local economic development, industrial economy, and energy economy. National Academy of Development and Strategy of Renmin University of China relies more on discipline advantages and stresses theoretical innovation. It has established four major research areas: economic governance and economic development, political governance and legal construction, social governance and social innovation, and public diplomacy and international relations. Compilation and Translation Bureau of the CPC Central Committee focuses on five key research areas, including Marxist theory and contemporary practice and frontier issues of contemporary socialism. It has set up 10 special divisions to carry out researches in different areas.

On the whole, however, high-end think tanks still face problems such as low research orientation and insufficient foresighted and in-depth researches. It is necessary to keep in mind that the central task of high-end think tanks is serving central policy-making. They should focus on major issues concerning overall situation and exerting long-term influence, study urgent issues, and find solution to problems the country will face in the future needs. While enhancing basic researches, they need to strive to make research achievements with strategic vision, thought depth, and credibility.

1.3.3 Actively Serve Major National Strategic Tasks

The essential role of high-end think tanks is serving central policy-making. While focusing on the country's major strategies, tasks and works, they must carry out in-depth, forward-looking, targeted, and preparatory policy researches. Over the past four years, based on the 13th Five-Year Plan, the Belt and Road Initiative and national security, pilot institutions have made a large number of in-depth research achievements with practical value, contributing significantly to central policy-making.

Actively participate in major projects of the 13th Five-Year Plan. The first year of the 13th Five-Year Plan coincides with the official launch of the pilot work of the national high-end think tanks. In order to gather the intelligence of think tank experts and widely collect opinions on planning, the central government commissioned 42 institutions to assist in the planning of the 13th Five-Year Plan. In the end, thirty-one 13th Five-Year major projects and 117 special research reports were completed. Think tanks that participated include DRC, the Chinese Academy of Social Sciences, the Chinese Academy of Sciences, NSD and many other pilot institutions. Of the 17 research projects undertaken by DRC in 2015, 10 were major projects related to the planning of 13th Five-Year Plan. In March 2016, chief experts from 4 national high-end think tanks—NSD, Shanghai Academy of Social Sciences, National Institution for Finance and Development of the Chinese Academy of Social Sciences and National Defense University, actively shared their opinions and gave suggestions to the government work report and the draft of layout plan of the 13th Five-Year Plan.

Work together to help the construction of the Belt and Road Initiative. The "Silk

Road International Forum" and "Silk Road International Think Tank Network" initiated by the DRC are early attempts to build a Belt and Road think tank cooperation network on a global scale. China Institute of Fudan University established the Digital Belt and Road Research Center (DBRC) to study the Belt and Road Initiative from the perspective of new technologies and industries. Since 2013, the Chinese Academy of Sciences has led the way to create a Belt and Road sci-tech cooperation system combining "talent, platform, and projects", and implement the "Development Project of Science and Education Cooperation of Developing Countries" and the Belt and Road Initiative Sci-Tech Cooperation Action Plan. It also launched Alliance of International Science Organization (ANSO) of the Belt and Road Initiative and organized science and education institutions from over 40 countries or regions to join it. The Chinese Academy of Engineering has established cooperation with 32 countries along the Belt and Road, set up a basic framework for "Belt and Road" international engineering cooperation in science and technology, and gathered more than 100 academicians in the Academy to carry out researches. The Shanghai Academy of Social Sciences has better served the construction of the Belt and Road Initiative through the founding of the Silk Road Information Network, the "Belt and Road" Shanghai Forum, English Periodicals on Belt and Road Research and the "Belt and Road" large database. CCIEE has made more outstanding contributions on policy-making during the construction of the Belt and Road Initiative. It was commissioned by National Development and Reform Commission to finish major tasks such as the "Bangladesh-China-India-Myanmar", "China-Laos" and "China-Myanmar" economic corridors. Some leaders from CCIEE were directly involved in the work of the "Belt and Road" project. Meanwhile, CCIEE has published a series of "Belt and Road" books, making contribution to the Belt and Road Initiative and realization of high-quality development.

"Second Innovation" in the integration of military science and technology. The Academy of Military Sciences readjusted some key scientific researches, like researches on war and battle and the revision of laws and regulations. It cut research projects that deviated from the main business while adding projects on actual military combats, such as war forms and combat modes. It put forward overall layout of "multi-point park" collaborative innovation and preliminarily established a work situation of military joint, open and cooperative researches. The National Defense University strives to build a high-end think tank of national security. It has built platforms such as the National Laboratory for Safety Engineering, China National Security Research Center, and the Research Center for Military-Civil Integration In-depth Development. It conducts researches, strategic research and judgment, personnel training and international exchanges based on major strategic needs of the Party, the country, and the army.

1.3.4 Involve in Policy-Making Process to Directly Serve National High-End Decision-Making

According to Pilot Working Plan, pilot institutions of national high-end think tanks can report results of their findings directly to the central government through *National High-end Think Tank Report* sponsored by the National Planning Office of Philosophy and Social Science, so as to involve in policy-making process through direct channels. At the same time, pilot institutions are allowed and encouraged to report important findings to relevant departments through its own channels. For example, the Shanghai Academy of Social Sciences has set up three special reports: *New Think Tank Special Report*, *International Issues Special Report* and *Public Opinion Information* to provide more comprehensive suggestions for decision-making to leaders of the central government, and Shanghai municipal Party committee and government. Institute of Science and Development of the Chinese Academy of Sciences has also established three internal journals—*Technology Think Tank Report*, *Sci-Tech Decision Reference*, *Sci-Tech Frontier Development*, and two wall bulletins—*Frontier Reports of Science and Technology* and *Reports of Technology Policy and Consulting* to support decision-making services. The Institute of Guangdong, Hong Kong and Macao Development of Sun Yat-sen University submits findings through internal references like *Special Report of Guangdong*, *Hong Kong and Macao Research*, *Social Condition*, *Public Opinion and Development of Hong Kong and Macao*, *Short Reports of Guangdong*, *Hong Kong and Macao Research Viewpoints*, and *Development of Global Bay Areas*.

In addition to submitting internal references, high-end think tanks can also involve in the policy-making process by participating in document drafting and internal symposiums, establishing cooperation platforms and temporary transferring and exchanges of personnel to provide intellectual support for central decision-making. For example, the Chinese Academy of Sciences and the State Council Research Office jointly set up China Innovation Strategy and Policy Research Center with the support of Institute of Science and Development of the Chinese Academy of Sciences. It relies on channels for results utilization and transformation of the State Council Research Office and integration platform of comprehensive researches of CASISD to provide more foresighted and constructive consulting suggestions for national innovation strategies and macro policies. The Institute of Guangdong, Hong Kong and Macao Development of Sun Yat-sen University invites famous retired or former Party or government officials with rich experience in decision-making consulting to join the board of directors, designates a deputy administrative dean in charge of communication, and occasionally invites officials from relevant departments to give lectures. Experts of the Institute proactively provide consultations and suggestions to policy-making departments, participate in making of plans, and jointly organize expert symposia. It selects young scholars to work temporarily at policy-making departments, or to join in work departments of Hong Kong and Macao for short-term researches.

1.4 Diversified Subjects Have a Strong Voice, Guide Public Opinion Rationally and Forcefully

1.4.1 Brand Matrix Gradually Takes Shape

Building unique think tank product system has gradually become a key driving force for national high-end think tanks to do something new and enhance the social influence of think tanks. At present, pilot institutions continue to integrate superior resources, promote the release and transformation of outstanding achievements by organizing academic forums, establishing quality books, compiling serial books, and building special platforms, with the aim to create a unique think tank brand matrix.

First, host or undertake major national academic forums. For example, since 2000, DRC has hosted several times High-Level Forum of China's Development, a large national-level international forum. This forum is also an important platform for high-level dialogues and discussions among government officials, business leaders, experts and scholars from both China and abroad. Since 2009, CCIEE has held five sessions of Global Think Tank Summit consecutively, on which participants can have in-depth exchanges on topics, such as global governance, economic globalization, and the building of the Belt and Road Initiative. The Chinese Academy of Sciences holds the High-Level Forum on Strategy and Policy-Making and Lecture Hall on National High-End Sci-Tech Think Tanks, a brand construction activity of high-end think tank, on a regular basis, initially forming a multi-tiered high-level academic exchange system made up of academic annual conference and academic forum of Academic Divisions, frontier forum of science and technology, and small-sized high-end forums. Since 2013, the Chinese Academy of Engineering has held, at regular intervals, Strategic Forum of Emerging Industries Cultivation and Development in Shenzhen every year, and released annually Development Report of Strategic Emerging Industries in China, which has aroused warm responses in the industry. NSD has organized three think tank brand activities—China Economic Observation Seminar, Exploration of Politics and National Development Forum, and led the organization of China-US Economic Dialogues and China-US Dialogues on Health. It started to hold Youth Forum of National Development since 2010 to provide a communication platform for young talents of think tanks. AMR has formed a series of academic brands, such as AMR Macroeconomic Forum, AMR Lecture Hall, AMR Academic Teahouse, effectively promoting the innovation of macroeconomic theory with Chinese characteristics.

Second, found quality books and special topic books. For example, the Chinese Academy of Engineering has developed two comprehensive academic journals in engineering—*Engineering* and *Chinese Engineering Science*. The latter is an important display window for the achievements of national high-end think tank of the Chinese Academy of Engineering. AMR has developed 6 academic journals, including *Macroeconomic Research*, *Chinese Energy* and *Digest of Economic Management*, and displayed the results of think tanks in the form of academic series, annual collected works and annual reports. NSD has set up two major journals, *Economics* (Quarterly) and *China Economic Journal*, providing a platform for the display and exchange of achievements made at home and abroad to boost the development of China's economics. CDI has established two special journals—*National High-End*

Think Tank Observation ; *China Economic Monthly* and *CDI Newsletter* (its research development in English), sending them to relevant domestic government departments, key think tanks, international think tanks and multinational companies. This has enhanced its impact both at home and abroad. It also issues a series of publications in the form of annual reports, CDI series, CDI reference, open guidance, and CDI reports.

Third, organize special events and build an index platform. CDI has launched the activities of Silver Lake Salon and CDI Capital Salon. The latter is a high-end, professional, niche, and closed exchange platform. It has also jointly compiled the Global Financial Center Index with the British Z / Yen Group and released *China Financial Center Index* (*CDI CFCI*) *Report*. In addition, NSD has also built a series of index platforms, such as China Investor Sentiment Index, China Consumer Confidence Index and China Regional Innovation and Entrepreneurship Index, to show China's economic development in the form of index reports.

1.4.2 Experts from Think Tanks Act Actively

More and more high-end think tanks have appeared on important international occasions to clarify China's views and make China's proposals. This has become an indispensable and important force in China's public diplomacy. The international influence and popularity of Chinese think tanks have also continuously enhanced. For example, on April 4, 2018, the U. S. government announced a list of 1,333 items worth about $50 billion exported to the U. S. from China, on which it planned to levy additional tariffs. The following morning, experts from CCIEE and AMR discussed the Sino-US economic and trade relations and expressed their opinions. Moreover, CCIEE held a high-end seminar on Sino-US economic and trade relations, during which Zeng Peiyan, director-general of CCIEE, analyzed Sino-US economic and trade issues objectively and rationally and refuted the wrong views with a tough tone. Fan Gang, director of CDI, accepted the interview with CCTV International to interpret the various topics of the G20 Hangzhou Summit. He has also been interviewed by Bloomberg TV for several times to analyze RMB exchange rate and issues related to capital control. Moreover, he has shared his views at Boao Forum for Asia and Peking University's 120th Anniversary Ceremony in London and other mainstream media. CAITEC embraces a "trinity" publicity mode—giving opinions actively, and through external forces and cooperation. It has set up a committee of specially invited experts from the political, commercial, academic and media professionals to enhance the effectiveness and pertinence of external discourse system. Through researches on China-US, China-Europe, China-Japan and China-South Korea dialogues, CCIEE responds actively to the complex and changing international economic and trade situation, firmly safeguards national interests, and strives to make a Chinese voice.

1.4.3   Form of Publicity Gets Richer

Over the past 4 years of construction, national high-end think tanks have, through such media platforms as newspapers, websites, and WeChat official accounts, widely publicized important achievements of think tanks and experts with outstanding contributions, continuously enhancing the influence and credibility of think tanks. As a research center of public policy of Xinhua News Agency's national high-end think tank, Liao Wang Institute has gradually formed a new-type transmission mode of think tanks with research teams of public policy and research committees of serial policies as foundation, research-based internal references, such as *Liao Wang Research Reports*, as the core, and Think Tank Client Cluster as new form of publicity and interaction matrix. AMR has opened its WeChat official accounts—AMR High-End Think Tank, and built internal website, external Chinese website and external English website. China Institute of Fudan University put forward the idea of three platforms generating forces together, meaning that holding the offline activity of Thinkers Forum, building the online platform of Observer Network and creating the short video brand of Watch Video. The three platforms work together to build a "'Internet plus' plus think tank" mode. The Shanghai Academy of Social Sciences has set up an office to publicize scientific research achievements, found its network, newspaper, and WeChat official account, and launched special columns and customized channels. It has given full play to the integration of traditional and emerging media, forming an influential publicity network. CDI has opened three commentary columns using new media: CDI National Policy, CDI Observation and Pengpai Asking Policies, calling on participation of the public to expand social influence and public transmission.

2 Building Progress of New Provincial & Municipal Key Think Tanks

In order to further implement the *Opinions* issued by General Office of the CPC Central Committee and the General Office of the State Council, provinces (autonomous regions and municipalities) , led by national high-end think tanks, have continued to explore reform plans that suit the development of local think tanks and tried to cultivate and develop a number of new provincial-level key think tanks and industry-based think tanks, gradually forming a matrix of provincial-level key think tanks with reasonable structure and complete functions.

2.1 Gradually Improved Management Systems of Think Tanks

2.1.1 Basic Documents for Building New-Type Think Tanks Are Introduced

After issuance of the *Opinions* by the General Office of the CPC Central

Committee and General Office of the State Council, provinces (autonomous regions and municipalities) have formulated guidelines for the construction of new-type local think tanks based on local development, providing basic guidelines for building provincial key think tanks. According to statistics (as of December 2019), about 30 provinces (autonomous regions and municipalities) have issued opinions on the construction of new think tanks, most of which were issued between 2015 and 2017. The think tanks are mainly managed by Provincial Party Committee Publicity Department or Advisory Committee (Office). For example, *Opinions on Strengthening the Construction of New Think Tanks in Jiangsu Province* issued by the Province points out that "By 2020, efforts will be focused on building a group of professional high-end think tanks supporting national and regional development". As one of the first provinces in China to issue local basic documents for construction of new-type think tanks, Jiangsu Province has made quick responses, started early and introduced lots of measures, setting an example for other provinces and municipalities to accelerate the construction of new-type think tanks. *Opinions on Strengthening the Construction of New Think Tanks in Henan Province* issued by the Province states that "By 2020, endeavor to build 2 to 3 national professional high-end think tanks, and 5 to 8 professional think tanks having influence in the central and western regions or even the whole country". Its goal is clear, and attitude firm.

With the successive introduction of opinions on the construction of new-type local think tanks, some regions have begun to set the goal for building provincial-level key think tanks. As a result, corresponding construction plans and management measures have been released, such as those by Jiangsu, Heilongjiang, Yunnan and Shandong provinces. Jiangsu Province has formulated *Interim Measures for the Construction and Management of New-Type Think Tanks in Jiangsu Province*, offering specific provisions in terms of management mechanisms, tasks and projects, personnel, funds, assessment and motivation. This has provided guidance for standardized management and operation of the think tanks in the province. Hubei Provincial Party Committee Publicity Department released *Construction Plan of New-Type Think Tanks in Hubei Province* on June 3, 2016. Ten new-type and key think tanks relying on Wuhan University, Huazhong University of Science and Technology, Hubei Academy of Social Sciences, Provincial Party School and other six institutions were included. General Office of the Hunan Provincial Party Committee and General Office of the Hunan Provincial Government jointly issued *Opinions on Strengthening the Construction of New Think Tanks in Hunan Province* on July 14, 2015, pointing out that "building a number of provincial-level key think tanks having influence in the province and even the whole country". In September of the same year, the Publicity Department of the Hunan Provincial Party Committee issued *Management Measures of Provincial Key Think Tanks in Hunan Province*. Moreover, policies and documents, such as *Management Measures of Provincial Key Think Tanks in Anhui Province (Trial)* and *Construction and Management Measures for Capital Pilot Institutions of High-End Think Tanks*, have clarified duties, tasks, submission of results, fund management, assessment and evaluation of local high-end think tanks.

2.1.2 Industrial Policies and Documents of Think Tank Follow Up Closely

According to the *Opinions* by General Office of the CPC Central Committee and General Office of the State Council, efforts should be made to coordinate the development of think tanks of Party and government departments, Chinese Academy of Social Sciences, Party School of the CPC Central Committee (National School of Administration), universities, armed forces, scientific institutes, enterprises and society, so as to form a new-type think tank system with Chinese characteristics, which has clear position, distinctive features, proper scale and reasonable layout. At the national level, the Ministry of Education has issued *Plan for Promoting the Construction of New-Type University Think Tanks with Chinese Characteristics*, nine ministries, including Publicity Department of the CPC and the Ministry of Civil Affairs, have jointly released *Several Opinions on the Healthy Development of Social Think Tanks*, and China Association for Science and Technology has issued *Opinions on Building High-End Sci-Tech Innovation Think Tanks*. Local governments have followed the pace of the country closely and successively formulated major plans for cultivating and building university, sci-tech innovation, society, Party schools think tanks. For example, Education Department of Liaoning Province issued *Construction Plan for New-Type University Think Tanks in Liaoning Province (Trial)* and announced the first 20 new-type university think tanks of Liaoning Province in January 2019. In 2018, Education Department of Shaanxi Province issued *Management Measures for New-Type University Think Tanks in Shaanxi Province*. Later on, through selection and recommendation by universities and review by the Education Department, 22 new-type university think tanks were identified in 2018. In April 2018, *Management Measures for Constructing and Operating of Sci-Tech Innovation Think Tanks in Yunnan Science (Trial)* drafted by Department of Science and Technology of Yunnan Province was officially implemented, aiming to cultivate 24 major sci-tech innovation think tanks in Yunnan Province. Meanwhile, Education Department of Yunnan Province issued *Construction Plan for New-Type University Think Tanks in Yunnan Province (Trial)*. In the second half of 2014, 14 think tanks were approved for construction, and 3 think tanks were approved for cultivation. During the construction, fiscal department of the province would offer 800,000 to 1 million RMB as construction fund.

2.1.3   Supporting Policies for Think Tanks Are Quickly Formulated

In order to further improve the internal governance of provincial key think tanks, provinces have also formulated and issued a series of special management measures and enforcement regulations, mainly covering management of special funds, expert team construction, assessment and evaluation, which offer professional guidance and supervision for the standardized management and operation of key think tanks.

The first is management policies of special funds of new-type think tanks. Proper use of think tank funds affects standardized operation and management effectiveness of new-type think tanks. Under the general guidance of *Management Measures of Special Funds of National High-End Think Tanks (Trial)* issued by the Ministry of Finance, Beijing, Heilongjiang, Jiangsu and Anhui provinces and Ningxia Hui Autonomous Region have successively introduced management measures of special funds suited to local development and clarified the limit of subsidizing, scope of expenditure, budget management and supervision. In addition, Guangxi, Hubei, Chongqing, Hebei and other provinces have established achievement reward for policy-making consulting, which is mainly given to researches on application of countermeasure.

The second is team construction policy of experts of new-type think tanks. Talent team is the core competitiveness of think tank construction. In order to further strengthen the construction and management of talent teams of provincial key think tanks and give full play to the main role of think tank experts in policy-making, some provinces (autonomous regions and municipalities) have formulated talent funding plans or management methods. For example, Shandong Province has issued *Opinions on Building High-End Talent Teams of Think Tanks*, Education Department of Heilongjiang Province has formulated *Management Measures for "Supporting*

Heilongjiang Scholars", and Henan Province has issued *Management Measures for Scholars in Henan Province*. All these have clarified recruitment criteria and scope, duties, reward mechanism and achievement evaluation of think tank experts.

The third is evaluation and assessment policy of new-type think tanks. In order to effectively monitor and evaluate the effectiveness of the construction of provincial key think tanks, provinces and municipalities have formulated work plans for the evaluation of think tanks and improved supervision and evaluation mechanisms, including detailed index system of evaluation and mechanism for dynamic adjustment of key think tanks and back-up think tanks. For example, at the symposium of dealing No. 221 Key Proposal of Zhejiang Provincial Political Consultative Conference, *Index System of Evaluation of New-Type Think Tanks in Zhejiang Province* was deliberated and approved, gradually forming a framework for working of think tanks in Zhejiang. In December 2016, Jiangsu Province issued *Trial Measures for the Management and Assessment of New Think Tanks in Jiangsu Province*, which stipulates that evaluation of the think tanks is in the charge of Think Tank Construction Office of Jiangsu Province and that major high-end think tanks shall be evaluated every 5 years while key cultivated think tanks shall be evaluated every 3 years. These evaluation mechanisms are dynamic, clarifying the evaluation indicators and specific enforcement rules.

In general, the policies of think tanks are improving continuously. However, the implementation of policies in different provinces and municipalities is quite different, and measures and efforts to promote reforms are also different. The phenomenon of "last mile" exists in policy implementation. In terms of formulation of policies, due to the restrictions of development of society and economy, construction foundation of think tanks, and ideological perception, planning for the construction of key think tanks has not yet been implemented. In some regions, supporting policies and measures for key provincial think tanks have not been improved, and management measures clarifying access conditions, construction standards, fund management, evaluation methods, and elimination mechanisms of key think tanks have not been formulated. In terms of implementation of policies, local departments often fail to implement policies due to insufficient and poor communications. Therefore, the construction of think tanks should not become formalistic. Rather, it should focus on content innovation and improvement of quality, make full use of institutional advantages, deepen the reform of institutional mechanisms, and provide better decision-making support for major national strategies and local economic development.

2.2 Give Play to Actual Effect of Management Mechanism of Think Tanks

2.2.1 Provincial Board of Directors of Think Tanks Endeavor to Ensure Good Planning and Coordination

As management department of provincial key think tanks, the local board of directors of think tanks is generally organized by provincial management departments of think tanks. It is responsible for receching out to provincial think tanks and coordination and management like coordinating policies, advancing tasks, making strategic plans, assessing and evaluating. According to incomplete statistics, about 14 provincial governments have established management departments for the construction of new-type think tanks, and 6 of them have provincial boards of directors of new-type think tanks. For example, in 2017, a board of directors of new-type think tanks is organized by the Publicity Department of the Jiangsu Provincial Party Committee, it is a deliberative and appraisal agency for construction of new-type think tanks in the province. The directors of the board include members from departments of provincial party committee and provincial government and heads of 9 key high-end think tanks and 15 key cultivated think tanks in Jiangsu Province. In 2018, Beijing set up Capital Board of Directors of High-End Think Tanks and formulated *Rules of Procedure of Capital Board of Directors of High-End Think Tanks*. Meanwhile, Peking University, Beijing Administration Institute (Beijing Municipal Party Committee School), National Academy of Development and Strategy of Renmin University of China and other pilot high-end think tanks in Beijing have also established boards of directors. Hebei Province has established Leading Group of Hebei Provincial Philosophy and Social Sciences Work (New Think Tank Construction) and the Board of Directors of New-Type Think Tanks. The former is responsible for coordinating and handling major issues related to the development of philosophy and social sciences, while the latter has deliberation and decision-making as its main functions and is in charge of coordinating forces of social sciences in the province to pool wisdom and efforts for the construction of think tanks.

It can be seen that provincial boards of directors of think tanks have been established one after another to fully play the roles in development planning, decision-making guidance, assessment and evaluation of think tanks. Next, provincial think tank authorities including boards of directors should strengthen connection between supply and demand and channels and establish a comprehensive project claim system oriented to decision-making departments. They should make achievement-making as the first goal in guiding the selection and supervision of think tank research teams, managing and evaluating works, and assisting think tanks to provide high-quality policy-making consulting. In addition, while ensuring the overall coordinated development of think tanks, provincial think tank authorities should enhance targeted guidance and management, striving to form a batch of back-up teams of think tanks construction with reasonable structure and distinctive characteristics.

2.2.2 Submission Channels for Key Think Tanks Become More Stable and Smooth

Apart from offering advice through compiling books, publishing research reports, hosting internal discussions, and accepting media interviews, provincial key think tanks submit their research results to the provincial party committee research office, government research office, Publicity department of government departments through specific channels. The channels generally include, first, internal references designated by management departments of think tanks. For example, *Capital High-End Think Tank Reports* run by the Secretariat (Association of Social Sciences) of the Capital Board of Directors of High-End Think Tanks, *Think Tank Special Reports* run by Think Tank Office of the Publicity Department of Jiangsu Provincial Party Committee for provincial key high-end and cultivated think tanks, *Consulting Digest* co-run by Advisory Committee of Liaoning Provincial Party Committee and Provincial Government and Policy Research Office of Liaoning Provincial Party Committee, and *Special Reports of Think Tank Achievements* run by Leadership Group Office of Sichuan Second, exclusive internal publications of provincial key think tanks. Take Jiangsu Province as an example. The Provincial Federation of Social Sciences releases *Reference for Policy-Making* with the support of 39 research bases for decision-making consulting and famous experts in the field, Sichuan Academy of Social Sciences edits and issues *Special Reports for Policy-Making Consulting*, Sichuan Party Committee School (Sichuan Administration Institute) compiles *Research Reports*, and Yangtze Industrial Economic Institute issues *Reports on Yangtze Industrial Economic Policy-Making Consulting*. It can be said that key provincial think tanks can rely on designated internal references and self-created internal journals to submit research results in a more standardized, orderly, and direct manner, fully playing their role in actively serving central and local policy-making.

Apart from involving in policy-making process through traditional internal references, provincial key think tanks need to expand new channels to serve policy-making and actively undertake scientific researches entrusted and assigned by policy-making departments. They should also actively draft documents, give lectures and trainings, investigate public opinions, conduct international exchanges, integrate their researches into policy-making and serve for it.

2.3 Development Ideas of Provincial Key Think Tanks Become Clearer

2.3.1 Cultivation Patterns of Think Tanks Are Characteristics

Policy pilot is a Chinese characteristic measure to implement policies and an effective way to carry out national strategies and policy ideas. At the 35th plenary session of the Leading Group of Comprehensively Deepening Reform, General Secretary Xi Jinping made clear requirements for promoting pilot reforms, stressing "pilot projects first, then extension" and "do a good job in system design, and deploy pilots with targets". This shows that doing a good job in pilot project is a key measure to the reform and innovation, which has profound meaning to the overall reform. According to preliminary statistics (as of December 2019), 21 provinces (autonomous regions and municipalities) have carried out pilot projects of cultivating new-type key think tanks, guided by Provincial Planning Offices of Philosophy and Social Sciences, Publicity Departments of Provincial Party Committees, Provincial Advisory Committees of Policy-Making, and Provincial Associations of Social Sciences. The construction period is 3 to 5 years, with funds ranging from 100,000 to 1 million RMB per project. See Table 1.1.

The multilayered governance structure of modern local governance requires the participation of different types of think tanks with different hierarchies. Looked vertically, the systems of provincial key think tanks can be divided into two modes. One is a singular "emphasis/ cultivation" mode. This mode is used by think tanks in most provinces and autonomous regions, typical examples including Liaoning, Heilongjiang, Guangdong, Ningxia, etc. The other is "emphasis-cultivation" mode. Jiangsu, Anhui and other provinces have followed a mode of "first training, then selecting"—choosing a group of professional think tanks urgently needed by the central and local governments for policy-making and having good foundations to give support, forming a construction structure of provincial key think tanks with reasonable layout and concentrated advantages. According to the key think tanks officially announced by the provinces (autonomous regions and municipalities) and CTTI, university think tanks have the largest proportion, followed by think tanks of party committees or government departments and think tanks of the Academy of Social Sciences. The pattern is basically same as the development pattern of new-type think tanks in different provinces.

Table 1. 1   Constructions of Provincial-Level Key Think Tanks

Provinces	Names of Think Tanks	Governing Bodies	Numbers
Beijing	First Pilot Institutions of Capital High-End Think Tanks	Council of High-End Think Tanks in the Capital	14
Heilongjiang Province	Key Cultivation Think Tanks of Heilongjiang Province (two batches)	Publicity Department of Heilongjiang Provincial Party Committee	20+6
Jilin Province	Pilot Institutions of New-Type Think Tanks of Jilin Province	Publicity Department of Jilin Provincial Party Committee	8
Liaoning Province	First Pilot Institutions of New-Type Key Think Tanks of Liaoning Province	Policy-Making Consulting Commission of Liaoning Provincial Party Committee and Government	27

Continued

Provinces	Names of Think Tanks	Governing Bodies	Numbers
Jiangsu Province	Key High-End Think Tanks of Jiangsu Province	Led by the Publicity Department of Jiangsu Provincial Party Committee and Guided by the Planning Office of Jiangsu Philosophy and Social Sciences	9
	Key Cultivation Think Tanks of Jiangsu Province		15
Shandong Province	First Pilot Institutions of New-Type Think Tanks	Planning Office of Philosophical Science of Shandong Province	15
Anhui Province	Key Think Tanks of Anhui Province	Publicity Department of Anhui Provincial Party Committee	10
	Key Cultivation Think Tanks of Anhui Province		5
Hebei Province	First Pilot Institutions of New-Type Think Tanks of Hebei Province	Planning Office of Philosophical Science of Hebei Province	9
	Key New-Type Cultivation Think Tanks of Hebei Province		5
Hubei Province	Top Ten New-Type Think Tanks of Hubei Province	Publicity Department of Hubei Provincial Party Committee	10
	Top Ten Reform Think Tanks of Hubei Province	Policy Research Office of Hubei Provincial Party Committee (Provincial Reform Office)	10
Hunan Province	First Provincial Key Think Tank Construction Unit in Hunan Province	Publicity Department of Hunan Provincial Party Committee	7
	Professional and Special Think Tanks of Hunan Province		26
Jiangxi Province	First Pilot Institutions of Key Think Tanks of Jiangxi Province	Publicity Department of Jiangxi Provincial Party Committee	17
Guangxi Zhuang Autonomous Region	Key Think Tanks of Guangxi Characteristic New Think Tank Alliance	Policy-Making Consulting Commission of Guangxi Zhuang Autonomous Region	22

Continued

Provinces	Names of Think Tanks	Governing Bodies	Numbers
Chongqing	Pilot Institutions of Comprehensive High-End Think Tanks of Chongqing	Publicity Department of Chongqing Municipal Party Committee	6
Sichuan Province	First New-Type Think Tanks of Sichuan Province	Publicity Department of Sichuan Provincial Party Committee	22
Zhejiang Province	Pilot Institutions of High-End Think Tanks of Zhejiang Province	Led by the Publicity Department of Zhejiang Provincial Party Committee and Guided by the Joint Meeting of Zhejiang Provincial New Think Tanks, the Secretariat is set up by Zhejiang Provincial Union of Social Science and Technology	5
	New-Type Key Professional Think Tanks of Zhejiang Province		13
	Key Cultivation Think Tanks of Zhejiang Province		8
Yunnan Province	First Pilot Institutions of Key Think Tanks of Jiangxi Province	Publicity Department of Yunnan Provincial Party Committee	30
Qinghai Province	Key Think Tanks of Qinghai Province	Publicity Department of Qinghai Provincial Party Committee	5
Ningxia Hui Autonomous Region	First Key Cultivation Think Tanks of the Autonomous Region	Publicity Department of Ningxia Hui Autonomous Region Party Committee	3
Guangdong Province	Key Think Tanks of Guangdong Province	Publicity Department of Guangdong Provincial Party Committee	15
Guizhou Province	First New-Type Special Think Tanks of Guizhou Province	Publicity Department of Guizhou Provincial Party Committee	4
Inner Mongolia	First Pilot Institutions of Inner Mongolian High-End Think Tanks	Publicity Department of Inner Mongolia Autonomous Region Party Committee	6

Note: 1. Due to the different degrees of publicity of key think tank construction lists in each province, the "quantity" in the table is incomplete statistics, and the duplications in the think tank lists are not taken into account. The accurate data are mainly from the officially released lists.

2. The "Governing Bodies" in the table refers to the administrative departments that play an overall coordinating role in publishing units, releasing units of the list of key think tanks, and units responsible for the selection of key think tanks, etc. , according to the actual situation.

2.3.2 Development System of Provincial Key Think Tanks Formed Gradually

Facing the complicated international and domestic situations, the policy-making tasks undertaken by think tanks are also highly comprehensive. No single discipline or institution can handle them independently, and the tasks call for different types and levels of think tanks to participate. Against such background, the construction of multi-level and diversified think tank development systems is crucial. At present, the system construction of new think tanks is facing difficulties, such as insufficient motivation, unbalanced development of think tanks, insufficient research motivation and cooperation of think tanks, and poor connecting mechanisms. Provinces have accelerated top-level design and overall planning to build new-type key think tanks hierarchically and based on different categories, so as to gradually form a development system that conforms to operation rules of local think tanks.

In terms of overall pattern, some provinces and cities have established a new development pattern for provincial think tanks, which is led by national high-end think tanks, supported by provincial key think tanks, and supplemented by university think tanks, sci-tech innovation think tanks and social think tanks. For example, Jiangsu Province has set up a strategic pattern of "10 key high-end think tanks plus 16 key cultivation think tanks plus 50 research bases of policy-making consulting", basically forming a pattern with distinctive characteristics and diverse research fields, which enables joint development of comprehensive and professional think tanks.

Hunan Province proposed that by 2020, a system of new-type think tanks will be formed, which is led by provincial key think tanks and supplemented by university think tanks, sci-tech innovation think tanks, enterprise think tanks and social think tanks. Guangxi Province has set up a "1 + 1 + 6 + 4" special system of new-type think tanks organized by policy-making consulting committee, coordinated by alliance of think tanks, focusing on building six types of think tanks, and supported by four service platforms.

In order to promote coordinated development of different types of think tanks, provinces (including autonomous regions and manicipalities) have selected think tanks from different industries urgently needed by central policy-making and relevant to overall development to give them support and special training. Take university, sci-tech innovation and social think tanks as examples. Based on incomplete statistics (as of December 2019), 13 provinces (including automomous regionsand municipeilities) have announced provincial new-type university think tanks, and 7 provinces (including automomous regions and municipalities) have announced provincial sci-tech innovation think tanks or research bases. They have strived to build a deeply integrated pattern of professional think tank, carry out policy-making consulting and activities of giving advice and suggestions, and provide efficient services for party committees, the government and local economic development.

First, the constructions of provincial key university think tanks. As the special management departments of provincial key university think tanks, provincial Education Departments or provincial Education Committees are responsible for selection, identification and guidance of provincial key university think tanks. It can be seen from Table 1. 2 that Yunnan, Liaoning, Gansu and other provinces have announced the first batch of provincial key new-type university think tanks. For example, Shanghai has built a network of university think tanks featuring "inner ring-middle ring-outer ring" relying on coordinating mechanism of university think tanks in Shanghai. The inner ring includes 30 university think tanks funded by the Shanghai Municipal Education and Health Working Committee and Education Commission. The middle ring is university think tanks selected for connotation construction (think tanks for cultivation), and outer the ring is other active think tanks. Zhejiang Province launched the construction of new-type university think tanks in 2016. So far, 15 university think tanks have been selected as the first batch for 2016 and 13 as the second batch for 2018, gradually forming a system of new-type provincial university think tanks with distinctive characteristics, reasonable layout, and regional features.

Table 1. 2   Constructions of Provincial-Level Key University Think Tanks

Provinces	Names of University Think Tanks	Numbers
Zhejiang Province	New-Type University Think Tanks of Zhejiang Province (two batches)	15+13
Jilin Province	New-Type University Special Think Tanks Construction Institutions (two batches in 2015 and 2016)	22(2015) 18(2016)
	New-Type University Special Think Tanks Cultivation Institutions (two batches in 2015 and 2016)	9(2015) 7(2016)
Jiangsu Province	Off-Campus Research Bases of Humanities and Social Sciences of Jiangsu Province	20
	Cultivation Spots of Off-Campus Research Bases of Humanities and Social Sciences of Jiangsu Province	15
Yunnan Province	New-Type University Think Tanks Construction Projects of Yunnan Province	14
	New-Type University Think Tanks Cultivation Projects of Yunnan Province	3
Shaanxi Province	New-Type University Think Tanks of Shaanxi Province	22

Continued

Provinces	Names of University Think Tanks	Numbers
Anhui Province	University Think Tanks of Education Department of Anhui Province	16
Liaoning Province	New-Type University Think Tanks of Liaoning Province	20
Ningxia Hui Autonomous Region	New-Type University Think Tanks of Ningxia Hui Autonomous Region	8
Gansu Province	University Think Tanks for Targeted Poverty Alleviation of Gansu Province	5
	New-Type University Think Tanks of Gansu Province (humanities and social sciences)	20
Shanghai	Shanghai University Think Tanks	30
Tianjin	Tianjin University Think Tanks (two batches)	12+8
Jiangxi Province	Key University Based of Jiangxi Province	53
Fujian Province	New-Type University Special Think Tanks of Fujian Province (three batches)	9+15+20

Note: The "Numbers" in the table is incomplete statistics, and the duplication in the think tank list (such as Jilin) is not considered. The accurate data shall be subject to the official list.

The second is the construction of provincial key sci-tech innovation think tanks. In order to implement the decision and deployment of the central and provincial party committees and based on requirements of the Chinese Association of Science and Technology, provincial departments of science and technology or provincial associations of science and technology should build a batch of high-level sci-tech innovation think tanks or research bases (see Table 1. 3) in cooperation with provincial-level academies and institutional, university and enterprise science associations. For example, in May 2017, *Opinions on Building High-End Sci-Tech*

Innovation Think Tanks by Shandong Association of Science and Technology pointed out that by 2020 it plans to build a system of Sci-Tech Innovation Think Tanks with Shandong Institute of Innovative Strategy as the "small center", surrounded by provincial-level academies, city-level sci-tech innovation think tanks and universities and research institutes in strategic cooperation. In September 2017, the Shaanxi Provincial Department of Science and Technology issued *Construction Plan of Shaanxi Sci-Tech Think Tank System*, proposing a plan of "platform + base + center". It aims to build a system of sci-tech think tanks relying on Shaanxi Research Institute of Scientific and Technical Intelligence and supported by 11 provincial soft science research bases. Since 2018, Jilin Provincial Association of Science and Technology has dedicated itself to the construction of provincial sci-tech think tanks and wisdom exchange project. By now, it has basically formed a system of policy-making consulting services composed of 20 bases.

Table 1. 3　Constructions of Provincial-Level Key Sci-Tech Innovation Think Tanks

Province	Names of Key Sci-Tech Innovation Think Tanks	Numbers
Jiangsu Province	Sci-Tech Innovation Think Tank Bases of Science Association of Jiangsu Province (three batches)	13+18+10
Yunnan Province	First Sci-Tech Innovation Think Tanks of Yunnan Province	24
Jilin Province	Sci-Tech Innovation Think Tank Bases of Jilin Province (two batches)	12+8
Shaanxi Province	Research Bases of Soft Sciences of Shaanxi Province	11
Heilongjiang Province	Sci-Tech Innovation Think Tank Bases of Heilongjiang Province	16
Guangxi Zhuang Autonomous Region	Sci-Tech Think Tanks of Guangxi Zhuang Autonomous Region	5
Chongqing	Pilot Institutions of New-Type Sci-Tech Think Tanks	19

The third is the construction of provincial key social think tanks. On the whole, the construction of social think tanks by provinces (including autonomous regions and municipalities) has just begun or is still in exploration, with a small number and scale of social think tanks. However, some provinces (including autonomous negions and municipalities) have started to attach importance to the construction of social think tanks and have incorporated the healthy development of social think tanks into the development system of new-type think tanks. For example, in March 2018, Jiangsu Provincial Department of Civil Affairs and other 8 departments jointly issued *Opinions on the Healthy Development of Social Think Tanks in Jiangsu* to explain task requirements and measures for developing social think tanks in the province. At the same time, Jiangsu Province implements "dual management system" for social think tanks as it does for organizations of social sciences. Under the system, both the Department of Civil Affairs and the governing bodies are responsible for and should join in their management. Shandong Provincial Department of Civil Affairs drafted *Opinions on Promoting the Healthy Development of Social Think Tanks (Exposure Draft)*, which decided that pilot construction of provincial key social think tanks should be carried out in 2019, and about 10 provincial key social think tanks should be cultivated by 2020. For that to happen, local governments should make more favorable policies on social think tanks and support well-established social think tanks, so as to provide better external conditions for social think tanks to get involved in social governance system.

2.3.3　Provincial Think Tank Alliance Begins to Show its Scale

The provincial think tank alliance is a think tank consortium co-sponsored by units including the provincial committee and government, provincial key universities, party and government departments, enterprises, etc. With the method of platforms co-construction, resources sharing, and collaborative research, the alliance aims to coordinate and integrate the advantageous resources of alliance members and to promote the coordinated development of government, industry, research, academy and media, and the benign interaction between think tanks and government. Typical examples include Hunan, Shandong, Heilongjiang, and Guangxi. For example, with the approval of the Shanxi Provincial Civil Affairs Bureau, the first provincial think tank industry association in China, namely Shanxi Provincial Think Tank Development Association (Sanjin Think Tank Alliance), was established. It is a public and non-profit independent association corporation that is in the charge of Shanxi Academy of Social Sciences and constituted by provincial key universities, scientific research institution, state-owned enterprises, and experts and scholars from all walks of life. More than 40 think tanks from 25 party and government offices, colleges and universities, science and technology enterprises, industry associations, and news media institutions in Gansu Province voluntarily and jointly initiated the establishment of the province's first new type of think tank alliance with scientific and technological innovation as its main purpose—Gansu Provincial Think Tank Alliance of Science and Technology Innovation. In January 2019, Henan Provincial Universities Think Tank Alliance was inaugurated. It is a research platform of the application of countermeasures in which the provincial universities' think tanks voluntarily participated. The first batch consisted of 65 think tanks from 46 universities in Henan Province. It aims to build a cooperation platform of information sharing, scientific research collaboration, and achievement communication. Shandong Academy of Social Sciences cooperated with provincial key think tanks and various municipal academies of social sciences to establish the Shandong Think Tank Alliance. It also opened up the Shandong Think Tank Alliance website, WeChat public account and Weibo, established the *Think*

Tank Exchange monthly magazine, and hosted the "Taishan Think Tank Forum", which has provided an effective channel for alliance members to communicate and share resources. The Policy Research Office of the Party Committee of Guangxi Zhuang Autonomous Region and the Development Research Center of the Government of the Autonomous Region led the formation of a new type of think tank alliance with Guangxi characteristics. The alliance operaties a joint meeting system. It has six haison offices, including university think tank and enterprise think tank. A comprehensive alliance system consists of 16 director units, 22 Guangxi key characteristic think tanks, 160 think tank alliance member units and 106 think tank experts.

3　Suggestions on the Construction of New National High-End and Provincial Key Think Tanks

After more than four years of construction, national high-end and provincial and municipal key think tanks have made important progress and achieved significant results, fully showing their demonstration effect and leading role as pilot units. While the socialism with Chinese characteristics enters a new era, China's think tanks should seize the important period of strategic opportunities, bravely undertake missions, and demonstrate greater accomplishments. Faced with the new situation and new tasks, the construction of new think tanks with Chinese characteristics should focus on two concepts: "Chinese characteristics" and "new types". "Chinese characteristics" is to solve practical problems in China's development, and "new types" is to require think tanks of breakthroughs in the innovation of systems and mechanisms. The construction of new think tanks can achieve greater results only by using the thoughts of modern think tanks, centering on the central work of the Party and country, major decisions and arrangements of Party Central Committee, and social hot issues, continuing to deepen the reform of management systems of think tanks in human and material management, scientific research organization, project management, achievement evaluation and application transformation, international exchange and cooperation, etc.

3.1   Clarify Function Positioning, Focus on Content Innovation

General Secretary Xi Jinping pointed out: "The construction of think tanks should lay emphasis on improving research quality and promoting content innovation. " Clarifying function positioning is the primary task of strengthening the connotative construction of new think tanks. It is necessary to grasp the right direction, clarify the function positioning, reflect Chinese and socialist characteristics, focus on deepening the research on major issues, and adhere to high-standard positioning and high-quality development. On the one hand, the positioning of think tanks should reflect "Chinese characteristics", focus on the overall situation, find the correct positioning, firmly grasp the correct political direction and value orientation, firmly focus on the outstanding contradictions and problems faced by the cause of Party and country, carry out in-depth strategic and forward-looking research, pay attention to investigation and research, reinforce basic research, accurately meet the needs of the central decision-making, and provide accurate strategies for national macro-strategic planning and local reform and development. On the other hand, the positioning of think tanks should manifest the "new types", start with solving fundamental problems such as "stressing institutions, establishments and levels", and regard the reform of institutional mechanisms as the focal point for new breakthroughs in think tanks. Most think tanks are subordinate to the secondary units of entities, and their management systems are strictly controlled by the parent units. Therefore, only by being independent from parent units and carrying out substantive construction to fully release the autonomy of scientific research, personnel, and finance management can the true development of think tanks be realized.

3.2 Fully Enter Decision-Making Service, Achieve Seamless Communication Between Think Tanks and Government

Doing a good job in the smooth joint of decision-making is the key for China's think tanks to be national high-end and to better serve the central and local decision-making, and it is also an important link to promote the construction of a decision support system with Chinese characteristics. First, give full play to the role of the Council in policy coordination and decision guidance, deepen communication with the decision-making department, urge the decision-making department to take more active and effective measures in information disclosure, project procurement, personnel exchanges, and result feedback, and achieve the bidirectional influence between supply and demand. The decision-making department should be happy to "intellectual borrowing" to improve the government information disclosure system and result feedback mechanism, occasionally convey the central spirit and decision-making demands to think tanks, change the "high-profile" role of decision-making department, and facilitate the research of think tanks; think tanks should be adept in "way finding" to actively enter the decision-making department, expand new service and decision-making channels, actively carry out work like document drafting, plan planning, public opinion research, lectures and training, and international exchanges, so that the research of think tanks can be fully integrated into decision-making and serve decision-making. Second, know how to seize the opportunity effectively and regard "timeliness as the priority" as the key criterion for think tanks to make internal statements and speak out to the outside world. Prompt result promotion can effectively improve the chances of high impact of think tank results, quickly gain the attention and recognition of the decision-making department and the public, and realize the rapid transformation of think tank results.

3.3　Improving the Mechanism for Selecting, Employing, and Retaining People Is the Priority

Talent is the first resource for the construction of think tanks and also the internal driving force for the long-term development of think tanks. China's think tanks should take talent cultivation as a basic project, establish and improve a scientific and reasonable mechanism for selecting, employing, and retaining people, and fully activate intellectual resources. First, encourage think tanks to actively introduce high-end external talents. It is necessary to explore and solve the problem of flexible establishment of traditional scientific research units, allow think tanks to introduce high-end experts or urgently-needed professionals within a certain overstaffing range, and exploit green channels for special urgently-needed professionals; in addition, it is necessary to improve the selection criteria and management of introducing talents, focus on employing some expert officials and overseas experts of think tanks with rich experience in decision-making consultation, and effectively improve the level of decision-making services. Second, establish a flexible and efficient employment mechanism. Chiefly, focus on cultivating a group of industry leaders and give full play to the demonstration and leading role of high-end talents such as chief experts and young backbones; next, use research projects as a link to strengthen self-construction, build a professional and innovative team, and improve the ability to respond quickly to emergency decisions. Third, make innovation in talent evaluation and motivation. In the first place, implement the reform of the talent evaluation mechanism by category and strengthen the support and recognition of the achievements of talents' suggestions, excellent newspaper articles, and participation in foreign affairs and publicity of think tanks; in the next place, focus on the compensation of high-end results, provide the fair treatment of professional title evaluation and other aspects, and open up a high-quality room for the growth of think tank researchers; finally, increase the non-material rewards of outstanding talents, mobilize the enthusiasm of think tank talents by sending them overseas for exchanges, supporting project fund, equipping them with scientific research assistants, giving priority to recommending them and other measures, and form a clear direction of more pay for more work, and better pay for better work.

3.4　Strengthen the Construction of Global Cooperation Network of Think Tanks

Across the whole country, the "go global" pace of China's think tanks is accelerating. Strengthening the deep cooperation of think tanks on a global scale is a necessary element of "opening think tanks and opening to the outside world", and is also an effective way for China's think tanks to integrate into the world discourse system and participate in global governance. First, China's think tanks should center on important international conferences such as the "Belt and Road" International Cooperation Summit Forum, China Development Forum, and China International Import Expo, and actively organize multi-type and multi-level thematic activities of think tanks, carry out multilateral international exchanges and cooperation, and bring out "Chinese products", "Chinese thoughts", and "Chinese voices". Second, support qualified think tanks to set up branches or research bases overseas, and provide overseas exchange and internship opportunities for outstanding think tank talents. Both parties actively organize international academic forums and strengthen cooperation with internationally renowned media to expand China's power of discourse and influence in the international arena. Third, build think tank cooperation organizations and exchange platforms at home and abroad, such as the "Belt and Road" International Think Tank Cooperation Committee, use institutionalized partnership to open up channels of national information sharing and talent exchange, and provide organizational guarantees for promoting global governance, facilitating multi-track diplomacy, and strengthening global thinking dialogue. Fourth, aim at hot, main, and difficult issues at home and abroad, support extensive research, commissioned research, and joint research with overseas think tanks under the framework of a cooperative network, and provide the "Chinese Approach" for global governance. Fifth, aim at major issues with foresightedness, predictability, and emergency, actively participate in the activities of international academic organizations, take the lead in organizing international major scientific projects, encourage the introduction of internationally renowned think tank experts, build a global network of interpersonal connections, and communicate with a number of trustworthy and useful international friends, realize thoughts gathering, information sharing, and data interconnection, so that China's think tanks can contribute more Chinese thoughts, Chinese values, and Chinese power to the construction of a community of shared future for mankind.

3.5　Break through Obstructions Caused by Certain Systems and Mechanisms and Improve Governance Efficiency

The Fourth Plenary Session of the Nineteenth CPC Central Committee has highlighted the general requirements for adhering to and improving the system of socialism with Chinese characteristics, and promoting the modernization of the national governance system and governance capabilities. The new type of think tanks with Chinese characteristics, as an important component of the modern national governance system, should put the reform focus on the breakthroughs of blockages in systems and mechanisms, find the entry point from the aspects of institutional setting, function transformation, and organizational adjustment, increase the intensity of research and reform in systems and mechanisms in key fields, and help solve deep-seated contradictions and problems. It is required that China's think tanks must quickly dismantle the barriers in systems and mechanisms such as "the low transform rate of scientific research, difficulty in introducing and retaining talents, solidification of professional title system, and limitation of productivity caused by organizational system", fundamentally activate the internal power of scientific research units, and form an energetic, efficient, and modern management system of think tanks which is in line with the operation characteristics of think tanks. Therefore, several attempts can be made: select a batch of non-substantial research institutes (institutions, centers) of different types, carry out special reform pilot work, give these pilot institutions independent legal person qualifications as public institutions, exclude them in the scope of verification of the organization establishment, manage them with the help of "market contracting", assume sole responsibility for their profits and losses, and achieve enterprise-style management and market-oriented operation. This kind of modern corporate governance structure can fully release the autonomy of think tanks in terms of institution setting, expert selection and employment, employee recruitment, and salary distribution, which is more conducive to the transformation of scientific research results and the maximization of social benefits, stimulating the vitality of think tanks and the creativity of scientific researchers, improving the governance efficiency, and promoting the "rule of China" to a new level.

Topic 2   New Types of Think Tanks Become an Emerging Force of Decision-Making Consultation

Opinions on Strengthening the Construction of New Think Tanks with Chinese Characteristics was reviewed at the 6th meeting of China's leading group for overall reform on 27th October, 2014. General Secretary Xi Jinping stressed that, our governing of the country should take advantage of combining wisdom and pooling the strength of all sources. The more arduous the task of reform and development is, the greater the need for stronger intellectual support. We need to make it a major and urgent task to build new types of think tanks with Chinese characteristics by adopting scientific and democratic decision-making, modernizing the governance system and governance capacity, as well as enhancing national soft power. *Opinions on Strengthening the Construction of New Types of Think Tanks with Chinese Characteristics* (The *Opinions*) was issued by the General Office of the CPC Central Committee and the General Office of the State Council on 20th January 20, 2015. They made it clear that new types of think tanks with Chinese characteristics are a major prop for the law-based decision-making of the Party and the government, an important content of the modernization of the governance system and governance capacity, and a significant part of the country's soft power. This has pointed out the direction for the construction of new types of think tanks with Chinese characteristics and decision-making consultation services. For five years in a row, new types of think tanks with Chinese characteristics have taken the responsibility of providing guidance to build consensus, offering political consultation services and exerting edifying influence on the public. Impressive achievements have been made during this period. Think tank organizations at all levels have worked hard to recognize decision-making needs and integrate themselves into policy-making process to serve decision-making. Many think tank products have been translated into public policies and social productive forces. All of these have suggested that think tanks have become an important member of the policy-making community and an important supplement to China's consultative democracy and scientific decision-making process. They have to a large extent made tremendous contributions to the modernization of the country's governance system and governance capacity as well as to the building of soft power.

1　Offering Consultation Services Is the Main Function of New Types of Think Tanks

Seeking political consultation from people of wisdom has been one of China's traditions since ancient times. Think tank systems such as hangers-on of aristocrats, counselors, private assistants, assistants to ranking officials or generals, expostulators, critics and think tank institutions such as the imperial academy were long-established. "If everyone's strength is pooled, even the heaviest thing can be lifted. If everyone's wisdom is combined, even the most difficult task can be achieved." This old saying has illustrated the importance of pooling the strength of the public and establishing think tank systems. Ancient scholars and officials took it as their responsibility to offer consultation services and make political suggestions, and they were so proud of their work. The declaration "If someone is to rule the world, who but myself can do it" showed their courage; "Pay attention to home, national and global affairs" showed their concern for their country; "Bending back to the task until the dying day" showed their spirit of utter devotion. As the think tanks for emperors, they mapped out strategies and even directly involved in the decision-making of the states by drawing on their knowledge, experience and wisdom, changing the direction and process of historical development. This long-established tradition has laid a good cultural foundation and created an atmosphere for the development of modern consultation services. The current new types of think tanks come down in a continuous line from ancient think tanks. They can be regarded as the inheritance of China's tradition of seeking political consultation from people of wisdom, the development of ancient scholars' spirit of devotion, and the result of learning and drawing on Western consultative mechanisms.

At present, the overall deepening reform has entered a crucial stage. Economic growth has gone into a transitioning phase. And with the modernization of the national governance system and governance capacity, as well as the transformation of the functions of the government, governments at all levels show increasing demands for democratic, scientific and law-based decision-making and greater decision-making accuracy. Many governments have chosen to seek consultation services and intellectual support in light of China's peaceful rise, the increasingly complex global environment, and the constantly changing domestic economic and social structure. For instance, in order to reinforce epidemic prevention, Ying Yong, the provincial Party Secretary of Hubei province, held several seminars to seek opinions and suggestions from medical workers and experts in the fields of medical treatment, psychological crisis intervention, emergency management and law services. At the expert think tank seminar on February 25, 2020, he noted clearly that "As the top priority for epidemic prevention and control, Hubei and Wuhan need to seek experts' opinions comprehensively and from various angles. " "Borrowing wisdom" from external forces can help the government cope with the complex decision-making environment and improve the decision-making level. And think tanks are an important part of these external forces.

The *Opinions* has pointed out that "New types of think tanks with Chinese characteristics are non-profit research consultative institutions. Their main research objects are strategic issues and public policy, and their purpose is to serve the Party and the government's scientific, democratic and law-based decision-making." It has made it clear that new types of think tanks with Chinese characteristics serve the functions of "offering consultation services, making suggestions, making theoretical innovation, influencing public opinion, serving society and maintaining public diplomacy", and that "We will improve the decision-making support system with Chinese characteristics, strengthen the development of think tanks, support scientific decision-making with scientific consultation, and guide scientific development with scientific decision-making". New types of think tanks with Chinese characteristics, therefore, are essentially decision-making consultation institutions. Their primary function is to offer consultation services and make suggestions, and their key tasks are to focus on the strategic issues in economic and social development and policy-making, carry out in-depth analyses and research based on a solid theoretical foundation and scientific research methods, and provide support for the Party and the government's decision-making.

China, at a new historical stage of overall deepening reform, has provided fertile soil for the development of new types of think tanks. The Third Plenary Session of the 18th CPC Central Committee has pointed out the direction for the development of think tanks from the perspective of top-level design and system construction, providing a broader stage for the development of think tanks. The construction of think tanks at various levels has made remarkable achievements in the last five years. The governance structure, system construction and research team building of think tanks continue to improve. Innovation has been made on their scientific research organizing and managing modes, and their inner impetus for development keeps growing. A think tank system has gradually developed. It has become a consensus for think tanks, especially high-end think tanks, to focus on overall interests and serve decision-making. Think tanks offering consultation services have focused their research areas on decision-making needs, taken initiative to achieve national major strategic tasks, and actively involve themselves in the decision-making process to offer better services. New types of think tanks have been integrated into the open platform of national decision-making and become a part of China's policy decision-making system.

2　New Type of Think Tanks Have Become an Important Member of the Policy-Making Community

Policy support is a prerequisite for think tanks to participate in the decision-making process and to promote the construction of think tank system. In the first chapter, we have made an in-depth analysis of the think tank management system at all levels. At present, the basic policies, industry documents and supporting documents for the construction of think tanks are being developed. The policy environment for the development of think tanks including the decision-making consultation services system keeps improving, encouraging think tanks to offer consultation services and make suggestions. The *Opinions* has noted that we will establish and improve supporting systems such as "the government's information disclosure system, the system for seeking opinions for major policy decision-making, the policy evaluation system and the system of purchasing decision-making consultation services", in order to lay a foundation for new types of think tanks to participate in the government's decision-making. Based on that, some provinces and cities have established their decision-making consulting systems. For example, Shandong province has issued *The Working Rules of Specially Appointed Experts Offering Consultation Services to the Decision-Making of Shandong Province Government* [Lu (2018) No. 205]. It defines the responsibility scope, work specification and other relevant rules for experts offering consultation services to participate in the government's decision-making. And some provinces and cities have included think tank services into the list of government procurement. For example, *The Regulations on Purchasing Decision-making Consultation Services of Hebei Province (trial)* issued in 2016 has put forward that "The provincial government's purchase of decision-making consultation services should follow the fundamental principles of purchasing according to needs, setting fees according to the nature of matters, selecting people openly according to their merits, and running management by contracts." It has clearly defined the purchase subjects, the undertaking subjects and the purchasing contents.

The constantly improved system of think tank decision-making consultation services has expanded the channels of think tank decision-making services and increased the involvement of think tanks in the decision-making process. Despite the differences in various think tanks' nature, characteristics and the breadth and depth of their involvement in the government's decision-making, overall, they have become an important member of the policy-making community. Different types of think tanks have played an increasingly important role in decision-making through tapping their full potential and shouldering their responsibilities. In this chapter, we will analyze the roles of think tanks and their relationship with other participants in the policy-making community according to the three structural levels of public policy-making participants and think tanks' influence (decision-making/core influence, elites/central influence and public/marginal influence).

2.1　Offering Direct Services to Core Decision Makers

2.1.1　Inviting Experts to Deliver Lectures and Training

China has developed a well-organized learning and training system for leadership from central to local levels. Nationally, the collective learning system of the Political Bureau of the Central Committee has been established since the 16th Party Congress. 139 collective learning classes have been organized since 2002, which means there are on average one class every 40 days. About 200 top experts and scholars in different fields have gathered at Zhongnanhai and given lectures to these special classes. Since the 19th Party Congress, 19 collective learning sessions of the Political Bureau of the Central Committee have been held, and many experts have been invited. For instance, on November 29, 2019, professor Xue Lan from Tsinghua University gave a lecture and put forward his opinion and suggestions on the management and capability building of China's emergency system. Experts and scholars invited to become the lecturers of the collective learning classes of the Political Bureau of the Central Committee have combined decision-making needs with current affairs, brought their research expertise into full play, and explained theories or presented think tank products to the central decision-makers with profundity and in an easy-to-understand approach.

Regular leadership training sessions at local levels are usually organized by party schools. Party schools at all levels (including think tanks of the local Party school or administrative college) often set up training sessions and seminars on major national and local policies and documents for officials. For instance, on the day before a major national policy is launched, the Party School of the Central Committee (National Academy of Governance) usually holds seminars for provincial and ministerial-level officials to discuss the construction of the Party and the route, guidelines and policies of the governing party in order to offer general guidance to their governing philosophy and decision-making. Besides, special training sessions inviting experts to interpret current affairs have also become an option for quite a few local governments. Think tank experts who are actively engaged in these training sessions can also establish a direct dialogue with decision-makers, offering consultation services and making political suggestions. For example, at the invitation of the People's Congress of Inner Mongolia Autonomous Region, experts from the Institute of Economics of Shanghai Academy of Social Sciences gave a lecture on the Belt and Road Initiative at the information work training session. Their effort has enhanced the overall consciousness of carrying out information research work in Inner Mongolia, guided the attention to hot topics and difficulties, and prompted better information research work in the region, which as a result has promoted scientific decision making.

2.1.2 Presenting Internal Reference Reports on Decision-Making Consultation

Combining their research expertise with current affairs, producing research results and submitting internal reference reports have become one of the most prominent ways for think tanks to get involved in decision-making reference. According to the statistics of internal reference reports and feedback of 706 source think tanks in CTTI, by March 2019, the system had included 7976 internal reference reports and 2005 feedbacks. Since General Secretary Xi Jinping gave major instructions on the construction of new types of think tanks with Chinese characteristics in 2013, the submission and feedback of internal reference reports have increased annually.

And in particular, the submission of internal reference reports has seen exponential growth after the launch of *Opinions on Strengthening the Construction of New Think Tanks with Chinese Characteristics* in 2015 (as shown in Fig 2. 1).

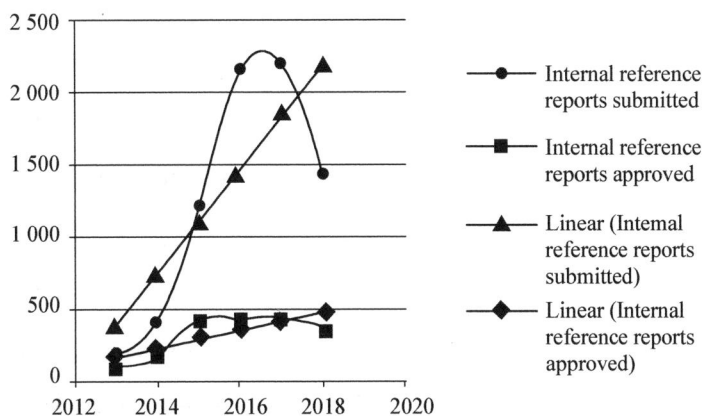

Fig 2. 1   The Annual Number of Internal Reference Reports Submitted and Approved

University think tanks (accounting for over 65% of CTTI source think tanks) have the largest number of internal reference reports submitted and approved (the specific number of internal reference reports submitted by different types of think tanks and the number of internal reference reports approved are shown in Fig 2. 2). For example, since 2016, the National Academy of Development and Strategy of Renmin University has submitted 1, 000 internal reference reports to the central government through channels such as the university's direct information reporting to the General Office of the Communist Party of China. According to incomplete statistics, 200 of them were approved by leaders of the Party and the country, and about one-third of the products were adopted by related departments and translated into major national policies. The following university think tanks are think tanks of Party/government organization, think tanks of academy of social sciences and think tanks of the Party school or administrative college. The average submission/approval ratio of these three types of think tanks is higher than that of university think tanks, which is due to the fact that they have a closer relationship with government departments. For example, the Chinese Innovation Strategy and Policy Research Center co-established by Chinese Academy of Sciences and the Research Office of the State Council based on the Institute of Science and Development of Chinese Academy of Sciences has put forward constructive and forward-looking suggestions on national innovation strategies and macro policies by making full use of the translation channels of the Research Office of the State Council and the research integration platform of the Institute of Science and Development. And the Shanghai Academy of Social Sciences has established a research and consultation docking mechanism with many central departments to further improve the regular consultation services of think tanks. The internal reference journals such as *Ideological and Theoretical Internal*

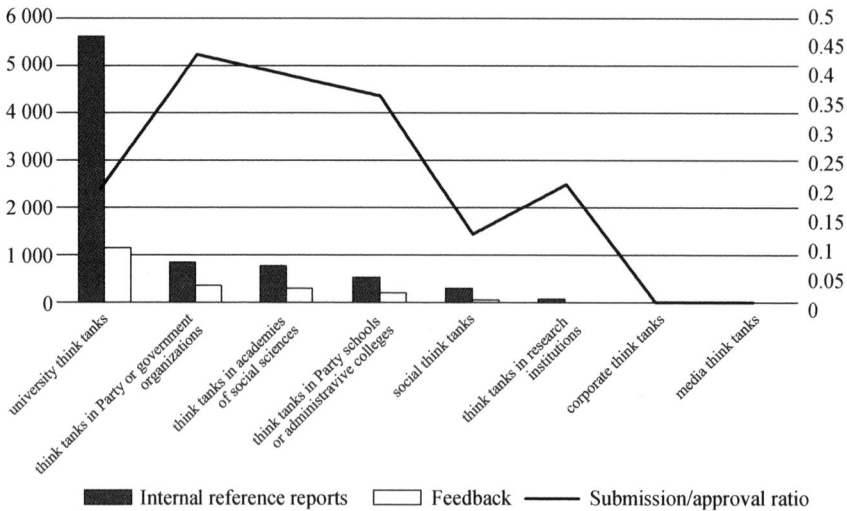

Fig 2. 2　The Number of Internal Reference Reports Submitted and Approved and the Submission/Approval Ratio of Different Types of Think Tanks

Reference Reports and *Research Reports* from the Party School of the Central Committee can be directly submitted to central decision-makers such as the Political Bureau of the Central Committee, the Secretariat of the Central Committee, the General Office of the Communist Party of China and the General Office of the State Council of the People's Republic of China.

2.1.3   Undertaking Government Consultation Projects

Government consultation projects undertaken by think tanks can be divided into two types. The first type is projects instructed by officials, which submit research products directly to officials for reference. Many provinces and cities have this kind of projects. For example, experts from Guizhou province have carried out research on instructed projects through the provincial Academy of Social Sciences by combining the application of projects instructed by provincial officials, public bidding and administrative entrustment. Guangzhou Planning Office of Social Sciences launches an annual event for projects instructed by officials and presents project products directly to officials concerned. The second type of projects are entrusted by government departments, which submit research products directly to entrusting departments and related officials. For instance, the Western Region Tourism Development Research Base of China Tourism Academy (School of Geography and Tourism, Shaanxi Normal University) has been entrusted by Xi'an government's Decision-Making Consultation Expert Committee with the major project on *Study on the Implementation of Rural Vitalization Strategy through Cultural Tourism*. Research has been conducted on how to make effective use of culture and tourism to achieve rural revitalization. Undertaking projects enables think tanks to offer individualized and customized consultation services, deepening think tanks' communication with decision-making departments. By doing this, governments can better convey their decision-making needs to think tanks, and think tanks can get more decision-making information and receive product feedback in time, realizing the match between supply and demand and providing better-targeted services. For example, when the Western Region Tourism Development Research Base of China Tourism Academy was carrying out research and writing reports, it communicated with departments such as Xi'an government's Decision-Making Consultation Expert Committee, Xi'an Municipal Administration of Culture and Tourism and Xi'an Municipal Administration of Rural Work to make sure that the reports are tailed to decision-making needs.

2.2 Engaging Directly in the Decision-Making Process

2.2.1 Engaging in Policy Documents Drafting

Think tanks of Party/government organization, such as provincial and city governments' development research centers and policy research offices, are the main drafters of major local policy documents. By the end of 2019, the CTTI database has included 69 think tanks of Party/government organization, who are responsible for making major local policies, conducting theoretical research and drafting documents. For example, for the last three years, Shandong Academy of Macroeconomic Research has undertaken or participated in drafting 400 major documents or planning ideas, and taken part in 200 provincial governments'; major research events, providing strong intellectual support for the provincial government's decision-making and making great contributions to the region's economic construction and social development.

The rise of third-party in government legislation drafting in recent years means that other types of think tanks have become more involved in drafting policy documents. The Center for Cultural Policy and Management Research of National Academy of Governance has undertaken the drafting of important documents in the field of culture, such as *Public Cultural Services Guarantee Act*, *Public Libraries Act*, *Guidelines on Promoting the Development of Characteristic Cultural Industries*, *Implementation Opinions on the Opinions of the State Council on Promoting Further Development of Cultural Creativity and Design Services and Integration of Related Industries*, and *Opinions of the General Office of the Communist Party of China and the General Office of the State Council of the People's Republic of China on Accelerating the Construction of a Modern Public Cultural Services System*. More than 10 research institutes, including the Chinese Academy of Engineering, 32 academicians, and hundreds of staff members have participated in the drafting of *Outline for Building National Strength in Transportation Infrastructure*. The Research Base of National Intellectual Property Strategy Implementation of Tianjin University was invited to take part in the drafting of *Outline for Building National Strength in Intellectual Property* (2021—2035). It has carried out research on improving intellectual property services and completed related policy documents, providing a solid and comprehensive theoretical support and data support to the drafting of the *Outline*.

Besides, there are many new attempts and explorations made in the field of third-party legislation. For example, Guizhou province has developed *Drafting and Evaluation Methods for Third-Party Legislation of Guizhou Provincial Government* to specify the procedures and norms for third parties to participate in government legislation. Local governments often entrust the drafting of local legislation and policy documents to think tank teams, such as university think tanks or social think tanks through direct entrustment or public bidding. On March 1st, 2018, the Development and Reform Commission of Hunan Province signed *Contract of Legislation Entrustment Services of the Conservation Regulations on Hunan Dongting Lake* with

Hunan Normal University. The Research Center of Rule of Law for Environmental Protection, Hunan Normal University was entrusted with the legislation drafting work. Based on previous research results, the think tank team went to cities, such as Changde, Yueyang and Yiyang, to carry out legislative research. Their product, the *Conservation Regulations on Hunan Dongting Lake (draft)* was approved by the standing committee of Hunan Provincial People's Congress in the first stage in July 2019. Another example is the Research Institute of Environmental Law of Wuhan University. Its report on *Risk-based Research on Multi-Governance System of Environmental Treatment* has provided important references for the consideration and adoption of relevant legislation, law enforcement and judicial documents and draft programs on multi-faceted environmental co-governance. And its consulting report *Draft and Compilation Illustration of Implementation Plan Reform of Qinghai's Ecological Environment Damage Compensation System* was adopted by Qinghai Provincial Committee of the CPC and the General Office of Qinghai government.

2.2.2 Providing Experts' Opinions of Consultation

In addition to joining think tank teams and getting involved in the decision-making process as team members, experts can also make their contribution through the following two means. First, they can be included in the governments' consultation database of experts. To better promote their decision-making and management capability, local governments have set up various types of decision-making consultation database of experts. There are comprehensive expert databases that provide consultation services to provinces' major decision-making involving fields like economy, culture and ecology, such as Shandong provincial government's decision-making consultation database of distinguished experts and the database of legislative experts of Sichuan province. There are also professional expert databases, such as the

Hainan Tourism Expert Database, which mainly deals with tourism. Think tank experts in governments' consultation database of experts can put their talent into good use and perform their duty by demonstrating the proof of rationality of policy options and helping governments' decision-making. For example, since its establishment, the decision-making consultation database of experts of Guangzhou City has participated in more than 1,000 seminars, review meetings and consultation meetings held by the municipal Party committee and departments of the municipal government, and made thousands of suggestions, which provides strong support to the improvement of the quality of government's decision-making. Second, they can attend consultation and demonstration meetings. To better pool the wisdom of people and listen to people's opinions, legislation institutions hold consultation and demonstration meetings before their decision-making. They would ask for opinions through hearings, information-sharing meetings and seminars, during which experts' opinions are often valued. For example, experts are often invited to participate in special work meetings of the departments of Guangzhou municipal government to offer opinions on policy document discussion, policy feasibility analysis and policy risk assessment.

2.3   Participating in Shaping Policy-Making Environment

Scholars, experts, media and the public are the participants of public decision-making. When offering direct services to policymakers is not available, other forms of participation become the option for many think tanks. Some think tanks publish their research products in the forms of books, journals and reports, and establish public dialogue in the forms of meetings and forums, spreading their ideas, drawing attention and sparking discussion from other participants of the decision-making community, including scholars, media and the public. By doing this, they have promoted participation and exerted influence on public opinion, which indirectly achieves the goal of serving governments' decision-making by offering consultation and making suggestions.

First, they have developed and issued quality publications, such as books, journals and special reports. Publishing books, reports and issuing journals is one of the most important ways to give the public access to think tanks' products and spread their ideas. For example, the Academy of Macroeconomic Research of National Development and Reform Committee has altogether issued 6 academic journals, including *Macroeconomics* and *Economy and Management Digest*, and interpreted many macroeconomic questions to display their products in the forms of academic book series, annual proceedings and annual reports. The Chinese Academy of Engineering has started two comprehensive academic journals on engineering—*Engineering* and *Engineering Sciences*. The latter opens up an important window for displaying the products of the national high-end think tank of the Chinese Academy of Engineering. The Think Tank of Pangu has published academic books on the Belt and Road Initiative, such as *30 Essential Questions on the Belt and Road Initiative* and *A Study on the Attitudes of Node Countries under the Belt and Road*, and produced special research reports to provide professional and in-depth interpretations of problems encountered in the process of international cooperation, which has promoted the Belt and Road cooperation and understanding of the Belt and Road Initiative.

Second, they have hosted events of exchanges, such as academic conferences and academic forums, which are important platforms for showcasing think tanks' products. Participants can share their ideas in in-depth exchanges, explore solutions to issues to build consensus, make their voices heard, and influence public opinion. A series of continuous activities can also bring better branding and scale advantages, further expanding think tanks' social influence. For example, the Chinese Academy of

Sciences regularly holds the High-Level Forum on Strategy and Decision-Making and the National High-End Science and Technology Think Tank Lecture Hall, a branding activity for high-end think tanks. A multi-level quality academic exchange system consisting of annual academic conferences, frontier forums of science and technology, small high-end forums and academic forums of various faculties is initially developed. Since 2016, the Shanghai Global Think Tank Forum has been held annually by Shanghai Academy of Social Sciences, National High-End Think Tank of Xinhua News Agency, Fudan Development Institute, Center for China and Globalization (CCG) and SASS Think Tank Foundation. The forum brings together think tanks and experts from more than ten countries in the world to discuss the hot issues of globalization and think tank development, offering an opportunity for them to exchange ideas, pool wisdom, build consensus and bring greater influence.

Third, they work together with media platforms to achieve a win-win situation. The shortage of the media's ability to conduct independent analyses of major policies makes it necessary for it to take advantage of think tanks' research products and opinions in news reports and comments. Meanwhile, compared with the media, think tanks lack mass communication ability and public influence. Since the cooperation between think tanks and the media can bring about a win-win situation, they both show a strong willingness to work together. On the one hand, the media may take the initiative to seek support from think tanks. For example, People. cn, Guangming. cn and other media platforms have a column for experts' interpretations of policies. They have invited think tank experts to analyze policies and paid attention to seeking and reprinting information on excellent think tank products. On November 12th, 2019, many media platforms, including People. cn, Ifeng. com and China News Service, reported the release of the product "China County Social Governance Index Model and the Top Ten Counties in Zhejiang Province of Good Social Governance 2019" by the Social Governance Research Institute of Zhejiang University. On the other hand, think tanks also make good use of media platforms. For example, the National High-End Think Tank / China (Shenzhen) Development Institute has set up three opinion columns on media platforms, i. e. , "Comprehensive Research on National Policies", "Comprehensive Research on Observation" and "the Paper's Opinion on Politics", calling for public engagement to expand its social influence and mass communication ability. The active cooperation between think tanks and the media has made think tanks the source of professional opinions of the media, and the media a carrier and a driving force for spreading think tanks' policy proposals and ideas, which helps to create a social atmosphere that drives decision-making.

3   Think Tanks Are Integrated into Policy-Making Process to Promote Scientific and Regulated Policy-Making

In the complicated and long process of public policy-making, especially in the major decision-making process, governments provide a variety of opportunities for think tanks to participate in putting forward issues and providing contents at the initial stage, implementing policies at the middle stage, and evaluating policies and giving feedback at the last stage. New types of think tanks strive to be included in the whole process of public decision-making to offer consultation services, playing their role in giving intellectual support, influencing public opinion and bridging communication. The following is an analysis of new types of think tanks' role in the public policy-making process at the three stages of policy formation, policy implementation and policy evaluation.

3. 1   Promoting Democratic and Scientific Policy-Making

Think tanks have become an indispensable part of governments' decision-making

process, but for now think tanks play a consulting role mainly at the stage of policy

formation. As of March 2019, manual indexing and analysis of the corresponding

policy stages of internal reference reports and feedback of CTTI source think tanks

(excluding 1,131 confidential internal reference reports and 25 pieces of feedback

whose contents or abstracts are not accessible) had revealed that the system includes

6,665 internal reference reports and 1,980 pieces of feedback. Among them, internal

reference reports about the process of agenda-setting and policy recommendation

account for over 93%, and feedback for over 94%. It can be seen that the current

focus of think tanks' decision-making consultation is laid on policy formation. Think

tanks play their role in inspiring agenda setting, guaranteeing democratic decision-

making and promoting scientific decision-making. They have contributed to the

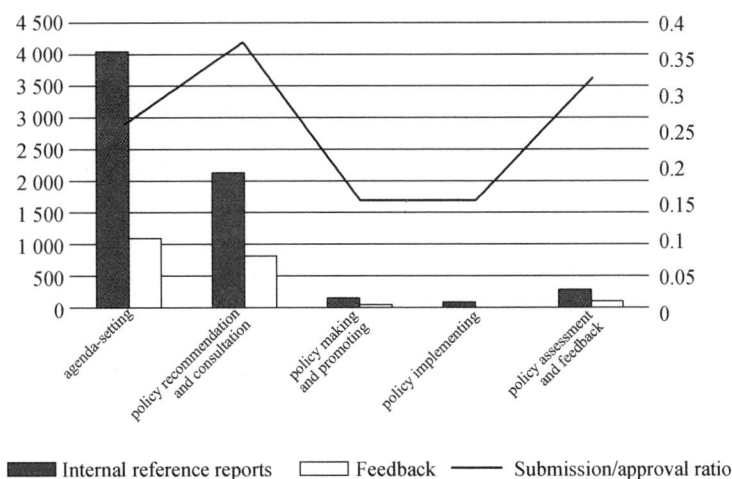

Fig 2. 3   The Corresponding Policy Stages of Internal Reference Reports and Feedback of CTTI Source Think Tanks and Submission/Approval Ratio

promotion of scientific and democratic decision-making by guiding attention to social issues to inspire agenda setting, providing scientific basis and solutions, and offering experts' consultation in policy demonstration and deliberation.

3.1.1 Having Two-Pronged Participation in Agenda-Setting

Policy agenda setting is the initial stage of the decision-making process and one of the most important steps. Limited government resources mean that only some of the issues can be included in the formal policy agenda. To get issues that are of public concern and that social development needs to be included is think tanks' consultation task at the agenda-setting stage. Policy agendas generally include government agendas and public agendas, and think tanks inspire the setting of public policy agendas through playing their parts in these two types of agendas.

First, they participate in government agendas. Government agendas are formal official agendas that pay attention to certain social issues and then incorporate them into the policy-making discussion. Official or semi-official think tanks directly participate in government agendas, accept government entrustment, or conduct independent research and present their research results to government departments in various forms such as internal reference reports, projects, suggestions and proposals so that these results can be included in government agendas. For example, the report " Exploration and Development of the System of Procurators' Participation in Adjudication Committee" by Xu Hanming, an expert of the Research Center of Law Development and Judicial Reform of Zhongnan University of Economics and Law, was adopted by the Supreme People's Procuratorate's journal *Leadership Reference* and was incorporated as important legislative proposals.

Second, they guide public agendas. Public agendas refer to the process in which social issues attract public attention and then affect the setting of government agendas. For example, the vaccine incidents in recent years have attracted widespread public attention and promoted the promulgation of the "Vaccine Administration Law of the People's Republic of China". Policy research helps to redefine the boundaries of issues and dimensions of interventions before the issue is formally discussed. Think tanks play a role similar to "enlightenment" and "focusing attention" on public agendas. They clarify relevant concepts from a professional perspective, focus attention and define issues, guide the public's values, creating a public opinion atmosphere for issues to be adopted by policymakers.

3.1.2   Speaking for the Public to Promote Democratic Consultation

Public opinion is the activated carbon in the decision-making process, which can remove harmful impurities that affect decision-making, i. e. , hidden risks and undetectable hidden dangers. Increasing transparency and public participation are the requisites for democratic decision-making. Some governments have established a variety of democratic consultation methods, including proposals, meetings, seminars, hearings, public announcements, consultations and polls. But despite their efforts to make down-to-earth and public-oriented decisions, some problems still exist in the expression of public opinion. For example, the channels for expression cannot be accessed conveniently, and public opinion is inconsistent, unsystematic, and difficult to be adopted by governments.

Think tanks can serve as a bridge, filter and lubricant in collecting and expressing public opinion. By carrying out public opinion surveys, they can serve as a bridge between governments and the public. They collect information in a more comprehensive and targeted manner and increase channels for public opinion transmission. They sort out and analyze public opinion and social realities based on science, which helps them to filter out ineffective opinion, produce streamlined and professional research reports, and communicate effectively the interests of the public to governments. Thus, they have made possible the rational communication of the three forces of governments, the public and experts. For example, in 2018, the Anhui University Management Big Data Research Center carried out a teacher and student satisfaction survey taken by a total of 15,051 students and 1,355 teachers at 27 universities of Anhui Province. The survey analyzed students' and teachers' satisfaction with the quality of higher education and organized comprehensively and systematically data on the policy formulation and implementation of higher education, management, teaching, support and services, which helped to effectively convey policy stakeholders' opinion. Likewise, to investigate food safety issues, the research team of food safety and risk governance of Jiangnan University conducted field surveys in more than 90 prefecture-level cities of over 20 provinces (including autonomous regions and municipalities) and interviewed 40,000 community-level officials and masses as well as over 400 food production and marketing enterprises. Their survey report *From the Farm to the Table : How to Ensure Food Safety ? Analysis on China's Food Safety Risk Management and Situation* was reprinted by the journal *Xinhua Digest*, included *by Situation Report* (volume 128, 2018), a journal issued by the General of Office of Editor in Chief of *Guangming Daily* and submitted to the General Office of the Central Committee of the CPC and the General Office of the State Council to convey the voice of the people to the government. It was also retweeted more than 1,000 times by mainstream online media and major new media platforms, which has aroused public attention and discussion, further increased public participation, and promoted public opinion expression in a wider scope.

3.1.3 Making Scientific Suggestions Based on Research

With the increasing demand for scientific decision-making, expert consultation and demonstration have become a necessary part of governments' decision-making. Many governments have established expert consultation teams before the formulation of policy documents. For example, in October 2019, the Guangdong provincial government established "the 14th Five-year Plan" Development Planning Expert Committee consisting of 38 well-known domestic experts, scholars and entrepreneurs. The committee is responsible for providing opinions and suggestions on the promotion of high-quality development of Guangdong province, and offering consultation and demonstration of the implementation of the development plan, in an effort to improve the scientific formulation and implementation of the development plan of Guangdong Province.

In addition, think tanks have seized the opportunity to provide services. They are actively involved in legislative investigations, document drafting, and program planning and other works, integrating think tank research fully into the decision-making process to serve it. They pay close attention to major policies and take the initiative to undertake government projects based on their solid professional research foundation, providing a basis for decision-making and even decision-making schemes. For instance, when China's new round of tax reform was officially launched in 2018, China Household Finance Survey (CHFS) and China Micro and Small Enterprise Survey (CMES), two research results provided by the Survey and Research Center for China Household Finance offered an objective basis for policy formulation. Shaanxi Economic Research Center undertook and completed the legislative research report of *Regulations on Tongchuan Air Pollution Prevention* and *Regulations on Tongchuan Drinking Water Source Protection*, which provided foundation for the legislation of Tongchuan city.

At the First International Import Expo in Shanghai in November 2018, General

Secretary Xi Jinping stressed that supporting the regional integration of the Yangtze River Delta has become a national strategy. Since then, based on their research foundation, the Yangtze Industrial Economics Institution of Nanjing University, the Yangtze Delta Research Institute of Fudan University, the Research Center of Yangtze River Delta Regional Integration of East China Normal University, China Academy for Rural Development of Zhejiang University and other think tanks have proposed schemes on Yangtze River Delta integration construction from various perspectives, such as the establishment of a regional innovation community, the promotion of rural integration in the Yangtze River Delta and the accessibility of government data in the Yangtze River Delta. The collection of alternative programs is itself a policy selection process that helps simulate scientific decision-making. And different think tanks' researches on the same theme can help expand governments' decision-making ideas, greatly promoting comprehensive, feasible and scientific decision-making. Think tanks can also give full play to their professional advantages, gain the attention and recognition of decision-making departments, and realize the rapid translation of think tank products during this process. For example, the expert team of the Yangtze Industrial Economics Institution of Nanjing University, which focuses its attention on the research of the Yangtze River Delta integration for more than 20 years, has conducted a series of in-depth studies on "Yangtze River Delta Integration Development Strategy" in recent years. Their studies have brought many professional and operational schemes. Two of their specific proposals, i. e., "Establishing the Shanghai-Nanjing Industrial Innovation Belt" and "Building a Regional Equity Exchange Market of Integrated Development", were adopted by the *Outline of the Yangtze River Delta Regional Integration Development Plan*, and their consultation report *Unified Market Construction: Mission and Task of the*

Yangtze River Delta Integration was published on the journal *National Social Science Fund Project Achievements* (volume 39) in 2019 and was reported to the central leadership.

3.2   Policy Education Brings Wider Social Consensus

The reason why some policies fail to achieve the expected results lies not in policies themselves, but in that the policies cannot be understood by the public and cannot be implemented properly. *Opinions on Strengthening the Construction of New Think Tanks with Chinese Characteristics* put forward that we should bring into play "think tanks' positive role of explaining the Party's theory, interpreting public policies, researching and judging public opinion, guiding social hot topics, and channeling public sentiments. " It is the responsibility of think tanks to carry out policy publicity and interpretations to enhance public recognition.

3.2.1   Focus on Policy Hot Topics and Guide the Public

Many think tanks, especially high-end think tanks, take it their responsibility to analyze and interpret the Party and the country's major policies comprehensively and from various angles. For example, the National Academy of Development and Strategy of Renmin University of China, using *Policy Observation* and *Everything in a Picture* as their platforms, pays close attention to and offers exclusive interpretations on national policies, the spirit of important conferences and the trends of various ministries and commissions. Think tanks' scientific interpretations can guide the public's attention to what is in line with policy objectives, the overall situation of social stability and development, and people's interests. For example, when the 19th CPC National Congress was held, China. com and Pangoal Institution jointly launched "working hard with perseverance and opening a new chapter", a series of interpretation reports on the 19th CPC National Congress. They interpreted the report and relevant issues of the 19th CPC National Congress from angles, such as law-based governance and green development, and published several interpretation reports, including *The 19th CPC National Congress Will Be a Milestone in Bringing New Millennium Achievements*, the *19th CPC National Congress Report: What's the Role of Law-Based Governance in the Construction of Socialism with Chinese Characteristics* and *Practicing the Concept of Green Development and Establishing a Long-term Mechanism for Environmental Protection*, which helped to attract the public's attention to new development concepts raised at the 19th CPC National Congress.

3.2.2 Interpret the Policy Provisions to Help the Public Understand Them

The Internet era gives rise to a variety of policy interpretations, but we need high-end think tanks to play their role and provide authoritative and accurate policy interpretations. Think tanks can give full play to their professional and authoritative advantages and offer accurate policy interpretations by publishing monographs and research reports, setting up opinion columns, and conducting interviews with media as experts. By doing this, they can help the public get a comprehensive, accurate and deep understanding of policies and thus promote policy implementation. Among the channels for policy interpretations and dissemination, publishing interpretation reports and expressing expert opinions through the media are the most efficient means. Think tanks can rephrase obscure policies into points that are easier for the public to understand and find the footholds for policy publicity in public opinion through their own media platforms or the expert policy interpretation columns of major platforms, such as People. cn and Guangming. cn. For example, when *Outline of the Yangtze River Delta Regional Integration Development Plan* was launched, experts from China Institute of Regulation Research had an interview with the Xinhua

News Agency right away to interpret some highlights in the outline.

3.2.3   Build Social Consensus and Create a Good Policy Atmosphere

The professionalism and authority of think tanks (and the independence of most think tanks) have made it easier for their policy publicity to win trust and recognition from the public than governments', thus achieving better results in guiding public opinions. Many think tanks carry out in-depth research and analysis on major policies and issues, and some issues may become the choices of several think tanks. The 2019 CTTI think tank product collection reveals that topics such as "poverty alleviation", "the Belt and Road Initiative" and "rural revitalization" have attracted many think tanks' attention. Think tanks' in-depth and all-round research on the same issue can help explain policy concepts and facilitate the public's understanding of the purpose and significance of policies, building consensus and creating a good policy atmosphere. For example, between 2017 and 2019, the Center of Economic Development Research of Wuhan University and *Guangming Daily* jointly held three think tank forums of Wuhan University under the themes of "New Era, New Concept, New System", "the Strategy of Developing a Strong Culture in the New Era" and "Global Governance System Reform and China's Proposal". The forums were launched in the forms of keynote speeches and round-table discussions, focusing on the urgent needs of the country and major decision-making arrangements of the central government. They helped to establish a correct conception of history, the overall picture, and the role we play in response to the changes in the global situations, prompting economic and social innovation and development.

3.3   Make Policy Evaluation to Promote Timely Policy Adjustment and Improvement

Public policy evaluation is an indispensable part of the modernization of national governance. China's public policy evaluation got off to a late start and is still being explored. Since the 18th CPC National Congress, policy evaluation has received more attention from the central government and local governments at all levels, as well as from all sectors of society. The report of the 18th CPC National Congress and *Resolution of the Central Committee of the Communist Party of China on Major Issues Concerning Comprehensive Law-Based Governance* adopted by the Third Plenary Session of the 18th CPC Central Committee clearly stated that "The social stability risk assessment mechanism for major decision-making should be improved. " The Fourth Plenary Session of the 18th Central Committee identified " risk assessment" as an important step in the statutory procedures for major administrative decisions. The Fourth Plenary Session of the 19th CPC Central Committee's adoption of *Resolution of the Central Committee of the Communist Party of China on Major Issues Concerning Upholding and Improving the Socialism with Chinese Characteristics to Promote the Modernization of National Governance and Governance Capability* put forward that we should " improve the decision-making mechanism, strengthen investigation and research, scientific demonstration and risk assessment of major decisions, and reinforce execution, assessment and supervision of decision-making" .

The idea of "risk assessment" proposed by the 18th CPC National Congress and the Third and Fourth Plenary Sessions of the 18th CPC Central Committee is a prior assessment of decision-making. It refers to the assessment of the feasibility of a policy before its implementation in order to make the policy scheme more considerate and feasible, which is similar to the consultation and demonstration of policy at the implementation stage. For example, the high-end think tank of Public Health and Safety and Medical Reform Strategy Research of Heilongjiang Province built a medical insurance system simulation model based on ProModel. They simulated the improvement of the medical insurance system under the implementation of different policy schemes to explore the means and policy options for multi-objective improvement of the medical insurance system. The idea of the execution, assessment and supervision of decision-making raised at the Fourth Plenary Session of the 19th CPC Central Committee, on the other hand, is post-assessment on decision-making. It refers to the assessment of the effect of a policy after its implementation in order to provide the basis for policy changes, policy improvement and new policy formulation, help governments optimize the allocation of policy resources and ensure scientific and accurate policy operation. This is the policy evaluation we are going to discuss in this section.

The analysis of the corresponding policy stages of internal reference reports and feedback of CTTI source think tanks shows that, by March 2019, internal reference reports made at the stage of policy evaluation account for less than 5%, but the submission/approval ratio of internal reference reports at this stage is much higher than that of other stages. This means that our government's demand for think tanks to participate in policy evaluation and policy feedback is still on the rise. And in response, think tanks have made many efforts and attempt to engage in policy evaluation to make improvement in recent years.

3.3.1   Keep Tracking to Effectively Evaluate the Effect of Policy Implementation

The effect of public policy implementation requires long-term follow-up evaluations made by professional teams. The capacity and level of policy evaluation show decision-making consultation institutions' ability to make suggestions to governments, which means that the evaluators are expected to have strong professional competence. Think tanks' talent teams and policy involvement experience have given them a competitive edge in policy evaluation. University think tanks, social think tanks and other non-party and non-government think tanks have the potential to become excellent third-party policy evaluators. At present, many think tank teams have been invited or have volunteered to participate in the follow-up evaluation of the policy effect. For example, entrusted by the Gansu Provincial Food and Drug Administration, the School of Management of Lanzhou University, as a third-party evaluator, has made an evaluation of the food and drug safety governance performance of Gansu Province since the implementation of the "13th Five-Year Plan". Based on the intermediate assessment of the implementation of the "food and drug safety" engineering project of *165 Major Engineering Projects in the National Outline of the 13th Five-Year Plan*, the intermediate assessment of the implementation of the food and drug safety traceability system raised by the "Safe Gansu" engineering project of *Gansu Provincial Outline of the 13th Five-Year Plan*, and the intermediate assessment of the goals and tasks of *Gansu Provincial Plan on Food and Drug Safety According to the 13th Five-Year Plan*, the evaluation team carried out field surveys and produced the report entitled *Intermediate Evaluation Report on the Food and Drug Safety Governance Performance of Gansu Province during the 13th Five-Year Plan*. The report made a scientific, comprehensive and objective assessment of the Food and Drug Safety Governance Performance of Gansu Province, listed out existing problems, identified the new impetus for development at the late stage of the 13th five-year plan, and proposed specific and well-targeted solutions and suggestions. Between 2013 and 2016, the Center for Experimental Economics in Education of Shaanxi Normal University conducted a number of follow-up surveys on 243 teachers and about 10,000 fifth-grade students they taught in 216 rural primary schools of 16 impoverished counties in the west of China. They investigated the implementation of performance-based salary policy for teachers in rural primary schools of poverty-stricken areas and produced a report entitled *Suggestions on Improving the Performance-Based Salary Policy for Teachers in Rural Primary Schools of Poverty-Stricken Areas.* The report published in the think tank's own journal *Policy Research Briefs* has gained the attention of the Ministry of Education and thus has provided a basis for the reform of teachers' performance-based salary system. Examples above show that think tanks can give full play to their professional advantages when they investigate the match between public policies and practical needs of the grassroots and evaluate the adaptability and performance of public policies scientifically and openly and based on extensive and comprehensive research.

3.3.2 Carry Out In-depth Research to Explore the Reasons for the Poor Implementation of Policies

Although the ability of governments at all levels to make scientific decisions and carry out law-based administration continues to improve, there are still many public policies that are improperly formulated and implemented or have become outdated due to changes in the social and economic environment. Think tanks can sort out and analyze the collected data and materials based on comprehensive and objective research, produce policy evaluation reports, give feedback of the attitudes of the relevant responsible parties, summarize and analyze the pros and cons of the policies, deduce and study the reasons for the failure, propose opinions on revision and adjustment, and even directly participate in subsequent work of policy adjustment. Their efforts can resolve conflicts among stakeholders promptly, further promote the formulation of fair and democratic policies as well as improve policy efficiency. For example, Guangdong Institute for International Strategies and Center for Enterprise Research of Peking University jointly conducted a survey on the lack of participation of private enterprises in the construction of the Belt and Road Initiative, covering

14,500 private enterprises, 21 prefecture-level cities and 29 cities or districts (counties) in Guangdong Province. Based on their first-hand data of micro-enterprises, they made an in-depth analysis and summary of the present situation of private enterprises' participation in the construction of the Belt and Road Initiative, their willingness to participate, existing problems and the reasons behind them. Their report *Private Enterprises' Participation in the Construction of the Belt and Road Initiative : Reasons and Solutions for Strong Willingness But Little Progress* has put forward solutions and suggestions for the development of practical industry-university-research platforms and the establishment of a one-stop management model for China's overseas investment, which will help to bring private enterprises' role in the construction of the Belt and Road Initiative into full play and achieve win-win cooperation. Likewise, the Party School of the Guizhou Provincial Party Committee gave questionnaires and had in-depth interviews with people at resettlement sites in Banqiao Town, Sinan County to identify the problems in the implementation of poverty alleviation and relocation policy in inhospitable areas like Sinan County of Tongren City. Their report *Real Problems of Poverty Alleviation and Relocation in Sinan County of Tongren City and the Solutions* was adopted by the provincial internal reference journal *Decision Consultation of Guizhou Province* (volume 1, 2019), and received feedback from Sun Zhigang, Secretary of the Guizhou Provincial Party Committee, and Luo Ning, Vice Chairman of Guizhou Provincial Political Consultative Conference. It has provided the reference for subsequent policy formulation of poverty alleviation and relocation in different places.

3.3.3 Make a Comprehensive Analysis to Sum Up the Successful Experience for Reference

When making public policy evaluation and giving feedback, think tanks not only identify the problems and deficiencies of existing policies and make suggestions for improvement, but also summarize innovative and successful policy experience and make recommendations on promotion based on local conditions. Their timely evaluation and feedback on the pilot policies will help further improve the policy and promote the rapid spreading of policy experience. For example, six months after the pilot work of the construction of a medical and health community in counties of Zhejiang Province, the research team of the Social Governance Research Institute of Zhejiang University, based on the performance, capacity, organization, system and other dimensions of the medical and health community in counties of Zhejiang Province, made a third-party independent evaluation, summarized the successful experience of the pilot work, and put forward policy suggestions to promote the construction of the medical and health community. 9 of their policy suggestions were adopted by *Opinions on Comprehensive Construction of a Medical and Health Service Community at County Level* launched by Zhejiang Provincial Committee of the CPC and the General Office of Zhejiang government. Their advanced experience was fully acknowledged and was quickly translated into public policies.

4   Summary

After several years of development, new types of think tanks continue to enrich and improve their means of offering decision-making consultation to governments. They have played an increasingly important role in public policy processes, such as agenda-setting, policy formation, implementation, evaluation and feedback. Now they have become the important brainpower for the Party and government's scientific and democratic decision-making, and an important adviser for social reforms. They have carried out in-depth surveys to serve the grassroots, gathered public opinion to serve the masses, conducted advanced and professional research to serve development, and focused on hot issues and difficulties to serve the overall situation. They have become an important member of the policy community and an important intellectual supporter for the modernization of the national governance system and governance capacity. In the future, faced with the new situation of globalization and China's rapid economic and social development, new types of think tanks should further improve their level and ability of decision-making consultation services, create competitive new types of think tank brands with Chinese characteristics at home and abroad and continue to contribute to the promotion of the modernization of the national governance system and governance capacity.

Topic 3   Communication Abilities of New Type Think Tanks Embody Remarkable Progress

Opinions on Strengthening the Construction of New Think Tanks with Chinese Characteristics (The *Opinions*) was issued as a guiding document for the development of new-type think tanks, by the General Office of the CPC Central Committee and the General Office of the State Council in January 2015, which refers to "encouraging think tanks to utilize mass media and other multiple methods for spreading mainstream ideological values and grouping social positive energy", "strengthening overseas publicity and discourse system construction of new-type think tanks with Chinese characteristics, improving competitiveness and influence of our national think tanks in international community". These two sentences from the *Opinions* on one side made clear the disseminating function of new-type think tanks, and on the other side indicated requests from two facets for new-type think tanks dissemination: the first is to look to domestic dissemination, take the responsibilities as assistants to the Party and government administration, complete job tasks, such as theoretic explanations, policy elucidation, public opinions studies and judgement, counsel the public sentiments; the second is to look abroad and strive for international dissemination and exert functions of public diplomacy: "New-type think tanks with Chinese characteristics should be capable of providing favorable conditions for international cooperation and communication." For one aspect, Chinese new-type think tanks through their fruits spread China's voice and shape China's image, promote the credibility from national populace and international media systems to official agencies as well as domestic media; for another aspect, Chinese think tanks by means of disseminating activities can scientifically generate issues at both home and abroad, therefore boost China's discourse power, exert effects on public opinions and serve state's strategic deployment.

1   The Significance of Communication Energization of Think Tanks

1.1   Communication of Think Tanks Help Assemble Agreements in Policies

As policy studies and advisory agencies, think tanks need to draw support from various channels to disseminate think tanks' thoughts, and therefore achieve aims include guiding public opinions, enlightening civilian intellects, influencing decision-making and building up think tanks brands. The dissemination of think tanks contains aspects such as awareness, contents and channels for dissemination, which can penetrate into the complete process from administration consultation, government decision-making to national governance.

Communication awareness of think tanks is the premise for them to take disseminating actions. Before making decisions, think tanks dissemination on the one hand through long-time collection of novel ideas and concepts proposed by think tanks' experts, gathers and analyzes a great deal of realistic, scientific, objective data information, by aid of effective research means like data mining tools and statistical analysis techniques improves policy research levels, and provides favorable database, professional advice and authorized consultation for decision-making; on the other hand, directed by scientifically theoretic approaches "penetrates into reality and community level, goes deep among the masses and listens to their voices, learns the real situations, studies extensively and concentrates on researches", through collectively gathering and studying mass wisdom reflects for sure the will of people, generally collects the wisdom of people, provides a new scope for the decision-making of both the Party and government and influences their decision-making to a certain extent.

The contents of think tanks' communication bear opinions of think tanks. During the decision-making process, think tanks for one aspect belong to a moderately stable policy research and consulting organization, an important participant during the policy-making process, through participating in drafting significant resolutions and policies, investigating and surveying can directly provide suggestions for government's decision-making, and the communication contents of think tanks show up rather high-level academic soundness, specialty, credibility and reliability which have immediate impacts on decision-making; think tanks on the other hand communicate with the general public, correctly interpret major decisions, complete public policy discourse transforming work, enhance the public's trust and understanding of major decisions, lead folk intelligence and social force to take part in government's decision-making in length, reduce disharmonious factors by constructing various balance mechanism to advance government's pace of democracy, hence actively put the policies into practice, realize the maximization of policy-making benefits, so as to facilitate economic growth and social progress.

The communicating effects of think tanks date from the disseminating channels of think tanks. After decisions were made, to achieve the disseminating effects at social, popular and universal levels of think tanks, on one side the think tank communication exploits new media technology, takes advantage of social media like network platform, mainstream media and third-party platform, puts up diversified disseminating channels, spreads think tanks' ideas in affectionate ways and channels to the people, provides interactive platforms for audience, thus to achieve goals of influencing the public and give auxiliary support for implementing policies; on another side, during interaction with the public, think tank communication realizes the expressions and delivery of the public's interests, corrects shortsighted, single-faceted or extreme viewpoints in the public opinions, and reflects the people's opinions back to the government, amends political schemes further, which can make it easier to gain consensus from society and shape social opinions that are more probable to be adopted by decision-makers as policies, hence has an impact on government's public policy and helps enforcement of policies after being issued.

The role think tank communication plays in the earlier, middle and late phases of decision-making is an important one that functions as a bridge as well as a bond—it's not only beneficial for perfecting national governance system, improving state's governance capabilities, but also through novel disseminating approaches like the Internet and new media, it maximally strives for support to public policies from the will of people, which can generate impacts like assisting governance, enlightening civilians, explaining theories, elucidating policies, counseling public sentiments and so on.

1.2 Communication of Think Tanks Concentrate on Telling Good Chinese Story

Chinese think tanks are to disseminate China's voice, portray China's image, undertake the responsibility as an important role of the nation's communication soft power outwards, enhance national soft power, enlarge our influence and discourse rights in international community, play their parts as thoughts' engines in outbound communication, and establish a benign international environment for development of our society and economy. Currently, international communication of think tanks basically participates from the following three aspects in the construction of global governance system:

The first is constructing "China's Discourse System". Through the years in China's disseminating practices, mainstream official media have been holding their positions as core bodies for action. But under the influences of elements like politics, ideologies, culture and religions, especially the inadequate trust from the international community, the Western society has more than enough doubts toward the objectiveness, authenticity and completeness of the contents from Chinese official media, which leads to a good deal of reduction of effects and efficiency of outbound communication. This on the one hand reserves some space for think tanks to come into play. On the other hand, the subjective initiatives of Chinese think tanks are to be further elevated. Over the past two decades, the world-famous Davos Forum, Shangri-La Dialogue, and Fortune Global Forum are always leaked by top-notch think tanks and relative organizations from Europe and America. Chinese think tanks need to put to practice subjective initiatives by means of building up think tanks at the level of national strategic dissemination, scientifically setting up international policy agenda, promoting discourse power in global stage, influencing the trend of international public opinions and so forth.

The second is carrying out "going abroad" strategy. Think tanks communication should spread the voice of China to the globe, tell good Chinese story, integrate global resources and take part in worldwide governance system. By approaches of equivalent dialogues, rational communication, eradicating irregularities and building up reasonable rules, think tank communication proactively responds to concerns of international community; grasps opportunities in opportune occasions for outbound communication, exerts positive influence on international public opinions before and after major diplomatic events; based on giving full play to their own research advantages participates vigorously in international academic theories discussions and construction of academic discourse rights, as well as investigation of global subjects; disseminates national values to the globe and serves the implement of national strategic goals.

The third is building up international brands. Chinese think tanks should erect awareness for the whole world and own brands, integrate think tanks' construction into the macro system of national diplomatic strategy for operation, establish increasingly sound schemes and mechanism for the development of think tanks, explore for a road for the development which is compatible with China's national conditions, in order to enhance dissemination of think tank communication across the world and strive for a voice of think tanks in the international stage. Through brand construction, making use of brand effect and brand influence, communication of think tanks improves dissemination of think tanks in global area and thus exerting direct influence on think tanks' capabilities of coping with worldwide issues and dealing with cross-border affairs. It is specially noted that the scope for think tanks research should extend to international topics, through forming global or regional think tanks network incessantly enlarging their own global impacts. China plays an active role in propelling construction of shared community of human destiny, facilitates the Belt and Road Initiative international cooperation, joins hands in and leads reforms of global governance system. Therefore, completing the international communication of think tanks and developing their public diplomatic functions are important methods for the world to learn China, know China, accept China, as well as to strengthen China's discourse power and continuingly improve national soft power.

2 Status Quo Analysis of Communication of CTTI Source Think Tanks

The improvement of influence of think tanks and their obtainment of speaking rights are closely related to dissemination from think tank organizations. Diversification in both channels of issuing results and propaganda & promotion enhances communicating chances among think tank organizations, decision-making institutes, academic research institutions and the public at home and abroad. With more and more organizations and people learning about research results of think tanks, ideas of think tank organizations, the goal of achieving decision-making counselling and participation in governance will come true at last.

At present, the Internet has become the major medium of information dissemination. Think tank organizations by virtue of conventional websites and new media platforms disseminate research results, make full play of the strengths of Internet platforms like interactivity, timeliness and applicability, which accelerates disseminating efficiency and increases the brand influence of think tanks. CTTI database embodies data information of a good deal of channels of communication, mainly consisting of: related coverage platforms (printed media, news websites, television), websites of organizations, new media platforms (Weibo, WeChat, etc.). This report chooses constructions of 706 websites and new media platforms that were nominated as CTTI source think tanks of 2018 for analysis.

2.1   Statistical Analysis of Communication Platforms

According to statistics, amid 706 think tank organizations of CTTI database, 503 of them have exclusive websites, 339 have established their WeChat official accounts and 101 have official Weibo accounts.

Table 3.1 reflects statistical situations of different types of think tanks including websites, WeChat and Weibo. In terms of think tanks of party/government organizations, party schools, Academies of Social Sciences, the construction of their traditional websites starts early and takes a relatively high proportion under the influence of conditions like government affairs going public. Corporate think tanks, private think tanks, media think tanks have preponderant strengths of using WeChat platform for publicity compared with other types of think tanks. Apart from media think tanks, all other types of think tanks have large room for improvement in employment of the Weibo platform.

The construction of omnimedia communication platforms can satisfy tailored policy research needs, and at the same time can improve communication of professional think tanks which enjoy international reputation. As one unit for priority development of China Top Think Tanks, one of the first key think tanks of Jiangsu, by constructing the new multi-channel communication method, Yangtze Industrial Economics Institution constantly develops operation capabilities of self-media platforms, timely exchanges the newest academic messages and research results, and successfully builds up the brand image of think tanks. By December 12, 2019, its official websites in total had released 409 news notifications, 298 chief articles, 514 expert views, 149 essays related to roundtables, 101 media articles, 7 research reports and resources of 45 serial works—its official WeChat account totally had released 419 original articles, each having over 1200 pageviews on average.

Ideas of communication of private think tanks are rather more flexible and changeable compared with other types of think tanks. Take the Pangoal Institution as an example. Its propagation matrix of multiple platforms, stereoscopy and high efficiency provide powerful protection for the home and abroad propaganda of think tanks. The professional media team of Pangoal builds up fine channels for cooperation with both domestic and foreign mainstream media, which can manoeuvre a number of influential Internet celebrities and self-media to speak up, deploy various media resources to support its think tanks. Since the establishment 6 years ago, Pangoal

Institution has put up propagation matrixes including Pangoal Think Tanks, India Research Center of Pangoal Institution, Northeast Asia Research Center of Pangoal Institution, Aging and Future, Think Tanks Academy, and cultivated a good number of young scholars "who can speak up" and superior audience "who love reading". For the moment, the Pangoal Institution altogether has 13 self-media platforms, over 50 cooperative mainstream media, more than 100 self-media, connections with 350 plus experts, fans in Internet platforms adding up to 3. 39 million, 1. 55 million news articles in Baidu, 663 thousand articles in both English and Chinese in Google, 132 thousand coverage and reprints from other media and 8,000 articles from its self-media platforms. This kind of communication platform matrix, with bountiful transversal propagation platforms and many crosswise propagation platforms, is becoming the leading configuration of media and private think tanks.

Table 3. 1　Situations of Construction of CTTI Source Think Tanks Websites,

WeChat, Weibo Platforms (by types)

Think tanks of	CTTI Source Think Tanks Total Number	Websites		WeChat		Weibo	
		Number	Ratio	Number	Ratio	Number	Ratio
Party/government organizations	69	63	91. 30%	38	55. 07%	14	20. 29%
Academies of social sciences	51	47	92. 16%	24	47. 06%	12	23. 53%
Party schools	48	34	70. 83%	23	47. 92%	2	4. 17%
Universities	441	301	68. 25%	200	45. 35%	40	9. 07%
Armed forces	6	1	16. 67%	2	33. 33%	0	0%
Research institutions	34	23	67. 65%	12	35. 29%	7	20. 59%
Corporations	8	5	62. 50%	6	75. 00%	3	37. 50%
Society	36	24	66. 67%	23	63. 89%	14	38. 89%
Media	13	5	38. 46%	11	84. 62%	9	69. 23%

Table 3. 2   Statistical Constructions of CTTI Source Think Tanks' Websites,

WeChat, Weibo Platforms (by provinces)

Names	CTTI Source Think Tanks Number	Official Websites		WeChat Official Accounts		Weibo		All three channels are accessible
		Number	Ratio	Number	Ratio	Number	Ratio	
Beijing	207	147	71. 01%	104	50. 24%	44	21. 26%	31
Tianjin	41	27	65. 85%	16	39. 02%	2	4. 88%	2
Hebei	19	13	68. 42%	7	36. 84%	1	5. 26%	1
Shaanxi	3	1	33. 33%	0	0. 00%	0	0. 00%	0
Inner Mongolia	6	4	66. 67%	2	33. 33%	1	16. 67%	1
Liaoning	14	9	64. 29%	4	28. 57%	0	0. 00%	0
Jilin	13	8	61. 54%	6	46. 15%	1	7. 69%	1
Heilongjiang	12	8	66. 67%	5	41. 67%	1	8. 33%	1
Shanghai	81	57	70. 37%	45	55. 56%	13	16. 05%	11
Jiangsu	43	31	72. 09%	21	48. 84%	7	16. 28%	4
Zhejiang	17	15	88. 24%	11	64. 71%	3	17. 65%	3
Anhui	7	5	71. 43%	2	28. 57%	0	0. 00%	0
Fujian	10	8	80. 00%	0	0. 00%	0	0. 00%	0
Jiangxi	15	11	73. 33%	4	26. 67%	1	6. 67%	1
Shandong	15	13	86. 67%	6	40. 00%	1	6. 67%	1
Henan	5	3	60. 00%	3	60. 00%	1	20. 00%	1
Hubei	27	21	77. 78%	17	62. 96%	4	14. 81%	4
Hunan	28	19	67. 86%	13	46. 43%	3	10. 71%	2
Guangdong	24	20	83. 33%	23	95. 83%	5	20. 83%	5
Guangxi	5	5	100.00%	2	40. 00%	1	20. 00%	1
Hainan	10	6	60. 00%	1	10. 00%	0	0. 00%	0
Chongqing	18	15	83. 33%	7	38. 89%	2	11. 11%	1

Continued

Names	CTTI Source Think Tanks Number	Official Websites		WeChat Official Accounts		Weibo		All three channels are accessible
		Number	Ratio	Number	Ratio	Number	Ratio	
Sichuan	16	11	68.75%	5	31.25%	5	31.25%	2
Yunnan	12	6	50.00%	5	41.67%	0	0.00%	0
Guizhou	5	2	40.00%	2	40.00%	1	20.00%	0
Tibet	3	3	100.00%	1	33.33%	0	0.00%	0
Shaanxi	24	17	70.83%	9	37.50%	2	8.33%	1
Gansu	16	9	56.25%	11	68.75%	2	12.50%	2
Qinghai	4	4	100.00%	2	50.00%	0	0.00%	0
Ningxia	4	3	75.00%	4	100.00%	0	0.00%	0
Xinjiang	2	2	100.00%	0	0.00%	0	0.00%	0

Table 3. 2, Fig. 3. 1, Fig. 3. 2, and Fig. 3. 3 statistically show construction situations of websites, WeChat and Weibo of CTTI source think tanks by provinces. From perspective of sheer number, Beijing and Shanghai have outstanding advantages in possessing websites, WeChat and Weibo platforms of think tanks organizations at the same time, which conforms to the reality of the development tendency of new-type think tanks; from the perspective of ratio in construction, websites of provinces display a better situation in construction compared to WeChat, and the construction of Weibo platform remains to be strengthened.

Fig. 3. 4 shows the effect picture of contemporary constructions with websites, WeChat and Weibo of CTTI Source think tanks from all national provinces (including municipalities and regions). The darker the color, the more comprehensive the disseminating channels are. Its method of calculation is: the total amount of think tanks that have established all three channels divides the total number of think tanks.

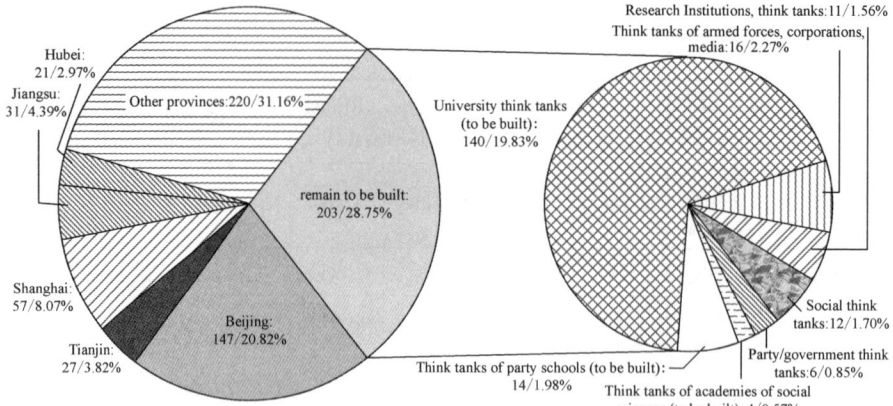

Fig. 3.1 Construction Situations of CTTI Source Think Tanks' Websites

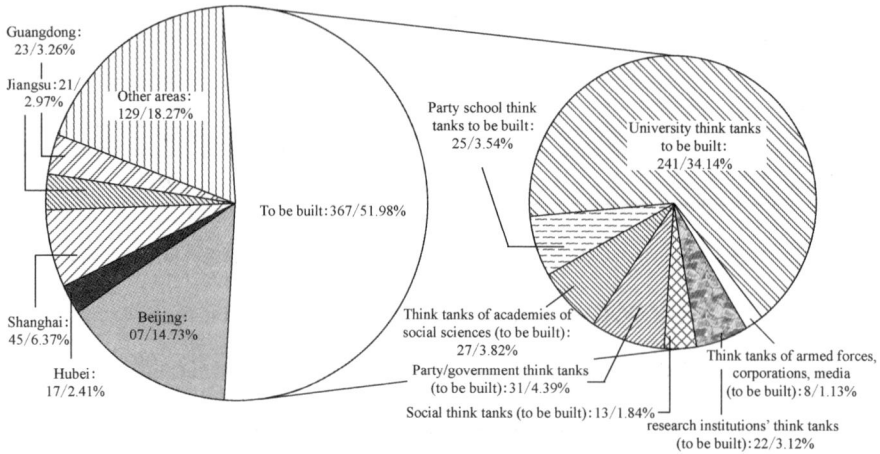

Fig. 3.2 Statistical Construction of CTTI Source Think Tanks' WeChat

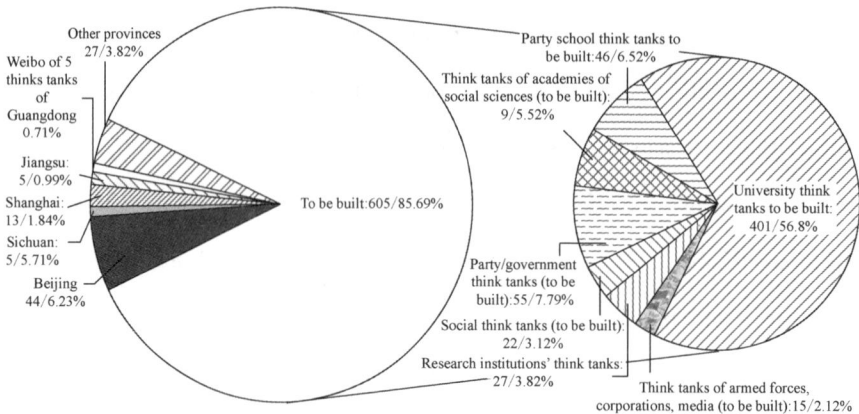

Fig. 3.3 Statistical Construction of CTTI Source Think Tanks' Weibo

Table 3. 3 shows the statistical conditions of Websites, WeChat, Weibo of units for priority development in national top think tanks and the construction of national top think tanks. Compared to all CTTI Source think tanks' average data, the first group of national top think tanks have gone through several years of construction, taken the obviously leading position in constructing disseminating channels, and possessed relative data that is rather high than the average figures. Units for priority development of national top think tanks' construction have a moderately better construction in disseminating channels than the average figures, an unapparent one. In terms of specific construction of platforms, Weibo platform construction remains to be further strengthened. In contrast, overseas think tanks' new media platforms are adept in employing platforms such as Twitter and Facebook to enhance communication and influence public opinions and government decision-making. These new media platforms own fast speed in communication, targeted audience, immediate interactions and feedbacks—characteristics shared with Weibo platform.

Table 3. 3   Statistical Construction of Websites, WeChat and Weibo of Units for Priority Development of National Top Think Tanks and National Top Think Tanks Construction

Types	Total Number of Think Tanks	Websites		WeChat		Weibo	
		Number	Ratio	Number	Ratio	Number	Ratio
All CTTI Source Think Tanks	706	503	70. 94%	339	47. 81%	101	14. 25%
National Top Think Tanks	25	23	92. 00%	17	68. 00%	10	40. 00%
Units for Priority Development of National Top Think Tanks	15	15	100. 00%	9	60. 00%	2	13. 33%

The ideas of communication to the public from noted overseas think tanks at the same time have impacts on ideas of our national new-type think tanks. Chongyang Institute for Financial Studies of Renmin University of China, for instance, pays equal attention to research and communication and operation persists that think tanks are more than just ideas serving the leadership, and also should disseminate the information from think tanks to the public. The Chongyang Institute for Financial Studies has been painstakingly managing its Chinese and English official websites, and meanwhile, has been trying to expand and improve operating abilities to its own self-media platforms, building the communication matrix of "Chongyang Institute for Financial Studies of Renmin University of China" in platforms including WeChat official accounts, Sina Weibo and so on, timely disseminating and updating the newest and most authoritative research results of academies. Ever since the creation of its WeChat official accounts, 144 original articles had been published by December 12, 2019, with each article having more than 1,000 pageviews. The Weibo Platform of the institute has over 900 thousand fans and more than 10 thousand pageviews every day, making think tanks have more significant influence in larger populations.

2.2 Comprehensive Evaluation and Analysis of Dissemination Power of Communication Platforms

Source of the evaluation sample of this report comes from data of construction conditions of 706 websites and new media platforms of 2018 CTTI Source think tanks. The evaluation index system consists of two grades, containing 3 primary indicators (communication through official websites, WeChat official accounts, Weibo) and 14 secondary ones including indexes like whole website IP average per day, whole website VP average per day, average reading of WeChat official accounts, number of fans of Weibo, the number of times articles have been forwarded, etc. (see

Table 3. 4). Approaches of analytical hierarchy process together with entropy weight method were adopted—analytical hierarchy process is a method of systematically decision-making targeting at multiple goals and complicated questions, judging the small or huge impacts of each index to objects of research based on subjective experience and determining the weight of indexes, having comparatively high subjectivity; entropy weight method decides the objective weight according to variance of indexes, using information entropy for calculating entropy coefficients of indexes, thereby making adjustments of index weights deducted from the analytical hierarchy process, so as to get evaluation results that are objective and applicable to realistic needs. Reconduct revises determined weights from analytical hierarchy process with entropy weight method, making the weights more reliable.

Table 3. 4　Comprehensive Evaluation Index System of Think Tank Communication

Comprehensive Evaluation Index System of Think Tank Communication		
	Indexes	Single index
Evaluation of Think Tank Communication	Official websites	Whole website average IP per day
		Whole website average VP per day
		Baidu weight
		Mobile weight
		Baidu traffic anticipation
		Quantity of index
		Baidu records
		Baidu backlinks
	WeChat official accounts	Average pageviews
		Number of original articles
	Official Weibo	Average number of likes
		Average number of forwards
		Number of fans
		Average number of comments

Specific procedures:

Step one: analytical hierarchy weighting

(1) construe pair judgment matrixes (compare pair by pair the importance of indexes, namely, judge which one of the two indexes g_i and g_j is more important; the importance of g_i divides that of g_j is r_{ij})

$$\begin{bmatrix} r_{11} & r_{12} & \cdots & r_{1n} \\ r_{21} & r_{22} & \cdots & r_{2n} \\ \cdots & \cdots & \cdots & \cdots \\ r_{n1} & r_{n2} & \cdots & r_{nn} \end{bmatrix}$$

(2) judge in pairs the standardization of matrixes.

$$\overline{r_{ij}} = \frac{r_{ij}}{\sum\limits_{k=1}^{n} r_{kj}} \quad (i,j = 1,2,\cdots n)$$

(3) plus line by line the standardized matrixes.

$$\overline{w_i} = \sum\limits_{j=1}^{n} \overline{r_{ij}} \quad (i = 1,2\cdots n)$$

(4) standardize the matrix $\overline{w} = (\overline{w_1}, \overline{w_2}, \cdots, \overline{w_n})$

$$w_i = \frac{\overline{w_i}}{\sum\limits_{j=1}^{n} \overline{w_j}} \quad (i = 1,2,\cdots,n)$$

Step two: entropy weight method weighting

Now m programs are to be evaluated, n indexes for evaluation, together forming the kernel data matrix $A = (a_{ij})_{m \times n}$

$$A = \begin{bmatrix} a_{11} & a_{12} & \cdots & a_{1n} \\ a_{21} & a_{22} & \cdots & a_{2n} \\ \cdots & \cdots & \cdots & \cdots \\ a_{m1} & a_{m2} & \cdots & a_{mn} \end{bmatrix}$$

Of which, a_{ij} is the value of evaluation under No. j index of the No. i program.

For a certain index for evaluation, the information weight is:

$$e_j = -k \sum_{i=1}^{m} p_{ij} \cdot \ln p_{ij} \quad (i = 1,2,\cdots,m; j = 1,2,\cdots,n)$$

Of which, $e_j = -k \sum_{i=1}^{m} p_{ij} \cdot \ln p_{ij} \quad (i = 1,2,\cdots,m; j = 1,2,\cdots,n)$

Provided with basic principles of information weight, the information effect value of index depends on subtraction of this index weight with 1, thus entropy weight of the index is:

$$W_j = (1-e_j)/\sum_{j=1}^{n}(1-e_j) \quad (j = 1,2,\cdots,n)$$

So, the entropy weight vector of evaluation index is: $W = (W_1, W_2, \cdots, W_n)$

Step three: combination weight

Combine the strong and weak points of analytic hierarchy process (AHP) and entropy weight, draw together their merits and conclude the combination weight of evaluation indexes:

$$\overline{W} = \left\{ \frac{W_1 w_1}{\sum_{j=1}^{n} W_j w_j}, \frac{W_2 w_2}{\sum_{j=1}^{n} W_j w_j}, \cdots, \frac{W_n w_n}{\sum_{j=1}^{n} W_j w_j} \right\} = (\overline{W_1}, \overline{W_2}, \cdots \overline{W_n})$$

Obviously, combination weight $\overline{W_j}$, w_j and W_j should be as close as possible, according to the principle of minimum relative information entropy, we can get:

$$\min M = \sum_{j=1}^{n} \overline{W_j}(\ln \overline{W_j} - \ln w_j) + \sum_{j=1}^{n} \overline{W_j}(\ln \overline{W_j} - \ln W_j)$$

The Lagrange multipliers solve the above issue of optimization and obtain the optimal combination weight:

$$\overline{W} = \left\{ \frac{(W_1 w_1)^{0.5}}{\sum_{j=1}^{n} (W_j w_j)^{0.5}}, \frac{(W_2 w_2)^{0.5}}{\sum_{j=1}^{n} (W_j w_j)^{0.5}}, \cdots, \frac{(W_n w_n)^{0.5}}{\sum_{j=1}^{n} (W_j w_j)^{0.5}} \right\}$$

$$= (\overline{W_1}, \overline{W_2}, \cdots \overline{W_n})$$

The calculating results of AHP-entropy weight indexes weight are:

Whole website average IP per day	0.49
Whole website average VP per day	0.49
Baidu weight	0.79
Mobile weight	0.77
Baidu traffic anticipation	0.71
Quantity of index	0.57
Baidu records	0.97
Baidu backlinks	0.60
Average pageviews	0.74
Number of original articles	0.84
Average number of likes	0.27
Average number of forwards	0.25
Number of fans	0.82
Average number of comments	0.36

Step four: calculating scores of evaluations

Substitute the produced optimal combination weight into the following formula, and obtain score results of evaluation of m to be evaluated programs:

$$F = A^* \overline{W} \quad (i=1,2,\cdots,m; j=1,2,\cdots,n)$$

Of which, $\overline{W}$ is optimal combination weight; A^* is the index value of evaluation of think tank communication capabilities.

Due to the differences of units of measurement in separate evaluation indexes of comprehensive evaluation index system, dimensions of evaluation indexes should be unified at the first place before constructing indexes. This research nondimensionalized the adopted data, made 1 the maximum value of values of separate indexes, and calculated other data according to their ratio to the maximum value. Multiply the standardized data with weight of the index, summarize and produce Internet communication comprehensive indications of every sample of think tanks (the specific scores of communication abilities of think tanks organization remained unexposed). Table 3.5 shows scores and ranks of different types of think tanks. The coefficient to

Table 3.5　Statistic Sectioned Ranks Table of Disseminating Power Evaluation of CTTI Source Think Tank Communication Platforms

Types of think tanks		Party/government	Academies of social sciences	Party school or administrative college	University	Armed forces	Research institutions	Corporation	Society	Media
Population		69	51	48	441	6	34	8	36	13
Ratio		9.77%	7.22%	6.80%	62.46%	0.85%	4.82%	1.13%	5.10%	1.84%
Rank 1~100	Number	18	7	2	49	1	5	3	8	7
	Ratio	18.00%	7.00%	2.00%	49.00%	1.00%	5.00%	3.00%	8.00%	7.00%
	Efficient to population	1.84	0.97	0.29	0.78	1.18	1.04	2.65	1.57	3.80
Rank 1~200	Number	31	14	14	104	1	11	4	13	8
	Ratio	15.50%	7.00%	7.00%	52.00%	0.50%	5.50%	2.00%	6.50%	4.00%
Number of all types	Coefficient to population	1.59	0.97	1.03	0.83	0.59	1.14	1.77	1.27	2.17
Rank 1~300	Number	49	22	28	157	1	12	4	17	10
	Ratio	16.33%	7.33%	9.33%	52.33%	0.33%	4.00%	1.33%	5.67%	3.33%
Number of all types	Coefficient to population	1.67	1.02	1.37	0.84	0.39	0.83	1.18	1.11	1.81

Continued

Types of think tanks		Party/government	Academies of social sciences	Party school or administrative college	University	Armed forces	Research institutions	Corporation	Society	Media
Rank 1~400 Number of all types	Number	57	40	33	215	2	15	6	20	12
	Ratio	14.25%	10.00%	8.25%	53.75%	0.50%	3.75%	1.50%	5.00%	3.00%
	Coefficient to population	1.46	1.38	1.21	0.86	0.59	0.78	1.32	0.98	1.63
Rank 1~500 Number of all types	Number	60	49	39	283	2	21	7	27	12
	Ratio	12.00%	9.80%	7.80%	56.60%	0.40%	4.20%	1.40%	5.40%	2.40%
	Coefficient to population	1.23	1.36	1.15	0.91	0.47	0.87	1.24	1.06	1.30
Rank 1~600 Number of all types	Number	69	51	48	356	2	25	7	30	12
	Ratio	11.50%	8.50%	8.00%	59.33%	0.33%	4.17%	1.17%	5.00%	2.00%
	Coefficient to population	1.18	1.18	1.18	0.95	0.39	0.87	1.03	0.98	1.09
Rank 1~706 Number of all types	Number	69	51	48	441	6	34	8	36	13
	Ratio	9.77%	7.22%	6.80%	62.46%	0.85%	4.82%	1.13%	5.10%	1.84%
	Coefficient to population	1.00	1.00	1.00	1.00	1.00	1.00	1.00	1.00	1.00

the population can display the overall construction conditions of communication platforms of think tanks in sectioned ranks.

Among think tanks that rank 1~100, scores of disseminating ability from high to low are: media think tanks, corporation think tanks, party/government think tanks, social think tanks, think tanks of research institutions, thinks tanks of academies of social science, university think tanks, party school or administrative college think tanks. Among think tanks that rank 1~200, scores of disseminating ability from high to low are: media think tanks, corporation think tanks, party/government think tanks, social think tanks, think tanks of research institutions, party school or administrative college think tanks, think tanks of academies of social sciences, think tanks of armed forces. Among think tanks that rank 1~300, scores of disseminating ability from high to low are: media think tanks, party/government think tanks, party school or administrative college think tanks, corporation think tanks, social think tanks, think tanks of academies of social sciences, university think tanks, think tanks of research institutions, think tanks of armed forces. With general analysis, scores of media think tanks, party/government think tanks, corporation think tanks are comparatively higher, scores of university think tanks, and armed forces think tanks are comparatively lower.

3   Existing Problems of Think Tank Communication, Countermeasures and Suggestions

3.1   Existing Problems

3.1.1   The Awareness of Communication of Think Tanks Themselves Is Not Strong Enough

On the basis of present conditions, the majority of think tanks still have inadequate recognitions of the importance of communication and relatively weak awareness of it—they often pay too much attention to reporting and publicity of research results and ignore the introduction and communication of think tanks themselves. Therefore the general public have rather few chances to learn about them.

It is worth noting that communication awareness and characteristics show big differences in properties and areas. In relation to properties of think tanks, because university think tanks can directly draw support from communication platforms and systems of their own universities, they are highly employed by sorts of media with the most coverages among all think tanks. Think tanks of the party, government, armed forces, research institutions are closer to the core of decision-making, and their research results are confidentially limited, so coverages from relative media are rather less and are prone to channels like confidential reference and submission for improving influence. Compared to other types of think tanks, the number of society think tanks is the least, but they are the most flexible and free ones in operating new media and the Internet. In the areas where think tanks locate, districts whose economies are prosperous tend to lay more emphasis on the construction of new-type think tanks. Development of think tanks are therefore provided with favorable outside environment and stable capital source. In these areas, awareness of communication is comparably strong, the utilization percent of media is higher, and approaches and contents of communication are more various and flexible.

A distinctive difference between think tank organizations and absolute academic institutions is that the later emphasize "sitting at the academic chair still last for ten years", "caring nothing outside windows of research buildings", caring less about construction of public relations. However, apart from few think tanks whose properties are confidential, the rest majority are all required to play the functions of communication, building up cooperative relations between think tanks and the public, government, corporations, media and academic organizations. Communication ability is the lifeline of think tanks; the high or low efficiency in communication is directly related to the survival and development of think tanks. But now, when media have highly developed, huge differences in awareness of communication should not be caused by properties or areas.

3.1.2   The Level of Communication Remains to be Improved

3.1.2.1   Powerless Efforts in Establishing Dissemination Mechanism Based on Positioning of Self-Functions

Recent years have witnessed substantial development of think tank construction. With some completely unqualified profit organizations whitewashing themselves as "think tanks", the generalization of think tanks becomes a phenomenon, which to a great extent influences the construction quality of new-type think tanks. Some think tanks are yet to position their future direction for development, still lingering at the stage of "research on whatever are hot spots" and "just follow the tasks". These all reflect that the self-recognitions of partial think tanks are not comprehensive, and that positioning is not clear, let alone improving communication of themselves with plans and emphasis.

3.1.2.2   The Output of Disseminating Contents Doesn't Match Perfectly with Practical Needs

At present, the domestic and foreign situations are of extreme complexity and variety, and more than several key fields like diplomacy and army are longing for more professional intelligence support—it is a significant opportunity for think tanks to actively respond to national needs and attract the public attention. But part of think tanks still cannot escape ties of conventional research paradigms, thus having less breakthroughs of methodology of think tank research, less comprehensive and deep scope for research, inadequate quantity of high-quality professional think tanks and rather fewer influential contents of communication.

3.1.2.3   The Expressiveness and Attractiveness of Communication Contents Are Not Strong

At present, the communication contents of some think tanks are mainly manifested by press releases, which can easily cause the issue of homogenization. Thus basic developments of academic output, activities like meeting can only be displayed in simplicity, and core characteristics of think tanks like ideological function, system of ideas and research features can't be disseminated with substantiality.

3.1.3   The Disseminating Channels Are Single, the System for Dissemination Is Yet to be Promoted

Although the development of new media has created a huge space for communication, part of think tanks still have limited choices of disseminating channels. In terms of the types of think tanks, influenced by cost of capital, ability of communication and properties of think tanks, the construction of self-media of think tanks is slow and depends too much on Internet platforms, especially news portal websites. In terms of ranks, the majority of think tanks tend to choose mainstream media as disseminating channels, which often have a certain extent of influence and credibility—that in turn leading think tank communication to a more popular and social path.

The contradiction between the variety of communication channels and monotony of realistic practice reflects that currently, our national think tanks can't utilize various media platforms in a flexible and overall way, and that both the self-media construction of think tanks and the cooperation with mainstream media have problems like inadequate, partial and unimpressive employment.

3.2　Countermeasures and Suggestions

As the age of convergence media is coming, if think tanks cannot adapt to the brand-new media environment and make use of multiple channels for improving dissemination efficiency, then the communication effects would be very poor and thus unable to satisfy the building requirements of new-type think tanks.

3.2.1　Improve Communication Awareness of Think Tanks

Conscious awareness of communication is the premise for new-type think tanks to carry out all disseminating activities. Think tanks in Europe and America realize not only the importance of communication, but also sound cooperative relations with media. Moreover, they also strive to strengthen cooperation and combination with media, proactively send their newest movements in research and understandings of policies to media through their own public relation departments. Many of their researchers also show up usually in news media, openly comment on current affairs, policies and events as well as launch dissemination activities.

Firstly, designate specialized departments or personnel for communication. Think tanks commonly choose to set special departments, normally set think tanks director which is responsible for generally coordinating with think tank communication affairs, and put into a great deal of resources for exposure in media, aiming at improving the public images of think tanks. Brookings Institution, for example, has an experienced team for dissemination who spend a lot of time and energy updating information on its websites and monitor their real-time data flow so as to ensure high exposure of their think tanks in renowned media. Among our new-type think tanks, the publicity of Party/government think tanks, Party school think tanks and think tanks of academies of social sciences are usually duties of publicity departments or staff who are in charge of publicity. Neither is totally responsible for think tank communication. University think tanks are usually inner administrative organizations of universities or colleges and are not capable of professional publicity. Thus the work of think tank communication becomes part-time job of official workers in university think tanks. Society media have flexible operation mechanism, and the work of communication is normally shouldered by special workers.

Secondly, craft multi-disseminating scenarios for think tanks. Think tank communication contains not only releasing research reports, but also think tanks' participation in government investigation and survey activities, decision-making activities and policies road show activities, and so forth. By means of various kinds of think tanks' activities and participation in the government's decision-making scenarios, think tanks can comprehensively learn about causes and effects of policies published and build up fine relations with government—a situation that produces positive effects for disseminating think tanks' opinions. For another side, through crafting such disseminating scenarios for think tanks, information about government departments can be known and direction of the following research can therefore be prepared. Many speeches of government leaders are of two versions—one is spoken on the scene, while the other is written on paper. Sometimes there are huge differences between the two versions—many important messages, opinions and ideas are expressed by leaders in their speeches while they are not suitable to be disclosed to the public. If think tank researches are only conducted based on written scripts, a lot of "misinterpretations" and "misjudgments" would undoubtedly be brought about. Thus, multi-disseminating scenarios created for think tanks are also effective sites for think tanks and government to exchange information with each other.

Thirdly, enlarge cooperation and exchanges with media. Think tank organizations and scholars should all pay attention to their relations with media, so as to think tanks brand. Think tanks should deliberately take advantage of media publicity, learn and utilize think tank page of media, paper and newspaper, and enlarge influence of themselves in order to realize a win-win situation between think tanks and media. That think tank organizations and experts become the interviewees of media appears usually at two periods: one is when generally concerned issues progress with new changes, and the other is when brand new hotspot events come out. Think tank experts spread their research results and opinions through media, and think tanks also can recommend the latest research results to mainstream media at any time. Coverages of mainstream media can attract attention of audience and generate huge impacts, which can highly improve the disseminating level of think tanks.

3.2.2　Promote the Quality of Think Tank Communication Contents

High-quality think tank communication content is a core element of think tank communication promotion. For one side, think tank communication content should take bases from social atmosphere and needs of audience, should impact the decision-making level and also emphasize close contact with the social public of different levels and groups. For instance, *People's Daily* often adopts straightway forms of picture-illustrating news, comic news, short film news, etc. for interpreting profound think tank research reports in order to get them across to broader groups. For another side, timeliness of communication content should be watched closely. For example, when crucial moments appear, such as major international events, significant turnover of a certain situation, think tanks can disseminate influence by issuing articles and receiving interviews from media.

To promote the quality of think tank communication contents, efforts can be put into practice from the following three aspects:

First, take shape of think tanks research field with distinctive features. National comprehensive think tanks, such as Chinese Academy of Social Sciences, Development Research Center of the State Council (DRC) and so on, have professional research teams, abundant resources and extensive research fields. The majority of the rest think tanks should take their strengths into good consideration and concentrate their resource advantages on building up think tanks' research field brands. Yangtze Industrial Economics Institution devotes itself to researches in economic area, focuses on six strategic directions for development: China's economic operation, industrial economy, financial development, China' s macroeconomy, open economy and enterprise development. By long-time research of Yangtze River Delta in domestic economies, the institution grasps the trends and tendencies of economic development and can specifically articulate answers to issues brought about by the development of economy. The chartered "roundtable meeting" covers key matters like domestic economics' hotspot topics and discussions, exploration and analysis of China's development pattern, integration with international development. Together the institution forms a new-type think tank communication pattern whose field is specific, framework is clear and hierarchy is distinct.

Second, continue to bring out premium smart products. Settings of smart products should fully reflect three "combinations": combination with hotspot policies, combination with significant strategy, combination with external demand. *Development Plan for Regional Integration of the Yangtze River Delta* was just issued by the government in December, 2019. Soon Yangtze Industrial Economics Institution released analysis and research papers on related economics, exploring the importance and implementation strategies of the regional integration of the delta area from the perspective of our own and even the whole globe. Actions of the Institution are divergently different with those of some foreign think tanks who publish "slimming" articles in high frequency, use a lot of pictures, ignore academic strictness and care only about taking the lead of gaining attention. Chongyang Institute for Financial Studies of Renmin University of China keeps up with the Belt and Road Initiative of the central party and government for five consecutive years and keep releasing research results of the Initiative. From the *Eurasian Age : Silk Road Economic Belt Construction Blue Book 2014 - 2015* in 2014, to *The Belt and Road Initiative and New Pattern of International Trade: Silk Road Economic Belt Think Tanks Blue Book 2015—2016* in 2016, until *The Five Years Story of the Belt and Road Initiative* in 2019, Chongyang Institute not only offers advice and suggestions for the Belt and Road Initiative, but also shows the journey how China, as an emerging major country, drives countries along the silk road to jointly construct infrastructures, and how these countries learn from and blend with each other in economy and culture to the world, so as to effectively contribute to the image of the implementation of the Belt and Road Initiative.

Third, enhance control over the communication content. Forming distinctive research areas for deciding content of communication is a source problem, bringing out high-quality intelligent products is presentation of results, and the middle process of controlling over contents is a path for implementation. Control over dissemination contents contains not only control over documents such as research papers, but also process control of think tank activities' products like conferences and meeting affairs, since small problems reflect inadequate capabilities in controlling of contents. Even minor problems can affect the professionalized brand image and the influence of think tanks. Managements and control over documents are indispensable steps for brand construction. In fact, for a think tank research report or a think tanks program, records of activities and documents during the whole process from beginning and implementation of work are all valuable for reservation, and (both written and electronic materials) should be stored and checked by special personnel and places designated by think tanks. These forms of documents should be arranged and deposited in certain archive modes, for the convenience of references for the next consultation work.

3.2.3 Build Up Multiple Channels for Communication

Facing chances in communication environment of "Internet ＋" era, think tanks should take measures which are close to the public, directly exchange with them, learn about tendencies and satisfy the need of the common people. Brookings Institution of America, RAND Corporation, and British Overseas Development Institute have all gone through developing process from policy circle, to academic circle, and then to the popular circle. Efforts should be put to perfect traditional unitary communication platforms, putting up new-type stereoscopic ones, integrating entity communication platforms and social online communication platforms, increasing users' degree of participation and experience, so as to realize comprehensive optimizing of think tank communication platforms. For one thing, official website construction of think tank organizations should be attached more importance since the websites are battle grounds for disseminating information. From the collected data we can see that official websites of many think tank organizations lie in "paralyzed" condition and belong to zombie websites. Inaccessible pages, delayed updates, etc. often turn up, and some think tanks even have no official websites of their own. Compared to overseas famous think tank organization, Chinese think tanks have many potentials for improvement in number of interlinkages from other sites, total linkages, web page views and visits rate, still have a long way to go in terms of website, construction. For another thing, work should also be done to establish think tanks' media platforms with characteristics, immediately update research results, release contents in multiple kinds of languages, classify contents to break up language barriers, attract audience from all over the world, constantly enhance functions of WeChat official accounts and official Weibo, and add keyword search, social media and customized service functions. Platforms should be open to reflective information from audience, exchange ideas timely with users, improve degree of participation of audience, simply to a great extent the ways of releasing information—which is simple and highly interactive. Therefore, the communication area of think tanks can be enlarged, browsing histories of audience can be tracked, their reading tendencies can be analyzed, point-to-point individualized service could be provided to satisfy demands, and the disseminating capabilities of websites and new media can be promoted.

Topic 4 Think Tanks Play an Important Role in External Relations

In November 2014, General Secretary Xi Jinping's speech at the Central Conference on Work Relating to Foreign Affairs clearly defined the position of China's major-country diplomacy, which marks that China has entered into a new era of major-country diplomacy. Since the 18th CPC National Congress, the Central Committee of CPC with Xi Jinping as its general secretary has grasped the new changes in the international situation, actively promoted the innovation of China's diplomacy in both theory and practice, and put forward a series of new ideas, new concepts and new measures, to make new ground in promoting major-country diplomacy with distinctive Chinese features. Think tanks, as "advisers" and "pioneers" in external relations, undertake important missions, such as publicizing national policies, participating in international affairs and guiding public opinion. Under the new situation of major-country diplomacy with distinctive Chinese features, think tanks in our country have accelerated their pace of internationalization, deepening international cooperation and paying attention to the study of global issues in many fields, such as economy, politics, military affairs, science, education and culture. By making suggestions for major-country diplomacy, think tanks have gradually become an important bridge for communication between countries and provided intellectual support for major-country diplomacy.

1　New Changes of Diplomatic Strategy in the New Era

With the great increase of China's comprehensive national strength, China has become an important force in the platform of global governance, which not only provides a rare historical opportunity for China to participate fully and deeply in global governance, but also brings China with pressure, risks and challenges from economic globalization. With the development of worldwide multi-polarization, economic globalization, social informatization as well as cultural diversity, the imbalance in global development has intensified, and the gap between the rich and the poor is widening. The ideological trends like hegemonism, power politics, new interventionism, protectionism, populism, terrorism and racism are rampant, regional conflicts and local turmoil occur frequently, and complex problems, such as illegal immigration, food security, climate change, shortage of energy resources, network security as well as nuclear proliferation require immediate solutions. All these drawbacks lead to the continuous generation and accumulation of global problems, resulting in the state of world disorder. In order to effectively solve the crisis, cope with global challenges and change the deadlock in institutions, it is necessary for the international community to make substantial changes to the global governance system and promote the construction of a global governance system that is consistent with economic globalization.

The Fourth Plenary Session of the 19th CPC Central Committee made an incisive exposition on "upholding and improving the independent foreign policy of peace and helping build a global community of shared future". This is not only a strategic choice to promote the change of global governance pattern and enhance China's international voice, but also an inevitable requirement for responding to the expectations of the international community and assuming the responsibility of a major country. General

Secretary Xi Jinping has a profound insight into the general trend of global governance and reform, and he proposes the concept that "We will proceed from the overall interests of world peace and development, contribute China's wisdom in handling contemporary international relations and China's plan to improving global governance, and make our own contribution to human society's response to various challenges in the 21st century. " He has also launched a wealth of practical activities in the fields of politics, economy and diplomacy.

First, in the political field, China actively promotes new ideas of China's global governance and governance programs. At the G20 Summit held in Hangzhou in 2016, General Secretary Xi Jinping proposed China's solution to the issues of world economy, finance and poverty management, and explained China's philosophy of global governance. In 2017, General Secretary Xi Jinping proposed at the opening ceremony of the Davos Economic Forum that "We must keep pace with the times and build a fair and reasonable governance model. " Schwab, founder and executive chairman of the World Economic Forum, also said that "The world is entering the transformation period of multi-polarization, and Davos Forum is looking forward to China's voice as well as listening to President Xi's interpretation of how China exerts responsible leadership in international affairs". At the 2017 summit of BRICS leaders in Xiamen, General Secretary Xi Jinping pointed out that "The reform of global economic governance should be accelerated, the representation and voice of emerging market countries and developing countries should be improved, and a good external environment should be created for the development of all countries. " In 2018, at the BRICS Business Forum held in Johannesburg, South Africa, General Secretary Xi Jinping put forward the idea of "upholding multilateralism and improving global governance". In 2019, at the closing ceremony of the Sino-French Global Governance

Forum, General Secretary Xi Jinping pointed out that "We should adhere to the concept of global governance of achieving shared benefits through extensive consultation and joint contribution, insisting that global affairs should be dealt with through consultation by the people of all countries, and actively promote the democratization of global governance rules. "

Second, in the economic field, China advocates that international economic and financial organizations should effectively reflect changes in the international landscape, more representation and a greater say for emerging market countries and developing countries should be secured, and a better global governance system should be promoted, so that the vital interests of most countries are represented. In recent years, China has put forward a number of initiatives such as the Belt and Road Initiative, the construction of the New Development Bank, the construction of the Asian Infrastructure Investment Bank, the establishment of the Silk Road Fund, and the introduction of the ten cooperation plans between China and Africa. The establishment and operation of these multilateral institutions not only help maintain the stability of the international financial order, but also provide important financial guarantees to the domestic infrastructure construction in developing countries. For example, the Belt and Road Initiative acts as China's proposal to improve the system of global economic governance and promote global common development and prosperity. By the end of August 2019, China had signed 195 cooperation agreements under the framework of the Belt and Road Initiative with 136 countries and 30 international organizations, most collaborators being developing countries. In a sense, the rise of multilateral institutions reflects the general trend of the mass rise of emerging countries, reflects the profound changes in the world political landscape, and also indicates that the international order and global governance system are ushering in a major change.

Third, in the diplomatic field, Chinese leaders scientifically analyze the current international situation and rationally define China's international position, and on this basis, they timely adjust China's foreign policy and strategy, and formulate an international strategy in line with the national and world situation. In November 2014, at the Central Conference on Work Relating to Foreign Affairs, General Secretary Xi Jinping put forward that "China must have its own major-country diplomacy with distinctive Chinese features to fully demonstrate our distinctive vision, style and way of conducting diplomacy." This means that China has officially defined the position of major-country diplomacy, and China has entered a new era of major-country diplomacy. In the aspect of theoretical innovation, China has put forward the concept of Chinese dream and profoundly elaborated its significance for the whole world. It has proposed the ideas like building a new type of international relations and a global network of partnerships, building a community with a shared future for mankind, and establishing right approach to justice and interests. In the aspect of practical innovation, China strives to build a global network of partnerships, expand the layout of multi-faceted diplomacy, and participate deeply in global governance. China actively contributes China's proposal to the world, strengthens public diplomacy and people-to-people exchanges, and enhances the country's soft power.

It is noteworthy that public diplomacy, as an important aspect of diplomatic work, has also received unprecedented attention under the guidance of Xi Jinping's thought on socialist diplomacy with distinctive Chinese characteristics in the new era. The report of the 18th National Congress of the Communist Party of China puts forward that "We will take solid steps to promote public diplomacy as well as people-to-people and cultural exchanges." Afterwards, the report of the 19th National

Congress of the Communist Party of China further puts forward that "We will strengthen people-to-people and cultural exchanges with other countries, giving prominence to Chinese culture while also drawing on other cultures. We will improve our capacity for engaging in international communication so as to tell China's stories well, present a true, multi-dimensional, and panoramic view of China, and enhance our country's cultural soft power. " China has carried out various activities in the field of public diplomacy for publicity and promotion. China has conducted an all-round analysis from all levels of major issues, such as participating in the modernization of global governance and promoting the reform of the global governance system, so that the international community could have a thorough and comprehensive understanding of China's global governance concepts as well as its actions and role in global governance in the new era. At the same time, in the system of public diplomacy, think tank diplomacy often plays an important role as a center of intelligence and information. It is called the "brain", "idea factory" and "agenda setter" of public diplomacy, and is entrusted with such important missions as publicizing the national image and policies, and participating in public affairs as well as public opinion and propaganda. Under the new situation, Chinese think tanks have accelerated the pace of internationalization and deepened international cooperation. They attach importance to the study of global issues such as regional security and international economic issues, continuing to open up new platforms in the process of exchanges and cooperation.

2　Take an Active Part in Diplomatic Activities by Exerting Its Advantages

The complicated international situation and the fact that China has played an increasingly important role in the international platform have put forward new requirements for think tanks. This part, taking the classification method used in *The 2018 Annual Report on CTTI Think Tanks* as a reference, analyzes the positive roles that these different kinds of think tanks have played in diplomatic activities like think tanks of party and government organizations, think tanks of academies of social sciences, think tanks of party schools and administrative college, corporate think tanks, private think tanks and media think tanks.

2.1 Think Tanks of Party and Government Organizations

In the construction of a new type of think tanks with distinctive Chinese characteristics, think tanks of party and government organizations hold the balance. Since the Third Plenary Session of the 18th CPC Central Committee, think tanks of party and government organizations have actively followed the central government's spirit of strengthening the construction of a new type of think tanks with distinctive Chinese characteristics, and in combination with their own positioning and professional expertise, they have actively studied the research in foreign policy and the participation in public foreign affairs.

For example, in the field of foreign policy research, for a long time the China Institutes of Contemporary International Relations has been actively carrying out comprehensive and special research on international strategy, world politics and economy, bilateral diplomacy between China and other countries, as well as international issues related to China's Taiwan, Hong Kong and Macao. Since 2001, the institute has issued, for 19 consecutive years, a strategic beige book called *Strategic and Security Review*, which comprehensively combed, systematically summarized and profoundly explained the international situation and worldwide hot issues, providing reference for the formulation of China's foreign policy and the implementation of foreign strategy. In addition, the institute also hosts well-known publications, such as *Contemporary International Relations* and *International Research Reference* to regularly output research results in theory and offer suggestions to the Party Central Committee and the State Council.

In terms of participation in affairs of public diplomacy, the Development Research Center of the State Council has carried out international exchanges with the delegation of Organization of Islamic Cooperation, China-Japan Economic Association, National Institution for Transforming Indian(NITI Aayog) and other institutions to exchange opinions on China's development experience, multilateral trading system and the cooperation between institutions of both sides, so as to give full play to the role of public diplomacy. And the Shanghai Institute for International Studies held a seminar with the World Bank on "World Bank Group Engagement in Upper-Middle-Income Countries: Evidence from IEG Evaluations", and was entrusted by the Ministry of Foreign Affairs to hold a seminar on "The Way Out and Prospect of the Syrian Issue". It also held the Fifth Seminar of the North Pacific Arctic Research Community in cooperation with the Third Trilateral High-level Dialogue on the Arctic. The Shanghai Institute for International Studies played its role of a think tank in serving the country's overall diplomacy and Shanghai's local foreign affairs.

2.2   Think Tanks of Academies of Social Sciences

As an institution under the leadership of party committees and governments specializing in philosophy and social sciences, the Academy of Social Sciences has unique advantages in building a new type of think tanks. With the state's full deployment of new type of think tanks with distinctive Chinese characteristics, the Chinese Academy of Social Sciences as well as provincial and municipal academies of social sciences have actively participated in the activities of public diplomacy, playing the role of "idea tank" and "brain trust".

For example, in terms of theory construction, the Chinese Academy of Social Sciences has focused on China's the Belt and Road Initiative and conducted a series of theoretical studies. A series of special studies have been published successively, such as *The Belt and Road : Orientations, Contents and Challenges*, *The Belt and Road Initiative and ASEAN's Regional Integration*, *The Belt and Road Initiative and the Reconstruction of Asian Integration Model*, *The 21st Century Maritime Silk Road : Target, Implementation and Policy Suggestions*, and *Comparative Studies on Silk Road Strategy Between China and USA*. Comprehensive and in-depth study and analysis of different countries have been carried out on the national conditions, economy, investment and bilateral relations of the countries along the Belt and Road, providing important references for the implementation of the Belt and Road Initiative. On the other hand, the Institute of International Studies of the Guangdong Academy of Social Sciences has completed, in combination with regional economic characteristics, more than 40 major decision-making consultation tasks of the Guangdong provincial level, including *The Further Strategy Study of Guangdong-ASEAN*, *The Study on Building the Guangdong-Hong Kong-Macao Greater Bay Area into a World-Class City Cluster*, *Comparative Research of the Culture of Guangdong-Hong Kong-Macao Greater Bay Area*, and *Research on Major Issues of Guangdong's Ocean Economy*. Many research results have been positively instructed by the main leaders of the Guangdong Provincial Committee of the CPC and government, and been translated into government documents for implementation. At the same time, the institute has compiled more than 20 books such as *Blue Papers on the Construction of the Guangdong-Hong Kong-Macao Greater Bay Area* (2018, 2019) and *Research on South Asia's Capital Cooperation*, steadily increasing its influence on academy and society.

In terms of information assurance services, the Shanghai Academy of Social Sciences, as one of the first batch of national high-end think tank pilot units, cooperated with the Hong Kong Trade Development Council to jointly issue *The Report on the Development of Sino-Foreign Cooperation Parks of the Belt and Road Initiative*. Based on the local characteristics, this report discussed the background and concrete results of the construction of economic and trade cooperation zones established by mainland enterprises in the relevant countries of the Belt and Road Initiative, and put forward ideas and policy suggestions to further promote the development of China's overseas economic and trade cooperation zones. At the same time, the institute actively exerts its advantages as a high-end think tank platform, by cooperating with China Center for International Economic Exchanges to build the Big Database of the Belt and Road Initiative (also known as Silk Road Information Network), which covers relevant countries and numerous cities of the Belt and Road Initiative, including 9 sub-databases such as Silk Road National Database, Silk Road City Database, Literature Database, Statistical Database, Investment Project Database, Economic Operation Report Database, and China National Policy Database, providing information platforms for governments at all levels, enterprises, and countries participating in the construction of the Belt and Road Initiative.

2.3 Think Tanks of Party Schools and Administrative College

Think tanks of party school are an important part of the new type of think tanks with distinctive Chinese features in the new era as they play an increasingly prominent role in serving the Party committees and governments for scientific decision-making, and promoting the modernization of the national governance system and governance capacity. Some think tanks of party schools and administrative colleges have become platforms for publicity, foreign exchange and cooperation as well as international cooperation of high-end think tanks, by playing their role of publicity in a series of diplomatic activities.

Taking the Party School of the Central Committee of Communist Party of China as an example. By various forms, such as seminars, forums, think tank discussions, exchange of students, speeches and media conferences, the party school actively introduces diplomatic concepts such as the Belt and Road Initiative to foreign political circles, academic circles as well as all other sectors of society, and introduces China's practice of governing the country and relevant achievements of reform and opening up. During the meeting of BRICS leaders in 2017, the party school successfully held the BRICS Seminar on Governance with the Publicity Departments of the Communist Party of China in Quanzhou, Fujian and Johannesburg, South Africa. In addition, the party school has actively built a platform for international cooperation and exchange of high-end think tanks. It continuously expands channels for external communication of think tanks and establishes relations for communication and cooperation with relevant well-known think tanks of major neighboring countries, countries along the "Belt and Road" and the BRICS countries. The party school has always been promoting the implementation of China's foreign policy and diplomatic strategy.

Local party schools combine " coming-in " with " going-out " in international exchanges, to give full play to the positive effects of spreading China's diplomatic ideas and external policies. The think tank of Zhejiang Party School of the CPC Committee of CPC has maintained a long-time partnership with renowned universities overseas such as the University of New South Wales in Australia, Sciences Po in Paris and the Civil Service College of Singapore. In the aspect of "coming-in", the school has received many groups of foreign delegations from the United States, Russia,

France and other countries. In the aspect of "going-out", the school leaders have led many delegations to the United States, Australia, Czech Republic and other countries to carry out official exchanges and special research and to participate in international academic conferences.

2.4   University Think Tanks

As an important part of the new type of think tanks with distinctive Chinese features, universities have certain advantages in academic research resources, reserve of teachers and talents, and construction of public diplomacy platform. Based on their own superior resources, some university think tanks have established a number of professional diplomatic think tanks. For example, Fudan University's Center for American Studies, East China Normal University's Research Center for Co-development with Neighboring Countries, Sichuan University's Institute of South Asian Studies, Zhejiang Normal University's Institute of African Studies and other institutions have achieved fruitful results in their respective fields.

For example, the Center for American Studies of Fudan University, based on its own advantages on academic resources, focuses on six research directions, namely, American politics and diplomacy, arms control and regional security, American society and culture, security strategy of America and Asia-Pacific areas, American economy as well as relations between America and China. It holds the strategic dialogue on China-US relations and regional security, in cooperation with the US Pacific Forum every year, and has established a database of research on America and a database of research on international relations, fulfilling a lot of foundation work of preliminary research and theoretical research for China on US foreign strategy and foreign policy.

Another example is the Institute of Korean Peninsula Studies established by

Yanbian University based on its geographical advantages. As one of the earliest research institutions of Korean Peninsula established in China, it focuses on various issues in research fields of the Korean Peninsula and creates *Dongjiang Journal*. And it has established a wide range of academic exchange and cooperation mechanisms with well-known universities and academic institutions at home and abroad, such as Kim Ⅱ-Sung University of DPRK, Seoul National University of South Korea, the Academy of Korean Studies, and Waseda University of Japan. The Inner Mongolia University of Finance and Economics, on the other hand, has made full use of its geographical advantages to establish " China, Mongolia and Russia Economic Corridor" and "Economic Belt on the Prairie Silk Road" and carry out research. At the same time, it has set up a number of international cooperation platforms and research centers, such as the China-Mongolia Cooperation Research Institute and China-Mongolia Business School, so as to better promote China's Belt and Road Initiative.

2.5 Media Think Tanks, Corporate Think Tanks and Private Think Tanks

Comprehensive think tanks, such as media think tanks, corporate think tanks and private think tanks, play their own roles in the development process of China's foreign strategy from their respective perspectives. For example, media think tanks use their own advantageous resources and media networks to spread China's voice on the global stage, playing an important role in shaping the country's image, disseminating China's policies and promoting foreign strategies. Compared with government think tanks and university think tanks, the biggest advantage of media think tanks is to understand the grassroots, to be close to practice, and to own a strong communication platform with rich communication experience. Through effective communication, media think tanks can enhance the popularity of their products and expand the influence of their achievements. Xinhua News Agency is committed to building a discourse system that integrates China and foreign countries. It has established high-level contacts with 18 United Nations agencies, recruited some experts and scholars as key contacts of think tanks, and set up a national high-end think tank forum, so as to continuously increase its international influence and strengthen international think tank cooperation. Global think tank perspective communication platform by absorbing thousands of scholars and brain trustors on international issues and international economy as well as more than 100 overseas observers and launching three text columns of *The Pioneer*, *The Strategist* and *Dialogue with the World* as well as a video column called *Phoenix International Time*.

As a corporate think tank, Ali Research, starting from the consumption field, uses big data technology to study the development status of global e-commerce, so as to provide guidance for Chinese enterprises to "go out" and to do overseas market research for the promotion of China's Belt and Road Initiative. CNPC Economics & Technology Research Institute has summarized the research results of overseas investment environment for many years and published a series of books called *The Oil and Gas Cooperation Report of the Belt and Road Countries*, providing an important reference for the energy investment and cooperation research of countries along the "Belt and Road".

In addition, the Charhar Institute, as a private think tank, actively participates in the setting of international issues. It held the Shanghai Peace Forum with the Korean Association of International Security Exchange, the International Forum on Public Diplomacy with Clingendael Institute (the Netherlands Institute of International Relations) and Institute for Foreign Cultural Relations, as well as the

Charhar Round Table Conference with the theme being *Crisis Management in Sino-Japanese Conflict in the East China Sea* with the Stockholm International Peace Research Institute. According to the cases of CTTI source think tanks, the Pangoal Institution has collected practical experience that has been serving the Belt and Road Initiative for a long time and published *30 Essential Questions on the Belt and Road Initiative* to guide and help Chinese enterprises and institutions to carry out international cooperation.

3   The Main Ways for Think Tanks to Serve Diplomacy

As an important carrier of national soft power and a key factor of international competitiveness, think tanks aim to enhance China's soft power and international influence. For domestic affairs, think tanks need to "serve decision-making" and to be "half a step early" and "moderately advanced" in research, so as to improve the quality of foreign policy and serve the national strategy. In recent years, under the guidance of Xi Jinping's socialist diplomacy with distinctive Chinese features in the new era, the new type of think tanks with Chinese characteristics has shown its advantages in giving advice on diplomatic work, participating deeply in diplomatic activities, and actively guiding international public opinion, which has injected fresh strength into opening up new ground for major-country diplomacy with distinctive Chinese features.

3.1   Think Tanks Provide Advice on Work Relating to Foreign Affairs in the New Era

3.1.1   Think Tanks Work as an Incubator of Foreign Policy in the New Era

To be in a dominant position in international relations, a country should not only attach importance to traditional hard power, but also should pay adequate attention to soft power. Public diplomacy is actually a competition for soft power in all the countries around the world, and think tanks, as the source of idea and innovation, are the source of a country's soft power. The frequent and smooth public diplomacy of think tanks in international relations can provide innovative and forward-looking strategic ideas for the country's overall diplomacy. Think tanks help decision-makers to fully demonstrate and evaluate policies by actively giving full play to their resource superiority in knowledge processing and production, thus reflecting the scientization of diplomatic decision-making mechanisms, and in this way think tanks serve as incubators in the formulation of the country's foreign strategy.

In the formulation of foreign policies, the academic achievements of many think tanks have been adopted and reflected in China's foreign policy. For example, as a professional research institution directly under the Ministry of Foreign Affairs of the People's Republic of China, the China Institute of International Studies has published successively in recent years *Putin's Great Diplomacy : Russia's Foreign Strategy for the 21st Century 1999 – 2017*, *Evolving International Order and Major-Country Diplomacy with Chinese Characteristics*, *The CIIS Blue Book on International Situation and China's Foreign Affairs* (*2019*), *The CIIS Research Report*, and sponsored the journal *China International Studies* (Chinese and English versions) and other theoretical achievements with great influence at home and abroad. On the other hand, the Charhar Institute conducts in-depth research on the development of China's public diplomacy's theory and practice and private think tanks of international relations through periodicals such as *Public Diplomacy Quarterly* and *Charhar Newsletter*, and a series of books of Charhar Diplomacy and International Relations. And the Charhar Institute actively acts on the Korean Peninsula issue, bilateral relations between China and North Korea as well as South Korea, and Sino-Japanese relations. In addition, China Institute of International Studies and Shanghai Institutes for International Studies have also actively served Chinese leaders in their diplomatic decisions on a number of diplomatic issues, including China's policy on the European debt crisis. They have driven the China-EU Strategic Dialogue in 2015 and laid the foundation for the joint statement of the 17th China-EU leaders' meeting.

Think tanks, as incubators for foreign policy, also promote consultation and communication through proposing and applying new ideas. Take think tanks' serving in the Belt and Road Initiative as an example. In July 2016, Chongyang Institute for Financial Studies of Renmin University of China and the Deutsche Gesellschaft für Internationale Zusammenarbeit (GIZ) jointly organized the Think Tank Dialogue of the Belt and Road Initiative Between China and Kazakhstan and carried out a series of exchange activities, which have made good achievements. The China (Shenzhen) Development Institute provided planning and consulting services for a number of projects such as the Kirifi Special Economic Zone in Mombasa, Kenya, the Jinfei Cooperation Zone in Mauritius and the Nanpu Comprehensive Bonded Zone in DPRK, and helped Chinese enterprises to participate in the Belt and Road Initiative.

3.1.2 Think Tanks Become a "Senior Advisor" in Coping with Major Events

As a specialized policy research institution, think tanks have provided theoretical guidance and research preparation for foreign policy response and given strategic ideas and policy recommendations, through analysis of the international situation and field research.

Taking the role of think tanks in Sino-US relations as an example. In recent years, the international situation has undergone historic changes, and Sino-US relations are facing a major juncture of making important choices. For instance, the US strategic community is increasingly anxious about China, and the Trump government is exerting constant pressure on China. In view of this, Chinese think tanks must put forward corresponding measures, so as to strengthen the conceptual guidance for the sound development of Sino-US relations. For Chinese think tank scholars, on the one hand, they should strive for cooperation with the groups knowing China well and friendly to China to jointly balance the expansion of hawkish people that do not like China; on the other hand, they should take the initiative to resolve misunderstandings in the US attitude towards China and maintain dialogue and mutual trust between Chinese and US think tanks. For example, think tanks such as the Center for China & Globalization (CCG), the China Institute of International Studies, the China Institutes of Contemporary International Relations, the Carnegie-Tsinghua Center for Global Policy, the Charhar Institute, and Intellisia Institute have continued to express their views on the New Deal of Trump-era in the United States and a series of topics of public concern, held seminars and forums, and written survey reports, combing the ruling context of the Trump administration and making suggestions for China's policy towards the United States.

Li Cheng from Brookings Institution said: "If the economic interdependence between China and the United States is the ballast stone of the relations between the two countries, the academic exchange is the coordinate instrument for the development of the relations, and the communication between think tanks of the two countries would be the alarm, buffer and pressure regulator of the relations." For example, the Institute of International and Strategic Studies Peking University in cooperation with the Brookings Institution of the United States, has launched the North Pavilion Seminar. Former domestic and foreign dignitaries and well-known experts with rich political experience, profound academic accomplishment and broad strategic vision have been invited to Peking University to jointly discuss the international situation and the prospect of world politics, to discuss whether China and the United States can "unhook" connections with each other economically and technically in the future, as well as to discuss major strategies and hot issues such as the changing global order. In addition, the Pangoal Institution has recorded Trump's preparations for administration in detail through the publication of *An Outlook for the Domestic and Foreign Policies of the New Administration of the US (Observations over the President-Elect Trump before Inauguration)* and held seminars such as the one called General Pattern of Sino-US Relations and Prospect of Sino-Japanese Relations, to discuss the impact of Sino-US relations on the world pattern. It has been reported to the upper levels through think tank reports and other channels and has received the attention of relevant decision-making departments.

Taking the issue of Brexit as an example. Chinese Academy of International Trade and Economic Cooperation under the Ministry of Commerce paid close attention to hot spots in a timely way. Its timely report *The Impact of Brexit on China's Changing Rights and Obligations in the Economic and Trade Field* received the attention and affirmative instructions of the central leadership. On the other hand, the China Center for International Economic Exchanges has held many seminars on Sino-European trade relations after Brexit and published the research results in its internal publications *Think-Tank's Voice* and *Research Report* so that relevant decision-making departments would learn about them. In addition, think tanks such as the Shanghai Institutes for International Studies have also launched a series of forward-looking academic discussions on Brexit and have formed multi-angle and multi-level research results, providing strong intellectual support for China's decision-making departments in response, emergency response and policy formulation.

3.2 Think Tanks Participate Deeply in Diplomatic Activities

3.2.1 Think Tanks Become a "Pioneer" in the Activities of Major-Country Diplomacy

Since the 18th National Congress of the Communist Party of China, in the face of the complicated and changeable international situation, the new type of think tanks with distinctive Chinese characteristics has become a participant and promoter in the major-country diplomacy with distinctive Chinese features. It not only can make suggestions for the government on foreign affairs, but also needs to actively participate in foreign affairs. Through communication, dialogue and exchange with foreign think tanks, it can actively participate in various official diplomatic dialogues, thus shaping a good image for China, boosting China's concept to spread around the world and enhancing China's international voice and appeal.

In recent years, many think tanks, especially high-end national think tanks, have taken advantage of the situation and played an increasingly prominent role in many international think tank cooperation mechanisms. For example, the Chinese Academy of Social Sciences has set up a network of think tank cooperation with 16 countries in Central and Eastern Europe, formed a fixed think tank exchange mechanism with ASEAN countries, and also established a regular cooperation mechanism with well-known think tanks of the member countries of Group of 20 (G20), Shanghai Cooperation Organization, BRICS and so on. For example, on the Conference on Dialogue of Asian Civilizations that was held in 2019, the Chinese Academy of Social Sciences and relevant national think tanks launched a multilateral cooperation initiative to promote the plan of Building Partnership of Think Tanks for the Asian Community with a Shared Future, signed the letter of intent called Partnership of Think Tanks for Building Asian Civilizations Exchange and Mutual

Learning with relevant units, and carried out the first batch of multilateral joint research projects with relevant national think tanks, including the mutual learning of Asian civilizations, the construction of the community with a shared future for mankind, the Belt and Road Initiative and the construction of the Community of Asian Civilizations. These cases fully demonstrate that think tanks have actively participated in the field of foreign affairs and become important participants in the implementation of China's foreign strategy.

3.2.2 Think Tanks Become one of the Main Forces of the Two-Track Diplomacy

In the diplomatic field, the status of diplomatists is generally important, formal, authoritative and sensitive, and at the same time there are also many restrictions. Both sides are often subject to some tacit natural restrictions due to the formal and sensitive status. However, think tanks have greater flexibility and professionalism compared to official diplomacy and non-governmental exchanges. As an important complement to government diplomatic activities, through actively undertaking the two-track diplomatic function, they promote communication and consultation on major interest issues between countries or regions, provide ties for dialogue and cooperation, and strive to find constructive solutions in conflicts and disputes.

In recent years, think tanks of China have accumulated a lot of useful experience in assisting public diplomacy. For example, in the process of various large-scale multilateral international conferences, the new type of think tanks actively acts as a supporting organization for international think tank conferences, which provides important intellectual support for the successful holding of the conference through providing equal exchanges, consensus building, atmosphere building and suggestions. Centering on these diplomatic agendas, Chinese think tanks have also initiated the establishment of an international think tank consortium to cooperate with relevant national think tanks to carry out research projects and jointly hold seminars.

In the G20 summit, T20 (the summit of the think tanks from the G20 members) served as the "goodwill ambassador" of the G20 leaders' summit. Since 2013, T20 meetings have been held consecutively. The meetings have attracted more than 1,000 scholars from global think tanks, and several rounds of meetings were held around the world. Relevant research results have sent effective information to decision-makers, which laid a good foundation for the G20 meeting and attracted extensive international attention. For example, as the co-leading think tank for the summit of the think tanks from the G20 members (T20), the Chongyang team of National Academy of Development and Strategy of Renmin University of China actively cooperated with leaders to participate in major home diplomacy and high-level visits of leaders such as the G20 summit and was invited to comment in major official media.

In BRICS cooperation, think tank forums are usually held before the BRICS summit, and the think tank forum is hosted by the countries hosting the leaders' meeting, with relevant members of think tanks from all countries participating to discuss the future development path of BRICS cooperation and deepen the BRICS cooperation mechanism. According to the *Durban Declaration*, the BRICS Think Tank Council was established in March 2013 by the five think tank leaders during the summit. Since 2014, the Council has held annual meetings before the BRICS summit. For example, the Chinese Council in the BRICS think tank cooperation is the Chinese leading unit of the BRICS think tank Council, currently covering 88 directors and 90 governing units, which includes both official think tanks and private think tanks. Since its establishment, the Chinese Council has established the Wanshou Forum, hosted more than 10 BRICS cooperation-related seminars and released the think tank BRICS series, making the voice of think tank cooperation a beautiful harmony of

BRICS cooperation. The think tank forum not only conducts joint research and academic exchanges with think tanks in BRICS countries, but also devotes itself to exchanges and cooperation with think tanks in other emerging market countries and developing countries to continuously promote the achievement of new South-South cooperation.

3.3 Think Tanks Actively Guide International Public Opinion

General Secretary Xi Jinping once pointed out that "We should build up our capacity in international communication, carefully construct the foreign discourse system, and make good use of emerging media, so as to enhance the creativity, charisma and credibility of foreign discourse, and to tell Chinese stories well, disseminate Chinese voices and explain Chinese characteristics." Our think tanks adhere to China's position with worldwide vision, strengthen strategic thinking and keep up with the world's leading edge. They actively face the world and move towards the world, and open up think tanks in an open way. Think tanks actively carry out international exchanges and cooperation, as well as various forms of think tank diplomacy and think tank publicity, so as to help the country to enhance its public diplomacy capability, enhance its international influence and make it have a greater say on international platform.

3.3.1 Think Tanks Spread the Diplomatic Concept in the New Era and Shape the National Image in the New Era

As a beautiful name card for the communication between the country and other countries, the national image can reflect the position of the country in the international community to a certain extent. Carrying out public diplomacy through think tanks is an important and efficient way to improve the national image. In recent years, all kinds of think tanks in China have been actively interacting with the international community, telling a good story about China and explaining China's plan. They deeply participate in answering questions and try to show the world the true, comprehensive and open image of China.

In recent years, through all-round diplomacy which treats each country as equals, China has stood in the center of the world stage with a brand-new international image. It has also participated in global governance with its own successful development experience and shared its development achievements with the world, for example, the inception, implementation and fruition of the Belt and Road Initiative. China has gradually become one of the boosters of world economic recovery. Since the Belt and Road Initiative was put forward in 2016, as an important part of the people-to-people communication work of the Belt and Road Initiative, think tank communication has developed vigorously in the past few years, playing a unique role in promoting policy communication, enhancing people-to-people communication and promoting practical cooperation, and increasingly becoming a beautiful scenery line in the construction of the Belt and Road. In April 2015, International Department, Central Committee of CPC led the establishment of the think tank cooperation alliance of the Belt and Road Initiative. Up to May 2019, the alliance had 138 domestic member units and 114 foreign member units. The secretariat of the think tank alliance and its member units have visited more than 60 countries along the Belt and Road and jointly held all kinds of seminars of various scales, specifications and themes with other think tanks to systematically introduce the development of the Belt and Road Initiative, so as to make all parties realize that the Belt and Road Initiative is not only beneficial to China's development, but also beneficial to the development of countries along the Belt and Road, relevant countries and even the whole world. In addition, the alliance also invited experts from well-known foreign think tanks to come to China to hold special seminars, and encouraged experts and scholars at home and abroad to further discuss the Belt and Road Initiative and deepen people's in-depth understanding of the Belt and Road Initiative in countries along the Belt and Road.

In the spreading process of the diplomatic concept of the "community with a shared future for mankind", Xinhua News Agency, as a high-end national think tank, organized experts from think tanks right away to let them speak out and interpret on a series of foreign strategies and important diplomatic activities in China. And Xinhua News Agency comprehensively used omnimedia communication modes to give full play to the advantages of overseas communication. Key articles were published in mainstream media in 19 countries of G20 member countries, such as the United States, Britain, France and Germany. On the other hand, the Chunqiu Institute for Development and Strategic Studies launched the website called Guancha Syndicate, which takes "Care from China, with Global Vision" as the slogan. It invites famous Chinese political scholars, economists, and well-known media as well as foreign guests, and creates China's own voice channel through in-depth reports and exclusive comments. However, many media think tanks, including the YICAI Research Institute, the Cover Institute, the Phoenix International Think Tank, the Guangming Think Tank, and the Liaowang Institute, have also used omnimedia technology to "tell Chinese stories well", and to promote China's national image overseas, create hot topics, and create a good atmosphere for international public opinion.

According to the data of CTTI source think tanks, there are currently 17 think tanks that engage in the research field of the Belt and Road Initiative, involving international tourism resources development, high-end personnel training, China's foreign trade and cultural exchanges, international business cooperation and other research directions. Among them, national think tanks, such as the Chinese Academy of Social Sciences, the China Institute of International Studies, the Chinese Academy of Sciences, the State Information Center, and the Academy of Macroeconomic Research have released a series of theoretical research results, providing theoretical support to relevant decision-making departments, and they have held a series of international academic seminars, becoming one of the main forces in the dissemination of the Belt and Road Initiative. In addition, media think tanks such as the Phoenix International think tank have also become new channels of think tank communication for the Belt and Road Initiative, using foreign language websites, WeChat and other self-media platforms to continuously enhance their international influence.

3.3.2   Think Tanks Participate in International Policy Debates and Guide International Public Opinion

In the era of globalization, whether a country is welcomed by the general public in other countries is closely related to the ideas and values it conveys as well as the communication strategies it adopts. Under the complicated new international situation, Chinese think tanks have the courage to stand on the international stage and clarify China's ideas. They transfer information to society through certain media of public opinion and actively improve the dissemination, guidance, influence and credibility of public opinion.

For example, in the trade friction between China and America, Chinese think tanks offered advice and suggestions to relevant decision makers from various fields, such as international relations, economy and trade, international law, and analyzed the Sino-US trade friction. They predicted the trend of the Sino-US situation, expressed China's stance, and effectively counterattacked the unreasonable provocation by the US. Faced with the provocation and unreasonable demands of the

United States, experts and scholars from think tanks, such as the Academy of Macroeconomic Research and the Development Research Center of the State Council, have written articles or given media interviews to analyze the economic and trade situation between China and the United States, effectively easing the panic in the market. Internally, they help to stabilize the hearts and minds of the people and enhance the confidence of the market, and externally, they demonstrate China's firm determination of not being afraid of pressure and strive to get international understanding and respect. In the situation where the Western media dominated by the United States advocate the "China threat theory", Chinese think tanks could use overseas communication channels to convey China's real image, to break the Western media's attempt to demonize China, and to spread the concept of peaceful development, and by this way, they can guide public opinion and create a stable international development environment for China. At the same time, by making use of the platform of omnimedia, think tank experts have carried out various publicity and promotion activities through monographs, papers, interviews, documentaries and other forms, to help Western people objectively understand China and to show their national image.

In the South China Sea crisis, many think tanks, including the Chinese Academy of Social Sciences, the National Academy of Development and Strategy of Renmin University of China, and the Wuhan University Institute of International Law, all stood up to defend China's territorial sovereignty from the perspectives of history and international law authority. In diplomatic practice, think tanks could respond quickly so as to strike first to gain the initiative, and they use radio, television, Internet, social networking platforms and other channels to proactively express their opinions so as to create an international public opinion that is conducive to our country. For example, during the South China Sea arbitration, the China Institute of Fudan University and the Guancha Syndicate jointly launched a video called *The Truth of* the *South China Sea Arbitration*, which was broadcast through platforms, such as Youku and Tencent, and received nearly 5 million hits in a few days. The English version was uploaded to YouTube, published by the *Huffington Post*, which is the largest Internet media in the United States, and reprinted by websites of many countries including the Philippines. From the perspective of military strategy, experts from think tanks of the National Defense University and the Academy of Military Sciences have exposed the unreasonable demands of the United States and the Philippines in the South China Sea arbitration. A series of articles called *Ten Questions and Ten Answers to the South China Sea Arbitration* have been widely reproduced on the Internet. The new type of diplomatic think tanks used domestic and foreign media to "speak out" and effectively reversed the international community's prejudice against China on the South China Sea arbitration. In addition, Fu Ying, chief expert of the National Institute of Global Strategy of the Chinese Academy of Social Sciences, also reversed the international misunderstanding of the South China Sea issue at that time by publishing a long article *On the Nansha Islands Dispute and the Causes of Tension in the South China Sea*, which was widely reproduced by domestic and overseas media.

4　Suggestions

"Cultivate harmony within the world, and harmony becomes ubiquitous." As the guiding thought of China's foreign affairs in the new era, Xi Jinping's diplomatic thoughts are the fundamental guidelines for promoting major-country diplomacy with distinctive Chinese features. The construction of Chinese think tanks should follow the guidance of Xi Jinping's diplomatic thoughts, continuously explore and innovate in practice, and strive to contribute to the major-country diplomacy with distinctive Chinese features. The following suggestions are hereby put forward.

4.1 Enhance Brand Building of Think Tank Serving for Public Diplomacy

Brand building is one of the important ways to promote the high-quality development of think tanks, and think tank brand is the embodiment of its quality and credibility, with high degree of identification. In the process of serving public diplomacy, a good think tank brand can be more convenient to connect with the outside world, and can gain mutual recognition and trust of international community, so as to promote cultural exchange and mutual learning in the global context. The brand building of think tanks serving public diplomacy should be based on professional and high-quality research results and quality-oriented, and it should constantly open ground for new horizons, ideas and patterns, injecting new momentum into the development of think tanks serving public diplomacy. First, brand awareness should be established, and brand image should be shaped. Grasp the standard, rigorous and professional positioning of the think tanks serving, public diplomacy, actively establish and cultivate brand awareness in public diplomacy practice, and actively shape and maintain brand image. The core values of the think tank brand serving public diplomacy should be fully grasped, and run through the whole process of brand building. Second, brand advantages should be highlighted and brand characteristics should be demonstrated. Use China's unique diplomatic theory and practical experience as support to carry out long-term and in-depth research on public diplomacy issues, and to conduct in-depth discussions and repeated refinements on the achievements of public diplomacy. Based on its research expertise, a think tank should develop advantageous disciplines, create competitive products, and play the role of opinion leader in the field of public diplomacy. Strive to form a brand of think tanks with Chinese characteristics, conforming to China's national conditions and conforming to the mainstream of the times. Third, brand competitiveness should be enhanced, and brand influence should be expanded. Hire talents, take in experts and scholars in the field of public diplomacy at home and abroad, and build a talent reserve echelon of a general type of public-diplomacy think tanks. Actively publish research results and internal references for decision-making, broaden the channels for the transformation of decision-making and consultation results, and form high-quality public-diplomacy think tank products. At the same time, a think tank should broaden its vision, by focusing on global issues, innovating its thinking, and keeping pace with the times. In the field of public diplomacy, the brand building of think tanks serving public diplomacy should have talents as its core, have products as its support, and have innovation as its lead.

4.2   Boost the Use of Omnimedia for Think Tanks

Boosting the use of omnimedia for think tanks is a new focus for the construction of think tanks in our country. Diversified communication channels of omnimedia can provide more opportunities for the promotion of research achievements of think tanks. First, think tanks should decide the overall planning and design for the omnimedia. Based on China's strategy and overall development situation, think tanks should build a research system, define the research direction, and innovate the dissemination mechanism of research results. They should establish a long-term growth mechanism and a sustainable development mechanism, and at the same time they should establish management standards in accordance with laws and regulations and carefully treat the dissemination of think tank results. Second, think tanks should make innovation in communication means and carriers. Think tanks should create a communication platform of omnimedia and improve the communication efficiency of think tank, through the development of websites, App and mini programs, and the opening of various forms of online media communication channels, such as microblog, WeChat, Facebook, Twitter and YouTube as well as the production of electronic publications, in addition to the traditional paper media, conferences, forums and scholars' visits. Third, think tanks should reshape the achievements and services. Connecting with traditional media and flexibly using the communication platform of network media, think tanks gather the wisdom of all resources as well as absorbing and integreting data resources, to carry out systematic and in-depth research and to develop into data achievements. So think tanks form a production mode of think tank achievements integrating production and dissemination and can better serve the government's decision-making needs.

4.3 Establish an All-around Mechanism of Dialogue and Cooperation Between Domestic and Foreign Think Tanks

Think tank dialogue is playing a more and more important role in China's work relating to diplomacy. By establishing an all-round mechanism of dialogue and cooperation between domestic and foreign think tanks, international exchanges and cooperation will be further deepened, and this will help to draw on the experience and wisdom of other countries, to widely disseminate the voice of China and to promote the development of public diplomacy. On the one hand, exchanges and cooperation between domestic think tanks can be strengthened. Through strengthening interdisciplinary cooperation, the channels of dialogue and cooperation between experts and scholars from domestic think tanks in various fields and all kinds of talents can be unblocked, the achievements of think tanks can be jointly built and shared, and an academic community in relevant research fields can be built. On the other hand, exchanges and cooperation between domestic think tanks and international think tanks should be strengthened. For example, through interactive dialogue on social media, the ideological achievements and insights of Chinese think tanks can be expressed in foreign online media in a timely and accurate manner, and the scope of dialogue and exchange among think tanks would be expanded. It is also possible to establish a cooperation platform, which advocates an equal dialogue and cooperation mechanism, attracts foreign think tank experts and scholars to come in and encourages our think tank experts and scholars to go out, so as to carry out in-depth cooperative research on issues of common concern.

4.4　Enhance the Ability to Participate in and Set Up International Issues

In recent years, China has participated more actively in the process of global governance and has shown the world China's wisdom and style. Enhancing their ability to participate in and set up international issues, think tanks can improve the communication ability, emotional appeal and influence of Chinese think tanks in international community, so as to encourage the world to view China comprehensively and objectively and make the world have understanding, resonance and empathy for China's diplomatic ideas. First, strengthen cultural self-confidence and expand global vision. Through innovative service methods, think tanks can strengthen the dynamic research of global public opinion, improve the policy supply capacity, and actively put forward China's views and China's initiatives to contribute China's solutions to global problems. Second, strengthen the awareness of "China participates in" and "China creates". China should actively serve as the rotating chairman of international organizations or provide conference preparation and policy suggestions for international organizations, actively participate in and lead the agenda setting of multilateral mechanisms, and set up a platform for think tank exchanges and cooperation, actively gaining discourse space in the international arena. Third, widely distribute research institutions and improve the pertinence of issues. Think tanks should learn from the operation mode of excellent foreign think tanks, set up overseas branches of relevant think tanks in our country, and conduct in-depth research on target audience countries' hot spots under the current background of international relations. Think tanks should expand research fields that are forward-looking, produce prospective products of ideas, and put forward targeted issues that meet the current world situation and the concerns of the international community.

Topic 5 Formation of New Type Think Tank Community:
Think Tank Network and Communication Progress

Community refers to a group that has common interests and values to profoundly act on its members. The emergence and development of think tank community is based on the boom as different kinds of think tank institutions have sprung up in China, since President Xi Jinping put forward the proposal for "constructing new-type think tanks with Chinese characteristics". As the flourish of think tank institutions, diversified think tanks with different themes in various areas gradually form the local think tank network of a certain scale in the field. Meanwhile, think tanks interact and exchange more frequently with decision-makers, think tank institutions, social organizations, media and the public. The communication between the think tank network and think tanks mutually promotes the formation and development of think tank community. The think tank network vertically and horizontally converges the force of think tanks to make the foundation for the formation of think tank community. The communication among think tanks can pool their intellectual power, capability and experience to multi-dimensionally energizes themselves and motivates the development of think tank community. The construction of think tank community and integration of think tank elements and platforms further improve the system of new-type think tanks and upgrade the quality and efficiency of growth.

1 Full Cohesion: Think Tank Network Laying the Foundations for Think Tank Community

The rapid development of new-type think tanks in China promotes the formation of think tank network, which can be regarded as a form of the combination of think tanks and related policy research institutions. The think tank network, as an important platform to maintain the relation among think tanks, is able to give necessary service and safeguard to their development, and plays a critical role in enhancing their communication, providing financial support, organization and management advice, and sharing resources and information, so as to boost the construction of think tank community. According to the development of new-type think tanks, the think tank network can be divided into government-leading, systematic, platform-mediated and coalition forms, each with different characteristics.

1. 1 Government-Leading Network Gathering Top Intellectual Power

It is an important opportunity that the government values and encourages the construction of new-type think tanks, because "constructing new-type think tanks with Chinese characteristics" has been highlighted as a national strategy. Now therefore, the think tank network led and built by the government is a big part of the think tank development in China. "Government-leading network" is a net form, mainly represented by China Top Think Tanks (CTTT) and provincial and municipal key think tanks. With official approval, such think tank network enjoys high resource guarantee, breaks boundaries of regions, properties and subjects, and keeps high stability. The network aims to achieve the goal for "mainly building a batch of influential and international top think tanks". Most of the members are handpicked, leading in the world of think tanks with good development or great potential, strong strength and relatively high conversion rates. That's the reason why the government-leading network becomes a kind of think tank network to gather high-level elites as think tank resources.

1.1.1　CTTT Network Gathering Advanced Think Tanks

The CTTT network consists of pilot units and cultivated units for CTTT construction, getting advanced think tanks in all areas in China together. In early 2015, "The Plan of Pilot Projects for China Top Think Tanks" was formulated by the Publicity Department of CPC Central Committee based on in-depth research. On December 1st, 2015, the Pilot Projects for CTTT Conference was held in Beijing, marking the beginning of the construction. The conference emphasized building a batch of top think tanks that the state is in urgent need of, each being unique in its own way for institutional innovation and leadership in development, pushing the construction into a new stage of development. In 2017, the Publicity Department of CPC Central Committee announced 13 cultivated units for CTTT construction. In party and institutional reform in 2018, both responsibilities of Party School of Central Committee of CPC and Chinese Academy of Governance were integrated to become one brand-new party school of Central Committee of CPC (Chinese Academy of Governance), and the 25 pilot units decreased to 24. Thus, the structure of CTTT network is composed of "24+13" (24 pilot units plus 13 cultivated units), including many sorts of think tanks, such as comprehensive research institutions directly under the CPC Central Committee, the State Council or the Central Military Commission, specialized think tanks affiliated to universities or research institutions, corporate think tanks and private think tanks. And the research encompasses many key fields, such as politics, economy, ideology, science and technology, military, law, and internationalization.

To increase think tanks' autonomy in internal governance, improve the efficiency of resource allocation and pep them up, the departments like the Publicity Department of CPC Central Committee published a series of policies to build the preliminary fundamental institutional framework for the pilot projects. In 2015, the Publicity Department of CPC Central Committee studied and drafted *Tentative Measures for the Administration of China Top Think Tanks*, and jointly with the Ministry of Finance enacted *Tentative Measures for the Management of Special Funds for China Top Think Tanks* as basic rules to manage the operation of top think tanks and specialized funds. In January 2016, the National Office for Philosophy and Social Science under the Publicity Department of CPC Central Committee issued *Introduction to First Batch of Pilot Units for China Top Think Tanks Construction* to present their institutions, research teams, fields and achievements, platforms for achievement transformation, conditions to support research, structure and management system, as well as international cooperation and communication, so that the central decision-making departments can learn about CTTT, specifically assign research projects and match supply with demand effectively.

At the same time, in order to strengthen coordination and management of CTTT and serve the innovative development, the National Leading Group for Philosophy and Social Sciences, approved by the central government, established the CTTT Council as the deliberation and evaluation agency for CTTT construction. The establishment of CTTT Council has important implications for CTTT development and think tank network cohesion, because it fully displays abilities of guidance, management and overall coordination, actively opens the channel of political consultation, and reinforces the link among think tanks. In October 2016, the second plenary session of CTTT Council was held to know the work reports of all pilot units, evaluate them and make request for the nest phase. To make the political consultation research more targeted, effective and practical, the Council solicited and researched subjects from a dozen or so central decision-making bodies, formed and issued *Research Direction and Key Subjects for CTTT in 2016*. In January 2017, for the better CTTT brand image, extended social impact and down-to-earth and deep expansion for the CTTT pilots, the Council organized and designed a logo for CTTT, and released *CTTT Logo Regulation* to specify when and where to use it. In June 2019, the National Office for Philosophy and Social Sciences held the meeting to exchange experience for CTTT construction in which the principals further studied and implemented President Xi Jinping's remarks on the construction of new types of think tanks with Chinese characteristics, fully communicated and discussed their own practice like decision-making services, public opinion guidance and foreign exchange, and experience on the reform of system and mechanism.

As the "national team of think tanks", the CTTT network assembles the strongest think tanks' which are diversified, extensive and featured, and it is also equipped with the substantive council and working conferences, strict organization and management systems, as well as steady financial support, so as to accumulate valuable experience and build up a good model for the construction of new-type think tanks in China.

1.1.2 Provincial and Municipal Key Think Tank Network Concentrating on Regional Superior Power

As *Opinions on Strengthening the Construction of New Think Tanks with Chinese Characteristics* came out and the pilot work for CTTT construction was carried out, all provinces began to launch their new-type think tanks and develop regional key think tanks. From this, the provincial key think tank network was formed. For instance, Publicity Department of the CPC Hebei Provincial Committee approved and established 9 pilot units of new-type think tanks at first in April 2016. In September 2016, Publicity Department of the CPC Shandong Provincial Committee issued *Notice on Announcing the List of Key Pilot Units for Shandong Think Tank Construction* and selected 15 think tanks as the first key pilot units. In December 2017, Jiangxi Provincial Association of Social Sciences published *Notice on Selecting the First Batch of Provincial Key Think Tanks*, made by Publicity Department of the CPC Jiangxi Provincial Committee, and released the list of 17 key think tanks in 2018. In August 2017, Publicity Department of the CPC Heilongjiang Provincial Committee organized and carried out the development of their key think tanks, and finally decided to set up 20 pilot units of key think tanks at first. In September 2018, it openly launched the second selection of key think tanks in the whole province and announced the second batch of 6 key think tanks in November. In May 2018, Zhejiang Province started to select the key think tanks, and in September, published 13 think tanks as key specialized think tanks of new types, and 8 key cultivated think tanks that can be developed as key think tanks in five years. Thus the complement pattern between the two kinds of think tanks was formed. Places like Beijing, Jiangsu, Hunan, Guangdong, Anhui, Hubei, Chongqing and Sichuan, all formulated *the Opinions* or *the Plan* in their own areas to launch the pilot work, so that the provincial key think tank network took shape. Besides the provincial network, the key think tanks of some counties and cities also formed their think tank network. For instance, in May 2017, Chuzhou declared 4 key think tanks and 4 key cultivated think tanks; in March 2018, Lianyungang announced the first batch of 9 key think tanks; in April 2018, Nanjing made public the first batch of 6 key think tanks.

In addition, some provinces and cities set up agencies to instruct and manage the construction of key think tanks. For instance, Jiangsu established the committee for guiding the construction of new-type think tanks and the office dealing with the matter, and in May 2017, it founded the new-type think tank council of Jiangsu Province as the deliberation and evaluation agency for the construction. Sichuan set up the leading group for the construction of new-type think tanks under the leadership of the provincial committee and government, the deliberation and coordination institutions in charge of the work, and the committee of experts as the specialized academic consultation agency for the leading group.

A series of policies have been formulated by provinces and cities to promote the construction and development of their new-type think tanks. Consequently, like CTTT, the provincial and municipal key think tank network also possesses fund and policy support to a certain extent, relatively perfect management and evaluation systems and more open channel for political consultation. The formation of the provincial and municipal key think tank network is the strong guidance and model for the construction of local new-type think tanks in order to gain experience on the one hand, and contributes to gathering the superior think tank power and resources in the area to boost the local think tank community so as to achieve greater synergy and serve the local government's decisions more effectively on the other hand.

1.2   Systematic Network Gathering Industrial Intellectual Power

Systematic think tank network mainly consists of think tanks in one system (industry), advocated and established by national ministries or relevant institutions. The *Opinions* proposes that the construction of new-type think tanks with Chinese characteristics should have appropriate sizes and sensible configuration, and divides them into seven types: party and government departments, academies of social sciences, Party schools or administrative colleges, universities, armed forces, research institutions and private think tanks. Think tanks in different types own different features and affiliations, while think tanks of the same type have large similarities. Therefore, in the boom of building new-type think tanks in China, different types of think tanks in different systems connect with each other and form the systematic network. With the management system in "vertical fragmentation", not like the government-leading network in block form, the systematic network "vertically" takes shape. For instance, Development Research Center of the State Council (DRC) and development research centers (labs) in some provincial cities, cities specially designated in the state plan and provincial capitals, jointly launch the mechanism of national policy consultation, information communication and collaboration, establish the system of "joint session", and hold the working conference of policy consultation every year so as to promote such exchanges and cooperation.

Systematic think tank network has quite strong industry attributes and is constituted with think tanks in the same field or industry, so there are more concentrated focuses in network policies and smaller gaps in industries and disciplines among think tanks, as well as relatively high network stability. It often aims to boost the relevant systematic work and industrial development, under the guidance of related departments. For instance, *Promoting Plan to the Construction of New-type University Think Tanks with Chinese Characteristics*, issued by the Ministry of Education in 2014, mentions that it should be based on the construction of 2011 collaborative innovation centers and key research bases of humanities and social sciences to vigorously build up a batch of national think tanks, which can be regarded as the think tank network in education system. Besides the national think tank network in education system, some provinces and cities also set up their think tank network. In 2015, Gansu Education Department (college working committees) began to construct think tanks for targeted poverty alleviation in colleges and announced five college think tanks for targeted poverty alleviation in Gansu, aiming at the deep research work of targeted poverty alleviation and elimination in the whole province and providing intellectual support for relevant decision-making of the government. In August 2018, Fujian Education Department selected 20 new-type think tanks with Chinese characteristics in Fujian colleges (15 in A level, 5 in B level).

In education system, there is the think tank network in one field. For instance, the national and regional research record centers of the Ministry of Education make up the think tank network of the national and regional research in education system. In November 2011, the project of the national and regional research training bases was launched. In January 2015, the Ministry of Education published *Interim Measures for the Training and Development of National and Regional Research Bases*, and issued *Guideline for the Construction of National and Regional Research Centers* (*Tentative*) in March 2017. In November 2018, the Fourth Meeting of National and Regional Research Record Centers & the Workshop of Africa Center Construction were held at Zhejiang Normal University. Participants were the department heads, such as the Department of African Affairs of Ministry of Foreign Affairs, the Department of International Affairs of Ministry of Education and the Ministry of Education of Zhejiang Province, and directors and scholars of 147 national and regional research record centers. The construction of national and regional research record centers is aimed to serve national diplomacy strategies, provide consultation for national diplomacy development by researches of universities, and make them become "brain trust" or "thinking bank" for important decisions in China.

In addition to the think tank network of education system, such networks also exist in systems like culture, science and technology, transport and so on. For instance, in April 2016, the Office of Ministry of Culture carried out the annual project application of cultural and art think tanks, in which form it contributes to the development of cultural and art think tank system. And in November, the collective proposal conference of cultural and art think tank projects, organized by the Department of Culture and Technology of Ministry of Culture, was held in Guizhou, when four projects were firstly approved, marking the official launching of "the project of cultural and art think tank system". What's more, Ministry of Culture set up "contact points of think tanks" by corresponding selection procedure, and relied on eligible provincial art academies to gather their research strength from all parties. Later, in 2017 and 2018, Ministry of Culture continued to carry out the application and relied on the cultural and art think tank system to form the cultural and art think tank network, which can provide decision-making consultation for local cultural and art development and decision-making reference for national cultural and art development depending on typical and demonstrational research achievements. In February 2018, Ministry of Transport published *Opinions on Promoting the Development of New-type Think Tanks in Transport*. It specified that the classified guidance and advancement for think tanks should be in the order of affiliation, industry and social spheres, striving to build up a batch of new-type think tanks in transportation fields, such as railway, motorway, water transport, civil aviation and postal service in five years, and developing new-type think tank pilots at the ministerial level. Thus, the think tank network in transport system was formed.

1. 3   Platform-mediated Network Gathering Wide-Ranging Intellectual Power

Platform-mediated think tank network is based on one platform, greatly affecting the think tank networking in stability, cohesion of network members, qualification and so on. Thus, it also leads to uncertainty partly compared with the above two types of network. For this reason, the platform-mediated think tank network could be comfortably scaled up and gather think tank resources more widely. The emergence of the platform-mediated think tank network benefits from the development of information technology and the strong support of party and government as the result of the increasing number of think tanks in different types, upgraded structure of the system, enhanced quality and the mutual development of research and evaluation institutions. And it can be divided by various functions, such as research and evaluation platforms, service-oriented platforms and management platforms.

The network of evaluation platforms is formed, taking advantage of relevant evaluation institutions. In December 2016, Conference on Chinese Think Tank Governance 2016 was launched in Nanjing, hosted by Guangming Daily Press and Nanjing University and undertaken by Think Tank Research and Release Center of Guangming Daily Group and China Think Tank Research and Evaluation Center of Nanjing University, in which Chinese Think Tank Index (CTTI), the first vertical search engine and data management platform in China, published the list of the first batch of think tanks. By December 2019, there have been 848 think tanks in CTTI integrating themselves into the think tank network, developed, governed and shared by all, with online and offline benign interaction. At the same time, Guangming Daily Press and Nanjing University have consecutively held the Conference on Chinese Think Tank Governance three times since 2016, accumulating thousands of participants. Linked by the Conference on Chinese Think Tank Governance and the CTTI, the network of 848 think tanks in CTTI mutually facilitates the construction of new-type think tank community. What's more, Think Tank Research Center of Shanghai Academy of Social Sciences introduces the series of *Chinese Think Tank*

Report, in which the alternative pool including 509 think tanks also forms a think tank network linked by research and evaluation platforms.

The network of service-oriented platforms is based on service platforms, making use of their services and functions. In the case of Sina think tank platform, the launch of Sina platform, attracting dozens of excellent think tanks, not only provides the cooperation of think tanks on Sina Net with independent display space of value-added service, but also sets up an effective channel docking projects of think tanks, government and enterprises, building the "online + offline" integrated service system so as to transform intellectual resources into products of information value-added service to better serve the society.

The network of management platforms is often advocated and built by competent authorities of think tanks, which are supported by relevant information platforms to manage, serve and guide the development of think tanks. For instance, in September 2018, Civil Aviation Administration issued *Implementation of Improving New-type Think Tanks of Civil Aviation of Administration* and put forward the information construction of the new-type management platform of Civil Aviation Administration. Based on the website development of Civil Aviation Administration, the platform has five functions of releasing policy research needs, registering think tank members, applying for research projects, publishing information, managing and evaluating projects. To build an open pattern of new-type think tanks, the Civil Aviation Administration implements registration administration for think tank members that are divided into units and individuals to register on the platform and complete certification after review. The platform can make public the policy research trend, strengthen information exchange, share resources and improve the communication and joint research among think tank members. It is also the platform to borrow and attract intelligence for decision-making departments and communicate with them, as well as spread and transform think tank achievements. The units or individuals on the platform make up of the think tank network linked by the new-type management platform of Civil Aviation Administration. With certain management and strict registration and certification system, the network of management platforms has higher cohesion than others.

1. 4   Coalition Network Gathering Specialized Intellectual Power

Coalition is a form of network in which multiple actors pool resources and actively communicate with each other to achieve their common goals in the joint action. Since the 18th CPC National Congress, the construction of new-type think tanks has been placed on the important agenda by the Central Committee of the party and the central government on the level of the national governance system and modernization of the governance capacity. The construction of new-type think tanks gives an impetus to the development of think tank coalitions. And the good momentum in recent years prompts think tank coalitions to become one of network forms that are most common and distribute widely. The aim or purpose of the coalition think tank network is clear, which is spontaneously built by think tanks in order to gather the strength and resources of one area, industry or even discipline, and to set up the communication and cooperation platforms for sharing think tank information, resources and achievements. It can mutually promote the development in the region or field and will be of great value to integrate regional think tank resources, absorb specialized think tank power and promote the construction of think tank community. For instance, directed by Nanjing CPPCC, Nanjing Think Tank Coalition was established in January 2014, running independently under the rules of the Coalition. As a non-profit and loose think tank community, the high-end Nanjing

Think Tank Coalition is joined by different members, whose major works include decision-making consultation, communication, information sharing, research cooperation, political affairs management and discussion, decision evaluation, talent training and foreign exchanges. It has important implications for the integration of think tank resources in Nanjing area and even the Yangtze River Delta region. In April 2015, the "Belt and Road" Think Tank Coalition was established and aimed to build an exchange platform for research institutions to share information, resources and achievements, and improve the research level of the "Belt and Road". It also has the high-level think tank functions of analyzing policies, providing advice and consultation, and promoting communication.

Unlike the government-leading network and systematic network, most coalition network has no government background, but quite complete organization and structure. Generally speaking, the membership limit of coalition network is relatively small, with varied scales and concentrated research fields, so the cohesion and stability are higher than those of platform-mediated network. As the network is spontaneously formed by think tanks, it has fewer restrictions on the form and frequency of activities. Nowadays, the present development of think tank coalitions in China can be divided into many types by areas, research fields, industries, disciplines and think tank attributes to form different coalition network. Overall, the features of the present development of think tank coalitions are presented as follows.

1.4.1 Rapid Growth of Think Tank Coalitions

In general, the number of think tank coalitions has made significant breakthroughs in recent years. Guangdong Think Tank Coalition and Wuhan Think Tank Coalition, as the early organizations of think tank coalitions in China, were established in 2010 and 2012 respectively. After 2013, the think tank coalitions experienced explosive growth, like Fig 5. 1. With the publishing of *the Opinions* and *The Plan of Pilot Projects for China Top Think Tanks*, the think tank coalitions enter a period of high-speed development, based on the steady advance in the process of the construction of new-type think tanks. In the four years from 2015 to 2018, more than 70 think tank coalitions had been set up. In the first half of 2019, think tank coalitions, such as Think Tank Coalition of Vietnam Studies, Think Tank Coalition of Henan Universities, New Think Tank Coalition in Jiangsu and Think Tank Coalition of Party Schools (Administrative Colleges) in the Yangtze River Delta region, were established. Up to December. 2019, there are more than one hundred think tank coalitions in China, providing a platform of exchange and cooperation for different types of think tanks in different regions or fields, so as to break intellectually separate islands and improve abilities of collaborative innovation and policy service among think tanks. From the aspect of think tank forms, different think tanks, such as university think tanks, private think tanks, party, government and military think tanks, and corporate think tanks, can make up different types of think tank coalitions, such as national or provincial university think tank coalitions, coalitions of party schools (e. g. Shandong Think Tank Coalition of Party Schools, Cooperative Think Tank Coalition of Party Schools in the Yangtze River Delta and Pearl River Delta), corporate think tank coalitions (e. g. Think Tank Coalition of Central Enterprises) and private think tank coalitions (e. g. the platform of Research and Development International). The coalition with the same type of think tanks not only facilitates information communication among think tanks in one system, but also leads to the vertical fragmentation against interaction and cooperation on a larger scale.

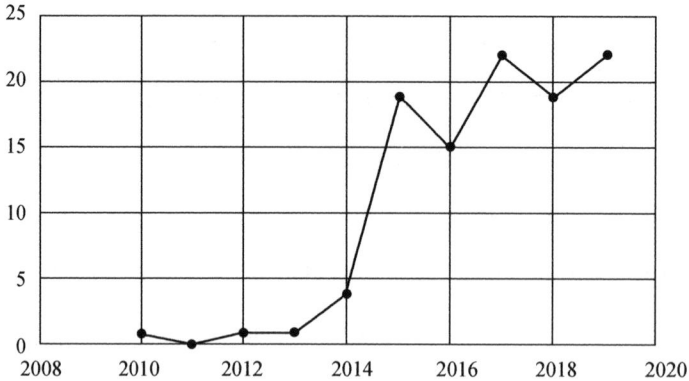

Fig 5. 1   Annual Quantity of Think Tank Coalitions from 2010 to 2019

1.4.2   Regional Features of Think Tank Coalitions

In terms of areas of think tank coalitions, there are national, provincial, regional, municipal and county-level, as well as international think tank coalitions. International think tank coalitions are advocated and established by think tanks in China, joined by foreign think tanks. Regional think tank coalitions are constituted by think tanks from different provinces and cities. The specific number of the coalitions is shown in Fig 5. 2. Regionally, provincial think tank coalitions are mainly distributed in Guangdong, Guangxi, Yunnan, Hunan, Shandong, Jiangsu, Guizhou and Gansu. Cities like Nanjing, Suzhou, Wuhan and Heihe, establish municipal think tank coalitions, and even some counties and districts have their own think tank coalitions. For instance, in 2015, Policy Research Office of Xiangshan County CPC Committee of Ningbo, Zhejiang, Xiangshan Research Institute of Ningbo University of Technology and Tianyi Think Tank of Xiangshan co-sponsored and built up Xiangshan Think Tank Coalition as the first county-level think tank coalition in China. In 2018, Baoan District of Shenzhen set up Baoan Think Tank Coalition.

Besides them, there are some cross-regional think tank coalitions, such as Strategic Coalition of New-type Think Tanks of Coastal Provinces and Areas in China, Think Tank Coalition of Chinese Cities along the "Belt and Road", Think Tank Coalition of Nanjing, Zhenjiang and Yangzhou, and think tank coalitions of areas like Yangtze River Delta, Pearl River Delta and Beijing-Tianjin-Hebei region.

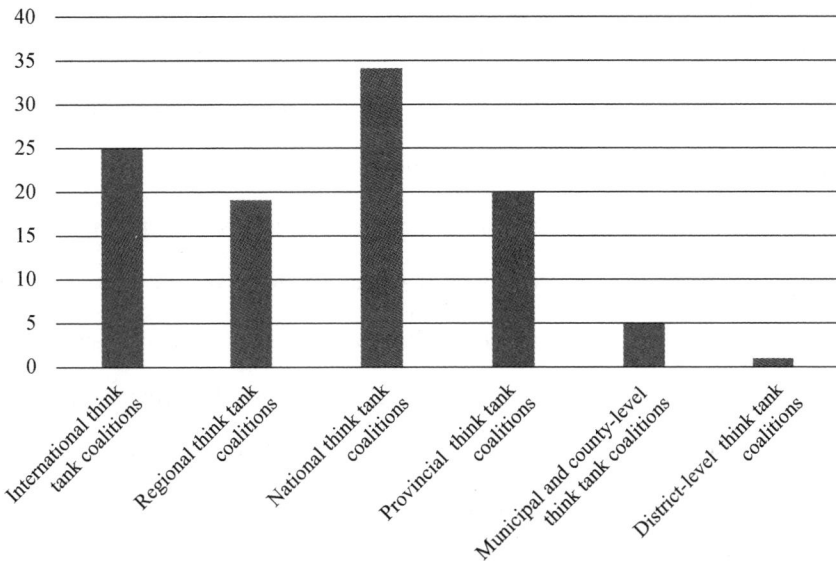

Fig 5. 2   Regional Features of Think Tank Coalitions

1.4.3   Weakness in the Operating Mechanism of Think Tank Coalitions

Think tank coalitions can effectively avoid the disadvantages of "separation" and "isolation" for one single think tank, overcome shortcomings and produce win-win cooperation. However, most think tank coalitions are offline entities at present in China, and there are no special websites of think tank coalitions but a few online communitive and cooperative platforms based on offline coalitions. It means considerable gaps compared with many think tank coalitions in foreign countries. In the form of entities, the offline think tank coalitions are easily limited by positions, time, funds, number of people and so on. And numerous different types of think tank coalitions have several or hundreds of members, which is inconvenient for the management and operation of coalitions. The activities of think tank coalitions are held, confined to the form of meetings or forums. Since most think tanks are new and some meetings are held every two or three years, the link among members of think tank coalitions is weak. It must be taken into account how to make sure the cohesion of think tank coalitions and strengthen the sense of belonging of their members, especially for the think tank coalitions with wide regions and many members. Some think tank coalitions have announced the rules and goals of think tanks in their early days, but haven't established suitable mechanisms to evaluate, accept and transform the outcomes. It's not enough to rely on the meetings every year or more in order to improve the cooperation, talent exchange and outcome transformation among think tanks. The think tank coalitions are not veritable, because their communication and cooperation still stay on the surface, contrary to their intention and leading to the waste of intellectual resources in some degree.

2 Multidimensional Empowerment: Think Tank Communication Strengthening Think Tank Community

With the progressively deepening construction of new-type think tanks in China and the increasing think tank institutions, the think tank network gradually takes shape, and the communication among different types of think tanks in different areas, and between think tanks and other institutions becomes more and more frequent and common. The main ways for think tank communication include think tank forums, meetings, training and research. The think tank communication is the key step to broaden mutual understanding and maintain harmonious and sustainable think tank development. In the construction of new-type think tanks, the formation of think tank network lays the foundation for new-type think tank community, and the enriching think of tank communication strengthens the development of think tank community.

2.1   Emerging Brands of Think Tank Forums, Strengthening Potential Energy

It ushered in the spring since *the Construction of New Types of Think Tanks with Chinese Characteristics* was put forward by President Xi Jinping as the initiative in 2013. Particularly, when *the Opinions* was published in 2015, all kinds of think tank institutions sprang up in the support of the Party and government. Think tank communication usually closely follows think tank development. At the beginning of the development, part of the think tank forums were successively set up. After several years, with the increasing participants and expanding scale of some forums year by year, the brand effect began to emerge. Under the direction of the DRC and its goal of building "international top think tanks" as well as its full commitment, Development Research Think Tank (DRTT) Forum of China was hosted by China Development Press, the directly affiliated institution of the DRC, undertaken by DRTT (Guoyan Culture and Media Inc.) and China Development Observation Press, and comprised of DRTT Annual Conference, DRTT New Year Forum, DRTT Monthly, Industrial or Local Forum and DRTT International Dialogue. Since its founding, it has held dozens of high-level forums, giving full play to think tanks and contributing to interpretation of national policy, think tank publicity, scientific decision-making and healthy development of economic society. The previous forums have scored fruitful results and created the good social impact, so the DRTT Forum has become iconic in the think tank field of China and its omnimedia influence has been top-ranked in the list of influential academic forums in China.

To drive the management of think tanks more modern, specialized and scientific, China Think Tank Research and Evaluation Center of Nanjing University and Think Tank Research and Release Center of Guangming Daily jointly initiated the establishment of Conference on Chinese Think Tank Governance and decided to hold the annual conference in every December. Each conference will invite leaders of central, provincial and municipal administrative departments of think tanks, celebrated experts and scholars of think tanks in CTTI and researching field, and some media. It has accumulated more than 21000 people to take part in since 2016 and become the "Aspen Ideas Festival" in China's think tank field. The Conference on Chinese Think Tank Governance is not only an academic feast but also an idea gathering, as well as a presentation of outcomes from think tanks in CTTI. Since 2017, the Conference on Chinese Think Tank Governance has solicited outstanding works from think tanks, and it aims to show the value pursuit and impressive performance in consultation, inspiration and suggestion for people and government by means of selecting and recommending excellent outcomes of think tank research. It notes particularly that the sources of entry works are not limited and can be completed individually or collectively. It also encourages think tank coalitions and the cooperative network to actively participate in. The results will be published by special reports of relevant administrative departments. The conference's honor mechanism is to be a significant part of motivating think tanks, sharing advanced experience and enhancing the cohesion of think tank network.

The "Luojia Think Tank Forum" was jointly organized by Wuhan University and Guangming Daily. It has been held for three consecutive sessions since 2017. The conference was held in the form of keynote speeches and round-table dialogues, focusing on the urgent needs of the country and the major decision-making arrangements of the central government. Based on the discipline and scientific research advantages of Wuhan University, it built a platform for linking think tank services with policies, and actively promoted economic and social innovation and development. Every year, experts and scholars from academic circles, political circles, business circles, financial circles and think tanks gather in Luojia Hill to jointly plan a new era of China's development. To promote the construction of China's new think tank system, we need to focus on strengthening the ability of think tanks in agenda setting, public opinion propaganda, overall coordination, etc. It is inseparable from the cooperation between think tanks and the media. The think tank forum is one of the representatives of the cooperation between well-known universities in China and the mainstream media in the central government.

China South Think Tank Forum is a vital part of implementing the *Guangdong Outline Development Plan for Powerful Cultural Province* (2011—2020) and the *Development Program of "Twelfth Five-Year Plan" of Guangdong Philosophy and Social Sciences* published by CPC Guangdong Provincial Committee and People's Government of Guangdong Province, and one of important projects of constructing the powerful cultural province as well as an important item in cultural development field of Guangdong and a great event in the development of social sciences. China South Think Tank Forum mobilizes the social sciences field in Guangdong and invites national and international experts to join in the annual forum in Guangdong, which has been held for eight times, forming its own features of "new" (new beginning, trend, mechanism and advantages), "distinguishing" (Guangdong's and Chinese characteristics) and "high-level" (the level of theories, decision-making and research). It has gradually built the public credibility and influence of its think tank brand and become a major platform for political, commercial and academic communication and exchange so as to make due contributions to achieving the overall goal of "Three Guiding, Two Leading".

In addition, there are many other influential forums in China, such as the Forum of Constructing New-type Think Tanks with Chinese Characteristics jointly hosted by China Executive Leadership Academy Pudong and Guangming Daily Press, Shanghai Global Think Tank Forum held by institutions like Shanghai Academy of Social Sciences, and China University Think Tank Forum held by Fudan University and Secretariat of Think Tank Forum. In the view of current situation, the think tank forums in China have maintained strong continuity and become more common as the number of people, units and institutions taking part in the forums increases year by year. Particularly, some think tank forums established early have gained rich experience, formed mature mode, and emerged obvious brand effect in think tank field and even the whole society, based on the development for years. Therefore, the branding think tank forums on which all eyes in think tank field focus, are the important platforms for ideas and thoughts about think tanks to communicate and play a significant role in guiding and pooling strength to constantly strengthen potential energy for the development of think tank community.

2.2 Diversified Think Tank Conferences Gathering Driving Force

Besides the forums of high-end brands drawing attention of the entire think tank field, there are many kinds of think tank conferences in diversified scales and topics held by institutions in different regions, such as annual conferences, forums, seminars, advisory sessions and symposiums. It's flexible and highly initiative that "one conference focuses on one theme" to make sure widely covering the subjects in the think tank construction and research, and adapting to the important, difficult and popular concerns of society.

Some provinces and cities actively hold think tank conferences in the region to build their platforms for think tank communication and exchange. Jiangsu Think Tank Summit is a high-level communicative platform for think tanks in Jiangsu, held by Publicity Department of CPC Jiangsu Provincial Committee and Jiangsu Federation of Social Science Associations. As an annual "idea feast" in Jiangsu think tank field, it has been successively held four times since 2016. It aims at strengthening communication and cooperation among think tanks, improving their research quality and promoting the development of new-type think tanks in Jiangsu. Since the third summit, it has organized and selected excellent cases in think tank practice and research so as to make them bring more impressive achievements.

The industrial think tank conferences focus on the development trend in their own industries and fields, gathering the intellectual power of think tanks. For instance, the "Internet and National Governance Think Tank Forum" has been held six times since 2014 and began to publish *Annual Report on Internet and National Governance* in 2015. It aims to push forward the academic research and decision-making service in the field of internet and national governance, establish the long-term mechanism for interdisciplinary communication and cooperation and give full play to social service and specific think tanks in relevant field.

Cross-industry and interagency think tank conferences gradually becomes an important platform to break down industrial barriers and exchange think tank resources in different fields. China Zhoushan Zhili Center (CZZC) sponsored and launched "Saturday & Sunday Zhiku Salon" (SZS) as a new intellectual platform on March 10th, 2019. Through endless exploration and practice, SZS is held every half month, each time about 25 people joining in, and becomes one of the seminars with CZZC characteristics. CZZC has successfully held SZS eleven times so far, of which each salon has heated discussions and brilliant views, reflecting the intellectual level of think tanks. The salon not only pays attention to studying and discussing national strategies, measures and hot political topics, but also focuses on analyzing and solving the difficulties in the development of Zhoushan Archipelago New Area, which really plays an important role as a "new-type university think tank" in providing intellectual support and suggestions.

What's more, non-regular symposiums, seminars and advisory sessions flexibly make up for the limitation of time fixed and topics for annual conferences. In the formation of new-type think tank community, diversified think tank conferences are one of the most important and common forms in think tank communication and become the major platform to gather the strength of think tanks in the same field or area and accelerate the circulation of think tank resources.

2.3 Pragmatic and Efficient Think Tank Training Improving Skills

In the construction of new-type think tank in China, some think tank institutions have accumulated amount of experience, formed mature operation modes and emerged in a large number of experts with advanced ideas and concepts. Training is the process to teach experienced or inexperienced trainees essential cognitive thinking, basic knowledge and skill in order to accomplish something. Think tank training is not only an important way for think tank experts to pass on think tank ideas and concepts to think tank practitioners or institutions, but also a significant form for the communication of think tank community. For instance, Jiangsu Think Tank Research and Exchange Center, founded by Jiangsu Federation of Social Science Associations, performs functions of carrying out research of think tank theories, promoting the development of research bases, organizing communication of think tank achievements and talent training, guiding and supporting the provincial and municipal think tank construction of social science associations. It has helped to organize Jiangsu Think Tank Summit for three times, which is held by Publicity Department of CPC Jiangsu Provincial Committee and Jiangsu Federation of Social Science Associations. It also held three training courses and fifteen salons for Jiangsu young think tank scholars so as to introduce their many achievements via media both inside and outside the province and boost the development of new-type think tanks in Jiangsu. In November 2019, Seminar of Jiangsu High-Level Think Tank Experts was held at School of Continuing Education of Tsinghua University, instructed by Publicity Department of CPC Jiangsu Provincial Committee, sponsored by Jiangsu Federation of Social Science Associations and organized by Jiangsu Think Tank Research and Exchange Center. It attracted near sixty persons to participate, including chief or backbone experts from Jiangsu key high-level think tanks, Jiangsu key think tanks and Jiangsu research centers for decision-making and consultation, and heads of functional departments of Jiangsu new-type think tank councils, such as research centers of CPC Jiangsu Provincial Committee and Government, Jiangsu Development and Reform Commission and Industry and Information Technology Department of Jiangsu.

Senior Seminar on Think Tank Capability and New-type Think Tank Construction, sponsored by the editorial board of *Think Tank Theory and Practice* which is published by National Science Library of Chinese Academy of Sciences, has been successfully held for four times, whose teachers include think tank experts or scholars from national departments, corporortions, research institutions, and universities. It centers on the development of core capability of new-type think tanks to deeply explain and make interaction, aiming at promoting the improvement of core capability and modernization for national governance system and ability, and solving new problems about theory and practice in the development of new-type think tanks.

The first High-Level Seminar on World-Leading Think Tank was held in 2017, sponsored by Center for China and Globalization (CCG), TTCSP and Penn Wharton China Center, co-organized by China Think Tank Research and Evaluation Center of Nanjing University. It has been held three times and aims to prompt deep communication between experts in China think tank and academic circles and world-leading experts, and enhance specialization, management and innovation in the construction of Chinese think tanks, by learning the world-class think tank management experience and strategic planning.

In recent years, institutions in many regions run training classes and invite celebrated think tank experts as lecturers, or visit famous think tanks to study experience and skills about think tank development, or initiate deep dialogues about major problems of new-type think tank development, such as "making use of think tanks", "new-type think tank construction and research", "think tank transmission" and "talent training of think tanks". That means think tank training has become a communitive activity for think tank community to strengthen connection and convey ideas.

2.4 Mutual Think Tank Investigations Inspiring Potential

Mutual visits, inspections and Investigations are important ways to communicate among institutions. As various new-type think tanks are successively established, the investiations and surveys among think tanks, or between think tanks and other institutions become more frequent and serve as a great way to promote the communication and cooperation of new-type think tanks. The features of mutual think tank researches are as follows:

First, mutual investigations and surveys among think tanks. It is an effective and common approach to learn from each other, communicate information and cooperative projects, and exchange personnel. Think tanks know well about the system, mechanism, operation modes, team climate and research achievements of their own new-type ones, so by learning from each other, they can absorb and gain more inspiring experience of new-type think tank construction to transform and upgrade the traditional think tanks, and build consensus for think tank development and research, so as to lay the foundation for pragmatic cooperation.

Second, investigations and communication between think tanks and other institutions, such as universities and corporations. The wisdom of think tanks comes from the nation and people, so the communication between think tanks and other institutions is the prerequisite to fully realize the functions of think tanks. For example, Chongyang Institute for Financial Studies of Renmin University of China visits and welcomes different research institutions, universities and media in China dozens of times every year. These activities are the important way to build contacts between think tanks and other institutions and understand each other for further cooperation.

Third, ivestigations and surveys between government departments and think tanks. The main purposes of government departments' inspection for think tanks consist of surveying the construction of new-type think tanks, listening to the experience and finding out difficulties, or making policy consultation for think tank institutions. Some competent authorities of provincial and municipal think tanks organize specialized think tank research group to regularly research and evaluate the construction of think tanks in the administrative area. For instance, Shanghai established a research group for the construction of new-type think tanks, led by Shanghai Planning Office of Philosophy and Social Science and allied with different departments, such as CPC Committee of Shanghai Education and Health Work,

Office of Shanghai Decision-making Consultant Commission. The group made a survey about the development of Shanghai university think tanks. And according to the communication in research, the government authorities learned more about the achievements and difficulties of university think tanks and also built a bridge between think tanks and the government.

Fourth, mutual visits of think tanks at home and abroad. With improved international influence of Chinese think tanks and increasingly expanded "friend circle" in the world, Chinese think tanks visit and welcome international institutions and experts more and more frequently, contributing to actively making connection with international think tanks, learning advanced think tank concepts and research focuses, and timely acquiring the trend of international think tanks. For instance, CCG has received visiting missions from many countries and areas, such as Germany, Japan, India, the U. S. , Cuba, Britain and Israel from 2015 to 2019. At the same time, it has been also actively "going abroad" by visiting many foreign agencies, such as United States Chamber of Commerce, United States Department of Commerce, British Institute of Development Studies and Center for American Progress, getting more about the form of foreign think tanks and communicating experience with them.

An important objective of think tank investigations is to strengthen mutual understanding. On the basis of drawing lessons, making cooperation or learning about the achievements, pains and difficulties, it is helpful for them to fully recognize the situation of think tank construction, learn from each other and mine potential so as to facilitate the formation of think tank community and further promote the development of new-type think tanks.

3   Collaborative Development: Think Tank Community Upgrading Think Tank Construction

In the process of building new-type think tanks in China, the formation of think tank community has important implications for integrating think tank elements, blending think tank platforms, and formulating the classified, hierarchical and coordinated development system of new-type think tanks. The think tank community is not only partly immune to homogenization, fragmentation and other problems in think tank research so that the think tank resources can be maximized, but also gathers high-quality think tank resources in different regions, departments, systems, disciplines and industries driven by project research and academic discussion as a tie to make joint efforts of think tanks, make up for the shortage and weakness of one think tank and build diversified, coordinated and new mechanisms of think tank construction with "powerful combination, complementary advantages, openness and harmonization", as a result of producing "a whole greater than the sum of the parts" and creating a new pattern for think tank development.

3.1   Think Tank and Government Exchange, Seeking Strength and Advantages from Political Consultation and Suggestion

Different types of think tanks are conducive to livening up the think tank industry in China and generating "catfish effect", but they will present different developmental states affected by many elements, such as property, resources and areas, for instance, in the new-type think tank system, Party, government and military think tanks and research institutes are closer to decision-making centers, grasp more think tank resources and have more accessible channels for political consultation than university think tanks and private think tanks. On the one hand, the think tank community effectively reduces differences between individual think tanks and build a bridge for communication and cooperation between government and think tanks so as to facilitate their exchanges. On the other hand, as think tank "plus", when providing the service of political consultation, the think tank community has to catch up with current events, focus on the major trends, adapt to the change of social environment, and make adjustment apt for national policies and strategies. Only the political consultation and advice focusing on how to seek strength and advantages can give full play to the think tank community.

For instance, on November 25th, 2019, University Think Tank Coalition of Henan Province held a conference to present 122 outcomes submitted by 43 think tanks of 32 universities, in order to further make full use of the platform for "mutual negotiation, development and sharing", display the research outcomes of university think tanks and better serve economic and social development of Henan Province. The conference offers the think tanks an opportunity to get face-to-face connection and communication with practical departments, breaking down the long-term "separation" and "isolation" between think tanks and their practices, which are chronic problems and obstacles in the think tank development, and reducing the predicament of some think tanks to do enclosed research, make their own efforts and even satisfy their own achievement. Therefore, the conference held by University Think Tank Coalition of Henan Province builds the bridge and bond between government and think tanks. Based on this, if every ministry can make connection and establish long-term cooperation with some think tanks, interdependently and collaboratively, the difficulties of think tank development could be largely overcome.

Another example is that in order to promote high-quality development of China-South Korea (Yancheng) Industrial Park, Think Tank of Coastal Development initiatively connected with the Park and built communitive and cooperative mechanisms. Based on the effective communication ways, such as joint sessions, field research, expert discussion, publicity and promotion, both of them put forward many advisory suggestions and jointly built China-South Korea Center for Industrial Cooperation. *Plans of China-South Korea (Yancheng) Industrial Park Construction*, as the advisory suggestion, was posted and confirmed by Jiangsu Provincial People's Government. At the same time, Think Tank of Coastal Development worked together with China-South Korea (Yancheng) Industrial Park to set up various national and international forums so as to share information and jointly advance high-quality development of the Park.

3.2   Think Tank and Media Connection, Guiding Public Opinions and Timely Speaking

The development of communication technologies and media platforms is one of the important characteristics of the present society. Think tanks are spread by taking full advantages of media. Think tanks can publish their outcomes more rapidly and widely, through the partnerships with media platforms, enhance and expand their influence and popularity, and further bring their functions into full play. Nowadays, the coalition cooperation and even combination between think tanks and media have become a major trend of the think tank development in the age of media convergence. In practice, the new-type think tank media community in China actively cooperates with media and network platforms and builds "online + offline" transmission of think tanks.

Take Guangzhou Think Tank for G-H-M Greater Bay Area (GGBA) for example. It is supported by four universities and six key bases of humanities and social sciences in Guangzhou, pooling the intellectual power of universities so that based on its scientific research advantages and characteristics of research fields, it can work as a whole to carry out decision-making research so as to provide solid safeguard for high-quality results. Meanwhile, it pays much attention to the innovation of linkage mechanism between think tanks and media, actively guiding public opinions. It also strengthens cooperation with media, such as *Guangming Daily*, *Chinese Social Sciences Today*, *Guangzhou Daily*, Guangming Online and Dayoo, and explores the linkage mechanism of "think tank + media". Consequently, it centers on relevant themes of Guangzhou-Hong Kong-Macao Greater Bay Area construction in the form of special pages, topics and columns, organizes and arranges expert interviews so as to make the voice of think tanks heard and guide the mainstream of social opinions. On February 18th, 2019, *Outline Development Plan for Guangdong-Hong Kong-Macao Greater Bay Area* was published, and GGBA organized experts like Zhang Xichun, Party Secretary of South China University of Technology, to give a special interpretation on February 21st, and devoted a full-page *GBA: Building the Most Competitive International Scientific and Innovative Center*, published on the "Guangming View" of *Guangming Daily*, showing the sensitivity of think tanks and vigorously playing the role of explicating policies to people.

3.3　Think Tank and Academic Institutes Helping Each Other, Advocating Think Tank Research

Think tanks are not simply academic research institutes. Although academic research provides theoretical and academic foundations for think tank research, which takes professional thinking as the starting point, the latter does better in application and practice than the former. Therefore, in the development of think tank community in China, it's important for think tank studies and academic research to complement and reinforce each other, and further pay attention to learning about the practice, policies, foresightedness and strategies of think tank studies based on academic research. For instance, in order to respond to national strategies, facilitate the reform to multimodal transport structure and promote the transformation of multimodal transport with railways at the core, the branch of multimodal transport of Shanghai Transportation Trade Association and China Institute of FTZ Supply Chain jointly advanced "the research on the comprehensive evaluation index system of multimodal transport based on railway transportation". Under the leadership of multimodal transport association, they established a leading group of evaluating the comprehensive evaluation index system of multimodal transport based on railway transportation and jointly conducted with railway freight yards and management departments of three provinces and one city in the Yangtze River Delta region. From the perspective of railways, the research evaluated the situation of multimodal transport development in the context of transport structural adjustment, made analysis and suggestion based on the actual transport data in this region, and offered insights for the multimodal transport development in China by means of industry-university-research combination.

Moral Development Institute of Southeast University held "a series of monthly activities" to promote communication among government, scholars and the public, strengthen exchanges among students, young scholars and senior experts, and increase self-awareness of young scholars to serve the country. On the core issue of "cultural strategy of ethical and moral development", one after another, Moral Development Institute conducted Distinguished Young Scholar Think Tank Forum on "'Chinese Problems' and Forefront Theories about the Ethical and Moral Development in the Last 70 Years of New China", Changjiang Scholar Think Tank

Forum on "Cultural Track and Law of the Ethical and Moral Development in the Last 70 Years of New China", and International Moral Development Think Tank Forum on "Cultural Strategies of the Ethical and Moral Development". These activities are a series of dialogues based on the scope of ethics and beyond, with the depth of the thoughts, the width of the content and the height of the strategy, encouraging broad participation of government decision-makers, young scholars, national experts and overseas scholars, who supply precious decision-making suggestions and intellectual support to develop think tanks.

3.4 Think Tank Building International Prestige, China and Foreign Dialogues Emerging

Opinions on Strengthening the Construction of New Think Tanks with Chinese Characteristics puts forward "strengthening the ability of international communication and the development of discourse system for new-type think tanks with Chinese characteristics, increase international competitiveness and influence of our think tanks, build the mechanism of communication and cooperation with celebrated international think tanks, make research on international cooperation projects, and actively join in the conversation on the international think tank platforms". In general, the international influence of Chinese think tanks has been largely improved through the development of years. The formation and development of new-type think tank community in China significantly play the role of public diplomacy and contribute to having a say for Chinese think tanks on the world stage.

Shanghai Global Think Tank Forum has been held five times since 2014. 2019 Shanghai Global Think Tank Forum was jointly held by Shanghai Academy of Social Sciences, the "Belt and Road" Think Tank Coalition, Academy of Macroeconomic Research, Fudan University, Shanghai Top Think Tanks and Wan Li Think Tank. It focused on "China's New Open and Global Think Tank's Innovation", attracting nearly 200 experts and scholars of over 70 think tanks to join in the discussion. The activities, such as Global Think Tank Summit held by China Center for International Economic Exchanges, China-Russia Top Think Tank Forum hold by Chinese Academy of Social Sciences and Russian International Affairs Council, and "Forum on Chinese Think Tank's International Influence, all gave out "China's voice" and told "China's story" so as to accelerate the exchanges of think tanks between China and foreign countries, promote and lead important academic brands and communication platforms for think tank research and innovation.

In addition to such exchanges as conferences and forums, Chinese think tanks also actively make "China's propositions". In order to build the global biosafety community of shared future, Center for Biosafety Research and Strategy of Tianjin University formulated the norms for biological scientists and undertook many national and international meetings. Through continuous endeavor, "model of norms for biological scientists" has been the agenda of the expert conference of UN's *Biological Weapons Convention* and been officially included into the working plan to demonstrate our abilities and guide in global biosafety governance.

Moreover, Chinese think tanks actively act and positively initiate and establish international think tank coalition to establish international cooperation. Take Center of BRICS Countries Studies of Fudan Development Institute for example. Since the center took on the work of Secretariat of BRICS Universities League, leaders of universities and the Institute, director of the Center and other workers held meetings together to make working arrangement and plans and set priorities for the year. With the hard work of the whole year, the Secretariat made breakthroughs in the formulation of rules and regulations, structural governance, representative platforms and core products so as to stably operate the League. It has exerted great influence on major partners, further consolidated and improved China's reputation and influence in education of BRICS, which is the most representative field in the League.

The prosperous development of new-type think tanks, deepening communication among think tanks and increasingly expanded think tank network lay the foundations for the formation of new-type think tank community. Building a new-type think tank community is an integral part of enriching the system of new-type think tanks with Chinese characteristics. It is conducive to taking advantages and pooling think tank resources, enhancing the ability of coordinated innovation among think tanks, serving the major social demands, providing the government with policy advice, and promoting the good interaction between think tank research and government decision-making. However, the think tank community in China is still in the early stages of development, and it is necessary to own legal identity, develop the community system, seek support from platforms free from the network shackle, and improve the weak cohesion and functions of the community. The development of new-type think tank community and think tanks complement each other. As a long-term systematical work, it needs to break the limits of areas, disciplines, properties, fields, institutions and forms, so as to fully play the role of aggregation, communication and political consultation as a whole.

Topic 6 Countries and Academy: Progress of Think Tank Research in the New Era

The strategic positioning of one country's development is closely related with updated academic changes. National demand, a driving force for the development in philosophy and social science, also has an important role to play in encouraging leading academic researches to be innovative. To meet the demand of our country, the intellectual community responds warmly to each policy issued by Chinese government, and pools all efforts and brings into full play diverse scientific research resources to serve for major projects of our country, which makes unpopular research sphere popular and turns some marginalized research fields to cutting-edge ones. Since the 18th National Congress of the Communist Party of China, President Xi attached great importance to think tank building and made crucial instructions on speeding up the development of new-type think tanks with Chinese characteristics. He made the point that we should put heads together and unite people from all walks of life to govern our country. The more assiduous task of reform and development needs stronger Chinese think tanks to provide intellectual support. At the Fourth Plenary Session of the 19th Central Committee of the CPC, Chinese government released *The Decision of the Communist Party of China (CPC) Central Committee on Some Major Issues Concerning How to Uphold and Improve the System of Socialism with Chinese Characteristics and Advance the Modernization of China's System and Capacity for Governance*. This report stresses developing new types of think tanks with distinctive

Chinese features will further improve the system of socialism with Chinese characteristics and advance the modernization of China's system and capacity for governance. The progress of think tank researches in the new era fully simplifies that our country and academic community work together to achieve mutual benefit. In addition, their cooperation helps think tank knowledge system to develop in an institutionalized way and ushers a new era driven by knowledge system for think tanks.

1 National Demand Drives Academic Development

The whole society and science researchers should pay close attention to national policies because they are a mirror of the imminent demands of society, which means academic researches are entwined with national policies and they promote each other. It's not rare to see that changes in political environment and national policies benefit the frontier development of philosophy and social science, which can be proved by changes in "think tank researches". This subject, once being a marginalized one, now takes the lead in academic community.

1.1 Major National Strategic Need—Developing New-Type Think Tanks with Chinese Characteristics

On April 15th, 2013, President Xi Jinping made important instructions ("The 4 · 15 Instruction") on the building of think tanks and made a major strategic layout—developing new-type think tanks with Chinese characteristics. *The Decision on a Few Major Issues in Further Reform in Different Areas* adopted by the Third Plenary Session of the 18th CPC Central Committee in November 2013, makes it clear that "We should cement the construction of think tanks and develop an all-round consulting and decision-making system." Besides, it incorporated those important messages of "The 4 · 15 Instruction" into important files of the Central Committee. In this context, academic and think tank community regard the year 2013 as the inception of developing new think tanks with distinctive Chinese features. In 2014, General Office of the CPC Central Committee issued the No. 65 document of *Opinions on Strengthening the Construction of New Think Tanks with Chinese Characteristics*, but the document has never been publicized for the whole society. What we mentioned frequently today is *the Opinions* disclosed by General Office of the CPC Central Committee and the General Office of the State Council on January, 20th, 2015. The *Opinions* presents that new types of think tanks with Chinese characteristics as important backups for the CPC and Chinese government to make scientific, democratic and law-based decisions. They are also important divers for improving national governance system and modernizing governing capabilities and a key part of national soft power. The *Opinions* is the first special file of Central Committee on developing new types of think tanks with Chinese characteristics and mapped out a new blueprint for intensifying the construction of Chinese think tanks, deepening reform in governance system, improving institutional guarantee system and enhancing organizing capabilities and the art of leadership. To carry out principles of the *Opinions*, *Tentative Measures for the Management of Special Funds for China's Top Think Tanks* (Department of Finance and Education, [2015] No. 470) and *The Plan of Pilot Projects for China's Top Think Tanks* (Publicity Department, [2015] No. 37) was adopted successively by China's Ministry of Finance and Publicity Department of the CPC Central Committee in November 2015. Generally speaking, the above-mentioned files lay a theoretical basis for the construction of new-type think tanks with Chinese characteristics, basically expound who should and how to develop new think tanks and demonstrate in details the management measures on human, financial and material resources. In response to this, ministries and commissions at provincial, municipal level and those in autonomous regions proceeded from respective regional conditions, embarking on the construction of new think tanks, and some of them issued documents on developing new-type think tanks after 2015. The Fourth Plenary Session of the 19th Central Committee of the CPC deliberated and adopted *The Decision of the Communist Party of China (CPC) Central Committee on Some Major Issues Concerning How to Uphold and Improve the System of Socialism with Chinese Characteristics and Advance the Modernization of China's System and Capacity for Governance (The Decision)*. *The Decision* makes a summary of epic achievements made in Chinese national system and governance system since the founding of People's Republic of China. It summarizes remarkable advantages of socialism with Chinese characteristics and China's governance system, proposes the general requirements and goals of adhering to and improving socialism with Chinese characteristics and further modernizing national governance system and governance capability, and deploys a major task—upholding and improving fundamental, basic and important systems supporting socialism with Chinese characteristics. It's actually a political proclamation and an action plan for upholding and improving the system of socialism with Chinese characteristics and advancing the modernization of China's system and capacity for governance. *The Decision* urges us to "improve the decision-making mechanism, make efforts to do surveys, research, scientific validation and risk assessment when making significant decisions and pay heed to assessment and oversight when implementing decisions", which plays a direct and significant role in the construction of new-type think tanks. The wave to develop new think tanks, spurred by national policies, swept through the whole country and reached a zenith, which encouraged theoretical researchers and academic community to commit to emergency research on theoretical and practical study as well as case study concerning the construction of think tanks.

1.2   National Research Fund Contributes to Frontier Think Tank Research

Diverse research fund programs set to express national demand to intellectual community steered think tank research in China. According to the guidelines and approved projects issued by the National Social Science Fund of China and the Social Science Fund of the Ministry of Education from 2011 to 2018, the number of think tank research subjects has increased rapidly (see Table 6. 1). Related think tank project guidelines mainly focus on Library and Information Science (34%), international studies (19%), management (15%) and political science (13%) (see Table 6. 1). Projects related to think tanks are widely distributed among those approved. Different from Table 6. 1, many new subjects concerning think tank research, such as "publishing" "law" "medicine" "computer science", are listed in Table 6. 2. The above statistics indicate that, under the guidance and support of national policies and state-driven academic development tools, scholars from different disciplines have taken the initiative to do think tank research and pushed think tank research, previously a marginalized interdisciplinary subject, to walk onto the center of academic, theoretical and media stage in many aspects.

Table 6. 1   Statistics of Think-Tank-Research-Related Projects Issued by the National Social Science Fund and the Social Science Fund of the Ministry of Education

Think tank research Project guidelines/ Projects approved	Year	2011	2012	2013	2014	2015	2016	2017	2018
The National Social Science Fund	Project guidelines	1	1	3	3	14	6	9	3
	Projects approved	3	2	1	10	21	8	10	9
The Social Science Fund of the Ministry of Education	Project guidelines	0	0	1	0	0	0	1	0
	Projects approved	0	0	7	3	14	1	5	3

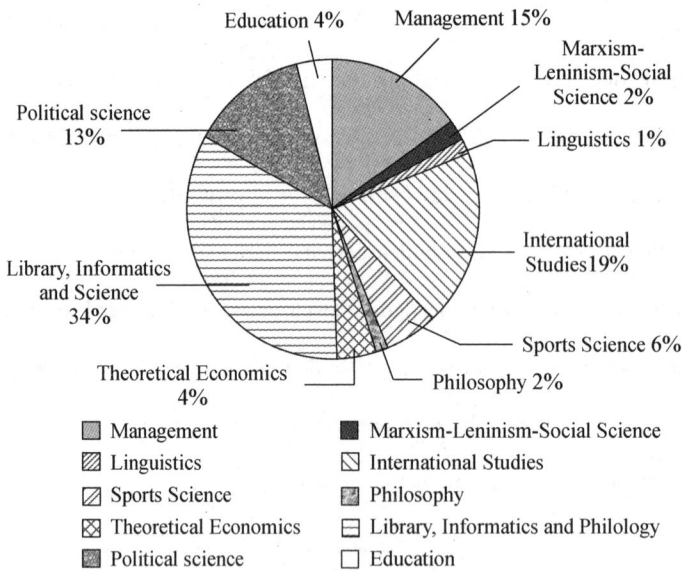

Education 4%   Management 15%
Marxism-Leninism-Social Science 2%
Political science 13%
Linguistics 1%
International Studies 19%
Library, Informatics and Science 34%
Sports Science 6%
Theoretical Economics 4%
Philosophy 2%

- Management
- Linguistics
- Sports Science
- Theoretical Economics
- Political science
- Marxism-Leninism-Social Science
- International Studies
- Philosophy
- Library, Informatics and Philology
- Education

Fig. 6. 1   The Categories of Think-Tank-Related Subjects in Project Guidelines of the National Social Science Fund of China and the Social Science Fund of the Ministry of Education

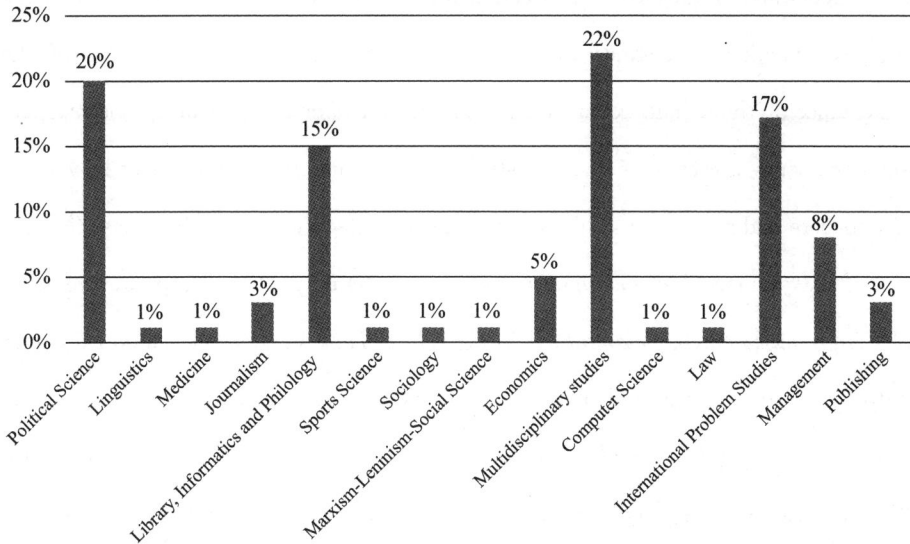

Fig. 6. 2   The Categories of Think-Tank-Related Subjects in Projects Approved by the National Social Science Fund of China and the Social Science Fund of the Ministry of Education

1.3   Party Newspapers and Magazines Publish More Think Tank Research Findings

Party newspapers and magazines play an important role not only in advocating theories, statements and policies of the CPC but also in showcasing major academic achievements. On June 16th, President Xi wrote a congratulatory letter to commemorate the 70th anniversary of the founding of *Guangming Daily*. The letter writes, "During the past 7 decades, *Guangming Daily* consistently upheld the CPC's leadership, pursued truth, kept pace with the times, and united, communicated, guided and served the intellectual community, which made great contributions to such fields as political construction, theoretical innovation, moral leadership, education enlightenment, cultural transmission and publicity of scientific information. ", party newspapers and magazines, an effective driver for the implementation of national policies, function as engines to make the general public be more aware of the importance of think tank construction. The CNKI database of Chinese newspapers and documents presents us the statistics of think tank findings published by party newspapers and magazines. Chinese party newspapers began to publish these findings since 2003, among which *Guangming Daily* consistently published important remarks of think tank research. *Guangming Daily. Think Tank Version* opened on December 25th, 2014 served as a vital platform for think tank researchers to exchange ideas. Later, *Xinhua Daily, Think Tank Version* was launched on June 9th, 2015, with "communicating with social science experts, eyeing social science news and updating think tank reports" as its core ideas, and it later opened many new columns like "Think Tank Publishing", "Social Science Experts", "Think Tank Forum" and "Decision-Making Eyes". *Economic Daily* not only created website especially for think tanks, but also developed an app called "Chinese Economic Think Tank" for handset users, which expanded the influence of think tank as well as spread its thoughts. Think tank research findings published by central and local party newspapers and magazines reached an all-time height in 2015, which fully reflects that they are enough prompt in following political hot-button topics and informing related information (see Fig. 6. 3). Top priority being given to publishing think tank research findings by party newspapers and magazines that are important tools for the CPC to publicize party principles, ways and policies, means a lot. On the one hand, it shows that major media agencies speak highly of high-quality fruits of think tank research and believe these fruits will benefit new-type think tank construction and encourage more innovative talents in intellectual community to devote themselves to its construction. On the other hand, think tanks secure a prominent place in national development strategic layout. The think tank is instrumental to enhance national governance and government decision-making capabilities and to entrench its role in steering the social media.

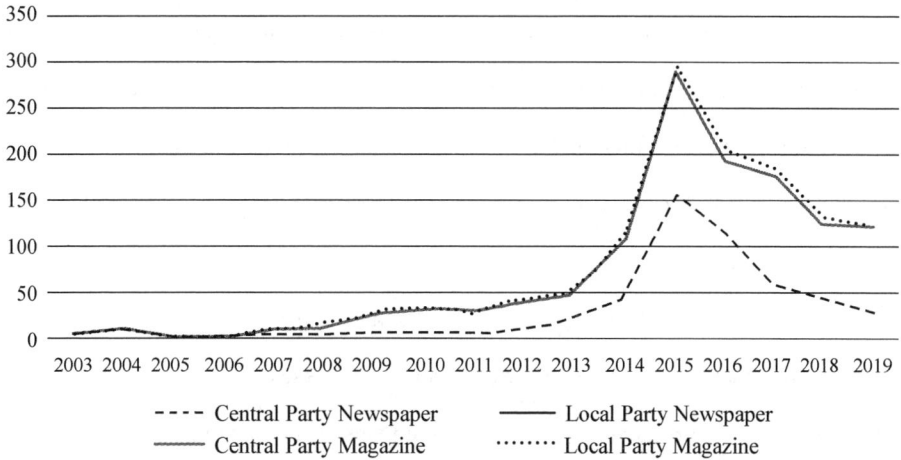

Fig. 6. 3   Statistics of Think Tank Research Findings Published in Central/Local Newspapers or Magazines

2   Academic Development Caters for National Policies—Think Tank Research Makes Breakthrough Achievements

Studies on philosophy and social science are closely bonded up with national politics in China. They should, based on pragmatic needs and policies of our country, allocate research resources, with a top priority being given to pressing topics. The transformation of think tank research from a marginalized subject to a frontier one in academic community fully proves that. Statistics of literature and monographs on think tank research clearly reflect this dramatic change.

More than 7, 000 papers can be found by retrieving CNKI database with keywords "think tank" "think factory" "think bank" "internal brain" and "Brookings Institution". After weeding out repeated and irrelative ones and news release, we can get 6,359 effective documents. We find the past few years saw a remarkable change in the number and growth rate of documents on think tank research. Table 6.2 shows Chinese scholars have been making think tank research since early 1980s, but the number of related documents remained low until 2008, which tells us less attention has been directed to this marginalized subject. Though the number was on a rapid rise from 2009 to 2014, it cannot compete with that from 2015 till now. The total number of papers on think tank research in 2015 almost doubled that of 2014 and it stayed high from then on. Fig. 6.4 displays that, around January 20th, 2015, when central government adopted *the Opinion*, the number of theses on think tank research experienced an impressive growth. This implies that national policies helped demarginalize think tank research and strongly pushed it to be a frontier subject. Meanwhile, intellectual community poured research resources into it and contributed to its sustainable development.

Table 6.2   The Year Distribution of Think Tank Research Literature Published

Year	Number of literature	Total number of literature	Year	Number of literature	Total number of literature
1981	1	1	2001	6	127
1982	3	4	2002	9	136
1983	2	6	2003	12	148
1984	4	10	2004	37	185
1985	2	12	2005	24	209
1986	4	16	2006	37	246
1987	5	21	2007	28	274
1988	6	27	2008	40	314

Continued

Year	Number of literature	Total number of literature	Year	Number of literature	Total number of literature
1989	3	30	2009	107	421
1990	2	32	2010	130	551
1991	2	34	2011	102	653
1992	6	40	2012	159	812
1993	5	45	2013	224	1 036
1994	7	52	2014	388	1 424
1995	12	64	2015	718	2 142
1996	11	75	2016	1 110	3 252
1997	6	81	2017	1 127	4 379
1998	9	90	2018	1 140	5 519
1999	17	107	2019	840	6 359
2000	14	121			

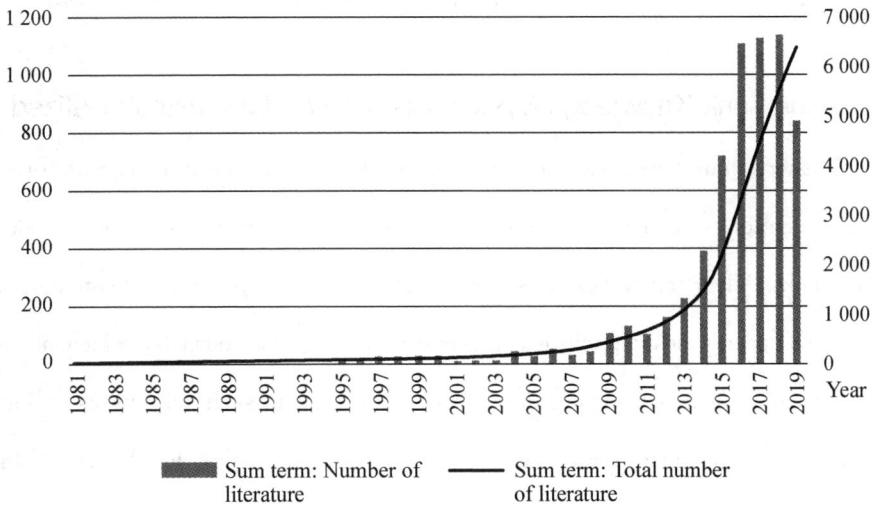

Fig. 6. 4   The Growth Tendency of Think Tank Research

The year distribution of changes in the number of think tank research monographs based on statistics from Duxiu database are presented in Fig. 6. 5. The number of monographs on think tank research met a considerable growth compared with previous statistics. The breakthrough growth of literature and monographs on think tank research indicates that intellectual community realized the value of think tank research on enhancing a country's decision-making consultation capabilities.

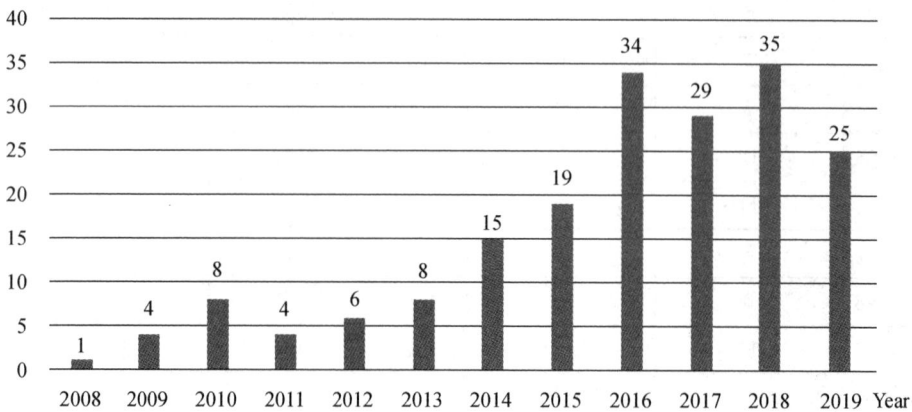

Fig. 6. 5   The Year Distribution of Think Tank Research Monographs Published

3   Think Tank Knowledge System Should Be More Institutionalized

Western think tank researches have already been institutionalized because of the development of professional decision-making and consultation and progress of modern think tanks. Their researches are supported by hundreds of professional core authors with 70% papers being published in world-class academic journals, which attract close attention of master or doctoral students majoring in such subjects as political science, public administration, education, library and informatics. Furthermore, they will hold international academic meetings regularly and discuss professional issues of think tanks. All of these contribute to a rising influence of Western think tank research across the globe. The institutionalized think tank research in Western countries means two things: one is that think tank research is concerned with political science and public administration so it's actually an academic activity and its rich theoretical connotations should be explored; another is that think tanks get improved through practice so we should detect ways and means to enhance their management. Western think tank research has been an indispensable part of dominant social science, and it's common to do such researches. Institutionalized and normalized think tank researches provide a breeding ground for the growth of think tanks.

3. 1   Knowledge on the Basic Construction of Think Tank Knowledge System Is the Primary Basis

The important speeches President Xi Jinping made on the forum on philosophy and social science on May 17th, 2016 underscored: "We, aiming to quicken the construction of philosophy and social science with Chinese characteristics, should proceed from national conditions and draw strengths of other countries, learn from historical lessons and cater for needs of modern times, as well as take account of people's demand and future development. Chinese characteristics, styles and visions should be integrated into its guiding thought, discipline, academic and discourse system. " Chinese philosophy and social science will gain its own features and advantages only by building discipline, academic and discourse system with our own characteristics.

The think tank is not only an academic institution, but also a vital part of modern consulting. High-level think tanks should develop a shifting mechanism to apply theoretical findings to production and help governments to make political decisions in a more scientific and reasonable way, so as to bring into full play the five functions of think tanks: providing suggestions to government decision-making, developing theoretical innovation, guiding public opinion, conducting public diplomacy and offering social services. We should do researches on all points of think tank development and encourage the construction of an institutionalized think tank knowledge system in order to provide backups for government's decision-making and consultation. Think tank knowledge system is an organic combination of think tank discourse, career development, discipline and academic systems. Firstly, the construction of think tank discourse system should intermix the history and practice of Chinese think tank development, step up our efforts to have a say on international stage in terms of think tank, and fully reflect what President Xi has stressed: the Chinese characteristics, styles and visions. Secondly, in terms of the construction of think tank discipline system, we should expand research realms, make it part of basic subject system, devise core curriculum of think tank research, compile related textbooks, cultivate high-caliber talents and push its research onto the dominant stage of academic communities so that we can lay a solid foundation for the development of Chinese modern think tanks. Thirdly, developing an academic system composed of academic institutions, journals and activities. We should set a think tank research academic committee to do duties like planning, organizing and coordinating national or local think tank research and evaluation; provide a platform for the publication of think tank research results to help topics on think tank research to be major research directions in mainstream academic journals in a long-term and stable way; organize think tank academic activities regularly and constantly to expand academic influence of think tanks and to enhance their popularities among media, and to institutionalize think tank academic activities. Fourthly, fostering a think tank career development system to cultivate numerous top talents for government organs, research institutions and think tanks so that think tank management will be more institutionalized, normalized and scientific.

Think tank knowledge system will be established in four aspects, the discourse, discipline, academic and career development system, to fuel the think tank development, achieve the goal of building a modern think tank, modernize the national governance system, intensify efforts to make political decision-making more reasonable, enhance the level of modern national governance and push the national decision-making and consultation strategy forward steadily.

3.2   The Construction of Think Tank Discourse System Obtained Primary Progress

Establishing think tank discourse system with Chinese characteristics can invoke the sense of developing independent Chinese think tanks. Though the earliest think tank development can date back to the 1980s, which was marked by the founding of such decision-making consultation institutions as Development Research Center of the State Council (1980), Policy Research Office of the CPC Central Committee (1981) and China Institutes of Contemporary International Relations (1980), it's hard to only rely on a decision-making consultation model centered by think tanks within the party committee and government to improve the modernization of governance capabilities. Therefore, it's imperative to resort to information policy research model, carry out evidence-based policy research and vigorously develop the construction of professional high-end think tanks. When the construction of think tanks swept through the whole China at the beginning of 2015, the domestic difficulties was that an extreme shortage of think tank knowledge reserve and poor understanding of the historical development of think tanks and the operation and management of modern think tanks.

We, taking 2015 as the watershed, compares the changes of key words of think tank research in different stages from 1981 to 2014 and from 2015 to 2019, and analyzes the evolutionary path of domestic think tank research. According to the statistics of keywords frequency and the 80/20 Rule, we found that the number of co-occurrence of high-frequency keywords in the former stage is 15 or more, and that of the latter stage is 60 or more. The UCINET software was used to draw the clustering map of the co-occurrence of high-frequency keywords in different stages in Fig. 6.2, and the clustering statistics of high-frequency keywords were made accordingly (see Table 6.3). By calculating the network density and the degree centrality of keywords in two graphs presented in Fig. 6.6, we can find that the network of co-occurrence of high-frequency keywords in the former stage (network density is 0.4397) is looser than that in the latter stage (network density is 0.6677). By calculating the degree centrality of high-frequency keywords in each stage and observing Fig. 6.6 and Table 6.3, we can find that, from 1981 to 2014, think tank research mostly focused on foreign think tanks, especially those in the United States and Japan, and probed into such issues as the basic functions of think tanks, the relationship between think tanks and the government, and the innovation and development of new think tanks. Around 2013, China's intellectual communities held a number of think-tank-related conferences, forums and seminars, which produced some important conference literature review. From 2015 to 2019, a new trend of think tank research was on vogue, which made think tank research cluster more concentrated. University think tank research secured a place, and libraries played an important role in think tank service. Furthermore, think tank development kept in step with times and paid heed to hot social issues such as "big data" and the Belt and Road Initiative. The research categories have become more differentiated with the construction of technological, social and non-governmental think tanks being the focus of the intellectual community.

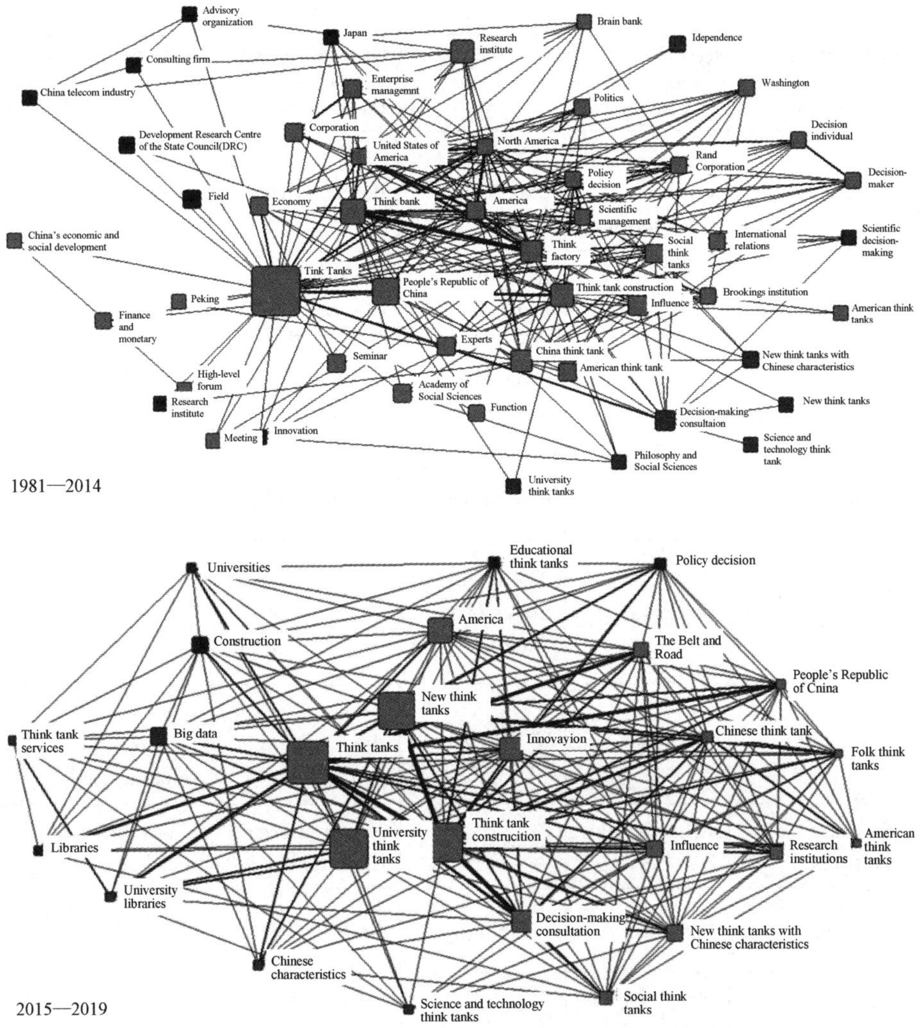

Fig. 6. 6 The Clustering Map of High-Frequency Keywords Co-occurrence of Think Tank Research at Different Stages

Table 6. 3 Clustering Tables of High-Frequency Keywords of Think

Tank Research at Different Stages

1981—2014

Cluster 1	Cluster 2	Cluster 3		Cluster 4
advice agencies	Chinese socio-economic development	brain bank	decision-making	independency
China's telecom industry	Beijing	research institutes	RAND Corporation	scientific decision-making
consulting agencies	finance	enterprise management	individual decision-maker	new-type think tank with Chinese characteristics
Japan	top forums	enterprises	decision-makers	new-type think tank
Development Research Center of the State Council	seminars	The United States of America	scientific management	decision-making consultation
fields	meetings	North America	think tank	science and technology thinking bank
research institutes	Academy of Social Sciences	politics	non-governmental think tank	philosophy and social science
innovation	functions	Washington	diplomacy	university think tank
	American thinking bank	economy	think tank construction	
		thinking bank	The People's Republic of China	
		America	think tank	
		Chinese think tank	specialists	

Continued

1981—2014

Cluster 1	Cluster 2	Cluster 3		Cluster 4
		American think tank	influence	
		Brookings Institution		

2015—2019

Cluster 1	Cluster 2	Cluster 3		
universities	think tank services	America	innovation	university think tank
education think tank	big data	the Belt and Road Initiative	Chinese think tank	think tank construction
decision-making	university libraries	The People's Republic of China	non-governmental think tank	influence
construction	Chinese characteristics	new-type think tank	think tank	research institutes
libraries	science and technology think tank	American think tank	decision-making consultation	new-type think tank with Chinese characteristics
		social think tank		

The primary study during the past four years enabled Chinese intellectual communities to have a better knowledge of the think tank's basic elements, including its attribute, characteristic, historical development and evolution and the past and current situation of Western think tanks. Chinese think tank research begins to focus on building a specialized think tank system, which requires think tanks to be institutionalized, self-managed and authoritative. Research on how to build an institutionalized think tank helps think tank institutes to make difference between basic and special functions so as to define the basic nature, feature, duties and rights of think tanks. Think tank "self-management" research provides momentum for the establishment, management and operation of institutions and urges these institutions to set up basic functional institutions, such as academic committees, advisory committees and councils. Developing an authoritative think tank reassures the lofty social responsibility think tanks bear, that is winning the international discourse right for the country and offering scientific and objective advice for the social construction. But the above-mentioned researches have not yet affected international intellectual communities. Compared with Western think tank research theories like think tank independency, "Revolving Door Mechanism" and "the fifth power", which exerted huge influence on Chinese think tank research, China has not yet developed a new-type think tank discourse system featuring Chinese characteristics, styles and visions.

3.3 Think Tank Subject System Is Developed on a Wide Interdisciplinary Basis

Think tank research is cross-disciplinary with many subjects involved, including such first-level disciplines as politics, management, communication, international relations, science of library, information and archival, history and education. Therefore, think tank research subject system should be based on multi-disciplinary basic theories and research methods and then gradually take shape into its independent core knowledge and training system. To establish a think tank subject system is an important path to develop a think tank knowledge system. Besides, it helps to stabilize the leading position of think tank research, constantly cultivate high-end talents of this field and integrate it into dominant social science.

The statistics from CNKI database of master's and doctoral theses show that 233 papers were closely related to think tank research from 2004 to 2019. This figure saw a substantial increase since 2015. From 2015 to 2019, 179 postgraduates and doctoral students make studies of think-tank-related topics (see Fig. 6. 7). They major in different and differentiated subjects, among which the political science subjects such as administration management, public management and international relations account for the largest proportion. Education (including educational economy and management, higher education, comparative education, etc.), science of library information and archival as well as media communication follow (see Table 6. 4). The head subjects related to think tank research hold a large share, and the tail subjects are dispersed with a small proportion. According to the Long Tail Effect, think tank research embodies typical characteristics of pre-disciplinary stage.

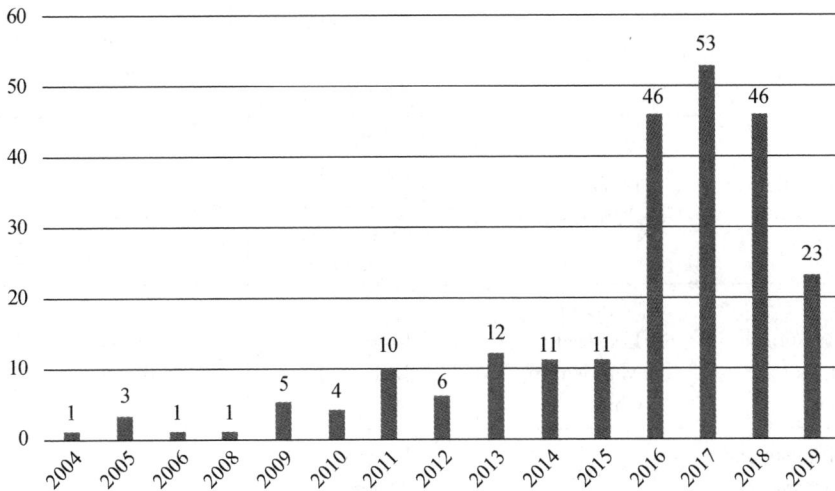

Fig. 6. 7　Year Distribution of Master's and Doctoral Theses on Think Tank Research

Table 6.4 Statistics of Subject Distribution of Master's and Doctoral Theses on Think Tank Research(N^* = number of theses)

Subject	N^*	Subject	N^*	Subject	N^*	Subject	N^*
Administration Management	64	Political Theory	5	History of Education	2	Sociology	1
Public Management	41	Archival Science	4	Science of Comparative Institution	2	Ideological and Political Education	1
International Relations	18	World History	3	Science of Law and Policy	2	Humane and Sociological Science of Sports	1
Educational Economy and Management	12	English Language and Literature	3	Comparative Politics	1	Philosophy	1
Higher Education	11	Science of Law	2	Philosophy of Science and Technology	1	Political Science	1
Information Science	10	Business Administration	2	Scientific Socialism and International Communist Movement	1	Chinese and Foreign Political Institution	1
International Politics	8	Study of Localization of Marxism in China	2	Marxist Jurisprudence	1	Science of Public Security	1
Journalism and Communication	8	Diplomacy	2	Marxist Theory	1	Law	1
Library Science	7	Education Science	2	Agricultural Information Management	1	German Language and Literature	1
Comparative Education	6	Management Science and Engineering	2	Software Engineering	1		

It is necessary for experts and scholars of mainstream disciplines, first-class universities and famous research institutes to attach importance to it and make joint efforts to develop think-tank subject system, embed think-tank research into mainstream disciplines such as political science, management, library and information science, economics and education and encourage think tank research to be part of the mainstream academic circle.

We analyzed the authors of 6,359 think-tank research papers published since 2015 when the number of think tank research papers saw a breakthrough growth. Price's Law was used to ascertain core author groups in different periods. As Table 6.5 shows, the number of core authors of think tank research from 2015 to 2019, compared with the previous stage, has greatly increased from 42 to 90. Scholars such as Xue Lan, Zhu Xufeng (both working in Tsinghua University), Wang Wen and Wang Lili from Renmin University won high reputation in the field of first-tier discipline research. The cooperative network density of core authors before 2015 is 0, indicating that the core authors of think tank research have not yet formed a cooperative network during this period. Instead, that figure from 2015 to 2019 is 0.0058. Though it's not high, it means core authors have begun to cooperate on a small scale. Fig. 6.8 proves that there are at least 7 types of small group networks in the core author collaboration network. The domestic think tank research community has formed a certain scale, and the scale is expanding, which will lay a foundation for the institutionalization of think-tank research. They will become important consultants for the construction of the think tank knowledge system and the operation and management of the think tank.

Table 6. 5   Comparison of Core Authors at Different Stages

(CA=core authors, N* =number of theses)

	CA	N*	CA	N*	CA	N*	CA	N*	CA	N*	CA	N*
1981 — 2014	Wang Lili	15	Xue Lan	7	Li Shulin	5	Chen Guangmeng	4	Li Zhen	3	Wang Huiyao	3
	Wang Wen	13	Chen Qi	6	Zhang Zhiqiang	5	Chen Xiangyang	3	Wu Tianyou	3	Zhu Youzhi	3
	Xu Xiaohu	9	Wei Lei	5	Wang Li	4	Li Anfang	3	Li Jing	3	Fu Xi	3
	Li Wei	8	Wei Siyu	5	Zhang Xinxia	4	Li Guang	3	Wang Chunfa	3	Liu Yidong	3
	Zhu Xufeng	8	Wang Ronghua	5	Wang Ying	4	Zhu Yikai	3	Zhao Kejin	3	Wang Dingfeng	3
	Chen Yixin	7	Jin Jiahou	5	Xia Chunhai	4	Cui Shuyi	3	Gao Shangquan	3	Wang Xiaohai	3
	Li Guoqiang	7	Wang Dingfeng	5	Cao Shengsheng	4	Hu Leming	3	Zi Shi	3	Sun Zhiru	3
2015 — 2019	Wang Wen	29	Li Qinggang	8	Shi Mingrui	7	Guo Hua	6	Tian Shanjun	6	Xu Weiying	5
	Li Gang	29	Zhu Xufeng	8	Hou Shuyi	7	Sun Hongfei	6	Chen Kaimin	5	Liu Dake	5
	Zhang Xu	13	Wen Shaobao	8	Wu Ying	6	Zhang Guanghui	6	Bu Xuemei	5	Zhou Hongyu	5
	Shen Shaojing	13	Ding Xuankai	8	Yang Zaifeng	6	Guo Zirui	6	Bai Bicheng	5	Shen Jinjian	5
	Zhang Shundong	12	Cheng Yu	8	Wang Lili	6	Li Guoqiang	6	Zhang Dawei	5	Wang Weiguang	5
	Li Ling	12	Miao lv	8	Peng Yan	6	Yang Guoliang	6	Liu Chunyan	5	Wan Jinbo	5
	Cao Ruzhong	11	Qiu Junping	8	Yu Fengyuan	6	Zheng Junwei	6	Chen Yunchang	5	Li Li	5
	Li Wei	10	Ma Yan	7	Wu Huijuan	6	Wang Linggui	6	Huang Changwei	5	Zhang Hongbao	5
	Ren Fubing	9	Fu Rui	7	Fu Guangwan	6	Yang Qian	6	Pan Yanting	5	Yu Henan	5

Continued

CA	N*	CA	N*	CA	N*	CA	N*	CA	N*	CA	N*
Ren Heng	9	Chen Haibei	7	Han Wanqu	6	Yang Baoqiang	6	Zhou Xiangzhi	5	Li Hong	5
Wang Huiyao	9	Yi Bensheng	7	Wei Lei	6	Huang Dongsheng	6	Liang Xiaomeng	5	Pan Jiaofeng	5
Tan Yu	9	Liu Zhiguang	7	Zhang Tao	6	Wang Shiwei	6	Zhang Xianglin	5	Xue Huifeng	5
Zhuo Xiangzhi	9	Zhao Rongying	7	Yang Dongsheng	6	Zhang Shucun	6	Zhang Dongmei	5	Xu Ye	5
Yi Lin Diandian	9	Xu Lu	7	Hu Yan	6	Liu Ying	6	Wang Qinglian	5	Ding Yuanzhu	5
Zhao Xueyan	9	Lian Lijun	7	Yuan Xilin	6	An Jingyi	6	Chu Jiewang	5	Zheng Rong	5

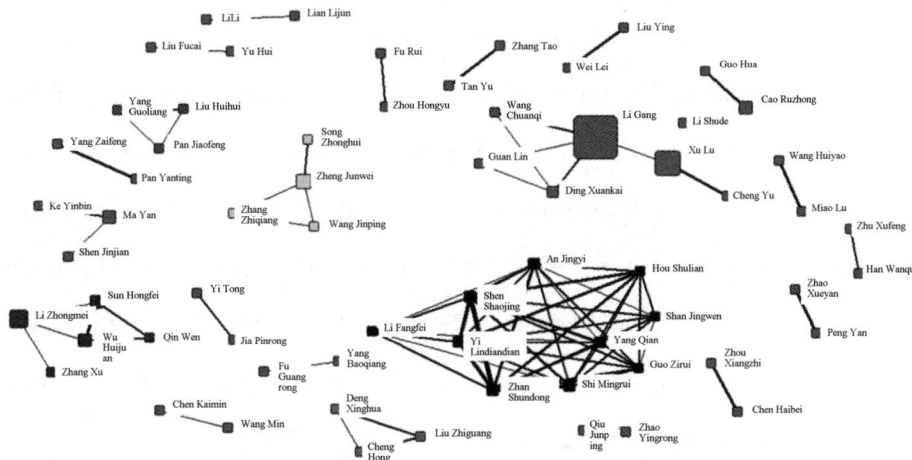

Fig. 6.8   The Co-occurrence Clustering Map of Cooperative Network of the Core Authors on Think Tank Research from 2015 to 2019

According to statistics, the number of institutions (2,708) to which the authors belong from 2015 to 2019 is more than three times that of the previous stage (821). Scientific research institutions, universities and government departments at all levels began to catch the wave of think tank research with a hundred or even a thousand institutions sharing their academic findings on think tank research. Fig. 6. 9 presents us the top 20 institutions in terms of the number of papers published at different stages. By analyzing the overall situation of the publishing institutions, we can find colleges and universities played an increasingly important and dominant role in the publishing institutions from 1981 to 2014. In particular, "Double First-Class" universities actively promote and support relevant colleges and research centers to carry out think tank research. Although the number of papers issued by national and local academies of social sciences and research institutes has increased by a large margin, the proportion has dropped. On the contrary, non-governmental research institutions and other institutions account for an increasing proportion in terms of paper publishing, but the total number is less than that of the former. Nanjing University, Chongyang Institute of Finance of Renmin University of China, Think Tank Research Center of Shanghai Academy of Social Sciences, Development Research Center of the State Council, China Center for International Economic Exchange and others had a tradition to carry out think tank research, while institutions like the Chinese Academy of Sciences and its subordinate institutions, Wuhan University, Jilin University and the editorial department of *Think Tank*: *Theory & Practice* began to do such researches after 2015.

From 1981 to 2014, the cooperation network of think-tank research institutions was very loose, which means they basically did researches independently rather than cooperatively. Among these institutions, the centrality of the School of Public Administration of Tsinghua University and the Department of Public Management of the School of International Relations was the most prominent. Different departments of Zhejiang Provincial CPC Committee maintained frequent cooperation. So did

Institute for Southeast Asian Studies, Guangxi... ▉▉▉▉ 4
The Institute for the History of Natural Sciences... ▉▉▉▉ 4
Zhejiang Provincial Committee of the CPC ▉▉▉▉ 4
Zhou Enlai School of Government, Nankai University ▉▉▉▉ 4
School of Information Management, Nanjing... ▉▉▉▉ 4
School of Journalism and Communication, Renmin... ▉▉▉▉▉ 5
Institute of Marxism of Chinese Academy of Social... ▉▉▉▉▉ 5
Think Tank Research Center of Shanghai Academy... ▉▉▉▉▉ 5
Editorial Department of Chongqing Social Science... ▉▉▉▉▉ 5
Chinese Academy of Sciences... ▉▉▉▉▉ 5
School of Public Communication, Renmin Universit... ▉▉▉▉▉ 5
International Relations Institute, Nanjing University... ▉▉▉▉▉ 5
National Academy of Development and Strategy,... ▉▉▉▉▉ 5
School of Law, Hebei Normal University ▉▉▉▉▉ 5
Taiyuan Heavy Machinery Institute ▉▉▉▉▉▉ 6
College of Economics and Management, Nanjing... ▉▉▉▉▉▉▉ 7
School of Public Policy & Management, Tsinghua... ▉▉▉▉▉▉▉ 7
Development Research Center of the State Council... ▉▉▉▉▉▉▉▉▉▉▉ 11
Chongyang Institute of Financial Studies, Renmin... ▉▉▉▉▉▉▉▉▉▉▉▉▉ 13
China Center for International Economic Exchanges ▉▉▉▉▉▉▉▉▉▉▉▉▉▉▉▉ 16

0　2　4　6　8　10　12　14　16　18

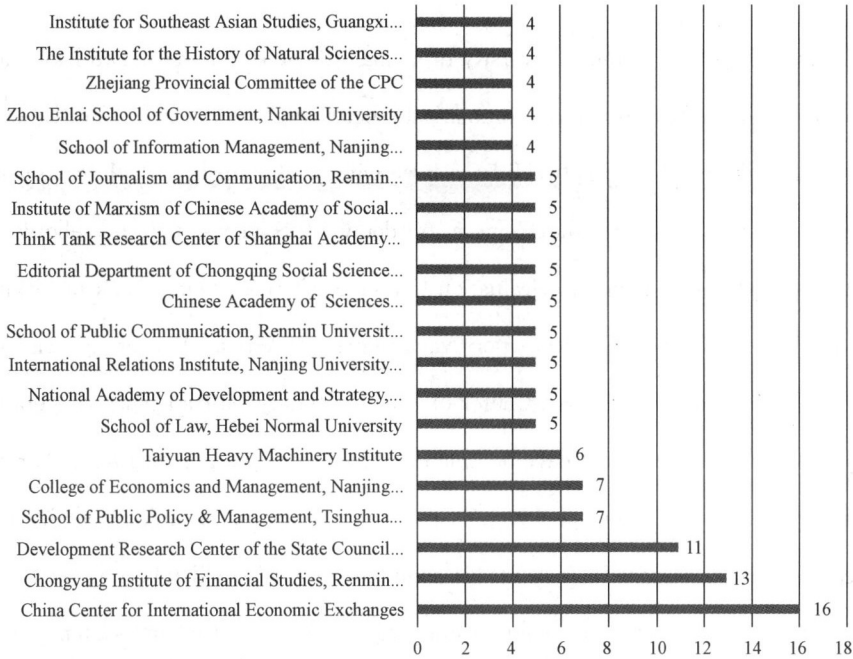

Fig. 6. 9 - 1　Statistics of Publishing Institutions on Think Tank Research at Different Stages 1981 - 2014 Statistics of Publishing Institutions (top 20)

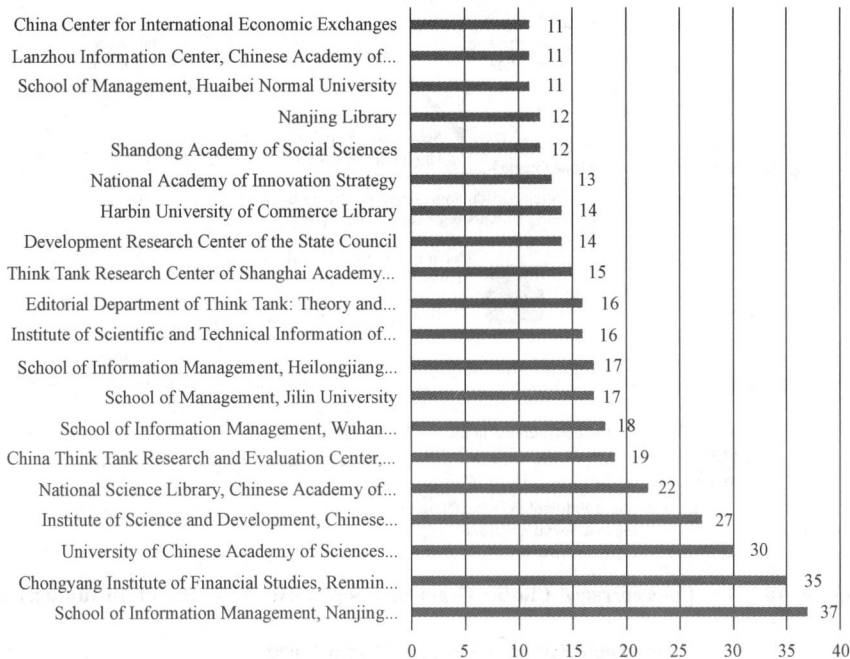

China Center for International Economic Exchanges ▉▉▉▉ 11
Lanzhou Information Center, Chinese Academy of... ▉▉▉▉ 11
School of Management, Huaibei Normal University ▉▉▉▉ 11
Nanjing Library ▉▉▉▉ 12
Shandong Academy of Social Sciences ▉▉▉▉ 12
National Academy of Innovation Strategy ▉▉▉▉▉ 13
Harbin University of Commerce Library ▉▉▉▉▉ 14
Development Research Center of the State Council ▉▉▉▉▉ 14
Think Tank Research Center of Shanghai Academy... ▉▉▉▉▉ 15
Editorial Department of Think Tank: Theory and... ▉▉▉▉▉ 16
Institute of Scientific and Technical Information of... ▉▉▉▉▉ 16
School of Information Management, Heilongjiang... ▉▉▉▉▉▉ 17
School of Management, Jilin University ▉▉▉▉▉▉ 17
School of Information Management, Wuhan... ▉▉▉▉▉▉ 18
China Think Tank Research and Evaluation Center,... ▉▉▉▉▉▉ 19
National Science Library, Chinese Academy of... ▉▉▉▉▉▉▉ 22
Institute of Science and Development, Chinese... ▉▉▉▉▉▉▉▉ 27
University of Chinese Academy of Sciences... ▉▉▉▉▉▉▉▉▉ 30
Chongyang Institute of Financial Studies, Renmin... ▉▉▉▉▉▉▉▉▉▉ 35
School of Information Management, Nanjing... ▉▉▉▉▉▉▉▉▉▉ 37

0　5　10　15　20　25　30　35　40

Fig. 6. 9 - 2　Statistics of Publishing Institutions on Think Tank Research at Different Stages 2015 - 2019 Statistics of Publishing Institutions (top 20)

different colleges of Renmin University of China. The cooperation network of think
tank research institutions changed dramatically between 2015 and 2019. The network
density and the number of network links have witnessed a surge with the emergence
of small groups, such as the Chinese Academy of Sciences and its subordinate
institutions, the Research and Evaluation Center of Chinese Think Tank of Nanjing
University, the School of Information Management of Wuhan University, and the
Information Resources Research Center of Jilin University. Intra-agency cooperation
and inter-agency cooperation have become more frequent (see Fig. 6. 10). According
to the current development trend, it is not difficult for think tank research to be
integrated into the mainstream academic communities but it will take time to be the
mainstream social science, to build an improved think tank discipline system and to
publish professional core textbooks.

Political Research Office
of Zhejiang Provincial
Party Committee

Institute of National Development and
Strategy, Renmin University of China

Zhejiang Provincial
CPC Committee

Marxism Leninism Teaching and
Research Department of Shijiazhuang
University

School of Journalism, Renmin
University of China

College of Ideological and Political Education,
China University of Geosciences (Beijing)

Department of Public Administration,
School of International Relations

School of Law and Politics, Hebei
Normal University

International Relations College

Zhou Enlai School of Government,
Nankai University

Political Research Office
of Zhejiang Provincial
Party Committee

School of Public Administration,
Tsinghua University

Zhejiang Provincial CPC Committee

Institute of Political Science, Chinese
Academy of Social Sciences

1981—2014

**Fig. 6. 10 - 1   Co-occurrence Cluster Gram of Cooperative Networks of Institutions on
Think Tank Research and at Different Stages**

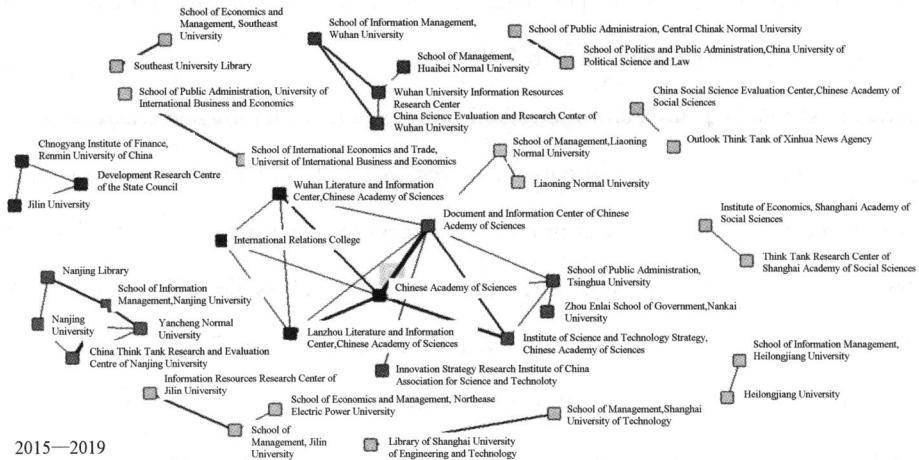

Fig. 6. 10 - 2   Co-occurrence Cluster Gram of Cooperative Networks of Institutions on Think Tank Research and at Different Stages

3. 4   The Academic System and Career Development System of Think Tanks Kicked a New Start

Efforts should be made to build an academic system of think tanks, establish relevant academic organizations and journals, organize academic activities of think tank research regularly, help researchers and administrators working in think tanks to further improve their career development systems, and provide the fundamental guarantee to ensure that the knowledge system of think tanks could be institutionalized and sustainable.

At present, we have not yet founded a national first-level think-tank research institute, nor a professional committee for think tank research under Chinese Association of Political Science, Society of Management Science of China or Library Society of China. Works conducted in research and evaluation of national think tanks, such as their planning, activity-organizing, coordination and development should be more uniform and legitimate. The think-tank academic research organizations, which saw zero development, remained to be developed. More high-quality resources and strength should be poured down to establish professional, uniform and scientific think tank academic organizations on national or regional scale. The construction of think tank academic organizations can provide a platform for think tank researchers across the country to exchange ideas, spur the innovation and application of think tank research results to maximize the effectiveness of these academic findings.

Think Tank: Theory & Practice, founded in February 2016, is the only professional think tank research journal in China. It dedicated to exploring the theory of think tanks, backing the construction of think tanks, guiding the practice of think tanks, and publicizing the research findings of think tanks. The journal has published more than 300 think tank research papers during the past more than three years, serving as a professional publishing platform for think tank research. Nevertheless, it's too hard for the only professional journal to attract a stable group of authors for a long time so it is difficult to form an institutionalized high-level publishing platform.

According to statistics, a total of 612 journals published papers on think tank research, among which 117 journals were CSSCI from 1981 to 2014, and the figure is 1,226 and 173 respectively from 2015 to 2019. It can be seen that the publication of think tank research literature attracted attention from many domestic academic journals at different levels, especially those in library, information and philology, management, political science, economics, education and comprehensive social science, for instance, *People's Tribune*, *Library Tribune*, *Chinese Public Administration*, *Economic Perspectives* and etc. (see Table 6. 6). High-quality academic publications put emphasis on think tank research and recognize the scientific and standardized research methods so the research results have an important influence. It lays a solid foundation for the construction of the theoretical system of the think tank, provides a theoretical basis for expanding the influence of its academic system, offers an important reference for strengthening the construction of the think tank discipline system, and points out the direction for planning its career development system.

Table 6. 6 Statistics of the Number of Think Tank Research Literature Published in CSSC Journals at Different Stages (top 30) (CSSCI=CSSCI core journals, N* =the number of literature)

2015—2019				1981—2014				
CSSCI	N*	CSSCI	N*	CSSCI	N*	CSSCI	N*
People's Tribune	89	Library & Information	12	People's Tribune	19	International Economic Review	4
Journal of Intelligence	61	Publishing Research	11	Social Sciences Abroad	17	Red Flag Manuscript	4
Library and Information Service	26	Journal of Higher Education Management	10	Chinese Public Administration	12	Information Science	4
Journal of Modern Information	22	Jiangsu Higher Education	10	Studies of Marxism	9	Information Studies: Theory & Application	4
Information and Documentation Services	21	China Higher Education	10	Global Review	8	Library and Information Service	4
Library Tribune	21	Journal of Chongqing University (Social Science Edition)	10	Information and Documentation Services	8	Social Sciences in Yunnan	4

Continued

2015—2019				1981—2014			
CSSCI	N*	CSSCI	N*	CSSCI	N*	CSSCI	N*
Educational Research	20	Nanjing Journal of Social Sciences	9	Contemporary International Relations	8	China Higher Education	4
Information Studies: Theory & Application	20	Social Sciences in Ningxia	9	Economic Perspectives	6	Forum on Science and Technology in China	4
Higher Education Exploration	19	Journal of National Academy of Education Administration	8	Social Science Front	6	China Soft Science	4
Information Science	18	Social Sciences Abroad	8	Foreign Affairs Review	6	Journal of Higher Education Management	3
Research on Library Science	16	Research in Educational Development	8	Research in Educational Development	5	Journal of Management	3
China Public Administration	16	Science-Technology & Publication	8	World Economics and Politics	5	International Forum	3
International Economic Review	15	Comparative Economic & Social Systems	7	China Higher Education Research	5	Chinese Journal of Journalism & Communication	3
Tourism Tribune	14	Scientific Management Research	7	Comparative Education Review	4	Administrative Tribune	3
China Higher Education Research	13	Academic Journal of Zhongzhou	7	Contemporary World and Socialism	4	Comparative Economic & Social Systems	3

The China Think Tank Governance Forum, founded by *Guangming Daily* and Nanjing University, is a continuous national meeting aimed at think tank research and professional construction of think-tanks. The forum has been successfully held for three times, each with nearly 800 participants. It is an annual event for think tank industry. Statistics of the forum attendees from 2016 to 2018 (see Table 6.7) shows that most of them come from think-tank management departments; national high-end think tanks and party; government and military think tanks; party schools; administrative colleges and social science academies; university think tank management departments; social, media, science and technology and corporate think tanks; and university think tanks. The number of participants at all levels and from different departments has increased every year. This signifies that the "China Think Tank Governance Forum" is becoming increasingly influential and radiating. Some think-tank forum participants are shouldering the responsibility to carry out think-tank research, operation and construction, and there is a career development path for them.

Table 6.7   Statistics of the "China Think Tank Governance Forum"

Attendees from 2016 to 2018

Attendees Work Units	2016	2017	2018
Think tank management department	32	36	35
National high-end think tanks and party, government and military think tanks	37	51	100
Party schools, administrative colleges and social science academies	72	75	82
University think tank management departments	48	50	54
Social, media, science and technology and corporate think tanks	74	72	78
University think tanks	498	476	394
Academic support unit	26	29	33
Foreign experts	1	1	1

National demand and academic development are intermixed and interdependent. The CPC Central Committee continued to formulate policies and adopt actions to vigorously promote the development of philosophy and social science since the founding of the People's Republic of China. Philosophy and social science are important tools for people to understand and transform the world and an important force to promote historical development and social progress. Its development reflects a country's progress in thinking ability and spiritual civilization, demonstrating a country's comprehensive national strength and international competitiveness. The development of a country depends not only on the degree of natural science development, but also on philosophy and social sciences. In this aspect, a country without advanced natural sciences cannot be in the forefront of the world, nor can a country without booming philosophy and social science. It's a must for us to adhere to and develop socialism with Chinese characteristics in terms of practice and theory and to apply the ever-changing theory to practical actions. In this process, philosophy and social science assume an irreplaceable role in fulfilling the needs of our country, while national demand is also a key driving force for the development of philosophy and social science.

This is a chance for think tank research to incline to national policy, meet the strategic needs of national development, and push the research onto the leading stage. The think tank research in the new era has made a significant stride, with the breakthrough growth of the think tank research, the continuous expansion of the research communities and research networks, the constant advancement of research themes to the forefront and the deepening of research intersection. This is an important embodiment of the continuous development of think tank research guided by national policy. The think tank research in the new era must, in accordance with the national policy and the development strategy of philosophy and social science, constantly promote the construction and innovation of discipline, discourse, career development and academic system, and make use of knowledge system to promote the construction of new-type think tanks in our country.

Part Two

**Chinese Think Tank Index Source
Think Tanks Report**

1. A Brief Introduction to the Three Phases of CTTI System

1.1 The Construction Process of CTTI System

In order to comprehensively describe and collect think tank data and equip the think tank with the function of data processing, data search, data analysis and data application, so as to better serve the construction of new think tank with Chinese characteristics, under the guidance of the Publicity Department of the Jiangsu Provincial Committee of the Communist Party of China, China Think Tank Research and Evaluation Center(CTTREC) of Nanjing University took the lead in proposing the idea of developing Chinese Think Tank Index (hereinafter referred to as CTTI), and Think Tank Research and Release Center (TTRRC) of Guangming Daily responded actively to this. Since 2015, they have used their strengths to work together to develop the CTTI system.

After preliminary system development, CTTI already had relatively complete data fields, and it was officially launched on September 28, 2016. It is open to all source think tanks included for data entry. In the course of more than a year's operation, CTTI has collected a large number of actual needs from various think tanks and management departments, and found that the lack of information management tools for think tanks has seriously restricted the daily management of think tanks. Therefore, in May 2017, the China Think Tank Research and Evaluation Center

(CTTREC) of Nanjing University and the research team of Think Tank Research and Release Center of Guangming Daily decided to further improve the CTTI data fields and optimize system functions to support solutions to these needs. These two centers proposed to jointly create an enhanced data information tool for IT management of think tanks, and the CTTI Plus version came into being. CTTI Plus focuses not only on the quantitative evaluation of think tanks, but also on the business needs of think tank information management. With the joint efforts of the research team, CTTI Plus was updated and tested online at the end of 2017 and was put into use in 2018. In May 2017, the "2017 CTTI Think Tank Best Practice Awards (BPA) Release and Think Tank Evaluation System Seminar" was held in Nanjing, jointly sponsored by Think Tank Research and Release Center of Guangming Daily and China Think Tank Research and Evaluation Center of Nanjing University. The release and launch ceremony of CTTI Plus system, which was specially held in this event, once again attracted great attention of domestic think tank peers, experts and scholars. And the new version of the system was also widely promoted and utilized.

After the first two phases of construction, the CTTI system already had the functions of think tank search, expert search, product search, activity search and MRPAI evaluation. Through the online filing mechanism, a large amount of think tank construction and product data have been collected so far. However, with the deepening of CTTI system construction and the participation of more and more people from the think tank circle, it is found that there is still room for improvement in CTTI construction. After repeated investigations and explorations, we have determined the construction objectives of CTTI Phase III. The focus of research and development is to improve user friendliness and practicability of system functions. At the same time, we will vigorously build internal evaluation of cloud think tank, and on the basis of collecting data from think tanks, retrieving data from think tanks and evaluating think tanks, we will realize horizontal evaluation and comparison between management organizations and experts of cloud think tanks. In order to maintain the stability of the system and the reliability of existing data, the core functions of CTTI Phase III will continue to use the design of the previous two phases of CTTI. It will further strengthen SaaS service, upgrade retrieval functions and improve data export function. Besides, it will optimize the function of data statistics and management, and add convenient data analysis tools.

1.2   The Overall Architecture of CTTI System

At present, apart from local main system, the overall architecture of CTTI also includes two other aspects: cloud management of think tanks and the think tank community mechanism. It features a multi-level star topology for user rights assignment, and the topology of user ID and rights description is shown in Fig. 7.1.

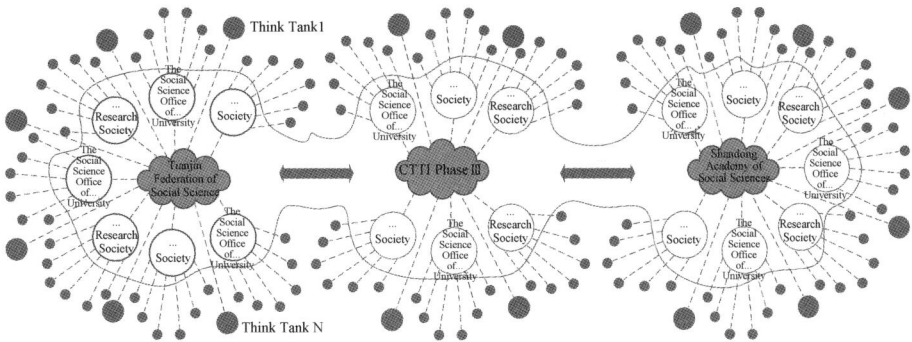

Fig. 7.1   Topology of CTTI Phase III's Functional Architecture

The central area demarcated by the curved line represents the think tank community users and cloud think tank users, and the dots outside the curved line stand for the cloud think tanks. CTTI will provide an online information sharing platform for the Chinese Think Tank Community, and it further describes the levels of think tank management through the think tank cloud function.

CTTI Phase III also reserves a synchronous data entry for the self-built systems of various think tanks, supporting the integration of the self-built systems of various think tanks into the CTTI system through customized development.

1.2.1 The Community of CTTI System

The Think Tank Community (TTC) mechanism has been incorporated into CTTI for the construction of an online alliance of new types of Chinese think tanks to share the achievements in think tank development. The Think Tank Community is meant to offer a substantiated network resource platform for think tanks and administrative authorities that are committed to promoting exchange and cooperation among new Chinese think tanks. The Think Tank Community members will mainly consist of government authorities, public institutions, and non-profit legal persons. The members will have access to all the data and functions of the system. Meanwhile, CTTI will assist them in deploying local systems and creating local think tank clouds and ensure the daily refreshing of intra-system data, as shown in Fig. 7.2.

As for think tanks added by community members, they can be recommended to CTTI's pool of supplementary resource through intra-system process and they will be properly weighed. The local data of community members can be divided into two parts: the data of institutions and experts included in the CTTI system that will be refreshed on a daily basis to community members by CTTI, and the data of institutions and experts created by members themselves that will be locally maintained so as to ensure the security and privacy of data. When the think tank recommended by community users is included in the CTTI source think tank list, CTTI will

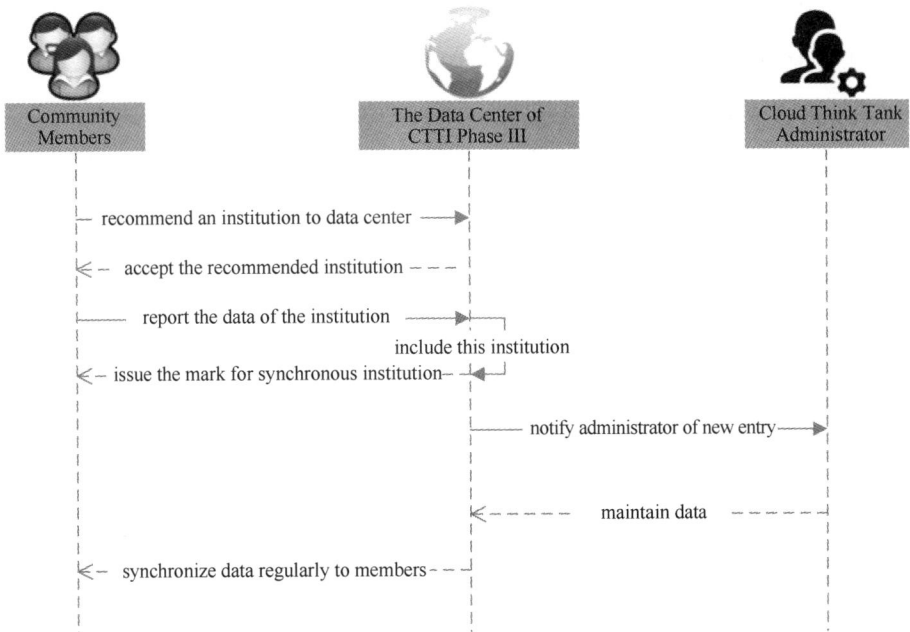

Fig. 7. 2   The Data Interchange Mechanism of CTTI Phase Ⅲ

incorporate all its data at one time and refresh such data on a daily basis, together with those of other source think tanks, to the TTC's local system.

In consideration of compatibility with TTC members' existing information management systems, we also support customized front interfaces for member units and provide data exchange interfaces so as to facilitate connection and data exchange with existing systems. In the meantime, single sign-on will be adopted for log-on by foreground users under the control of all TTC members.

At present, Tianjin Federation of Social Scientists and Shandong Academy of Social Science have become members of the CTTI think tank community, and local system deployment has already been completed.

1.2.2　The Think Tank Cloud of CTTI System

To meet think tank administrative departments' business needs in practical work, CTTI system has added the think tank cloud function after visits to a large number of think tanks and think tank administrative units and the summary of previous experience. Think tank cloud function provides institutions or departments that have data management needs with access to the CTTI system's well-developed think tank data fields, advanced database schema, and scientific assessment algorithm. By means of online big data resource trusteeship platform, it offers data management service to think tank institutions and administrative departments, with an aim to provide well-developed think tank management and index service to users that are incapable of designing and developing think tank data management system. Access to think tank clouds can endow common institutions and units with CTTI system's data management and evaluation functions (as shown in Fig. 7.3).

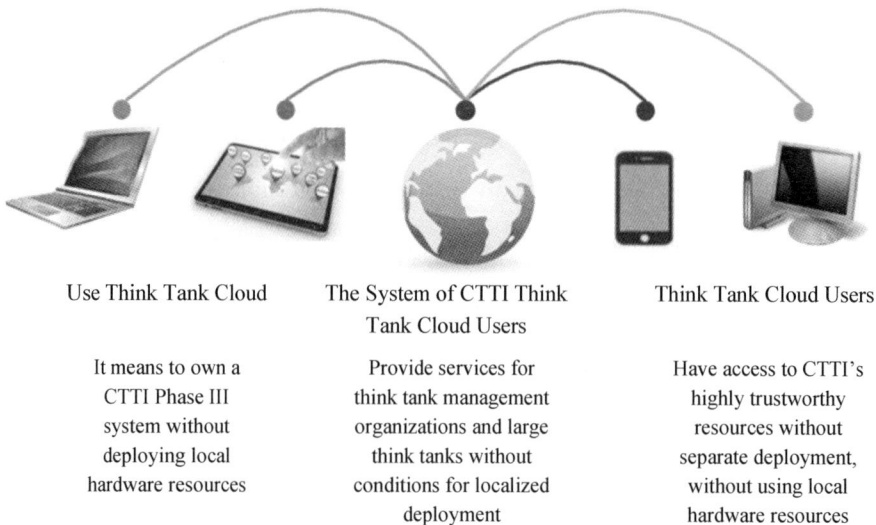

Use Think Tank Cloud	The System of CTTI Think Tank Cloud Users	Think Tank Cloud Users
It means to own a CTTI Phase III system without deploying local hardware resources	Provide services for think tank management organizations and large think tanks without conditions for localized deployment	Have access to CTTI's highly trustworthy resources without separate deployment, without using local hardware resources

Fig. 7.3　The Management System of Think Tank Cloud

Think tank cloud users can add institution users and expert users by themselves so as to realize the management of people that under their control, and meanwhile, they will have access to CTTI's highly trustworthy resources without separate deployment or using local hardware resources. Besides, they have access to all the updates and upgrades of CTTI. However, it should be emphasized that in order to ensure data security, all data among think tank clouds are independent of each other. That is to say, all data belonging to the users of any think tank clouds are only accessible to the think tank accounts within the framework of that particular cloud rather than to the public. Think tank cloud administrators can incorporate subordinate think tanks and experts into think tank clouds for centralized management by creating a cloud think tank. Having access to the cloud think tank account is equivalent to establishing a private space in CTTI, and users can independently maintain the contents of think tank construction such as institutions, experts, projects, products and activities, and manage, evaluate and assess the institutions and experts in the cloud think tank. Every cloud think tank administrator can have a clear view of the construction of think tanks within their jurisdiction (as shown in Fig. 7.4)

CTTI will assist all cloud think tanks to carry out their daily work in an all-round and fair manner, from its overall perspective by making contributions for every think tank. With the full roll-out of the think tank cloud, the think tank community will gradually form a unified data management standard, which seamlessly interfaces with the CTTI evaluation algorithm, so that the think tank evaluation can effectively play a role in the daily management of think tanks, thus achieving mutual promotion between evaluation and management and the double helix rise of evaluation methods and management level.

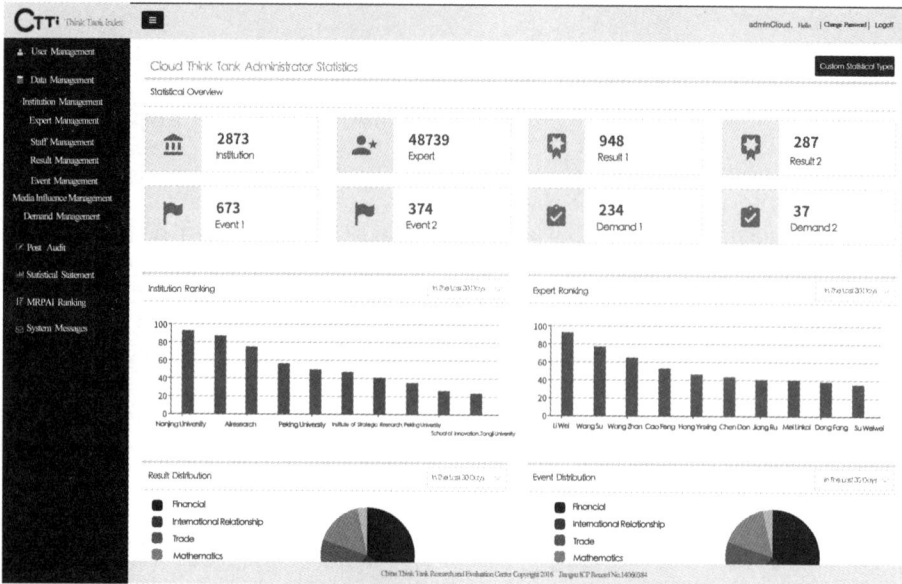

Fig. 7. 4   The Management Interface of Think Tank Cloud

1.3   Main Functions of CTTI

1.3.1   Retrieval Function

The home page of CTTI system mainly realizes the function of retrieval, which covers the retrieval tasks including institution retrieval, expert retrieval, project retrieval, product retrieval, activity retrieval, demand retrieval, etc. Since the CTTI system was launched, it has received extensive attention from the think tank community. On the basis of fully investigating the needs of experts and scholars in the think tank circle, CTTI Phase III has made a brand-new upgrade in its search function. CTTI Phase III strengthens the function of advanced search, by refining the granularity of retrieval according to different retrieval objects and increasing operations, such as fuzzy matching, precise matching, and/or relation combination, so as to help users to retrieve the target objects more quickly and accurately and build a font search engine that conforms to the retrieval habits of scholars.

CTTI's retrieval mode supports fuzzy retrieval, precise retrieval and the retrieval of combined multi-conditions.

For multi-value retrieval with a single retrieval condition, search can be achieved by separating key words by a blank space. As for logical relationships among multiple values, the system will automatically default to "OR" operation. Search fields of all input types provide the choice of fuzzy and precise retrieval. The retrieval of combined multi-conditions enables users to select logical relationships among multiple conditions—all "AND" or all "OR", with all "AND" indicating that the query results are displayed with all conditions matched and all "OR" indicating that the query results are displayed with any one of the multiple conditions matched.

In addition, in the retrieval of products, activities and demands, CTTI Phase III will support multi-category retrieval and single-category retrieval. In multi-category retrieval, the retrieval field only displays the common attribute fields of all products. However, when users search in a single category, richer fields will be displayed for users to search accurately.

The final retrieval result of CTTI is displayed as a list, and the result items are sorted according to the hit weight, which means that the matching rate of retrieval field is ranked from high to low.

In consideration of the characteristics of think tank research, CTTI Phase III also supports searching institutions or experts according to a certain policy research field. Take the institution search task for example. If users want to search organizations in a certain policy research field on the front page of CTTI system, they can check the corresponding research field in the list on the left and then carry out relevant search (as shown in Fig. 7.5).

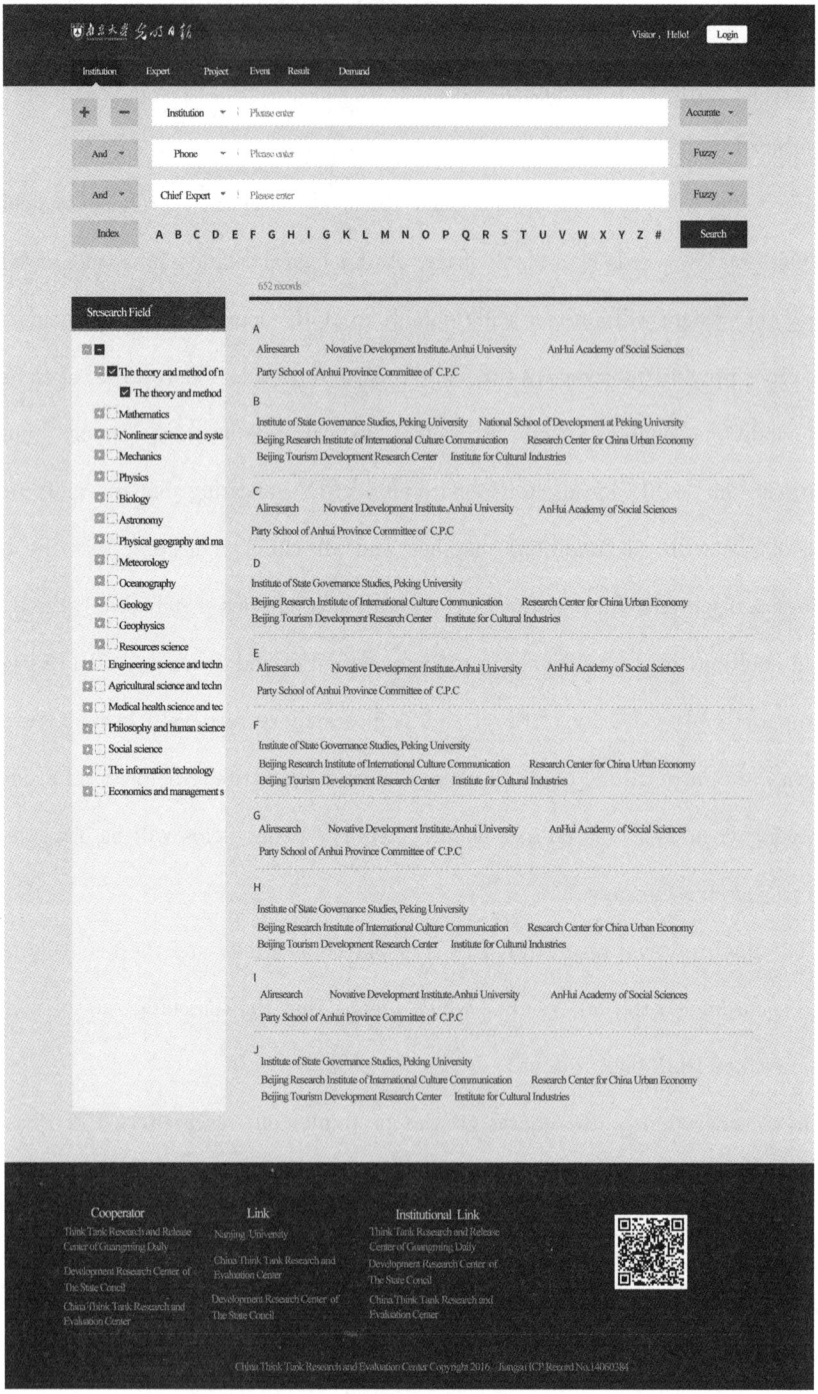

Fig. 7.5 The Diagram of Search Interface

1.3.2　The Function of Data Management

1.3.2.1　Data Processing

The main functions of the data processing flow include data entry, modification, review, release and maintenance (as shown in Fig. 7.6). The "data" includes not only the data of institutions, experts, projects, products and activities, but also peripheral data, such as news and demand information. Data comes from manually collected network or paper information sources. In the data processing process, institutional users and experts can log in to the system through different portals to enter data of corresponding fields. These data will be released or open for retrieval after being reviewed by the system administrator. The system administrator has the highest authority for auditing and data management. The audited data can be displayed to users according to the retrieval rights of users at different levels.

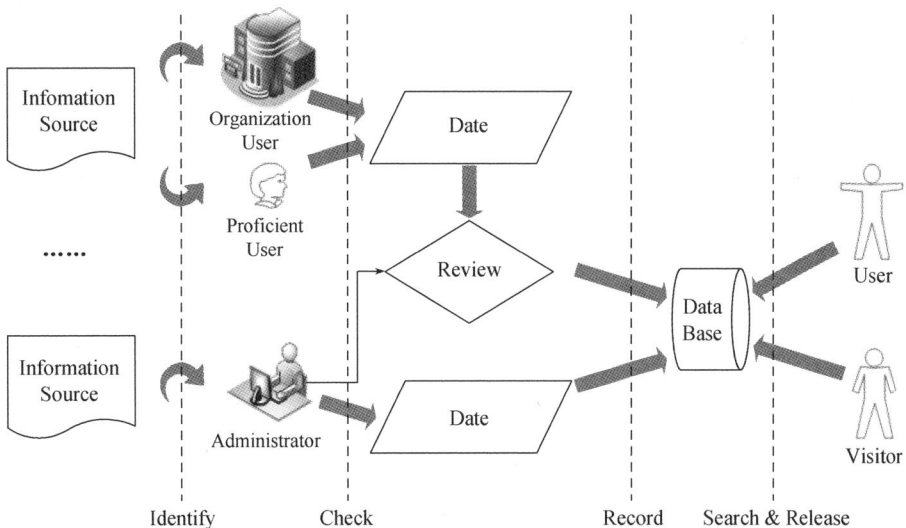

Fig. 7.6　The Diagram of Data Processing Flow

In order to meet the daily business needs of institutions and experts, CTTI Phase III strengthened the design of data export. Horizontal and vertical dual-path export is available for 38 types of data, such as institutions, experts, projects, products, activities and influence. Institutions and experts can not only easily fill in data, but also export the filled data with one click for other business scenarios.

1.3.2.2 Data Statistics and Management

CTTI is committed to serving the new think tank community and becoming a good helper in dealing with data management for all think tanks and think tank experts. CTTI Phase III has greatly upgraded the function of data statistics and management, hoping that by providing a variety of different types and dimensions of statistical results, the data recognition effect will be enhanced, effective information will be transmitted, and to finish daily management work, institutions and experts will be able to observe data status more intuitively and manage data more conveniently and quickly. Think tanks from various sources and their think tank experts can use CTTI Phase III system to directly see the statistics of various data, such as projects, products and activities, and they can choose to generate corresponding statistical charts according to their actual needs. Taking the account of an institution for example. After logging into the system, the administrator of the institution can not only directly and clearly see the statistical information of experts, projects, papers, activities, demands and other data collected by the institution, but also select different types of data to generate trend graphs or distribution graphs according to the actual situation of the institution (as shown in Fig. 7. 7). These statistics and charts could help the busy organization managers free themselves from complicated information and analyze the construction status and development trend of their think tank more quickly and efficiently.

1.3.2.3 The Personal Knowledge Management of Experts

CTTI has been exploring the way to better serve think tank experts and help

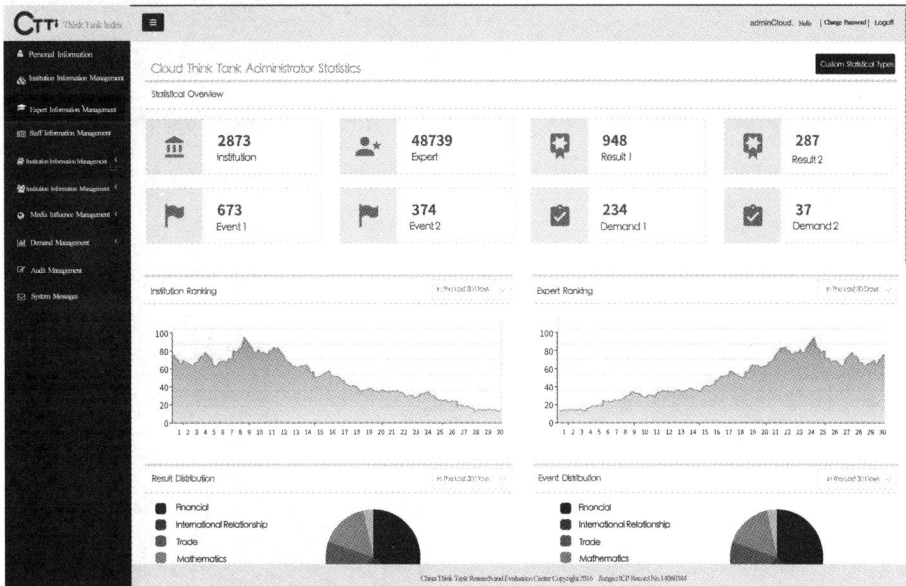

Fig. 7. 7   Organization's Interface of Data Statistics and Analysis Function

experts to conveniently manage the intellectual property of their own think tank construction. Therefore, CTTI Phase III has added the function of experts' personal knowledge management, and experts can learn their own contribution to think tank construction through the CTTI system.

Experts not only can conveniently input relevant data in CTTI system, but also can export system data according to their own needs, and they can generate personal knowledge management interface with one click for various qualification declaration or assessment requirements. For example, experts can freely choose the data of the past year or several years, and they can freely choose the basic information and results types needed to be displayed, and then match to generate their own resumes (as shown in Fig. 7. 8 and Fig. 7. 9)

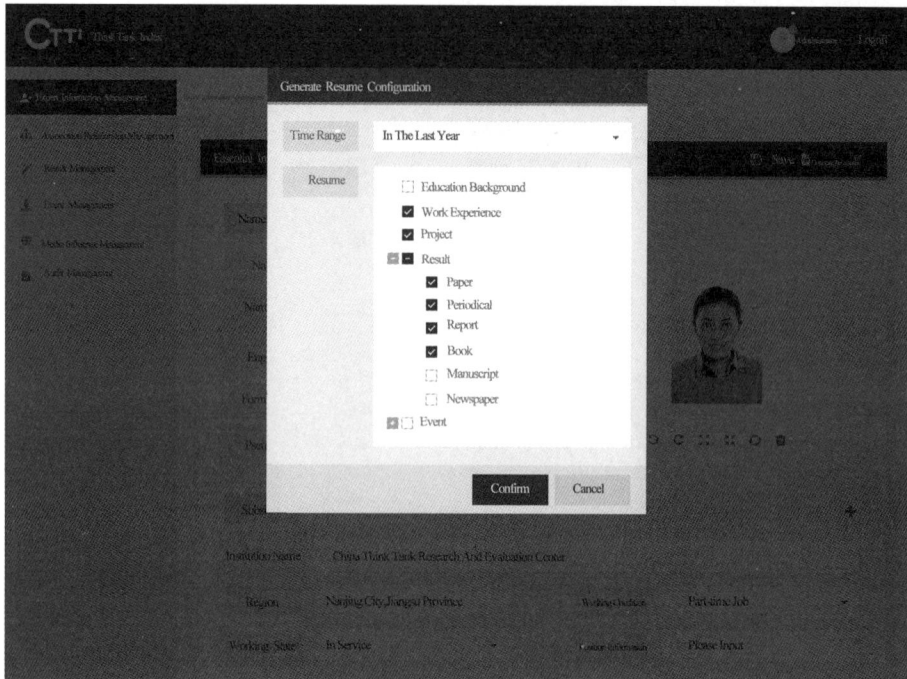

Fig. 7. 8   The Display Interface of Experts' Personal Knowledge Management

1.3.2.4   The Data Analysis of Cloud Think Tank

The CTTI system adopts mainstream big data analysis technology and has realized the function of offline data statistics, analysis and mining for think tank data. It strives to objectively evaluate and rank think tank institutions and experts from different angles, mainly including horizontal comparison among think tanks, horizontal comparison among experts, and development trends of think tanks and experts themselves in various fields, so as to provide decision-making services for the party and government and provide data support for policy consultation in designated fields. The examples of charts provided by CTTI are demonstrated in Fig. 7. 10.

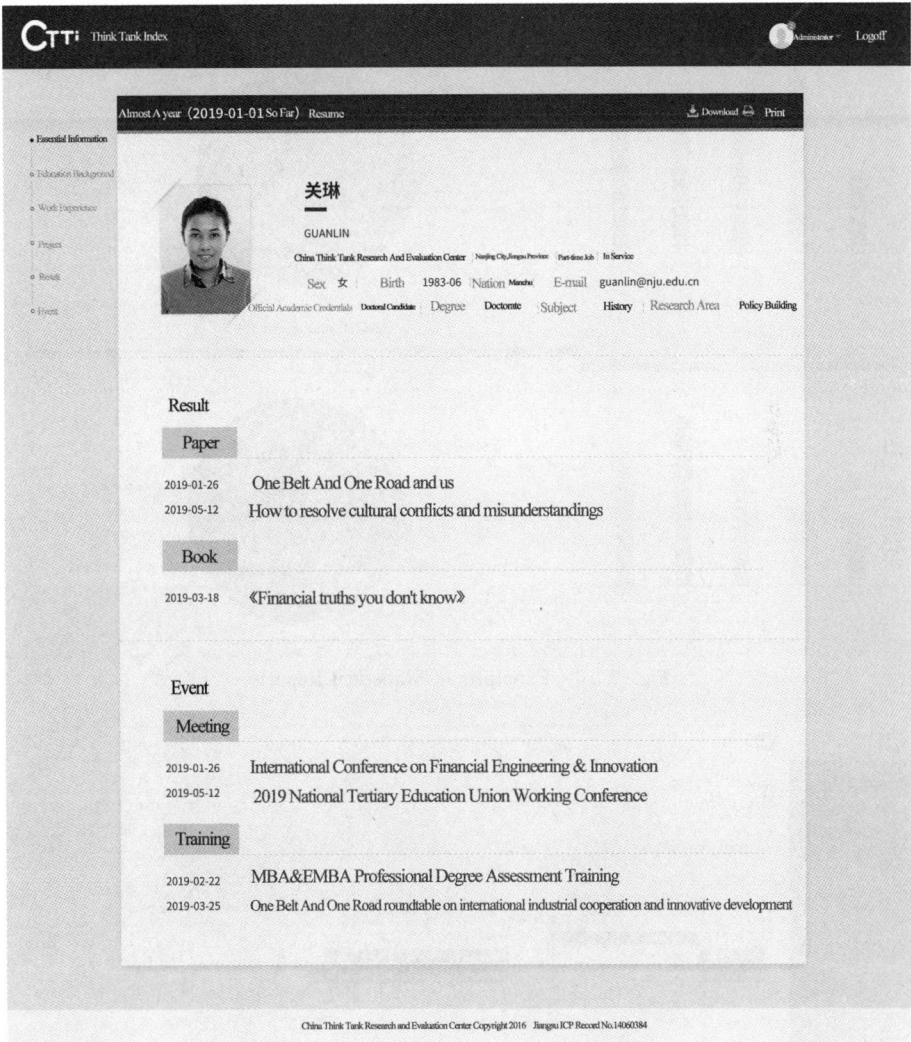

Fig. 7. 9   The Display Interface of Experts' Personal Knowledge Management

CTTI Phase III continues to optimize its data analysis function, and on the basis of the original statistical reports, it develops a convenient query and statistics tool based on page operations. Think tank researchers could conduct more targeted special analysis and research through combined queries (as shown in Fig. 7. 11).

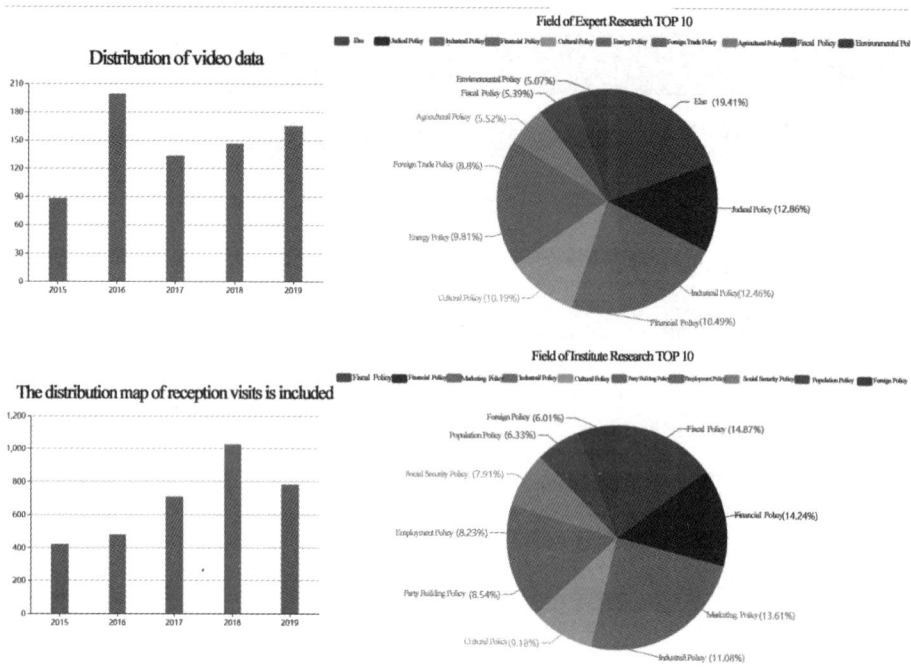

Fig. 7. 10 Examples of Statistical Reports

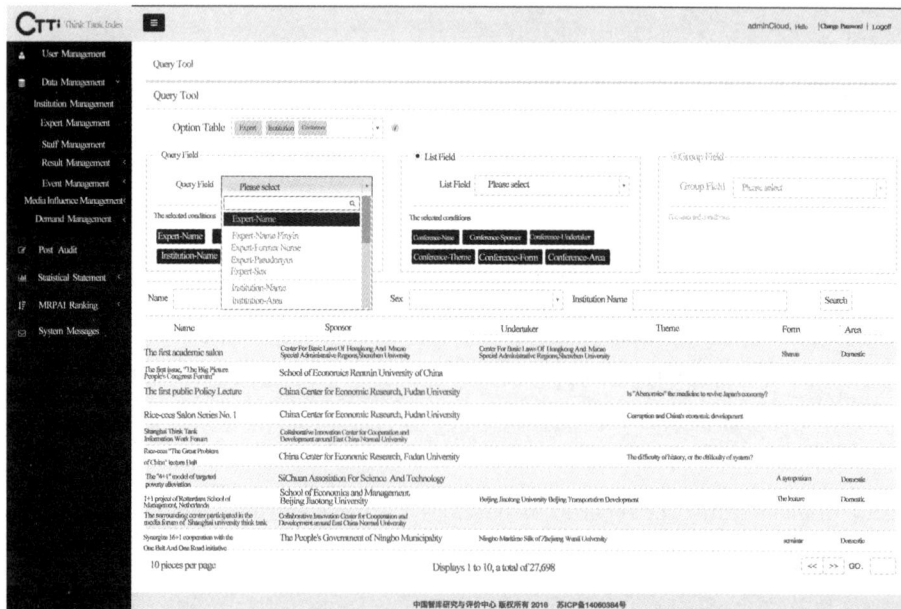

Fig. 7. 11 The Display Interface of Combined Query Tool

1.3.3 Diversified Evaluation Functions

1.3.3.1 CTTI's Basic Principles of Evaluation

CTTI think tank evaluation is process-result-oriented evaluation of think tanks in terms of their capability and efficiency of resource utilization with the think tank being a third party. In the implementation of the project, we draw on relevant methods of the fourth-generation evaluation theory, and at the same time, combining the specific reality in the field of think tank evaluation, we establish the following points as the basic principles of think tank evaluation.

① The purpose of implementing this evaluation is to provide professional services for think tanks to improve management quality, rather than generate right of governance or speech.

② Evaluation is a process in which the evaluator learns from the evaluated object and a process of dialogue and exchange. The evaluator and the evaluated need to participate in the evaluation process together, instead of unilateral discipline and regulation.

③ Evaluation is a systematic analysis based on data, and without data, the measurement is impossible to be fulfilled. Think tanks whose data are not available are not included in the evaluation scope. The interpretation of the data in evaluation should be objective and accurate, and the results of the evaluation and analysis should not be distorted.

④ The evaluation process must be fair and open, with the results being verifiable and repeatable, and social accountability should be responded to in a timely manner. At the same time, evaluators should have essential professional qualifications.

⑤ Business secrets should be respected, individuals' privacy should be protected, and basic security requirements of state secrets should be strictly observed.

⑥ Everything is built for public benefit, and the evaluation outcome should be publicly shared in non-profit ways within a certain range.

1.3.3.2 MRPAI Evaluation Indicators

CTTI database fields are "portraits" of think tank institutions, experts, projects, products, activities and media influence. They are metadata formats and standard "vocabulary" for describing think tanks. Theoretically speaking, the richer the vocabulary, the more accurate the "portrait". Based on these data fields, we hope to carry out quantitative and qualitative analysis of the data from CTTI source think tanks with a combination of expertise in data science and specialized knowledge about modern think tank management, and offer the results to the think tank community. It should be noted that when selecting and determining the evaluation indicators, we do not cover every data field in the database, but make some choices. Specifically, we focus on the following principles when determining the evaluation indicators.

① The granularity of the indicator data must suit their availability. Although some achievements have been made in the construction of new think tanks in our country, think tanks differ enormously in their way of doing things, with various forms of raw data. Besides, China's think tanks have low data cumulativeness, and the awareness of data management is lacking. Most think tanks do not have long-term data archives except for the key centers under the Ministry of Education, which have standard data filling procedures. In view of this situation, in order to encourage think tanks to apply for inclusion in CTTI and reduce the difficulty of filling in data, most database fields are specially set with a reasonable number of required data items. Therefore, when selecting MRPAI indicators, we must consider the availability of the actual data of CTTI field and specifically follow the following procedures:

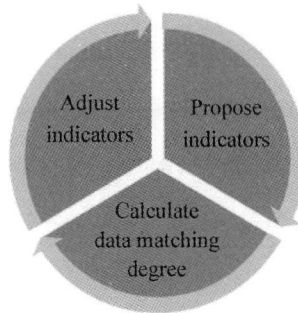

Fig. 7. 12   The Selection Procedure of MRPAI Indicators

At the beginning, the proposed indicators were entered into the system one by one to match, and if data availability were below 80%, the granularity of indicators would be abandoned or lowered. Take the "think tank expert" indicator for example. We had expected to evaluate experts' professional titles and age structure, but data matching showed that we had not acquired enough data in this field. However, the number of experts and the annual budget had been reported by 90% of the think tanks. So these two values were selected as basic indicators for measuring a think tank's resource (R).

② Indicator data must be highly critical, typical and expressive. The selected indicators must be key and representative fields that reflect the attributes of think tanks. The attributes of think tanks are mainly reflected in the well-developed structure of governance, strong tendency of policy influence, active use of forums and meetings for greater public influence, in-depth and pragmatic research and survey. Therefore, more indicators were selected from fields that can reflect such attributes as internal reference, written instructions or comments, research reports, projects, meetings, and investigations, reflecting the tendency of indicators to highlight the attributes of think tanks.

③ Indicators should be objective and systematic. The objectivity of indicators has two meanings. Firstly, indicators, like CTTI data fields, reveal the true attributes of think tanks and are synthesized from the most objective fields. Secondly, it refers to the objectivity of index values, which are not subjective values such as valuation. That indicators should be systematic refers to the existence of rigorously logical relationship between various indicators. For example, the five primary indicators of MRPAI reflect the performance logic of input and output. Only such indicators can make up what is called an indicator system.

④ The indicator system must be conductive to promoting the development of think tanks through evaluation and it should suit the current situation of the construction of new think tanks. If the construction of new types of think tanks with Chinese characteristics has achieved certain results in the past five years since 2013, then the next three years will be the crucial stage for the construction, the key stage for achieving high-quality development of new think tank construction. But at the same time, we should also admit that there are still many problems, such as inadequate understanding of the rules governing the construction of think tanks, lack of standardization and imperfect operation procedures. Therefore, we cannot measure the think tank according to international standards or standards that do not match the present construction of China's think tanks. Otherwise, the enthusiasm of the evaluated think tank would be easily dampened, and it would be difficult to play its encouraging and affirmative role in promoting the establishment of think tanks by evaluation.

According to these principles, we have selected 5 primary indicators and 24 secondary ones. The 5 primary indicators are M (management structure), R (resources of the think tank), P (products of the think tank), A (activities of the think tank) and I (media influence of the think tank), and they are named as the MRPAI evaluation indicators. As a result-oriented system for assessing the effectiveness of think tanks, MRPAI can evaluate think tanks from two dimensions— one is the amount of resources occupied, the other is the effect of resource utilization, that is, efficiency. It can measure a think tank's size and output, its effectiveness, as well as the intensity of its attributes. Therefore, the MRPAI system conforms to the principles for indicator selection and could be used for effective measurement of CTTI source think tanks.

In terms of secondary indicators, when we focus only on R indicators, we can measure the amount of a think tank's budget and personnel. There is no doubt that a well-funded think tank with abundant experts and administrative personnel is a think tank of large scale. When we focus only on P indicators, we can measure the number of a think tank's research findings. Obviously, a think tank with fruitful findings is a good one. When we only look at A indicators, we can measure the number of events organized by a think tank. Though a think tank cannot be considered a good one just because it holds many events, one that rarely does so could hardly be a typical think tank. Such think tanks are more like research centers in universities or the government's policy research offices. Although having a certain academic and policy influence, the think tank attributes might be weak. When we focus only on I indicators, we can measure the number of media reports of this think tank and its social impact. Media influence is one of the ways for think tanks to play their role in providing consultation for governments and educating the public, and it is also an important indicator to evaluate the level of think tanks.

An institution is usually considered to have strong think tank attributes when it has high values in P1, P2 and P5 of P indicators and a high total value in the A and I indicators. MRPAI can also be used to measure the effectiveness of a think tank, for its output having divided by its resources equals its effectiveness.

Table. 7. 1   MRPAI Think Tank Assessment Indicators and Their Assigned Values

Primary Indicators	Code	Secondary Indicators	Code	The Scoring Rule	Points
Management Structure	M	Council (Board of Directors)	M1	assign value if yes	15
		Academic Committee	M2	assign value if yes	10
		Consultative /Advisory Committee	M3	assign value if yes	10
		Management Team/ Chief Expert	M4	assign value if yes	10
		China Top Think Tank	M5	assign value if yes	100
Resources of Think Tank	R	Annual Budget	R1	≤1 million	20
				assign value for each additional sum of 100,000 yuan	1
		Scientific Research Staff	R2	≤10 persons	40
				multiplied by value for each additional person	2
		Administrative Staff	R3	≤5 persons	20
				Multiplied by value for each additional person	1
		Cyber Resources	R4	has a portal in Chinese	20
				has a portal in English	8
				has a WeChat public account	8
				has an official Weibo account	5
				has a dedicated data acquisition platform	10
Products of Think Tank	P	Single Internal Reference Reports (with or without leaders' comments)	P1	assign value for each title	2

Continued

Primary Indicators	Code	Secondary Indicators	Code	The Scoring Rule	Points
		Internal Reference Reports Commented by Leaders	P2	state level/per comment	30
				sub-state level/per comment	20
				provincial or ministerial level/per comment	10
				sub-provincial or ministerial level/per comment	5
		Journals Sponsored/ Run by Think Tanks	P3	each CSSCI source journal	20
				each common journal	10
				each bulletin/collection of internal reference reports	8
		Books (officially published)	P4	assign value for each report	2
		Research Reports	P5	assign value for each report	4
		Articles Published in the Theoretical Edition of *People's Daily*, *Guangming Daily* or *Seeking Truth*,	P6	assign value for each article	5
		Academic Papers	P7	each paper in CSSCI source journal	1
				each paper included in SSCI/A&HCI	2
				each paper included in CSCI/EI	1
				each of other papers	0. 5
		Vertical Projects	P8	vertical: major projects supported by National Social Science Fund or Social Science Fund of Ministry of Education	10

Continued

Primary Indicators	Code	Secondary Indicators	Code	The Scoring Rule	Points
				vertical: key projects supported by National Social Science Fund or National Natural Science Fund	6
				vertical: common/young scholar projects supported by National Social Science Fund	4
				vertical: provincial/ministerial level projects	2
				vertical: others	0.5
		Horizontal Projects	P9	basic points for each project+1 mark point for every 100,000 yuan	
Activities of Think Tank	A	Conferences and Meetings	A1	each national conference sponsored or organized	10
				each conference at the level of province, municipalities or autonomous region	5
				each international conference	10
				other meetings	3
		Training	A2	each national training program	8
				training on other levels	2
		Surveys and Observations	A3	each survey by leaders/experts at or above the sub-state level	15
				each survey by leaders at or above the provincial/ministerial level	5

Continued

Primary Indicators	Code	Secondary Indicators	Code	The Scoring Rule	Points
				each survey by leaders/ experts at other levels	2
				outbound visits for survey or observation	1
Media Influence of Think Tank	I	Newspaper Coverage	I1	central level	5
				provincial or ministerial level	4
				local level	3
				overseas media	2
				other media	1
		Television Coverage	I2	central level	5
				provincial or ministerial level	4
				local level	3
				overseas media	2
				other media	1
		Internet Coverage	I3	central level	5
				provincial or ministerial level	4
				local level	3
				overseas media	2
				other media	1

There are many ways to allocate the weight of indicators. MRPAI adopts direct assignment method, which is easy to understand, intuitive and open, and can be rechecked. The evaluated party can directly check whether the obtained value is accurate according to an established algorithm, which makes for effective dialogue between the evaluator and the evaluated. However, the requirements for evaluation are relatively high. Not only should the values assigned be reasonable, the assessment system also should guarantee precision. Otherwise it would be impossible to give timely response to the query of the evaluated party.

The Delphi Method was adopted for value assignment in Table 7. 1. Four rounds of expert surveys were conducted successively, with a total of 98 leaders and experts receiving the questionnaire. The following is a description of value assignment method.

The following circumstances have been taken into consideration when the values are assigned to the secondary MRPAI indicators in Table 7. 1:

① The structural assessment of think tanks from M1 to M4 only examines whether there are internal management institutions, without examining whether these institutions are functioning properly. This is compatible with the status quo of new think tanks in China. We will first see whether the internal institution exists or not, and then we will see whether it works properly or not when we measure it later. As a result, the value assigned is not high, with the full score being only 45 points. M5 is a special value assigned to what has been listed among China's Top Think Tanks, and this is a recognition of such prestige.

② R1 investigates the annual budget. Considering that the general size of Chinese think tanks is small with a normal annual budget being one million yuan, there is no need to differentiate between think tanks with an annual budget below one million. Twenty points are assigned to each of such think tanks, with one extra point for each additional sum of 100,000 yuan.

③ R2 and R3 consist of staff indicators and their values. We do not distinguish between full-time and part-time personnel because of the reform of personnel system, as part-time employees may also be full-time employees. Moreover, it would be hard to say if think tank experts are full-time or part-time since most of them have flexible work hours. In view of this, 40 points are assigned to each institution that has 10 or fewer researchers, with 2 extra points for each additional person. There will be 20 points for each administrative team with 5 or fewer persons, with one extra point for each additional person. With the increasing standardization of system data, this part of the data may need to provide corresponding certification materials in the future, and each think tank should prepare the recruitment contracts as soon as possible.

④ R4, or network resources, actually can also be considered as outcomes of think tank development. We see websites and other network resources as basic settings like work places. Since today's think tanks are not demanding when it comes to work places, there would be no way to verify whether they really have offices if they choose not to enter any data on this feature. Therefore, with respect to staff, funds, equipment and network resources, R4 focuses on network conditions while omitting measurement of physical working conditions. All these indicators are verifiable and feasible. Considering that most Chinese think tanks have not paid enough attention to website construction and are quite unfamiliar with the use of social media, value assignment to this indicator is only based on presence or absence, without considering the quality.

⑤ Among the P indicators, high values are assigned to internal reference reports, leaders' instructions and comments, as well as research reports. The experts questioned commonly believe that these are major indicators reflecting the decision-making influence of think tanks, and that the score should be increased. In fact, they also reflect the main purpose of building think tanks. The current points have been heightened according to experts' opinions. Since it is not easy for most provincial-level think tanks to obtain comments from state leaders, points for such comments from the leaders at the national level do not make much difference for the total points of common think tanks as most think tanks cannot get them. Such value assignment is relatively fair since MRPAI evaluation focuses on classification and sorting, comparing and ranking think tanks on the same levels. In order to encourage the writing of internal reference reports, values are assigned to any piece published in collections of such reports at or above the provincial or ministerial level (internally submitted serial publications), such as *Guangming Internal References*, with or without leaders' comments. The assignment of high values to the P6 indicator shows the special prestige of *People's Daily*, *Guangming Daily* and *Seeking Truth* in the Chinese system of policy discourse. Publishing articles in any of them means the expansion of influence on policy and the public.

⑥ The MRPAI evaluation indicator system has given think tanks' activities a relatively high status. High-level and high-caliber forums and conferences are important means for think tanks to exert their influence, and this is also a crucial feature that sets think tanks apart from traditional research institutions. Almost all of the world's famous think tanks are conference centers and major platforms for road shows of significant policies. As a result, high values are assigned to national or international conferences held by think tanks. There might be the undesirable practice of "erecting platforms and inviting celebrities", but this is only true for a very small number of think tanks. In addition to spreading information, conferences also become one of the major channels by which think tanks can extend their research and policy networks.

Survey and investigation are research methods with Chinese characteristics for think tanks. There is no right to speak without investigation and research, and big data analysis cannot replace field survey. Therefore, high values are assigned to this type of activity in the MRPAI indicators.

⑦ The focus of the I indicator is the media influence of a think tank. Whether it is at home or abroad, media influence has always been the focus of the think tank community. The citation rate of national or international newspapers, magazines, television and other media is also the most common public evaluation. This is because think tanks are different from traditional academic research institutions, as communication is as important as research for think tanks. Therefore, appearances or expressing opinions on television, newspapers, and the Internet are considered as important manifestations of think tanks' influence. At present, we only include the coverage disseminated in newspapers, television and on the Internet as the application and influence of these three media in think tank communication are more extensive and they also have certain quality guarantees. Different values are assigned according to different levels of reports, and as the central level is the most authoritative, it is assigned the highest value. The values are successively decreased as the level of the report decreases.

(3) MRPAI Evaluation System

MRPAI evaluation system is a back-end system of CTTI system. The MRPAI evaluation system involves a deep understanding of the MRPAI indicator system, value assignment, and ranking rules. An advanced ranking algorithm has been employed and some basic machine-learning functions have been included for real-time evaluation of source think tanks. The ranking of MRPAI evaluation system can be done comprehensively or according to different types.

In addition, the MRPAI evaluation system can be searched and is capable of statistical analysis of data. It can not only accurately pinpoint each think tank and expert, but also calculate the specific scores of the MRPAI indicators of each think tank and expert. In this way, the proportion between the scores of the source think tanks can be clearly analyzed, and it can reveal the strengths and weaknesses of the think tanks in management, resources, products, activities and other specific aspects, which is of great help to improve the management of think tanks.

CTTI system has set up a flexible, configurable and customized evaluation function—the points in the MRPAI indicators are in the form of adjustable parameters. In this way, after logging into the system, the evaluators (which may be think tank management departments, researchers or users with special needs) can choose their own data dimensions and invoke different algorithms according to the evaluation objectives and emphases, thus obtaining different personalized ranking results.

It should be noted that the MRPAI evaluation system is currently arranged in the background and cannot be consulted at the foreground for the time being, which can better protect the safety of institutions and experts' evaluation data and also shows respect to the privacy of experts. The CTTI project team will never disclose the detailed evaluation results to any third party without the consent of institutions and experts themselves.

(4) The Function of Subjective Evaluation

The CTTI evaluation is a multi-factor evaluation model, which includes dozens or even hundreds of factors, to maximize the authenticity of think tank evaluation. As for think tank evaluation, experts' subjective evaluation of think tanks is also an indispensable dimension. Therefore, CTTI system introduces experts' subjective evaluation on the basis of MRPAI algorithm.

The CTTI system has now included more than 10,000 experts, and these experts are all included in the think tank's resource pool of subjective evaluation. The CTTI system has developed a questionnaire survey function in the background. The list of think tanks to be evaluated and the dimensions of this evaluation will be sent in the form of questionnaire links to experts through e-mails. The experts could log into the system to score these think tanks. Then senior users or system administrators will make a comprehensive calculation of subjective evaluation results and objective quantitative evaluation results, and then make a complete comprehensive evaluation of these think tanks.

1.4　The Main Characteristics of CTTI System

CTTI's user groups include governments, enterprises and institutions, social organizations, etc. These users have a large number of policy research and consulting needs, but they may not know who the most appropriate solution provider is. And think tanks often cannot find the target customers, which limits the function of think tanks. One of the goals of CTTI is to solve this information asymmetry. As a "vertical search engine" (professional search) of a think tank, CTTI, supported by complete fields, displays the results of the query in a comprehensive way through multi-angle query. It realizes a three-dimensional display of think tank institutions from internal structure to external activities, from personnel composition to results release, and it realizes an intelligent analysis of all kinds of information of think tanks, so as to quickly and accurately retrieve target information, such as finding experts for topics and finding topics for specialists, thus eliminating "information asymmetry" between think tanks and users. The successful launch of CTTI has filled in the gaps in the data management and online evaluation tools in China's think tanks, provided basic data for the evaluation work of think tanks in our country, clarified the complicated work of the new type of think tank evaluation which includes organization evaluation, product evaluation, personnel evaluation and activity evaluation, and guided the work to become rational and objective. However, it should be pointed out that the purpose of CTTI evaluation is to serve source think tanks. We have always regarded selection, data collection and evaluation as the process of learning and communication from source think tanks. And the evaluation results are meant to provide some reference for source think tanks, management departments and academia.

At the same time, CTTI is not an imitation of a mature western product, but an independent innovation based on China's institutional advantages. It is embodied in the following aspects.

1.4.1 Design Concepts

1.4.1.1 Data Collection

CTTI has established a data collection mechanism for co-construction and sharing and attaches great importance to the objectivity and accuracy of data. At present, there are three ways for the system to collect data: ① relying on independent reporting by source think tanks and experts; ② manual collection by China Think Tank Research and Evaluation Center of Nanjing University; ③ automatic capture of online data. The first method is mainstream. The data are entered by the think tank administrator or experts themselves and submitted to CTTI background for review. Each piece of data cannot be submitted to the database until it is verified by the background. This kind of data collection mechanism seems labor-intensive. In fact, due to the adoption of the most popular "crowdsourcing" (crowdfunding) model, the data are jointly built and shared, and the data collection cost of data collection is shared among each participant, making it relatively low. However, due to the artificial mode, the accuracy and objectivity of the data are greatly enhanced. In order to reduce the situation in which the data is interfered, the impact value of each expert in each think tank of the CTTI is calculated automatically based on the data filled in except for a few fields filled in by the background administrators.

1.4.1.2 Functional Layout

CTTI has innovated a user-tiered service model. The CTTI users cover not only the policy research institutions of the party and government that need to use think tanks, the bureaus of civil affairs and publicity departments that are responsible for the registration and guidance of the think tank, internal users, such as think tank administrators and experts, but also academic publicity units like universities, media, research institutes, companies and other profit-making departments as well as the general public. CTTI has designed a layered service solution for different levels of users, providing targeted services. Users of different levels have access to the different levels and types of data. For example, various statistical icons and statistical tools are designed in consideration of the needs of the administration departments. In the aspect of data presentation and export, the needs of think tanks are fully taken into consideration. Think tanks and experts can easily manage and export data in CTTI. For example, in order to facilitate the risk emergency management for system administrators, CTTI provides the function of instantly closing all data of one think tank without affecting data of other think tanks. In this way, even if the data of an individual think tank is sensitive, there is no need to shut down the whole system.

1.4.2 Data System

CTTI has established a statistical indicator system and metadata standards for new types of think tanks with Chinese characteristics in a certain sense. After three periods of repeated investigations and starting from the actual needs of community members, users and think tank management departments, we have again expanded, reformed and improved the data system for all kinds of object fields, aiming at sharing the existing management systems with users to the greatest extent. For example, linking with the "National Information System for Research and Management of Humanities and Social Sciences in Colleges and Universities" would lay a foundation for the establishment of an internationally accepted industry data standard for think tanks in the future. At present, the CTTI system includes thousands of fields to achieve a comprehensive coverage of various attributes of the basic information, expert information, project information, product information, activity information and influence information of the think tank, and gives a three-dimensional portrait of each element of the think tank. These data fields can be used as metadata for the development of other think tank systems in the future.

1.4.3 Flexibility

CTTI system has considerable flexibility to deal with the complex characteristics of think tanks. One is flexible, configurable and customized evaluation. The algorithm of MRPAI evaluation system, which can independently assign value, enables time range, evaluation indicator and score weight to be configurable. Senior users, such as community members and think tank cloud members or system administrators, can automatically configure MRPAI algorithm according to actual needs. Second, the data dictionary can be dynamically expanded. Think tanks involve a great number of fields, and many fields have inaccurate and imperfect definitions in the construction process. Therefore, the extensibility of fields is of great significance to the maturity and perfection of the system and accurately and fully describing the think tank. CTTI Phase III system develops intelligent normalization function of think tank field data, which supports automatic extraction of the user's input of think tank dictionary and automatically converts qualified input text into mapped data dictionary according to mapping settings of administrators, thus realizing the dynamic expansion of data dictionary.

1.4.4 Security

CTTI system and data security of CTTI have reached the level of quasi-financial data security. In the deployment scheme, CTTI deploys the application server and the data server separately and adopts the internal and external network isolation scheme. Public network users can only access the application server and cannot directly access the data server, which ensures data security. In terms of communication protocol, CTTI uses https SSL encryption protocol of https to ensure that all request data is encrypted during transmission, preventing attackers from illegally accessing the system by intercepting the tampering with the request content. Due to the large amount of data collected by CTTI, in order to prevent the system data from being easily stolen, CTTI has also made a corresponding design in the aspect of anti-theft network, adopting B/S architecture and scientific permission setting as well as role allocation to ensure the availability and controllability of information. Generally, visitors can only query the most basic data in the access system and cannot see the complete picture of the system.

After years of construction and upgrading, CTTI has now developed into an integrated information management system integrating the functions of think tank retrieval, think tank data management and online intelligent evaluation. With the increasing influence of CTTI at home and abroad as well as the increase of think tank community members and think tank clouds, the system data increment will surely usher in a stage of rapid development. At that time, with the resources of the academic community composed of more than 10,000 experts and together with the objective and quantitative evaluation function that can be customized flexibly, CTTI will become an important tool with retrieval, management and evaluation functions in the think tank community, helping the construction of new types of Chinese think tanks to move forward.

2. Certificate Renewal of Source Think Tanks and Addition of New CTTI Think Tanks in 2019

2.1 Certificate Replacement of CTTI Source Think Tanks

Since the first batch of source think tanks of "Chinese Think Tank Index" (CTTI) was released in December 2016, our center has recorded 706 source think tanks by December 2018 after two times of addition in 2017 and 2018. For the think tanks officially selected in the list of source think tanks, our center and Think Tank Research and Release Center of Guangming Daily jointly issued credentials. It is worth noting that the catalogue of CTTI source think tanks is a dynamic system and will be partially adjusted after a certain period of time, whose adjustment is based on the timeliness of data update. The validity of the certificates (from January 2017 to December 2018) of the first batch of source think tanks (selected in 2016) and additional think tanks (added in 2017) expired. Therefore, the center launched certificate renewal of CTTI source tank in March 2019. After four months' contact and communication with various source think tanks, we had received 207 copies of *Basic Information Form for CTTI Source Think Tank Certificate Renewal* by July 2019. After audit, all 207 think tanks could actively fill in data to CTTI, which fully ensured the timeliness and integrity of CTTI data. Then, plaques were issued to these think tanks in September 2019 by mail, whose period of validity was from January 1, 2019 to December 31, 2022, as shown in Figure 8.1.

Fig. 8. 1   Plaque of CTTI Source Think Tank

2.2   Addition to Catalogue of CTTI Source Think Tanks in 2019

New types of think tanks with Chinese characteristics are an important part of the national governance system, and the construction of modern think tanks is in the ascendant. Insisting on the nonprofit nature of CTTI, Nanjing University and Guangming Daily Group are committed to promoting the construction of a new type of Chinese think tank community that is jointly built and shared, and serving the modernization construction of national governance system and governance capacity. In order to enable the CTTI source think tank catalogue to more accurately reflect the development trend of new think tanks, it is decided through research to start the 2019 addition work of CTTI source think tanks. The method of voluntary application by think tanks, data submission, expert review and diagnostic research is still used to strictly control the quality of supplemental think tanks and strictly implement their selection procedures and requirements.

2.2.1 Requirements for Addition

Adhere to the same standards that were applied to the selection of the first batch of think tanks, and think tanks that expect to be added will be considered in terms of the following seven aspects, as shown in table 8.1, with particular focus on whether they operate as substantial entities and whether they are highly capable of policy research and advice as indicated by successful products. Those that have been identified by provinces, cities, ministries and commissions as provincial and ministerial-level key think tanks and think tanks for priority development (policy research bases) are preferred.

Table 8.1   Benchmarks for the Selection of Source Think Tanks

	Details	Quantitative Indicator
Political Requirement	Compliance with state laws and regulations	
Academic Foundation	Full-time think tank researchers have published papers in academic journals in the past two years	In the past two years, each full-time researcher has published at least one paper in any CSSCI source journal, *People Daily*, or the theoretical edition of *Guangming Daily*
Area of Research	Having a long-studied area for decision-making consultation with distinct characteristic	
Form of Organization	A relatively stable and well-regulated research entity	Having official documents of approval for establishment or other documentary evidence
	A sound management structure	Having articles of association and such organization as a board of directors and an academic committee

Continued

	Details	Quantitative Indicator
Support in Resources	A certain number of full-time/ part-time researchers and administrators	Having one or two pacesetters, at least five full-time researchers, and at least five part-time researchers and research assistants
	Guaranteed and sustainable source of funds	At least 300,000 yuan of annual funds
	Fixed work place and basic equipment	An independent office with a size of at least 50 m²
Operation and Products	Regular research, consultation and meetings	Holding at least three events per year
	Submission of research products	Officially releasing (or submitting to users) at least three research reports and three journal articles per year
	Website and new media	Having an independent website and a new media public account in WeChat or Weibo
	Serial publications	Having such printed or electronic publications as periodicals and internal references
International Cooperation and Exchange	Qualified for international cooperation and exchange with certain international impact	

2.2.2 Rules of Addition

The think tanks of a university can be recommended by the university's research supervision department or by themselves. In the latter case, they should still obtain approval from that department. We have limited the number of CTTI source think tanks from each college or university in order to ensure fairness in the assessment of source think tanks. However, such restrictions are not applicable to strong and highly active university think tanks that have distinct characteristics, abundant products, and flexible mechanisms. Besides, for regions, categories and policy areas in which smaller numbers of think tanks have been selected, we will give them full consideration and an appropriate measure of preference during the adding process.

2.2.3   Addition Procedures

i) Think tanks expecting to be added should fill out the application form

ii) Qualification Review

iii) Create CTTI accounts for think tanks that are up to the standard

iv) Think tanks that have passed the primary selection fill in the data

v) Data review

vi) Screen out the think tanks up to the CTTI criteria for the quality and quantity of data

vii) CTTI expert panel review

viii) Announce the addition list and issue the CTTI source think tank certificate.

2.2.4   Process of Adding Think Tanks

The adding process was officially initiated when the CTTI team issued "2019 Notice on the Addition of CTTI Source Think Tanks" on the official website (https://cttrec.nju.edu.cn/) on September 16, 2019. Think tanks expecting to be added were required to fill out "2019 CTTI Source Think Tank Addition Application Form" and provide their evidentiary materials. The application form focuses on the institutional level, policy research field, human and financial resources, flagship achievements and activities, and the recommendation of the scientific research management department of the competent or parent unit, which can comprehensively investigate the operation of think tanks. The adding efforts of source think tanks received strong support from think tanks and research management departments. Scientific research departments of universities, such as Wuhan University, South

China University of Science and Technology, Southwest University, and Shaanxi Normal University, planned properly, carried out publicity, organization, screening and submitted application forms to the CTTI Addition Work Group with the university as a unit. By October 20, 2019, the working team had received 371 electronic and paper materials. The CTTREC of Nanjing University and the TTRRC of Guangming Daily made an initial selection of 133 qualified think tanks after joint surveys, discussions and reviews. Many think tanks were not selected because of their insufficient attributes. The main reasons were the insufficient number of researchers, too few internal reference and instructions, lack of policy research areas, and only academic achievements being included.

After the primary selection, the Work Group issued the account number and password of CTTI to the primary think tanks and sent a letter to invite the primary think tanks to collect data. The quantity and quality of filled data are not only one of the important bases for the secondary evaluation, but also the important basis for each think tank to use CTTI for data self-management in the future. Therefore, most think tanks attach great importance to them and are carefully filled in with data. At the same time, in the face of the massive data submitted by hundreds of think tanks, a number of staff of our center were organized to audit the data one by one in the background of CTTI, ensuring the rationality, effectiveness and correctness of the data. Thanks to efforts from all quarters, by November 30, 2019, these think tanks had entered large amounts of precious data, including organizations, experts, activities and products in a responsive and meticulous manner, which gave strong support to the CTTI addition efforts.

As soon as data collection was over, the Work Group organized a team of experts for a second evaluation of the think tanks that had attended the primary selection, based on the data they filled in, their application forms and the survey results, by the standard of how scientific and complete the data were and the corresponding competitiveness. 3 think tanks, which had failed to provide adequate and valid data for expert review, would be excluded from the addition list by the work group.

Through the above work, it is finally determined that 130 CTTI think tanks have been added this year, with a passing rate of 35%. Such an addition process with a high standard and strict requirement helps powerful think tanks to stand out and be added successfully and ensures that the quality of CTTI source think tanks always remains at a high level. According to the types of think tanks, 119 think tanks of universities, 2 think tanks of party and government departments, 2 think tanks of scientific research institutes, 2 think tanks of media, 2 think tanks of enterprises, 2 think tanks of society and 1 think tank of administrative college of Party school have been added; according to the level of institutions, there are 4 national high-end (high-end cultivation) think tanks, and 59 think tanks at provincial and ministerial levels (preferential cultivation), 1 key research base of philosophy and society of the Ministry of Education, and 8 national research bases of the Ministry of Education.

On the other hand, Tianjin Federation of Social Science (TFSS), Nanjing University and Guangming Daily have been in strategic cooperation since 2016. In accordance with the three-party strategic cooperation agreement, the 2019 addition of CTTI source think tanks in Tianjin was organized and implemented by TFSS. The three phases of data reporting, addition reporting and addition review have got positive response from think tanks and superior supervisory units in Tianjin. TFSS launched the work of CTTI-TJ data reporting in the second half of 2019. By the end of November, think tanks in Tianjin had rigorously and meticulously entered a large amount of data of their basic information, experts, activities, products, etc., strongly supporting the follow-up addition review work. Based on it, TFSS, in accordance with the addition requirements of CTTI source think tanks and the actual situation of Tianjin, determined the principles of the addition application and carried out the work of addition application. By the end of the application work, a total of almost 30 application forms from 9 units had been received, covering the major universities and social think tanks in Tianjin. After formal review, preliminary approval, and modification, candidate think tanks were selected to participate in the addition review. In order to ensure the fairness and impartiality of the addition review, TFSS has repeatedly deliberated and formulated a detailed review plan. Through the qualification review, quantitative scoring, and MRPAI scoring, the top 12 think tanks are recommended as CTTI source think tanks after discussion in the meeting.

Finally, there are 848 existing official think tanks on the list of CTTI source think tanks, including 706 original source think tanks, 130 source think tanks added this year, and 12 think tanks recommended by Tianjin.

2.2.5 Features of Newly-Added Think Tanks

This year's work of adding think tanks has received warm response from all walks of life, and the number of application forms for addition is the highest in the past years. Compared with previous years, this year's newly-added think tanks have the following distinctive characteristics:

First, excellent academic foundation. It is estimated that 8. 6 national scientific research projects and 19. 4 provincial and ministerial scientific research projects have been completed, and 9. 9 monographs and 53. 9 CSSCI source journals have been written by newly-added source think tanks on average in the past three years. Without doubt, there are contributions of university think tanks. At the same time, it is glad to find that non-university think tanks attach great importance to the value of academic research in think tank construction. For example, Energy Development Research Institute of China Southern Power Grid Co. , Ltd. has 29 projects at provincial and ministerial level or above, 4 monographs and 9 high-quality papers in recent three years. However, how to combine the theoretical research with the application research of countermeasures to produce the research results with strong rationality and high practical value are still worthy of consideration.

Second, establish for a long time. According to statistics, 22 new think tanks have existed for 5 – 8 years, 28 for 8 – 15 years, and 11 for more than 15 years. Most of these think tanks with a long history are university think tanks and research institute think tanks, which have been deeply involved in a specific field for a long time and accumulated rich research resources to play an important role in specific policy research fields. For example, Yunnan Institute of Environmental Science founded in 1976 takes "support decision-making and serve society" as its mission, and forms professional advantages in water pollution prevention and control, air and soil environment protection, ecological protection and restoration, heavy metal pollution prevention and control, environmental planning, coping with climate change and other fields, and some of research results reaches the advanced level in China.

Third, strong consultation ability. It is estimated that 19.5 internal references have been written and 8.0 written instructions or comments at provincial and ministerial level and above have been obtained by newly-added think tanks on average in three years. Although a few think tanks have improved the average value by their own efforts, for example, the Institute of International Studies, Fudan University writes 232 internal references and obtains 33 written instructions or comments at provincial and ministerial level or above, the average value can still prove that newly-added think tanks are powerful and fruitful, which play an important role in CTTI source think tanks.

Fourth, a wide range of influence. On the one hand, according to statistics, the newly-added think tanks have hosted or undertaken nearly ten national or provincial and ministerial meetings on average in the past three years, which shows that these think tanks have certain charisma and influence in the domestic industries and are committed to building a platform for learning and communicating among peers. On the other hand, 41 of the newly-added think tanks have joined the think tank alliance, which indicates that a think tank community of positive interaction is forming in China. Moreover, a few think tanks have joined international think tank alliances. For example, the Development Research Center of the State Administration for Market Regulation has joined " the Belt and Road " international think tank cooperation alliance, and the Institute of Overseas Chinese, Huaqiao University has joined the Indonesia research alliance. They tell China's stories on the international stage, which reflects new types of think tanks with Chinese characteristics play an important role in the public diplomacy.

2.3   Information Perspective of CTTI Source Think Tanks after Addition

2.3.1   Regional Distribution of CTTI Source Think Tanks

Firstly, the regional distribution of the CTTI source think tanks is shown in Fig. 8. 2, according to the administrative division of China. Overall, North China and East China show a noticeable superiority in number. Source think tanks in these two regions account for more than a half of all the selected think tanks. North China has 305 selected think tanks, accounting for 36. 0% of all the selected organizations; East China followed closely, owning 227, accounting for 26. 8%; ranking the third,

Central China has 87, accounting for 10. 3%; the distribution of source think tanks is relatively even in other regions. In the addition work in 2019, the reserve forces of think tanks in East China and North China are sufficient, once again expanding the quantitative advantage; think tanks in South China University of Technology, Guangdong University of Foreign Studies and Jinan University in Guangdong Province are successfully added, and the proportion of think tanks in South China is increased significantly from 5. 92% in 2018 to 7. 4%, jumping from the seventh in 2018 to the fourth.

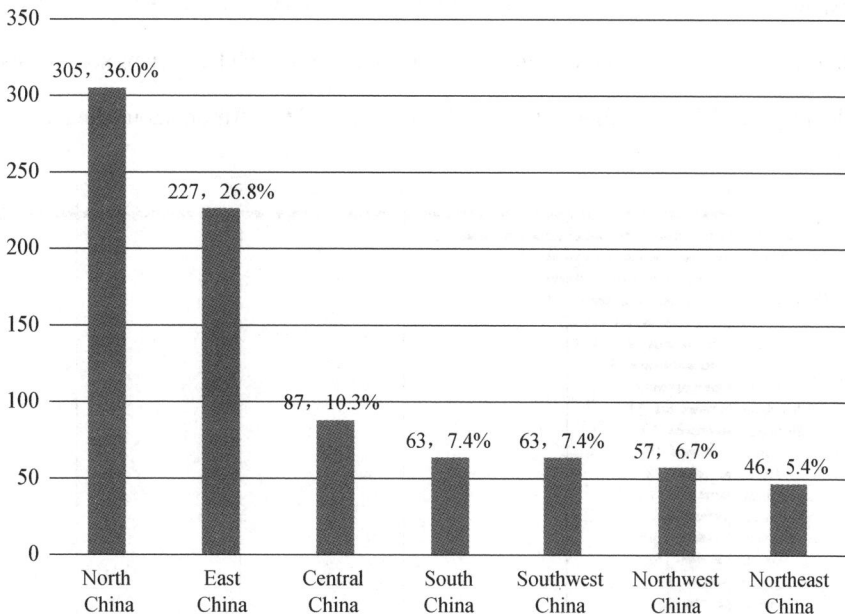

Fig. 8. 2   Regional Distribution of the CTTI Source Think Tanks

Secondly, as is shown in Fig. 8. 3, compared with previous years, the regional distribution of the top 4 source think tanks is basically unchanged, still in Beijing, Shanghai, Tianjin, and Jiangsu. Among them, a total of 197 think tanks were selected in Beijing, and the number of newly-added think tanks ranked the first of all provinces in 2019. Now there are 219 source think tanks in Beijing, further consolidating its top position. This is inseparable from Beijing's special political, economic and cultural status. The rankings of Shanghai, Tianjin and Jiangsu closely followed. Hunan Province ranked sixth from the previous fifth place, and Guangdong Province ranked in the top five. This is related to South China University of Technology and Guangdong University of Foreign Studies mentioned above. In 2019, 20 source think tanks were added in Guangdong, which achieved a breakthrough in quantity. At the same time, Hubei, Shaanxi, Zhejiang and Chongqing also continued to expand their think tanks, with the number of selected think tanks reaching more than 20. In addition, think tanks in Shandong, Jilin, Hebei, Jiangxi, Yunnan, Heilongjiang, Fujian, Anhui, Hainan, Henan, and Tibet Autonomous Region were

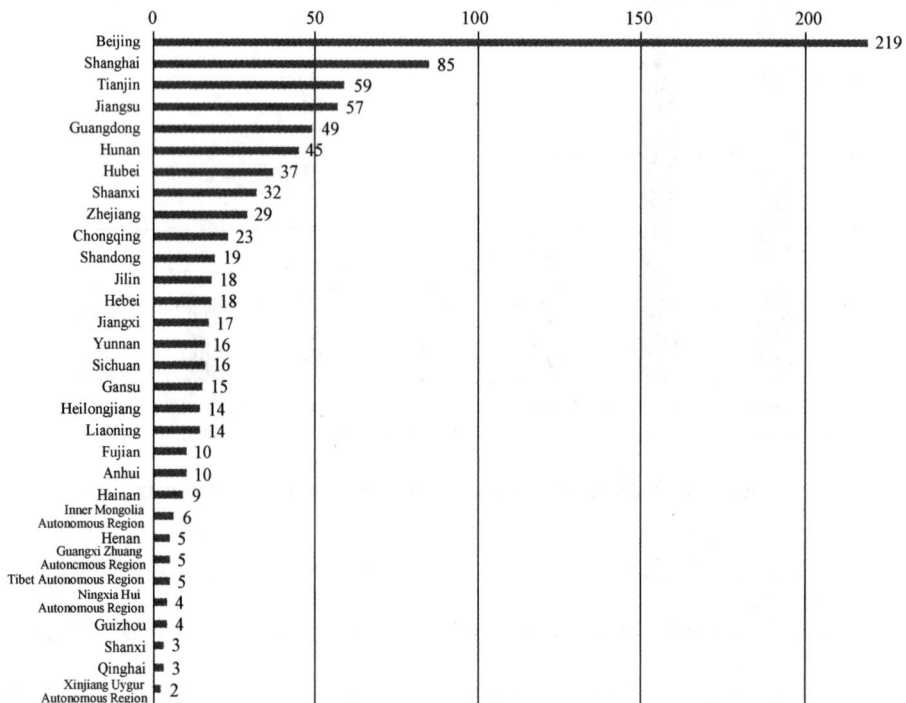

Fig. 8.3 Distribution of the CTTI Source Think Tanks by Province (Region/City)

added in 2019, so the number of think tanks increased to some extent. There were no newly-added think tanks in Sichuan, Gansu, Liaoning, Inner Mongolia Autonomous Region, Guangxi Zhuang Autonomous Region, Ningxia Hui Autonomous Region, Guizhou, Shanxi, Qinghai and Xinjiang Uygur Autonomous Region, so the number of think tanks is the same as last year. Obviously, there are many higher-level universities in provinces with more think tanks, while there are some deficiencies in the number and quality of universities in provinces with less think tanks. That is to say, although this map is the distribution map of source think tanks, it also reflects the distribution of science and education resources.

2.3.2   Distribution Analysis of CTTI Source Think Tanks by Type

According to Fig. 8.4, the university think tank is still the most important type in the source think tank, with a total of 572 and accounting for 67%. There are

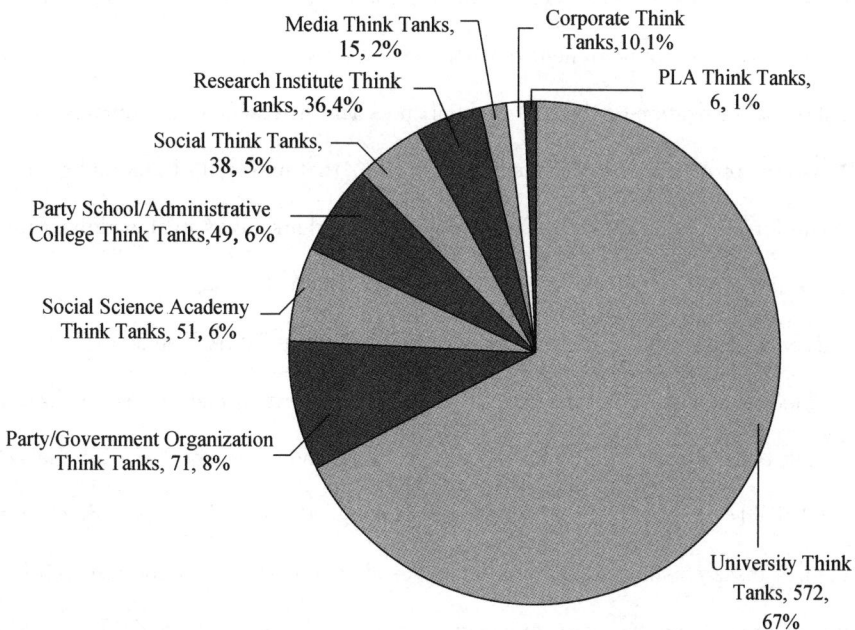

Fig. 8.4   Distribution of CTTI Source Think Tanks by Type

71 (8%) think tanks in Party or government organizations, 51 (6%) in academies of social sciences, 49 (6%) in Party schools or administrative colleges, 38 (5%) society think tanks, 36 (4%) in research institutions, 15 (2%) media think tanks, 10 (1%) corporate think tanks, and 6 (1%) in the armed forces.

From the overall distribution of think tank types, the proportion of all kinds of think tanks has hardly changed much. Compared with last year, only the proportion of university think tanks has increased, from 62% to 67%. As mentioned above, university think tanks are the main force of newly-added source think tanks in 2019. South China University of Technology, Guangdong University of Foreign Studies and Wuhan University all have more than 5 newly-added source think tanks, once again expanding the group of university think tanks. Compared with university think tanks, the proportion of social think tanks, media think tanks, enterprise think tanks and military think tanks remains unchanged, and the number of newly-added think tanks in 2019 of party and government departments, the Academy of Social Sciences, the school of administration or the party school and scientific research institutes is small in 2019, so the proportion has declined. This reflects that university think tanks are still the main force of think tanks in China, followed by think tanks in the administrative system, and private think tanks are still members of small groups.

2.3.3 Research Field Analysis of CTTI Source Think Tanks

The direction of think tank development is specialization and professionalization, and think tank research's division of labor is more and more detailed. By analyzing research fields of source think tanks and ranking research fields according to the number of research subjects of think tanks, as shown in Fig. 8.2, the research fields of source think tanks are very extensive, involving 53 research fields. It should be noted that these source think tanks include not only think tanks researching in a

Table 8. 2 Research Fields of CTTI Source Think Tanks

	Party/ Government Organization Think Tanks	Social Science Academy Think Tanks	Party School/ Administrative College Think Tanks	University Think Tanks	PLA Think Tanks	Research Institute Think Tanks	Corporate Think Tanks	Social Think Tanks	Media Think Tanks	Summary
Industrial Policy	15	25	7	121	0	10	5	15	4	202
Financial Policy	14	21	8	98	0	3	2	13	4	163
Cultural Policy	6	23	8	90	0	1	1	9	6	146
Fiscal policy	17	14	7	69	0	4	3	11	3	128
Market Policy	8	16	6	62	0	3	4	9	4	112
Diplomatic Policy	3	8	2	78	1	1	1	11	2	107
Social Security Policy	11	21	5	45	0	1	0	6	1	90
Science and Technology Policy	6	5	3	41	1	18	3	9	3	89
Social Construction and Social Policy	4	4	7	63	0	1	0	4	2	85
Judicial Policy	4	11	2	59	0	1	1	2	2	82
Resource Policy	8	7	4	48	0	6	1	5	2	81

Continued

	Party/ Government Organization Think Tanks	Social Science Academy Think Tanks	Party School/ Administrative College Think Tanks	University Think Tanks	PLA Think Tanks	Research Institute Think Tanks	Corporate Think Tanks	Social Think Tanks	Media Think Tanks	Summary
Foreign Trade Policy	8	8	2	50	0	1	2	7	1	79
Agricultural Policy	5	18	4	41	0	5	1	3	1	78
Environmental Policy	8	6	3	47	0	5	1	4	1	75
Security Policy	2	3	0	57	2	0	1	5	0	70
Ideological Policy	2	12	21	29	0	0	1	1	1	69
Urban and Rural Construction Policy	5	12	2	34	0	3	0	7	1	64
Party Building Policy	4	8	34	18	0	0	0	0	0	64
Population Policy	6	13	3	36	0	2	0	3	0	63
Higher Education Policy	4	2	0	51	0	1	1	2	1	62

Continued

	Party/Government Organization Think Tanks	Social Science Academy Think Tanks	Party School/Administrative College Think Tanks	University Think Tanks	PLA Think Tanks	Research Institute Think Tanks	Corporate Think Tanks	Social Think Tanks	Media Think Tanks	Summary
Ethnic Policy	0	7	4	41	0	0	0	4	0	58
Internet Management Policy	1	3	3	34	0	2	4	5	4	56
Employment Policy	7	12	5	25	0	0	1	3	3	56
Service Industry Policy	4	8	1	23	0	3	2	7	2	50
Energy Policy	6	4	0	30	0	3	3	3	1	50
Consumption Policy	4	8	1	27	0	0	1	4	2	47
Industrial Policy	4	10	0	22	0	3	1	4	1	45
Religious Policy	1	8	2	28	0	0	0	3	1	45
Network Security Policy	1	2	3	25	0	3	1	3	2	40
Basic Education Policy	5	2	0	25	0	1	1	4	1	39
Labor Policy	3	8	2	21	0	0	0	3	1	38

Continued

	Party/ Government Organization Think Tanks	Social Science Academy Think Tanks	Party School/ Administrative College Think Tanks	University Think Tanks	PLA Think Tanks	Research Institute Think Tanks	Corporate Think Tanks	Social Think Tanks	Media Think Tanks	Summary
Health Care Policy	6	5	2	20	0	1	1	2	1	38
High-End Manufacturing Policy	6	6	1	15	0	4	0	5	0	37
Housing Policy	1	8	2	16	0	1	1	5	0	34
Civil Administration Policy	4	6	3	17	0	1	0	0	0	31
Marine Policy	4	1	0	16	0	4	0	5	0	30
Transport Policy	2	2	0	19	0	1	0	3	1	28
National Defense Policy	0	2	1	14	4	0	0	4	0	25
Press Policy	1	2	0	14	0	0	0	0	8	25
Forestry Policy	1	4	0	11	0	3	1	1	1	22
Military Policy	0	0	0	8	5	0	0	2	0	15
Personnel Policy	2	3	2	8	0	0	0	0	0	15

Continued

	Party/Government Organization Think Tanks	Social Science Academy Think Tanks	Party School/Administrative College Think Tanks	University Think Tanks	PLA Think Tanks	Research Institute Think Tanks	Corporate Think Tanks	Social Think Tanks	Media Think Tanks	Summary
Health Policy	1	3	0	7	0	1	1	0	1	14
Publishing Policy	2	1	0	8	0	0	0	1	1	13
Food Policy	2	2	0	8	0	0	0	0	0	12
Hong Kong, Macao and Taiwan policies	0	0	1	8	0	0	0	3	0	12
Radio and Television Policy	1	2	0	7	0	1	0	0	1	12
Water Policy	0	2	0	3	0	3	0	2	0	10
Supervision Policy	1	0	1	8	0	0	0	0	0	10
United Front Policy	2	1	2	4	0	0	0	1	0	10
Audit Policy	1	3	1	4	0	0	0	0	0	9
Drug Policy	0	1	0	4	0	2	0	0	0	7
Public Security Policy	2	0	0	4	0	0	0	0	0	6

specific filed but also think tanks researching in multiple fields. Industrial policy, financial policy, cultural policy, fiscal policy, market policy and diplomatic policy are relatively popular research fields, and more than 100 think tanks focus on these field, each of which reflects the research power of different types of think tanks. This shows that most of the source think tanks pay much attention to major issues' such as economy, culture and diplomacy, which are obviously related to the development of China's national conditions: taking economic construction as the center is the foundation of the country and the fundamental requirement of the country's prosperity and long-term stability; culture, especially ideology, is the soul of a country and a people, so we should strengthen cultural self-confidence; with the improvement of China's international status, we need to tell Chinese stories well to the outside world. Moreover, social security policy, science and technology policy, social construction and social policy, judicial policy, resource policy, foreign trade policy, agricultural policy, environmental policy and security policy have also attracted the attention of more think tanks. But there are few think tanks studying water conservancy policy, supervision policy, united front policy, audit policy, drug policy and public security policy. The development of think tanks of different fields is not sufficient, and the level of policy research in these industries will not be improved. For example, a film about drugs exposed the problem of the high price of imported drugs and promoted the revision of the *Drug Administration Law*, which to a certain extent reflects the lack of attention and influence of think tanks on drug policies. Therefore, the construction of think tanks in some important fields still needs to be strengthened.

According to the types of think tanks, university think tanks have a large number of intellectual resources by virtue of their disciplinary and professional advantages and have different degrees of research on various policies. In contrast, military think tanks mainly focus on military policy, national defense policy, security policy, diplomatic policy, science and technology policy and other research fields, and the research of think tanks gradually shows the characteristics of refinement. Think tanks, such as enterprise think tanks, social think tanks and media think tanks, are involved in most research fields except a few fields, such as party building policy, supervision policy, and public security policy, which reflects the universality and diversity of think tank research.

3. Features of the Human Resources of Source Think Tanks

3.1 General Introduction of the Human Resources of Source Think Tanks

Intellectual resources are the most precious resources of a country and a nation and the most important resources to build think tanks. John Thornton, former chairman of the board of the Brookings Institution, said, "The success of any think tank depends first and foremost on the capability of the experts it has. " Think tanks rest on wisdom, which in turn counts on best experts, first-class and efficient research teams and researchers from diverse backgrounds. The personnel include both leading figures and outstanding talents, providing authoritative, scientific and constructive opinions for decision-making and consultations and promoting the researches of think tanks, and stable operating teams, ensuring that the daily work of think tanks is effectively carried out.

Table 9. 1 Types of Personnel and Their Educational Backgrounds in CTTI

The average number of people in each think tank	Full-/Part- time	Types of personnel	Educational backgrounds	Proportions
14. 3	Full-time	Researchers	Doctor	78%
			Master	14%
2. 4	Part-time		Bachelor	7%
			Others	1%
0. 9	Full-time	Administrative staff	/	

According to the background data of CTTI, as shown in Fig. 9. 1, CTTI includes two types of think-tank personnel—administrative staff and researchers (or experts). And the researchers include both full-time and part-time ones.

As shown in the table above, each think tank has on average 14. 3 full-time researchers and 2. 4 part-time researchers. In terms of educational backgrounds, researchers with doctoral, master's, bachelor's and other degrees account for 78%, 14%, 7%, and 1% respectively. The distribution of educational backgrounds forms an inverted pyramid. On the one hand, this indicates that most experts from the source think tanks have received long-term and systematic academic training, enjoy salient advantage in terms of intelligence and are dedicated to professional research fields, who are capable to provide stable and continuous intellectual support for the think tanks to play their role. On the other hand, this implies that many university think tanks have high requirements for the academic qualification of researchers. In the research process, however, many preliminary works, such as information collection, questionnaires, and data analysis can be done by people without a doctoral degree. The distribution of educational backgrounds of a research team should resemble a pyramid, just like many well-known foreign think tanks, whose senior researchers have several research assistants to carry out basic works. In this way, human resources are rationally allocated to improve utilization efficiency of personnel. Therefore, by comparison, it can be said that the source think tanks have overstressed the importance of academic qualifications of researchers and ignored the significance of maintaining a proper talent ratio, thus causing the problem of waste of talents to some extent.

As the table above indicates, each source think tank has only 0. 9 full-time administrative staff on average. This is probably because many think tanks have not filled in the information of their administrative staff or have not included them all. The actual number might be a little bit larger. Given that the number is so small, the information of their educational backgrounds will not be compiled here. In the United States, the ratio of administrative staff to researchers in think tanks is about three to one, whereas in China, the opposite is true—the number of administrative workers is much smaller than that of researchers. This has made administrative workers too busy to do any non-research work. It is worth noting that the strength of administrative workers in think tanks cannot be underestimated. Only by employing a certain number of professional administrative workers can a think tank carry out internal operation and management and engage in external communication and publicity. In the CTTI system, a total number of 49 full-time administrative workers from Center for China and Globalization have been included. Based on reasonable division of labor, they are in charge of financing, operation, new media, etc. to maintain the sound operation of Center for China and Globalization, and enable think tanks to play their role in China and the world at large.

3.2   Analysis of Research Fields of the Specialists

As shown in Table 9. 1, the specialists have altogether 13 research fields. Two thirds of them are from economics, law and management, accounting for 26%, 23% and 17% respectively. Humanities and engineering each account for 7%, history and philosophy each 5%, and pedagogy, natural science, medical science, arts, agronomy, and military science all account for less than 5%. It can be said that the divisions of disciplines of these specialists are rather concentrated, with humanities and social sciences taking up the main part while natural sciences and studies of cutting-edge technologies occupying a small part. In other words, the majority of the think tanks' specialists are scholars of humanities, and technology-driven researches of the think tanks and sci-tech problems would be hard to deal with. This will lead to the lack of research findings in terms of both quantity and quality in the corresponding policy study areas, which doesn't fit into the background of revitalizing the country through science and technology. The good news is that searching "blockchain" in CTTI, 13 records of activities and 59 records of achievements would come out. Blockchain is a novel concept, which does not exist in the research field. But the search results indicate that some specialists can sensitively find hot topics, free themselves from the restraint of their study fields, and conduct timely interdisciplinary and multi-industry researches. Doubtlessly, it is very important for specialists of think tanks to do more researches in their fields. At the same time,

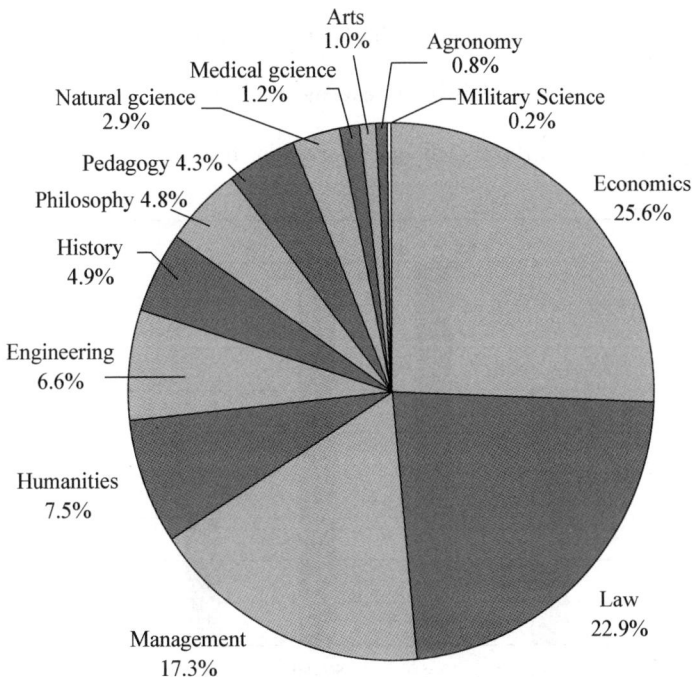

Fig. 9. 1   Research Fields of the Source Think Tanks' Specialists

however, they must also follow closely the current events, pay attention to the latest research trends, and work as governments' eyes and ears, vanguards and advisers.

3.3   Analysis of Ages of the Specialists

After the filling and submitting of data in 2019, CTTI has included 14,241 specialists. Of the 13,802 specialists whose data are valid, information of ages has been compiled, as shown in Table 9.2. Their ages are, on the whole, normally distributed, with an average age of 48.3. The number of specialists at the age between 40 and 50 is the largest, accounting for about one-third, followed by those at the age between 50 and 60, accounting for about 30.6%. There are also a certain number of specialists at the age between 30 and 40 or between 60 and 70. Specialists under 30 or above 70 are small in number, which is similar to that of the think tanks in other countries. In the United States, most of the experts in think tanks are university professors or officials who once served in the governments and are about 50

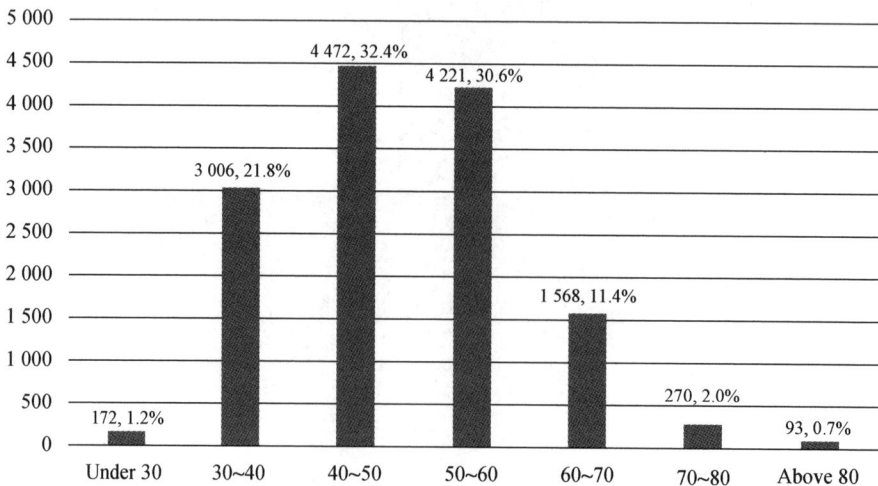

Fig. 9. 2   Ages of the Source Think Tanks' Specialists

years old. On the one hand, think tank researchers need to have some social experience to think, to have insights on major issues in economic and social development and to carry out strategic, forward-looking and comprehensive research. On the other hand, increase in age means accumulation of interpersonal network, which can help to broaden channels and ways of think tank services and shorten the time for research results to enter decision-making. Therefore, middle-aged experts are the backbone of think tanks. Of course, as the mainstay of the future, young experts, with profound knowledge, huge potential, and readier reaction to new things and current events, are also an important part of researches.

4. Analysis on Output Database of CTTI Source Think Tanks

By December 6th, 2019, CTTI has included 848 institutions, 142,943 achievements and 23,907 events. This means that the system has covered various types and a large amount of think tank data, which on the whole can meet scholars' different needs and uses of think tank information retrieval.

4.1 Analysis on Product Database of CTTI Source Think Tanks

4.1.1 Overall Analysis on Product Database of Source Think Tanks

According to the statistics of all the data in each sub-database of CTTI, we found that the product database contains the largest volume of information, covering products of the greatest number of types and fields. Among them, 69,469 papers make up nearly half the volume of the whole product database. It is followed by projects, newspaper articles, single internal references and reports, accounting for 17.83%, 9.32%, 7.60% and 7.32% respectively (as shown in Fig. 10.1), which in total represent 90.67% of all the data. It can be concluded that the products of think tanks are still presented in the most mainstream way and in relatively fixed but abundant forms.

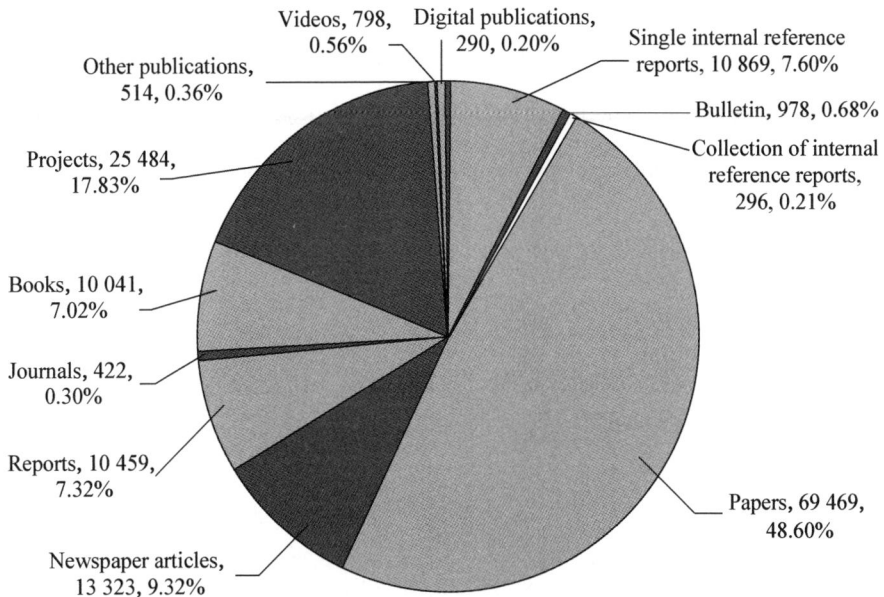

Fig. 10. 1   Product Types of Source Think Tanks

4.1.2   Detailed Analysis on Product Database of Source Think Tanks

At present, CTTI has 13 think tank products. In the following section, a detailed analysis will be made on five major products, namely, papers, single internal references, projects, reports, as well as newspaper articles.

4.1.2.1   Analysis on Papers in Product Database

Papers have always been the main product of source think tanks. In this section, we will review all the data on papers in CTTI and analyze them in detail according to the distribution of types, levels, disciplines and the geographical locations of issuing institutes. Since a paper may be included in different core journal catalogues at the same time, we only count the number of papers included in each core journal catalog.

According to the distribution of paper types, 97. 11% of these papers are journal publications, and the rest are conference proceedings and academic theses, accounting for 2. 53% and 0. 36% respectively (as shown in Fig. 10. 2). The great proportion of journal publications means that most experts tend to present their results in the form of journal publications. The activities of scholars to promote the exchange of think tanks in the form of conference papers are still relatively small.

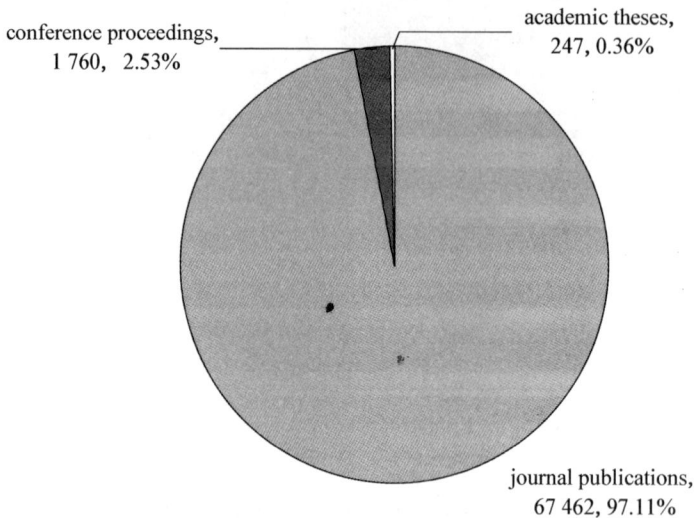

Fig. 10. 2   Paper Types of Source Think Tanks

According to the distribution of paper levels, CSSCI has the largest number of papers included, accounting for 54. 04%, more than half of all the papers. It is followed by papers published in general journals, which stand at 36. 53%, and in SCI, SSCI and EI, which make up 1% to 5% (as shown in Fig. 10. 3). Compared with the statistical results of papers in source think tanks of 2018, the number of papers from CSSCI, SCI and SSCI has increased. Thus, it should be recognized that source think tanks have laid a solid foundation for and shown great strength in academic research and fundamental theoretical research. But it also reveals that the evaluation of scierslific research level of think tanks in China is still based on papers and awards, the pheromenon of comment on papers by publications still exists, and the work of "breaking five only" is still the key to speed up the construction of quality-oriented acoolemic evaluation governance system.

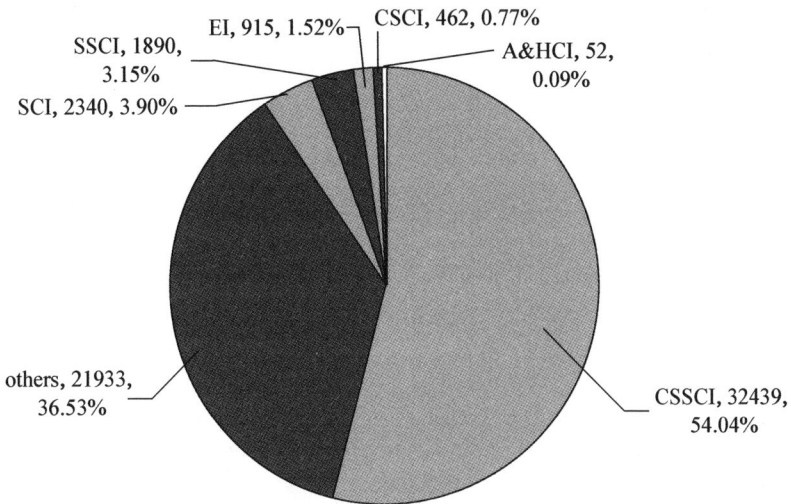

Fig. 10. 3   Paper Levels of Source Think Tanks

Two conclusions can be made as to the distribution of paper disciplines. First, the field of disciplines is relatively concentrated. Most of the published papers of source think tanks concern disciplines such as management, economics, law, education and politics, with more than 1,000 papers, accounting for over 65. 7%, coming from the top three disciplines. Second, papers included cover a wide range of disciplines, including disciplines of natural science such as transportation engineering, energy science and technology, materials science and aerospace technology. Though papers of these disciplines only take a small proportion, their existence shows the expansion of types and scopes of papers included in source think tanks (as shown in Fig. 10. 4). The construction of new type think tanks involves not only exclusive research in the field of philosophy and social sciences, but also important topics in interdisciplinary exchanges made by experts and scholars in various fields in the whole

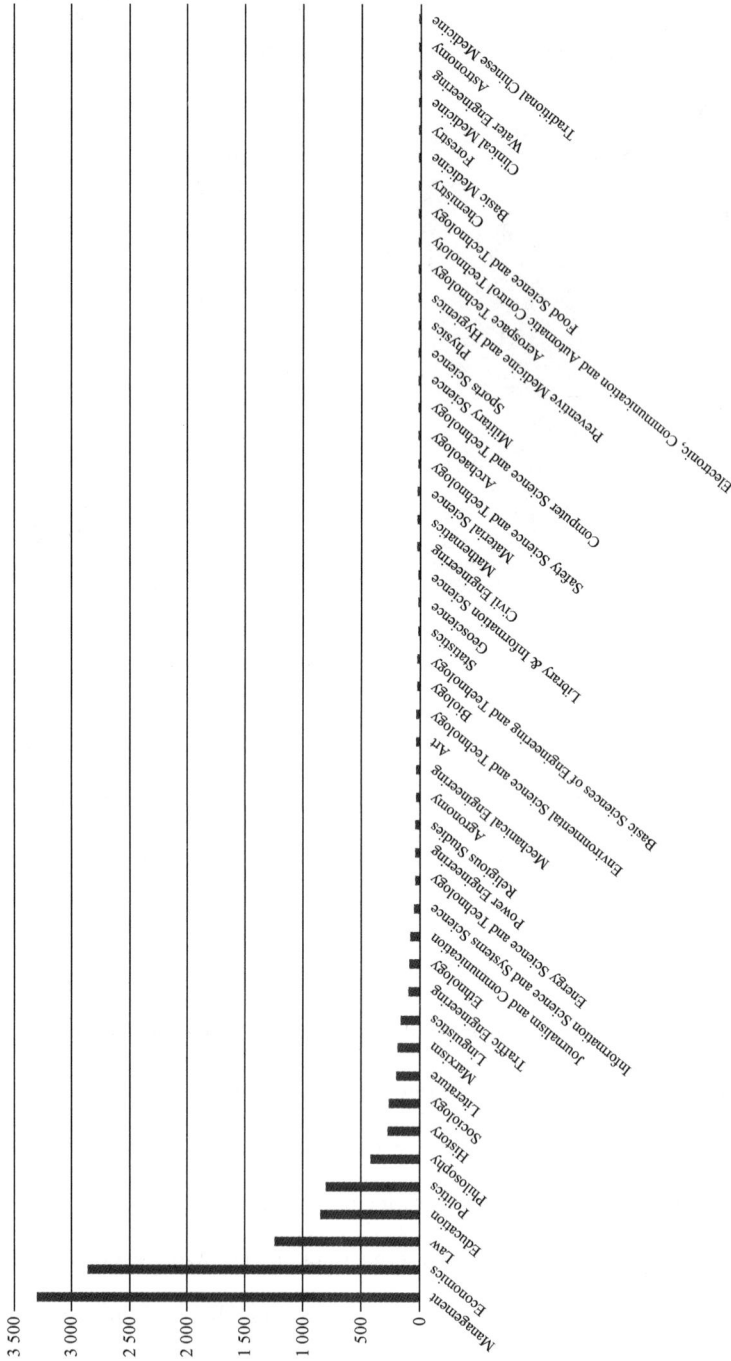

Fig. 10. 4　Paper Disciplines of Source Think Tanks

society. It requires joint discussion, exchanges and cooperation from nationwide and even global experts, who show an interest in the construction of think tanks. Their concerted efforts will help advance the building of think tanks of a shared future.

According to the statistics of the geographical locations of issuing institutes, institutes of Beijing and Hubei Province have the largest number of papers included, both exceeding 4,000. The next are institutes of Shanghai, Hunan Province, Tianjin and Guangdong Province, each having 2,000 to 3,000 papers, which are closely followed by those of Jiangsu Province, with about 2,000 papers. Nationally, most papers included are issued by institutes in the central regions, particularly Hubei and Hunan provinces, institutes in the eastern regions, particularly Jiangsu and Anhui provinces, institutes in the northern regions, particularly Beijing and Tianjin, and institutes in the southern regions, particularly Guangdong Province. Institutes in western regions, such as Sichuan, Yunnan and Guizhou provinces, have a relatively small number of papers included. Therefore, institutes of northwestern northeastern and some southern provinces should further strengthen their research on the construction of new-type think tanks and draw on the experience of other provinces with excellent performance through shared platform, joint conference and external experts, as a way to promote the research and development of think tanks.

4.1.2.2　Analysis on Feedback on Single Internal Reference Reports in Product Database

The internal reference reports are the most striking characteristic and most important decision-making consultation product of China's think tanks. According to the current think tank evaluation system, feedback on single internal reference reports is a key indicator of think tanks' ability to offer services to the central government's decision-making and regional development. According to the statistics of the internal reference reports of source think tanks, CTTI has included 10,869 single internal reference reports. Since a single reference report may receive feedback from several officials, we only count the number of single reference reports that receive feedback from different levels of officials. Among them, 185 (6.72%) were approved by the state level, 263 (9.55%) by the sub-state level, 1,975 (71.71%) by the provincial and ministerial level, and 292 (10.60%) by the bureau/department level. And 8,283 internal reference reports failed to get a response after submission. The factor of confidentiality cannot be ruled out, which explains why some reports may have been commented on but no feedback was given to think tanks. It can be concluded that the quality and the consultative ability to decision-making of internal reference reports submitted still remain to be improved. There is a certain mismatch between the supply of policy research and decision-making needs.

It is worth noting that, up to now, CTTI has included a total of 69,469 papers and 10,869 internal reference reports. The ratio between them is about 6 to 1. It is evident that papers are still the most important product of think tanks. This is due to the fact that think tanks of colleges and universities represent a major part of China's think tanks, and most experts of think tanks are professors. The system is built with distinct Chinese characteristics, but such characteristics may also bring challenges. The construction of university think tanks still relies heavily on research institutes and research centers at faculty level, the second brand of academic institutions. The role of academic institutions is to teach students, carry out research and provide social service, while think tanks serve the function of offering consultation services, making suggestions, making theoretical innovations, influencing public opinion, serving society and maintaining public diplomacy. Therefore, academic institutions should never be confused with think tanks, for there is a significant difference between them. In the past, universities evaluated professors' performance basing only on papers. At present, whether universities can make innovative changes to the mechanisms of resource allocation, achievements allocation, performance appraisal and awards assessment is a key factor in arousing experts' research enthusiasm and bringing policy research output.

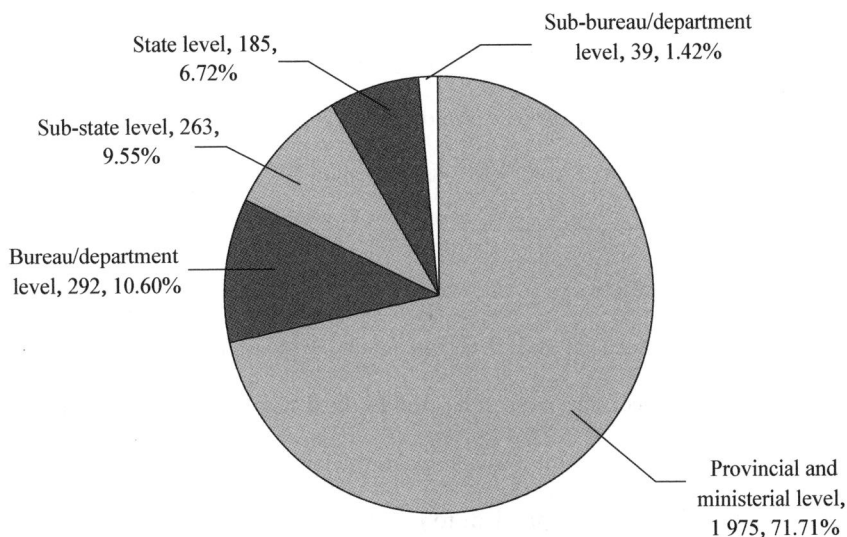

State level, 185, 6.72%

Sub-bureau/department level, 39, 1.42%

Sub-state level, 263, 9.55%

Bureau/department level, 292, 10.60%

Provincial and ministerial level, 1 975, 71.71%

Fig. 10. 5   Feedback on Single Internal Reference Reports of Source Think Tanks

4.1.2.3   Analysis on Research Projects in Product Database

Research projects are a series of complex, systematic and interrelated scientific research activities carried out by think tanks, which generally include vertical research projects supported by governments horizontal research projects jointly completed by enterprises and institutions, and research projects funded by institutions themselves. According to the statistics of vertical and horizontal research projects in CTTI, the system includes vertical projects, with the number of provincial and ministerial level projects being the largest, accounting for 47. 16%. It is followed by common/young scholar projects (15.54%) and major projects supported by the National Social Science Fund or the Social Science Fund of the Ministry of Education (7.08%), roughly keeping with the statistics of 2018. Among the 6,992 horizontal projects included, the total number of social science projects far exceeds natural science: the former is more than four times the latter. Among social science projects, projects at or above 50,000 RMB constitute the majority, followed by those at or above 10,000 RMB and at or above 150,000 RMB. Among natural science projects, projects at or above 20,000 RMB take the largest proportion, followed by those at or above 100,000 RMB and at or above 250,000 RMB (as shown in Fig. 10.6). Source think tanks' enthusiasm for undertaking horizontal projects, mostly small-scale projects under 200,000 RMB, is on the rise (as shown in Fig. 10.7). In the future, source think tanks need to remain focused and dedicated to their research in order to lay a solid foundation for basic theoretical research. And to those new-type think tanks aiming at offering consultation services for decision-making, how to translate scientific research projects into products is still a problem to be addressed.

4.1.2.4 Analysis on Reports in Product Database

Scientific research reports are a form to present think tank products systematically and also an important carrier of products in source think tanks. According to the statistics of reports in product database of CTTI, Scientific research reports in source think tanks consist of research reports, consulting reports, survey reports and others. Among them, research reports take the largest proportion (55.16%), followed by consulting reports (39.53%) and survey reports (4.72%) (as shown in Fig. 10.8). The number of research reports is still significant, and the proportion of consulting reports has increased compared with that of last year. Source think tanks' awareness of offering consultation services to decision-making has been

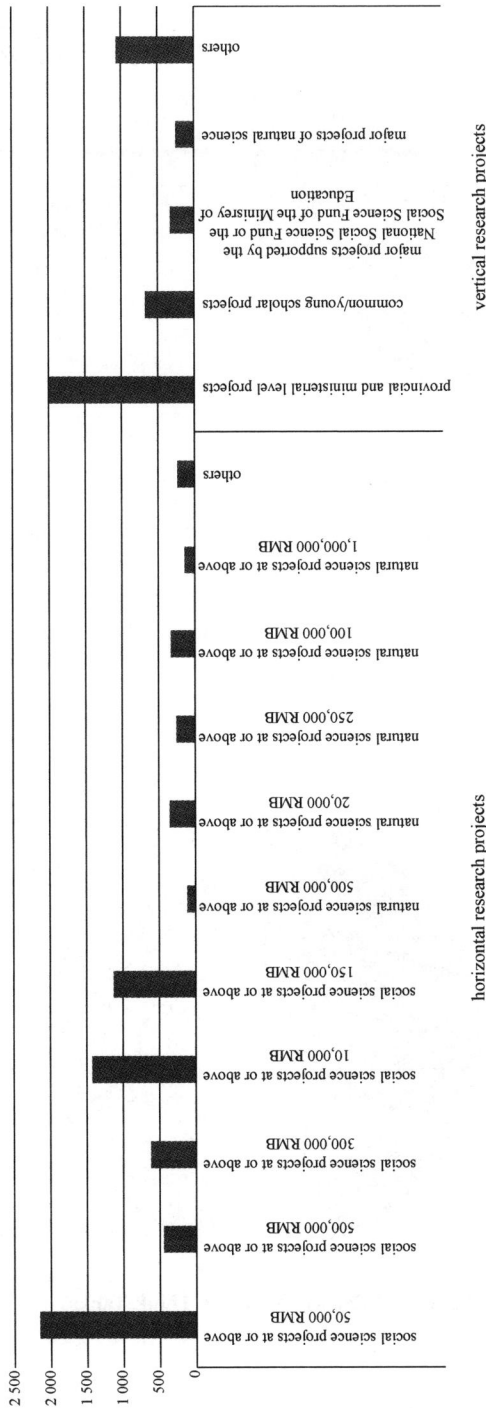

Fig. 10. 6 Research Projects of Source Think Tanks

Note: The chart lists only horizontal and vertical research projects, not self-financing and other types of research projects.

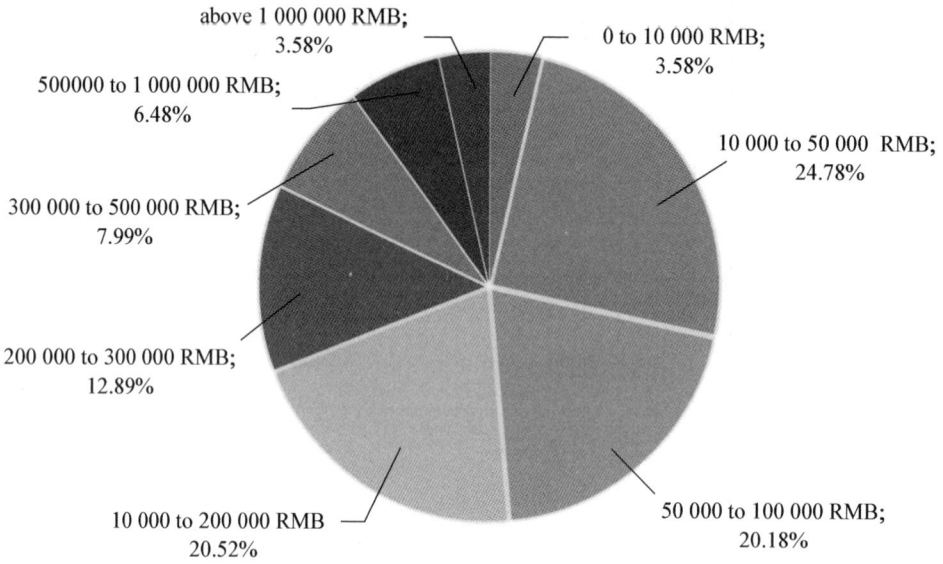

Fig. 10. 7   **Project Funds of Source Think Tanks**

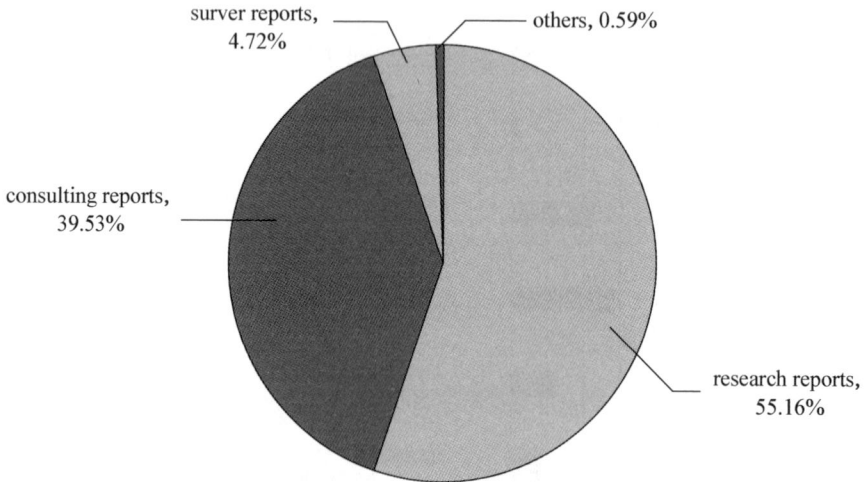

Fig. 10. 8   **Reports of Source Think Tanks**

strengthened. In the near future, improving the quality of consulting reports and the effective translation rate of report results will remain to be the most important steps in the construction of high-quality think tanks.

4.1.2.5 Analysis on Newspaper Articles in Product Database

As the mouthpiece of the party and the government, newspapers are an important window for China's international cultural exchanges and also the main media platform for think tanks to voice their opinions worldwide in a timely manner. According to the statistics of newspaper articles in product database of CTTI, 13,323 newspaper articles are included. Among them, *Guangming Daily* has the largest number of articles, with 729 newspaper articles. The next are *People's Daily* (495 articles) and *Economic Daily* (171 articles), closely followed by *Chinese Social Sciences*, *Procuratorate Daily*, *Global Times* and *Wenhui Daily* (as shown in Fig. 10. 9). Newspaper articles in the system come from a wide range of sources, including newspapers at the state level, at provincial or ministerial level and at regional level. The top three are all newspapers at the state level. But the number of newspaper articles is still far smaller than that of papers. Thus, source think tanks need to take the initiative to share views and influence public opinion through traditional media such as newspaper. By doing that, they can tap into the power of media to spread the achievements of think tanks and therefore have more influence on decision-making and social discourse.

4.2 Analysis on Event Database of CTTI Source Think Tanks

4.2.1 Analysis on Event Types in Source Think Tanks

According to the statistics of events in sub-database of CTTI, events in the source think tanks consist of four types, namely, institutional meetings, surveys, trainings, receptions and visits. Among them, 12, 961 meetings constitute the

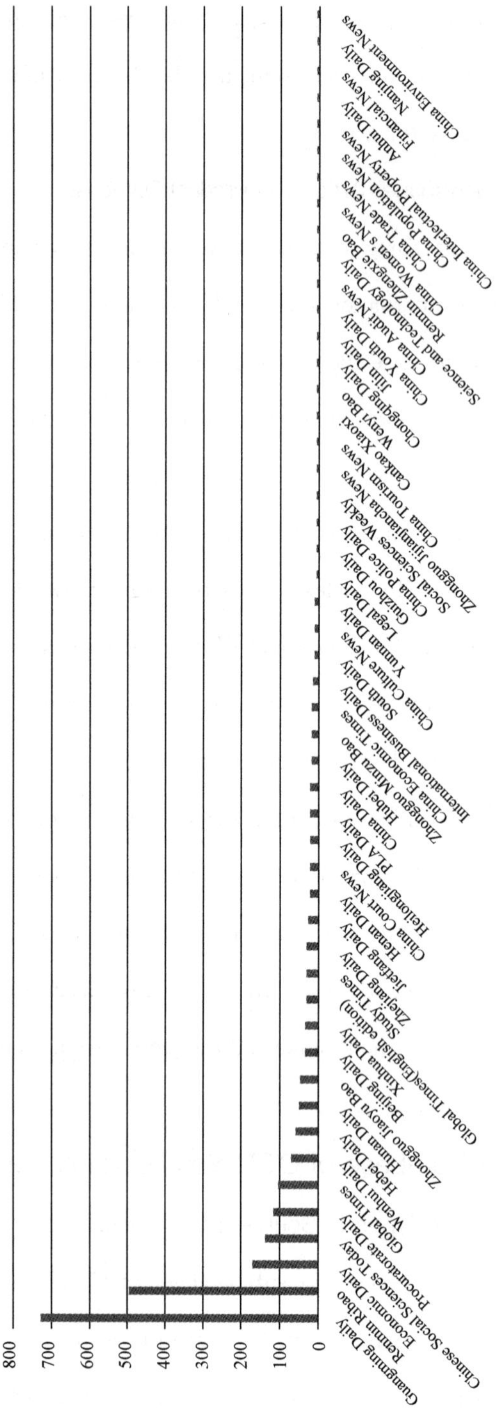

Fig. 10. 9 Newspaper Articles of Source Think Tanks(Top 50)

majority, accounting for 54. 21%, followed by 4,017 surveys (16. 8%), 3,768 receptions and visits (15. 76%) and 3,161 trainings (13. 22%) (as shown in Fig. 10. 10). It can be concluded that source think tanks remain to be highly motivated in holding various events. By doing that, they can enhance exchanges and cooperation with other think tanks or experts, and thus they can make more resource contribution and realize coordinated and healthy development.

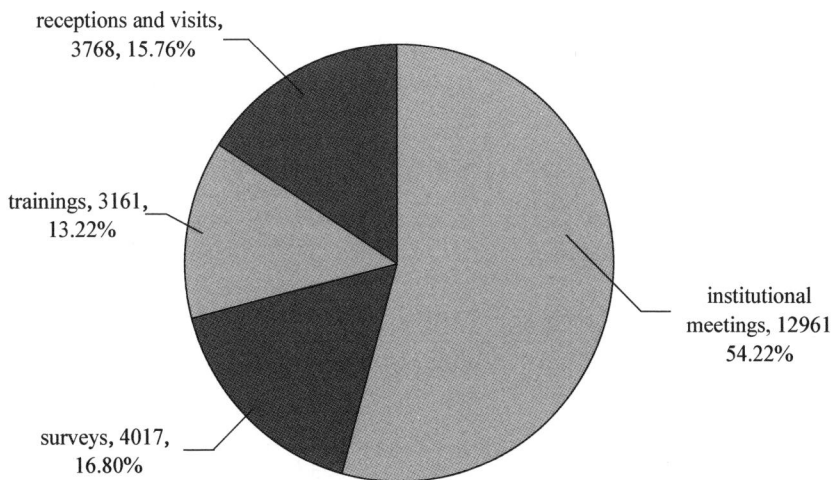

Fig. 10. 10   Event Types of Source Think Tanks

4.2.2   Analysis on Meeting Types in Source Think Tanks

According to statistics mentioned in the above section, meetings constitute the major events in source think tanks. An analysis on global/national meeting types reveals that national meetings are mainly presented in the forms of lectures, seminars and forums, some of which are symposia, workshops and professional meetings. The meeting types are diverse and widely distributed. Global meetings on the other hand are mainly presented in the forms of seminars and forums, but there are overall fewer of them around. In addition, some source think tanks are trying to set up new-type platforms for exchanges, such as summits, banquets, salons and launch events, offering experts from different fields of think tanks different opportunities and experiences to share ideas and communicate. However, brainstorming expert meetings for policy research and development are still few, which affects the depth and breadth of policy research and development to a certain extent. Think tanks still need to pay more attention to improving research quality and promoting content innovation.

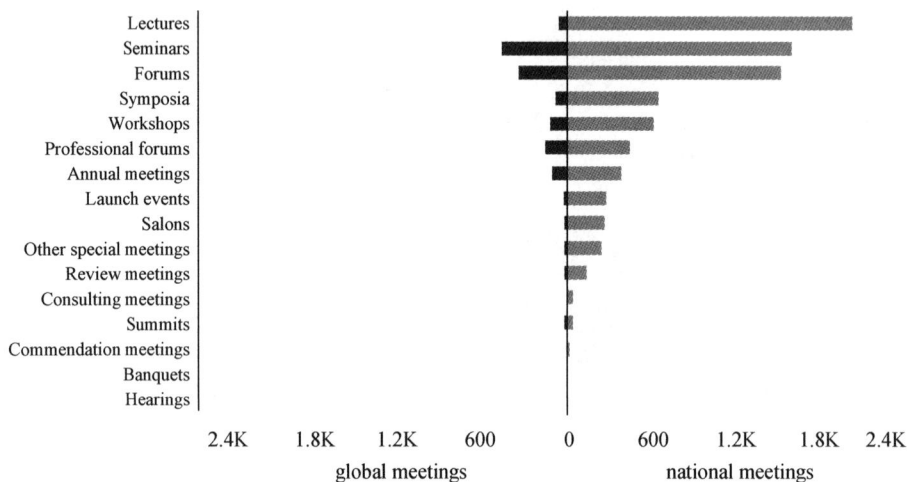

Fig. 10. 11 Global/National Meeting Types of Source Think Tanks

In summary, the products of CTTI source think tanks are presented in a wide range of forms. The number of papers published in top-level journals keeps growing. Papers included cover about 47 disciplines, such as management, economics and Sociology. Feedback on a single reference report has increased, with the number of a single reference report approved by the provincial and ministerial level or above reaching a new high. Source think tanks have showed greater enthusiasm for undertaking horizontal projects, and the number of small-scale horizontal projects under 200, 000 RMB has greatly increased. Compared with that of last year, the number of consulting reports rises, which means that think tanks' awareness to provide consultative services to decision-making has been strengthened. The number of articles published in newspapers has improved, but experts of source think tanks still lack initiative and enthusiasm for sharing opinions in state-level newspapers. Source think tanks are actively engaged in all kinds of events. Lectures, seminars and forums are the most popular meeting forms. Meanwhile, new-type meetings such as summits, banquets and salons have emerged, gradually transforming the traditional interactive situation of current think tank event market. These changes can help to build a better communication environment and fuel sustainable and healthy development of new-type think tanks.

5. Data Scanning of CTTI Source Think Tanks in Different Policy Areas

The research of think tanks is professional, scientific, forward-looking and political, which forms the key factors that decide the influence of think tanks and becomes the cornerstone for think tanks to perform functions and deliver ideas. At present, the research on new types of think tanks focus on major social events and keep close track of national policies, involving many fields, becoming more professional and presenting its own characteristics. Following the principles of the previous year and taking CTTI source think tanks as examples, this report, supported by the scientific and reasonable evaluation system and the data filled out by source think tanks, shows the influence of new types of think tanks in different policy areas from 17 aspects, such as "macroeconomics and international trade", "industry and finance", "regional and national research fields", and summarizes advanced experience. This evaluation is mainly guided by the output impact. The three indicators of product, activity and media impact are assigned and calculated according to the proportion of 5 : 3 : 2, and the result value, output impact, i. e. , PAI (Output Impact Value) $= 0.5 \times P$ (Product) $+ 0.3 \times a$ (Activities) $+ 0.2 \times I$ (Impact), is the basis for ranking the output impact of think tanks in various policy areas. The time frame of this evaluation is from January 2017 to December 2019. All the data filled out by CTTI source think tanks within that time frame are analyzed, and the data of 650 think tanks are relatively sufficient and accurate. Based on the principles of data availability and accuracy, these 650 think tanks are the major objects of this evaluation. The PAI value in each table is calculated according to the formula "PAI=0.5×P+0.3×A+0.2×I", with P, A and I being original values.

In order to protect the information of the think tanks, we only publish the evaluation and analysis results of think tanks with high output impact values in various areas, and the data released this time is only the values of primary indicators, not involving the specific values of the secondary ones, and the relevant data will never be released to the third party. For more details, think tanks can send a formal letter in the name of the organization to ctti@nju.edu.cn. The CTTREC of Nanjing University will export the results for them.

5.1 Macroeconomy and International Trade

As China's economy has shifted from high-speed growth to high-quality development, high-quality economic development has become an important starting point for policy-makers to formulate economic and foreign trade policies. In order to meet the needs of the Party and the government to formulate policies, think tanks of their own fields, by focusing on issues, such as regional economic growth and international or regional trade, and using their own resource advantages, have carried out a large number of investigations and studies on hot-button issues and challenges and have produced lots of excellent results, such as Research Institute of Chinese Economy, Fudan University's *Libra is unsafe : China Should Put Commercialized Cryptocurrency Under Strict Supervision*, Center for Quantitative Economics of Jilin University's *Changing Political Ecology : Fundamental Way to Revitalize Northeast China* and *Policy Suggestions on Coordinated Promotion of Economic Revitalization and Poverty Alleviation in Northeast China*. Table 11.1 shows 20 think tanks with high PAI values in this area.

Taking scientific research as its foundation, Institute of International Economy, University of International Business and Economics focuses on basic theoretical study, national policy research and business consulting services, and it mainly involves many fields, such as world economy and China's foreign economic and trade. There are nine research centers under the institute, namely, Research Center of Asian Economy; Research Center of Taiwan, Hong Kong and Macao Economy; Research Center of European Economy; Research Center of China-Russia CIS; Research Center of China-ASEAN economy; Research Center of Processing Trade; Research Center of International Development and Innovation; Research Center of China's Capital Operation and Research Center of International New Energy Strategy. With an international perspective and an open mind, the institute actively carries out internal and external exchanges and cooperation. The *Report on International Competitiveness of China's Export Industry* it publishes every year has been widely recognized by and received good reviews from the academia, government and society.

In promoting the development of the new types of think tanks, Shandong Academy of Macroeconomics Research Institute has always adhered to the value pursuit of serving decision-making. Following the scientific research philosophy of "Being good at finding solutions and making achievements" and "intellectual support for policies" and the style of correlating theory with practice, the institute, with "the think tank to support party committees and governments to make decisions in a scientific way" and "the helper to serve the development and reform of the whole province" as its roles, takes a distinctive path of giving regional measures, gets deeply involved in the decision-making process of the government, comprehensively improves the influence of think tanks, and directly participates in the research, demonstration, formulation, interpretation and publicity of major decisions, so as to continue to enhance the practical application of research results, raise the level of serving decision-making, continuously extend the functions of think tanks, improve the development pattern of think tanks, and actively serve society and communities at grassroots level. In order to further promote exchanges and development, the institute, together with 20 well-known domestic think tanks, including Chinese Academy of Macroeconomic Research, jointly launched "Chinese Macroeconomic Think Tank Alliance" in 2018. In the past three years, the academy has participated in over 200 research activities, and its 45 special reports have been accepted by the provincial Party committee and government. A large number of scientific research results have been approved by leaders at the provincial level, and many research results and opinions have been adopted by government departments and used in relevant policy documents, providing strong intellectual support for the decision-making of the provincial Party committee and government, and making positive contributions to Shandong's industrial and regional growth and social development.

Table 11. 1   Top 20 Think Tanks in Macroeconomy and International Trade According to Performance in PAI Assessment

(in alphabetical order according to the first letters of their names in pinyin spelling)

Names of Think Tanks	PAI	P	A	I
National Academy of Economic Security, Beijing Jiaotong University	172. 4	103	371	48
Institute of International Economics, University of International Business and Economics	261. 5	523	0	0
The Academy of China Open Economy Studies, University of International Business and Economics	118. 95	299. 5	127	2

Continued

Names of Think Tanks	PAI	P	A	I
China Institute for WTO Studies, University of International Business and Economics	118. 95	232. 5	9	0
Research Institute of Chinese Economy, Fudan University	512. 6	970	92	0
Macroeconomic Research Institute in Hebei Province Development and Reform Committee	293	586	0	0
Peikang Chang Institute for Development Studies, Huazhong University of Science and Technology	137	274	0	0
Center for Quantitative Economics of Jilin University	465. 55	779. 5	220	49
Institute of Guangzhou Nansha Free Trade Test Area Research, Jinan University	232. 05	436. 5	46	0
Center for Studies of Political Economy of Nankai University	176. 45	320. 5	54	0
Shandong Macroeconomics Research Institute	270	516	30	15
Chinese Academy of International Trade and Economic Cooperation	170	340	0	0
Shanghai Center for Global Trade and Economic Governance, Shanghai University of International Business and Economics	560. 5	1121	0	0
China Institute of FTZ Supply Chain, Shanghai Maritime University	241	482	0	0
Tianjin Academy of Free Trade Area, TUFE	279. 2	538	34	0
The Center for Economic Development Research of Wuhan University	151. 25	254. 5	80	0
Digital Economy Development Research Center in Xi'an, China	139	278	0	0
Shaanxi Collaborative Innovation Research Center of Macroeconomics and Economic Growth Quality, Northwest University	129. 1	141	66	194
China Academy of Fiscal Sciences	256	506	10	0
China's Income Distribution Research Center	185. 8	329	71	0

5.2 Industry and Finance

Industry and finance focus on the process of industrial structural transformation, which appears in the process of the integration of modern financial system. During the transformation, finance lease and real economy are closely intertwined. With the successive introduction of "the 13th Five-Year Plan", "supply-side structural reform", "the Belt and Road Initiative", "Made in China 2025" and other guiding policies, real economy and the financial sector are getting closely integrated, and finance lease has provided a strong impetus for the structural transformation of the industry. It is an important task for think tanks in the area of industry and finance to continue to realize the deep integration of industry and finance from the major practical needs of China's economic development, and to solve the integration problems in the process of guiding practice by theories. According to the data filled out by think tanks in the industry and finance area, the system automatically calculates the values of 20 think tanks in this area with high PAI values, as shown in table 11. 2.

The fourth plenary session of the 19th CPC Central Committee called for accelerating the improvement of the socialist market economy, strengthening the basic system of the capital market, improving the modern financial system that is highly adaptable, competitive and inclusive, and effectively preventing financial risks. China Business Working Capital Management Research Center, supported by its original "business working capital management theory based on channel management" and "innovative analysis system of capital efficiency and financial risk", continues to carry out investigations on capital efficiency and financial risks of Chinese listed companies, leading the development of capital management theory innovation. On this basis, the research center strives to integrate science and education, coordinate industries and integrate theory and practice, giving full play to the pathfinding role of theoretical innovation in both talent training and social services, and it has become the "literature base", "information base" and "case base" in China's capital management.

Chongyang Institute for Financial Studies, Renmin University of China, also a university think tank, is also the secretariat of the Green Finance Committee of China Society for Finance and Banking. It aims to make suggestions on green production and consumption, green finance development and promotion of market-oriented green technology innovation. Led by Renmin University of China and Industrial and Commercial Bank of China, *2018 Research Report on China's Green Finance* released by the institute conducted an in-depth research on major theories, policies and hot topics in various fields of China's green finance at various stages, and reviewed historical experience for the future development of green finance. In Table 11. 2, the A value of Chongyang Institute for Financial Studies, Renmin University of China is 1, 122, which indicates that Chongyang Institute attaches great importance to implementing its own work, which is supported by intelligence through engaging in activities such as decision-making consultation meetings, and that it holds influential think tank forums and summits to spread new ideas of think tanks and improve the influence of think tanks.

In addition to the university think tanks, there are enterprise think tanks in this area. As a first-class representative of enterprise think tanks, Suning Institute of Finance is a practical think tank in this area. It provides strategic support for the Suning Corporation internally and customized research consulting services for third parties externally. Suning Institute of Finance, as an enterprise-led and market-oriented technological innovation system that brings together firms, universities, and research institutes, is of guiding significance to promote the basic industrial capabilities and modernize industrial chains. In addition, Suning Institute of Finance has set up a dedicated daily-work post for data management, assigning personnel to update and maintain the information of the data systems and information platforms in the think tank, thus realizing the modern management of think tank information.

Table 11. 2   Top 20 Think Tanks in Industry and Finance According

to Performance in PAI Assessment

(in alphabetical order according to the first letters of their names in pinyin spelling)

Names of Think Tanks	PAI	P	A	I
The HSBC Financial Research Institute at Peking University	144. 5	64	375	0
Research Base of Beijing Modern Manufacturing Development, Beijing University of Technology	330. 75	661. 5	0	0
National Research Center for Economic Comprehensive Competitiveness, Fujian Normal University Branch	159. 3	291	46	0
Institute of De Rong, Hebei Finance University	264	306	370	0
Guangzhou Financial Services Innovation and Risk Management Research Base, South China University of Technology	112. 45	171. 5	89	0
Research Institute of Machinery Industry Economics & Management	797	1 594	0	0
Development Strategy Research Base of IOT Industry, Jiangnan University	89. 85	106. 5	114	12
Modern Services Think Tank, Nanjing University of Finance & Economics	136	272	0	0
Yangtze Industrial Economics Institution, Nanjing University	1 371. 45	1 051. 5	2,575	366
College of Economic and Social Development, Nankai University	526. 1	760	459	42
Suning Institute of Finance	952. 05	1,735. 5	281	0
Business Management Research Center of TUFE	133. 4	244	38	0

Continued

Names of Think Tanks	PAI	P	A	I
Collaborative Innovation Center for Intangible Asset Evaluation, TUFE	395. 8	704	146	0
Coordinated Innovation Center for Binhai Finance in China, TUFE	230. 4	426	48	15
Modern Service Industry Development Research Center, Tianjin University of Commerce	239. 5	479	0	0
Survey and Research Center for China Household Finance, Southwestern University of Finance and Economics	379. 15	467. 5	150	502
China Academy of Cross-border E-commerce, Zhejiang University	108. 25	69. 5	243	3
China Business Working Capital Management Research Center, Ocean University of China	4,923. 9	9,804	29	66
Chongyang Institute for Financial Studies, Renmin University of China	821. 05	966. 5	1,122	6
Collaborative Innovation Center of Industrial Upgrading and Regional Finance (Hubei), Zhongnan University of Economics and Law	1,203. 25	1,518. 5	956	786

5.3 Regional and National Research

Regional and national research is one of the important preconditions for a comprehensive and objective view of the external world issues and for scientific and reasonable international comparison, and it is inevitable in China's development from a regional major country to a global one. University think tanks have been strengthening their sense of mission and responsibility to serve the overall interests of China, providing intellectual support for the formulation of national development strategies, policies and measures by giving full play to their important disciplines, such as language, economy and trade as well as their geographical and talent advantages. These think tanks have become a major force in the area of regional and national research. Table 11. 3 shows 12 think tanks with high PAI values in this area.

The Institute of African Studies of Zhejiang Normal University, founded in 2007 with the support of the Ministry of Education and Ministry of Foreign Affairs, is the first comprehensive substantive African research institute of Chinese universities. After more than 10 years of development, it has become an influential Chinese African research institution and national think tank on African affairs. Focusing on the overall situation of national development and the general trend of China-Africa cooperation, the institute has carried out in-depth research on basic theories and application measures with the focus on "contemporary African development issues" and "China-Africa cooperation in the new era". Focusing on brand building, the institute has edited and published *Annual Report on the Development of Africa*, an annual report of philosophy and social science of the Ministry of Education and the professional journal *African Studies*. It has also hosted a series of influential international academic conferences such as China-Africa Think Tanks Forum and China-Africa Media &. Think Tanks Symposium to build an important brand of Chinese research on Africa and make it more recognized. The institute has also made great efforts to carry out academic research, consolidating the foundation for the development of think tanks and activating think tank research through academic research, and has published various academic works under *Library of African Studies*, as well as articles on important journals at home and abroad. Based on all its efforts, the institute has always had a strong think tank output capability. It took the initiative to submit various advisory reports to ministries and commissions of the country, many of which were approved by state leaders or included by *Special Journal of University Think Tanks of the Ministry of Education*.

Approved by the Ministry of Education to be one of the Key Research Institutes of Humanities and Social Sciences in Universities by the Ministry of Education in December, 2000, the Middle East Studies Institute of Shanghai International Studies University is the only key institute in this university. Attaching great importance to team building, the institute gradually builds up a research team with advantages and characteristics while combining application measures research with basic research, and social science research with humanities research. It not only maintains regular contact and communication with relevant ministries and commissions of the central government, but also promotes the overall construction of Arabic studies and Islamic studies with Chinese characteristics. In addition, the institute has laid a good academic foundation while continuously promoting achievement transformation. In the past three years, the institute has published nearly a hundred academic papers, as well as important academic works, such as *Research on Economic Modernization of Islamic Republic of Iran*, *Clinical View on the Hot-Button Issues of the Middle East* and *The Research on the National Security System and Mechanisms of Main Countries in the World*. In addition, over the past three years, the institute has submitted more than 60 internal references, actively offering suggestions and providing advisory services for decision-making.

Table 11. 3   Top 12 Think Tanks in Regional and National Research According to Performance in PAI Assessment

(in alphabetical order according to the first letters of their names in pinyin spelling)

Names of Think Tanks	PAI	P	A	I
G20-BFSU Center, Beijing Foreign Studies University	100. 95	142. 5	99	0
National Research Center for Canadian Studies, Beijing Foreign Studies University	103. 3	119	146	0

Continued

Names of Think Tanks	PAI	P	A	I
British Studies Centre, Beijing Foreign Studies University	166. 25	253. 5	109	34
Center for American Studies, Fudan University	482. 15	304. 5	819	421
Center for Russian Studies of ECNU (CRS)	170. 3	223	196	0
Center for Northeast Asian Studies, Jilin University	152. 4	303	3	0
Center for Turkish Studies, Shanghai University	106. 6	69	173	101
Middle East Studies Institute, Shanghai International Studies University	918. 75	822. 5	487	1,807
German Studies Center, Tongji University	172. 9	179	278	0
Institute of Korean Peninsula Studies, Yanbian University	214. 9	410	33	0
Institute of Myanmar Studies, Yunnan University	103. 9	119	148	0
Institute of African Studies, Zhejiang Normal University	622. 8	635	927	136

5.4   International Relations and Foreign Policies

Globalization has closely linked countries in politics, economy, culture and other fields, and cooperation and competition among countries are deepening. Some think tanks conduct research on international affairs, international hot-button issues and foreign policies and offer policy references to decision-making organs, exerting important influence on foreign policies. Table 11. 4 shows 10 think tanks with high PAI values.

Research Center for Co-Development with Neighboring Countries, founded in 2012, is a collaborative innovation platform launched by East China Normal University and co-built by Peking University and Fudan University. It also established a collaborative relationship with Shanghai Institutes for International

Studies. Over the years, the center has focused on regional and national research on China's neighboring areas, emphasizing the integrity of this research field, and providing data support for the integration of decision-making consultation and academic research through a combination of specialized historical databases and two professional databases. In addition, the center attaches great importance to international academic exchanges and cooperation and has set up studios in Wilson International Center for Scholars in the US and in Russia's National Research University—Higher School of Economic. Center for Russian Studies, also affiliated to East China Normal University, was established in 1999 and became a key research base on humanities and social sciences designated by the Ministry of Education in 2000. In the past ten years, the center has undertaken 44 scientific research projects, with a total fund of 11 million yuan, published 50 academic monographs and more than 300 papers on core journals, and won 15 provincial and ministerial awards for outstanding achievements. The center has formed its research characteristics in the history of Soviet Union, history of research on Russian and Soviet literature, Russian transformation, Russian diplomacy and other aspects, and its achievements are widely acknowledged.

Center for China and Globalization (CCG) is an organization think tank brand registered by China Globalization Think Tank Foundation. It is a leading global research institution of non-government think tank in China. Founded in 2008 and headquartered in Beijing, CCG has nearly 10 branches or overseas representatives at home and abroad. With "Global Vision for China" and "Chinese Wisdom for the World" as its visions, CCG has nearly 100 full-time researchers and personnel that are committed to the research in the fields of China's globalization, global governance, talent internationalization and enterprise internationalization. CCG is a member of the

"Belt and Road" Think Tank Alliance, a National Talent Research Facility designated by Central Coordination Group for Talent Work, the site of the China International Professional Committee for Talents of the Ministry of Human Resources and Social Affairs, a founding member of the "American Research Think Tank Alliance" established by the Ministry of Finance and a national postdoctoral program research center. It also holds United Nations "Special Consultative Status". CCG publishes over ten research works every year, including the blue books jointly published by Social Sciences Academic Press with domestic and foreign influence, such as *Report on Chinese Enterprises Globalization*, *Report on the Development of Chinese Students Studying Abroad*, *Report on the Development of Chinese Returnees*, *Report on Chinese International Migration*, *Report on Overseas Chinese Professionals and Report on China's Regional International Talent Competitiveness*. It also undertakes the research projects of many national ministries and commissions and holds multiple forums and think tank seminars, which makes it influential.

Table 11.4 Top 10 Think Tanks in Regional and National Research According to Performance in PAI Assessment

(in alphabetical order according to the first letters of their names in pinyin spelling)

Names of Think Tanks	PAI	P	A	I
Center for Public Diplomacy, BFSU	137.15	239.5	58	0
China-ASEAN Research Institute, Guangxi University	187.95	313.5	104	0
Intellisia Institute	424.1	401	726	29
Centre for National Discourse Ecology Studies, East China Normal University	175.65	217.5	211	18
Research Center for Co-Development with Neighboring Countries, East China Normal University	3,068.85	5,011.5	1,877	0

Continued

Names of Think Tanks	PAI	P	A	I
Academy of Overseas Chinese Studies in Jinan University	305. 05	507. 5	159	18
The Pangoal Institution	985. 5	384	2,523	183
Center for China & Globalization	2,362. 7	2,878	2,021	1,587
Central for Global Public Opinions, SISU, Shanghai International Studies University	442	884	0	0
Center for China's Neighbor Diplomacy Studies, Yunnan University	724. 9	1,386	85	32

5.5 Party Building and National Governance

Since the 18th National Congress of the Communist Party of China, great changes have taken place in the situation and tasks of the Party building in organs. The Party Central Committee with Xi Jinping at its core has made a series of important plans to see Party self-governance exercised fully and with rigor and strengthen Party building in organs, and has made significant progress in organ Party building. In particular, after the 19th National Congress of the Communist Party of China, think tanks of the area of Party building and national governance have continued to focus on the important topics such as "Party building in the new era", "upholding and strengthening the overall leadership of the Party", "seeing Party self-governance exercised fully and with rigor", and "strengthening the Party's long-term governance capacity and its advanced nature and purity", and promote the theoretical innovation of Party building and strengthen to review the work of Party building at the community level. According to the data filled out by think tanks in the area of Party building and national governance, the system automatically calculates the scores of 20 think tanks with higher PAI values, as shown in table 11. 5.

In terms of national governance, think tanks in this area closely focus on the important topic of "modernization of national governance system and governance capacity", dealing with system building and the theoretical basis and the path towards the modernization of national governance. Focusing on national strategies and the important tasks undertaken by Shanghai as it is at the forefront of deepening reform in all areas, Shanghai Academy, centering on the major theoretical and practical issues of reform and development, has been working hard to build itself into a high-end think tank, high-end talent training center, high-end international exchange and cooperation platform, and high-end national conditions research center. The academy attaches great importance to its publicity work and its leading role, and has actively published many articles on *People's Daily*, Guangming Online, *Jiefang Daily*, *Wenhui Daily Po*, Xinhuanet and other media, focusing on national strategies, deepening reform in all areas and other important issues. The academy has also built think tank brand lectures "High-End Lectures of Humanities and Social Sciences" and "Think-tank Lecture Hall of Shanghai Academy". These lectures help deepen think tank services, build their own image, becoming an effective way to spread humanistic knowledge and exchange think tank ideas. In addition, the academy actively participates in international exchanges. For examples, it has hosted the China-Korean Humanities Forum, co-hosted the high-level dialogue on China-Japan Marxist Studies, international academic seminars on population aging, hospice and social policies. It also engages in visits and exchanges in Turkey and Greece and signed a memorandum of understanding with University of Bath. By building platforms for international exchanges, it continuously strengthens foreign-oriented publicity, learns about foreign situations and studies the international situation.

As a university think tank, the Institute for the Development of Socialism with

Chinese Characteristics of Southeast University has effectively played its role as a high-end think tank, with outstanding performance in decision-making consultation, theoretical innovation, media communication and other aspects. It has undertaken one major national engineering program and nearly 10 general programs funded by the National Social Science Fund of China. Shortly after the 19th national congress of the CPC, a series of theoretical articles written by the institute on political progress in the new era were published on the full page of Page 12 of *Guangming Daily* on October 24, 2017 At present, the Institute has published more than 20 theoretical articles in top newspapers in related fields such as People's Daily, Guangming Daily and Economic Daily, and nearly 40 theoretical articles were published on *Xinhua daily*, *Qunzhong* and other provincial-level media. The institute also lays emphasis on strengthening theoretical publicity. Through making use of new media, accepting media interviews, participating in policy interpretation, holding seminars and symposia and other ways, it helps promote the theoretical publicity to the public. For example, a number of theoretical articles published by the institute's experts have been reposted and disseminated by xuexi. cn and other media and "Micro Class of Ideological and Political Education", a series of videos, were launched on xuexi. cn and jschina. com. simultaneously. Besides, two experts participated in a series of interviews of "Building a moderately prosperous society in all respects at a high level by innovation with joint efforts and focus on enriching people: think-tank experts and media bosses in Jiangsu". They had face-to-face communication with Party secretaries of people's government of Xuzhou and Huaian respectively to discuss industrial upgrading, innovation and entrepreneurship, city construction and other issues, and put forward policy suggestions. In addition, the institute has held 7 large-scale high-level forums and more than 40 seminars on the topics of new urbanization with

Chinese characteristics, technological and industrial innovation, and the Fourth Plenary Session of the 19th CPC Central Committee, among which 2 activities were reported on the full page of the think tank edition of *Xinhua Daily*, which had a broad social impact.

The Institute of State Governance Studies of Peking University, also a university think tank, is a co-innovation unit jointly operated by Peking University, Fudan University, Jilin University, Sun Yat-sen University, and the Institute of Fiscal Science of the Ministry of Finance (later renamed Chinese Academy of Fiscal Science). Research on State Governance Series are the representative achievement of the institute. At present, 11 of them have been published. They are research works on the special issues of national governance and deepening reform as the institute and the center implement co-innovation research tasks and promote the transformation and application of relevant outstanding achievements. Centering on the overall goal of deepening reforms in all areas and the major urgent needs of the modernization of state governance, the Institute of State Governance Studies of Peking University, through its own research strength, works closely with all sectors of society to promote multi-disciplinary integration and undertake scientific research on major issues, such as government governance, market governance, social governance and even global governance, providing intellectual support for national-governance-related personnel training, discipline building and social services. It strives to build itself into a new type of world-class think tanks with Chinese characteristics and advanced institutions that are urgently needed by the country and make outstanding achievements and contribute to the modernization of state governance and the development of "Double First-Class" initiative.

Table 11.5 Top 20 Think Tanks in Party Building and National Governance

According to Performance in PAI Assessment

(in alphabetical order according to the first letters of their names in pinyin spelling)

Names of Think Tanks	PAI	P	A	I
Institute of State Governance Studies, Peking University	565.85	803.5	547	0
Beijing Institute of Letters to Government	601.15	1,014.5	313	0
Institute for the Development of Socialism with Chinese Characteristics, Southeast University	742.4	1,423	103	0
National Corruption Prevention and Punishment Research Center of Hunan University	77.65	95.5	99	1
The Institute of State Governance, Huazhong University of Science and Technology	150.85	186.5	192	0
Center for Anti-Corruption Research and Education of Jilin University	181.2	246	194	0
Research Center of the Management-Decision Evaluation of Jiangxi Normal University	218	371	71	56
Collaborative Innovation Center for China Economy, Nankai University	156.45	289.5	39	0
Chinese Government and Politics Unite Research Center, Nankai University	189.85	309.5	63	81
The Development Research Center, Shanghai Municipal People's Government	101.5	158	75	0
Collaborative Innovation Center for Security and Development of Western Frontier China, Sichuan University	149.7	294	9	0
Tianjin Research Base of Rule of Law and Letters to Government, Tiangong University	89.6	130	82	0
Research Institute of Governance, Tianjin Normal University	183.55	144.5	371	0
Emergence Management Research Center of Tianjin Normal University	123.5	247	0	0

Continued

Names of Think Tanks	PAI	P	A	I
Institution of Inner-party Laws and Regulations, Wuhan University	96.5	147	62	22
Research Center of Economic Reform Innovation and Assessment, Xi'an Jiaotong University	115.75	207.5	40	0
Ethnic Issues Think Tank Construction Team, Yunnan University	165	330	0	0
China Institute of Regulation and Public Policy Research, Zhejiang University of Finance and Economics	125	196	90	0
China Society of Administrative Reform	129.75	85.5	22	402
Shanghai Academy	702.55	688.5	967	341

5.6 Social Governance and Social Security

Since the 19th National Congress of the Communist Party of China, the Central Committee has put forward four requirements for the modernization of social governance in the new era, namely, making it more social, intelligent, specialized and developed under the law. Progress has been made in actively building a social governance pattern of pursuing shared growth through social collaboration and governance, enabling the people to have more direct and real sense of gain, happiness and security. Think tanks in the area of social governance actively respond to the new requirements of the Party and the government for social governance. By focusing on medicine, health, social security and other important issues, they have carried out study on social governance, people's livelihood and public policies, providing intellectual support for solving practical problems. Table 11.6 shows the 20 think tanks with high PAI values in this area.

With "public opinion and social mentality" as its main research interests, Zijin

Media Think Tank of Nanjing University focuses on the changes of public opinion and social mentality after the key events and the introduction of major domestic and foreign policies. It conducts long-term follow-up research on the issues of China's Internet and media development, social risks and public crises and makes accurate and efficient suggestions, boosting China's economic, social and cultural development. In the past three years, the think tank has successively held a number of brand forums, such as Zijin High-Level Forum on Addressing Public Complaints, Zijin Qingjiao Forum and Zijin Media Forum, influencing the domestic think tank circle. It has also produced a series of think tank products with "big data" research as the core competitiveness, such as *Report on China's Stock Market 2015*, *Report on Chinese Economic Confidence Index (2015—2016)*, and *Report on the Innovation Index of China's A-share Listed Companies (2016)*.

As the social security research and innovation center of the programs in the second phase of China's 985 Project, Social Security Research Center of Wuhan University has a significant output impact. Centering on the research interests of medical and health and work injury compensation insurance, aged-care insurance, social welfare and aid, and integration of medical and elderly care services, the research center takes the lead in raising brand awareness, creating its own flagship products *Report on the Reform and Development of China's Social Security and Social Security Studies*, and a CSSCI source journal, Social Security Studies and important activity Luojia Graduate Forum on Social Security by combining the university's characteristics, the subject characteristics and its advisory interests and making use of its professional advantages. The reputation and social impact of its think tank brand have been improved through flagship products and brand activities.

Relying on the advantages of its traditional research, the Public Opinion Big Data

Research Center of Guangzhou of Jinan University focuses on strengthening the building of technical platforms. Centering on major theoretical problems, major practical challenges and major social concerns, it strives to build a unified "data lake" and subdivided "data warehouses", improve the "data governance" of modern organizations and push for better "information welfare" of the public. The research center regularly compiles "Guangdong Public Opinion Trends", cooperating with Kaidi network information to publish Public Opinion Observer, and has published a series of "yellow books on public opinion and social management". It has released some survey results, including series of surveys on the National Day parade, the public opinion survey on World Expo, series of surveys on Asian Games, the cognition and evaluation survey on Gary Locke as ambassador to China, and the survey on data-based finance and economics, all of which have received extensive attention from many media at home and abroad. As one of the units directly reporting public opinion information to the Publicity Department of the Communist Party of China, the research center has submitted many pieces of information to the Department, and more than 80 were adopted. In terms of serving the local government, the research center has held Guangdong Governance Forum with the Research Institute of Nanfang Public Opinion Data for many years. *New Progress on the Governance of Guangdong*, edited and published by researchers, gives a comprehensive introduction of the achievements of Guangdong, a frontier of the reform and opening up, in promoting the modernization of government governance capabilities.

Table 11. 6   Top 20 Think Tanks in Social Governance and Social Security

According to Performance in PAI Assessment

(in alphabetical order according to the first letters of their names in pinyin spelling)

Names of Think Tanks	PAI	P	A	I
Huazhong University of Science and Technology School of Health Policy and Management	111. 4	157	95	22
The Public Opinion Big Data Research Center, Jinan University	258	345	185	150
Institute for Economic and Social Research, Jinan University	199. 5	141	430	0
Jiangxi Provincial Research Center	359. 6	712	12	0
Collaborative Innovation Center of Chinese Society Transformation Research, Jiangxi Normal University	391. 1	747	28	46
Evidence-Based Social Science Research Center of Lanzhou University	184. 25	280. 5	130	25
Zijin Media Think Tank, Nanjing University	486. 4	784	276	58
Jiangsu Academy of Talent Development, Nanjing University of Science & Technology	300. 85	594. 5	12	0
Institute of Healthy Jiangsu Development, Nanjing Medical University	311. 55	424. 5	213	177
Center for Health Management and Policy, Shandong University	281. 75	419. 5	240	0
Research Center for Local Governance, Shanghai University	274. 65	442. 5	178	0
The Center for Third Sector, Shanghai Jiao Tong University	140. 95	126. 5	259	0
Institute of Public Opinion Research, Shanghai Jiao Tong University	172	344	0	0
National Sport and Fitness Research Think Tank, Tianjin University of Sport	127	227	45	0
Global Health Institute, Wuhan University	404. 25	484. 5	500	60

Continued

Names of Think Tanks	PAI	P	A	I
Center for Social Security Studies of Wuhan University	353. 75	641. 5	98	18
Research Center for Social Governance and Social Policy Collaborative Innovation, Xi'an Jiaotong University	115. 1	155	22	155
Hebei Provincial Public Policy Evaluation and Research Center, Yanshan University	605. 2	1,202	14	0
Academy of Social Governance, Zhejiang University	164. 7	258	119	0
Human Resources Research Center of Central South University	188. 05	314. 5	68	52

5.7   Urban and Rural Development and Regional Coordinated Development

In recent years, China has made remarkable progress in balancing urban and rural development and promoting new urbanization, but there are still problems to be solved. For example, the flow of urban and rural factors is not smooth, and the allocation of public resources is not reasonable. Some think tanks focus on the experience and problems in the process of urban and rural development and have carried out relevant policy research. In terms of regional coordination, *13th Five-year Plan for National Economic and Social Development* (*2016—2020*) has placed regional coordinated development in a prominent strategic position, reflecting the central government's important judgment on the current regional development situation. Since then, some think tanks have carried out theoretical research and practical discussion on promoting regional coordinated development and regional integration in their own professional fields. Table 11. 7 shows the 25 think tanks with high PAI values in this area.

Among them, the Center for Modern Chinese City Studies of East China Normal

University has a good performance. In the past three years, the center has actively applied for important projects. Based on projects, it has been engaged in theoretical research on urban geography, urban society and other disciplines, contributing in academic works, consulting reports, journal papers, and making suggestions on media. In the first half of 2019, the center published 7 academic works and more than 40 papers in Chinese and foreign languages and received interviews with important media such as *Guangming Daily* and *Xinhua Daily* giving expert suggestions. For example, *Report on Index of Urban Coordinated Development Capability in the Yangtze River Economic Belt* (*2019*), an important research achievement of the center, makes a systematic analysis of the coordinated development capacity of 110 cities of prefecture-level and above in the Yangtze river economic belt, and puts forward some measures and suggestions to improve the coordinated development capacity of the cities. It is highly recognized by the academic, political and business circles and wins the second prize of the "Outstanding Achievements of the 14th Shanghai Philosophy and Social Science Theory of Socialism with Chinese Characteristics". Its main research conclusions have also been widely reported by domestic mainstream media such as CCTV, xinhuanet. com, people. cn, sina. com. cn, ifeng. com and released by other domestic and foreign academic journals, such as *Erdkunde*, *Reform*, *People's Tribune and Resources* and *Environment in the Yangtze Basin*.

The Think Tank of Coastal Development of Yancheng Teachers University focuses on the coastal high-quality development goals, and, on the basis of doing a good job in theoretical research, does more in practical work, and constantly promotes the transformation of theoretical research results to the practical level. In terms of theoretical research, the think tank focuses on the theoretical innovation of marine economy and coastal industry development and has published 17 articles on *People's Daily*, *Guangming Daily*, *Qunzhong* and other journals, 5 monographs including *Research on Marine Economic Development Strategy of Jiangsu Province*, and 5 consecutive issues of *Journal of Coastal Development* through Social Sciences Academic Press. As for practical work, the think tank also explores its multiple functions in serving the high-quality development of China-South Korea (Yancheng) Industrial Park, fully participating in the building of the industrial park. It has organized specialized teams of the forces of government, firms, universities, and research institutes, signed formal agreements with the industrial park, and established a cooperation mechanism for smooth and effective cooperation. After that, focusing on the research of "industrial transformation and upgrading, environmental protection and utilization, park development and institutional mechanism innovation", the think tank has submitted a series of decision-making advisory reports to the think tanks of Yancheng municipal Party committee and government and the publicity department of Jiangsu provincial Party committee, putting forward practical suggestions and measures, and assisted the construction office of China-South Korea (Yancheng) Industrial Park to draft and submit the *Implementation Plan of the Construction of China-South Korea (Yancheng) Industrial Park*, playing an important role in service consultation.

As a research institute of regional development led by the publicity department of Guangdong provincial Party committee and jointly built by a number of government agencies and social groups, the Academy of Greater Bay Area Studies has gathered the top forces of Guangdong, Hong Kong and Macao's governments, firms, universities, research institutes and capital, striving to build a world-famous and domestic first-class high-end think tank so as to help the Guangdong-Hong Kong-

Macao greater bay area become an international first-class bay area and a world-class city group. Against the backdrop of internationalization, according to the laws of economic development in the greater bay area and relying on the resource advantages of the provincial development and reform commission, the provincial Hong Kong and Macao affairs office and the provincial academy of social sciences, the academy has built a scientific research and service platform, together with the expert teams of famous domestic and international universities and scientific research institutions, offering references for the decision-making of the regional governments and strengthening the scientific decision-making capability. At present, the academy has published a blue paper and a white paper on the Guangdong-Hong Kong-Macao greater bay area and opened a dedicated channel for the studies of the bay area.

Table 11.7   Top 20 Think Tanks in Urban and Rural Development and Regional

Coordinated Development According to Performance in PAI Assessment

(in alphabetical order according to the first letters of their names in pinyin spelling)

Names of Think Tanks	PAI	P	A	I
Institute of Anhui Economic and Social Development Research, Anhui University	973.1	1,687	428	6
Innovative Development Institute, Anhui University	995.55	1,861.5	216	0
Institute of Beijing Studies, Beijing Union University	253.2	462	48	39
Research Center for Economy of Upper Reaches of the Yangtze River, Chongqing Technology and Business University	257.1	363	252	0
Chongqing Think Tank	164.35	327.5	2	0
Guangdong Institute for International Strategies, Guangdong University of Foreign Studies	1,066.9	1,847	436	63
Institute of Studies for the Great Bay Area (Guangdong, Hong Kong, Macao), Guangdong University of Foreign Studies	298.4	404	276	68

Continued

Names of Think Tanks	PAI	P	A	I
Guangzhou Development Research Institute, Guangzhou University	205. 35	326. 5	101	59
Research Center of Yangtze River Delta Regional Integration, East China Normal University	245. 95	423. 5	114	0
The Center for Modern Chinese City Studies, East China Normal University	1,070. 35	1,377. 5	1,000	408
North Jiangsu Development Research Institute, Huaiyin Institute of Technology	336. 1	671	2	0
China (Henan) Innovation and Development Institute, Huanghe Science and Technology College	534. 4	478	540	667
Institute of Modernization, Jiangsu Provincial Academy of Social Sciences	341. 85	644. 5	60	8
Jiangxi Institute of Economic Development of Jiangxi Normal University	165. 95	274. 5	95	1
Soviet Area Revitalization Institute of Jingxi Normal University	455. 1	764	129	172
Jiangsu Yangtze Economic Belt Research Institute, Nantong University	418. 05	602. 5	116	410
Development Research Center of Inner Mongolia Autonomous Region	1,263. 3	2,339	198	172
Institute of Modernization	272. 5	545	0	0
West Tourism Development Research Base of China Tourism Academy, Shaanxi Normal University	187. 2	353	33	4
China Institute for Urban Governance, Shanghai Jiao Tong University	403. 45	423. 5	575	96
Economic Development Research Center of West China, Northwest University	193. 15	276. 5	121	93
Think Tank of Coastal Development, Yancheng Teachers University	255. 5	466	65	15
China Academy of West Region Development, Zhejiang University	377. 45	644. 5	184	0

Continued

Names of Think Tanks	PAI	P	A	I
The Co-Innovation Center for Social Management of Urban and Rural Communities in Hubei Province, Zhongnan University of Economics and Law	8,934.3	15,181	3,364	1,673

5.8 Law and Judicial Policies

General Secretary Xi Jinping mentioned at the first session of the Central Committee of Comprehensively Advancing the Rule of Law, "We must focus on the key links of comprehensively advancing the rule of law, improve the legislative system and the quality of legislation. We should promote strict law enforcement, straighten out the law enforcement system, improve administrative law enforcement procedures, and fully implement the responsibility system for administrative law enforcement. We should support the judicial organs to exercise their duties and powers independently according to law and improve the institutional arrangements for the division of responsibilities, cooperation and mutual restriction of judicial powers. We need to increase the efforts of improving public awareness of laws, and foster a legal environment in which the whole society acts in compliance with the law, and uses the law to resolve problems and conflicts. " We need to promote the rule of law through scientific legislation, strict law enforcement, fair administration of justice and law-abiding of the whole people, which have always been important measures for the modernization of national governance. Think tanks in the area of law and judicial policy research have carried out studies and decision-making consultation based on relevant professional disciplines on various important topics of legislation, justice, law enforcement and law-abiding. Table 11.8 shows 20 think tanks with high PAI values.

There are many think tanks in this area that study the macro strategy of enhancing the rule of law. The Center for the Development of Rule of Law and Judicial Reform Research of Zhongnan University of Economics and Law is one of the important representatives. Enjoying a high starting point, attaching great importance to progress, collaboration and system-building, it strives to provide high-quality consulting services for the legislation and decision-making of the central and local governments. The center focuses on studies on the rule of law in social governance, the rule of law in basic public services, legal protection in public security, the law of network social governance, the evaluation of the rule of law, the reform of the judicial system and other important research interests, producing many important results. *Exploration and Development of the Chief Procurator Attending the Judicial Committee*, one of the important achievements of the center, gives a thorough study on the system of the chief procurator attending the judicial committee and other important issues, providing a useful guide for deepening the implementation of this system. The paper was adopted by *References for Leaders* of the Supreme People's Procuratorate.

The Institute for China Legal Modernization Studies of Nanjing Normal University is also one of the important think tanks studying the macro strategy of rule of law development. Focusing on the important theoretical and practical issues of promoting the rule of law in China and enhancing the rule of law in Jiangsu Province, the institute has carried out in-depth theoretical and decision-making consulting research on the development strategy of the rule of law, the rule-of-law government, society under the rule of law, judicial reform and modernization, and the investigation of the situation of the rule of law in China. The institute has not only published theoretical articles on *China Daily*, *Guangming Daily*, qstheory. cn and other national mainstream media, but also organized important activities such as the think tank symposia of "Studying and Implementing the Guiding Principles of the 19th CPC National Congress", "Integrating Core Socialist Values into the Rule of Law" and "Making the Rule of Law Become an Important Symbol of the Development of Jiangsu's Core Competitiveness" and the high-level think tank forum "The Profound Change in the Prominent Challenge of Society in the New Era and the Modernization of Legal System", increasing the visibility and influence of the think tank.

In addition, some think tanks, relying on their own advantages, continue to develop towards the aim of being more specialized and accurate. They strive to be precise in researching, providing strong intellectual support for specialized legal fields, such as intellectual property research and environmental law research. The Center for Studies of Intellectual Property Rights of Zhongnan University of Economics and Law is one of the outstanding representatives of intellectual property research. It actively engages in the national and local legislative and judicial consultation, undertakes the application research projects of the departments, and provides legal services and legal consultation for society in various forms, striving to build itself into a "think tank" for national intellectual property research. Research Base for the Implementation of National Intellectual Property Strategy of Tianjin University, Guangdong Zhong Ce Intellectual Property Research Institute, Intellectual Property Research Institute of Xi'an Jiaotong University, the Research Center of Intellectual Property Development in Jiangsu etc. are also important think tanks in the field of intellectual property. The excellent achievements of these think tanks have provided important references for making China strong in intellectual property. In terms of studies on environmental law, the Research Institute of Environmental Law of Wuhan University has made remarkable achievements. As an important think tank in promoting environmental law-based governance, it has played an extremely important role in advancing the law-based governance in the environment. It has successively undertaken important projects entrusted by National People's Congress, National Development and Reform Commission, Ministry of Environmental Protection, Ministry of Land and Resources, and Ministry of Water Resources, and regularly presented the latest research results and relevant information on foreign environmental law to national legislature, executive and judiciary. It also closely follows the trends of international environmental conventions and negotiations and on many occasions sends personnel to participate in on-site negotiations on issues related to international treaties, such as *United Nations Convention on the Law of the Sea*, *Convention on Biological Diversity* and *International Mercury Convention* and engages in preparing relevant counterproposals. The institute has also become an important force in the academic exchange of environmental law in China. It has successively established "Luojia Environmental Law Forum", "Luojia Lecture Series on Environmental Law", "RIEL Alumni Salon" and other high-level platforms for academic exchange. In addition, the Research Center of the Rule of Law on Ecology and Environment of Hunan Normal University also focuses on the study of environmental law. Recently, it is actively proposing the comprehensive legislation for Dongting Lake to integrate the development and protection of the basin, realizing the comprehensive, scientific, standardized and efficient operation, so as to better provide legal guarantee for the Lake.

Table 11. 8   Top 20 Think Tanks in Law and Judicial Policies According

to Performance in PAI Assessment

(in alphabetical order according to the first letters of their names in pinyin spelling)

Names of Think Tanks	PAI	P	A	I
Institute for International Intellectual Property of Peking University	179. 55	202. 5	261	0
Center for Regional Integration for Rule of Law, Guangdong University of Foreign Studies	200. 5	342	97	2
Institute for Land Legal System Studies, Guangdong University of Foreign Studies	155. 35	128. 5	303	1
China Strategy Institute for Intellectual Property	165. 85	275. 5	55	58
East China University of Political Science and Law	118. 4	226	18	0
Guangdong Local Legislation Research Evaluation and Consultation Base, South China University of Technology	143. 2	286	0	1
Jilin University Crime Governance Research Center	137. 25	274. 5	0	0
The Research Center of Intellectual Property Development in Jiangsu, Nanjing University of Science and Technology	117. 5	134	161	11
Institute for Chinese Legal Modernization Studies, Nanjing Normal University	1,336. 05	2,410. 5	436	0
Center for Basic Laws of Hong Kong and Macao Special Administrative Regions, Shenzhen University	537. 4	435	569	746
Research Base for the Implementation of National Intellectual Property Strategy, Tianjin University	374. 3	353	654	8
Institute of International Law, Wuhan University	2,330. 8	4,616	76	0
Research Institute of Environmental Law, Wuhan University	385. 75	663. 5	180	0
Center for the Development of Rule of Law and Judicial Reform Research of Zhongnan University of Economics and Law	873. 9	998	379	1,306

Continued

Names of Think Tanks	PAI	P	A	I
Center for Studies of Intellectual Property Rights, Zhongnan University of Economics and Law	936. 4	1,437	599	191
Legislative Research Base for Education of Central South University	122. 7	177	114	0
Human Rights Center of Central South University	123. 85	130. 5	148	71
Institute of Medical and Health Law, CSU	118. 75	136. 5	157	17
Intellectual Property Research Institute of Central South University	248. 2	269	249	195
China Center for Cultural Law Research of Central South University	261. 3	364	225	59

5.9 Public Security

Public security is an important part of the overall national security, with the core goal of ensuring people's life and property security, social stability and order, and the sustainable operation of the economic and social system. General Secretary Xi Jinping points out that ensuring public safety is of great realistic and far-reaching significance for building a harmonious society, promoting the building of a moderately prosperous society in all respects, and even for the great rejuvenation of the Chinese nation. In this context, focusing on the major needs from the national or regional public security area, some think tanks make use of their own advantages and characteristics to make suggestions for the decision-making of public security and provide theoretical support and set the technical development direction for solving public security problems. Table 11. 9 shows the 5 think tanks with high PAI values in this area.

Jiangsu Public Security Institute of Jiangsu Police Institute gives full play to the institutional advantages of the close contact between public security think tanks and organs of public security and politics and law, highlights its professional strengths and the value proposition of serving the real-world practice, so as to promote the high-quality development of the think tank. The institute has made great efforts to build a distinctive brand of research on international law enforcement security cooperation and overseas interest protection, finishing 14 research reports on national conditions analysis, security risks and law enforcement security cooperation and 3 reports on national police system. In addition, through the brand activity "China Modern Policing Reform Forum" for domestic policing research and exchanges, the institute has become an important platform for gathering think tanks from all sides to contribute ideas and suggestions for the public security work. The institute also attaches great importance to theoretical innovation and public opinion guidance, strengthens cooperation with the media and makes efforts in ensuring a safe and secure China. It holds think tank seminars centering on major events, such as the 19th National Congress of the Communist Party of China, National Public Security Work Conference, and the Fourth Plenary Session of the 19th CPC Central Committee, and organizes experts to make their voice heard in a timely manner to effectively guide public opinion.

With the rapid development of China's economy and society, ensuring food safety is one of the important contents of implementing the Scientific Outlook on Development and building a harmonious society, which is also a very urgent task of public safety management. Committed to studies on food safety risk management, the Institute for Food Safety Management of Jiangnan University, based on real-life scenarios and specific problems and through empirical investigation and case analysis, has carried out a series of studies, scoring a series of important achievements. Series of *How to Ensure the "Safety of Every Bite of Food" from Farmland to Dining*

Table—Analysis of China's Food Safety Risk Management and Situation give a

comprehensive review of the concrete actions and innovative measures of China's food

safety management, give an in-depth analysis of the severe challenges faced by food

safety, and give relevant measures and suggestions. The full text was published on

Guangming Daily and later reposted by qstheory. cn, *Xinhua Digest*, huanqiu. com

and other important media, having a broad impact.

Table 11.9   Top 5 Think Tanks in Public Security According to Performance in PAI Assessment

(in alphabetical order according to the first letters of their names in pinyin spelling)

Names of Think Tanks	PAI	P	A	I
Institute of Modern Policing Reform, Ministry of Public Security	631. 6	904	560	58
Institute for Food Safety Risk Management, Jiangnan University	800. 6	1,187	239	677
Jiangsu Public Security Institute, Jiangsu Police Institute	925. 8	1,440	596	135
Food Safety Strategy and Management Research Center of Tianjin University of Science and Technology	104. 85	138. 5	92	40
Center for Capital Social Safety, People's Public Security University of China	162. 4	275	79	6

5.10   Culture Policy

Culture is an important force for the survival and development of a nation. Since

the 18th CPC National Congress, the CPC Central Committee headed by General

Secretary Xi Jinping has been sticking to the path of advanced socialist culture,

vigorously accelerating China's establishment as a country with a leading socialist

culture with a firm cultural self-confidence and a high degree of cultural

consciousness. Focusing on the new problems and requirements of cultural development, think tanks in this area carry out policy research on national culture, local culture, language culture, architectural culture, media, history and other aspects, and make suggestions for strengthening cultural confidence, forging ahead and making innovations, and promoting in-depth reform of the cultural system. Table 11. 10 shows 20 think tanks with high PAI values.

Based on the cross-over research and theoretical integration of humanities, social sciences and natural sciences, the Moral Development Institute of Southeast University focuses on "moral national conditions and moral frontiers" to study and solve major theoretical and practical problems in the development of ethics in China. Since its establishment, the think tank has achieved fruitful outcomes in the fields of government decision-making consultation, high-level theoretical research, moral national surveys, high-level research reports, international cooperation and exchange, and high-level academic forums. The most iconic original achievement is the project of constructing China's National Ethics Databases, which includes China Ethics Development Database and Evaluation System of Moral Development in Jiangsu Province. At the same time, in order to better absorb the theoretical suggestions of senior experts and scholars at home and abroad, listen to the decision-making opinions of government departments and discuss the practical problems of moral development, the think tank held Monthly Series of Think Tanks of Moral Development, spreading the influence of its theoretical achievements and diversifying ways of the transformation of their achievements.

Hubei Collaborative Innovation Center for Chinese Culture Development of Hubei University is a provincial collaborative innovation center for carrying forward culture. In recent years, focusing on cultural development, the center has constantly gathered academic teams, built collaborative innovation platforms, and developed six brands, including the blue book series of *Report on the Development of Chinese Culture*, collected papers of cultural development, series of ideological and cultural history, *Suggestions on Governance*, culture development forums and large-scale academic conferences, and the development of the think tank platform for Chinese cultural development. Taking culture development forums and large-scale academic conferences as examples, the center has successfully held World Culture Development Forum for 7 times, China Culture Development Forum for 6 times and Hubei Culture Development Forum for 3 times. At the same time, more than 70 high-level international and domestic academic conferences were held, including the first International Summit Forum on Virtue, Charrette on Further Carrying Forward and Developing Fine Chinese Traditions in Hubei, Symposium on Building a System of Philosophy and Social Sciences with Chinese Characteristics, the 2nd Summit Forum of Chinese Social Science and Ethics and International Value Philosophy Forum.

With a high degree of cultural mission and cultural consciousness, Soochow University Think Tank actively undertakes the important mission of carrying forward and developing the culture of Suzhou and Jiangnan. In recent years, in order to protect and rescue Suzhou's existing cultural resources, Soochow University Think Tank has adopted the method of oral history studies to record interviews with famous Suzhou experts and make feature films. It has launched more than ten series of books and documentaries, including "Soochow Masters: Artists Series" and "Soochow Masters: Famous Doctors Series". In addition, the "Dialogue with Suzhou" series of activities are the brand activities of the think tank, aiming to strengthen the effective communication between the academic community and the practical one, and realize the direct dialogue and exchange between scholars, Party and government leaders and entrepreneurs. It has been held for five years, becoming an important academic advisory platform for Suzhou municipal Party committee and government to establish development strategies, formulate development plans, and realize scientific decision-making. It is also an important brand to promote the dialogue and interaction between think tanks and the government and advance the innovative development of Suzhou.

Table 11. 10   Top 20 Think Tanks in Culture Policy According

to Performance in PAI Assessment

(in alphabetical order according to the first letters of their names

in pinyin spelling)

Names of Think Tanks	PAI	P	A	I
National Center for Research into International Communication of Arts, Peking University	142. 7	128	75	281
Beijing Cultural Exchange Research Center, Beijing Foreign Studies University	177. 8	262	156	0
International Institute of Chinese Studies, Beijing Foreign Studies University	916	1,424. 5	680	0
National Research Centre for State Language Capacity, Beijing Foreign Studies University	242. 15	443. 5	68	0
Moral Development Institute, Southeast University	606. 85	993. 5	337	45
Hubei Collaborative Innovation Center for Chinese Culture Development, Hubei University	192. 2	274	184	0
Center for Studies in Moral Culture of Hunan Normal University	417	627	299	69
The Institute for Modern Chinese Thought and Culture, East China Normal University	183. 5	313	90	0
The Research Institute of Nanjing Massacre History & International Peace	492. 75	646. 5	551	21
Purple Academy of Culture & Creativity, Nanjing University of Arts	230. 05	216. 5	406	0
Center for Studies of Mongolia, Inner Mongolia University	173. 45	317. 5	21	42

Continued

Names of Think Tanks	PAI	P	A	I
Northwest Institute of Historical Environment and Socio-Economic Development, Shaanxi Normal University	114. 1	144	97	65
Research Center of Foreign Language Strategies, Shanghai International Studies University	122. 3	228	27	1
Soochow University Think Tank	457. 8	909	11	0
International Research Centre for the Chinese Cultural Heritage Conservation, Tianjin University	125. 25	250. 5	0	0
Institute of National Culture Development, Wuhan University	292	578	10	0
Center for Studies of Media Development, Wuhan University	741. 2	805	1,037	138
Center for Collaborative Innovation in the Heritage and Development of Tibet Culture, Tibet Minzu University	414. 05	795. 5	39	23
Research Center of Chinese Village Culture, Central South University	181. 55	344. 5	9	33
Research Base of Central South University of Chinese Writers' Association Network Literature Committee	104. 45	165. 5	45	41

5.11 Education Policy

As an important component of new types of think tanks with Chinese characteristics, educational think tanks play an important role in serving national educational decision-making and promoting educational reform and development. In the new era, new educational think tanks with Chinese characteristics play multiple roles, such as the think tank for educational decision-making, think tank for educational reform, commentator of educational policies, guide of educational practice, evaluator of educational development, pool of high-level personnel, liaison office of educational exchange and source of positive public opinion. Besides, they contribute to making suggestions on policies, theoretical innovation, practice guidance, talent training, data reserve, public opinion guidance and so on. Table 11. 11 shows 10 think tanks with high PAI value in this area.

Standing at the height of the national macro strategy and guided by national major needs, National Institute of Educational Policy Research of East China Normal University, aiming at the major issues, such as economic and industrial layout, social development and institutional innovation, has carried out comprehensive research on education issues from multiple perspectives, such as economy, industry, region and society. The institute has created publications including *International Education Policy Review* and *Education Information Review* and has written more than ten monographs such as *In the Area of Institutional Innovation in Higher Education Resource Distribution in a Transitional Economy*. In addition, supported by the national education decision support system, in recent two years, National Institute of Educational Policy Research has submitted more than 80 special reports on the targeted poverty alleviation of the "three regions" and the "three prefectures", research on teacher staffing issues, survey on the treatment of state and non-state employed teachers, research on the integration of education in the Yangtze River Delta, research on educational innovation in the Yangtze River economic belt, and analysis of national teacher data. It has got approval from state leaders, Ministry of Education and Shanghai municipal leaders for nearly 60 times, and more than 10 research reports have been adopted by all levels of government.

It is an important trend of current education reform and development to improve education practice based on education big data and give full play to the supporting role of education monitoring and evaluation in education decision-making. Entrusted by the Ministry of Education, Collaborative Innovation Center of Assessment for Basic Education Quality has been responsible for the quality monitoring of national compulsory education for many years. Through organizing professional forces to analyze the monitoring results of each province, discovering the main problems existing in each province, continuously providing the national and local education administrative departments with monitoring results reports, and actively exploring ways to promote governments at all levels to use the monitoring results to improve the level of educational governance and advance the development of educational connotations, it has formed a closed-loop mechanism of "monitoring-feedback-rectification-promotion", which has promoted the governance of local education by the provincial government.

Institution of China's Science, Technology and Education Policy, Zhejiang University has always aimed at the frontiers of international engineering education development and focused on the reform of engineering education based on the development of new domestic engineering, carrying out research on characteristic think tanks. *International Engineering Education : Frontiers and Progress* compiled by the center in cooperation with the Education Committee of the Chinese Academy of Engineering is the first domestic theme publication to translate the research progress of international engineering education. The contents are divided into five sections: Research Report, Frontiers Review, Conference Notice, Event News and Publication Digest, which report the latest development trend of foreign engineering education research and policy, and provide references for domestic experts, scholars, policy makers and relevant managers engaged in engineering education research and practice.

Table 11. 11 Top 10 Think Tanks in Education Policy According

to Performance in PAI Assessment

(in alphabetical order according to the first letters of their names

in pinyin spelling)

Names of Think Tanks	PAI	P	A	I
China Institute of Education and Social Development, Beijing Normal University	1,762. 9	3,524	3	0
Institute of International and Comparative Education, Beijing Normal University	249	453	75	0
Collaborative Innovation Center of Assessment for Basic Education Quality, Beijing Normal University	337. 65	313. 5	603	0
National Institute of Educational Policy Research, East China Normal University	848. 05	1,276. 5	480	329
Institute of Schooling Reform and Development, East China Normal University	300. 5	453	206	61
The Institute of Curriculum and Instruction, East China Normal University	464. 35	699. 5	382	0
Center for Higher Education Development of Xiamen University	380. 7	731	28	34
Research Institute for International and Comparative Education, Shanghai Normal University	249. 35	347. 5	252	0
Changjiang Education Research Institute	264. 9	522	13	0
Institute of China's Science, Technology and Education Policy, Zhejiang University	396. 1	682	163	31

5. 12 Ecological Conservation

To uphold and improve the system of ecological conservation and promote harmonious coexistence between man and nature is an important instruction made at the fourth plenary session of the 19th CPC Central Committee. To promote ecological progress is a millennium plan related to the sustainable development of the Chinese nation. We must be guided by the conviction that lucid waters and lush mountains are invaluable assets, remain committed to the basic state policy of conserving resources and protecting the environment as well as the principle of giving high priority to conserving resources, protecting the environment and promoting its natural restoration, and pursue a model of sustainable development featuring increased production, higher living standards, and healthy ecosystems, carrying out the Beautiful China initiative. Think tanks in this area constantly review the disadvantages in the traditional development process, innovate development ideas, and contribute intellectual support to the development of the system of ecological conservation. Table 11.12 shows 10 think tanks with high PAI values in this area.

Focusing on scientific, economic development and public policy issues of climate change and environmental governance, Research Institute of Climate and Environmental Governance of Nanjing University of Information Science and Technology has carried out academic research and provided decision-making consultation and policy services in six aspects of climate change, environmental pollution, smog governance, low-carbon development, climate policy and ecological culture, sending Jiangsu's message of contributing to climate and environmental governance to support state decision-making. The backbone of the think tank focuses on the globalization of climate change, views the impact of climate change and pollution prevention methods from an international perspective, and conducts in-depth research from legal, economic, moral and foreign policy perspectives. It has published nearly ten works through China Social Sciences Press, Science Press and other authoritative publishing houses, including *Just Emissions: The Moral Foundation of Global Climate Governance* and *On the Value of China's Participation in International Climate Cooperation*.

There are four research offices under China Institute for Marine Affairs, namely, Marine Rights and Interests and Law, Marine Policy and Management, Marine Economy and Science and Technology, Marine Environment and Resources and many research achievements have been made in marine development strategy, policy, law, and rights and interests, marine economy and environmental resources. For many years, the institute and its experts have been engaged in various bilateral and multilateral diplomatic consultations on marine legal affairs, providing legal and policy advisory services to relevant government departments. The institute organized experts to draft important documents such as *China's Marine Agenda 21*, *China's Marine Development*, *Outline of the National Plan for the Development of the Marine Economy*, *Hainan Marine Economic Development Plan*, *Study on Maritime Delimitation in Chinese Waters*, *Atlas of Exclusive Economic Zones and the Continental Shelf of the People's Republic of China* and *Collection of State Marine Police Studies*. In addition to publishing works and papers, the institute also releases *China's Ocean Development Report* and organizes the High-Level Forum on China's Ocean Development every year, which are highly valued by government agencies, academia and society.

Table 11. 12   Top 10 Think Tanks in Ecological Conservation According to Performance in PAI Assessment

(in alphabetical order according to the first letters of their names in pinyin spelling)

Names of Think Tanks	PAI	P	A	I
Think Tank on Natural Disaster Prevention and Geological Environment Protection, Chengdu University of Technology	383. 6	682	142	0

Continued

Names of Think Tanks	PAI	P	A	I
China Institute for Marine Affairs	126.5	250	5	0
Research Center of Rule of Law for Environmental Protection, Hunan Normal University	166.75	279.5	90	0
Research Center for Longshan Green Economy of University of Jinan	97.25	185.5	15	0
Research Center of Low Carbon Economy for Guangzhou Region, Jinan University	97.05	120.5	110	19
Institute of Resource, Environment and Sustainable Development, Jinan University	128.25	213.5	65	10
Jiangxi Center of Cooperative Innovation for Eco-civilization System, Jiangxi University of Finance and Economics	155.1	247	100	8
Research Institute of Climatic and Environmental Governance, Nanjing University of Information Science and Technology	168	303	55	0
Research Base on National Marine Rights and Strategy, Shanghai Jiao Tong University	89	64	150	60
Center for Ecological Civilization of Zhejiang Province, Zhejiang Sci-Tech University	435.05	686.5	272	51

5.13 Energy and Infrastructure

To innovate and develop the energy industry, we need to strengthen basic research, expand and implement several major scientific and technological projects, and highlight key common technologies and modern engineering technologies. The development of infrastructure is an important condition for regional economic development. In recent years, think tanks in this area actively carry out relevant research based on their own advantages. Table 11.13 selects eight think tanks with high PAI values.

Beijing

Beijing Transport Institute was established with the approval of Beijing municipal Party committee and government in January 2002. The main responsibility of the institute is to carry out research on the development strategy, policy and planning of Beijing's transport. The institute has established Beijing Key Laboratory of Simulation and Decision Support of Urban Transport, Beijing Key Laboratory of the Testing and Evaluation of Urban Transport Energy Conservation and Emission Reduction, Beijing International Science and Technology Cooperation Base of Urban Transport, and National Energy Measurement Center (urban transport) and got the ISO 9001 certification in 2006. With its strong technical strength and modern management, it has provided high-quality advisory services for Beijing municipal government and relevant departments, and provided strong technical support for Beijing to build a modern transportation system. Beijing Institute of Logistics, Informatics and Service Sciences, which also belongs to Beijing Jiaotong University, has undertaken more than 160 major and key projects of National Natural Science Foundation, National "973" Project, National "863" Plan and other projects, with a total scientific research fund of more than 34 million yuan. It has won 1 National Prize for Progress in Science and Technology (2010), 2 third prizes of Beijing Science and Technology Award (2012, 2003), 1 first prize for Progress in Commercial Science and Technology (2008) and other important awards. The institute provides decision-making advisory services for the formulation of Beijing's logistics development plan during the "10th Five-year Plan", "11th Five-year Plan" and "12th Five-year Plan", makes outstanding contributions to the major issues of service sciences in the field of logistics and informatics in China and Beijing, and gradually forms a distinctive logistics and informatics theory and method system—logistics management and engineering theory and methods under the emerging IT.

Registered and managed by the State Commission Office of Public Sectors Reform, Electric Power Planning & Engineering Institute is a state-level high-level advisory body with more than 60 years of development. It mainly provides government departments, financial institutions and energy and power enterprises with research on industrial policy, development strategy, development planning and new technologies, as well as the evaluation and advisory and technical service of engineering projects. It also carries out works on the standardization and IT application of scientific research as well as international exchange and cooperation. Considering its role of serving the government and the industry as well as its long-term development needs, the institute puts forward its development vision of "energy think tank, national think tank" and the strategic goal of building itself into a "national high-level energy advisory body and professional think tank". In recent years, it has completed major plans and studies, such as the 13th Five-year Plan on National Energy Development, special study on energy international cooperation in electric power development planning and energy development plan of Xiong'an New Area, engaged in studies on important national and local policies and policies on energy and power system reform, undertaken supporting tasks in energy and electric power supervision, organized and implemented major systematic projects in the industry and deeply involved in international energy cooperation, providing high-quality think tank research support for building a green, low-carbon, safe and efficient modern energy system. In the future, with wisdom as the core and innovation as the driving force, the institute will strive to become a world-class energy think tank and international consultancy, and work together with all walks of life to jointly promote the transformation of global energy to clean, low-carbon and sustainable development, so as to promote the sustainable development of mankind.

Table 11. 13   Top 8 Think Tanks in Energy and Infrastructure According

to Performance in PAI Assessment

(in alphabetical order according to the first letters of their names

in pinyin spelling)

Names of Think Tanks	PAI	P	A	I
Research Center for Beijing Transportation Development, Beijing Jiaotong University	1,338. 25	1,643. 5	1,721	1
Beijing Logistics Informatics Research Base, Beijing Jiaotong University	177. 25	210. 5	240	0
Electric Power Planning & Engineering Institute	715. 65	1,198. 5	388	0
State Grid Energy Research Institute	504. 05	914. 5	156	0
China Southern Power Grid	139. 75	210. 5	115	0
Shanghai International Shipping Institute, Shanghai Maritime University	840. 05	1,426. 5	350	109
APEC Sustainable Energy Center, Tianjin University	220. 95	188. 5	421	2
Shaanxi Economic Research Center, Xi'an Jiaotong University	139. 7	231	72	13

5. 14   Information and Technology

Since the beginning of the 21st century, facing the new situation of world's scientific and technological revolution and industrial transformation, standing at a new starting point of China's development, General Secretary Xi Jinping has made an important judgement that "to achieve China's strong and prosperous development, we must vigorously develop science and technology", emphasizing that "to realize the great goal of building China into a great modern socialist country and realize the Chinese dream of great national rejuvenation, we must have scientific and technological strength and the ability to innovate", and that "we should open up a green channel connecting basic research and technological innovation, and strive to promote breakthroughs in application technology through basic research". In recent years, through the implementation of the core technology strategy, China has made breakthroughs in research and development and application of a number of network information technologies. According to the data filled out by think tanks in the area of information and technology, the system automatically calculates the scores of 15 think tanks with high PAI values, as shown in table 11. 14.

Among them, Institute of Global Innovation and Development of East China Normal University, a university think tank, is committed to the strategic research on the globalization of science and technology and China's innovation, geo-technology and national security. In recent years, in response to China's major strategic needs, it has conducted in-depth, basic and forward-looking research and has always been ready to undertake national projects in related fields, serving the central and national scientific decision-making and providing theoretical support for the solution of major practical problems.

Evaluation Center for Think Tank of Industry and Information Technology of Nanjing University of Aeronautics and Astronautics, also a university think tank, conducts academic research on major issues of industrial and information systems and think tank evaluation and provides accurate data and decision support for important issues of industrial and information systems and performance evaluation of think tanks. By creating a new university think tank research platform, it effectively promotes the development of think tanks in industrial and information systems. In order to give full play to the advantages of its resources and information analysis, the center has carried out visual analysis on the external characteristics and content characteristics of more than 43,000 papers on artificial intelligence, deeply explored the development trend of the subject at home and abroad, providing accurate data and decision support for the development of artificial intelligence under the background of "Double First-Class" initiative. Some of the achievements of the research have been written on *Development and Innovation* of *Artificial Intelligence Research from the Perspective of ESI Highly Cited Papers*, which won the first prize of JSSTI Achievements and the second prize of Achievements of Science and Technology Information of East China in 2019.

Institute of Science & Technology Strategy of Jiangxi Academy of Sciences provides scientific and technological services, such as scientific and technological strategic research, scientific and technological consultation, scientific and technological innovation and intellectual property analysis and appraisal for all levels of governments, industrial enterprises, scientific research institutes, colleges and universities in response to the major decision-making of the provincial Party committee and the government and the demand of the economic and social development of Jiangxi Province for science and technology, providing effective support for the macro decision-making on the development of science and technology, economy and society in Jiangxi Province as well as its innovation-driven development.

At the same time, in order to provide better services, the institute has successively established cooperative relations with Institute of Science and Development of Chinese Academy of Sciences, Chinese Sciences Library of Chinese Academy of Sciences, and Chinese Academy of Science and Technology for Development, realizing the sharing of scientific and technological information resources, the interaction between experts and collaborative tackling of scientific research projects.

As an enterprise think tank, AliResearch draws on the massive data of Alibaba Group to make meticulous efforts in studying cutting-edge cases of small and medium-sized enterprises and gather global business wisdom, so as to build an influential business knowledge platform through open cooperation and co-creation. Its slogan is "Insight into data by AliResearch to create new knowledge". Since its establishment in April 2007, the institute has worked closely with top scholars and institutions in the industry, focusing on e-commerce ecology, industrial upgrading, macroeconomics and other research fields, jointly launched a number of innovative data products, such as aSPI-core, aSPI, aEDI, aCCI and data map, a large number of research reports in the field of information economy, and thousands of classic case summaries of small enterprises. In the face of the governance problems brought about by the development of digital economy, AliResearch, through holding the New Economic Think Tank Summit, focuses on key issues, such as new technology, new economy, new governance, new think tanks, new responsibilities, and big future, deeply considers the value measure, innovation and competition of digital economy, and exchanges ideas on and insights into digital economy and governance, providing theoretical support for the development of digital economy of Ali and even society.

Table 11. 14   Top 15 Think Tanks in Information and Technology According to Performance in PAI Assessment

(in alphabetical order according to the first letters of their names

in pinyin spelling)

Names of Think Tanks	PAI	P	A	I
AliResearch	91	176	10	0
Zhejiang Informatization Development Institute, Hangzhou Dianzi University	59	110	12	2
Hunan Science and Technology Strategy Research Center	58. 25	116. 5	0	0

Continued

Names of Think Tanks	PAI	P	A	I
Institute of Global Innovation and Development, East China Normal University	410. 6	761	87	20
Third-Party Evaluation Think Tank for Performance of Major Scientific Projects and Platforms, South China University of Technology	121. 8	231	21	0
Anhui Big-Data Research Center on University Management, Huaibei Normal University	104. 35	150. 5	97	0
China Research Center for Scientific and Technological Policies and Management, Jilin University	90	132	80	0
Jiangxi Academy of Sciences Institute of Science & Technology Strategy	519	1,017	35	0
Evaluation Center for Think Tank of Industry and Information Technology, Nanjing University of Aeronautics and Astronautics	177. 2	322	54	0
Research Center for Technological Innovation, Tsinghua University	60. 9	93	48	0
Institute of Science and Technology for Development of Shandong	124. 15	166. 5	89	71
Wuzhen Institute	103	142	100	10
Academy of Development of Wuhan University	96. 6	192	2	0
Institute of Science and Development, Chinese Academy of Sciences	50. 5	101	0	0
China Institute of Science and Technology	104	208	0	0

5. 15　Poverty Alleviation and Three Rural Issues

The report of the 19th National Congress of the Communist Party of China notes that issues relating to "agriculture, rural areas, and rural people" are fundamental to China as they directly concern our country's economy and our people's wellbeing and must always be the top priority of the whole Party. In 2019, the No. 1 central document emphasized that we should firmly formulate policies to give priority to the development of agriculture and rural areas, and make the implementation of the "four priorities" as the top priority in our work related to "agriculture, rural areas, and rural people" by giving priority to funding for agriculture, rural areas and rural people, and giving priority to providing rural public services. Table 11. 15 shows 10 think tanks with high PAI values in the area of poverty alleviation and three rural issues according to the data filled out by think tanks in this area.

Institute of China Rural Studies of Central China Normal University is a specialized academic institution engaged in research on issues related to rural areas and rural people, also one of the 100 key research bases on humanities and social sciences designated by the Ministry of Education. Based on field work and guided by empirical research, CCRS has undertaken a series of national major projects and produced a number of high-level research results. In particular, CCRS has published academic papers on the Social Sciences in China (Chinese and English versions) for seven consecutive years since 2010, among which 6 papers have been published in Chinese, accounting for 22. 2% of the total publications in the discipline of political science, having a large academic influence. At present, the institute has formed a field work system with a main structure of "One Principal and Three Secondary". The types of survey cover "observation of one hundred villages", village survey, household survey, oral history survey, etc. Meanwhile, it has established a data storage platform "Think Tank for China Rural Policies" with a large amount of rural survey data. It is a single academic institution in China with the longest continuous survey time, the most staff input and the most comprehensive categories.

China Academy for Rural Development, Zhejiang University was founded in 1999. Its full name is Center for the Agricultural and Rural Development, Zhejiang

University. It is called CARD in English. It is one of the first batch of national key research bases of humanities and social sciences designated by the Ministry of Education, as well as an interdisciplinary and open institution for education, scientific research and policy consultation directly under Zhejiang University. The development goal of CARD is as follows. Guided by Xi Jinping's Thought on Socialism with Chinese Characteristics in the New Era and the strategy of serving the development of China's "three rural issues" and taking platform building, personnel training, scientific research, institutional mechanism building, and cross disciplinary integration as main tasks, thriving in Zhejiang and aiming to serving the whole country and the whole world, we strive to promote the integration of agricultural and forestry economic management and related disciplines, and through years of efforts, build a research base of humanities and social sciences and a high-end professional think tank with world-class disciplines, first-class scientific research strength and first-class ability of providing social service.

On the Fourth Plenary Session of the 19th Central Committee of the Communist Party of China, it is proposed to deepen the reform of the rural collective property rights system, develop rural economy and improve the basic rural management system. Institute of Anhui's Agricultural and Modernization Research is a comprehensive intelligence service platform for "three rural issues" established by Anhui Agricultural University in cooperation with a number of research institutions by pooling multi-disciplinary intelligence resources. The institute closely follows the central government's thought on the issues of agriculture, rural areas and rural people, and actively makes suggestions on related problems based on relevant documents of the central government. For example, a number of research results have been produced centering on the No. 1 central document in 2017 and 2018, which have been recognized and adopted by the local government. The institute will further give play to the advantages of its interdisciplinary research, widely integrate all kinds of resources, form a high-end professional think tank integrating strategic planning, forward-looking research and judgment, resource and political enlightenment, policy evaluation and public opinion guidance, and strive to build itself into a think tank for decision-making consultation of the agricultural modernization of Anhui provincial Party committee and provincial government, as well as a think tank for Anhui provincial governments at all levels and relevant departments to formulate policies on "agriculture, rural areas and rural people".

Table 11. 15   Top 10 Think Tanks in Poverty Alleviation and Three Rural Issues

According to Performance in PAI Assessment

(in alphabetical order according to the first letters of their names

in pinyin spelling)

Names of Think Tanks	PAI	P	A	I
Institute of Anhui's Agricultural and Modernization Research	311. 25	616. 5	10	0
Modern Agricultural Development Research Center, Northeast Agricultural University	126. 75	201. 5	60	40
Research Institute of Rural Education, Northeast Normal University	176. 9	331	38	0
Rural Development Research Institute of Hunan	64	128	0	0
Institute of China Rural Studies, Central China Normal University	4,389. 3	8,391	626	30
Research Center for Poverty Alleviation and Development in Ethnic Minority Areas, Jishou University	52. 65	85. 5	33	0
Jin Shanbao Agricultural Modernization Research Institute, Nanjing Agricultural University	249. 5	499	0	0

Continued

Names of Think Tanks	PAI	P	A	I
Center for Targeted Poverty Alleviation & Regional Development Research, Northwest Normal University	54. 9	105	8	0
China Academy for Rural Development of Zhejiang University	645. 9	789	504	501
Center for China Farmers' Development, Zhejiang A&F University	67. 6	122	22	0

5.16 The Belt and Road Initiative

Since the Belt and Road Initiative was proposed, it has changed from an initiative to action, from an idea to practice, and has now become the world's largest international cooperation platform and the most popular international public product. The Belt and Road Initiative emphasizes connectivity and win-win cooperation and aims at promoting connectivity in the five priority areas as policy, infrastructure, trade, finance and people-to-people ties, pushing countries along the routes to deepen cooperation and exchanges in various areas. So far, the Belt and Road Initiative is still an important issue for national development, also a key topic for many think tanks. According to the data filled out by think tanks in the area of the Belt and Road Initiative, table 11. 16 shows the 10 think tanks with high PAI values in this area.

With "thriving in Western China to serve Shaanxi and China with a global vision" as its philosophy and supported by Shaanxi provincial Party committee and provincial government, XJTU Institute of the Belt and Road Pilot Free Trade Zone integrates high-quality intellectual resources at home and abroad and explores ways to create a multilateral, open and innovative ecological platform of shared benefit for resource and political enlightenment through institutional innovation and task-driven development. Relevant research results of the institute are submitted to relevant departments of the state, provinces and cities for reference through such channels as *Special Issue Report* and *Suggestions on Decision-Making* (special issue of XJTU Institute), which effectively promotes the implementation of the idea of building the Central Legal Services District and the Intellectual Property Securitization Exchange, advancing the key work of the free trade zone. In addition, in line with the philosophy of "openness, inclusiveness, innovation, coordination and complementarity", the institute holds the China (Shaanxi) Pilot Free Trade Zone Development Forum, building a high-end think tank exchange platform for government, industry, universities, research institutes and applications. It also organizes experts to attend seminars held by the Counsellors' Office of the State Council, China Economic Information Service of Xinhua News, Hainan Federation of Social Science Circles and government departments and research institutions at all levels, continuously providing high-quality decision-making advisory services.

China Academy of the "Belt and Road" Initiative of Beijing International Studies University directly serves the national strategy of the Silk Road Economic Belt and the 21st Century Maritime Silk Road, building a broad platform for international cooperation and exchanges. The academy conducts long-term research on national studies, investment and security, humanities and diplomacy, language strategy and long-term policy in countries and areas along the routes and serves central and national ministries and commissions and embassies and consulates in countries along the routes by publishing research briefs and blue books on the initiative, holding relevant forums and engaging in relevant tasks, giving full play to its role of decision-making consultation in the connectivity project of the Belt and Road Initiative and providing core support for the initiative.

Founded in 2013, Grandview Institution is one of the famous independent think tanks in China. The institution adheres to the development philosophy that a high level of mutual understanding in the international community is the key to promoting efficient and effective global governance and devotes itself to the security, prosperity and stability of China. It focuses on the Belt and Road Initiative, overseas investment, maritime strategy, blue economy, frontier governance and global counter-terrorism. Adhering to the "application research oriented and information research based" research thinking Grandview Institution has set up a research team of more than 100 people to give advice and suggestions to China's decision-makers through independent reports, government special reports, internal media reports and other forms, and participated in relevant major strategic research of the Ministry of Foreign Affairs, National Development and Reform Commission, State Oceanic Administration and many other departments of the central government. Its research results are highly recognized by the decision-makers. At the same time, as a think tank in the area of the Belt and Road Initiative, Grandview Institution has developed the first domestic research system and database of opinions of global marine strategy and actively promoted the series of dialogues on cooperation and development of countries along the routes to realize the integration of knowledge and action of its functions.

Table 11. 16   Top 10 Think Tanks in the Belt and Road Initiative According

to Performance in PAI Assessment

(in alphabetical order according to the first letters of their names

in pinyin spelling)

Names of Think Tanks	PAI	P	A	I
China Academy of Belt and Road Initiative, Beijing International Studies University	231. 85	286. 5	254	107

Continued

Names of Think Tanks	PAI	P	A	I
Fudan Institute of Belt and Road and Global Governance	142. 4	127	175	132
Grandview Institution	148. 3	110	235	114
Hainan University Belt and Road Research Institute	165. 05	116. 5	158	297
Institute of the Belt and Road, Jiangsu Normal University	209. 6	324	156	4
Collaborative Innovation Center for the Study on China, Mongolia and Russia Economic and Trade Cooperation & Construction of Economic Belt on the Prairie Silk Road, Inner Mongolia University of Finance and Economics	636. 1	1 031	402	0
XJTU Institute of "the Belt and Road" Pilot Free Trade Zone	367. 35	583. 5	142	165
Think Tank on Ethnic Issues of Countries along "the Belt and Road Initiative", Yunnan University	197. 75	386. 5	15	0
Ningbo Maritime Silk Road Institute, Zhejiang Wanli University	108. 9	101	194	1
China Silk Road iValley Research	310. 6	235	369	412

5. 17　Comprehensive Think Tanks

In addition to the 16 main research fields mentioned above, there is also a type of comprehensive think tanks, mainly composed of local Party schools/administrative colleges, academies of social sciences, etc. Different from think tanks in other areas, comprehensive think tanks often carry out interdisciplinary, multidisciplinary and comprehensive research. There are 51 comprehensive think tanks in CTTI source think tanks, and 61% of them are provincial academies of social sciences.

According to the important instructions of the central government of building philosophy and social sciences with Chinese characteristics and the requirements of

Tianjin municipal Party committee and guided by Xi Jinping's Thought on Socialism with Chinese Characteristics for a New Era, Tianjin Academy of Social Sciences puts think tank development in the first place and strives to build itself into a strong theoretical arena for Marxism, a research base for philosophy and social sciences, and a comprehensive high-end think tank. At present, there are 7 think-tank research centers under the academy, including Tianjin Research Center of the theoretical system of socialism with Chinese characteristics, Tianjin Research Center for Public Opinions, Center for City Studies, Tianjin Research Center for History and Culture, Research Center for Beijing-Tianjin-Hebei Coordinated Development, Research Center for Social Governance, and Research Center for Northeast Asia Regional Cooperation. Supported by a number of think-tank research centers, Tianjin Academy of Social Sciences has undertaken a large number of national and Tianjin research projects and has received various awards from the state and Tianjin for many times. In addition, the academy also attaches great importance to academic exchanges. It establishes extensive academic contacts with universities and scientific research institutions at home and abroad and carries out long-term and in-depth academic exchanges and cooperation with academic institutions of Northeast Asian countries, such as Russia, Japan and South Korea.

As the only comprehensive research institute of philosophy and social sciences in Ningxia Hui Autonomous Region, Ningxia Academy of Social Sciences is an important research base of philosophy and social sciences in the region. Ningxia Academy of Social Sciences has sponsored three academic journals, *Ningxia Social Sciences*, *Journal of Hui Muslim Minority Studies*, and *Tangut Research*, and two internal publications, *Ningxia Chronicle* and *New Think Tank*. *Decision-Making Consultancy* and *Submission* compiled and issued by the academy plays a role in giving decision-making suggestions and plays an irreplaceable role in reflecting the diversity and timeliness of think tank achievements and promoting the transformation of think tank results. After years of development, a social science research system has been gradually established, with Ningxia major practical issues as the brand, blue books as the platform, major projects as the support, the compilation and collation of history and ancient books as the key efforts, and academic journals as important carriers. At present, there are nine disciplines, i. e. , Hui studies, Tangut studies, local history and culture, applied economics, sociology, political science, law, ecological civilization, culture studies and ethnic literature studies, forming basic, key and supported disciplines that can give support, have strong advantages and generate bigger potentials, and setting up a multi-level and multidisciplinary echelon that is mainly composed of chief experts, pacesetters and the backbone of disciplines.

Hebei Academy of Social Sciences is a government-affiliated institution directly under Hebei provincial Party committee and provincial government. It is a societies-affiliating institution for social sciences research and theoretical publicity. In recent years, guided by Xi Jinping's Thought on Socialism with Chinese Characteristics for a New Era, the academy has attached importance to building up the discipline system and talent team and has actively given full play to its complete disciplines and intensive research talents. It sponsors three public publications, namely *Hebei Academic Journal*, *Economic Forum* and *Tribune of Social Sciences*, and other publications, such as *Hebei Social Sciences*, *Think Tank Report*, *Policy Reference* and *Decision Reference*. It also jointly sponsored *Theory Learning Newsletter of the Party Committee Central Group*, *Theory Information* and other internal publications with the provincial publicity department of the Party committee. It carries out extensive international academic exchanges and cooperation and constantly raises the level of scientific research and management. So far, it has established long-term and stable academic exchanges and cooperation with nearly 30 research institutions and universities in major countries, Hong Kong and China's Taiwan.

In order to promote regional development, various comprehensive think tanks have also carried out a number of surveys on local issues, and many excellent achievements have been approved and adopted by leaders of the provincial Party committee. These results include Party School of Heilongjiang Provincial Committee of CPC (Heilongjiang Academy of Governance)'s *Research on Measures for the Transformation and Development of Coal Cities in Heilongjiang Province* and *Suggestions on Promoting the Standard Development of New Types of Agricultural Businesses in Heilongjiang Province*, Anhui Academy of Social Sciences' *Research on Tracking Public Opinions of Major Decisions of the Central and Anhui Provincial Party Committees*, Party School of Shandong Provincial Committee of CPC (Shandong Academy of Governance)'s *Talents Recruiting Calls for Precise Efforts: A Case Study of Binzhou's Efforts in Attracting Graduates to Return*, Party School of Guizhou Provincial Committee of CPC (Guizhou Academy of Governance)'s *To Promote Private Investment : From Shenzhen's Practice to Guizhou's Suggestions* and Real *Problems of Poverty Alleviation through Relocation from Inhospitable Areas and Their Solutions*.

Think Tanks in CTTI (2019)

(in alphabetical order according to the pinyin spelling of names)

(Ⅰ) Think Tanks of Party or Government Institutions (71)

Beijing Institute of Letters to Government

Tariff Policy Research Center of Ministry of Finance of the People's Republic of China

International Economics and Finance Institute

Economic Information of Chongqing (Comprehensive Economic Institute of Chongqing)

China Center for Contemporary World Studies

Development Research Center of Fujian Provincial People's Government

Public Security Development Strategy Research Institute of the Ministry of Public Security

Public Security Development Strategy Research Institute of the Ministry of Public Security City Police Work Research Center

Institute of Modern Policing Reform of Ministry of Public Security

International Cooperation Center of National Development and Reform Commission

Academy of Macroeconomic Research of National Development and Reform Commission

China Institute for Marine Affairs

National Center for Education Development Research

Development Research Center of the State Administration for Market Regulation

Taxation Institute of State Administration of Taxation

China Institute of Sport Science

China National Health Development Research Center

National Institute of Hospital Administration

China Communication Research Center, State Administration of Press, Publication, Radio, Film and Television

National Center for Climate Change Strategy and International Cooperation

Intellectual Property Development Research Center of the State Intellectual Property Office

Strategic Research Center of Oil and Gas Resources, MLR

State Grid Energy Research Institute

Development Research Center of the State Council

The Institute of Fiscal Science and Policy of Hebei Province

Macroeconomic Research Institute in Hebei Province Development and Reform Committee

Research Institute of Machinery Industry Economics & Management

Development Research Center, the People' Government of Jilin Province

Research Institute of People' Government of Jiangsu Province

Jiangxi Provincial Research Center

Research Center for Social Science Development of Higher Education Institutions, the Ministry of Education

Development Research Center of Liaoning Provincial Government

The Research Institute of Nanjing Massacre History & International Peace

Development Research Center of Inner Mongolia Autonomous Region

Research Center for Rural Economy

National Society for the CPC Building Studies

Shandong Academy of Innovation Strategy

Shandong Macroeconomics Research Institute

Chinese Academy of International Trade and Economic Cooperation

Shanghai Academy of Development and Reform

Shanghai Academy of Educational Sciences

Shanghai Pudong Academy of Reform and Development (Institute of China (Shanghai) Free Trade Zone)

The Development Research Center of Shanghai Municipal People's Government

Policy Research Center for Environment and Economy, Ministry of Ecology and Environment of the people's Republic of China.

Ministry of Justice Crime Prevention Research Institute

Binhai Research Institute in Tianjin

Tianjin Innovation and Development Institute

Center for Studies of United Front

Zhejiang Development & Planning Institute (ZDPI)

Central Compilation & Translation Bureau

The Research of Marxism of Central Compilation & Translation Bureau

World Development Strategy Research of Central Compilation & Translation Bureau

Chinese Academy of Fiscal Sciences

China Center for Urban Development

China Institute of International Studies

Chinese Institute of Land and Resources Economy

National Institute of Education Sciences

Chinese Academy of Labour and Social Security

China Research Center on Aging

China Tourism Academy

Research Institute of Yangtze River Delta, China Executive Leadership Academy Pudong

Research Institute of Leadership, China Executive Leadership Academy Pudong

Research Institute of Socialism with Chinese Characteristics, China Executive Leadership Academy Pudong

China Youth & Children Research Center

Financial Institute of the People's Bank of China

Chinese Academy of Personnel Science

National Statistical Society of China

Chinese Academy of Cultural Heritage

China Institutes of Contemporary International Relations

Chinese Academy of Press and Publication

Ministry of Civil Affairs of the People's Republic of China

(Ⅱ) Think Tanks of Academies of Social Sciences (51)

Anhui Academy of Social Sciences

Beijing Academy of Social Sciences

Chongqing Academy of Social Sciences

Chongqing Center for Productivity Development

Institute for Innovative City

Fujian Academy of Social Sciences

Gansu Academy of Social Sciences

Guangdong Academy of Social Sciences

Guangxi Academy of Social Sciences

Guizhou Academy of Social Sciences

Hainan Academy of Social Sciences

Hebei Academy of Social Sciences

Henan Academy of Social Sciences

Heilongjiang Academy of Social Sciences

Strategic Research Institute for Northeast Asia, Heilongjiang Academy of Social Sciences

Institute for Social Development and Local Governance of Heilongjiang, Heilongjiang Academy of Social Sciences

Hubei Academy of Social Sciences

Hunan Academy of Social Sciences

Jilin Academy of Social Sciences

Jiangsu Academy of Social Sciences

Institute of Modernization, Jiangsu Academy of Social Sciences

Jiangxi Academy of Social Sciences

Liaoning Academy of Social Sciences

Nanjing Academy of Social Sciences

Inner Mongolia Academy of Social Sciences

Ningxia Academy of Social Sciences

Qinghai Academy of Social Sciences

Institute of Modernization

Shandong Academy of Social Sciences

Shaanxi Academy of Social Sciences

Shanghai Academy of Social Sciences

Sichuan Academy of Social Sciences

Tianjin Academy of Social Sciences

Tibet Academy of Social Sciences，TAR

Xinjiang Academy of Social Sciences

Yunnan Academy of Social Sciences

Zhejiang Academy of Social Sciences

Chinese Academy of Social Sciences(CASS)

National Academy of Economic Strategy，CASS

Marxist Political Economy Innovation Think Tank in Contemporary China，CASS

The Institute of Contemporary China Studies，CASS

National Institution for Finance & Development，CASS

National Institute of Global Strategy，CASS

Institute of European Studies of Chinese Academy of Social Sciences Shanghai Academy，CASS

National Institute of Social Development，CASS

Institute of World Economics and Politics，CASS

Taiwan Institute of Chinese Academy of Social Sciences

Ideological Research Institute of Chinese Academy of Social Sciences

China National Center for Cultural Studies，CASS

China-CEEC Think Tanks Network，CASS

（Ⅲ）Think Tanks of Party Schools or Administrative Colleges（49）

Research &. Assessment Center for Anhui Public Policy of Anhui School of Administration

Gansu Institute of Public Administration

Chinese Academy of Governance

E-Governance Research Center of China National School of Administration

Research Center for Development Strategy and Public Policy of China National School of Administration

Advisory Committee for Party Decision of China National School of Administration

Hebei Academy of Governance

Hunan Science and Technology Strategy Research Center

Shandong Academy of Governance

Shaanxi Academy of Governance

Institute for Leapfrog Development of Yunnan

Anhui Provincial Committee Party School of CPC

Party School of CPC Beijing Municipal Committee, Shanghai Administration College

Party School of Chongqing Provincial Committee of CPC, Chongqing Institute of Administration

Fujian Provincial Committee Party School of CPC, Fujian Administration College

Gansu Provincial Party School of CPC

Party School of the Guangdong Provincial Committee of CPC, Guangdong Institute of Public Administration

Party School of Guangxi Zhuang Autonomous Region Committee of CPC, Guangxi Institute of Public Administration

Guizhou Provincial Party School of CPC, Guizhou Administration College

Hainan Provincial Party School of CPC, Hainan Academy of Governance

Hebei Provincial Party School of CPC

Henan Provincial Party School of CPC, Henan Academy of Governance

Heilongjiang Provincial Party School of CPC, Heilongjiang Academy of Governance

Hubei Provincial Party School of CPC, Hubei Academy of Governance

Party School of the Hunan Provincial Committee of CPC, Hunan Academy of Governance

Party School of the Jilin Provincial Committee of CPC, Jilin Academy of Governance

Party School of the Jiangsu Provincial Committee of CPC

Party School of CPC Jiangsu Provincial Cornitlee, Jiangsu research institute of Porty Building Theory and Practice Innovation

Party School of the Jiangxi Provincial Committee of CPC, Jiangxi Academy of Governance

Party School of the Liaoning Provincial Committee of CPC

Party School of Inner Mongolia Autonomous Region Committee of CPC, Inner Mongolia Academy of Governance

Party School of Ningxia Hui Autonomous Region Committee of CPC, Ningxia Academy of Governance

Party School of the Qinghai Provincial Committee of CPC, Qinghai Academy of Governance

Party School of the Shandong Provincial Committee of CPC

Party School of the Shaanxi Provincial Committee of CPC

Party School of CPC Shanghai Municipal Committee, Shanghai Administration College

Party School of the Sichuan Provincial Committee of CPC

Party School of the Tianjin Municipal Committee of CPC, Tianjin Academy of Governance

Party School of the Tianjin Municipal Committee of CPC, Research Center of New-Era Innovative and Service-Oriented Government

Party School of the Tianjin Municipal Committee of CPC, Research Center of Tianjin New-Era Decision-Making of CPC

Party School of the Tianjin Municipal Committee of CPC, Research Center of New-Era Modern Economic System

Party School of Tibet Autonomous Region Committee of CPC, Tibet Autonomous Region Academy of Governance

Party School of Xinjiang Uygur Autonomous Region Committee of CPC, Xinjiang Uygur Autonomous Region Academy of Governance

Party School of Zhejiang Provincial Committee of CPC, Zhejiang Institute of Administration

Party School of Central Committee of CPC

Department of Party Building, Party School of Central Committee of CPC

Institutes for International Strategic Studies

China Society of Administration Reform (CSOAR)

Research Institute for the China's Political Party System of the Central Institute of Socialism

（Ⅳ）University Think Tanks（572）

Institute of Anhui Economic Development Research, Anhui University of Finance & Economics

Innovative Development Institute, Anhui University

Institute of Anhui's Agricultural and Modernization Research

Institute of Information and Strategy Studies, Peking University

Institute of International Intellectual Property of Peking University

National Center for Research into International Communication of Arts, Peking University

National School of Development, Peking University

Institute of State Governance Studies, Peking University

The HSBC Financial Research Institute at Peking University

Institute for Cultural Industries, Peking University

The Constitution and Administrative Law Research Center of Peking University

Research Center for China Urban Economy, Peking University

Beijing Research Institute of International Cultural Communication, Beijing International Studies University

Beijing Tourism Development Research Center, Beijing International Studies University

Beijing Research Institute of Cultural Trade of Beijing International Studies University

China Academy of Belt and Road Initiative, Beijing International Studies University

Research Center of Capital Garment Culture and Industry of Beijing Institute of Fashion Technology

Beijing Social Building Research Base, Beijing University of Technology

Research Base of Beijing Modern Manufacturing Development, Beijing University of Technology

Institute of Higher Education, Beihang University

MIIT Key Laboratory of Law Strategy and Management of Industry and Information Technology, Beihang University

China Aeronautical Engineering Science and Technology Development Strategy Research Institute, Beihang University

Beijing Center for Industrial Security and Development Research, Beijing Jiaotong University

Research Center for Beijing Transportation Development, Beijing Jiaotong University

Beijing Humanistic Transportation, Science and Technology Transportation and Green Transportation Research Centre, Beijing Jiaotong University

Beijing Logistics Informatics Research Base, Beijing Jiaotong University

National Academy of Economic Security, Beijing Jiaotong University

Capital University Students Ideological and Political Education Research Institute, Beijing Jiaotong University

Institute of Adapting Marxism to Chinese Conditions and Cultural Development, Beijing Jiaotong University

Sustainable Development Research Institute for Economy and Society of Beijing

Institute of Beijing Studies, Beijing Union University

Beijing Research Center for New Countryside Construction, Beijing University of Agriculture

Institute of International and Comparative Education, Beijing Normal University

Capital Economics of Education Research Base, Beijing Normal University

Beijing Institute of Culture Innovation and Communication of Beijing Normal University

Smart Learning Institute of Beijing Normal University

Collaborative Innovation Center of Assessment for Basic Education Quality, Beijing Normal University

China Institute of Education and Social Development, Beijing Normal University

China Institute for Income Distribution, Beijing Normal University

Winter Olympics Culture Research Center of Beijing Sport University

Sport Research Academy of General Administration of Sport of China, Beijing Sport University

China Wushu School (Research Institute of Traditional Chinese Sports), Beijing Sport University

Beijing Cultural Exchange Research Center, Beijing Foreign Studies University

G20-BFSU Center, Beijing Foreign Studies University

Center for Public Diplomacy, Beijing Foreign Studies University

International Institute of Chinese Studies, Beijing Foreign Studies University

National Research Center for State Language Capability, Beijing Foreign Studies University

Gulf Arab States Research Center, Beijing Foreign Studies University

National Research Center for Canadian Studies, Beijing Foreign Studies University

Center for Japanese Studies, Beijing Foreign Studies University

British Studies Centre, Beijing Foreign Studies University

Center for China-Germany People-to-People Exchange Studies, Beijing Foreign

Studies University

Center for Central and Eastern European Studies, Beijing Foreign Studies University

Center for Education Law, Beijing Foreign Studies University

Research Center for Knowledge Management, Beijing Information Science & Technology University

Beijing Literature Language and Cultural Heritage Center, Beijing Language and Culture University

Sichuan Mineral Resources Research Center, Chengdu University of Technology

Think Tank on Natural Disaster Prevention and Geological Environment Protection, Chengdu University of Technology

Research Center for Urban Green Development

Institute of Urban-Rural Construction and Development, Chongqing University

Center for Public Economy & Public Policy Research, Chongqing University

Legal Strategy Research Institute of National Cyberspace Security and Big Data, Chongqing University

Consilium Research Institute, Chongqing University

Institute for Sustainable Development Research of Chongqing University

Institute for China Public Service Evaluation and Research, Chongqing University

Research Center for Economy of Upper Reaches of the Yangtze River, Chongqing Technology and Business University

Chongqing's University Research and Consultation Center for Stability Maintenance

Think Tank for Yunnan Religious Governance and Ethnic Unity and Progress, Dali University

Belt and Road Initiative Research Institute, Dalian Maritime University

Northeast Asia Research Center, Dalian University of Foreign Languages

Daqing Spirit and Longjiang Western Economic and Social Development Research Center

Institute of Economic and Social Development, Dongbei University of Finance and Economics

China Academy of Northeast Revitalization, Northeastern University

Modern Agricultural Development Research Center, Northeastern Agricultural University

Institute of East Asian Studies, Northeast Normal University

Research Institute of Rural Education, Northeast Normal University

Moral Development Institute, Southeast University

Research Center for Anti-Corruption with Rule of Law, Southeast University

Research Center for the Juvenile of Jiangsu Province (Delinquency Prevention), Southeast University

Research Center for the Restoration of Community Correction of Jiangsu Province, Southeast University

Research Center for Traffic Rule of Law and Development, Southeast University

Judicial Big Data Platform of People's Court, Southeast University

Research Center for Modern Management Accounting Innovation, Southeast University

Southeast University Art Big Data and China Art Development Evaluation Research Center

China High Quality Development Evaluation Research Institute, Southeast University

Institute for the Development of Socialism with Chinese Characteristics, Southeast University

Institute of International Economics, University of International Business and Economics

The Academy of China Open Economy Studies, University of International Business and Economics

Institute of Education and Economy Research, University of International Business and Economics

Research Institute for Global Value Chains, University of International Business and Economics

China Institute for WTO Studies, University of International Business and Economics

National Research Center for Economic Comprehensive Competitiveness, Fujian Normal University

Fudan Development Institute, Fudan University

Institute of International Studies, Fudan University

Center for American Studies, Fudan University

Fudan University Center for Population and Development Policy Studies

Center for Think Tanks Research and Management in Shanghai, Fudan University

Center for Asia-Pacific Cooperation and Governance, Fudan University

Fudan Institute of Belt and Road and Global Governance

Center for Party Building and State Development Studies, Fudan University

Research Institute of Chinese Economy, Fudan University

China Institute, Fudan University

The Research Center for Investigative Theory and Application in Northwestern Ethnic Regions, Gansu Institute of Political Science and Law

National Economics Research Center, Guangdong University of Finance and

Economics

Collaborative Innovation Department Center of Pearl River Delta for Science, Technology & Finance Industries, Guangdong University of Finance and Economics

Guangdong Institute for International Strategies, Guangdong University of Foreign Studies

Center for International Migration Studies, Guangdong University of Foreign Studies

Center for Canadian Studies, Guangdong University of Foreign Studies

Center for Regional Integration for Rule of Law, Guangdong University of Foreign Studies

Institute for Land Legal System Studies, Guangdong University of Foreign Studies

Collaborative Innovation Center for Language Research & Service, Guangdong University of Foreign Studies

Institute of Studies for the Great Bay Area (Guangdong, Hong Kong, Macao), Guangdong University of Foreign Studies

Guangxi Research Institute for Innovation and Development of Guangxi University

China-ASEAN Research Institute, Guangxi University

Guangxi Development Research Institute of Intellectual Property, Guangxi University of Nationalities

Guangzhou Development Research Institute, Guangzhou University

Guizhou Research Institute of Big Data Industry Development and Application, Guizhou University

ASEAN Research Institute of Guizhou University

Institution of Public Market and Government Procurement, University of International Relations

Center for International Strategy and Security Studies, University of International Relations

Heilongjiang Regional Innovation Driven Development Research Center, Harbin Engineering University

"Belt and Road" Think Tank for Talent Strategy, Harbin Institute of Technology

Heilongjiang Innovation and Entrepreneurship Research Center, Harbin Institute of Technology

Think Tank of Public Health Security and Medical Reform Strategy of Heilongjiang, Harbin Medical University

Hainan University Belt and Road Research Institute

Hainan Policy and Industrial Reform Institute of Low-Carbon Economy, Hainan University

Hainan Institute of Development on International Tourist Destination, Hainan University

Research Center for Policy and Law of the South China Sea of Hainan Province, Hainan University

Development Strategy and Evaluation Research Center for Strong Province of Higher Education, Hangzhou Dianzi University

Zhejiang Informatization Development Institute, Hangzhou Dianzi University

Hebei Research Center for Eco-Environment Sciences, Hebei University

Hebei Cultural Industry Development Research Center, Hebei University

Intercultural Communication Research Center of Hebei University

Center for Beijing-Tianjin-Hebei Development Research, Hebei University of Technology

Institute of De Rong, Hebei Finance University

Hebei Research Center for Moral Culture and Social Development, Hebei University of Economics and Business

Collaborative Innovation Center for Beijing-Tianjin-Hebei Integrated Development, Hebei University of Economics and Business

Collaborative Innovation Center of Social Governance by Law and Virtue, Hebei University of Economics and Business

Research Base for Modern Service and Public Policy, Hebei Normal University

Research Center for Changcheng Cultural Security, Hebei Normal University

Academy of Hinterland Development, Henan University

Institute for Cultural Development and Strategy of Heilongjiang University

Institute for Longjiang Revitalization and Development, Heilongjiang University

Co-Innovation Center of Cultural Development and Strategy, Heilongjiang University

Co-Innovation Center of Sino-Russia Strategy, Heilongjiang University

Hubei Institute of Cultural Construction, Hubei University

Hubei Collaborative Innovation Center for Chinese Culture Development, Hubei University

Centre of Hubei Cooperative Innovation for Emission Trading System, Hubei University of Economics

South-central University for Nationalities Sub-center of Hubei Research Center of Socialism with Chinese Characteristics Theoretical System

International Trade Research Center, Hunan University

National Corruption Prevention and Punishment Research Center of Hunan University

Financial Development and Credit Management Research Center, Hunan University

Research Center of Honest Administration, Hunan University

Policy & Theory Research Base of Ministry of Civil Affairs, Hunan University

Research and Spread of National Studies in Yuelu Academy of Hunan University

China Industrial Finance Collaborative Innovation Center, Hunan University

China Center for Cultural Soft Power Research, Hunan University

Hunan Province Collaborative Innovation Center of Anti-Corruption, Hunan University of Technology and Sciences

Research Center for Cultural Exchange and Communication along "the Belt and Road"

Center for Studies in Moral Culture of Hunan Normal University

Human Research Institute of Chinese International Promotion, Hunan Normal University

Institute of Core Socialist Values of Hunan Normal University

Research Center of Rule of Law for Environmental Protection, Hunan Normal University

Institute of Ecological Civilization, Hunan Normal University

Beijing Energy Development Research Center, North China Electric Power University

Research Center for High Speed Railway and Regional Development, East China Jiaotong University

Center for Energy Economics and Environmental Management, East China

University of Science and Technology

Research Center for Social Work and Management, East China University of Science and Technology

Research Center of Yangtze River Delta Regional Integration, East China Normal University

Center for Russian Studies of ECNU (CRS)

Center for National Discourse Ecology Studies, East China Normal University

Institute for National Educational Policy Research, East China Normal University

Institute of Schooling Reform and Development, East China Normal University

Institute of Curriculum and Instruction, East China Normal University

Institute of Global Innovation and Development, East China Normal University

Shanghai Innovation Research Base of Population Structure and Development Trend, East China Normal University

Shanghai Municipal Institute for Lifelong Education, East China Normal University

Center for the Study and Application of Chinese Characters, East China Normal University

The Center for Modern Chinese City Studies, East China Normal University

The Institute for Modern Chinese Thought and Culture, East China Normal University

Research Center for Co-development with Neighboring Countries, East China Normal University

East China Institute of Prosecution, East China University of Political Science and Law

East China University of Political Science and Law

Center for Rule of Law Strategy Studies, East China University of Political Science and Law

Center of Public Diplomacy and Intercultural Communication Research, South China University of Technology

Institute of Public Policy, South China University of Technology

Guangdong Tourism Strategy and Policy Research Center, South China University of Technology

Guangdong Local Legislation Research Evaluation and Consultation Base, South China University of Technology

Center of Social Governance Research, South China University of Technology

Guangzhou Financial Services Innovation and Risk Management Research Base, South China University of Technology

Guangzhou Center for Research on Risk Governance in Megacities, South China University of Technology

Research Center of Financial Engineering, South China University of Technology

The Think Tank of Science & Technology Revolution and Technology Foresight, South China University of Technology

Guangzhou Think Tank for G-H-M Greater Bay Area, South China University of Technology

Center for Government Performance Appraisal, South China University of Technology

Third-party Evaluation Think Tank for Performance of Major Scientific Projects and Platforms, South China University of Technology

Institute of Overseas Chinese, Huaqiao University

Non-traditional Security Centre of Huazhong University of Science and Technology

The Institute of State Governance, Huazhong University of Science and Technology

Huazhong University of Science and Technology School of Health Policy and Management

Peikang Chang Institute for Development Studies, Huazhong University of Science and Technology

Central China Normal University National Research Center of Cultural Industries

Institute of China Rural Studies, Central China Normal University

Anhui Big-Data Research Center on University Management, Huaibei Normal University

North Jiangsu Development Research Institute, Huaiyin Institute of Technology

China (Henan) Innovation and Development Institute, Huanghe Science and Technology College

Entrepreneurship and Innovation Graduate School, Jilin University

Center for Northeast Asian Studies, Jilin University

Jilin University Crime Governance Research Center

Institute of International Studies, Jilin University

Center for Anti-Corruption Research and Education of Jilin University

Research Center for Social Justice and Governance of Jilin University

Center for Quantitative Economics of Jilin University

Judicial Statistics Application Research Center of Jilin University

China Center for Public Sector Economy Research at Jilin University

China Research Center for Scientific and Technological Policies and

Management, Jilin University

China Center for Aging Studies and Social-Economic Development, Jilin University

Chinese Culture Research Center, Jilin University

Research Center for Poverty Alleviation and Development in Ethnic Minority Areas, Jishou University

Research Center for Longshan Green Economy of Jinan University

Institute of Industrial Economics, Jinan University

Institute of Guangzhou Nansha Free Trade Test Area Research, Jinan University

Research Center of Low Carbon Economy for Guangzhou Region, Jinan University

The Public Opinion Big Data Research Center, Jinan University

Academy of Overseas Chinese Studies in Jinan University

Institute for Economic and Social Research, Jinan University

Jiangwei Economic Development Institute for the Great Bay Area (Guangdong, Hong Kong, Macao), Jinan University

Institute of Resource, Environment and Sustainable Development, Jinan University

Institute for Food Safety Risk Management, Jiangnan University

Development Strategy Research Base of IOT Industry, Jiangnan University

Jiangsu Institute of Educational Modernization, Jiangsu Second Normal University

Academy of Applied Maritime Talents of the Belt and Road, Jiangsu Maritime Institute

Jiangsu Public Security Institute, Jiangsu Police Institute

Institute of the Belt and Road, Jiangsu Normal University

Coordinated Innovation Center for Establishing an All-around Affluent Society in Jiangxi, Jiangxi University of Finance and Economics

Jiangxi Center of Cooperative Innovation for Eco-civilization System, Jiangxi University of Finance and Economics

The Collaborative Innovation Center of Strategic Emerging Industry Development of Jiangxi Province for Monitoring, Forecasting and Decision Supporting, Jiangxi University of Finance and Economics

Research Center of Nonferrous Metal Industry Development, Jiangxi University of Science and Technology

Research Center of the Management Decision Evaluation of Jiangxi Normal University

Jiangxi Industrial Transformation and Development Research Center, Jiangxi Normal University

Jiangxi Institute of Economic Development of Jiangxi Normal University

CPC Revolution Base Revitalization Institute of Jiangxi Normal University

Collaborative Innovation Center of Chinese Society Transformation Research, Jiangxi Normal University

Yunnan Integrated Transport Development and Regional Logistics Management Think Tank, Kunming University of Science and Technology

Research Institute of Kunming Scientific Development, Kunming University

Silk Road Economic Research Institute of Lanzhou University of Finance and Economics

The Center for Afghanistan Studies of Lanzhou University

Research Center for Silk Road Belt Construction of Lanzhou University

Center of Studies of Ethnic Minorities in Northwest China of Lanzhou University

Evidence-Based Social Science Research Center of Lanzhou University

China Research Center for Government Performance Management, Lanzhou University

Institute for Central Asian Studies, Lanzhou University

Collaborative Innovation Center of the Opening of Northeast China for Northeast Asia, Liaoning University

China Academy of Northeast Revitalization, Liaoning University

Research Center for the Economics and Politics of Transitional Countries, Liaoning University

MCA-ECNU Institute for Administrative Division

Jiangxi Development Research Institute of Nanchang University

Tourism Planning and Research Center of Nanchang University

Research Center for Central China Economic and Social Development of Nanchang University

Modern Service Industry Think Tank of Nanjing University of Finance and Economics

Yangtze Industrial Economics Institution, Nanjing University

Yangtze River Delta Economics and Social Development Research Center of Nanjing University

Institute of African Studies, Nanjing University

Huazhi Institute for Global Governance, Nanjing University

Interdisciplinary Center for Risk, Disaster & Crisis Management, Nanjing University

Collaborative Innovation Center of South China Sea Studies, Nanjing University

Zijin Media Think Tank, Nanjing University

Evaluation Center for Think Tank of Industrial and Information Technology, Nanjing University of Aeronautics and Astronautics

Jiangsu Academy of Talent Development, Nanjing University of Science and Technology

The Research Center of Intellectual Property Development in Jiangsu, Nanjing University of Science and Technology

Jin Shanbao Agricultural Modernization Research Institute, Nanjing Agricultural University

Institute for Chinese Legal Modernization Studies, Nanjing Normal University

Development Institute of Jiangsu New Area, Nanjing University of Information Science & Technology

Research Institute of Climate and Environmental Governance, Nanjing University of Information Science & Technology

Institute of Healthy Jiangsu Development, Nanjing Medical University

Purple Academy of Culture & Creativity, Nanjing University of Arts

Binhai Development Institute, Nankai University

Institute of Issues in Contemporary China, Nankai University

Research Center for Economic Integration and Global Governance, Nankai University

College of Economic and Social Development, Nankai University

Japan Research Center of Nankai University

Greece Research Center of Nankai University

APEC Study Center of Nankai University

Center for Studies of Political Economy of Nankai University

China Academy of Corporate Governance, Nankai University

Collaborative Innovation Center for China Economy, Nankai University

Chinese Government and Politics Unite Research Center, Nankai University

Jiangsu Yangtze Economic Belt Research Institute, Nantong University

Collaborative Innovation Center for the Study on China, Mongolia and Russia Economic and Trade Cooperation & Construction of Economic Belt on the Prairie Silk Road, Inner Mongolia University of Finance and Economics

Center for Studies of Mongolia, Inner Mongolia University

Center for Mongolian Studies, Inner Mongolia University

Donghai Institute of Ningbo University

Center of Marine Education Research, Ningbo University

Hui Institute of Ningxia University

China Institute for Arab Studies at Ningxia University

Qinghai Provincial Research Center, Qinghai University

Brookings-Tsinghua Center for Public Policy

Think Tank Research Center of School of Public Policy & Management, Tsinghua University

Institute of International Relations, Tsinghua University

Institute for Contemporary China Studies, Tsinghua University

Research Center for Technological Innovation, Tsinghua University

Carnegie-Tsinghua Center for Global Policy, Tsinghua University

Center for S & T Development and Governance, Tsinghua University

Institute for Global Sustainable Development Goals, Tsinghua University

Research Center for Contemporary Management, Tsinghua University

Center for Crisis Management Research, Tsinghua University

Center for China in the World Economy, Tsinghua University

Institute of Contemporary World Socialism, Shandong University

Center for Confucius Institute Studies, Shandong University

Shandong School of Development at Shandong University

Shandong Regional Financial Reform and Development Research Center, Shandong University

Center for Health Management and Policy, Shandong University

The Institute for Studies in County Development, Shandong University

Center for Judaic and Inter-Religious Studies of Shandong University

Research Institute of Political Parties, Shandong University

Cooperative Innovation Center for Transition of Resource-Based Economics, Shanxi University of Finance and Economics

Institute of Management and Decision of Shanxi University

Institute for the Study of Jin Merchants of Shanxi University

Central Asia Institute of Shaanxi Normal University

Poverty Alleviation and Assessment Research Center of Shaanxi Normal University

Center for Experimental Economics in Education at Shaanxi Normal University

Center for Turkish Studies, Shaanxi Normal University

Northwest Land and Resource Research Center, Shaanxi Normal University

Northwest Cross Border Ethnic Groups and Frontier Security Research Center, Shaanxi Normal University

Northwest Institute of Historical Environment and Socio-Economic Development, Shaanxi Normal University

Language Resources Development Research Center, Shaanxi Normal University

West Tourism Development Research Base of China Tourism Academy, Shaanxi Normal University

Institute for Western Frontier Region of China, Shaanxi Normal University

Institute for Public Policy and Governance, Shanghai University of Finance and Economics

Shanghai Institute of International Finance Center, Shanghai University of Finance and Economics

China Industrial Development Institute, Shanghai University of Finance and Economics

China Public Finance Institute, Shanghai University of Finance and Economics

Collaborative Innovation Center of China Pilot Free Trade Zone, Shanghai University of Finance and Economics

Center for Drug and National Security in Shanghai University

Research Center for Local Governance, Shanghai University

Center for Latin American Studies, Shanghai University

Center for Turkish Studies, Shanghai University

Think Tank Industry Research Center of Shanghai University

Shanghai Center for Global Trade and Economic Governance, Shanghai University of International Business and Economics

Shanghai WTO Affairs Consultation Center, Shanghai University of International Business and Economics

Shanghai International Shipping Institute, Shanghai Maritime University

China Institute of FTZ Supply Chain, Shanghai Maritime University

Institute of Urban Science in Shanghai Jiao Tong University

The Center for Third Sector, Shanghai Jiao Tong University

Center for Reform, Innovation and Governance at Shanghai Jiao Tong University

Research Base on National Marine Rights and Strategy, Shanghai Jiao Tong University

Cultural Industry Innovation & Development Academy, Shanghai Jiao Tong University

Center for World-Class Universities, Shanghai Jiao Tong University

Institute of Cultural Innovation and Youth Development, Shanghai Jiao Tong University

Institute for Public Opinion Research, Shanghai Jiao Tong University

China Institute for Urban Governance, Shanghai Jiao Tong University

China Strategy Institute of Ocean Engineering, Shanghai Jiao Tong University

Research Institute for International and Comparative Education, Shanghai Normal University

Institute of Silk Road Strategy Studies of Shanghai International Studies University (SISU)

Centre for British Studies, SISU

Middle East Studies Institute, SISU

Center for Global Public Opinions of China, SISU

Research Center of Foreign Language Strategies, SISU

Institute for the Security Studies of the Belt and Road, Shanghai University of Political Science and Law

SCO Research Institute, Shanghai University of Political Science and Law

Institute of Urban Governance, Shenzhen University

Center for Basic Laws of Hong Kong and Macao Special Administrative Regions, Shenzhen University

Institute of China Overseas Interests, Shenzhen University

Institute of Human Resource Development and Management, Shenyang Normal University

Beijing Economics and Social Development Policy Research Base, Capital University of Economics and Business

Beijing Basic Education Research Base, Capital Normal University

Institute of South Asian Studies, Sichuan University

The Faculty of Social Development and Western China Development Studies, Sichuan University

Collaborative Innovation Center for Security and Development of Western Frontier of China, Sichuan University

Center for Tibet Studies of Sichuan University

Soochow University Think Tank

Think Tank for Urban Development, Suzhou University of Science and Technology

Center for Economic Analysis of Law and Policy Evaluation, Tianjin University of Finance and Economics (TUFE)

Center for Public Economy and Management TUFE

Business Management Research Center TUFE

Research Center for Finance and Insurance, TUFE

Tianjin Academy of Free Trade Area, TUFE

Collaborative Innovation Center for Intangible Asset Evaluation, TUFE

Coordinated Innovation Center for Binhai Finance in China, TUFE

China Center for Economic Statistics Research, TUFE

Research Center for Urbanization and New Rural Construction of Tianjin,

Tianjin Chengjian University

Research Base for the Implementation of National Intellectual Property Strategy, Tianjin University

Center of Educational Science Research, Tianjin University

Center for Social Science Survey and Data, Tianjin University

Center for Biosafety Research and Strategy, Tianjin University

APEC Sustainable Energy Center, Tianjin University

Institute of Disaster Medicine, Tianjin University

Collaborative Innovation Center for Cultural Inheritance of China's Traditional Villages & Architecture Heritages, Tianjin University

Research Institute of China Green Development of Tianjin University

International Research Centre for the Chinese Cultural Heritage Conservation, Tianjin University

China Intelligent Rule of Law Institute, Tianjin University

Center for Information Service Evaluation and Governance of Tianjin Public Sectors

Research Center of Tianjin Letters of the Rule of Law, Tianjin Polytechnic University

Research Center of Energy Environment and Green Development, Tianjin University of Science and Technology

Food Safety Strategy and Management Research Center of Tianjin University of Science and Technology

Research Center of Circular Economy and Green Development, Tianjin University of Technology

Think Tank of Major Project and Technology of China "Going out" Investment

Model and Control, Tianjin University of Technology

Tianjin Rural Revitalization Institute

Tianjin University of Commerce Modern Service Industry Development Research Center

Research Institute of Governance, Tianjin Normal University

Research Center of Regional Development Institute for Strategy and Reform Studies, Tianjin Normal University

Emergence Managemene Research Center, Tianjin Normal University

Institute of Free Economic Zone, Tianjin Normal University

Tianjin Research Center for Basic Education Decisions and Service

National Sport and Fitness Research Think Tank, Tianjin University of Sport

Tianjin Institute for the Belt and Road Strategic Studies, Tianjin Foreign Studies University

Northeast Asia Research Center, Tianjin Foreign Studies University

Institute of Finance and Economics of Tongji University

German Studies Center, Tongji University

Sustainable Development and New-type Urbanization Think Tank, Tongji University

Institute for China & World Studies, Tongji University

Institution of Inner-party Laws and Regulations, Wuhan University

Academy of Development of Wuhan University

Wuhan University Institute of International Law

Institute of National Culture Development, Wuhan University

Hubei Institute of Political Construction, Wuhan University

Research Institute of Environmental Law, Wuhan University

The Center for Economic Development Research of Wuhan University

Wuhan University Center of Economic Diplomacy

Center for Studies of Media Development, Wuhan University

Center for Studies of Global Healthy, Wuhan University

Center for Social Security Studies of Wuhan University

Center for the Studies of Information Resources, Wuhan University

The Institute of Quality Development Strategy of Wuhan University

Wuhan University China Institute of Boundary and Ocean Studies

The Center for Studies of Chinese Traditional Culture of Wuhan University

National Institute of Chinese Language Matters and Social Development, Wuhan University

Institute for the Development of Central China, Wuhan University

The Mainstream Ideology Construction and Education Research Base of Wuhan University

XJTU Institute of "The Belt and Road" Pilot Free Trade Zone

Research Center of Economic Reform Innovation and Assessment, Xi'an Jiaotong University

Research Institute of Eurasian Economy and Global Development, Xi'an Jiaotong University

Shaanxi Economic Research Center, Xi'an Jiaotong University

Collaborative Innovation Centre for Social Governance and Policy, Xi'an Jiaotong University

Silk Road Institute for International and Comparative Law of Xi'an Jiaotong University

Collaborative Innovation Centre for Silk Road Economic Belt Legal and Polray

Studies, Xi'an Jiaotong University

New Media and Social Governance Center, Xi'an Jiaotong University

Intellectual Property Research Center of Xi'an Jiaotong University

China Digital Economy Development Research Center in Xi'an, China, Xi'an Jiaotong University

Research Centre of Chinese Management, Xi'an Jiaotong University

Collaborative Innovation Centre for Shaanxi Macroeconomics and Economic Growth & Quality, Northwest University

Research Institute of Silk Road Cultural Heritage Protection and Archeology, Northwest University

Institute of Middle Eastern Studies, Northwest University

Center For Studics of China Western Economic Development Research Center of West China, Northwest University

Research Center for Science, Technology and Industry Development for National Defense of Western China, Northwestern Polytechnical University

The Research Center for the Belt and Road Initiative and Education Development, Northwest Normal University

The Gansu Province's Construction and Research Center of Cultural Resource and Chinese Civilization, Northwest Normal University

Center for Targeted Poverty Alleviation & Regional Development Research, Northwest Normal University

Institute of Anti-Terrorism Studies, Northwest University of Political Science and Law

Institute of National Religion of Northwest University of Political Science and Law

Collaborative Innovation Center of Financial Security, Southwest University of Finance and Economics

Survey and Research Center for China Household Finance, Southwest University of Finance and Economics

Institute of Chinese Financial Studies of Southwest University of Finance and Economics

Western Center for Economic Research in China, Southwest University of Finance and Economics

Research Center of Russian-speaking Countries, Southwest University

The Research Center for Public Culture, Southwest University

Institute for Education Policy at Southwest University

Research Center of Rural Economy and Management, Southwest University

Research Center for Economic and Social Development of the Three Gorges Reservoir Region, Southwest University

Research Center for Urban and Rural Education Development, Southwest University

Center for Hellenic Studies, Southwest University

Center for Studies of Education and Psychology of Ethnic Minorities in Southwest China of Southwest University

Center for Iranian Studies, Southwest University

Research Center of Western Transportation Strategy and Regional Development, Southwest Jiaotong University

Sichuan Province Cyclic Economy Research Center, Southwest University of Science and Technology

Development Research Center of Oil and Gas of Sichuan, Southwest Petroleum

University

    Human Rights Institute, Southwest University of Political Science and Law

    Institute for Tibet Sustainable Development, Tibet University

    Institute of South Asian Studies at Xizang Minzu University

    Center for Collaborative Innovation in the Heritage and Development of Xizang Culture, Xizang Minzu University

    Center for Southeast Asian Studies, Xiamen University

    Center for Higher Education Development of Xiamen University

    Center for Macroeconomic Research, Xiamen University

    Graduate Institute for Taiwan Studies of Xiamen University

    China Institute for Studies in Energy Policy, Xiamen University

    Local Legislation and Social Governance Research Center, Xiangtan University

    Public Administration and Regional Economic Development Research Center of Xiangtan University

    The Studying Center of Mao Zedong Thought, Xiangtan University

    Government Performance Evaluation and Management Innovation Research Center of Xiangtan University

    Research Center of Revolutionary Spirit and Cultural Resources of the Communist Party of China, Xiangtan University

    Hebei Provincial Public Policy Evaluation and Research Center, Yanshan University

    Hebei Design Innovation & Industrial Development Research Center, Yanshan University

    Regional Economic Development Research Center of Yanshan University

    Institute of Korean Peninsula Studies, Yanbian University

Think Tank of Coastal Development, Yancheng Teachers University

Center for Advanced Study of Public Policy, Yunnan University of Finance and Economics

Research Institute for Indian Ocean Economics, Yunnan University of Finance and Economics

Yunnan Think Tank on Disaster Prevention and Mitigation, Yunnan University of Finance and Economics

Think Tank on Ethnic Issues of Countries along "the Belt and Road Initiative"

Frontier Ethnic Problems Think Tank of Yunnan University

Institute of Myanmar Studies, Yunnan University

Culture Development Institute of Yunnan University

Border Opening and Economic Development Think Tank, Yunnan University

Center for China's Neighbor Diplomacy Studies, Yunnan University

China Institute of Regulation and Public Policy Research, Zhejiang University of Finance & Economics

The Collaborative Innovation Center for the Belt and Road Initiative, Zhejiang University

National Institute for Innovation Management, Zhejiang University

Center for Non-Traditional Security and Peaceful Development Studies, Zhejiang University

Public Policy Research Institute of Zhejiang University

Institute for Public Policy of Zhejiang Univercity

Academy of Financial Research, Zhejiang University

Center for Research of Private Economy, Zhejiang University

Academy of Social Governance, Zhejiang University

Institute of China's Science, Technology and Education Policy, Zhejiang University

China Academy of Cross-border E-commerce, Zhejiang University

China Academy for Rural Development of Zhejiang University

China Academy of West Region Development, Zhejiang University

China Institute for Small and Medium Enterprises, Zhejiang University of Technology

Center for Economical Civilization of Zhejiang Province, Zhejiang Sci-Tech University

The Silk and Fashion Culture Research Center of Zhejiang Province, Zhejiang Sci-Tech University

Zhejiang Legislative Research Institute and Zhejiang University Legislative Research Institute

Center for China Farmers' Development, Zhejiang A & F University

Institute of African Studies, Zhejiang Normal University

Ningbo Maritime Silk Road Institute, Zhejiang Wanli University

Social Governance Collaborative Innovation Center of Henan Province, Zhengzhou University

National Center for Communication Innovation Studies, CUC

The Capital's Research Base of Media Economy (BJ Media), CUC

Institute of Marine Development of Ocean University of China

Center for Japanese Studies, Ocean University of China

China Business Working Capital Management Research Center

Anhui Province Key Laboratory of Big Data Analysis and Application, University of Science and Technology of China

Research Center of Anhui Science and Technology Innovation and Regional Development, University of Science and Technology of China

China Urban Public Security Management Think Tank, China University of Mining and Technology

Institute of Airport Economics, Civil Aviation University of China

Research Center for Environment and Sustainable Development of the China Civil Aviation, Civil Aviation University of China

Research Center for International Development, China Agricultural University

Institute of China Agricultural Economics and Rural Development, China Agricultural University

Center for Land Policy and Law, China Agricultural University

Chongyang Institute for Financial Studies, Renmin University of China

The National Academy of Development and Strategy, Renmin University of China

The Research Center of Civil and Commercial Jurisprudence of Renmin University of China

Population and Development Studies Center, Renmin University of China

Collaborative Innovation Center for Social Transformation and Social Governance, Renmin University of China

The Research Center of Criminal Justice at Renmin University of China

China Financial Policy Research Center, Renmin University of China

Center for Capital Social Safety, People's Public Security University of China

Center for Innovation and Development of Ideological and Political Work in the University of Chinese Academy of Social Sciences

School of Law-Based Government, China University of Political Science and Law

Institution for Human Rights at China University of Political Science and Law

Collaborative Innovation Center of Judicial Civilization of China, China University of Political Science and Law

China Society of Administrative Reform, China University of Political Science and Law

Collaborative Innovation Center of Industrial Upgrading and Regional Finance (Hubei), Zhongnan University of Economics and Law

The Co-Innovation Center for Social Management of Urban and Rural Communities in Hubei Province, Zhongnan University of Economics and Law

Center for the Development of Rule of Law and Judicial Reform Research of Zhongnan University of Economics and Law

Center for Counter-terrorism Studies, Zhongnan University of Economics and Law

Center for Studies of Intellectual Property Rights, Zhongnan University of Economics and Law

China's Income Distribution Research Center, Zhongnan University of Economics and Law

Institute for Local Governance of Central South University

Legislative Research Base for Education of Central South University

Institute of Metal Resources Strategy, Central South University

Collaborative Innovation Center for Resource Conserving & Environment-friendly Society and Ecological Civilization

Human Resources Research Center of Central South University

Human Rights Center of Central South University

Center for Social Stability Risk Assessment of Central South University (CSU)

Political Consultation Office of United Front Department, CSU

Institute of Medical and Health Law, CSU

Applied Ethics Research Center of CSU

Intellectual Property Research Institute of Central South University

Research Center of Chinese Village Culture, Central South University

China Center for Cultural Law Research of Central South University

Research Base of Central South University of Chinese Writers' Association Network Literature Committee

Green Development Institute of Hunan, Central South University of Forestry and Technology

Institute of State Governance, Sun Yat-sen University

Institute of South China Sea Strategic Studies, Sun Yat-sen University

Institute of Guangdong, Hong Kong and Macao Development Studies, Sun Yat-sen University

Institute of Public Procurement, Central University of Finance and Economics

International Institute of Green Finance, Central University of Finance and Economics

China Center for Internet Economy Research, Central University of Finance and Economics

Center for China Fiscal Development, Central University of Finance and Economics

Research Center for China's Banking Industry, Central University of Finance and Economics

Center for CPC Literature Translation Studies

Southeast University Center for Civil Prosecution of the Supreme People's

Procuratorate Research Base

(Ⅴ) Military Think Tanks (6)

Beijing System Engineering Research Institute

Research Center for Defense Technology and Civil Military Integration of National University of Defense Technology

National Defense Science and Technology Strategy Research Center of National University of Defense Technology

International Studies Center of National University of Defense Technology

National Defense University of People's Liberation Army, NDU, PLA

Academy of Military Sciences, PLA, China

(Ⅵ) Think Tank of Research Institutes (36)

Beijing Research Center for Science of Science

Surveying and Mapping Development Research Center, NASG

Rural Development Research Institute of Hunan

Jiangsu Information Institute of Science and Technology (Jiangsu Science and Technology Development Strategy Research Institute)

Jiangsu Suke Academy of Innovation Strategy

Jiangxi Academy of Sciences Institute of Science & Technology Strategy

International Engineering Education Center, United Nations Educational, Scientific and Cultural Organization

Research Center of Science and Technology for Development

Qindao Institute of Science and Technology Development Strategy

Institute of Science and Technology for Development of Shandong

Shanghai Institute for International Studies

Shanghai Institute of Science & Technology Policy (Shanghai Institute of Science & Technology Management)

Shanghai Institute for Science of Science

Capital Institute of Science and Technology Development Strategy

Development Research Center of the Ministry of Water Resources of P. R. China

Tianjin Research Institute of Economic Development

Western China Think Tank on Resources, Environment and Development

China Steel Development & Research Institute

Yunnan Institute of Environmental Science

Zhejiang Institute of Science and Technology Information (Zhejiang Institute of Science and Technology Development Strategy)

China Center for Information Industry Development

Chinese Academy of Engineering

China Aerospace Engineering Science and Technology Development Strategy Research Institute

Chinese Research Academy of Environmental Sciences

National Academy of Innovation Strategy

Chinese Academy of Science and Technology for Development

Institute of Scientific and Technical Information of China

Chinese Academy of Sciences

Institutes of Science and Development, Chinese Academy of Sciences

Center for Forecasting Science, Chinese Academy of Sciences

CASS Think Tank for Eco-civilization Studies

CNPC Economics & Technology Research Institute

China Academy of Information and Communication Technology

China Institute of Science and Technology Development Strategies on Information and Electronic Engineering

Chinese National Academy of Arts

Think Tank for Traditional Chinese Medicine, China Information Association for Traditional Chinese Medicine and Pharmacy

(Ⅶ) Corporate Think Tanks (10)

AliResearch

Beijing Greatwall Enterprise Institute

Electric Power Planning & Engineering Institute

Institute of China Development Bank

Economic Research Institute of State Grid Jiangsu Electric Power Co. , Ltd.

China Southern Power Grid

Suning Institute of Finance

Tengyun Think Tank

Advising Committee for China Academy of Management Science

CITIC Foundation for Reform and Development Studies

(Ⅷ) Private Think Tanks (38)

International Institute for Urban Development, Beijing

The Charhar Institute

Changjiang Education Research Institute

Institute of Industry Development Research, Changsha

Chongqing Think Tank

China Region Development &-Reform Institute (CRDRI)

South China Business Think Tank of Guangdong University of Finance and Economics

Asia-Pacific Innovation Economic Research Institute of Guangdong

China Strategy Institute for Intellectual Property (Guangdong ZHONGCE Intellectual Property Research Institute)

Grandview Institution

Intellisia Institute

Hainan Institute for World Watch

Research and Development International, Chinese Academy of Social Sciences

The Association of Soft Science Research of Liaoning

The Pangoal Institution

Center for China &- Globalization

Chunqiu Institute for Development and Strategic Studies

Shanghai FC Institute of Economics Forecast CO. , Ltd

Shanghai Academy of Huaxia Social Development Research

Shanghai Institute of Finance and Law

Shanghai Finance Institute

Shenzhen Innovation and Development Institute

Wuzhen Institute

Wanbo Institute

New Silk Road Economic Institute

Belt and Road 100 People Forum

Yuhuatai Red Culture Institute

Knowfar Institute for Strategic and Defense Studies

China Institute for Reform and Development

China Center for International Economic Exchanges

China Finance 40 Forum

China Society of Economic Reform

China Institute for Leadership Science

National Institute for South China Sea Studies

China Enterprise Reform and Development Society

China Silk Road iValley Research

China Institute of Science and Technology

China Development Institute

(IX) Media Think Tanks (15)

YICAI Research Institute

Cover Institute

Phoenix International Think Tank

Research Center of Cultural and Creative Industry at *Guangming Daily*

Guangming Think Tank

Guangzhou Daily Data & Digit Institute

Rednet Think Tank

China Economic Trends Research Institute

Liaowang Institute

Nanfang Media Think Tank

South Reviews Media Institute

Nanjing Institute of Government Affairs and Public Opinions

Shengjinghui Think Tank

People's Daily Online New Media Institute

Xinhua News Agency

图书在版编目(CIP)数据

CTTI 智库报告. 2019 / 李刚等主编. — 南京：南京大学出版社，2020.12

(南大智库文丛 / 李刚主编)

ISBN 978‐7‐305‐23982‐3

Ⅰ. ①C… Ⅱ. ①李… Ⅲ. ①咨询机构－研究报告－中国－2019 Ⅳ. ①C932.82

中国版本图书馆 CIP 数据核字(2020)第 227342 号

出版发行　南京大学出版社
社　　址　南京市汉口路 22 号　　　邮　编　210093
出 版 人　金鑫荣
丛 书 名　南大智库文丛
丛书主编　李　刚
书　　名　CTTI 智库报告(2019)
主　　编　李　刚　王斯敏　冯　雅　甘　琳
责任编辑　张　静

照　　排　南京南琳图文制作有限公司
印　　刷　南京玉河印刷厂
开　　本　718×1000　1/16　印张 46.25　字数 698 千
版　　次　2020 年 12 月第 1 版　2020 年 12 月第 1 次印刷
ISBN 978‐7‐305‐23982‐3
定　　价　138.00 元

网　　址：http://www.njupco.com
官方微博：http://weibo.com/njupco
官方微信：njupress
销售咨询：(025) 83594756